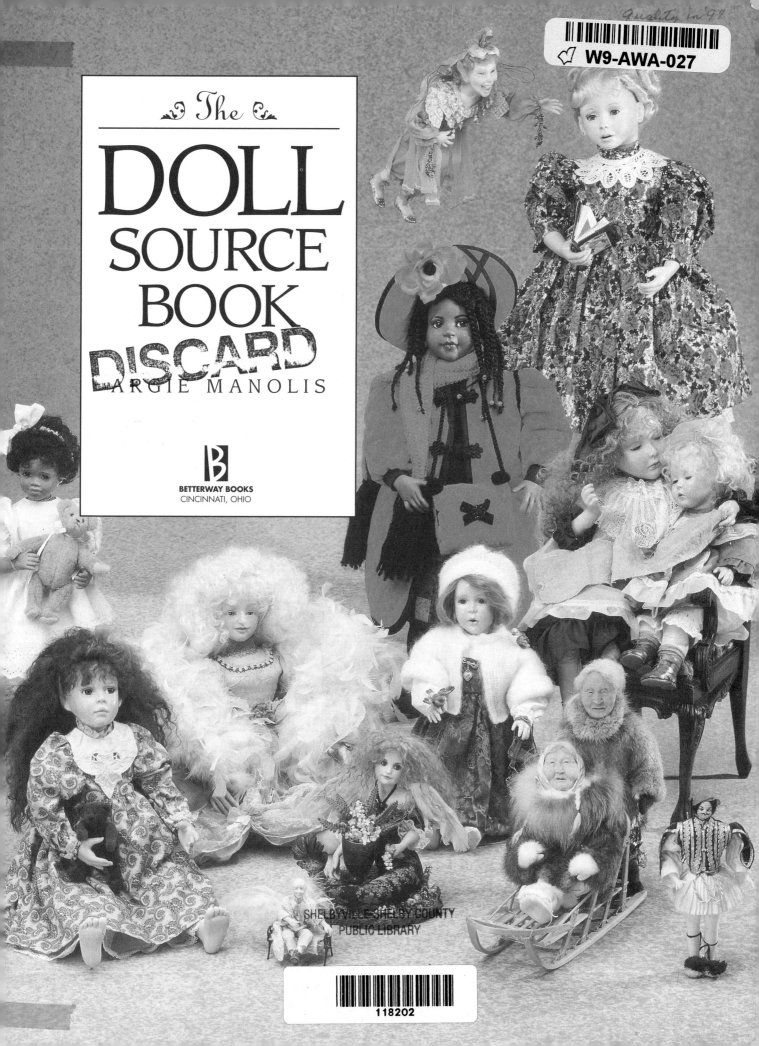

The

DOLL
SOURCE
BOOK

DISCARD

ARGIE MANOLIS

B
BETTERWAY BOOKS
CINCINNATI, OHIO

Other fine Betterway Books are available from your local bookstore
or direct from the publisher.

00   99   98   97   96   5   4   3   2   1

International Standard Serial Number: 1089-3180
International Standard Book Number: 1-55870-431-0

Edited by Argie Manolis
Designed by Sandy Kent
Cover photo by Pamela Monfort Braun/Bronze Photography

Betterway Books are available for sales promotions, premiums and
fund-raising use. Special editions or book excerpts can also be created to specification. For details, contact: Special Sales Manager,
F&W Publications, 1507 Dana Avenue, Cincinnati, Ohio 45207.

The following page constitutes an extension of this copyright page.

PHOTO ACKNOWLEDGMENTS

Pages 4-5: The Armand Marseille lady doll, the Little Orphan comic character doll and the low brow china doll were photographed by Judith Whorton from her collection.

Page 6: W. Donald Smith photographed Susanna Oroyan's "Gertrude" and "The Doll Peddler."

Pages 8-11: Carol-Lynn Rössel Waugh photographed all the dolls pictured in her article, including her own "Rosalind Golden," Sunnie Andress's "Prudence Kotten Bathing," Pam Hamel's "Georgia" and Barbara Giguere's "Tracey."

Pages 17-20: The examples of good and bad photos in Tracey Herring's article were taken by Barbara Giguere. The advertisements for Forever Dolls and Christie Cummins Dolls appeared in *Dolls—The Collector's Magazine*, and are used here with permission from the owner of Forever Dolls and from artist Christie Cummins.

Pages 43-46: All dolls pictured in Judith Whorton's article were photographed by Judith Whorton from her collection.

Pages 62-65: Kathy Wormhood's "Indian Maiden," Mavis Snyder's "Ricci," and Carol-Lynn Rössel Waugh's "Nosalie" were photographed by Carol-Lynn Rössel Waugh. Jack Johnston's Native American doll was photographed by Jack Johnston.

Pages 100-103: All dolls pictured in Barb Giguere's article were photographed by Barb Giguere.

Pages 195-196: Christina Wemmitt-Pauk's photos were taken by John Paul Pauk II.

Pages 241-243: Photos of the Yellow Brick Road Doll and Toy Museum were provided by Dorothy Tancraitor.

Pages 245-246: Photos of dolls in the Dolly Wares Doll Museum were provided by Sharon Smith.

Pages 255-262: Sue Shanahan, Judy Johnson and Norma Lu Meehan provided the paper dolls pictured along with Judy M. Johnson's article.

Pages 283-284: Jack Johnston provided the photos accompanying his interview.

ABOUT THE COVER

The dolls on the cover of *The Doll Sourcebook*, with the exception of Raggedy Ann and the Greek "Evzon" doll, were chosen by our designers from photos sent to us by the artists listed in this book. This cover is meant to reflect the many styles, mediums and cultures represented by doll artists today. The artists listed here generously offered to ship their dolls to us to be photographed for the cover of this book. Many were in the process of preparing for the Toy Fair and other shows during this time, and we are grateful for their generosity and trust. All the artists listed here have dolls for sale. Be sure to look for their listings in chapter four, where doll artists are listed alphabetically by last name!

Front Cover:

Karen Morley of Eau Claire, Wisconsin, created "Giggle-Fit," the aptly named red-headed fairy at top right.

"Brittainy," just to the right of "Giggle-Fit," is a lover of books, much like her maker, Barb Giguere. She comes from Scarborough, Maine.

Ann Jackson's "Mischief" is all bundled up with her red muff. She comes from Addison, Illinois.

Vancouver, Washington, is the home of Cindy McClure, who created "Cross Stitch." These two precious dolls sitting beside "Mischief" are busy at their craft.

"Abby," at far left, is adorable in her white dress with her little friend. She was made by Joan Ibarolle of Walnut Creek, California.

Christina Wemmitt-Pauk's beautiful woman wears an elaborate dress made of antique materials. Pictured near the center, she comes from Beech Mountain, North Carolina.

"The Bird Catcher," to the right of Christina's doll, was made with love by Cindy McClure. This little one has a couple of visitors.

The little brunette clutching her teddy bear, pictured at bottom left, is anxious to get back home to Huntington Beach, California, to be finished. Christie Cummins, her maker, allowed us to borrow her before her legs and shoes were done.

The little man on a park bench, sitting next to Christie's doll, is "My Guardian Angel" by Jill Nemirow-Nelson.

The thoughtful mermaid next to "My Guardian Angel" is "Evangeline," by Ann Jackson.

"Ochoopau" and her companion, "Parr," are on a sledding expedition, where they will use the working traps dangling from Parr's hand. Mary Ellen Frank carefully crafted this couple in Juneau, Alaska.

The "Evzon" at bottom right is a traditional Greek doll. Originally from Ikaria, Greece, he has been in the U.S. for the past fifteen years. He is owned by Argie Manolis.

Back Cover:

The soft-sculptured little girl with long, blond braids at top left, by Barbara Ogden, is named "Faye." She came to us from Hanover, Maryland.

"Albert," Faye's brother, is another soft-sculptured doll by Barbara Ogden. Pictured next to Faye, he is also from Hanover, Maryland.

The "Raggedy Ann" is from Cincinnati, Ohio. She is a childhood friend of Jennie Berliant.

Below "Raggedy Ann" is Jennifer Schmidt's "Evie," who looks cozy in her blue outfit, snuggling her bear. "Evie" comes from Mill Valley, California.

"Kapua," in her lively tie-dyed dress, was made by Ann Timmerman of Birmingham, Alabama.

"Granny Annie," just below "Kapua," is busy at the spinning wheel. Diana Martindale of Park City, Utah, is the proud artist.

"Kelly," the beautiful little girl with striking red hair at top right, is by Linda Henry. She's from Canal Winchester, Ohio.

"Peli" is an Amazon girl who just caught a frog. The artist is Hedy Katin of San Jose, California.

Hedy Katin is also the creator of "Muykul," the Aborigine hugging a koala.

Donna Schwellenbach's "Mist Princess" stands dignified in the mist with her flower basket at bottom right. Her home is Beloit, Wisconsin.

ACKNOWLEDGMENTS

So many people at Betterway Books contributed to the successful completion of *The Doll Sourcebook* that I could not name them all here. Special thanks go out to Amy Jeynes, the book's production editor; Tara Horton and Anne Bowling, who helped in more ways than I can count; designers Sandy Kent and Joan Heiob; and Anne Steely, Sharon Lee, Barb Brown, Michelle Frommeyer, Karen Gossage and others who typeset, proofread, and worked on the indexes.

David Borcherding, Alice Buening, Kristin Earhart and Cindy Laufenberg contributed interviews. Their time and effort made *The Doll Sourcebook* more interesting and lively.

Doll artists Christie Cummins, Mary Ellen Frank, Barb Giguere, Linda Henry, Joan Ibarolle, Hedy Katin, Ann Jackson, Diana Martindale, Cindy McClure, Karen Morley, Jill Nemirow-Nelson, Barbara Ogden, Jennifer Schmidt, Donna Schwellenbach, Ann Timmerman and Christina Wemmitt-Pauk generously allowed us to borrow their dolls to photograph them for the cover.

Thanks to expert contributors Susanna Oroyan, Carol-Lynn Rössel Waugh, Tracey Herring, Judith Whorton, Marnie Panek, Barb Giguere, Linda Henry, Christina Wemmitt-Pauk, Anna Mae Walsh Burke and Judy M. Johnson for their informative articles. Without their contributions, *The Doll Sourcebook* would never have been the diverse book that it is.

A very special thanks to consultants Barb Giguere, Linda Henry, Judy Johnson, Susanna Oroyan, Marnie Panek and Carol-Lynn Rössel Waugh for their tremendous contributions as consultants. They were with this project from its beginnings, giving suggestions on the table of contents and the industry questionnaires, gathering addresses for inclusion, and providing a great deal of insider information and support throughout the process. Without their contributions, *The Doll Sourcebook* would never have been published!

Finally, thanks to the more than 750 shop owners, antique doll dealers, artists, manufacturers, organizations, show organizers, museum directors and other doll enthusiasts who took the time to complete our detailed questionnaires for inclusion in *The Doll Sourcebook*. I have enjoyed getting to know so many of you at shows and over the phone, and have greatly appreciated your encouraging phone calls and notes. I hope this book is everything you imagined!

Argie Manolis
Editor
The Doll Sourcebook

Table of Contents

Welcome to The Doll Sourcebook! 1
BY JOHN FEY

Introduction for Doll Collectors 3
BY SUSANNA OROYAN

Introduction for Doll Artists 7
BY CAROL-LYNN RÖSSELL WAUGH

1 Retail Stores 13
* *A Guide to Chapter One* 14
* *Selling Your Dolls to Retail Stores* .15
  BY TRACEY HERRING
* *Retail Store Listings* 21

2 Antique Doll Dealers 40
* *A Guide to Chapter Two* 41
* *Collecting Antique German Dolls
  With Success* 42
  BY JUDITH WHORTON
* *Antique Doll Dealer Listings* 48
* *Auction Listings* 58

3 Supplies, Clothing and Accessories 60
* *A Guide to Chapter Three* 61
* *Choosing the Supplier that
  Best Suits Your Needs* 62
  BY MARNIE PANEK
* *Supplies, Clothing and Accessories
  Listings* 66

4 Doll Artists 95
* *A Guide to Chapter Four* 96
* *Marketing Yourself as Well as
  Your Dolls* 98
  BY BARB GIGUERE
* *Artist Listings* 104

5 Manufacturers 173
* *A Guide to Chapter Five* 174
* *From Artist to Designer:
  Working With Manufacturers* 175
  BY LINDA HENRY
* *Manufacturer Listings* 181

6 Shows 189
* *A Guide to Chapter Six* 190
* *Success on the Show Circuit* 191
  BY CHRISTINA WEMMITT-PAUK AND
  ANNA MAE WALSH BURKE
* *Show Promoter Listings* 198
* *Single Event Listings* 206
* *Exhibit Listings* 223

7 Organizations 224
* *A Guide to Chapter Seven* 225
* *Organization Listings* 226

8 Museums 239

- *A Guide to Chapter Eight* 240
- *Interview: Dorothy Tancraitor of the Yellow Brick Road Doll and Toy Museum.* 241
  BY ALICE P. BUENING
- *Interview: Sharon Smith of the Dolly Wares Doll Museum* 244
  BY KRISTIN EARHART
- *Museum Listings* 247

9 Paper Dolls 252

- *A Guide to Chapter Nine* 253
- *A Brief History of Paper Dolls* . . . 254
  BY JUDY M. JOHNSON
- *Interviews: Paper Doll Artists Today* 263
  BY JUDY M. JOHNSON
- *Paper Doll Publisher Listings* . . . 266
- *Paper Doll Dealer Listings* 266
- *Paper Doll Artist Listings* 269
- *Paper Doll Club Listings* 277
- *Paper Doll Publication Listings* . . 277

10 Additional Opportunities 280

- *A Guide to Chapter Ten.* 281
- *Interview: Jack Johnston* 282
  BY CINDY LAUFENBERG
- *Interview: Maryanne Oldenburg* . . 285
  BY DAVID BORCHERDING
- *Educational Listings* 287
- *Publication Listings* 295
- *Helpful Products and Services Listings.* 299

General Index 305

Geographical Index . 311

Brand Name Index 320

Supplies and Accessories Index . . . 325

*I*f you have ever loved a doll, this book is for you.

Maybe you have a childhood doll stored on a shelf in a hidden corner of your home, or paper dolls with dozens of costumes in a box in your closet. Perhaps you have been collecting for decades, with hundreds of dolls throughout your home. Maybe you've always wanted to make a doll or publish your paper doll sketches, but you don't know where to start. Perhaps you've been a doll artist for several years, designing and creating keepsakes meant to last a lifetime— and longer.

Regardless of your experience or skill level, if you love dolls, this book is for you. In it you will find all the resources you need if you collect or make dolls— or if you've always wanted to get started. *The Doll Sourcebook* includes more than 750 listings of retail stores; antique dealers; restoration and appraisal services; suppliers of materials, clothing and accessories for doll crafters and artists; doll artists; shows and exhibits; organizations; museums; paper doll resources; workshops; publications and much more. In addition, doll experts from across the continent share their knowledge of the world of dolls, providing friendly advice on everything from collecting antique dolls to building an image for yourself as a doll artist, from selling at retail stores to making the most of a doll show.

The Doll Sourcebook is perfect for beginning artists or collectors. Every resource beginners need to start a collection or a dollmaking business can be found among these pages. Experienced collectors and artists will find new resources here as well.

Betterway Books, the publisher of *The Doll Sourcebook,* is a part of F&W Publications, which also includes Writer's Digest Books, North Light Books and Story Press. F&W Publications has been providing directories for creative people for more than seventy-five years. *The Doll Sourcebook* is the latest addition to a line of twelve directories that includes *Writer's Market, Artist's and Graphic Designer's Market,* and, most recently, *The Teddy Bear Sourcebook.*

All of our directories, including *The Doll Source-book,* are all-inclusive. This means that listings are free, and that we do not take advertising. It also means that we are not necessarily endorsing a business by including them in this book. Rather, we want to make all possible resources available to you, allowing you to make the final decision about which businesses you will patronize, which shows you will attend, and which organizations you will join. Due to space constraints and the enormity of the doll industry, we have limited the listings to resources in the US and Canada. In addition, in certain cases where definitions were hazy, we have had to specify some requirements for inclusion in some chapters. In these cases, the requirements are described in the introductions that open each chapter.

This sourcebook was compiled by the editor as well as by consultants Barb Giguere, Linda Henry, Judy Johnson, Susanna Oroyan and Carol-Lynn Rössel Waugh. To compile the listings, we sent more than three thousand questionnaires to people and businesses who provide products and services for doll enthusiasts throughout the US and Canada. The more than ten different questionnaires, each aimed at a specific segment of the doll industry, were used to compile the information found in the detailed listings on these pages.

The Doll Sourcebook will be revised every two years. Some people and businesses may have been left out this time, either because they did not respond to the questionnaire mailed to them, or because we did not include them in the mailing. If you did not receive a questionnaire, I apologize. There will always be a few people missed in the first edition of any new directory. Please complete the form at the back of this book and mail it to me, and I will be sure to send you a questionnaire for the next edition. You can use the same form to share your comments with me. We are always looking for suggestions, as we want *The Doll Sourcebook* to be as useful and helpful as possible!

To make using this book simple, we have divided the listings by chapters for all the major segments of the doll industry. Each chapter starts with instructions on how to use the listings, and the listings are in alphabetical order in each chapter. In addition, there are four indexes at the back of the book to make your search simpler: a general index which includes all resources in the book, a geographical index divided by state or province, a brand name index to help you find a specific brand of doll, and a supplies and accessories index to help you find a specific type of supply.

For the sake of simplicity, we have used the following abbreviations throughout the book:

M = Monday, T = Tuesday, W = Wednesday, Th = Thursday, F = Friday, Sat = Saturday, Sun = Sunday.

SASE = self-addressed stamped envelope. An SASE should include 32 cents postage.

LSASE = large self-addressed stamped envelope. An LSASE should include four regular stamps, and should be at least 8½″ × 11″ in size.

b&w = black & white
AST = Atlantic Standard Time
EST = Eastern Standard Time
CST = Central Standard Time
MST = Mountain Standard Time
PST = Pacific Standard Time

Each listing is based on the information provided to us by the company or individual through the questionnaire. If a listing does not include a particular heading, it is because the business or person listed either did not offer any information about this on the questionnaire or does not offer the particular service or product. For instance, if a retail listing is missing the "modern manufactured doll" heading, it is because the shop does not carry modern manufactured dolls, or because the shop owner or manager did not include this information in the questionnaire they completed and returned to us.

We have no way of verifying if the information in the listing is correct. We have done everything possible to make sure these listings match the information provided to us by the business or individual. If you find that a business has supplied us with incorrect information, or if the information in a listing becomes outdated, please use the comment form at the back of this book to let us know!

We want to encourage you to consider proper business etiquette whenever you deal with a business or person listed in this book. Many people in the doll industry work out of their homes. All listings include information about the type of business—whether it is a mail order business, a business with a store location, or both. Pay careful attention to this before attempting to visit an address that is listed for mailing purposes only.

Unless an artist listing explicitly says that walk-ins are welcome, never drop in on an artist at home. (This may seem obvious, but I have heard of cases in which this actually happened!) Most artists do not have a selection of dolls on display at the address listed. Some artists do offer visits to their studios by appointment, but these appointments must be scheduled in advance.

In addition, if you are doing business or trying to get information over the phone, note the time zone listed directly after the phone number. Do not call or fax someone on the West Coast at 9 A.M. if you live on the East Coast—you'll probably wake them from a deep sleep! To be sure you are calling at a decent hour, check your telephone book for the hour differences between each time zone. Some listings include hours during which you may phone or fax. Others say only that phone and fax orders are "Available" or "Accepted." In either case, pay attention to the time zone.

When leaving a message, always leave your first and last name, address and phone number. Speak clearly, and include a brief message about the purpose of your call. Artists and those with home businesses often do not have the time or money to return long distance phone calls unless the call concerns an order. If you are calling to request a catalog or with a quick, simple question, leaving your address on an answering machine will make it easier for both you and the person you are calling.

I hope *The Doll Sourcebook* will bring you hours of pleasure as you read and re-read the articles and interviews on its pages and peruse the quotes scattered throughout the book. I also hope this book will eliminate the endless and often fruitless searches that all artists and collectors have gone through when trying to find that desperately needed supply or that perfect doll. Perhaps most importantly, I hope this book will make networking easier, putting you in touch with old and new friends who share your love of dolls!

Sincerely,

Argie G. Manolis

For Doll Collectors

BY SUSANNA OROYAN

Susanna Oroyan is one of the nation's best-known doll artists and collectors. She has been making dolls for more than twenty years. *Fantastic Figures,* published by Hobby House Press in 1994, is among the books she has written about dolls. She lives in Eugene, Oregon.

*W*hat makes us collect dolls? What is it that makes us dig for coins to pay for the rescue of a grim little figure buried in a thrift-shop bin? What makes our fingers tingle to hold a smiling baby doll or an elegant fashion lady figure?

It is, very simply, that dolls are small people. We identify with them. We love, appreciate and enjoy them because they represent us. A doll has the potential of being or becoming any aspect of the human condition, real or imagined.

A doll . . .

* can heal the sick and cheer the depressed
* can be your brother or sister
* can be your hero or heroine
* can make you soar with wings on flights of fancy
* can explore the outer limits, the extremes of the sublime and the ridiculous
* can make us laugh, cry, become angry or feel love
* can be a messenger of fashion trends
* can bring to life the pages of history
* can represent our ethnic backgrounds, festivals and holiday pastimes
* can demonstrate contemporary aesthetic interests
* can illustrate every stage of life from the innocence of childhood through the joys and frustrations of parenthood to the quiet reflection of old age.

Those who love and collect dolls share a common interest in the infinite variety of humanity. Just as we are social animals who like being surrounded with friends and family, once we get one or two dolls, we like to surround ourselves with more. And that's what makes us collectors!

Susanna Oroyan

A Long-Standing Hobby

Dolls, or representations of the human form and condition, have been with us since our beginnings. We see the doll form as religious sculpture, from small cult fetishes and charms to statuary in Greek and Roman temples to figures of Christian saints. We find the human form portrayed for purely aesthetic reasons in portrait sculpture in almost every culture. We see hints of the existence of the doll as a child's toy in forms found in Egyptian tombs and in the ash-covered remains of Pompeii. In the Middle Ages and early Renaissance, we see the play doll (then called a "baby") in the hands of children whose portraits were painted and in woodcuts showing dolls for sale in town markets. By the 1600s, we find fashion figures and mechanical mannequin toys being made for the amusement of well-to-do adults. At the same time, the Christmas crèche, or "Nativity scene," and the cabinet doll's house became popular for adult and family education and entertainment. All of these figures were individually handmade, usually from wood, wax, wire and cloth in various combinations. Some were made by watchmakers, some by dressmakers, and some by families for extra income.

All of these early dolls were separate phenomena. Although we would have no trouble considering any of these forms dolls, as late as the 1700s each type was considered to be a separate form made for a specific use. Some people may have owned more than one type; however, there does not seem to have been any element of collectibility associated with these figures in their times.

This rare closed-mouth Armand Marseille lady doll undoubtedly reflected the high fashion of the time.

The Industrial Revolution

What made these diverse items come together and form an area of collector interest? Several of the initial connections were made in the late eighteenth and early nineteenth centuries with the rapid expansion of industry and print communication.

Porcelain, which was an exotic Asian import prior to the nineteenth century, began to be made in Germany in 1710 after intensive experiments to perfect the formulas for clay mixtures and glazes. The process of using molds to mass-produce china was easily adapted to making china and porcelain doll parts—much easier work than carving individual figures of wood.

Spinning and weaving for cloth-making had been a labor-intensive home industry, but the Industrial Revolution changed this also. The speedy mechanized pro-

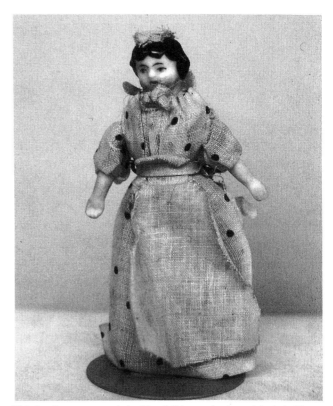

This low brow common hair china doll is wearing her original clothing.

duction methods introduced during this time made it possible to manufacture cheap cloth. Both homemakers and commercial interests could make cloth doll parts inexpensively.

The mechanized press and advancements in printing during the nineteenth century broadened the scope of communication, and this accelerated the growth of the doll industry too. Competing newspapers often printed paper dolls to attract readership. As it became feasible to print periodicals, the lady's fashion magazine emerged and had immediate success with patterns (including patterns for dolls) and paper toys for home use. Dolls printed on cloth yardage became available, ready for the homemaker to sew.

Finally, this same industrial expansion created a class of people who worked outside the home and off the farm, in either the factories that produced goods or the shops that sold them. This created a larger middle class that had hired household help, leisure time and a willingness to spend money on toys for their children. Even so, there were limits to what was considered acceptable for women to do, either at home or as businesspeople. Making dolls was a socially acceptable activity for leisure and for generating family income, and a few women such as Izannah Walker and Madame Montanari did develop dollmaking businesses.

The Birth of the Toy Industry

Many children still worked, often in far worse conditions in the factories than they had known previously at home in the city or on the farm. On the other hand, more middle-class children did not have to work. Instead of being considered small adults apprenticing with their parents in training for adult life, they were educated for professions or for domestic management and were given dolls and toys to fill their leisure time. For the first time in history, children, and their needs, became a market force. Manufacturers leapt to fill the void with books, toys and dolls created just for this market.

The result was that by the end of the Victorian era, the Western world had a very well-developed doll and toy industry. The middle-class nursery was filled with toys, and the more fortunate little girls had French or German dolls with extensive wardrobes. Even when family resources had to be watched carefully, mothers managed to save a quarter to buy a china head to make a doll, and children learned to salvage magazines to cut up for paper dolls. Almost every child born at the turn of the century had or wanted dolls, teddy bears and paper dolls. Mothers and grandmothers made dolls and even hired their dressmakers to sew for them.

From Toys to Collectibles

Very importantly for the development of doll collecting as a hobby, the Victorians were "keepers." They recycled their children's toys for their grandchildren and they kept them, either on display or in the attic, as memorabilia. Dolls and their related paraphernalia became collectibles when these children grew up. Adults either kept their old dolls or went searching in thrift shops to find the lost treasures of their childhoods. They found dolls, kept them for nostalgia, and then wanted to restore their treasures and learn more. By the 1940s, many of these early collectors began to organize themselves into doll-collecting clubs.

At the beginning of organized collecting, the major motivation was the "nostalgia factor"—the urge to find and preserve those dolls the collectors had as children. Fifty or more years ago, the dolls of the collector's childhood were the china and bisque dolls of the late nineteenth century. Today, the nostalgia factor reflects composition and vinyl dolls of the later twentieth cen-

This all-bisque Little Orphan comic character doll is an example of an early German doll.

tury. Nowadays, collectors recognize the value of preserving commercial and artistic production, and they purchase new dolls for posterity as soon as they arrive on the market.

The Magical Doll World

Those of us with an interest in dolls often refer to something called "the doll world." It sounds rather magical, and it is. Basically, the doll world is a loose network of all the people who create, care for and provide services for dolls. It encompasses collector and maker clubs, national organizations, commercial markets, retail sales, local doll shows, and services such as repair, costuming and accessories.

Because dolls represent people, it is easy for us to project them into a complete world of their own. They are "born" when a doll designer comes up with an idea and puts an assortment of miscellaneous materials together to bring a little person into tangible reality. They require a delivery system, and this is what we call the doll market. The doll market includes not only the large commercial world of international toy fairs, but also specialty shops and even mail-order businesses that operate from a dealer's dining table.

Dolls' needs, like people's, create systems: social, supply and educational. For instance, just as people need clothing, so do dolls. People with sewing experience, a love of fabric, and a desire to design become doll costumers. Those who like to teach provide books,

"Gertrude," a 24″ Paperclay doll by Susanna Oroyan, reflects the greater attempt by today's artists to represent a variety of ethnic and racial backgrounds through their work.

This 22″ Paperclay doll by Susanna Oroyan is named "The Doll Peddler." She reflects the wide range of life stages that can be captured by a doll.

lectures, publications and even symposia for learning and sharing doll information—a school system, if you will. The medical system, of course, is where preventive health maintenance, doll repair and restoration take place. Then, dolls may need adoption or reach retirement. This creates a whole system for marketing dolls that need to be moved into new homes—the secondary market, or the antique and collectible market. Dolls also need furnishings and accessories, and supply systems for these exist, too.

Do dolls need libraries, record keeping and accounting? Certainly. Specialized books and computer programs have been developed just to satisfy the doll collector's needs. How much is it worth? That question needs to be asked when a collectible goes on the market or a purchase is considered. We have auctions, price guides, dealers and appraisers to help us determine value. And then, dolls have their own "toys," too. The playability of teddy bears, miniatures and paper dolls makes those items just as enticing to the doll collector.

Accessing the Doll World

How does the collector access this world? As recently as twenty years ago, finding a key to open the door to the doll world was not easy. Only a dozen or so books on dolls existed—perhaps only one or two of which were in print and on bookstore shelves. A good library might have had a half dozen on the shelf. There were two or three non-newsstand doll publications, and one was available only to members of doll clubs. There were doll collector clubs, but unless they became "news" in the papers, where they met was a mystery. Nowadays, the collector who wants information can find doll publications on the magazine racks, and this usually becomes the first port of entry to the collecting world. However, the major part of the doll world is still made up of individual producers and suppliers. Only a small percentage of doll collector services and suppliers advertise in the periodicals. Today's collector likes "one-stop" shopping and easy access to information, and that is what this book provides.

Stepping into the doll world is just like stepping into a magical world. This book will help you take that step and keep you going through many hours of enjoyable collecting! ❧

For Doll Artists

BY CAROL-LYNN RÖSSEL WAUGH

Carol-Lynn Rössel Waugh has been creating original dolls and teddy bears for more than twenty years. Along with Susanna Oroyan, she co-authored *A Collector's Guide to Contemporary Artist Dolls,* published by Hobby House Press in 1986. She lives in Winthrop, Maine.

When you were a tot, did you "X" off the days till birthdays, Christmas or Hanukkah because you knew you'd be getting the thing you loved best—a doll?

Did dolls transport you to faraway times and fantasies?

Do they work that magic today?

This book is for you. As you leaf through its pages, you'll find almost anything a doll lover, artist or shop owner could want. Think of it as your phone book, "wish book" and passport to the world of dollmaking and collecting.

Like other passions, "doll love" seems to bypass the brain, targeting a bull's-eye in the heart. If this is the way dolls affect you, the best way to digest this book is in small bites. Nibble at a section on a subject you know. You'll find familiar names and sources plus a bundle of tempting new treats. There's enough new information here to offer a gourmet "read" to even the most experienced doll lover. If you arc a collector who has always wanted to make dolls, one of the most exciting discoveries you will find in this book may be the people who make art dolls and the suppliers who offer all the materials you need to create a handmade treasure. If you are an experienced doll artist, you will find new suppliers and hundreds of new marketing opportunities to fine-tune your business.

A History of Dolls as Art

If you are or want to be a doll artist, you are in good company. How long have doll artists been around? One could say forever. Every doll ever made, either by a commercial firm or in the home, had to be designed by someone. Sometimes one artist designed the doll;

Carol-Lynn Rössel Waugh

usually a team of artists worked together. But it wasn't until the early twentieth century that names of doll designers in the commercial world wcrc publicized. The first well-known American doll artist/designer of the twentieth century was Grace S. Putnam, who sculpted the famous "Bye-Lo Baby" doll, which was reproduced from her work by a firm in Germany in the early 1900s. Thirty years later, Dewees Cochran was the first high-profile American doll designer to create a line of dolls for an American doll company, Effanbee. These dolls were such a revolution that they made the cover of *Time* magazine just before America's involvement in World War II made their production impractical.

Notable among America's early noncommercial doll artists were Dorothy Heizer, Muriel Bruyere and Gertrude Florian, who worked in the 1930s, 1940s and 1950s. Their output was outstanding, setting a high standard for the doll art field. During the 1950s, more artists began to make dolls as art, doing their own sculptures and producing them in doll form.

Doll Artists' Organizations Are Born

At the end of the 1950s, a handful of artists formed the National Institute of American Doll Artists (NIADA). Magge Head Kane and Helen Bullard worked against great odds to establish recognition for original doll art, and it is because of their work through NIADA that the public began to be aware of the concept of doll art.

During the 1960s, doll artists were still scarce. In the early 1970s, artists in other media began discovering dolls as a focus. This explosion of interest probably had its roots in the crafts revival of the 1960s and early 1970s, which promoted originality and creativity and rejected mass-marketed plastic goods. Much of the crafts movement was based on the West Coast, and many early dollmakers worked there. The "something in the wind" infecting Californians began touching folks all over the continent. Newborn doll artists throughout the world began experimenting—most in isolation. They needed a way to communicate, sources of supplies, and support.

By 1975, two more United States dollmakers' organizations were in operation: the Original Doll Artists Council of America (ODACA) and the International Doll Makers' Association (IDMA). Dollmakers began to have conventions, shows, seminars, classes and impressive displays of their work. At this time, prices for increasingly scarce antique dolls took a tenfold leap. Collectors began seeing in the original art doll the collectible of the future.

Artist-Designed Dolls Become Popular

Beginning in 1978, commercial companies began using the talents of independent artists to sell name artist editions. The original doll had, by 1995, "come of age" in the collector's world. Between 1985 and 1995, many commercial firms tapped doll artists to design dolls. These firms ranged from direct-mail mints to agents working for television shopping channels. Most of these dolls are produced in sizeable editions under contract with the artist who created the doll. Some are produced under contracts that allow the artist little feedback or control. Some credit the doll to a two-dimensional artist whose work served to inspire a ghost artist, whose untold name is sometimes well-known.

These dolls have played a large role in the popularity of doll collecting today. Those selling these dolls have a hand in the general public's misunderstanding of doll terminology, however. Their advertisements give the impression that each of the ten thousand dolls in an exclusive "limited edition" was hand-signed by the person sculpting (or "inspiring") the doll's head. While these dolls are certainly collectible and often of very good quality, they are not truly art dolls, but artist-designed dolls. Every collector should recognize the difference.

By the early 1990s, new materials became available to doll artists. Some artists began subcontracting the production of their editions to technicians specializing in vinyl or resin casting. Some put these parts onto ready-made bodies, creating a new category of product: the artist-designed, artist-assembled doll. This doll is technically not an artist original doll. Lines between categories began blurring. No wonder the buying public was getting confused!

Rosalind Golden—"Goldie"—is a 29″ original by Carol-Lynn with a porcelain swivel head, hands and feet and an armatured cloth body.

Some Definitions for Doll Artists and Collectors

You say you're new at all this, and all the doll terms I've been using confuse you? You're not alone. Doll enthusiasts argue about them. In the early 1970s, everyone who made dolls was called a dollmaker. Today, people who make dolls are called "doll artists," "artisans," "designers" and "reproduction artists." So, what is a doll artist? What's the difference between an "original doll" and an "artist original?" How about an "artist-designed original?" Since knowing these sound-alike terms can save you money, not to mention saving your reputation in the doll world, here are some definitions. You might find yourself—or your dolls—among them.

Dollmakers

A *dollmaker* is anyone who makes dolls. The dolls can be of any material, from any source. They can be sewn using a pattern or design invented by the dollmaker or one bought in a five-and-ten. They can use parts purchased at a craft shop or whittled by the fire. The word "dollmaker" is a one-size-fits-all, generic term.

Artist Originals

Doll artists, on the other hand, are those who create original dolls. They design and sculpt or make the entire doll, including the head and body. Some doll artists also design and make the clothing, wig and accessories, although these may also be made by someone else or purchased ready-made. The types of dolls created by doll artists vary, as do the artists' roles in the dolls' production. The doll artist's creation is called an *artist original*, or sometimes an "original doll artist doll." Some people use the term "artist original" to refer to anything from one-of-a-kind to mass-produced dolls, as long as somewhere along the line, some artist was connected with the doll. But this term has a specific, important meaning. An artist original has been designed and made completely by the artist. No part of the doll comes from any source but the artist's brain and hands.

Doll artists making artist originals do not use patterns or molds invented by someone else. They do not remake someone else's design or use a mold of an antique doll. They do not use a casting (greenware) from a commercially available mold and re-paint it or re-wig it or re-dress it or put a new body on it and call it original. It is not. An artist original has to be completely original.

One should not design a new face and put it onto a composition or latex or fabric body from a doll supply company and call it an original doll. What you have is an original head, not an original doll.

Sunnie Andress's "Prudence Kotten Bathing" is a nylon needle sculpture doll on muslin.

Tweaking

Sometimes dollmakers buy a mold, cast it, remove the casting from the mold and then proceed to change the features on the greenware, figuring this is an easy way to achieve originality. It is not. What you have is an altered head from somebody else's mold. Anybody who knows anything about dolls will recognize it for what it is. This procedure is called *tweaking* and is one of the most dishonest, reprehensible things a so-called "designer" can do. It's illegal, and prosecutable. To knowing collectors, such dolls are not the cute transformations their makers believe. They are exercises in deception and as far from "original" as one can get.

Manufactured Designs

Sometimes, a doll artist chooses not to make duplicates of a sculpture or a cloth design herself. She prefers others, either a commercial company or apprentices or workers in her studio, to make duplicates. In this case, the artist is really a *designer*. Sometimes, the doll she designs never gets beyond the prototype stage before it is given to others for completion. A *prototype* is a model designed as a sample for other pieces to be copied from, usually for mass production. This model can be sculpted or sewn, and may be accompanied by a pattern if the doll is cloth. In this case, the original is the *artist's prototype* or *proof*. Dolls designed by doll artists for commercial production often reach only the sculpture stage—in wax or clay or, perhaps, fabric—in the studio. They are then produced by someone other than the artist/designer for public consumption in another medium, perhaps vinyl, porcelain or resin. Everything afterwards reproduced from the artist's original design is a *manufactured doll*. A manufactured doll should faithfully attempt to copy the original artist's intent—to reproduce it exactly as designed.

Sometimes the designer has full control over the final product's looks, but this seldom is the case. Depending on the contract, the manufacturer buying the artist's design may have great freedom to change the sculpture or painting or costuming. A manufacturer's reproduction of a doll artist's design often varies from the artist's intention; it may look nothing like the prototype. Sometimes the artist just sculpts the head. The limbs, body, painting and costuming may be the work of an uncredited design team. The quality of the doll may suffer if it is reproduced in huge editions.

In effect, each doll produced this way is a *reproduction doll* or *repro*. Usually we think of porcelain dolls and antiques when we talk of repros. But there are doll artists who only design repro dolls for commercial mold makers. There are famous doll designers who sometimes let mold makers offer their designs to crafters via molds in sizes different from the originals handmade by the artist. We call dolls from these molds *reproductions*. In no way can the crafter who makes these dolls from mold-poured greenware say they're "originals," even if she changes the painting or costuming or sculpting in the mold (this, again, is called "tweaking").

There has been a lot of discussion and disagreement—to put it mildly—about reproduction dollmaking and the freedom the reproductionist should be allowed. Look at the word. A reproduction is an attempt to copy someone else's work line for line. It is an exercise in trying to make things look like an already available example. Reproductions allow buyers to own, at reasonable cost, products of highly skilled artists. Sometimes these dolls are superb, sensitive statements. But there is no such thing as an "original reproduction." That is an oxymoron.

Doll Artisans

Most doll artists could never make enough originals to pay the rent; their patience with repetition is limited. This is why the *doll artisan* is important. Artisans are skilled craftspeople who delight in bringing to life dolls designed by others. They are reproductionists who usually work on designs created by contemporary doll artists, often under direct supervision.

Sometimes the group of artisans making an artist's edition is small. It can be a family affair. The degree of supervision artists give varies. It may be an apprenticeship situation, where an artisan learns techniques from the artist by helping to complete parts of his work. This situation is usually called a *collaboration*, and works out well, especially when an artist creates many designs and wants to make a small number of duplicates of each. Sometimes the apprentice-collaborator has special skills he contributes to the final design. This is the case when one person designs the doll and another dresses it. Such a doll cannot be called an artist original; it is not done by one artist. It is an *original collaboration*, even though the doll itself may be original. It should always be marked as such. Collaboration and apprenticeship are special, intimate opportunities for people to create artistic products, and one of the best ways to ensure that the skills of dollmaking are passed on.

Whatever role the artist has in dollmaking, she should be proud of the work she does, and that work should be given credit. Dolls should be signed. Clothing should be labeled with the designer's and the artisan's or craftsman's name or marked for future reference. Doll lovers of the future will want to know who created their treasures when these become "doll history."

Mainstream Acceptance

Unfortunately, the mainstream art world takes a different view from that of doll lovers. Doll art falls through cracks in its power structure. Much of the "legitimate art society" has never heard the term "doll artist," and, when introduced to it, dismisses it probably because of unfamiliarity. One never studies doll art in art history or studio classes. In addition, doll art combines so many media, so many techniques, it's hard to classify. Then there's the "toy syndrome." Dolls are toys—functional objects—aren't they? How can they be fine art? Where

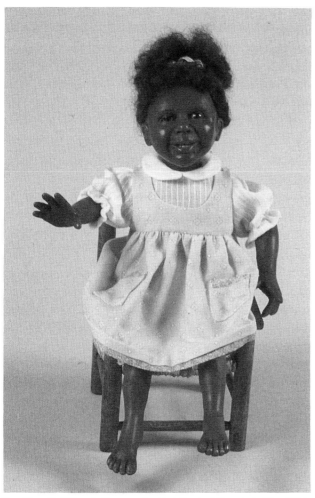

Pam Hamel's "Georgia," a one-of-a-kind Cernit doll made in May 1994, has a mohair wig and Glastic eyes.

Barbara Giguere's 28″ one-of-a-kind porcelain doll "Tracey" is an example of a portrait doll. Tracey wears a satin dress with lace and is a portrait of Barb's daughter on prom night.

and how would museums and galleries display them, anyway?

In Western art traditions, the doll has never been considered an art object. Yet in Japan, dollmaking is a revered art form. Doll artists are government-honored as living national treasures.

A doll artist's acceptance by the art world has a lot to do with how closely the work resembles what's shown by mainstream artists. Galleries look for new expressions or avant-garde work. They want pieces that cause controversy, creating sales and publicity. They stick with what has done well for them and what they understand. Most doll artists' work, running the gamut of artistic experiences and intentions, is alien and, at the same time, too tame.

By the mid-1990s, galleries in New York, in Chicago and on the West Coast successfully showcased art dolls as "art." With art doll auction prices rising, and the establishment of a couple of high-profile doll art museums, the field looks rosier now than it did in the mid-

1980s. This is leading to today's onslaught of "wanna-be" doll artists who imagine making dolls is a ticket to a seat on the next gravy train.

The Gravy Train

It doesn't work that way. Countless "doll artists" have come and gone (mostly gone). Those entering the doll world with dollar signs in their eyes neither last nor produce salable products. Why? What they make has no heart. Good dolls come from inspiration, from love, from an irrepressible need to create. If you don't have a mixture of talent and absolute passion for making dolls (and a bit of crazy blind faith), forget about entering the doll marketplace. Whatever you do, no matter how technically perfect it might be, won't sell. Buyers want a part of your emotions, a part of your soul. This is what gives your work life, what gives your buyers hope and dreams and something to pour love into: a doll is "a vessel for their souls."

So, You Still Want to Be a Doll Artist?

If you're convinced that, even if you're not going to make your bundle this way, you *must* make original dolls, this is *the* book—the bible, the encyclopedia—written for you. I wish that a book like this had been available when I began designing dolls in 1972.

If you're a beginner, I envy you. You have in your hands an overload of expertise and inspiration. Here you will find suppliers for everything from clay to wigs, eyes to fabric. If you want to learn more about the doll world or improve your skills, you will find books, magazines, videos and workshops listed here to help you. If you are selling your dolls—whether you're a new artist or a veteran—you will find shows and shops espe-cially for eager doll collectors who want to purchase artist dolls. Best of all, you will find organizations that give you the opportunity to network with other doll-makers and artists, so you don't go crazy on those long, gray February days when you're trying to make that mold all by yourself!

So brew yourself a cup of fragrant tea. Settle down in a cozy chair next to your favorite doll and begin paging through this book. I guarantee it'll become a favorite pastime and resource. Newcomer or old-timer, doll collector or dollmaker, the answers to your doll-making questions and quandaries are now just a page turn away!

1

Retail
Stores

A Guide to Chapter One

*I*n this chapter you will find listings of retail businesses that sell dolls. These businesses include the doll shops you already love that are filled with treasures from your favorite artists and manufacturers. They also include businesses that deal only in mail order. We have limited the businesses on these pages to those that deal solely or mostly in dolls. There are many shops, including galleries, toy stores and craft shops, that carry one or two manufacturers' lines or a few artists' creations. Due to space constraints, we could not have listed all of these businesses.

If you are a doll collector, it is to your advantage to buy from shops that specialize in selling dolls. After all, the owners of such shops are usually doll lovers themselves and can be wonderful resources. If you are interested in purchasing a certain manufactured or artist doll, and there is no store listed here in your area that carries that doll, you can use the listings in chapters four and five to contact the artist or manufacturer directly. They will be able to tell you if a shop in your area that is not listed here carries their product. Some manufacturers and artists sell their dolls directly to the customer, although it is always simpler to purchase from a local shop if one is available.

This chapter can also be used to find shops while you are traveling. Are you going to a show in another city, state or province? Why not check the geographical index to find the shops in that area, and visit them while you are there? Visits to doll shops are always fun additions to family vacations as well. Remember to call first if you are traveling a long distance to visit a shop. While we have tried to be as accurate as possible, hours are bound to change, and it is not uncommon for a shop to change locations. Please let us know if something is inaccurate. Use the comment form at the back of the book.

Finally, if you are a doll artist, you can use these listings to find businesses that might be interested in selling your work. Tracey Herring's article that follows will give you tips on how to choose the shops that are perfect for your work and how to go about contacting them.

The Listings

The listings in this chapter include the following information: the name of the business, location and contact information, business hours, year the business was founded, and information on the products the business carries. Each business had the opportunity to list the ten most popular or unique modern manufactured doll brands, retired manufactured doll brands and artist dolls they carry.

In addition, detailed business information is included. The "Type of business" heading will tell you whether the business has a store location, is mail order only, or offers both. Methods of payment accepted and policies on layaway, return/exchange and back orders are all included. In addition, if the shop has a catalog or price list, a description of this literature as well as how to get it is listed. Finally, if the shop allows phone, fax or mail orders, details about how these orders are handled are included. If the shop did not provide such details, but does accept these types of orders, the listing will simply say that such orders are "Accepted."

We hope this chapter expands your avenues for collecting and selling! ❧

Selling Your Dolls to Retail Stores

BY TRACEY HERRING

Tracey Lynne Herring was born into an artistic family, giving her a lifelong exposure to the arts and marketing. She grew up on the coast of southern Maine and was educated at the University of Maine and at Johns Hopkins University. Tracey has received several awards for her writing and has been published in several periodicals. In the doll world, Tracey has acted as judge and consultant, with emphasis on show presentations and advertising. She also makes dolls and teddy bears.

*S*o, you're doing something right with your dollmaking. You're attending shows, making sales, taking some orders. You even have a few local shops interested in your work. Perhaps some have bought your dolls. The local public likes what you do. You see the joy, the love, the connection that the collectors have with your creations. But you want more! You want to reach beyond your neighborhood and expand your customer base. Herein lies the big question— *how*? How do you reach the retailers who will buy your dolls, those who aren't in your backyard?

Advantages to Selling Wholesale

There are several avenues you can take to attract new retail stores, and through them, new collectors. But first, you need to know what to expect. Retail sales differ from wholesale sales in several ways. When you sell your doll directly to a collector, you sell that doll at a *retail* price. When you sell to a retail shop, they're buying your dolls so that they can sell them to collectors at a profit. Therefore, you're going to sell your work to the retail shop at a *wholesale* price. This of course means selling to the retail shop for less than you would if you were selling directly to the collector. After all, a retailer is not going to buy your dolls at full retail price and in turn mark the price up so that he makes a profit. No collector would buy from a shop when they could purchase the same doll directly from the artist for less.

You may be asking yourself, "Why should the retailer make 30, 40 or even 50 percent of the retail price

Tracey Herring

when I am the one who put time and dollars into creating each doll?" You must understand that the money the retailer puts out for your dolls will not be his sole investment in your work. The shop owner has several expenses tied up in your dolls. Besides the initial investment, there are costs associated with advertising and mail orders, shipping and handling costs, and displaying your dolls in their shops and at shows. When these costs are taken on by the retailer, you save both time and money, giving you more of both to do what you do best—make dolls! There are other risks involved for the retailer as well. The doll could be broken, even stolen. Keep in mind that the retailer must make a profit from the sale of your creations or there is no incentive for him to purchase from you. Remember that it costs money to make money. Also, keep in mind that you are striving toward a goal. If what you want is to reach a greater number of collectors with your dolls, then sharing profits with a retailer seems a small price to pay for the opportunity and the exposure.

How Do You Price Your Dolls?

You want to make money selling your dolls, whether you are selling them at wholesale or retail. But how can you be sure you're not losing money? You must recoup your investment and, of course, you want to make something for your time. The Executive Director of the Maine Society of Doll and Bear Artists, Barb Giguere, recommends that beginning artists use the following formula when pricing their dolls. Add the costs of all items you used to make each doll, using full retail prices only (*even if* you paid less). Include the cost for a normal-size spool of thread for each color you used—remember, if you didn't already have a color you needed, you'd have had to buy it! (You should not actually be paying full retail prices for materials such as eyes, wigs, fiberfill, armatures, fabric, etc. Instead you should be buying from sources that give discounts to original artists.) Total these expenses. Multiply the total by three for your minimum wholesale price. Multiply the same total by five for your minimum retail price. Using full retail prices for your materials, as opposed to the price you actually paid, adds in your per-hour earnings. The more dolls you make, the more time-efficient you become. You should be able to work faster as each step becomes more routine.

Who Are the Retailers, and How Do You Find Them?

Once you know what to expect, familiarize yourself with the different retailers. This requires that you do some homework. Who are the retailers? What do they sell? What are their price ranges? How do they attract their customers? What is their customer base? These are all important questions. Where do you begin? The answer is really quite simple. Begin with this book. Let it be your lifeline. Read through the pages and you'll find that the answers to many of your questions are right in front of you. Next, look to the various doll magazines. Three major publications are *Contemporary Doll Collector, Doll Reader* and *Dolls—The Collector's Magazine*. These magazines, and others, are listed in chapter ten, along with advertising information. Study these magazines.

Retailers advertise, and this is a good way to familiarize yourself with who's who and see each shop's advertising style and format. If a shop specializes in high-end play dolls or Barbie dolls, and you are making only artist originals, then this obviously would not be your market. Along these same lines, if a retailer sells only

artist originals priced in the $500 range, and your dolls retail for considerably more, this is also not the shop for your dolls. The retail listings in this chapter also provide information on the types of dolls each shop sells.

It is vital for you as the artist to target the right market. Your dolls must fit with what the retailer sells, as well as the price range in which the retailer deals. If your dolls don't fit, then they won't sell in that shop. The doll will become shopworn (remember, your work always represents you!). The shop owner will become frustrated, perhaps blaming you because the doll didn't sell. No one wins in this scenario.

How Do the Retailers Attract Their Customers?

Once you have decided what market best fits your needs, ask yourself how the various retailers attract prospective collectors. Do they use photographs in their ads? If so, are they full-page or small, color or black-and-white? Is there a single photo per ad, or are there several photos with each ad? Are the names of the dolls, the artists' names and the prices included with the photos? How do you want your dolls to be advertised? Again, these are all important questions. You want the coverage that is going to best sell you as well as your dolls. You want advertising that pleases *you*.

Reaching the Retailers

Now that you've targeted your market, how are you going to reach those retailers? Whom do you contact? You're going to need names. Most of the listings in this chapter include the name of the best person to contact. You want to reach the person in charge, the store owner. You will not get the desired results if you end up dealing with an employee whose sole responsibility is to ring up purchases. Find out who makes the buying decisions for each shop. Other doll artists can be helpful in this area. They may also be able to give you advice based on their own experience, such as which shops are better to approach. Record these names in a reference file specifically for retailers. This file can be a folder or series of folders, or one of the many databases available that can be customized to meet your needs. Use proper names in all correspondence rather than generalized salutations.

Corresponding With Retailers

Once you have established a list of store owners with whom you think you would like to do business, it is

Lisa Messier of Forever Dolls uses a consistent and easily recognized style for her advertisements. This ad, from *Dolls—The Collector's Magazine,* includes clear photographs with the artist's name under each photo. The doll's name and important facts, such as medium and one-of-a-kind or edition size, are also included. All photos are head shots, giving a uniform look to the advertisement.

time to decide how to reach them. One option is the telephone. This, however, may not be your best choice, since a store owner cannot see your work over the phone. Also, you may not have the owner's full attention if there are customers in the shop or another telephone line is ringing. Another option is to travel directly to these shops. This gives you the opportunity to see firsthand how the shop owner displays other artists' work. You meet the retailer face to face, and you can present your dolls in person. However, it is quite costly and time-consuming to travel across the country, even across the state, to meet with buyers. Unless you have the time and the resources, this probably isn't your best choice either.

Consider direct mail as a means of reaching retailers. This route will probably give you the greatest payback for the least amount of money. When using direct mail, you should start with a letter of introduction explaining who you are and what you are offering. Include two to four good-quality, clear photos showing samples of your dolls.

Be sure to show the range of your abilities. For example, do you make only babies or toddlers, or do you make adult dolls as well? Be sure to include the doll's name, medium, height, edition size, price and any other information that makes the doll unique. Tell the shop owner you'll follow up with a phone call (the telephone is more useful *after* the retailer has photos of your work in hand). A sample letter of introduction is shown on page 19.

It is a good practice to keep records of which photos you sent to each retailer, perhaps in your retailer files. Follow up with a phone call approximately two weeks later. Repeat the process about one month after that, being sure to include pictures of other examples of your dolls. You always want the retailers to have a good representation of your very best work. And remember, it's the squeaky wheel that gets the grease. You may also want to get referrals from other artists or retailers. Just because one retailer doesn't have the right collector base for your dolls doesn't mean that he doesn't know of another dealer whose collector base would be a perfect fit.

Magazine Advertisements

Placing your own ads in magazines is another alternative. This method presents your work to both retailers and collectors who might show your ads to the owner of their favorite shop. It would be wise to add the notation

Avoid common mistakes when taking promotional photographs of your dolls. There is a distinct shadow behind the doll, poor tone, and glare on the front of the costume. This looks like a mug shot!

This photograph of Barb Giguere's "India" (one in an edition of 25) is an example of a good photo. Details are easy to spot because there is adequate contrast between the background and the doll. There are no shadows.

"Dealer Inquiries Invited" to your ad. Also, be sure to list specifics such as the doll's name, height, medium and price. The drawback here is that advertising can be quite costly. You must continue to purchase ad space, or your name and your dolls run the risk of being forgotten once the next issue is out.

What About Trade Shows?

Trade shows are open only to retailers. The public is rarely permitted to attend, and if they do, they cannot buy. The best-known trade show is The American International Toy Fair, presented in New York City each February by the Toy Manufacturers of America. Nearly every artist has dreams of attending this show, yet few can comprehend the enormity of the facility and the number of exhibitors. Remember, this is first and foremost a toy show, not a doll show. Toys of every kind from around the world are presented here. Everything from the inexpensive bubble-packaged toys found at checkout counters to high-end educational toys are of-fered here. Booths range from simple tabletop displays to elaborate, larger-than-life-size toy buildings.

Another trade show is the International Doll Exposition (IDEX), held each January in Arlington, Texas. This show is a wholesale doll show. The shop owners have only dolls and bears to look at—no fighting their way to a crowded booth to discover that the vendor is offering the latest whirligig.

Considering Costs

Participating in shows is costly, but it's an excellent way to present your work to the greatest number of shop owners from across the country at one time. Show expenses are not limited to the cost of booth rentals. Back drapes, side drapes, tables, table covers, risers, lighting and even chairs can each be added expenses.

When considering this type of show, realize that you will be transporting your dolls from your studio to the show site. How will you be traveling to the show? Can you take your dolls with you or will you have to ship

Dear (Shop owner's name):

Perhaps you have read the Closing Comments article about me published in the November issue of *Dolls* magazine. One of my collectors asked me to send you photos of my dolls. I have always believed this is one of the best recommendations! I'm enclosing photos of two of my newest dolls.

Amy is a young girl from the 1940s ready for her first day of school. She stands 22″ tall and has hand-blown glass eyes, an auburn mohair wig and artist-made leather shoes. Her clothing was made from vintage fabrics. She is one of a porcelain edition of ten. Amy's wholesale price is $450.

Zachary is a 24″ one-of-a-kind Cernit doll. His hazel paperweight eyes sparkle with anticipation of his first overnight camping trip. I made his blond human hair wig and his outfit. His wholesale price is $990.

I'll call you in about two weeks to see if you're interested in placing my work in your shop. I look forward to talking with you soon.

Sincerely,

(Artist's signature here)

A sample letter of introduction from a doll artist to a retail shop. See pages 16-17 for tips on contacting retailers.

Sallie Jean
25"

Christie Cummins Dolls
one-of-a-kind porcelain
714·843·6734

Doll artist Christie Cummins believes that the doll should command the advertising space. She writes over the photo, letting the doll be the focus, not the frill.

them? Where will you stay? How much will you spend on food and lodging? Will you be able to walk or take a free shuttle from your hotel to the show location each day, or must you also include the cost of public transportation or cabs?

Gather these figures, total them and then talk to artists who have exhibited at these shows. Get their input. You can benefit from networking in every aspect of this industry. Do you know an artist with an umbrella organization where you could present your dolls at a more reasonable cost? If you can possibly attend a show before making your decision, you will learn much valuable information. I cannot emphasize enough just how different a trade show is from a retail show. The expenses are far greater for these shows as well. I'm not trying to discourage you, just listing the things you should consider to make an informed decision. You're turning your avocation into a vocation. That means you're now a businessperson with full responsibility for how well your business runs.

Focusing Your Efforts

There are distinct advantages to selling wholesale as opposed to retail, although the price per item is lower. When you are making your dolls to fill an order, each doll has already been sold. You can develop micro-manufacturing techniques that fit your studio space and the dolls you make to reduce the time involved in each doll. Less time means you can get more dolls completed. Your efforts are more focused. You're selling the items you're making, and your bank account should reflect this—as will the smile on your face! ❧

Retail Stores

THE ALCOVE

1801 Shell Beach Rd.
Shell Beach, CA 93449
Phone: For orders: (800)438-9527
For info: (805)773-3563
Fax: (805)773-9744
Hours: M-Sat, 10-5. Sun, 10-4 (extended summer hours).
In business since: 1991

PRODUCT INFORMATION:

Modern manufactured dolls: About 15 brands, including Ruth Treffeisen, Helen Kish, Seymour Mann, Daddy's Long Legs, Annette Himstedt, Barbie (Mattel), Susan Wakeen—Georgetown

Retired manufactured dolls: Daddy's Long Legs, Helen Kish, Ruth Treffeisen, sigikid, Barbie

Artist dolls: Mary Shaeffer, Virginia Keith, Alexandra, Linda Gill

Special orders: Special orders require ½ down and balance on delivery. Custom-designed (special clothing or resemblance) orders require additional charge depending on work involved.

Related products: Doll furniture, doll display cabinets, doll clothing

BUSINESS INFORMATION:

Type of business: Dolls sold at store location and by mail

Accepts: Cash, check, money order, Visa, MC, DC, AE

Discounts: On Tuesdays, seniors (over 55) get a 10% discount. On Thursdays, juniors (under 55) get a 10% discount.

Layaway: ⅓ down, 3-6 payments (depending on amount). Special terms arranged by request. No refunds.

Return/exchange policy: No return or exchange on sale items. No return on mail order items without authorization number. A 15% restocking fee will be charged (after 3 days).

Back order policy: Back orders continue for a maximum of 6 months unless cancelled by manufacturers or customer.

Price list: Free

Mailing list: Call or write to be included

Phone orders: Anytime on order line

Fax orders: Include name, delivery address (no P.O. box), telephone number, credit card number and expiration date. Will hold product a maximum of 2 weeks for check or money order.

Mail orders: Will ship to US, Canada, overseas. Include name, address (no P.O. Box please), telephone number, credit card number or method of payment. Prepayment required, or COD.

Shipping information: Prepayment is required. Please add $6 per doll for shipping. Dolls shipped via UPS or method preferred by customer. Allow 3-6 weeks for delivery.

ADDITIONAL INFORMATION:

The Alcove has scheduled signings by artists. Holds special drawings at Christmas and holidays. Private sales to doll clubs are available. Arrangements should be made at least 2 weeks in advance.

ANGIE'S DOLL BOUTIQUE, INC.

Lynne Reid or Frankie Lyles
1114 King St.
Alexandria, VA 22314
Phone: (703)683-2807 EST
Hours: T-Sat, 11-5:30.
In business since: 1976

PRODUCT INFORMATION:

Modern manufactured dolls: About 15 brands, including Alexander, Hamilton, Götz, Annette Himstedt, Vogue Ginny, Dynasty, Seymour Mann, Kingstate, Mattel (Barbies), Daddy's Long Legs, Georgetown, Delton

Retired manufactured dolls: Alexander, Daddy's Long Legs, Vogue Ginny

Artist dolls: Sonja Hartman, Annette Himstedt, Karen Germany, Robert Tonner, Ping Lau, Chris Malone

Special orders: ⅓ of the payment is required and nonrefundable if client changes mind. Balance due upon receipt. 30 days minimum.

Related products: Antique dolls, reproductions

BUSINESS INFORMATION:

Type of business: Dolls sold at store location.

Accepts: Cash, check, money order, Visa, MC, DC, AE

Return/exchange policy: Store credit only

Mailing list: Write to be included.

Phone orders: Call during business hours.

Mail orders: Will ship to US. Prepayment is required.

Shipping information: Shipped via FedEx or UPS, whichever the customer prefers. Allow 4-6 weeks for delivery.

ADDITIONAL INFORMATION:

Special features: This store offers two annual sales: the Christmas in July sale and the Christmas sale from November 1-December 31. Both feature savings of 20-60% off.

ANNA'S COLLECTIBLES

920 Walnut St.
Philadelphia, PA 19107
Phone: (215)627-2900 EST
Fax: (609)667-4241
Hours: Oct.-June: T-F, 9:30-5:30. Sat, 9:30-4. July-Sept.: M-F, 9:30-5:30.

PRODUCT INFORMATION:

Modern manufactured dolls: About 12 brands, including Barbies, Alexander, Ashton-Drake, Daddy's Long Legs, Annalee, Middleton, Seymour Mann and more

Retired manufactured dolls: Barbies, Alexander, Ashton-Drake, Daddy's Long Legs, Annalee, Middleton, Seymour Mann and more

Special orders: No added cost.

Related products: Figurines, Precious Moments, All God's Children, Cherished Teddies, Bearstones Bears, Raikes, Boyds, Muffy

BUSINESS INFORMATION:

Type of business: Dolls sold at store location.

Accepts: Cash, check, money order, Visa MC, DC, AE

Layaway: Small deposit required, three months to pay. No extra charge.

Return/exchange policy: No cash returned. Store credit only.

Phone orders: Call during regular business hours.

ADDITIONAL INFORMATION:
Anna's Collectibles is located inside Robert Anthony Jewelers.

BEAR-A-DISE LANDING

Jeanne Orlando
1310 Boston Post Rd.
Guilford, CT 06437
Phone: (203)458-2378 EST
Fax: (203)458-2378
Hours: T-Sat, 10-5. Sun, 11-3.
In business since: 1993

PRODUCT INFORMATION:

Modern manufactured dolls: About 12 brands, including Alexander, Effanbee, Bradlee, Lee Middleton, Johannes Zook, Götz, Heidi Ott, Jeckle-Jansen, RottenKids, Susan Wakeen

Special orders: On lines of dolls already carried; 50% deposit required. Nonrefundable.

Related products: Doll strollers, trunks, furniture, hair brushes, clothes, stands, books

BUSINESS INFORMATION:

Type of business: Dolls sold at the retail store location and by mail.

Accepts: Cash, check, money order, Visa, MC, DC, AE

Layaway: 25% down, 30 days

Return/exchange policy: Exchanges or store credit within 30 days of purchase

Mailing list: Write or call to be included.

Phone orders: During regular business hours

Fax orders: Include name, address, phone number and method of payment.

Mail orders: Will ship to US, Canada, overseas. Contact store first. Prepayment is required.

Shipping information: Shipping is added to cost of doll depending on destination. Shipped via method preferred by customer. Allow 3-7 days for delivery.

BIGGS LIMITED

Donna Biggs
5517 Lakeside Ave.
Richmond, VA 23228
Phone: For orders: (800)637-0704
For info: (804)266-7744 EST
Fax: (804)266-7775
Additional locations: Biggs Limited Editions, 1601 Willow Lawn Dr., Richmond, VA 23230. (804)282-0282
Hours: Lakeside: M-F, 9-5; Sat, 9-3. Willow Lawn: M-Sat, 10-9; Sun, 12:30-5:30.
In business since: 1985

PRODUCT INFORMATION:

Modern manufactured dolls: About 50 brands, including Alexander, Johannes Zook, Annette Himstedt, Bolden, Monika, Tonner, Lawton, Katrina, FayZah Spanos

Retired manufactured dolls: Lawton, Elke Hutchen, Gadco, Monika, Robert Tonner

Artist dolls: Elke Hutchen, Marilyn Bolden, Paul Crees, Gloria Tepper, Lorna Miller, Charlene Thanos, Jan McLean, Dolls By Jerri

Special orders: ½ deposit, balance when order is in. No refunds, but will gladly give store credit.

BUSINESS INFORMATION:

Type of business: Dolls sold at retail store location, by mail.

Accepts: Cash, check, money order, Visa, MC, DC, AE

Layaway: No refund on down payment after 10 days. Balance due in 30, 60 or 90 days.

Return/exchange policy: May return within 10 days for full refund and within 30 days for store credit.

Back order policy: Will call when available, no deposit required.

Catalog/price list: Color, free

Mailing list: Write or call to be included.

Phone orders: M-Sun, 9 A.M.-10 P.M.

Fax orders: Credit card number, name, address, phone number, title and information on piece desired.

Mail orders: Will ship to US, Canada, overseas. Include credit card number, name, address, phone number, title and information on piece desired. Prepayment is required.

Shipping information: Call for shipping expense. Shipped via UPS or method

preferred by customer. Allow an average of 10 working days.

ADDITIONAL INFORMATION:

Special features: The owners have been DOTY Judges. They will search for any doll and locate it, sparing the customer the expense.

> "START COLLECTING SLOWLY. TASTES CHANGE, AND A DOLL ON LAYAWAY MAY NO LONGER BE DESIRABLE. IF YOU ORDER A DOLL AND NO LONGER WANT IT, PLEASE GIVE THE DEALER THE COURTESY OF CANCELING."
>
> *Josie Jessup, Regina's Doll Heaven, Seattle, WA*

BLEVINS PLATES 'N' THINGS

Susan Williams, manager
Stella Blevins, owner
301 Georgia St.
Vallejo, CA 94590
Phone: For orders: (800)523-5511 PST
For info: (707)552-9345
Fax: (707)557-0679
Hours: M-F, 10-6. Sat, 9-5.
In business since: 1983

PRODUCT INFORMATION:

Modern manufactured dolls: About 12 brands, including Ashton-Drake, Barbie, Georgetown, Kingstate, Alexander, Hamilton, Seymour Mann, Lawton

Retired manufactured dolls: Ashton-Drake

Artist dolls: Jennifer Schmidt, Susan Krey, Maree Massey, Virginia Turner

Special orders: 20% deposit required. Can go on layaway when it arrives.

Related products: Clothes

BUSINESS INFORMATION:

Type of business: Dolls sold at the retail store location, by mail.

Accepts: Cash, check, money order, Visa, MC, DC, AE, Diner's Club

Layaway: 20% down, 3 months to pay; over $300 to $500, 6 months; $500-1,000, 9 months.

Return/exchange policy: Must be returned in 30 days—credit issued. Mail order dolls may be returned if customer calls immediately. Shipping not refunded unless doll is damaged.

Back order policy: Will check with customer to see if she wants to wait.

Price list: Available

Mailing list: Write or call to be included.

Phone orders: During regular business hours

Fax orders: Send name, address, phone number, name of doll, company, method of payment.

Mail orders: Will ship to US, Canada, overseas. Send name, address, phone number, name of doll, company, method of payment. Prepayment is required.

Shipping information: Prepayment is required. Please add $6-7 for shipping, $2 each additional doll. Shipped via UPS. Allow 7-10 working days to East Coast.

ADDITIONAL INFORMATION:
Shop sponsors doll signings once or twice a year and goes to local doll shows.

BODZER'S COLLECTIBLES

Dolly Bodzer
White Marsh Mall
8200 Perry Hall Blvd.
Baltimore, MD 21236
Phone: For orders: (800)776-0201 EST
For info: (410)931-9222
Fax: (410)661-1948
Hours: M-Sat, 10-9:30. Sun, 12-6.
In business since: 1982

PRODUCT INFORMATION:

Modern manufactured dolls: Ashton-Drake, Hamilton, Georgetown, Lawton, Alexander

Retired maufactured dolls: Ashton-Drake, Hamilton, Georgetown

Artist dolls: Available

Special orders: Deposit required

BUSINESS INFORMATION:

Type of business: Dolls sold at retail store location and by mail.

Accepts: Cash, check, money order, Visa, MC, DC, AE

Layaway: ⅓ down, 30 days; up to 90 days if total sale is $300 or more.

Return/exchange policy: Available with receipt

Catalog: Color, free

Mailing list: Write to be included.

Phone orders: During regular business hours

Mail orders: Should be on regular order forms. If sending check, include driver's license number and D.O.B. on

front of check. Prepayment is required.

Shipping information: Please add $5 for the first doll, $1 for each additional doll for shipping. Shipped via UPS. Delivery time depends on location. Most orders leave warehouse within 1-3 days.

ADDITIONAL INFORMATION:
Store sponsors Award Winning Dealer, hosts open houses for famous artists.

BROWNS GALLERY

12585 Tenth Line
Stouffville, Ontario L4A 7X3
CANADA
Purchases: Coreen
Sales: Coreen or Anne
Phone: (905)642-3606 CST
Fax: (905)642-4952
Hours: W-F, 11-5. Sat, 10-4. From Nov. 15-Dec. 24: Sun, 12-4.
In business since: 1992

PRODUCT INFORMATION:

Modern manufactured dolls: About 20 brands, including Ashton-Drake, Georgetown, Mattel, Bello, Hamilton, Lee Middleton, FayZah Spanos, Annette Himstedt, Götz, Paul Crees, Good-Krüger, Julie Rueger, Johannes Zook, Horseman, Effanbee, Nascar

Retired manufactured dolls: Ashton-Drake, Mattel, Good-Krüger

Artist dolls: Julia Rueger, Johannes Zook, Good-Krüger, Middleton, Fayzah Spanos, Annette Himstedt, Paul Crees, Philip Heath, Bello, Götz

Special orders: Deposit required

Related products: Books, cases, stands

BUSINESS INFORMATION:

Type of business: Dolls sold at retail store location and by mail.

Accepts: Cash, check, money order, Visa, MC, AE

Layaway: Usually 3 months; up to 1 year for higher-end dolls

Return/exchange policy: 10% restocking fee with store credit

Price list: Free

Mailing list: Write or call to be included.

Phone orders: During regular business hours

Fax orders: Include name, address, phone and fax numbers, method of payment.

Mail orders: Will ship to US, Canada and

overseas. Include name, address, phone and fax numbers, method of payment. Prepayment is required.

Shipping information: Shipping is included in the cost of the doll. Please add $5 per doll for special requests only. Shipped via UPS. Allow 1-10 days for delivery.

ADDITIONAL INFORMATION:
The shop offers artist appearances, good service, access to international markets for Barbies, and a knowledgable, friendly staff. The staff has judged DOTY awards.

C & W ENTERPRISES

Mary Ann Cook
P.O. Box 610
Salem, VA 24153
Phone: (540)389-9384 EST
Fax: (540)389-2832
E-mail: dolltime@bev.net
In business since: 1965

PRODUCT INFORMATION:

Modern manufactured dolls: About 10 brands, including Barbie, Effanbee, Alexander, Sasha, Kewpie, Faith Wick, Steiff, Gund, Hantel and more

Retired manufactured dolls: Barbie, Sasha, Alexander, Effanbee, Kewpie, Faith Wick, Steiff, Gund, Hantel

Artist dolls: Wick, Kolesar, Brohms, Gunzel, Annette Himstedt

Related products: Doll stands, Enesco Barbie products, related paper items, Christmas ornaments, paper dolls

BUSINESS INFORMATION:

Type of business: Dolls sold by mail, at shows and conventions

Accepts: Cash, check, money order, Visa, MC

Return/exchange policy: 5 days to return

Back order policy: Will call customers when they arrive.

Catalog/price list: b&w and color, $1 each plus LSASE. Some cost more. Price list—$1 plus LSASE.

Mailing list: Call or write to be included.

Phone orders: M-Fri, 9-4:30; some weekends and evenings.

Fax orders: Include all necessary info.

Mail orders: Will ship to US, Canada, overseas. Include all necessary info.

Shipping information: Prepayment required. Please add $5 per doll for shipping. Method preferred by customer. Allow 10 days or more for delivery.

CARRIAGE HOUSE COLLECTIBLES

Susan Powers
14 Shore Rd.
N. Brookfield, MA 01535
Phone: (508)867-7298 EST
Hours: M-T, 12-5. W-Sat, 10-5.
In business since: 1991

PRODUCT INFORMATION:

Modern manufactured dolls: About 25 brands, including Gadco, Götz, sigikid, Tonner, Kish and Co., Wakeen, Good-Krüger

Artist dolls: Lynne Randolph, Ann Timmerman, Maggie Iacono, Jeanne Singer, Christine Heath-Orange, Karen Alcaro, Jan McLean

Special orders: Available

BUSINESS INFORMATION:

Type of business: Dolls sold at store location and by mail.

Accepts: Cash, check, money order, Visa, MC

Layaway: Flexible, to fit customer's budget. Usually require 25% down.

Return/exchange policy: 15% restocking fee for returned/cancelled merchandise.

Phone orders: Call during business hours.

Mail orders: Will ship to US, Canada. Prepayment required.

Shipping information: Shipping is included in the cost of the doll. Dolls shipped via UPS. Allow 7-10 days from receipt of payment to furthest locations.

A CENTURY OF DOLLS

Karen D'Onofrio
2360 Middle Country Rd.
Centereach, Long Island, NY 11720
Phone: For orders: (800)90-DOLLS
For info: (516)981-0727 EST
Fax: (516)981-0727
Hours: T-Th, 10-5. F, 10-8. Sat, 10-6. Sun, 11-5.
In business since: 1994

PRODUCT INFORMATION:

Modern manufactured dolls: Lawton, European Artist Dolls, Alexander, Susan Wakeen, Effanbee, Käthe Kruse, Lee Middleton, Good-Krüger, R. John Wright, Crees and Coe, Georgetown, Barbie

Retired manufactured dolls: Ideal, American Character, Effanbee Com-

position, vintage Barbie Dolls, Lenci, Vogue Ginny, vintage composition dolls, dolls from the 1950s and 1960s

Artist dolls: Maggie Iacona, Blythe and Snodgrass Fairy Dolls, R. John Wright, Crees and Coe, Jan Mclean, Lawton

Related products: Teddy bears, educational doll books, patterns for dolls, doll wigs, doll clothing and shoes, accessories

BUSINESS INFORMATION:

Type of business: Dolls sold at retail store location and by mail.

Accepts: Cash, check, money order, Visa, MC, DC, AE

Discounts: Very Important Customer program

Layaway: 20% down, monthly payments of $100-150

Return/exchange policy: All new dolls. 7 days for refund; 3 days for antique and composition dolls. Credit available after time for refund expires.

Mailing list: Write or call to be included.

Phone orders: Call during business hours.

Mail orders: Will ship to US, Canada, overseas. Send your payment, name, address and product. Prepayment required.

Shipping information: Orders of more than $100 are shipped free. Shipped via FedEx. Allow 3-10 business days.

ADDITIONAL INFORMATION:

A Century of Dolls also sells antique, composition and modern dolls. This is a very unique store. It represents a full history of dolls, including new dolls that are currently manufactured.

CEDAR CHEST DOLL SHOPPE

Ruth C. Daniels
318 Third Ave.
Blue Anchor, NJ 08037-9531
Phone: (609)567-4505 EST
Fax: (609)561-1897
Hours: T-Sat, 10-5. Special hours for Christmas, small groups, appointments
In business since: 1991

PRODUCT INFORMATION:

Modern manufactured dolls: About 40 brands, including Virginia Turner, Götz, Hildegard Gunzel, Good-

Krüger, Johannes Zook, Middleton and more

Artist dolls: Ruth Treiffesen, Vera Scholz, Hildagard Gunzel, Julta Kissling, Mitzie Hargrave, Sonja Hartman and more

Special orders: Available

BUSINESS INFORMATION:

Type of business: Dolls sold at retail store location and by mail. Offers special prices when possible.

Accepts: Cash, check, money order, Visa, MC, DC, AE

Discounts: Available at owner's discretion at time of sale.

Layaway: 20% down; 3 months, no exchanges, no returns

Return/exchange policy: At owner's discretion

Phone orders: During regular business hours or at owner's home. Call (609)561-8549.

Fax orders: Accepted

Mail orders: Prepayment is required.

Shipping information: Shipped via UPS or US mail.

ADDITIONAL INFORMATION:

Shop has over 1,500 dolls on display. Ruth says, "Customers become my friends. I like having a word of mouth type business and helping customers whenever I can."

CELIA'S AND SUSAN'S DOLLS AND COLLECTIBLES

Celia Neadel
800 E. Hallandale Beach Blvd.
Hallandale, FL 33009
Phone: (305)458-0661 EST
Fax: (305)458-5609 EST
Hours: T-Sat, 10-5.

PRODUCT INFORMATION:

Modern manufactured dolls: About 17 brands, including Ashton-Drake, Effanbee, Georgetown, Lawton, Alexander, Mattel, Hamilton, Enesco, Ruth Treffeisen, Annette Himstedt, Jan McLean, Paul Crees, Yolando Bello Originals and more

Retired manufactured dolls: Ginny Dolls, Alexander, Robin Woods, Ideal Toy Co. and more

Artist dolls: Paul Crees, Jan McLean, Ruth Treffeisen, Annette Himstedt, Blythe and Snodgrass

Special orders: ⅓ deposit required

Related products: Books, magazines, doll furniture

BUSINESS INFORMATION:

Type of business: Dolls sold at store location and by mail.

Accepts: Cash, check, money order, Visa, MC, DC, AE

Layaway: ⅓ down, 90 days

Return/exchange policy: 5 day return policy. Store credit only. No returns on sale items or layaways.

Catalog/price list: b&w, $5. Price list, SASE.

Mailing list: Write to be included.

Phone orders: During regular business hours

Fax orders: Include name, address, order, phone number and credit card number.

Mail orders: Will ship to US, Canada, overseas. Send name, address, order, phone number and credit card number.

Shipping information: $5.95 first doll, add 50¢ each additional doll. Will ship via UPS or US mail. Allow 7 days delivery.

CHARLENE'S DOLLS AND COLLECTIBLES

Charlene Werderman
11395 Folsom Blvd.
Rancho Cordova, CA 95670
Phone: (916)933-1514 PST
Hours: 10-6.
In business since: 1991

PRODUCT INFORMATION:

Modern manufactured dolls: Annalee, The Doll Factory, Georgetown, Great American Doll Co., Good-Krüger, Götz, Royal Vienna, sigikid, Susan Wakeen

Retired manufactured dolls: Annette Himstedt, Barbie, Annalee

Artist dolls: S. Catherine Anderson, Shirley Baran, Amy Burgess, Sonja Bryer, Uta Brauser, Peggy Dey, Inge' Enderle, Grossle-Schmidt, Jan Hagara, Janie Bennett, Hedy Katin, Sandi McAslan, Marie Massey, Lorna Miller, Janet Ness, Susie Pitt, Juanita Montoya, Olga Roberts, Virginia Turner

Special orders: 20% nonrefundable deposit required

BUSINESS INFORMATION:

Type of business: Dolls sold at the retail store and by mail.

Accepts: Cash, check, money order, Visa, MC, DC, AE, Diners, all Novus

Layaway: Flexible; usually 20% down, up to 10 months

Return/exchange policy: Store credit only, no cash refunds; 20% restocking fee on special orders

Price list: Free

Mailing list: Write or call to be included.

Phone orders: During business hours

Mail orders: Will ship to US, Canada. Send name, address, method of payment, telephone number. Prepayment is required.

Shipping information: Shipping is included if the cost of the doll is over $250. Otherwise, customer must cover shipping cost. Please add $8 per doll for shipping. Shipped via UPS. Allow 15-20 working days for delivery.

> "DOLL QUALITY IS MORE IMPORTANT THAN DOLL QUANTITY."
> *Karen D'Onofrio, A Century of Dolls, Centereach, Long Island, NY*

THE COUNTRY SAMPLER

2874 Calgary Trail South
Edmonton, Alberta T6J 6V7
CANADA
Purchases: Donna Payne or Kathleen Bouwmeester
Sales: Donna, Kathleen or Norma
Phone: (403)435-2013 MST
Fax: (403)463-8829
Hours: M-Sat, 10-5:30. Sun, 12-5.
In business since: 1986

PRODUCT INFORMATION:

Modern manufactured dolls: Daddy's Long Legs, Sarah's Attic Dolls

Retired manufactured dolls: Daddy's Long Legs, Sarah's Attic Dolls

Special orders: Additional charge for postage

Related products: Figurines

BUSINESS INFORMATION:

Type of business: Dolls sold at store location and by mail.

Accepts: Cash, check, money order, Visa, MC, AE

Layaway: 20% down, 30 days. For large orders, balance in 2-3 payments.

Return/exchange policy: Exchanges only; no returns. No exchanges on sale merchandise.

Mailing list: Write or call to be included.

Phone orders: During business hours

Fax orders: Include payment intentions, charge card number

Mail orders: Will ship to US, Canada, overseas. Send name, address, phone, item, payment info. Prepayment required.

Shipping information: Prepayment required on shipping cost. Will ship via parcel post or method preferred by customer. If item is in stock, allow 1-2 weeks. If we must order item, 4-6 weeks.

DEERE CROSSING

Connie Frank
1902 Broadway
Scottsbluff, NE 69361
Phone: (308)635-3337 MST
Hours: M-Sat, 9-5:30. Christmas season: M-F, 9-8. Sat, 9-5:30. Sun, 1-5.
In business since: 1985

PRODUCT INFORMATION:

Modern manufactured dolls: About 20 brands, including Mattel (Barbie and Himstedt), Kish and Co., Alexander, Virginia Turner, Precious Moments, Jeckel-Jansen, Berjusa, Käthe Kruse, Sonja Hartman, Sweetmms, Vogue Ginny, Good-Krüger

Retired manufactured dolls: Same as above

Artist dolls: Jo Clair West

Special orders: No tax on out-of-state orders. Customer pays postage.

Related products: Doll clothes, doll dishes, teddy bears, collectible toys, Boy Scout, Girl Scout and Campfire supplies, figurines, music boxes, plush animals

BUSINESS INFORMATION:

Type of business: Dolls sold at retail store location and by mail.

Accepts: Cash, check, money order, Visa, MC, DC, AE

Layaway: 10% down, 10% of balance per month

Return/exchange policy: Returns and exchanges accepted with receipt.

Catalog/price list: b&w, free

Mailing list: Write or call to be included.

Phone orders: During business hours

Mail orders: Will ship to US, Canada,

overseas. Enclose description and payment. Shipping is included in the cost of the doll.

Shipping information: Shipping is included in the cost of the doll. Shipped via FedEx, UPS, US mail or method preferred by customer. Allow 5 days for delivery.

DOLL AND MINI NOOK

Peg Szekely
336 W. Broad St.
Quakertown, PA 18951
Phone: (215)536-4242 EST
Fax: (215)536-4242 after 4 P.M.
Hours: T-Th, Sat, 10-4. F, 10-6.
In business since: 1983

PRODUCT INFORMATION:

Modern manufactured dolls: About 50 brands, including Alexander, Mattel, Effanbee, Mann, Heidi Ott, Susan Wakeen, FayZah Spanos, Pittsburgh Originals, Good-Krüger, Johannes Zook, Middleton and more

Special orders: No added cost, 50% down

Related products: Doll houses, miniatures, doll clothing, accessories, furniture

BUSINESS INFORMATION:

Type of business: Dolls sold at store location and by mail.

Accepts: Cash, check, money order, Visa, MC, DC

Discounts: 20% off next purchase when you buy a doll for $50 or more

Layaway: 20% down

Return/exchange policy: Always cheerfully accepted with receipt.

Mailing list: Write or call to be included.

Phone orders: During regular business hours

Fax orders: After 4 P.M.; include name, phone number

Mail orders: Will ship to US, Canada. Include name, address, phone, method of payment, check or credit card info. Prepayment required.

Shipping information: Prepayment required on shipping cost. Shipped via UPS, US mail, or method preferred by customer. Allow 1 week for delivery.

> "DOLLS KEEP YOU YOUNG AND HAPPY!"
> *Young at Heart Doll Shop, Preston, CT*

THE DOLL GALLERY

Nan Radford
675 NW Gilman Blvd.
Issaquah, WA 98027
Phone: (206)392-4684 PST
Hours: T-F, 10:30-4:30. Sat, 11-4:30.
In business since: 1989

PRODUCT INFORMATION:

Modern manufactured dolls: Barbies (Mattel), Dynasty

Retired manufactured dolls: Sometimes available on consignment.

Artist dolls: Princess Radford Dolls

Special orders: Will order dolls and add shipping charges to price if necessary.

BUSINESS INFORMATION:

Accepts: Cash, check, money order, Visa, MC

Discounts: Quantity discounts available to wholesale customers.

Layaway: 1-3 months, depending on cost

Return/exchange policy: Returns and exchanges accepted with receipt.

Mailing list: Write or call to be included.

Phone orders: During business hours

Mail orders: Will ship to US, Canada. Prepayment required.

Shipping information: Shipping charges additional. Shipped via UPS or method preferred by customer.

THE DOLL GALLERY

Jan Scurto
7911 NW 72nd Ave. #106
Miami, FL 33166
Phone: For orders: (800)882-3655 EST
For info: (305)882-0086
Fax: (305)887-5084
Hours: M-F, 10-5. Sat, 12-5.
In business since: 1989

PRODUCT INFORMATION:

Modern manufactured dolls: About 40 brands, including Seymour Mann, Annette Himstedt, Barbie, Hamilton, Royal Vienna Collection, Götz, Zapf, Alexander and more

Artist dolls: Naber Dolls, Sandi McAslan, Sheila Michaels, Johannes Zook, Middleton, Good-Krüger, FayZah Spanos, GSR Art Dolls, Jeckel-Jansen, Jan Shackleford

Special orders: Depending on the doll and its cost, a deposit is required.

Related products: Manufactured and artist bears, doll furniture, doll stands and a few accessories

BUSINESS INFORMATION:

Type of business: Dolls sold at store location and by mail.

Accepts: Cash, check, money order, Visa, MC, DC, AE

Discounts: Repeat customer

Layaway: 4 equal payments, 3 months

Return/exchange policy: Store credit

Price list: Free

Mailing list: Write to be included.

Phone orders: During business hours, and most evenings and weekends

Fax orders: Include name of customer, shipping address, order and credit card number

Mail orders: Will ship to US, Canada, overseas. Include customer info., shipping instructions, order, check or money order. Prepayment required.

Shipping information: Prepayment required. Please add $6 per doll for shipping. (Could be more or less depending on cost and weight of doll.) Dolls shipped via UPS, US mail. Allow 1 week for delivery.

THE DOLL HOSPITAL, INC.

Mary Ann Pizzolato
419 Gentry St. #102
Spring, TX 77373
Phone: (713)350-6722 CST
Fax: (713)446-4165
Hours: T-Sat, 10-5. Sun, 1-5.
In business since: 1985

PRODUCT INFORMATION:

Modern manufactured dolls: About 20 brands, including Alexander, Effanbee, Hildegard Gunzel, Dynasty, Vogue Ginny, Robin Woods for Horseman, Let's Play Dolls, Royal Vienna, Middleton Dolls, Berjusa

Retired manufactured dolls: Alexander, Effanbee, Dynasty, Vogue Ginny, Robin Woods, Let's Play Dolls, Middleton Dolls

Artist dolls: Hildegard Gunzel

Special orders: 50% deposit, nonrefundable

Related products: Doll clothing, wigs, accessories

BUSINESS INFORMATION:

Type of business: Dolls sold at retail store location and by mail.

Accepts: Cash, check, money order, Visa, MC

Discounts: Frequent Buyer card, equivalent to a 15% discount. Call for details.

Layaway: ⅓ down, balance determines length of layaway.

Return/exchange policy: No cash or credit card refunds. Exchange or store credit only within 10 days with receipt.

Back order policy: Will cancel all back orders not filled by 12/31.

Mailing list: Write or call to be included.

Phone orders: During business hours

Fax orders: Include name, address, phone number (day and evening), credit card number, item number or description, signature

Mail orders: Will ship to US. Same requirements as fax orders. Prepayment is required.

Shipping information: Prepayment is required for shipping cost. Please add $5 per doll for shipping. Will ship via UPS. Allow 10-14 days for delivery.

ADDITIONAL INFORMATION:
Provides repair and restoration on all types of dolls, doll clothing, furniture, old toys, antique clothing and quilts.

DOLL WORLD AND SURROUNDINGS

Marge Dowdy
Mission Square
2901 University Ave., Suite 4
Columbus, GA 31907
Phone: (706)569-0905 EST
Hours: M-Fri, 10-6. Sat, 10-4.
In business since: 1993

PRODUCT INFORMATION:

Modern manufactured dolls: About 20 brands, including Effanbee, The Great American Doll Co., Alexander, Lee Middleton, WPM, Johannes Zook, Berjusa, Zapf and more

Retired manufactured dolls: A few are available.

Artist dolls: Nola Trollip, Valerie Pike, Karin Schmidt, Ruth Treffeisen, Virginia Keith, Sofia Lawiervzinsky

Special orders: Free shipping in US

Related products: Doll houses, miniature furniture, accessories, gifts

BUSINESS INFORMATION:

Type of business: Dolls sold at store location.

Accepts: Cash, check, money order, Visa, MC, DC, AE

Layaway: ¼ down, 90 days or more depending on availability

Return/exchange policy: All sales final

Mailing list: Write or call to be included.

Phone orders: During business hours

DOLLS AND FRIENDS

Penny or Kathy
15600 N.E. 8th St., Suite 0-11
Bellevue, WA 98008
Phone: (206)746-0244 PST
Hours: M-Sat, 10-7. Sun, 12-5.
In business since: 1994

PRODUCT INFORMATION:

Modern manufactured dolls: About 35 brands, including Ashton-Drake, Dynasty, Effanbee, Georgetown, Great American Doll Co., Lawton, Corolle, Alexander, Berjusa, Bradley, Furga, Götz, Hollywood, Kingstate, Lissi, Mattel, Pauline, Seymour Mann, Johannes Zook, Käthe Kruse, Kish and Co., Heidi Ott, Robert Tonner.

Artist dolls: Karen Alcaro, Julia Kruger, Gail Shumaker, Marilyn Bolden, Virginia Turner, Ruth Treffeisen

Special orders: Must be a current doll. Will charge for shipping and handling depending on location of buyer. Deposit required.

Related products: Doll clothing, furniture, trunks, hangers

BUSINESS INFORMATION:

Type of business: Dolls sold at store location and by mail.

Accepts: Cash, check, money order, Visa, MC, DC, AE

Discounts: Bonus card—for every $10 spent, customer gets 1 stamp on card. When card is full (approx. $200 in purchases), customer gets $20 off next purchase of more than $20.

Layaway: ¼ down, 3 payments, 3 months

Return/exchange policy: No cash refunds. Exchanges within 30 days with receipt; must be resalable. Store credit also given.

Back order policy: Will notify customer.

Mailing list: Write or call to be included.

Phone orders: Call during business hours.

Mail orders: Will ship to US. Send your name, address, phone number, payment information, product number, description. Prepayment required.

Shipping information: Prepayment re-

quired on shipping cost. Add approximately $6 per doll for shipping. Shipped via UPS, US mail, or method preferred by customer. Allow 2-3 weeks for delivery.

ADDITIONAL INFORMATION:
This store has a large selection of dolls in many price ranges, lots of accessories, and great customer service.

DOLLS BY DYAN

Dyan Lee
630 S. Loomis St.
Naperville, IL 60540
Phone: (708)420-2480 CST
Fax: (708)420-2480
Hours: M, T, W, F, 9-5. Th, 7-9 P.M.. Sat, 9:30-11:30 A.M.
In business since: 1995

PRODUCT INFORMATION:

Artist dolls: Dyan Lee

Related products: Supplies to make porcelain dolls: wigs, eyes, joints, molds, etc.

BUSINESS INFORMATION:

Type of business: Dolls sold at retail store location and by mail.

Accepts: Cash, check, money order

Layaway: Available

Return/exchange policy: As needed for customer satisfaction.

Mailing list: Write to be included.

Phone orders: During regular business hours

Mail orders: Will ship to US. Order via phone. Prepayment is required.

Shipping information: Prepayment is required. Please add $10 per doll for shipping. Shipped via UPS.

DOLLS BY JIM

JoAnn Pekar
4 Colonial Place
West Haven, CT 06516
Phone: (203)934-9629 EST
In business since: 1984

PRODUCT INFORMATION:

Modern manufactured dolls: About 100 brands, including Effanbee, Georgetown, Great American Doll Co., sigikid, Himstedt, Hartman, Hagara, Gunzel, Alexander, Good-Krüger, Barbie, Fiba, Lenci, Jerri

Retired manufactured dolls: Effanbee,

Alexander, Ideal, Lenci, Jerri, Good-Krüger

Artist dolls: Crees, Erff, From the Heart, Dali, Lasher, Hanna Hyland, McAslan, Fredericy, Bello, Gillie Charlson

Special orders: Substantial deposit required

Related products: Artist bears, doll furniture

BUSINESS INFORMATION:

Type of business: Dolls sold by mail.

Discounts: First time buyer, multiple purchase, frequent buyer

Layaway: 20% down, monthly payments. No longer than 2 years on expensive purchases.

Return/exchange policy: Within 10 days. If defective must return immediately.

Price list: $2

Mail orders: Will ship to US, Canada, overseas. Send name of doll, quantity, cost, deposit, balance, address. Prepayment is required.

Shipping information: Prepayment is required on shipping cost. Please add $5 per doll for shipping. Shipped via UPS.

DOLLS FROM THE HEART

Judy Donabauer
619 Mall Germain
St. Cloud, MN 56301
Phone: For orders: (800)865-3655 CST
For info: (320)656-0613
Fax: (320)656-0613
Hours: M-Th, Sat, 10-5. F, 10-7.
In business since: 1993

PRODUCT INFORMATION:

Modern manufactured dolls: About 20 brands, including Effanbee, Georgetown, Good-Krüger, Götz, Johannes Zook, Lee Middleton, Phyllis Parkins, Precious Heirloom, Susan Wakeen, Virginia Turner and more

Artist dolls: Karen Alcaro, Liz Clark, Linda Amadro-Valentino, Peggy Dey and more

Special orders: ½ upon ordering, ½ upon delivery. No returns

Related products: Muffy VanderBear and Gund Bears

BUSINESS INFORMATION:

Type of business: Dolls sold at retail store location and by mail.

Accepts: Cash, check, money order, Visa, MC, DC, AE

Layaway: Flexible, generally, ⅓ down and 2-4 monthly payments

Return/exchange policy: Return for exchange or store credit. No return on sale merchandise.

Back order policy: Shipped upon receipt in store

Price list: Free

Mailing list: Write to be included.

Phone orders: During regular business hours

Fax orders: Include name, address, phone number, fax number, name of item and artist, credit card type, number and expiration date.

Mail orders: Will ship to US, Canada, overseas. Send name, address, phone number, fax number, name of item and artist, credit card type, number and expiration date. Prepayment is required.

Shipping information: Shipped via UPS or method preferred by customer. Shipping is included in the cost of dolls over $100. Allow 2 weeks for delivery.

DOLLS UNLIMITED

Kristin Tipps and Amy Ritter
2025 S. MacArthur Blvd.
Springfield, IL 62704
Phone: (217)787-7733 CST
Fax: (217)546-8301
Hours: M-F, 12-9. Sat, 10-6. Sun, 1-5.
In business since: 1977

PRODUCT INFORMATION:

Modern manufactured dolls: About 20 brands, including Madame Alexander, Daddy's Long Legs, Hildegard Gunzel, Effanbee, Lissi, Berjusa, Kingstate, Faith Wick, Wimbledon, Heidi Ott.

Retired manufactured dolls: Alexander, Effanbee, Daddy's Long Legs, Hildegard Gunzel, Faith Wick

Artist dolls: Amy Ritter, Kristin Tipps—more than 300 styles of custom-made dolls

Special orders: Deposit required

Related products: Porcelain slips, wigs, eyes, molds, tools and brushes, paints, books, commercial and handmade clothes, trunks, beds, buggies, shoes, socks, doll stands, etc. Also dollhouses and miniatures and their accessories.

BUSINESS INFORMATION:

Type of business: Dolls sold at store location and by mail.

Accepts: Cash, check, money order, Visa, MC, DC, AE

Discounts: Occasional sales of 20% off. Clearances of 50% off.

Layaway: 20% down, 90 days. Arrangements can be made.

Return/exchange policy: Available

Back order policy: Accept until December 10

Mailing list: Write to be included.

Phone orders: During regular business hours

Fax orders: Include name, shipping address, item, phone number, charge card number or COD.

Mail orders: Will ship to US. Send name, shipping address, item, phone number, charge card number. Checks or COD.

Shipping information: COD or shipping is not included in the cost of the doll. Shipped via UPS, US mail or method preferred by customer. Allow 3-7 days for delivery.

ADDITIONAL INFORMATION:

Offers dollmaking classes by Seeley certified teachers and special seminars. The store has been "dollmaking" since 1980 and custom make over 300 styles of dolls. Also offers a doll hospital for all kinds of doll repairs and restoration.

THE DOLLMAKERS

505 S. Myrtle Ave.
Monrovia, CA 91016
Purchases: Pam Fitzpatrick
Sales: Jennifer Ranger
Phone: (818)357-1091 PST
Fax: (818)357-7261
Hours: M-Th, Sat, 10-6. F, 10-9. Sun, 11-4.
In business since: 1991

PRODUCT INFORMATION:

Modern manufactured dolls: About 10 brands, including Pauline Dolls, Effanbee, Middleton, Mattel, Seymour Mann, Victoria, Precious Moments, Sandy, Ginny, Robin Woods (Int'l Playthings)

Artist dolls: Rochelle Niemerow, Sharon Lee, Dollmaker Originals

Special orders: Available

Related products: Doll supplies, accessories (such as furniture, clothing, hats, luggage)

BUSINESS INFORMATION:

Type of business: Dolls sold at retail store location and by mail.

Accepts: Cash, check, money order, Visa, MC, DC

Discounts: Doll and Bear Club Membership available through store ($30/yr) gives 10% discount on all purchases (15% to seniors). Quantity discounts

Layaway: 20% down, 60 days. No additional charge

Return/exchange policy: 30 days with receipt

Mailing list: Write, call or sign guest book to be included.

Phone orders: During business hours

Fax orders: Send name, address, phone number, desired merchandise, price, desired delivery date.

Mail orders: Prepayment is usually required. Credit upon request and approval. Store bills actual costs.

Shipping information: Will ship to US, Canada, overseas. Shipped via UPS or US mail. Allow for delivery: in-stock items—1 week, special order—2-4 weeks.

ADDITIONAL INFORMATION:

Owners are commercial designers for the gift and doll industry. They specialize in custom orders, including handmade dolls in cloth, clay and wax, as well as porcelain. They custom-make doll clothes and do personalized/portrait dolls.

DOLLSVILLE DOLLS AND BEARSVILLE BEARS

461 N. Palm Canyon Dr.
Palm Springs, CA 92262
Phone: For orders: 1-800-CAL-DOLL, 1-800-GO-BARBIE, 1-800-CAL-BEAR EST
For info: (619)325-2241
Hours: M-Sat, 9-5.
In business since: 1980

PRODUCT INFORMATION:

Modern manufactured dolls: Ashton-Drake, Lawton, Barbie, Good-Krüger, Ellenbrooke, Federica, Johannes Zook, Pittsburgh Originals, Robert Tonner, Annette Himstedt and many more

Retired manufactured dolls: Barbie,

Robert Tonner, Good-Krüger, Annette Himstedt, Ellenbrooke

Artist dolls: Robert Tonner, Wendy Lawton, Federica, Connie Walser Derek

Special orders: Available

BUSINESS INFORMATION:

Type of business: Dolls sold at store location and by mail.

Accepts: Cash, check, money order, Visa, MC, DC, AE

Discounts: 10%-30% off regular prices to Golden Value Club members

Layaway: ⅓ down, ⅓ per month

Return/exchange policy: May exchange within 5 days, or return for store credit. Store credit lasts one year.

Catalog: Barbie News, Doll News or Bear-A-Log, b&w, $2 each

Mailing list: Write or call to be included.

Phone orders: During regular business hours

Mail orders: Will ship to US, Canada, overseas. $5 deposit if item is not in stock, balance due when shipped.

Shipping information: Free shipping to club members. Shipped via UPS. Allow 5-10 days for delivery.

ADDITIONAL INFORMATION:

Free exhibit of antique English bears and Gollys (Teddy's best friend in 1895) is part of the store.

EMPRESS DOLL BOUTIQUE

Pat Whaley or Karen Pugh
Rt. 3, Box 152I
Laurel, DE 19956
Phone: (302)875-9700 EST
Fax: (302)875-9700
Hours: T-F, 10-5. Sat, 10-4.
In business since: 1989

PRODUCT INFORMATION:

Modern manufactured dolls: About 100 brands, including Alexander, Ashton-Drake

Retired manufactured dolls: Alexander, Good-Krüger, Ashton-Drake, Dolls by Jerri

Special orders: Down payment required.

BUSINESS INFORMATION:

Accepts: Cash, check, money order, Visa, MC, DC, AE

Layaway: 20% down, 3 months

Return/exchange policy: Store credit on returns.

Mailing list: Write or call to be included.

Phone orders: During regular business hours

Fax orders: Information on doll, price, credit card number

Mail orders: Will ship to US. Include information on doll, price, credit card number. Prepayment required.

Shipping information: Shipping is extra. Shipped the next day.

> "BUY WHAT YOU LOVE."
> *Penny and Kathy, Dolls and Friends, Bellevue, WA*

FANTASIA DOLLS

Elna Meagher
1836 C St.
Sparks, NV 89431
Phone: (702)356-7583
Hours: M-Sat, 9-6.
In business since: 1975

PRODUCT INFORMATION:

Artist dolls: Fantasia Dolls by Elna

Special orders: Portrait dolls by Elna

Related products: Accessories, supplies

BUSINESS INFORMATION:

Type of business: Dolls sold at store location and by mail

Accepts: Cash, check, money order, DC

Discounts: "Bargain Basement" room of slow movers and discontinued dolls

Layaway: ¼ down, ¼ per month

Return/exchange policy: Returns accepted within 10 days of sale only.

Phone orders: During regular business hours

Mail orders: Will ship to US. For portrait dolls, include photo and $50 deposit. Balance must be paid before shipping. Prepayment is required on all mail orders.

Shipping information: COD. Shipped via UPS. Allow one month for delivery.

ADDITIONAL INFORMATION:

Special features: Shop has authentic antique reproductions and innovatively created modern doll reproductions. 200 to 300 dolls are usually on display. Shop specializes in porcelain portrait dolls and original sculptures. Regular in-shop classes are also available.

FOR THE LOVE OF DOLLS

Kay Rittenhouse
4359 Lovers Lane
Dallas, TX 75225
Phone: For orders: (800)35-DOLLS CST
For info: (214)528-LOVE (5683)
Fax: (214)528-7218
Hours: M-F, 10-6. Sat, 10-5.
In business since: 1992

PRODUCT INFORMATION:

Modern manufactured dolls: About 26 brands, including Mattel, Alexander, Ashton-Drake, Götz, KVK, Georgetown, Effanbee, Ginny, Johannes Zook, Susan Wakeen, Dolls by Jerri, sigikid

Retired manufactured dolls: Ashton-Drake, Georgetown, Dolls by Jerri, sigikid, Ginny, Johannes Zook, Effanbee, KVK

Artist dolls: Linda Steele, Nancy Spain, Marnie Panek, Pat Kolesar, Shirley Pick, Autumn Berwick, Patricia Crain, Marilyn Seeley

Special orders: 50% deposit, 4 month

Related products: Clothing, stands, cases, covers, furniture, bedding, doll jewelry, tea sets, paper dolls, bears

BUSINESS INFORMATION:

Type of business: Dolls sold at store location and by mail

Accepts: Cash, check, money order, Visa, MC, DC, AE

Layaway: 20% down, 20% per month—4 months

Return/exchange policy: No refunds on special orders. No returns or refunds on layaways after 10 days.

Catalog: b&w, $2, refundable with purchase or free with purchase

Mailing list: Write or call to be included.

Phone orders: During regular business hours

Fax orders: Include name, address, telephone, doll description, manufacturer, method of payment.

Mail orders: Will ship to US. Send name, address, telephone, doll description, manufacturer, method of payment. Prepayment is required, or autopay: After 3 credit card payments dolls will be shipped.

Shipping information: Prepayment is required for shipping costs. Add $5. Shipped via UPS or method preferred

by customer. Allow 6 working days for delivery.

ADDITIONAL INFORMATION:

Store sponsors several artist signings throughout the year. In 1995, artists included Linda Steele, Pat Kolesar, Anke Götz, Karen Germany and Robin Woods.

> "JUST AS WITH OTHER FORMS OF ART, WHEN BUYING A DOLL, KNOW THE SHOP OR DEALER AND THEIR REPUTATION. YOU ARE RELYING ON THEIR EXPERTISE TO HELP YOU MAKE SOUND CHOICES AND INVESTMENTS AND TO BE SURE YOU GET QUALITY, WELL-MADE WORK."
> *Nancie Mann, Mann Gallery, the Art of the Doll, Boston, MA*

HEAVENLY DOLLS

Yvonne Nosler
404 W. Meeker
Kent, WA 98032
Phone: (206)852-5643 PST
Fax: (206)852-1435
Hours: T-Sat, 9:30-4.
In business since: 1985

PRODUCT INFORMATION:

Retired manufactured dolls: Has an old doll section where dolls are accepted on consignment.

Related products: Antique reproduction dolls by Yvonne

BUSINESS INFORMATION:

Type of business: Dolls sold at retail store location and by mail.

Accepts: Cash, check, money order, Visa, MC, DC

Discounts: Wholesale dolls vary from 30 to 50%

Layaway: ⅓ down, 90 days

Return/exchange policy: Accepts returns

Mailing list: Write to be included

Phone orders: During business hours

Fax orders: Send name, phone number, address, items wanted and method of payment.

Mail orders: Will ship to US, Canada, overseas. Send name, phone, address, items wanted and method of payment.

Shipping information: Prepayment is required. Please add $20 per doll for shipping. Shipped via method preferred by customer. Allotted time for delivery varies with doll requested.

ADDITIONAL INFORMATION:

Special features: Most of the dolls are handmade porcelain dolls by Yvonne, including one-of-a-kind and limited edition dolls. Yvonne has been making porcelain reproduction dolls for 15 years.

HONEYDOLL'S COLLECTIBLES

Rosemarie or Margit
1075 Portion Rd.
Farmingville, NY 11738
Phone: (516)696-3005 EST
Fax: (516)732-8684
Hours: T-W, 11-6. Th-F, 11-8. Sat, 11-5.
In business since: 1994

PRODUCT INFORMATION:

Modern manufactured dolls: Ashton-Drake, Georgetown, Gadco, Seymour Mann, Kingstate, Lloyd Middleton, sigikid, Paradise Galleries, Hamilton

Artist dolls: Studio 7, Virginia Turner, Phyllis Parkins, Jamie Englert, Valerie Bunting, Teena, Zofia Majak, Linda Lee Sutton, Susan Wakeen, FayZah Spanos, Little Souls, Jan Shackelford, Lee Middleton, Federica, Amy Burgess

Special orders: ⅓ deposit

Related products: Wicker furniture, collectibles

BUSINESS INFORMATION:

Type of business: Dolls sold at store location and by mail.

Accepts: Cash, check, money order, Visa, MC, DC, AE

Layaway: ⅓ down, 30 days, unless special arrangements have been made.

Return/exchange policy: 30 days, store credit only

Mailing list: Write to be included.

Phone orders: Call during business hours.

Fax orders: Include address, phone number, doll, method of payment.

Mail orders: Will ship to US, Canada, overseas. Send name, address, phone number, doll, method of payment. Prepayment required.

Shipping information: Prepayment required for cost of shipping. Add $5 per doll for shipping. Shipped via UPS. Allow 5-10 days for delivery.

JUDY'S DOLL SHOP

Judy George
1201 A Hwy 70 East
New Bern, NC 28560
Phone: (919)637-7933 EST
Hours: M, T, Th, F, Sat, 9:30-5.
In business since: 1994

PRODUCT INFORMATION:

Modern manufactured dolls: Götz, Effanbee, Alexander

Related products: American Girl accessories

BUSINESS INFORMATION:

Type of business: Dolls sold at store location

Accepts: Cash, check, money order, Visa, MC, DC

Layaway: 30% down, 60 days

ADDITIONAL INFORMATION:

Special features: Large selection of antique and modern reproduction dolls

JULIA'S THE ULTIMATE COLLECTION

Julia Pollock
1016 SW Morrison
Portland, OR 97205
Phone: (503)274-9308 PST
Fax: (503)274-9308
Hours: M-Sat, 10-6.
In business since: 1987

PRODUCT INFORMATION:

Modern manufactured dolls: Daddy's Long Legs, Tahti

Retired manufactured dolls: Daddy's Long Legs

Special orders: No added cost or requirements

Related products: Doll furniture and accessories, doll house miniatures, Boyd's teddy bears

BUSINESS INFORMATION:

Type of business: Dolls sold at store location and by mail

Accepts: Cash, check, money order, Visa, MC, DC, AE

Layaway: 30% down, 30-60 days

Return/exchange policy: Store credit only

Back order policy: Will give approximate date when merchandise is expected.

Catalog/price list: Daddy's Long Legs catalog available, color, free. Price list, free.

Mailing list: Write or call to be included.

Phone orders: During business hours

Fax orders: Send name of doll, method of payment, name, address, phone number of buyer.

Mail orders: Will ship to US, Canada, overseas. Send name of doll, method of payment, name, address, phone number of buyer. Prepayment is required.

Shipping information: Prepayment is required for shipping costs. Please add $8 per doll for shipping. Shipped via UPS or method preferred by customer. Allow 2 weeks if doll is in stock.

KINDER HAUS—RETAIL AND WHOLESALE

Henri Startzel
Box 560
Cherry Valley, IL 61016
Phone: (815)547-4341 CST
In business since: 1975

PRODUCT INFORMATION:

Retired manufactured dolls: Ideal, Mego, Barbies, Alexander

Related products: Supplies, accessories

BUSINESS INFORMATION:

Type of business: Dolls sold by mail and at doll and toy shows.

Discounts: For dealers and teachers. Quantity discounts for orders of $200 or more.

Layaway: Flexible. Maximum 1 year.

Return/exchange policy: Returns within 3 days if merchandise has not been used or damaged.

Back order policy: No money collected. Ships when item becomes available.

Catalog/price list: b&w and color, $10. Price list included with catalog.

Mailing list: Write or sign up at a show to be included.

Phone orders: M-F, 7 A.M.-9 P.M.. Answering machine is on 24 hours. Please leave full name, address and phone number.

Mail orders: Will ship to US. Send full name and name of shop, address, phone number, tax number if dealer. Include MC or Visa number plus expiration date or check for approximate amount plus $4 postage.

Shipping information: COD. Shipped via UPS or priority US mail. Next day shipping usually available.

KMITSCH GIRLS

324 S. Main St.
Stillwater, MN 55082
Phone: For orders: (800)244-DOLL CST
For info: (612)430-1827
Fax: (612)430-2114
E-Mail: tdadak@aol.com
Hours: Holiday season and summer, M-Sat, 10-9. Sun, 11-6. Rest of year, M-Th, 10-6. F-Sat, 10-9. Sun, 11-6.
In business since: 1980

PRODUCT INFORMATION:

Modern manufactured dolls: About 100 brands, including Ashton-Drake, Lawton, Götz, Corolle, Alexander, Good-Krüger, sigikid, Johannes Zook, Barbie, Jerri, Berjusa

Retired manufactured dolls: Alexander, Gonpos, Shirley Temples, Nancy Ann and more

Artist dolls: Sonja Hartman, Maryanne Oldenburg

Special orders: Availability depends on cost of doll.

Related products: Antique dolls, doll clothes, furniture, cases, stands, accessories. Also Steiff and artist bears, pewter, crystal, Christmas collectibles, traditional quality toys (no violence toys), paper dolls, books.

BUSINESS INFORMATION:

Type of business: Dolls sold at store location and by mail.

Accepts: Cash, check, money order, Visa, MC, DC, AE, trade

Discounts: "Grandma discount" for those over 55 years. August thru November: buy 3 or more dolls at the regular price, get 15% off purchase.

Layaway: 25% down, 60 days (longer if purchase is more than $300). Regular layaway must be paid for in 120 days or deposit is lost. Layaway down payments can be applied to another purchase within 120 days.

Return/exchange policy: 30 days to exchange. No refunds unless defective.

Mailing list: SASE

Phone orders: Call during business hours.

Fax orders: Accepted

Mail orders: Will ship overseas. Send credit card info. Prepayment required.

Shipping information: Shipping is included for US orders over $100. Outside US or under $100, cost is added.

Shipped via UPS. Allow 5-7 days for delivery if in stock.

ADDITIONAL INFORMATION:
Hosts regular doll signings.

LESLIE'S AMERICAN HERITAGE, INC.

1311 Minnesota Ave.
Detroit Lakes, MN 56501
Purchases: Vernette Leslie
Sales: Scotty Leslie
Phone: (218)847-1908 CST
In business since: 1987

PRODUCT INFORMATION:
Modern manufactured dolls: Dolls with skin color and facial features ethnic to the Native American Nation. Doll bodies are imported from Italy. All clothing is authentic in style and designed and handmade by Vernette. The hair is rooted. Head, arms and legs are moveable, and eyes are hand set. Fur and deerskin used to make costumes.

BUSINESS INFORMATION:
Type of business: Mail order only
Accepts: Cash, check, money order
Layaway: 30% down, 3 months
Return/exchange policy: Will replace a doll if it's returned within 10 days and is in salable condition.
Catalog/price list: Color, $1. Price list—free.
Mailing list: Write to be included.
Phone orders: Accepted
Mail orders: Will ship to US, Canada, overseas. Send catalog order form. Prepayment required. Dealers given terms after they are established.
Shipping information: 8% shipping and handling fee. Shipped via UPS or method preferred by customer. Allow 10 days to 2 weeks.

LINDA'S LOV-LEZ HOUSE OF DOLLS AND BEARS, MORE

Linda Kemp
9103 Mentor Ave.
Mentor, OH 44060
Phone: (216)255-3655 EST
Hours: Sun, 12-4. M, F, 10-6. T, W, Sat, 10-5. Th, 10-8.
In business since: 1994

PRODUCT INFORMATION:
Modern manufactured dolls: About 10 brands, including FayZah Spanos, Ef-
fanbee, Ginny, Pittsburgh Originals, Middleton, LL. Knickerbocker, Barbie, Götz, Destiny and more
Retired manufactured dolls: Alexander, R. Woods, Barbie, Ashton-Drake, Susan Wakeen, Johannes Zook, Seymour Mann, Pauline
Artist dolls: FayZah Spanos
Special orders: Deposit required.
Related products: Bears, tea sets, jewelry, doll clothes, doll houses, miniatures, trunks, doll furniture, paper dolls

BUSINESS INFORMATION:
Type of business: Dolls sold at store location and by mail.
Accepts: Cash, check, money order, Visa, MC
Discounts: Monthly prize drawing, card holder (frequent buyer) discount
Layaway: ⅓ down, 2 months. Longer terms may be arranged for more expensive items.
Return/exchange policy: Returns available within 7 days with receipt for cash and credit card sales. Checks cannot be refunded until 10 days after they have cleared. No returns on special orders.
Back order policy: Will call when they arrive.
Mailing list: Write or call to be included.
Phone orders: During business hours
Mail orders: Will ship to US. Prepayment required.
Shipping information: Customer must pay cost of shipping. Shipped via method preferred by customer. Will be shipped immediately after payment.

ADDITIONAL INFORMATION:
Special features: Will provide any extra service needed to help the customer. Store takes on new artists whenever possible and takes items on consignment. Owner aims to help new and established artists. Doll and bear repair services also available.

"IF YOU ARE GOING TO COLLECT DOLLS, TAKE THEM OUT OF THE BOX OR CLOSET. DISPLAY THEM, LOOK AT THEM AND ENJOY THEM!"
Jeanne Orlando, Bear-A-Dise Landing, Guilford, CT

LITTLE SHOPPE OF DOLLS AND THINGS

Sue Fries
138 Main St.
Milford, MA 01757
Phone: For orders: (800)473-6867 EST
For info: (508)473-6830
Fax: (508)473-6830
Hours: M-Sat, 10-5, after hours and Sundays by appointment.
In business since: 1991

PRODUCT INFORMATION:
Modern manufactured dolls: Ashton-Drake, Alexander, Annette Himstedt, Barbie, Georgetown, Good-Krüger, Gadco, Lawton, Middleton, Johannes Zook
Retired manufactured dolls: Ashton-Drake, Naber Babies, Barbies, Good-Krüger, Gadco, Lawton, Himstedt
Special orders: Nonrefundable deposit required
Related products: Doll dresses, furniture, books, teddy bears, figurines, magazines

BUSINESS INFORMATION:
Type of business: Dolls sold at store location and by mail
Accepts: Cash, check, money order, Visa, MC, DC, AE
Discounts: Repeat customer discount
Layaway: 10% down, minimum $10, 3 months, one payment per month required. Extended terms can be arranged.
Return/exchange policy: Varies
Mailing list: Write or call to be included.
Phone orders: During regular business hours. After hours, orders can be recorded on answering service. Calls will be returned to confirm.
Mail orders: Will ship to US, Canada, overseas. Send name/description of doll ordered, customer's name, address and phone number. Prepayment or deposit required.
Shipping information: $5 for first doll, $3 each additional. Shipped via UPS. Allow 1-1½ weeks.

L.M. CROSSROADS

Lillie Shaw
Salem Mall Upper Level
5200 Salem Ave., Suite 2240
Trotwood, OH 45426
Phone: (513)837-0050 EST
Fax: (513)837-0050

Hours: M-Sat, 10-9. Sun, 12-6.
In business since: 1995

PRODUCT INFORMATION:

Modern manufactured dolls: About 20 brands, including Baby Cuddle-Kins by Bear Necessities, Dollmaker, Effanbee, Georgetown, Lee Middleton, Lloyd Middleton, Kingstate, Johannes Zook, Seymour Mann, FayZah Spanos, Marie Osmond, Daddy's Long Legs, Heidi Ott, Julie Good-Krüger

Retired manufactured dolls: Precious Moments, Lee Middleton, Victoria Impex

Artist dolls: Darlene Schlecty, Dolls by Jean

Special orders: 20% nonrefundable down payment required. Amount is refunded only if we are unable to secure the doll for the customer.

Related products: Doll stands

BUSINESS INFORMATION:

Type of business: Dolls sold at store location and by mail.

Accepts: Cash, check, Visa, MC, DC

Discounts: Dolls that are regularly priced and purchased in the store may be placed on Doll Club card. After 10 dolls are purchased, the 11th is free (taxes only).

Layaway: 20% down, up to 3 monthly payments, no refunds. Efforts are made to remind customers that they are overdue on their layaways.

Return/exchange policy: No cash refunds. Must have prior approval for exchange. Exchanges must be made within 30 days.

Mailing list: Write or call to be included.

Phone orders: During regular business hours

Fax orders: Send doll name, description, company selling doll.

Mail orders: Will ship within US. Send doll names, description, company selling doll. Prepayment is required. No mail orders taken on Baby Cuddle-Kins by Bear Necessities out of the Dayton, Ohio area (50 mile radius).

Shipping information: COD or customer may prepay. Shipped via UPS. Allow 4-12 weeks for delivery.

ADDITIONAL INFORMATION:

Baby Cuddle-Kins are unique, beautiful, porcelain doll-faced plush angels, bears, bunnies and cats. L.M. CROSSROADS is the distributor and sets up Certified Dealerships with protected territories throughout the US to doll, bear, and unique gift shops. Dealer inquiries are welcome; call (513)878-7555, M-F, 10-6.

LOVE OF COUNTRY

Sherrie McCarty
137 Ault Rd.
Urbana, OH 43078
Phone: For orders: (800)413-4120 EST
For info: (513)652-2620
Fax: (513)652-0105
E-Mail: bmcca4557@aol.com
Hours: M, T, F, Sat, 10-5. W, Th, 10-6.

PRODUCT INFORMATION:

Modern manufactured dolls: About 12 brands, including Ashton-Drake, Georgetown, Hamilton, Magic Attic, Effanbee, Seymour Mann, Pauline, Precious Moments Vinyl

Retired manufactured dolls: Ashton-Drake and Lee Middleton

Artist dolls: Virginia Turner, Lee Middleton, Val Shelton, Johannes Zook, Julie Good-Krüger, Kay MeKee (Tender Touch), Susan Wakeen, Ellenbrook (Linda Lee Sutton and Connie Walser Derek)

Special orders: Only from lines store carries. Nonrefundable 20% down. Balance due within 30 days upon receipt of doll.

Related products: *Dolls—The Collector's Magazine,* *Doll Reader,* *Collectors Price Guide,* doll record books and refills, bear record books and refills, doll-related small books, accessories, plush, magnets, cards, doll furniture, display cases, doll and bear dust covers, doll stands

BUSINESS INFORMATION:

Type of business: Dolls sold at store location and by mail.

Accepts: Cash, check, money order, Visa, MC, DC, AE

Discounts: Those who refer others to the store receive Bonus Bucks when those people purchase dolls. Bakers Dozen Club and Birthday Club allow customers to purchase certain dolls at a discount.

Layaway: Nonrefundable, 20% down. Under $100, 30 days; $100-300, 60 days; more than $300, 90 days with biweekly payments.

Return/exchange policy: All sales final on secondary dolls. Nonrefundable on layaways and special orders. Unconditional return with sales slip. Five days for exchanges, and 30 days with sales receipt.

Back order policy: Post card is sent when doll arrives or customer can arrange for store to charge and ship.

Catalog/price list: For Ashton-Drake and Middleton. Color, free. Price list for Middleton dolls and Indian dolls, free.

Mailing list: Those who make a purchase will be included.

Phone orders: Call during regular business hours. 800 number is answered at almost any hour.

Fax orders: Send name, complete address, charge card number, phone number, doll name, number (if available), price (if available).

Mail orders: Will ship to US. Include number and price if available, complete shipping address, phone number and method of payment. Prepayment is required.

Shipping information: $5 per shipment. Shipped via UPS. Will be shipped within 3 days of order if in stock.

ADDITIONAL INFORMATION:

When visiting the shop, be sure to bring a camera. Love of Country is located on a working farm with animals including mustangs, burros and buffalo. Love of Country has several open houses each spring and fall featuring several personal appearances by doll artists and doll exclusives.

MAGIC MOMENT

Judith Rudderham
116 Jefferson Dr.
Columbia, TN 38401
Phone: For orders: (800)763-4391 CST
For info: (615)388-7866
Fax: (615)388-8343
Hours: By appointment only.
In business since: 1994

PRODUCT INFORMATION:

Modern manufactured dolls: Only Naber Kids/Babies

Retired manufactured dolls: Naber Kids

Artist dolls: H.P. Naber

Special orders: Only Naber Kids

BUSINESS INFORMATION:

Type of business: Dolls sold at store location and by mail.

Accepts: Cash, check, money order, Visa, MC

Layaway: 10% down, 30 days.

Return/exchange policy: All sales final unless doll is found defective. Lifetime guarantee on parts.

Back order policy: Usually shipped within 10 days.

Price list: SASE

Phone orders: Accepted

Fax orders: Include credit card number, expiration date.

Mail orders: Will ship to US, Canada, overseas. Give UPS deliverable address. Prepayment is required.

Shipping information: Add $5 per doll for shipping. Canada and overseas will have an added charge. Shipped via UPS. If other means are desired by customer, there will be an additional charge. Usually 5-7 days for delivery.

MANN GALLERY, THE ART OF THE DOLL

Nancie Mann

39 Newbury St., Suite 208

Boston, MA 02186

Phone: For orders: (617)696-6666 EST
For info: (617)266-MANN

Fax: (617)696-6667

Hours: W-Fri, 9:30-6. Sat, 12-5.

In business since: 1992

PRODUCT INFORMATION:

Retired manufactured dolls: A few collectible high-end Barbies, recent years only

Artist dolls: All dolls are one-of-a-kind by artists from around the world. All dolls are completely handmade. Artists include NIADA (National Institute of American Doll Artists) as well as new, emerging local artists.

Special orders: No added costs—50% deposit at time of order—if refused, store credit is issued.

Related products: Miniature decorative boxes and chairs, jewelry, decorative art

BUSINESS INFORMATION:

Type of business: Dolls sold at the retail store and by mail.

Accepts: Cash, check, money order, Visa,

MC, DC, AE, Optima, travelers checks, Novus

Discounts: After first purchase, 10% discount guaranteed. Frequent customers get 15% to 20% discounts.

Layaway: Depending on cost of doll, between 20-30% down—very flexible, no additional cost.

Return/exchange policy: Refunds on damaged goods only.

Mailing list: Write or call to be included.

Phone orders: M-Sun, 8-7:30.

Fax orders: Send shipping address, payment information.

Mail orders: Will ship to US, Canada, overseas. Send payment information, shipping address. Prepayment is required.

Shipping information: Shipping is included in the cost of the doll. Shipped via method preferred by customer. Allow 2-3 weeks for delivery.

MARL AND BARBIE

Marl Davidson and Laurie Fetzer

10301 Braden Run

Bradenton, FL 34202

Phone: (941)751-6275 EST

Fax: (941)751-5463

E-Mail: marl@tsdg.com or marlbee@aol.com

Hours: By appointment only

In business since: 1987

PRODUCT INFORMATION:

Modern manufactured dolls: Barbies

Retired manufactured dolls: Barbies

Related products: Anything Barbie-related, including clothes, purses, jackets, phones, etc.

BUSINESS INFORMATION:

Type of business: Dolls sold by mail and at Joe and Marl shows

Accepts: Cash, check, money order, Visa, MC, AE

Layaway: ½ down, 30 days

Return/exchange policy: 5 days to return vintage Barbies and items. No other returns.

Back order policy: 20% deposit required

Catalog: $25 US, $30 Canada, $40 foreign. $7.50 sample.

Mailing list: Get a subscription to be included.

Phone orders: M-Sat, 10-6.

Fax orders: Include item, name, phone, address

Mail orders: Will ship to US, Canada, overseas. Send item, name, phone, address. Prepayment is required.

Shipping information: Add $7 per doll for shipping. Shipped via UPS, US mail or method preferred by customer. Allow 5-7 days for delivery.

ADDITIONAL INFORMATION:

Sponsors twelve Joe and Marl doll shows per year for Barbies only.

MID-OHIO HISTORICAL MUSEUM

Henrietta Pfeifer

700 Winchester Pike

Canal Winchester, OH 43110

Phone: (614)837-5573 EST

Hours: April through mid-December: W-Sat, 11-5.

In business since: 1884

PRODUCT INFORMATION:

Modern manufactured dolls: Barbies, Alexander

Retired manufactured dolls: Collectible dolls, 1950s-1980s

Artist dolls: Selection varies

Special orders: Doll searches for people looking for a special collectible doll.

Related products: Doll clothing, shoes, wigs and more

BUSINESS INFORMATION:

Type of business: Dolls sold at store location and by mail.

Accepts: Cash, check, money order, Visa, MC

Layaway: 20% down, 3 months. Will work with customers who need more time.

Price list: Free

Mailing list: Write to be included.

Phone orders: During business hours

MONTANA DOLLS and COLLECTIBLES

Lori Scheet

P.O. Box 429, 8000 Hwy. 35

Bigfork, MT 59911

Phone: For orders: (800)538-1587 MST
For info: (406)257-1985

E-Mail: mtdolls@netrix.net

Hours: M-Sat, 9:30-5:30.

In business since: 1995

PRODUCT INFORMATION:

Modern manufactured dolls: About 10 brands, including Georgetown, Hamilton, Alexander, Mattel/Barbie, Lee

Middleton, Lawton, Precious Heir-looms, Pittsburgh Originals

Artist dolls: Susan Wakeen, Julie Good-Krüger

Special orders: 50% downpayment required

Related products: Doll-related books, clothing, stands, furniture

BUSINESS INFORMATION:

Type of business: Dolls sold at store location and by mail.

Accepts: Cash, check, money order, Visa, MC

Discounts: To established customers

Layaway: 20% down, 90 days

Return/exchange policy: Exchanges only

Back order policy: Will notify customer, ship if they still want doll.

Price list: Free

Mailing list: Write to be included.

Phone orders: During business hours

Mail orders: Will ship to US, Canada. Include name, address, item and price. Prepayment is required.

Shipping information: Prepayment is required on shipping cost. Add $5 per doll for shipping. Shipped via UPS. Allow 1 week for delivery.

MY DOLL HOUSE OF HILLTOP

Gayle D. O'Neal

La Promenade Shoppes at Hilltop

1860 Laskin Rd.

Virginia Beach, VA 23454

Phone: (804)428-5900 EST

Fax: (804)461-4669

Hours: 7 days, 10-6.

In business since: 1985

PRODUCT INFORMATION:

Modern manufactured dolls: Alexander, Barbie, Corolle, *Gone With the Wind* display and Scarlett O'Hara doll collection

Artist dolls: Available

Special orders: Available

Related products: Playmobil and Brio educational toys, *Gone With the Wind* collectibles, collector videos, Muffy, Gund and Steiff bears

BUSINESS INFORMATION:

Type of business: Dolls sold at store location, cable TV ads using toll-free ordering number (800)637-2264.

Accepts: Cash, check, money order, Visa, MC, DC, AE, bank transfer

Layaway: Available

Catalog/price list: Free

Mailing list: Write or call to be included.

Phone orders: During regular business hours. Any time using toll free (800)637-2264.

Fax orders: Include name, shipping address, phone number, order number or description of doll/item, method of payment, type of credit card with expiration date and name on account.

Mail orders: Will ship to US, Canada, overseas. Send name, shipping address, phone number, order number or description of doll/item, method of payment, type of credit card with expiration date and name on account.

Shipping information: Varies with type of order. Shipped via method preferred by customer.

"MY DOLLS" DOLLS OF COLOR

Florine Cragwell

67 Lovell's Lane

Mashpee, MA 02649

Phone: (508)477-5100 EST

Hours: M-Th, 12-5. F, Sun, 12-4.

In business since: 1992

PRODUCT INFORMATION:

Modern manufactured dolls: About 8 brands, including Seymour Mann, Kingstate, Sandy, Daddy's Long Legs, Belle Dolls, Arnett Country Things, Opt 4 Kids

Special orders: ½ deposit, no refunds

Related products: All God's Children figurines, hand carved puppets, faceless rag dolls by My Dolls (Black)

BUSINESS INFORMATION:

Type of business: Dolls sold at store location and by mail.

Accepts: Cash, money order, Visa, MC, AE

Layaway: ⅓ down, 3 months

Return/exchange policy: Exchanges on broken dolls; otherwise, no returns.

Back order policy: Will ship as soon as it arrives at store.

Catalog: Color, free

Mailing list: Write or call to be included.

Phone orders: During business hours

Mail orders: Will ship to US. Orders should be on the regular order forms catalog. Prepayment is required.

Shipping information: Cost of shipping is on order blank. Shipped via UPS.

Allow 4-6 weeks for delivery.

ADDITIONAL INFORMATION:

This may be the most unique doll shop of its kind in the New England area, with African American dolls in abundance, and some Asian, Native American and Caucasian dolls. All who enter get quite an education.

NANALEE'S DOLLS AND GIFTS

Nancy L. McCabe

260½ Chestnut St.

Mifflinburg, PA 17844

Phone: (717)966-6355 EST

Hours: T-Sat, 10-5, holiday season: T-Th, 10-6. F-Sat, 10-7.

In business since: 1995

PRODUCT INFORMATION:

Modern manufactured dolls: About 10 brands, including Lee Middleton, Royal Vienna, Johannes Zook, Fay-Zah Spanos, Susan Wakeen, Good-Krüger, Georgetown, Hamilton, Virginia Turner-Vera Sholtz, Hildegard Gunzel

Related products: Carriages, some furniture and clothing. Also sells manufactured and local artist bears.

BUSINESS INFORMATION:

Type of business: Dolls sold at store location and by mail.

Accepts: Cash, check, money order, Visa, MC, DC

Discounts: Doll club discounts

Layaway: 30% down, 30% in 30 days, balance in 60 days

Return/exchange policy: Exchanges only

Mailing list: Write or call to be included.

Phone orders: During business hours

Mail orders: Will ship to US. Prepayment required.

Shipping information: Prepayment required on shipping cost. Add $4.50 per doll for shipping. Shipped via UPS. Allow 1-5 days or 3-4 weeks for special orders.

140 DOLL WORKS

Ruth A. Messier
Rt. 140, P.O. Box 994
Alton, NH 03809-0994
Phone: (603)875-6750 EST
Hours: Year-round by chance or appointment. Regular shop hours May-October: T-Sat, 10-4.
In business since: 1983

PRODUCT INFORMATION:

Retired manufactured dolls: Annalee, Effanbee, Horseman, Vogue Ginny, Dynasty and other brands occasionally

Related products: Dolls, old and new (antique, composition, collectible and modern); clothing and accessories; books and magazines; doll repair supplies

BUSINESS INFORMATION:

Type of business: Dolls sold at store location, by mail and at doll shows.
Accepts: Cash, check, money order, AE
Layaway: 20% down; number of payments depends on total amount and customer agreement.
Return/exchange policy: Items will be exchanged or accepted as returns only if in same condition as time of purchase. No penalties are charged.
Catalog/price list: Free
Mailing list: Write or call to be included.
Phone orders: Anytime
Mail orders: Will ship to US, Canada, overseas. Send name, address, telephone number, complete description of item ordered. Prepayment required.
Shipping information: Shipping is usually included in the cost of the doll. When not included in cost of doll, postage is negotiable depending on items purchased. Shipped via UPS or method preferred by customer. Items shipped 7-10 days after payment is received if by personal check. Other payments are shipped next day if possible.

THE ORANGE BLOSSOM

Joyce Brown
231 N. Lindell
Martin, TN 38237
Phone: For orders: (800)826-3629 CST
For info: (901)587-5091
Fax: (901)758-8646
Hours: M-F, 9-5. Sat, 10-4.

In business since: 1982

PRODUCT INFORMATION:

Modern manufactured dolls: About 3 brands, including Good-Krüger, Daddy's Long Legs, Ashton-Drake
Special orders: 50% deposit required

BUSINESS INFORMATION:

Type of business: Dolls sold at store location and by mail.
Accepts: Cash, check, money order, Visa, MC, DC, AE, Diners Club
Layaway: 20% down, 90 days
Return/exchange policy: Exchanges only
Mailing list: Write or call to be included.
Phone orders: During regular business hours
Mail orders: Will ship to US, Canada, overseas. Prepayment is required.
Shipping information: Shipping is included in the cost of the doll. Shipped via method preferred by customer. Allow 7-10 days for delivery.

PARIS DOLLS AND MORE SHOPPE

Madelene Grazaitis
700 E. Wood St.
Paris, IL 61944
Phone: (217)466-8500 CST
Fax: (217)466-8500
E-Mail: parisdol@comwares.net
Hours: By appointment only.
In business since: 1994

PRODUCT INFORMATION:

Modern manufactured dolls: About 10 brands, including Johannes Zook Originals, Lloyd Middleton Co., Lee Middleton, Seymour Mann, Timeless Creations—Mattel, Götz, Helen Kish (European Artist Dolls), Good-Krüger, White Horse Woman, FIBA
Artist dolls: Patricia Rose, Rose of Sharon Galleries
Special orders: 50% deposit required
Related products: Doll furniture, doll dresses, doll kits, reproduction porcelain dolls, wooden paper dolls, doll cases, doll stands, doll supplies (wigs). Also Russian nesting dolls, rag dolls, porcelain dolls

BUSINESS INFORMATION:

Type of business: Dolls sold at store location and by mail.
Accepts: Cash, check, money order, Visa, MC

Discounts: For $25 yearly membership fee—all dolls 10% off. Frequent sales.
Layaway: 6 month layaway (no other special requirements as long as doll(s) paid off in 6 months)
Return/exchange policy: Returns accepted within 1 month of purchase.
Back order policy: No payments required until order is available for shipment.
Mailing list: Write or call to be included.
Phone orders: Any hour or day. If no answer, leave message. Will return call.
Mail orders: Will ship to US, Canada, overseas. Send name, address, phone number, item and payment including shipping. Prepayment is required.
Shipping information: Prepayment is required. Please add $5 per doll for shipping. Shipped via UPS or method preferred by customer. Allow 1 week for delivery.

ADDITIONAL INFORMATION:

Special features: Also sells model trains, Russian collectibles, Bradford collectors' baskets, college monopoly games.

PATRICIA ALLGEIER BARBIE DOLLS AND COLLECTIBLES

Patricia Allgeier
R.D. 2, Box 378
Hawley, PA 18428
Phone: (717)226-0769 EST

PRODUCT INFORMATION:

Modern manufactured dolls: Mattel
Retired manufactured dolls: Mostly Barbie and family, some Tammy, Tressy and personality dolls and collectibles
Related products: New and vintage original Barbie doll and family clothing, structures and related

BUSINESS INFORMATION:

Type of business: Dolls sold by mail and occasionally at shows.
Accepts: Cash, check, money order
Return/exchange policy: 7 day return policy from date customer received items. Must call first for approval code. Must be in same condition as sent. Exchanges of equal value minus shipping costs.
Price list: $2
Mailing list: Write or call to be included.
Phone orders: M-Sat, 9-7.

Mail orders: Will ship to US, Canada, overseas. Send item number ordered and payment with shipping instructions. Prepayment is required.

Shipping information: Prepayment is required on shipping costs. Please add $5 per doll for shipping. Shipped via method preferred by customer. Allow 1-2 weeks for delivery.

ADDITIONAL INFORMATION:
Store offers lots of vintage and newer collectible Barbies with a nice mix of other dolls and collectibles at reasonable prices.

P.G.'S ENCHANTED DOLLS, INC.
Patricia Blasi
4360 W. Oakland Pk. Blvd.
Ft. Lauderdale, FL 33313
Phone: For orders: (800)783-1235 EST
For info: (954)739-9030
Fax: (954)739-9030
Hours: M-Sat, 10-5.
In business since: 1983

PRODUCT INFORMATION:
Modern manufactured dolls: About 20-30 brands, including Ginny, Alexander, Lawton, Effanbee, Robert Tonner, Kish and Co., H. Gunzel, Kingstate, Robin Woods, Horseman, Barbie, Ashton-Drake, Lee Middleton, Good-Krüger

Retired manufactured dolls: Alexander, Ashton-Drake, Barbie

Artist dolls: Marilyn Bolden, Kay McKey

Special orders: Deposit required.

Related products: Antique dolls, doll furniture, bears, shoes, socks and accessories, doll and bear cleaning products, books, magazines, Breyer horses

BUSINESS INFORMATION:
Type of business: Dolls sold at retail store and by mail.

Accepts: Cash, check, money order, Visa, MC, DC, AE

Discounts: V.I.P. Club available

Layaway: Deposit, 4 months

Return/exchange policy: Even exchange or store credit

Price list: LSASE

Phone orders: During regular business hours

Fax orders: Send name, address, home and work phone, product wanted, credit card number and signature

Mail orders: Will ship to US, Canada, overseas. Send name, address, home and work phone, product wanted, check, money order or credit card number and signature. Prepayment is required.

Shipping information: Shipped via UPS or US mail. Delivery time varies.

ADDITIONAL INFORMATION:
Special features: P.G.'s Enchanted Dolls Inc. sponsors artist signings. The shop is also a doll hospital.

REGINA'S DOLL HEAVEN
Josie Jessup
1000 NE 105th St.
Seattle, WA 98125
Phone: (206)523-0373 PST
In business since: 1989
Hours: By appointment only

PRODUCT INFORMATION:
Modern manufactured dolls: About 6 brands, including Götz, Jeckel-Jansen, Treffeisen, Kish and Co., Robert Tonner

Retired manufactured dolls: An occasional older Himstedt

Artist dolls: Maja Bill Buckwalder, Jan McLean, Marlena Blanford, Susan Krey, Melissa Wyatt, S&A Clark, Marilyn Bolden, Juanita and Monica Montoya, Donna Faville, Nicole West, Paul Crees

Special orders: ⅓ down, contract. No returns.

BUSINESS INFORMATION:
Type of business: Dolls sold by mail and in showroom.

Accepts: Cash, check, money order, Visa, MC, DC, AE

Discounts: 10% and 5% for cash on most dolls

Layaway: Usually 20% down, 8 months

Return/exchange policy: All sales are final on sale items and special orders.

Back order policy: Customer is frequently contacted.

Catalog/price list: Color copies of photos available for free with description of type of doll wanted, including price, height, medium, etc.

Mailing list: Write or call to be included.

Phone orders: 7 days, 9-9.

Mail orders: Will ship to US, Canada, overseas. Prepayment is required.

Shipping information: Shipped via UPS

or method preferred by customer. Shipping is included in the cost of the doll. Allow 10 days for delivery.

ADDITIONAL INFORMATION:
Josie generally includes teddies or chairs with doll. Special customers are first to see pictures of new dolls. Josie likes to maintain a friendly relationship with customers.

2ND TIME AROUND DOLL SHOP
D.J. Smith
112 Buckroe Ave.
Hampton, VA 23664
Phone: (804)851-7842 EST
Hours: By appointment only
In business since: 1978

PRODUCT INFORMATION:
Modern manufactured dolls: Several brands available

Retired manufactured dolls: Several brands available

Related products: Old and antique dolls, 1900-present

BUSINESS INFORMATION:
Type of business: Dolls sold at store location and at shows.

Layaway: Available

SHELLIE'S MINIATURE MANIA
Shellie Kazan
178 W. 25th Ave.
San Mateo, CA 94403
Phone: (415)341-7154 PST
Hours: M-F, 10-5:30. Sat, 10-5.
In business since: 1976

PRODUCT INFORMATION:
Modern manufactured dolls: About 5-6 brands, including Alexander, Helen Kirsh, Ashton-Drake, Dynasty, Effanbee

Retired manufactured dolls: Annette Hemstedt, Lawton, Middleton, McClure, Ashton-Drake, Alexander

Artist dolls: Dawn Adams, local artists

Special orders: Must meet minimum order requirements.

Related products: Doll clothes, doll furniture, doll foods and accessories, including antique accessories, furniture, antique dolls

BUSINESS INFORMATION:
Type of business: Dolls sold at store location.

Accepts: Cash, check, money order, Visa, MC

Layaway: 30% down, 60 days

Return/exchange policy: Returns within 10 days. Exchanges only; no refunds.

Mailing list: Write to be included.

Phone orders: During business hours

ADDITIONAL INFORMATION:

Special features: Shellie sells antique accessories, old collectible dolls and antique doll furniture.

> "WE HAVE 'CUSTOMERS' AS YOUNG AS SEVEN MONTHS ABSOLUTELY DETERMINED TO MAKE DOLL COLLECTING A LIFETIME HOBBY. FINDING A NEW DOLL IS BETTER THAN CHOCOLATE!"
> *Kmitsch Girls, Stillwater, MN*

SPECIAL OCCASIONS

Cindy

19171 Willamette Dr.

West Linn, OR 97068

Phone: (503)697-1765 PST

Additional locations: Country Peddler, 3 Monroe Pkwy., Suite J, Lake Oswego, OR 97035

Hours: M-F, 10-7. Sat, 10-6. Sun, 12-5.

In business since: 1984

PRODUCT INFORMATION:

Modern manufactured dolls: Lizzie High, Attic Babies and Daddy's Long Legs

Retired manufactured dolls: Lizzie High, Daddy's Long Legs

Special orders: Prepayment required.

BUSINESS INFORMATION:

Type of business: Dolls sold at store location.

Accepts: Cash, check, money order, Visa, MC

Layaway: ½ down, 30 days

Return/exchange policy: Exchanges available

Mailing list: Write or call to be included.

Phone orders: During business hours

STONE FENCE DOLL SHOPPE

Brenda Suiter

368 Southland Dr.

Lexington, KY 40503

Phone: For orders: (800)695-3590 EST
For info: (606)275-1962

Fax: (606)277-9231

Hours: M-F, 8-5. Sat, 9:30-4

In business since: 1993

PRODUCT INFORMATION:

Modern manufactured dolls: Wimbledon Collection, Gustave and Gretchen Wolff Designer Dolls

Artist dolls: Gustave F. Wolff, Gretchen M. Wolff

Related products: Little Gem teddy bears, Mary Meyer teddy bears, occassionally doll furniture

BUSINESS INFORMATION:

Type of business: Dolls sold at store location and by mail.

Accepts: Cash, check, money order, Visa, MC, DC, AE

Layaway: By mail order, 3-4 monthly payments. In store, 10% down, 10% every 2 weeks.

Return/exchange policy: By mail order, 30 day exchange or full refund. In store, no cash refund. May exchange only within 30 days of purchase.

Back order policy: Will be shipped upon arrival of merchandise.

Catalog: Color, $2, refundable with purchase

Mailing list: Write to be included.

Phone orders: During business hours

Fax orders: Fax regular order form.

Mail orders: Will ship to US, Canada. Send regular order form. Prepayment is required.

Shipping information: Dolls paid in full get free shipping. Dolls placed on layaway have $4.60 added to first payment. Allow 7-10 working days.

WEEFOKE EMPIRE

Nikki Menconi

619 4th St.

Bremerton, WA 98337

Phone: (360)792-9293 PST

Hours: M-F, 12-5, or by appointment.

In business since: 1960

PRODUCT INFORMATION:

Modern manufactured dolls: About 10 brands, including Dynasty, Franklin, Georgetown, Gadco, Johannes Zook, Global, Alexander

Retired manufactured dolls: Dynasty, Franklin, Georgetown, Gadco, Johannes Zook, Global, Alexander

Related products: Doll furniture, doll clothes, handmade dolls

BUSINESS INFORMATION:

Type of business: Dolls sold at store location.

Accepts: Cach, check, money order, Visa, MC, DC, AE

Discounts: 10% discount on cash sales only

Layaway: Flexible

Return/exchange policy: All sales final

Mail orders: Will ship to US. Prepayment is required.

Shipping information: Shipped via UPS. Allow 2 weeks.

WILD SPIRIT DOLL STUDIO

Nancy Pritchard

1235 Wampanoog Trail, Rt. 114

E. Providence, RI 02806

Phone: (401)433-1235 EST

Hours: T-Sat, 10-5.

In business since: 1995

PRODUCT INFORMATION:

Modern manufactured dolls: About 10 brands, including Seymour Mann, Johannes Zook, FayZah Spanos, Jeckel-Jansen, Dollmakers Originals, The Collectables, Mattel—Barbie and Himstedt, Sandi McAslan, Kingstate

Artist dolls: Peggy Dey, Karen Alcaro, Gail Hoyt, Christie Cummings, Gaskin, Nancy Pritchard, Pam Gray, Sue Walker

Special orders: Available

Related products: Dollmaking supplies, books on making dolls, doll clothes, Victorian doll furniture, large selection of teddy bears

BUSINESS INFORMATION:

Type of business: Dolls sold at store location and by mail.

Accepts: Cash, check, money order, Visa, MC

Discounts: 10% store club customer discount

Layaway: 25% down, 10% monthly. No additional cost.

Return/exchange policy: Equal value exchanges or store credit available

Back order policy: Deposit required. We contact customer.

Mailing list: Write, call or sign guest book to be included.

Phone orders: During business hours

Mail orders: Prepayment is required.

Shipping information: Shipped via RPS. Allow 4-6 days if in stock for delivery.

ADDITIONAL INFORMATION:

Special features: Dollmaking (sculpting) classes and workshops for adults and children available.

YOUNG AT HEART DOLL SHOP

Rt. 2
Preston, CT 06365
Phone: (203)887-6889
Hours: W-Sat, 10-5. Sun, 12-4.
In business since: 1981

PRODUCT INFORMATION:

Modern manufactured dolls: About 50 brands, including Alexander, Artist Collectibles, Berjusa, Bradley, Dynasty, Dakin, European Doll Artists, Furga, Gadco, Götz, Gunzel, Goebel, Good-Krüger, Hamilton Heritage, Himstedt, Kingstate, Legacy, Mann, Mattel, Middleton, Paradise Galleries, Precious Heirlooms, Tender Touch, Ultimate, Wakeen, World

Retired manufactured dolls: Available

Artist dolls: Local artists

Special orders: ⅓ down

Related products: Eyes, wigs, hats, clothes, stands, shoes, books, cards, prints, furniture

BUSINESS INFORMATION:

Type of business: Dolls sold at store location and by mail.

Accepts: Cash, check, money order, Visa, MC, AE

Discounts: 10% off for senior citizens. Many ongoing store discounts and specials.

Layaway: Available

Return/exchange policy: No cash refunds. Store credit offered.

Phone orders: During business hours

Mail orders: Will ship to US, Canada. Prepayment is required.

Shipping information: Shipped via UPS. Allow 10-15 days for delivery.

ADDITIONAL INFORMATION:

Special features: Ongoing museum display of 100 Shirley Temple dolls and memorabilia. 2,500 sq. ft. of 3,000 dolls for sale.

ZIP'S TOYS TO GO

Toni Volk
16 W. Lancaster Ave.
Ardmore, PA 19003
Phone: For orders: (610)649-2555 EST
For info: (610)649-8444
Fax: (610)649-8444
Hours: T, Th, F, Sat, 10-5. W, 10-8.
In business since: 1985

PRODUCT INFORMATION:

Modern manufactured dolls: Annalee, Lawton, Götz, vinyl dolls, Pauline, Good-Krüger

Retired manufactured dolls: Lawton, Annalee, Ginny (Old Meritas and Dakin), Good-Krüger, World Doll, Effanbee, Robin Woods

Artist dolls: Anna Avigail Brahams, Gail Lackey, Brigitte Deval, Fredricy, Linda Mason, Ruth Treffeisen, Wendy Froud, Blythe and Snodgrass, Jan Galperin, R. John Wright, GSR, Philip Heath, Yolanda Bellos, The Paul Crees Collection

Special orders: 50% deposit required. Doll must be accepted upon arrival, courtesy 20% reduction.

Related products: Old and new paper

dolls, doll clothes for modern dolls, plush and china accessories

BUSINESS INFORMATION:

Type of business: Dolls sold at store location and by mail.

Accepts: Cash, check, money order, Visa, MC, DC

Discounts: 10% prepayment discount on dolls over $1,000, 20% discount on dolls ordered and not in stock. In house collectors' clubs.

Layaway: 3 months, up to $500; 6 months, up to $1,000; 9 months, up to $1,500; 12 months, over $1,501. 20% nonrefundable deposit and equal monthly payments

Return/exchange policy: 7 days full cash or credit refund, 6 month exchange privileges

Back order policy: Deposits returned. Will call customer when item arrives.

Phone orders: During regular business hours

Fax orders: Send full name, address, phone, shipping instructions, credit card number and expiration date.

Mail orders: Will ship to US, Canada, overseas. Send full name, address, phone, shipping instructions, credit card number and expiration date. Prepayment is required.

Shipping information: Prepayment is required. Shipped via method preferred by customer. Allow 3 days-2 weeks for delivery.

ADDITIONAL INFORMATION:

Special features: The shop is "an art gallery, an antique shop, a bear shop, a full retail specialty import toy store, a major Steiff retailer and a lead miniatures dealer."

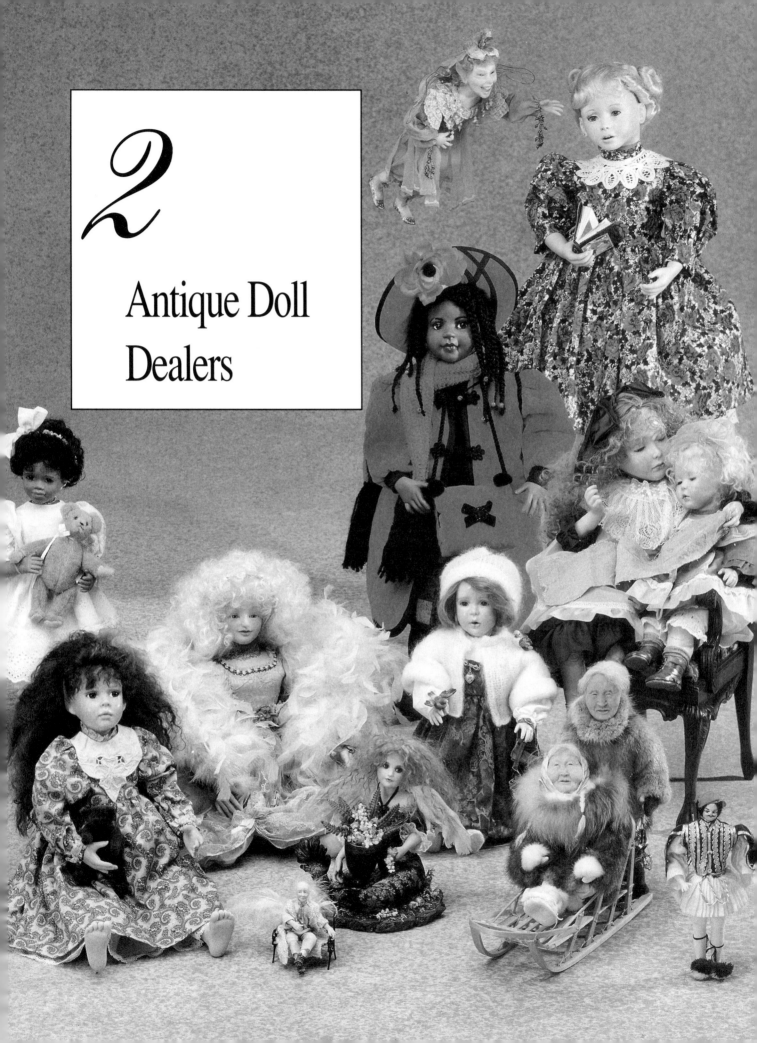

2
Antique Doll Dealers

A Guide to Chapter Two

The dolls of the past are witnesses to history. Look into their eyes. They have seen times that most of us cannot recall. They have survived wars and hardships and happy times and the hard love of children. Best of all, they never run out of love. They need collectors to take them in, care for them and pass them on to the next generation.

This chapter opens with an article by Judith Whorton that will give you an overview of the history of antique German dolls. The listings that follow will guide your search for antique dolls and the services they need to stay "healthy."

Some Definitions

There is much confusion over the correct use of the term "antique doll." It seems that there is no industry standard for this term. According to Judith Whorton, the U.S. government considers anything that is more than one hundred years old an antique. The United Federation of Doll Clubs uses the seventy-five-year mark as the dividing point between "old" and "antique." Judith thinks it makes sense to use World War II as the dividing point, although this is not considered an industry standard, since methods of production and distribution changed drastically after World War II. In this book, we use "antique" to describe any doll that is more than seventy-five years old (pre-1925), and "old" to describe anything manufactured before World War II but after the seventy-five-year cutoff point (1925 to 1945).

The Dealer Listings

The first section of the chapter includes dealers, restoration experts and appraisers. Because there is a great deal of overlap among these three segments of the industry, we have grouped all of these under single listings. In other words, someone who buys, sells, restores and appraises antique dolls will be listed once, with all this information included. We have not included separate listings for those who restore modern dolls, but most of the restoration experts listed here can also restore more recently made pieces. Call individual dealers for more information on these services.

The dealer listings include location and contact information, hours, and a description of the type of business. In addition, specific information about products and services, including areas of expertise, products bought and sold, and details about restoration and appraisal services are included. Finally, business details like methods of payment, discounts, layaway options, and details about phone, fax and mail orders are listed.

The Auction Listings

The second portion of the chapter lists auctions that offer antique dolls. We have included only individually sponsored auctions; auctions associated with a show are listed with the show in chapter six. If you are looking for modern doll auctions, you are more likely to find them in chapter six, although some of the auctions listed here also include dolls made more recently.

The auction listings include location and contact information, as well as how often the auction is held. In addition, the listing includes the times of year during which the auction is held, the duration of the auction, the cost of admission and average attendance. Finally, details on the types of items auctioned, how to get a catalog and how to be placed on a mailing list are also listed.

Collecting Antique German Dolls With Success

BY JUDITH WHORTON

Judith Whorton is a nationally known doll expert and collector. She won the *Dolls* Award of Excellence for her work as editor of *Doll News,* the official publication of the United Federation of Doll Clubs. She is a contributing editor for *Dolls,* where her column "Ask The Expert" is a popular feature. She has written for numerous magazines, including *Doll Reader, Spinning Wheel* and *Antique Trader.* The book *All Dolls Are Collectible,* which Judith co-authored with Genevieve Angione, is a practical guide to doll collecting. She has been a national judge for UFDC and the Modern Doll Convention and has lectured at several national conventions and universities. She is a graduate of Samford University in Birmingham, Alabama. She lives in Wilsonville, Alabama.

Judith Whorton

*T*he words "antique doll" have an almost magical connotation to the doll collector. Sooner or later, most collectors develop a yearning to own an old doll. Some collectors hesitate to move into the older doll field because they think it will be an expensive hobby. Actually, most collectors of new dolls probably could have a typical dolly-face German doll for what they have spent on newer dolls during the year. After all, several twenty-dollar Barbie doll purchases quickly add up.

One of the advantages of collecting older dolls is that their value and desirability have already been established. In contrast, the prices of newer dolls tend to fluctuate depending on the values assigned by speculators who have entered the doll market. Often the cost of newer dolls increases rapidly, then suddenly drops when the speculators lose interest. The 1995 Barbie is a good example. Before Christmas 1995, the doll was advertised for as much as $170. Later, Mattel sold vouchers for dolls to be delivered in the spring. Collectors who had purchased the doll at five times the retail price could have acquired the doll in the spring of 1996 for about $30. While the value of newer dolls depends on who is putting value on the doll, the accepted standards for determining the quality and value of antique and old dolls are widely recognized and accepted.

Several types of antique and old dolls are available to the collector. They vary widely in terms of country of origin, medium, availability and value. The collector's personal preference will determine if she chooses to specialize in a certain type of doll or to collect individual dolls that speak to her. If you are new at collecting antique and old dolls, visit your local bookstore or library and consult an expert, such as the dealers listed in this chapter, before deciding what you want to include in your collection. For more tips on collecting old dolls, see the list at the end of this introduction.

Because I could not cover all the types of antique or old collectible dolls in this introduction, I have chosen to focus on the history of old German dolls. Even if you decide that you would rather collect another type of old or antique doll, this introduction will give you an idea of the background information and distinguishing features that all collectors should consider.

This all-bisque doll has glass eyes and is wearing his original clothing.

Bisque: The Great Variety

Of all the materials used in producing old dolls, bisque is the most popular with collectors. China, parian and bisque all are mixtures of clay and other materials and are fired in a kiln. How the doll is finished determines the name of the material. A china doll has been finished with a glaze, like our china dishes. Parian dolls are left unglazed and without a tinted complexion. Bisque dolls have a tinted complexion with a matte finish.

Most bisque dolls were made in Germany from the late 1880s to the early 1930s, when economic depression drove most of the companies out of business. During these years, literally millions of dolls were produced, so collectors should not feel compelled to purchase the first old bisque doll they encounter. Many of the shops and dealers listed in this chapter will be able to help you locate a German bisque doll.

Not only are there many bisque dolls out there, but there is also a vast amount of information about them available to the collector. Fortunately, the majority of the bisque dolls are marked on the back of the head with names, symbols or numbers. Thanks to the excellent research of many historians and doll experts, we can identify the manufacturers of our dolls. Often the dolls can be dated as well. Mold numbers can help a collector identify the manufacturer and determine the rarity and value of a particular doll. Many dealers and shops listed in this chapter also offer appraisal services. Most listings include the types of dolls in which the dealer specializes and the cost of this service.

Dolly-Face Dolls and Character Dolls

Collectors will find more dolly-face dolls than any other kind of German doll. The typical dolly-face doll has sleeping eyes, an open mouth with teeth, and a placid expression. Besides these, there are also bisque character dolls (dolls with realistic-looking faces, often based on a real person), which were first made around 1910. These dolls often display fanciful features such as big, round googly eyes, or show strong emotions such as laughter or anger. These dolls range from cute children to haughty ladies like the Gibson girl. Some German character dolls are even more expensive than their French counterparts.

Most closed-mouth German bisque dolls were made before 1900, although some were produced as late as the 1930s. As a general rule, however, the closed-mouth dolls are older and rarer than the open-mouth dolls. Some of these dolls also have paperweight eyes, or eyes that remain open, which makes them especially valuable. A dealer who claims to have a doll with sleeping paperweight eyes is mistaken. Paperweight eyes have a clear glass dome around the eye, creating a feeling of depth and realism. These eyes are found in some German dolls, especially older ones, but are more common in French dolls. A good friend of mine used to say, "A good doll keeps her eyes open and her mouth shut."

Baby Dolls

The trend of baby dolls with realistic bent-limb bodies started in 1909. The German firm Kämmer and Reinhardt introduced a baby with the mold mark "100." Collectors have named this doll The Kaiser Baby, and it revolutionized the doll market. Until that time, bisque dolls were dressed as babies but did not look like them.

In 1923, the Bye-Lo became a sensation. This doll resembles a three-day-old infant and became the first doll to earn one million dollars in sales. Some collectors specialize in Bye-Los. These dolls are easy to identify as they are marked with the American designer's name, "Grace S. Putnam," on the back of the head.

All-Bisque Dolls

A collector with limited space might enjoy collecting all-bisque dolls. There is always room for one more of these little charmers. Most all-bisque dolls were manufactured between 1880 and the late 1930s and range in size from about eight inches to one inch or less. Most are unmarked, so collectors must look for other ways to determine quality. Swivel necks, glass eyes and detailed molding such as individual fingers and toes are desirable. Any extra production step adds to the value of the doll, including molded shoes with heels and straps. All-bisque dolls inspired by comic characters are particularly hot items at the moment.

China Dolls

Although some china dolls were made earlier, mass production of china dolls in Germany began in the 1840s. At one time collectors preferred china dolls to the now more popular bisque. Perhaps one of the reasons bisque overtook china in popularity is that the mold marks on the bisque can reveal a history, while it is more difficult to identify a china doll. Despite these difficulties, china dolls do add an old-fashioned charm to a collection.

China dolls are rarely marked, so collectors must rely on hairstyles to date them. Some styles were used for years, however, so even this is not necessarily a good guide. For example, the close-cropped low brow style was developed in the late 1880s, but this style continued into the 1930s.

The hairstyle is the most important feature of a china doll. Detailed curls, bows and bangs all add to the worth of a china doll. Black is the most common hair color. Even dolls with the low brow hairstyle usually have black hair; about two-thirds of such dolls were made with black hair, as opposed to blond. There are some very early brown-haired china dolls from the 1840s. Eyes can also be used to gauge the value of a china doll. Brown-eyed china dolls are rare and glass-eyed china dolls even more so.

Homemade bodies were very common, so do not choose a doll based solely on the quality of the body if you like the china head. Manufactured bodies with unusual features such as corsets add value, however. In the early 1900s, china dolls with cloth bodies printed with designs such as flags or multiplication tables became very popular. The heads on these bodies are usually the low brow style, so they do not bring as high a price as earlier china, but they are fun to have in a collection.

Parian Dolls

In the 1860s and 1870s, parian dolls were popular. While many of the china dolls depicted children, parian dolls were usually elegant ladies. A parian doll's complexion is left untinted, creating a striking white look. Accessories such as molded roses, ribbons and ruffles are hand-applied to the molded hair in the greenware

stage, after the porcelain slip (liquid porcelain) has set in the mold and been removed. Since the clay is still unfired, the heads are easily damaged. When finished, these dolls remind one of an elaborate birthday cake with white frosting and sugar decorations. Light brown or dark blond are the most common hair colors for parian dolls. A black-haired parian doll is rare.

German Firms: A Quick Look

Fortunately for collectors, most German bisque dolls are marked and can be identified. A thumbnail sketch of a few German firms may help you determine the value of a doll you are considering for your collection. Of course, you will want to consult an expert or one of the several doll price guides available as well.

This Armand Marseille 390 is dressed in his original clothing.

Armand Marseille

The firm with the French-sounding name, Armand Marseille, was the most prolific of the German manufacturers. This firm made inexpensive dolls for the mass market. The most common mark for the ball-jointed dolls is "390." The most common mark for kid bodies is "370." There is nothing wrong with acquiring a common doll; the price, however, should reflect that the doll is common. Special features on a "390" or "370" doll will increase its value and appeal. For example, I own a "390" in original soldier costume, which is one of the most impressive figures in my collection.

AM, as it is commonly known to collectors, did make some rarer dolls, such as a closed-mouth doll with a ball-jointed lady body, and a little girl marked "Just Me." Even though these dolls are marked with the common AM letters, they are rare and expensive today.

J.D. Kestner

Anyone collecting old German dolls should consider dolls made by the J.D. Kestner firm, one of the oldest of the German doll manufacturers. J.D. Kestner was the first firm to make both heads and bodies. The company produced bisque dolls after purchasing a porcelain factory in 1860. The bisque often has the delicate pale coloring so desired by collectors. This firm was so important to the German economy that one story alleges that J.D. Kestner, Jr. was given government permission to have two wives.

Practically all the Kestner dolls are of excellent quality, including the dolly-face dolls. The mold number "154" is among the most common. This firm made such classics as the Gibson girl, and it was among the first German firms to produce the Bye-Lo and the Kewpies. An interesting series of dolls were marked with a letter of the alphabet, the words "Made in Germany" and a size number. These dolls do not bear the Kestner name but are Kestner products and Kestner quality.

Gebrüder Heubach

Collectors are usually advised to consider the quality of body when purchasing a doll. Gebrüder Heubach dolls are an exception to the rule. This company made some of the finest character doll heads, but combined them with some of the cheapest cardboard bodies. As with the majority of German dollmakers, Heubach purchased bodies from an outside source. This seems to be one area in which Heubach cut corners. But given the dolls' wonderful lifelike heads, collectors don't mind.

Heubach did not start making doll heads until about 1910, the beginning of the character-doll era. The dolls often portray laughing, pouting or pensive children. Intaglio eyes are often found on Heubach dolls, although this was not the only company using this eye style. On intaglio eyes, the iris and the pupil are concave, creating a lively expression.

This beautiful Gebrüder Heubach doll has intaglio eyes.

Pre-coloring of the porcelain slip used for the heads was another interesting Heubach technique. Collectors usually prefer the more subtle tinted bisque, but the high coloring works well for Heubach, creating the image of an active, healthy child. The dolls are sometimes marked with a half-daisy or sunburst symbol and the initials "G" and "H" combined. The name "Heubach" in a square mold was also used.

Ernst Heubach

Markings are important because there were several other firms using the Heubach name, including Ernst Heubach. This firm often marked its dolls with the words "Heubach of Köppelsdorf." While some of the dolls are appealing, they do not compare with the artistic quality or value of Gebrüder Heubach dolls. Among the most common mold numbers for Ernst Heubach are "250" and "275." The ethnic dolls and the few character dolls from this company would be better additions to a collection than their dolly-face dolls.

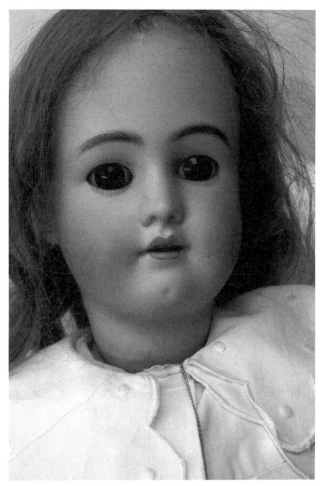

This doll is an example of a typical Simon & Halbig open-mouth doll.

Simon and Halbig

Simon and Halbig made a wide variety of beautiful dolls, from all-bisque to dolly-face to character dolls. This major company is well known for the quality of its bisque. The most common mold mark is "1079," but even this one is appealing. The company was established in 1869 and was sold to Kämmer and Reinhardt in 1920. As mentioned earlier, K&R, as it is known, made the first character baby. Most collectors would agree that this firm created the finest of character dolls. The baby doll with the mold number "126" is among the most common.

Carl Horn

The Carl Horn firm specialized in tiny all-bisque dolls dressed in crocheted clothing. Some of these little treasures are less than one inch tall. Yet they are jointed at the arms and legs and are completely dressed. One appealing plus is that most of these originally dressed dolls sell for less than $100 at the moment.

This list of firms is meant to whet a collector's appe-tite. There are hundreds more German firms that made appealing dolls. To learn more, read books and magazines, talk to experts, and keep in touch with other collectors of old and antique dolls.

Quick Tips for Successful Collecting

1. Antique and old dolls were mass-produced, so consider a doll carefully before purchasing it. If there are several flaws, you will probably be able to find a doll of the same mark and style that is of better quality.

2. Dealers who specialize in dolls, such as those listed in this chapter, are good sources. They generally will not overprice, as they wish to remain competitive.

3. Attend every show and museum exhibit you can. Looking at the actual dolls is a great learning experience, no matter how long you have been collecting dolls.

4. Tell everyone, including neighbors, friends and co-workers, that you are looking for old dolls. I acquired a prized Hilda baby through a friend of a friend.

5. Keep antique dolls away from direct sunlight. The fired bisque head will not suffer, but the clothing and composition (a very delicate molded material made of wood pulp, commonly used in earlier dolls) may deteriorate due to ultraviolet rays.

6. If a sleeping-eye doll must be stored in a drawer or chest, put the doll face down. Otherwise gravity will eventually harm the sleeping mechanism.

7. There is an old saying, "Buy what you like." Yet with dolls, a collector may become more discerning the more she learns. Study every doll carefully. Remember that old and antique dolls are major purchases that you plan to have for a long time.

8. Damaged dolls, especially those with head damage, are hard to resell. Unless a damaged doll is especially striking, pass it by. Another one will turn up.

9. Be alert for reproductions. Both old and new bisque have been sanded after the first firing. When sanded, newer bisque feels very smooth and slick to the touch, but the older bisque contains impurities which give it a slightly grainy texture even when sanded. Also, the painting is not always as good on reproductions. For example, many reproduction Bye-Los have stubby eyelashes and severely painted hairlines. The real Bye-Los have subtle painting with a soft hairline appropriate to a newborn baby. If you have a question, be sure to consult an expert.

10. Reference books and magazines are essential to successful doll collecting. If you are on a limited budget, visit a local library to review books and magazines before purchasing or subscribing to them. Many libraries will order a specific book or magazine if you request it.

11. You can learn a great deal from other collectors. Most serious collectors find it beneficial to join a doll club or become part of a national doll organization. Several clubs are listed in this book, along with detailed membership information. The United Federation of Doll Clubs publishes a national magazine, *Doll News,* four times a year. It also sponsors national and regional meetings. Members can rent slide and video programs from the national organization. For further information, contact The United Federation of Doll Clubs, 10920 North Ambassador Drive, Suite 130, Kansas City, MO 64153.

Doll collecting has many additional pleasures beyond that of acquiring an old object. You will make new friends and begin to see the world in different ways. After all, each old doll is a miniature three-dimensional lesson in our culture and history!

Antique Doll Dealers

ANN LLOYD—ANTIQUE DOLLS
Ann Lloyd
5632 S. Deer Run Rd.
Doylestown, PA 18901
Phone: (215)794-8164 EST
In business since: 1975

PRODUCT/SERVICE INFORMATION:
Area of expertise: Antique dolls
Buys: Anything pre-1930 that is salable.
Please send a slide or photo, write, or
call to set up an appointment.
Sells: Mostly bisque, but all types are included on list.
Appraisals: Cost varies. Will provide references on request. Customers must
provide the doll itself.
Other products/services: Sells Steiff,
some clothes, furniture, accessories,
books and original doll plates.

BUSINESS INFORMATION:
Type of business: Conducts business
from home, by mail, at shows.
Home Appointments: Mail order pre-
ferred. Occasionally by appointment.
Shows: Call to request list.
Accepts: Cash, money order, check
Layaway: 4 equal payments preferred,
but adjustments can be made.
Catalog/price list: b&w and color, 25¢
Mailing list: Write to be included.
Phone orders: 8:30 A.M.-11 P.M.
Buys through the mail: Send a letter
with a photo or slide and SASE. Will
pay with check. Policies are stated at
the bottom of list.
Sells through the mail: Call or mail a
request. Prepayment required.

ANNETTE'S ANTIQUE DOLLS
Annette Palm
P.O. Box 5227
Bellingham, WA 98227
Phone: (360)758-2476 PST
In business since: 1966

PRODUCT/SERVICE INFORMATION:
Area of expertise: Antique doll dealer for
the advanced collector.
Buys: French characters, German charac-

ters, early papier mâché, all dolls that
are 100+ years old.
Sells: Same as above
Appraisals: Negotiable

BUSINESS INFORMATION:
Type of business: Conducts business by
mail, at shows.
Phone orders: Accepted

ANTIQUE TREASURERS & TOYS
Jacqueline Henry
P.O. Box 17
Walworth, NY 14568-0017
Phone: (315)986-1424 EST
In business since: 1988

PRODUCT/SERVICE INFORMATION:
Area of expertise: Specializes in antique
bisque dolls and 1950s hard plastic
dolls (such as Tonies, Jennies, Curity).
Buys: Antique bisque and 1950s plastic.
The 1950s hard plastic should have
original clothes and the original box.
Sells: German and French
Appraisals: Negotiable

BUSINESS INFORMATION:
Type of business: Conducts business by
mail, at shows.
Shows: Those on mailing list will be no-
tified. Write to request a list of shows.
Send SASE.
Phone orders: Accepted

AUNT EMILY'S DOLL HOUSE
Emily Manning
6220 Rhode Island Ave.
Riverdale, MD 20737
Phone: (301)864-5561 EST
Additional locations: 4809 Ravenswood
Rd., Riverdale MD 20737 (301)864-
5561.
Hours: T-Sun, 12:30-5.
In business since: 1967

PRODUCT/SERVICE INFORMATION:
Buys: Antique dolls. Inexpensive collectibles and old dolls. Please schedule
appointment or send a slide or photo.
Sells: Collectible and general inexpensive antique and old dolls of all types.

Restorations: Cost is based on supplies
and time involved. If papier mâché is
wet, do not dry out. If a doll is torn
up, bring in all the pieces.
Appraisals: $5/doll. Will provide refer-
ences upon request. Customer must
provide the doll itself. Does not appraise French dolls unless they are
listed in *Blue Book of Dolls Value.*

BUSINESS INFORMATION:
Type of business: Conducts business at
home, by mail and at shows.
Home Appointments: Please schedule in
advance
Accepts: Cash, check, money order
Layaway: Usually ⅓ down, 2 months.
Flexible.
Mailing list: Write to be included.
Phone orders: During business hours
Buys through the mail: Send a photo or
slide and SASE. Will pay with check.
Will return within 1 week in original
condition if Emily does not want the
doll.
Sells through the mail: Use order form
in catalog/price list or mail a request.
Prepayment required.
Restores dolls through the mail: Call or
mail a request
Shipping information: Will ship to US,
Canada. Prepayment required.
Shipped via UPS or method preferred
by customer.

ADDITIONAL INFORMATION:
Also sells pre-made doll clothes, old
laces and clothes, new cotton lace and
ribbons, furniture and accessories.

> "DOLLS ARE HISTORICAL STATEMENTS. THEY ARE
> MADE AT A GIVEN TIME IN HISTORY AND REFLECT
> THAT ERA IN STYLE, MATERIAL AND
> WORKMANSHIP."
> *Henrietta Pfeifer, Mid-Ohio Historical
> Museum, Canal Winchester, OH*

BARBARA'S DOLLS

Barbara Spears
6916 Camp Bowie Blvd.
Ft. Worth, TX 76126
Phone: (817)738-0771 or (817)249-2069 CST
Hours: W-Sat, 10:30-4:30
In business since: 1972

PRODUCT/SERVICE INFORMATION:

Area of expertise: All old dolls, bisque to Barbies
Buys: Antique bisque, china, parians with no chips or cracks to heads, compositions, hard plastics, vinyls and older Barbies. All should be in good to mint condition. Please bring doll to shop, schedule appointment, send slide or photo of doll or send doll for offer.
Sells: Bisque, china, parian, papier mâché, composition, hard plastics, older Barbies and Barbie clothes—all older dolls
Appraisals: $5/doll at shop or $35/hour if Barbara travels to see dolls. Customer must provide the doll itself. Barbara will not appraise over the phone or by mail because there are too many factors involved, and even pictures do not always show flaws.
Other products/services: Doll stringing, clothes cleaning, hair fixing, doll cleaning

BUSINESS INFORMATION:

Type of business: Conducts business at store location, by mail, at shows and at antique mall.
Shows: Call or write to be included.
Accepts: Cash, check, money order, Visa, MC
Layaway: ⅓ down, 60 days for sales of $500 or less; ¼ down, 90 days for items $500-1,000; 6 months for items over $1,000.
Catalog/price list: Color, $5, refundable with purchase.
Mailing list: Send LSASE and $5 to be included.
Phone orders: During business hours; also (817)249-2069 8:30 A.M.-10 P.M. CST.
Buys through the mail: Call first, send a letter with a photo or slide and SASE or send dolls to get an offer. Barbara will return dolls she does not buy. Will pay with check or COD. Dolls bought with money up front may be returned for full refund.
Sells through the mail: Call or mail a request. Prepayment required.
Shipping information: Will ship to US, Canada, overseas. Prepayment required. Shipped via US mail, or method preferred by customer. Allow 1 month for delivery.

ADDITIONAL INFORMATION:

Barbara is a member of the National Antique Doll Dealers' Association.

THE BARBIE ATTIC

Sandi Holder
2491 Regal Dr.
Union City, CA 94587
Phone: (510)489-0221 PST
Fax: (510)489-7467
E-mail: sandihb4u@aol.com
Hours: By appointment only
In business since: 1989

PRODUCT/SERVICE INFORMATION:

Area of expertise: Vintage Barbie dolls, clothing and accessories.
Appraisals: $25/doll. Will provide references on request. Customer must provide the doll itself.

BUSINESS INFORMATION:

Type of business: Conducts business at store location, by mail, at shows.
Home Appointments: Schedule 1 week in advance.
Shows: Call or write to request a list of shows.
Accepts: Cash, check, money order, Visa, MC
Layaway: ½ down, 30 days
Catalog: b&w, $2 for sample or subscription rate of $15/yr.
Phone orders: 10-8.
Fax orders: Include name, address, city, state, zip, area code, phone number, credit card number with expiration date.
Buys through the mail: Call first or send a letter with a photo or slide and SASE. Will pay with check or money order.
Sells through the mail: Use order form in catalog/price list, call or fax a request. Prepayment required.
Appraises dolls through the mail: Call first. Prepayment is required.
Shipping information: Will ship to US, Canada, overseas. Will notify customer. Shipped via FedEx, UPS or method preferred by customer. Allow 1 day-1 week.

BILLIE NELSON TYRRELL'S DOLL EMPORIUM

Billie Tyrrell
13035 Ventura Blvd.
Studio City, CA 91604
Phone: (818)763-5937 PST
Hours: Th-Sat, 11-4:30.
In business since: 1995

PRODUCT/SERVICE INFORMATION:

Area of expertise: Antique dolls, older collectibles and movie star dolls
Buys: Antique and old dolls in fair or better condition, movie star dolls, older collectibles and related items. Please bring doll into shop, set up an appointment, or send a slide or photo.
Sells: Antique and old dolls in fair or better condition, movie star dolls, older collectibles and related items.
Appraisals: Free. Customer must provide the doll itself.

BUSINESS INFORMATION:

Type of business: Conducts business at store location, by mail and at shows.
Shows: Call for list.
Accepts: Cash, money order, check
Layaway: Full payment in 4 months; longer for more expensive dolls.
Phone orders: 7 days, 7 A.M.-9:30 P.M.
Buys through the mail: Call first or send a letter with a photo or slide and SASE. Will pay by money order. Must send doll for Billie to see. Will send bank or money order with postage to keep. If Billie does not want it, will return and pay postage both ways.
Sells through the mail: Call or order through ads in *Doll Reader* and *Antique Doll World*. Prepayment required.
Shipping information: Will ship to US, Canada, overseas. Prepayment required. Will ship via method preferred by customer. Allow 1 week after check clears.

ADDITIONAL INFORMATION:

Has a very large selection of antique and older collectibles like Shirley Temples and movie star dolls.

CAT'S CRADLE

Glen Rollins
P.O. Box 51442
Provo, UT 84605-1442
Phone: (801)374-1832 CMT
Additional locations: 1180 Columbia
  Lane, Provo, UT 84604
In business since: 1985

PRODUCT/SERVICE INFORMATION:
Area of expertise: Antique dolls, pre-
  1930s, bisque
Buys: All types, bisque, pre-1930s.
Sells: Pre-1930s, French and German
  bisque, papier mâché
Restorations: Cost range varies
Appraisals: Cost range varies

BUSINESS INFORMATION:
Type of business: Conducts business
  from home, at shows
Home Appointments: Schedule W-Sat,
  11-5.
Shows: Call to request a list of shows
Phone orders: Call W-Sat, 11-5.

A CENTURY OF DOLLS

Karen D'onofrio
2360 Middle Country Rd.
Centereach, Long Island, NY 11720
Phone: (800)90-DOLLS or (516)981-
  0727 EST
Fax: (516)981-0727
In business since: 1993

PRODUCT/SERVICE INFORMATION:
Sells: A Century of Dolls presents a full
  range of dolls for sale, including antique composition dolls and modern
  1950s and 1960s dolls, as well as new
  manufactured and artist dolls.
Appraisals: Available

BUSINESS INFORMATION:
Type of business: Conducts business at
  store location.

CHATTY CATHY'S HAVEN

Kelly and Jody McIntyre
19528 Ventura Blvd. #495
Tarzana, CA 91356
Phone: (818)881-3878 PST
Hours: 10-7.
In business since: 1989

PRODUCT/SERVICE INFORMATION:
Area of expertise: Mattel talking dolls;
  repair.
Buys: Mattel talking dolls. Please call.
Sells: Mattel talking dolls

Restorations: $35-45 for voice repair.
  Allow 2-3 weeks.
Appraisals: Free

BUSINESS INFORMATION:
Type of business: Conducts business at
  home and by mail.
Home Appointments: Call to schedule
  appointment.
Accepts: Cash, check, money order, Visa,
  MC, AE
Discounts: 20% for 5 dolls or more
Layaway: Available
Mailing list: Write or call to be included.
Phone orders: During business hours
Buys through the mail: Call first. Will
  pay with check.
Appraises dolls through the mail: Call
  first. Appraisal is free, but customer is
  responsible for shipping costs both
  ways.
Restores dolls through the mail: Call
  first. Customer will be billed.
Shipping information: Will ship to US,
  Canada, overseas. Shipping will be
  billed with doll repair, usually $5 for
  US. Shipped via UPS or method preferred by customer. Allow 5 days.

CHRISTIES

219 E. 67th St.
New York, NY 10021
Phone: (800)395-6300 EST, (212)606-
  0543
In business since: 1796

PRODUCT/SERVICE INFORMATION:
Area of expertise: Antique doll and bear
  consignment house
Appraisals: Free

BUSINESS INFORMATION:
Type of business: Conducts business at
  store location
Catalog: $10-20
Phone orders: M-F, 9-5.

CLARK'S ANTIQUE DOLLS

Joyce K. Clark
P.O. Box 6571
Kennewick, WA 99336
Phone: (509)582-5912 PST
In business since: 1990

PRODUCT/SERVICE INFORMATION:
Area of expertise: Large antique dolls
  with bisque heads
Sells: Antique dolls with bisque heads,
  especially large dolls. Both French

and German available. All dolls are
clean and beautifully dressed.
Other products/services: Doll furniture,
  doll clothes

BUSINESS INFORMATION:
Type of business: Conducts business by
  mail and at shows.
Shows: Write to request a list of shows.
Accepts: Cash, check, money order, Visa,
  MC
Layaway: Varies with the price of the
  doll
Price List: LSASE
Mailing List: Write to be included.
  Enclose LSASE.
Phone orders: Anytime
Sells through the mail: Mail a request
  with LSASE. Prepayment required.
Shipping information: Will ship to US,
  Canada, overseas. Prepayment re-
  quired. Shipped via method preferred
  by customer. Allow 7 days for
  delivery.

> "DECORATE WITH YOUR DOLLS. THEY ARE WORKS
> OF ART. DO NOT KEEP THEM TUCKED AWAY IN
> BOXES—LIFE IS TOO SHORT! SEE, TOUCH,
> ENJOY THEM!"
>
> *Ruth C. Daniels, Cedar Chest Doll Shoppe,
> Blue Anchor, NJ*

DEBRA'S DOLLS

Debra Falciani
45 S. Main St., Back Shop (at the Mews)
P.O. Box 705
Mullica Hill, NJ 08062
Phone: (609)478-9778 EST
Hours: W-Sun, 11-5.
In business since: 1991 went into busi-
  ness, 1995 opened shop.

PRODUCT/SERVICE INFORMATION:
Area of expertise: Antique dolls (circa
  1840-1920)
Buys: Antique dolls (circa 1840-1920) in
  person at the shop; also buys antique
  doll clothing and accessories. Please
  bring doll to shop. A call ahead is ad-
  visable but not necessary.
Sells: Antique dolls (circa 1840-1920),
  including French and German bisque,
  china, wax, papier mâché, etc. Also
  sells antique doll clothing, doll
  houses, accessories, books on antique
  dolls, antique doll and children's fur-

niture, etc. Age, attribution and physical condition of dolls is guaranteed in writing upon purchase.

Restorations: Please bring doll into shop for an estimate. Will provide references on request. Allow maximum of 3 months.

Appraisals: Please call for an estimate. Will provide references on request. Customer must provide the doll itself.

BUSINESS INFORMATION:

Type of business: Conducts business at the shop location, by mail, at shows.

Shows: Those on mailing list will be notified. Call or write to request a list of shows.

Accepts: Cash, check, money order, Visa, MC

Layaway: Available for up to 1 year. Prices are firm for all layaway purchases.

Catalog: b&w, free with SASE.

Mailing list: Write or call to be included.

Phone orders: During business hours.

Shipping information: Will ship to US, Canada, overseas. Shipped via UPS.

DEMPSEY & BAXTER

Sherri Dempsey
1009 E. 38th St.
Erie, PA 16504
Phone: (814)825-6381 EST
In business since: 1992

PRODUCT/SERVICE INFORMATION:

Area of expertise: Pre-1950, antique dolls

Buys: Pre-1950

Sells: Pre-1950

Restorations: Cost varies

Appraisals: Minimum $15

BUSINESS INFORMATION:

Type of business: Conducts business at store location, at shows.

Shows: Call to request a list of shows.

THE DOLL ATTIC

Sandi Holder and Cathe Rossi
2488 Regal Dr.
Union City, CA 94587
Phone: (510)489-0221 PST
Fax: (510)489-7467
In business since: 1990

PRODUCT/SERVICE INFORMATION:

Area of expertise: Vintage Barbie dolls and accessories.

Buys: Barbies
Sells: Barbies

BUSINESS INFORMATION:

Type of business: Conducts business by mail, at shows.

Shows: Call to request a list of shows.

Catalog: $15/year, subscription 6 issues.

Phone orders: 10-6.

THE DOLL DOCTOR

Mary Gates
P.O. Box 334
Pontiac, IL 61764
Phone: For info: (815)842-3442 CST
Additional locations: 1404 4H Park Rd., Pontiac, IL 61764
In business since: 1981

PRODUCT/SERVICE INFORMATION:

Area of expertise: Composition restoration, costume dressing

Buys: Send a slide or photo.

Restorations: Must see the doll, as each doll's condition and what needs to be done determines price. Mary lets the customer know what it will cost and will return the doll if they find it too costly. If the doll has been in a fire, will also include paper for insurance company if she gets the job. Allow 3-6 months, sometimes longer. She has worked on all types of dolls and has dressed most she has worked on. She makes her own patterns using pictures of the doll in its original costume.

Appraisals: With written papers for insurance purposes, $10. Customer must provide the doll itself. Mary has an extensive doll book library. She tries to locate the doll and writes down the source along with price.

Other products/services: She writes articles for a collector magazine and sells "how-to" sheets—such as "How to Remove Ink from Vinyl."

BUSINESS INFORMATION:

Type of business: Conducts business from home, by mail.

Home Appointments: Schedule 3 days in advance.

Accepts: Cash, check, money order

Layaway: Available

Restores dolls through the mail: Call first. Mail a request with photo and description. Prepayment is required.

Shipping information: Will ship to US, Canada. Prepayment required. Add $6

per doll. Sometimes she bills for exactly what it costs to ship. She pays for insurance. Dolls are shipped via method preferred by customer.

THE DOLL EXPRESS, INC.

Rae-Ellen Koenig
Rt. 272, Trains
P.O. Box 367
Reamstown, PA 17567
Phone: (717)336-2414 EST
Fax: (717)336-1262
Hours: M, T, Th, 10-5. F-Sun, 9-6.
In business since: 1992

PRODUCT/SERVICE INFORMATION:

Area of expertise: A 100-dealer cooperative. Acts as liason between buyer and seller and sells their dolls and bears for them. Sells dolls from the 1700s through contemporary.

Buys: All kinds of dolls and bears, both old and new. Set up an appointment, send a slide or photo, fax a list or call with info.

Sells: All types of dolls, antique through contemporary. All mediums, including bisque, wood, cloth, papier mâché, wax, composition, hard plastic, vinyl and porcelain.

Appraisals: $5/doll. Will provide references on request. Customers must provide the doll itself. Will do written appraisals for insurance purposes and estates. Collection appraisal charge available on request. Cost depends on travel, amount, etc.

Other products/services: Doll supplies; rent showcases, providing the shop, showcase, labor and other related services.

BUSINESS INFORMATION:

Type of business: Conducts business at store location.

Accepts: Cash, check, money order, Visa, MC, AE, DC

Layaway: 20% down, 30 days. All sales are final.

Mailing list: Write or call to be included.

Phone orders: During business hours

Fax orders: Accepted

Buys through the mail. Call first. Will pay with check.

Sells through the mail. Call, fax or mail a request. Prepayment required or COD.

Appraises dolls through the mail. Call

or send doll. Prepayment is required.

Shipping information: Will ship to US, Canada, overseas. COD or prepayment required. Shipped via UPS or method preferred by customer.

ADDITIONAL INFORMATION:

The shop is a recreated train station with 6 1930s cars and a depot station. "We stock more than 10,000 dolls," says Rae-Ellen.

THE DOLL GALLERY

Barb or Dan Giguere
P.O. Box 124
Scarborough, ME 04070-0124
Phone: (207)883-0822 EST
Fax: (207)883-0822
E-mail: bkhdgoa@prodigy.com
Hours: By appointment only

PRODUCT/SERVICE INFORMATION:

Area of expertise: Restoration of antique dolls

Restorations: Fee schedule for routing repairs. Individual quotes given on a doll by doll basis. Will provide references if requested. Allow 3-6 months.

Appraisals: $25. Will provide references if requested. Customer must provide the doll itself. All appraisals are for replacement value and do not reflect a "selling price." Accepted by major insurance companies.

Other products/services: Presentations on the history of dolls

BUSINESS INFORMATION:

Type of business: Conducts business from home, by mail.

Home Appointments: Schedule 24 hours in advance.

Shows: Call or write to request a list of shows.

Accepts: Cash, check, money order, Visa, MC

Price list: SASE

Appraises dolls through the mail: Mail the doll for appraisal. Pay on completion of work.

Restores dolls through the mail: Call first. Mail a request with photo and description. Customer will be billed when work is completed.

Shipping information: Will ship to US, Canada. Actual cost is added to bill. Will ship via method preferred by customer. Allow 2-3 business days for delivery.

THE DOLL GALLERY

Nan Radford
675 Gilman Blvd.
Issaquah, WA 98027
Phone: (206)342-4684 PST
Hours: T-F, 10:30-4:30. Sat, 11-4:30.
In business since: 1989

PRODUCT/SERVICE INFORMATION:

Buys: Old dolls and related items, including lace, bears and jewelry.

Restorations: All repairs, including restringing and rewigging.

BUSINESS INFORMATION:

Type of business: Conducts business at store location and by mail.

Accepts: Cash, check, money order, Visa, MC

Layaway: 1-3 months, depending on cost

Mailing list: Write or call to be included.

Phone orders: During business hours

THE DOLL HOSPITAL

Jane C. Messenger
6892 Route 291
Marcy, NY 13403
Phone: (315)865-5463 EST
Hours: Evenings and weekends, by appointment only.
In business since: 1978

PRODUCT/SERVICE INFORMATION:

Buys: Antique dolls, including bisque, composition, papier mâché, anything pre-1950 (all must be in good condition). Please bring doll to shop or schedule appointment.

Sells: Antique dolls, pre-1950

Restorations: Cost is determined by the amount of work that needs to be done. Will provide references on request. Allow 3-6 weeks. A price quote is given when doll is received. All repair work is covered under insurance. Receipts are given to owner for doll, cost of repairs and value of doll.

Appraisals: Cost varies. Will provide references upon request. Customer must provide the doll itself. For complete collection appraisal, all work is done on computer. Dolls are numbered, and description and value are included.

BUSINESS INFORMATION:

Type of business: Conducts business at home and at shows.

Home Appointments: Please schedule 24 hours in advance.

Shows: Those on mailing list will be notified. Write to be included.

Accepts: Cash and check

Layaway: ⅓ down, 90 days. Dolls over $1,000 can be extended to 6 months.

Mailing list: Write to be included.

Restores dolls through the mail: Call first. Prepayment required. Complete price quote is given to owner before any work is started. Will tell customer how long the repair will take.

Shipping information: Will ship to US. Prepayment required for shipping cost. Add $6 per doll. Shipped via UPS, US mail or method preferred by customer.

DOLL'TOR JEAN'S DOLL HOSPITAL

R.R. 2, Box 573
Chadbourne Ridge Rd.
West Buxton, ME 04093
Phone: (207)727-5385 EST
Hours: Appointment only.

PRODUCT/SERVICE INFORMATION:

Area of expertise: Repairing collectible and modern dolls and specializing in antique restoration and costuming.

Buys: All types. Call or, if necessary, make an appointment.

Sells: All types—composition, bisque, German, French, American, etc.

Restorations: The cost determination depends on the type of repair or restoration requested or needed. Jean has a complete book of before and after pictures, along with customer letters and testimonies. She always takes this book to doll shows, and it is in her home for inspection. She does not give out client names. She uses a number system (first come, first serve). Time also depends on the damage to be repaired or restoration required. She only does what is necessary to preserve the originality. All mail inquiries are answered with a letter of estimated repairs, cost as close as possible. Pictures are sometimes helpful and are returned with the estimate of repairs. A SASE is appreciated but is not required. When a doll is received a work order is sent out within 3 working days. Every work order includes: name, address and telephone number of the client. Description of the doll, exactly what repairs are to be made and cost along with the approximate turn-around time. This goes out to the client; if they are in agreement, then a check is sent in full. Once this is received the doll takes a number to be repaired. If work is not to be done, client sends a check for the shipping and insurance to have the doll returned to them.

Appraisals: $35 and up. Customer must provide the doll itself.

Other products/services: Written appraisal—must have doll for approximately 1 week.

BUSINESS INFORMATION:

Type of business: Conducts business from home and at shows.

Home Appointments: Schedule 1 week in advance.

Shows: Call to request a list of shows.

Accepts: Cash, check, money order

Discounts: Repeat customer

Layaway: ½ down, 30-90 days, depending on price of purchase.

Buys through the mail: Buy dolls through the mail sometimes. Call or send a letter with a photo or slide and SASE. Pays with check or by trade.

Appraises dolls through the mail: Call first. Must see doll. Prepayment is required.

Restores dolls through the mail: Call first. Mail a request with photo and description. Prepayment is required.

Shipping information: Will ship to US, Canada, overseas. Shipped via method preferred by customer.

DOLLY HEAVEN

Stevia Webster
502 Broadway
New Haven, IN 46774
Phone: (219)493-6428 EST
Hours: T-F, 10-4. Sat, 10-2.
In business since: 1982

PRODUCT/SERVICE INFORMATION:

Area of expertise: Broken bisque, china, composition

Buys: Bisque and china, some composition, dolls that need to be repaired. Please bring doll to shop or set up appointment.

Sells: Antique and modern dolls

Restorations: $25-85 to refurbish, clean, wig and string. Cost of other services are determined by time. Allow 2

weeks-1 year. 2 weeks to 2 months are required to refurbish a doll. It takes up to 1 year for a complete bisque repair.

Appraisals: $20/hour. Will provide references on request. Customer must provide the doll itself. Appraisals are based on blue book prices minus any restoration costs, including clothing.

Other products/services: Retail dolls, custom clothing, sewing, wigs, shoes, socks, stands

BUSINESS INFORMATION:

Type of business: Conducts business at store location and by mail.

Accepts: Cash, check, money order, Visa, MC

Discounts: Occasional sales on retail and/or repairs, seniors discount

Layaway: 10% down, 3-12 months, depending on price.

Phone orders: During business hours

Buys through the mail: Call first. Will pay with check.

Sells through the mail: Call or mail a request.

Appraises dolls through the mail: Call first. Mint price will be quoted. Customer will assume responsibility of price asked if staff cannot examine doll. Customer will be billed. Send in a double box and insure; will write an estimate and send back. Customer pays postage both ways.

Restores dolls through the mail: Call first. Customer will be billed. Upon receiving the doll (double-boxed and insured), staff evaluates the cost of restoration and sends a 2-part contract to the customer. Customer is asked to circle the restorations they wish completed. They mail back yellow copy with signature and 10% of cost, then staff begins work.

Shipping information: Will ship to US and Canada. Shipping is included in cost of doll. Shipped via FedEx, UPS or method preferred by customer. Allow 3-4 days for delivery.

DOLLWORKS

Eileen Mosteller
62-C Franklin St., Suite 107
Westerly, RI 02891
Phone: (401)596-4674 EST
In business since: 1987

PRODUCT/SERVICE INFORMATION:

Area of expertise: Mint and Mib cloth, composition and hard plastic dolls made between 1930-1970, especially Vogue Ginnys and Jills, Madame Alexanders, Ideal Tonis, Revelons and Shirley Temples, Arranbees, Effanbees and Hoyers.

Sells: Mint and Mib cloth, composition and hard plastic dolls made between 1930-1970.

BUSINESS INFORMATION:

Type of business: Conducts business by mail

Accepts: Money order, Visa, MC

Layaway: ⅓ down, 30 days.

Catalog: b&w, $2

Phone orders: 9-9 EST.

Sells through the mail. Call. Prepayment required.

Shipping information: Will ship to US, Canada, overseas. Prepayment required for shipping costs. Shipped via UPS. Allow 1-2 weeks for delivery.

THE FASHION DOLL

George Nelson
P.O. Box 32663
San Jose, CA 95152
Phone: (408)259-8287 PST
In business since: 1978

PRODUCT/SERVICE INFORMATION:

Area of expertise: Antique dolls and doll stands

Buys: Finest porcelain and composition. Will not buy if dolls are cracked or have been broken.

Sells: Finest porcelain and composition

Appraisals: Cost depends on value of dolls

BUSINESS INFORMATION:

Type of business: Conducts business from home, at shows.

Home appointments: Call first.

Shows: Call to request a list of shows.

Phone orders: Accepted

> "DON'T BUY LOTS OF DOLLS. BE SELECTIVE. OVER THE YEARS, THE PERSON WHO BOUGHT 10 GOOD DOLLS IS MUCH HAPPIER THAN THE ONE WHO IS STUCK WITH 100 LESSER ONES."
> *Donna Biggs, Biggs Unlimited, Richmond, VA*

GRANDMA'S ATTIC

Joyce Kekatos
3132 Ampere Ave.
Bronx, NY 10465
Phone: (718)863-0373 EST
Fax: (718)863-5312

PRODUCT/SERVICE INFORMATION:
Area of expertise: Antique bisque dolls
Buys: Antique dolls, French and German bisque.
Sells: French and German bisque antique dolls
Appraisals: Cost varies

BUSINESS INFORMATION:
Type of business: Conducts business by mail, at shows.
Shows: Write to request a list of shows.
Catalog: Free
Phone orders: Accepted

KARI HART

1623 E. 7th St.
Duluth, MN 55812
Phone: (218)728-1593 CST
In business since: 1984

PRODUCT/SERVICE INFORMATION:
Area of expertise: Barbie dolls, clothing, accessories
Buys: Barbie dolls, clothing, accessories
Sells: Vintage to modern Barbie dolls, clothing and accessories. Also sells replica Barbie jewelry, box liners, tiny rubber bands, 2″ × 2″ resealable zipper bags and much more.

BUSINESS INFORMATION:
Type of business: Conducts business by mail.
Price list: LSASE

HEIRLOOM DOLL, CUSTOMS AND RESTORATION

Mary Lytle
2806 E. 9th St.
Tucson, AZ 85716
Phone: (520)881-5545 MST
Fax: (520)881-5545 (call first)
In business since: 1991

PRODUCT/SERVICE INFORMATION:
Area of expertise: Bisque and china restoration. Full service restoration.
Sells: German, china dolls.
Restorations: Varies. Must inquire. Specialize in porcelain restoration.

BUSINESS INFORMATION:
Type of business: Conducts business from home.
Home Appointments: Flexible. Prefer 8-5.

> "DOLLS ARE MORE THAN JUST BEAUTIFUL OBJECTS TO ADMIRE. THEY REPRESENT OUR HISTORY, CULTURE AND ETHNIC DRESS."
> *Karen D'Onofrio, A Century of Dolls, Centereach, Long Island, NY*

MARY HERSH

2404 Pheasant
Farmington, NM 87401
Phone: (505)325-3864 MST
In business since: 1989

PRODUCT/SERVICE INFORMATION:
Buys: Antique bisque dolls. Send a slide or photo.
Sells: Antique bisque dolls

BUSINESS INFORMATION:
Type of business: Conducts business at home and by mail.
Home Appointments: Schedule at least 1 day in advance.
Accepts: Cash, check, money order
Layaway: ⅓ down, 3 months
Price list: Free
Mailing list: Write or call to be included.
Phone orders: Anytime before 10 P.M.
Buys through the mail. Call first or send a letter with a photo or slide and SASE. Will pay with money order or cashier's check.
Sells through the mail. Call or mail a request. Prepayment required.
Shipping information: Will ship to US, Canada, overseas. Shipped via method preferred by customer.

JUDY'S DOLL SHOP

Judy George
1201A Hwy. 70 E.
New Bern, NC 28560
Phone: (919)637-7933 EST
Hours: M, T, Th, F, Sat, 9:30-5.
In business since: 1984

PRODUCT/SERVICE INFORMATION:
Area of expertise: Bisque, china, and composition repair.
Buys: Antique dolls. Depends entirely on condition and price. Bring doll to shop.

Sells: Antique dolls. Ginnys, Alexanders, celluloids, bisque, compositions.
Restorations: Cost depends mostly on difficulty of repair; based on established guidelines. Will provide references on request. Allow 10 minutes-6 months depending on repair.
Appraisals: $10. Will provide references on request. Customers must provide the doll itself. Also appraises entire collections for insurance companies.

BUSINESS INFORMATION:
Type of business: Conducts business at shop location.
Accepts: Cash, check, money order, Visa, MC
Layaway: Accepted
Phone orders: Accepted
Restores dolls through the mail: Call first and mail a request with photo and description. Send doll, and Judy will call back with estimate.
Shipping information: Will ship to US. Shipping is included in cost of doll. Shipped via UPS. Allow 2 weeks for delivery.

KATE SMALLEY'S ANTIQUE DOLLS

Kate Smalley
P.O. Box 945
Branford, CT 06405
Phone: (203)481-8163
Fax: (203)481-8163
In business since: 1989

PRODUCT/SERVICE INFORMATION:
Area of expertise: French and German antique dolls.
Buys: Perfect antique French and German dolls that have no hairlines or repairs. Send a slide or photo, or call or fax with description and price.
Sells: Fine quality French and German antique dolls.

BUSINESS INFORMATION:
Type of business: Conducts business by mail or at shows.
Shows: Those on mailing list will be notified. Call or write to request a list of shows.
Accepts: Cash, check, money order, Visa, MC
Layaway: Terms discussed on an individual basis.
Catalog/price list: b&w, color, free. Price list, free.
Mailing list: Write or call to be included.

Phone orders: M-F, 9-8. Sat-Sun, 10-6.
Fax orders: Accepted
Buys through the mail: Call first or send a letter with a photo or slide and SASE. Will pay with check. Customers usually send the doll for inspection. If condition is as described, the sale is made.
Sells through the mail: Call, fax or mail a request. Prepayment required.
Shipping information: Will ship to US, Canada and overseas. Prepayment required for shipping cost. Shipped via UPS, US mail or method preferred by customer.

ADDITIONAL INFORMATION:
"Condition always guaranteed. We guarantee that our dolls have never had a hairline or repair. We select and sell only the finest quality antique dolls," Kate says.

KÄTHE KRUSE PUPPEN GMBH
Alte Augsburger Str. 9
Donauwörth 86609
GERMANY
Phone: 011 49 906 70678 0—6 hours ahead of EST
Fax: 011 49 906 70678 70
Additional locations: US address is Käthe Kruse Doll Co., 22 Westover Rd., Troy, NY 12180; phone, (518)273-0726; fax, (518)273-0754.
In business since: 1911

PRODUCT/SERVICE INFORMATION:
Restorations: Estimate mailed to customer upon receipt of doll and information of work requested. Allow 3 months. Käthe Kruse Puppen only repairs Käthe Kruse Dolls.
Appraisals: Customer must provide a clear photograph or slide of the doll. No guarantees on appraisals as the value changes, depending on supply and demand.
Other products/services: Manufacturer of dolls, plush toys, terry toys, and wooden toys; special orders; books relating to Käthe Kruse Company.

BUSINESS INFORMATION:
Accepts: Cash, check, money order

> "THERE ARE ONLY TWO KINDS OF DOLLS—THE ONES I HAVE AND THE ONES I WANT!"
> *Susan Williams, manager, and Stella Blevins, Blevins Plates 'N Things, Vallejo, CA*

JOAN KINDLER
P.O. Box 161
White Stone, NY 11357
Phone: (719) 767-2260 EST
Fax: (718)767-8794
In business since: 1966

PRODUCT/SERVICE INFORMATION:
Area of expertise: Antique dolls—early cloth, china and papier mâché.
Buys: Specializes in antique dolls (early cloth, china and papier mâché). Will buy any antique dolls pre-1950.
Sells: Antique (early cloth, china and papier-mâché) and pre-1950
Appraisals: Varies

BUSINESS INFORMATION:
Type of business: Conducts business at shows.
Shows: Call to request a list of shows.
Phone orders: Available, but usually after meeting at a show.

LINDA'S ANTIQUES
Linda Kellermann
8 Turley Ct.
North Potomac, MD 20878
Phone: (301)926-7771 EST
Fax: (301)926-7771 (call first)
In business since: 1984

PRODUCT/SERVICE INFORMATION:
Area of expertise: Antique French/German bisque dolls
Buys: Antique French/German bisque dolls
Sells: Antique French/German bisque dolls
Restorations: Minor repairs only. Charges vary.
Appraisals: Varies

BUSINESS INFORMATION:
Type of business: Conducts business from home, at shows.
Home Appointments: Call in advance.
Shows: Call or write to request a list of shows.
Phone orders: Accepted

MARILYN'S FOREST OF DOLLS
Laura Kilby or Marilyn Kilby
999 Glen Forest Way
Victoria, British Columbia V9B 5T7
CANADA
Phone: (604)478-2913 PST
Hours: By appointment only.
In business since: 1979

PRODUCT/SERVICE INFORMATION:
Area of expertise: German antique dolls.
Buys: German and French bisque hard plastic composition dolls in good condition. Will pay fair market price. Please schedule appointment to bring doll to shop.
Sells: German and French bisque composition, hard plastic and any collectible in stock; doll furniture; antique children's clothes suitable for dolls; toys.
Appraisals: $15/doll. Will provide references on request. Customer must provide a clear photograph or slide of the doll or the doll itself. Will provide replacement price and fair market price.
Other products/services: A small museum of antique dolls and toys

BUSINESS INFORMATION:
Type of business: Conducts business from home.
Layaway: Equal payments, 3 months, no interest
Catalog/price list: b&w, $2 refundable with purchase.
Mailing list: Write or call to be included.
Phone orders: Accepted
Home appointments: Call in advance
Buys through the mail: Send a letter with a photo or slide and SASE. Will pay with check.
Sells through the mail: Use order form on catalog/price list. Call or mail a request. Prepayment is required.
Appraises dolls through the mail: Mail a request with photo and description. Prepayment is required.
Shipping information: Will ship to US, Canada, overseas. COD. Shipping is included in cost of doll. Shipped via method preferred by customer. Allow 2 weeks for delivery.

DOROTHY A. MCGONAGLE
P.O. Box 323
Sudbury, MA 01776
Phone: (508)443-3527 EST
Fax: (508)443-5252
In business since: 1973

PRODUCT/SERVICE INFORMATION:
Area of expertise: Author, lecturer on antique dolls.
Buys: All types up to 1950s. Set up an appointment.
Sells: All types up to 1950s
Appraisals: Charges 0-10%. Will pro-

vide references on request. Customer must provide a clear photograph or slide of the doll.

Other products/services: Antique accessories

BUSINESS INFORMATION:

Type of business: Conducts business from home (by appointment), by mail and at shows.

Home Appointments: Please schedule in advance.

Shows: Call or write for list.

Accepts: Cash, check, money order

Layaway: 90 days

Discounts: Negotiable

Buys through the mail: Call first or send a letter with a photo or slide and SASE. Will pay with check, money order or cash.

Sells through the mail: Call, fax or send a request. Prepayment required.

Appraises dolls through the mail: No request necessary—send a photo, description and SASE. (In person is best.) Appraisal is free, but customer is responsible for shipping costs both ways.

Shipping information: Will ship to US, Canada, overseas. Shipped via FedEx, UPS, US mail or method preferred by customer. If shipped via US mail within the US, cost is included.

MCMASTERS

Sharon Harris
P.O. Box 1755
Cambridge, OH 43725
Phone: (800)842-3526 EST
In business since: 1976

PRODUCT/SERVICE INFORMATION:

Area of expertise: Any and all dolls.

Restorations: Cost will vary upon the dolls and their needs

Appraisals: Cost varies

BUSINESS INFORMATION:

Type of business: Conducts business from home, at shows and at auctions.

Home Appointments: Schedule an appointment between hours of 9-5.

MELTON'S ANTIQUE DOLLS

Julia and Bill Melton
4201 Indian River Rd.
Chesapeake, VA 23325
Phone: (800)736-6251 or (804)420-9226 EST

Fax: (804)420-1462
In business since: 1965

PRODUCT/SERVICE INFORMATION:

Area of expertise: All types

Buys: All types

Sells: All types

BUSINESS INFORMATION:

Type of business: Conducts business by mail.

Catalog: SASE.

Phone orders: 9-5.

RUTH A. MESSIER

Route 140, P.O. Box 994
Alton, NH 03809-0994

PRODUCT/SERVICE INFORMATION:

Restorations: Professional repair and costuming services available.

> "EVERY CHRISTMAS, EACH FEMALE IN MY FAMILY WAS GIVEN A DOLL AND A BOOK. NOW, THE LOVE OF DOLLS IS THE COMMON BOND THAT UNITES US ACROSS THE GENERATIONS."
> *Carol-Lynn Rössel Waugh, Winthrop, ME*

NEW YORK DOLL HOSPITAL INC.

Mr. Chase
787 Lexington Ave.
New York, NY 10021
Phone: (212)838-7527 EST
In business since: 1900

PRODUCT/SERVICE INFORMATION:

Area of expertise: Antique dolls—all types, French/German/mechanical. Also deals with antique toys and bears.

Buys: Discontinued antique dolls. Prefers collections. No new dolls.

Sells: Discontinued antique dolls. Prefers collections. No new dolls.

Restorations: Cost varies.

Appraisals: Cost varies. If travel is involved, a flat rate is charged. Large collections should have a typed list of items.

BUSINESS INFORMATION:

Type of business: Conducts business at store location.

THE ORILLIA DOLL HOSPITAL

Patricia Wimpory
271 Matchedash St. N.
Orillia, Ontario L3V 4V8
CANADA

Phone: (705)326-9719 EST

PRODUCT/SERVICE INFORMATION:

Other products/services: Established hospital welcomes repairs from all areas of Canada and US. Patricia has taken a certified course in the restoration of antique porcelains. She also mends mechanical dolls, soft toys and teddy bears, and will dress your doll if you wish.

BUSINESS INFORMATION:

Type of business: Conducts business at home and by mail. Customers should call for an appointment.

Shipping information: Will ship to US, Canada. Customer must pay cost of shipping.

PAMELA'S PLAYTHINGS DOLL HOSPITAL

Woodbury, CT 06798
Phone: (203)263-2220 EST
Fax: (203)263-2220. Call first.
In business since: 1983

PRODUCT/SERVICE INFORMATION:

Area of expertise: Antique doll repairs, costumes and identifying dolls.

Buys: Any German and French bisque

Sells: German and French bisque, cloth dolls and hard plastic from 1950s.

Restorations: Cost varies

Appraisals: Cost varies

BUSINESS INFORMATION:

Type of business: Conducts business from home.

Home Appointments: Schedule a few days in advance.

Phone orders: Accepted

EVELYN PHILLIPS

17 Loch Lane
Rye Brook, NY 10573
Phone: (914)939-4455 EST
Fax: (914)939-4569
In business since: 1971

PRODUCT/SERVICE INFORMATION:

Area of expertise: Antique bisque dolls, French/German, 1900s

Buys: Same as above

Sells: Same as above

Appraisals: Varies

BUSINESS INFORMATION:

Type of business: Conducts business by mail.

Catalog: Free

Phone orders: M-Sun, 9-5.

RICHARD WRIGHT ANTIQUES

Richard Saxman
Flowing Springs and Hollow Roads
Birchrunville, PA 19421
Phone: (610)827-7442 EST
Fax: (610)827-7939
In business since: 1981

PRODUCT/SERVICE INFORMATION:
Buys: Pre-1940 and other antique/old dolls
Sells: Pre-1940 antique/old dolls
Appraisals: Cost varies

BUSINESS INFORMATION:
Type of business: Conducts business at store location, by mail, at shows.
Shows: Call to request a list of shows.
Phone orders: T-Sat, 9-5 EST.

S & S DOLL HOSPITAL

Steve Schroeder
3100 Harvest Lane
Kissimmee, FL 34744
Phone: (407)957-6392 EST
Fax: (407)957-9427
In business since: 1981

PRODUCT/SERVICE INFORMATION:
Area of expertise: Resleeping eyes in traditional German way; dressing dolls in antique style clothing.
Restorations: Restorations, including clothing, cost about $50-70 for a 12″ or smaller doll, $150 for a 24″ doll and $175-255 for a 27-28″ doll. Allow 1-3 months
Appraisals: $10/doll. Customers must provide description of doll, including height and type of body. Photo helpful but not necessary.
Other products/services: Dr. Schroeder's miracle doll cleaner

BUSINESS INFORMATION:
Type of business: Conducts business at home, by mail and at shows.
Home Appointments: Please schedule 1 day in advance.
Accepts: Cash, check, money order
Discounts: 10% to dealers and retail shops.
Appraises dolls through the mail. Fax, call or mail a request. Customer will be billed.
Restores dolls through the mail. Fax, call or mail a request. Customer will be billed.
Shipping information: Will ship to US.

Prepayment required. Shipped via UPS and US mail. Allow 1-2 weeks for delivery.

SANDY'S DREAM DOLLS

Sandy Kralovetz
7154 N. 58th Dr.
Glendale, AZ 85301
Phone: (602)931-1579 PST
Fax: (602)931-5110
Hours: M-Sat, 10-4. 3rd Th of each month, Septemper-April, 10-9.
In business since: 1980

PRODUCT/SERVICE INFORMATION:
Buys: Antique, modern and collectible dolls. Bring doll into shop, set up an appointment, or send a slide or photo.
Sells: Antique French and German dolls.
Restorations: $10 and up, depending on doll. Will provide references on request. Length of time required varies.
Appraisals: $15 and up. Will provide references. Customers must provide the doll itself. Verbal and typed appraisals available.

BUSINESS INFORMATION:
Type of business: Conducts business at store location, from home, by mail or at shows.
Home Appointments: Please schedule in advance.
Shows: Those on mailing list will be notified.
Accepts: Cash, check, money order, Visa, MC, DC
Discounts: Occasional sales, repeat customer discount, doll club
Layaway: 25% down, 90 days
Mailing list: Write or call to be included.
Phone orders: During business hours
Fax orders: Accepted
Buys through the mail: Call first or send a letter with a photo or slide and SASE. Will pay with check or money order.
Sells through the mail: Use order form on catalog/price list, call, fax or mail a request.
Restores dolls through the mail: Call first.
Shipping information: Will ship to US, Canada, overseas. COD. Shipping is included in cost of doll. Shipped via FedEx, UPS or method preferred by customer. Allow overnight or 5 working days for delivery.

2ND TIME AROUND DOLL SHOP

D.J. Smith
112 Buckroe Ave.
Hampton, VA 23664
Phone: (804)851-7842
Hours: By appointment only
In business since: 1978

PRODUCT/SERVICE INFORMATION:
Area of expertise: Old and antique dolls, 1900-present
Sells: Old and antique dolls, 1900-present; also modern manufactured dolls

BUSINESS INFORMATION:
Type of business: Conducts business at store location and at shows.
Layaway: Available

SMALL WONDERS ANTIQUE

1940 Old Taneytown Rd.
Westminster, MD 21158
Phone: (410)875-2850 EST
Additional locations: Frizellburg Antiques, 1909 Old Taneytown Rd., Westminster, MD 21158. (410)848-0664.
Hours: F-M, 11-5.
In business since: 1976

PRODUCT/SERVICE INFORMATION:
Area of expertise: Toys and 1960 era
Buys: Any type of antique—single dolls and/or collections
Sells: Single dolls or collections
Restorations: Minor repairs only. Charge will vary depending on repair.

BUSINESS INFORMATION:
Type of business: Conducts business at store locations, at shows.
Shows: Call to request a list of shows.

THERIAULT'S

Catherine Rogers
P.O. Box 151
Annapolis, MD 21404
Phone: For orders: (410)224-3655 EST
For info: (800)638-0422
Fax: (410)224-2515
Hours: M-F, 8:30-5.
In business since: 1970

PRODUCT/SERVICE INFORMATION:
Area of expertise: 60 auctions annually in 25 cities of antique and collectible dolls and childhood ephemera.
Buys: Virtually all dolls prior to 1965. We will also consider some contemporary artists dolls. Please bring doll

to shop, schedule appointment or send slide or photo of doll. Call 800 number with questions.

Sells: All dolls and childhood ephemera from 1780 to 1965. Occasionally, modern artists dolls of high merit are also offered.

Appraisals: $9/doll by mail. Free of charge if on site in our office. Will provide references on request. Customers must provide a clear photograph or slide of the doll. Theriault's provides a complimentary doll identification guide to anyone inquiring regarding the value of their doll.

Other products/services: Theriault's provides outreach programs for clubs and nonprofit organizations to further understanding and education on antique and collectible dolls

BUSINESS INFORMATION:

Type of business: Conducts business at the store location, at shows.

Shows: Those on mailing list will be notified. Call or write to request a list of shows.

Accepts: Cash, check, money order

Catalog: 10-issue subscription, $154; individual, $33.

Price list: Includes after-sale prices realized.

Mailing list: Write or call to be included.

Phone orders: During business hours

Fax orders: Order forms are provided but not necessary.

Buys through the mail: Call first or send a letter with a photo or slide and SASE. Will pay with check, money order.

Sells through the mail: Customers receive the Gold Horse Guarantee on select premier dolls allowing the customer to return the doll at anytime during their lifetime after 12 months ownership. All dolls are guaranteed. There is no 10% buyers premium at premier cataloged auctions. Absentee bids through cataloged auctions. Use order form on catalog/price list, call, fax or mail request. Customer billed for absentee bids.

Appraises dolls through the mail: Reviewing appraisal guide. Prepayment required.

Shipping information: Will ship to US, Canada, overseas. Cost varies based on value of doll. Shipped via US mail. Allow 5-10 days for delivery.

TWIN PINES OF MAINE INC.

Nick Hill
P.O. Box 1178
Scarborough, ME 04070-1178
Phone: (800)770-DOLL or (207)883-5541 EST
Fax: (207)883-1239
In business since: 1991

PRODUCT/SERVICE INFORMATION:

Area of expertise: Makes materials for cleaning, restoration and preservation of dolls.

Restoration: Teaches people how to do the restoration.

BUSINESS INFORMATION:

Type of business: Conducts business at store location.

Catalog: Free

AUCTIONS THAT INCLUDE ANTIQUE DOLLS

ANN CHRISTINA'S REMEMBER WHEN COLLECTIBLES & AUCTIONS

Ann Walscher
5465 Rowland Rd.
Minnetonka, MN 55343
Phone: (612)931-1148 CST
In business since: 1995

BASIC INFORMATION:

Type of auction: Take place 2 times/year.

Location: Catalog auction. Bids are either mailed and/or telephoned in.

ITEMS FOR AUCTION:

Items: Modern collectibles—Barbie, American character, etc.

Catalog: b&w, $7, US; $11 outside US.

AUCTIONS BY NANCY

Nancy Farley
505 Trelawney Lane
Apex, NC 27502
Phone: (919)362-7235 EST
In business since: 1982

BASIC INFORMATION:

Type of auction: Monthly indoor events

Location: CC Jones Building, Holleman St., Apex, NC 27502.

Duration: 5 + hours

Admission: Free

Attendance: 100-125

ITEMS FOR AUCTION:

Items: Antique dolls, modern dolls, doll-related items, plush

Mailing list: Send $1 plus LSASE.

ADDITIONAL INFORMATION:

Member of UFDC, Sir Walter Raleigh Doll Club. Will also sell one doll or an entire collection.

BILL BERTON AUCTIONS

Bill Berton
2413-D Madison Ave.
Vineland, NJ 08360
Phone: (609)692-1881 EST
Fax: (609)692-TOYS (8697)
In business since: 1986

BASIC INFORMATION:

Type of auction: Held three times a year

ITEMS FOR AUCTION:

Items: Antique toys, banks and dolls

Catalog: Color, $30

ADDITIONAL INFORMATION:

Auctions 1,000-1,500 items. Allows absentee bidding through the catalog, as well as telephone bidding.

CHRISTENSEN AUCTIONS

1226 W. 5th St.
Santa Ana, CA 92703
Phone: (714)647-0294 PST
Fax: (714)647-0418
In business since: 1989

BASIC INFORMATION:

Type of auction: 1 public and 1 mail order auction per year

Location: Varies

Attendance: 100-200

ITEMS FOR AUCTION:

Items: Barbie dolls

Catalog: Full color, subscription $40-60; mail order b&w, subscription $5-10.

CHRISTIES

219 E. 67th St.
New York, NY 10021
Phone: (800)395-6300, (212)606-0543 EST

BASIC INFORMATION:

Type of auction: 2 times yearly in New York; 3 times in London

Location: U.S.: Christies, 85 Old Brompton Rd., S. Kensington, NY.

Attendance: Varies

ITEMS FOR AUCTION:
Items: Antique dolls only
Catalog: $10-20

THE DOLL EXPRESS, INC.

Rae-Ellen Koenig
Route 272, Trains
P.O. Box 367
Reamstown, PA 17567
Phone: (717)336-2414 EST
Fax: (717)336-1262
Hours: M, T, Th, 10-5. F-Sun, 9-6.
In business since: 1991

BASIC INFORMATION:
Type of auction: Indoor events that take place twice a year
Location: Varies
Time of year: May and November
Duration: Sat-Sun, 9-4.
Admission: Free
Attendance: 250

ITEMS FOR AUCTION:
Items: Modern collectible, contemporary, antique and artist dolls of all kinds
Catalog: b&w, $5
Mailing list: Write or call to be included.

ADDITIONAL INFORMATION:
About 1,000 dolls and bears are auctioned at each event.

COBB'S DOLL AUCTIONS

David M. Cobb
1909 Harrison Rd.
Johnstown, OH 43031
Phone: (614)964-0444 EST
Fax: (614)964-0444
In business since: 1983

BASIC INFORMATION:
Type of auction: Every 3 months, indoors
Location: In Columbus, Ohio, at various hotel facilities.

Time of year: February, May, August, November
Duration: Sat-Sun, 9-6.
Attendance: 150

ITEMS FOR AUCTION:
Items: Antique dolls and modern and collectible dolls. Modern dolls sold Saturday; antique dolls sold Sunday with a catalog.
Catalog: b&w and color, $26
Mailing list: Write, call or subscribe to catalog to be included.

ADDITIONAL INFORMATION:
Sometimes also holds 1-day modern doll auctions in between regularly scheduled 2-day auctions. Auctions also include teddy bears, doll and childrens' antique furniture and accessories, doll parts.

FRASER'S DOLL AUCTION

Barbara Fraser
Rt. 1, Box 142
Oak Grove, MO 64075
Phone: (816)625-3786 CST
Fax: (816)625-6079
In business since: 1983

BASIC INFORMATION:
Type of auction: 6 times/year
Location: Varies
Attendance: 150-250

ITEMS FOR AUCTION:
Items: Antique dolls, teddy bears and doll-related items
Catalog: $32; six issue subscription, $126; ten issue subscription, $189.

MCMASTERS DOLL AUCTIONS

Shari (Joyce for Barbies)
P.O. Box 1755
Cambridge, OH 43725
Phone: For orders: (800)842-3526 EST
For info: (614)432-4419
Fax: (614)432-3191
In business since: 1989

BASIC INFORMATION:
Type of auction: Monthly indoor events.

Location: Varies
Time of year: Varies
Duration: 4-6 hours
Attendance: 50-150

ITEMS FOR AUCTION:
Items: Barbies, modern dolls, collectible dolls, antique dolls and related items
Catalog: b&w and color. $30 single, $75 subscription to 4. For Barbies, $25 single, $60 subscription to 3.
Mailing list: Write, call or send money for a catalog subscription.

ADDITIONAL INFORMATION:
McMasters sponsors 3-4 general cataloged doll auctions per year, 3-4 cataloged Barbie auctions per year, and a monthly "Treasure Hunt" for uncataloged auctions.

THERIAULT'S

Catherine Rogers
P.O. Box 151
Annapolis, MD 21404
Phone: For orders: (410)224-3655 EST
For info: (800)638-0422
Fax: (410)224-2515
Hours: M-F, 8:30-5
In business since: 1970

BASIC INFORMATION:
Type of auction: These are 60 times annually, indoor.
Location: Varies, 25 cities nationwide.
Time of year: Year-round
Duration: 3-5 hours.
Admission: Free
Attendance: 100-200

ITEMS FOR AUCTION:
Items: Antique dolls and colectibles with childhood ephemera
Catalog: Color, 10-issue subscription $154, individual $33.
Mailing list: Write or call to be included.

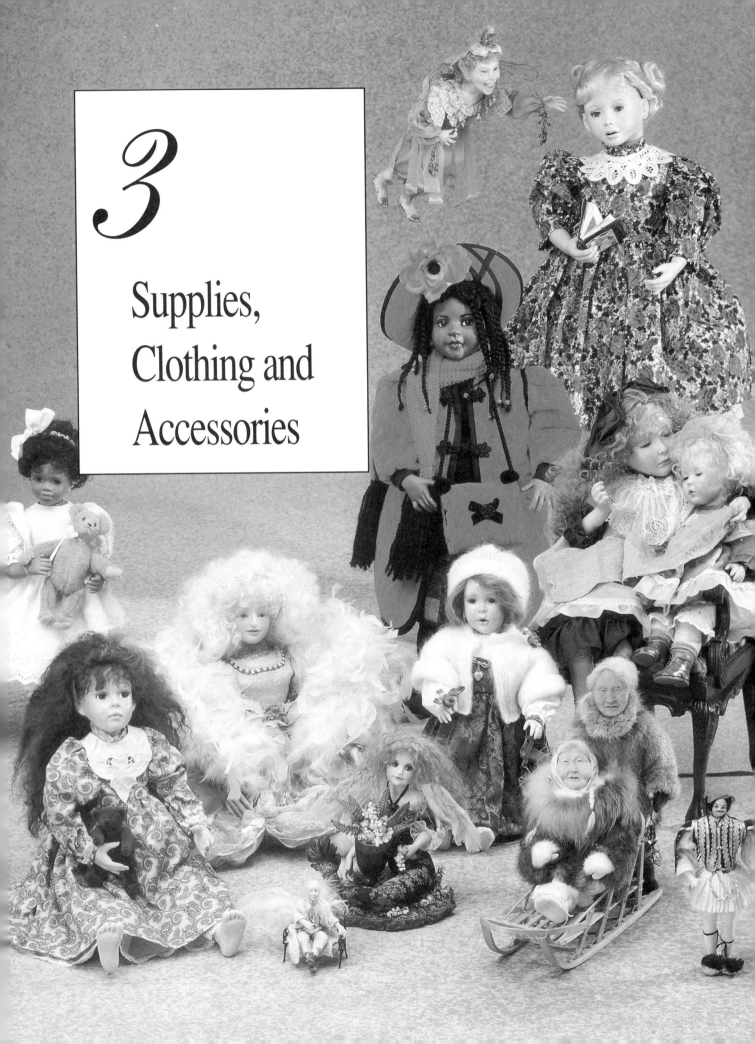

3

Supplies,
Clothing and
Accessories

A Guide to Chapter Three

*I*f you've always wanted to make dolls, but don't know where to start, this chapter will be very helpful. Suppliers of everything from clay to cloth, eyes to wigs, and shoes to dresses can be found on these pages. Even if you are an experienced doll artist, these listings will provide you with alternative suppliers to get you out of a jam, or more cost-efficient suppliers that you don't yet know about!

The listings in this chapter include businesses that sell supplies for making both art dolls and reproduction dolls. Sellers of clothing and accessories for dolls are also listed here. Due to space constraints, we could include only suppliers who specialize in items for dollmakers. There are several alternate suppliers available to dollmakers. For some additional ideas, and for more information on how to choose and handle a supplier, see the article by Marnie Panek following this guide.

A variety of businesses are included in this chapter: doll shops that also sell supplies; small shops that distribute supplies from a wholesale supply house; manufacturers or distributors of supplies like clay and stuffing; home-based businesses that sell specific supplies, accessories or clothing; and individuals who make clothing and accessories for dolls.

Some of the suppliers listed here sell wholesale only. They are listed so that shops can contact them about carrying lines of supplies in their stores. You may be eligible for wholesale discounts if you buy in bulk and have a vendor's number, which is acquired when you register your company with the government. Requirements for these discounts are also included.

We have tried to include as many suppliers as possible, but some of the manufacturers and wholesale suppliers may be able to tell you about a distributor in your area who is not listed in this book. It is best to call them directly for an updated list of such distributors.

The Listings

The listings include location and contact information for each business, hours and the year the business was founded. You will also find details on every type of supplies, clothing (supplies for making your own and ready-made clothing available) and accessories offered. Business information, including type of business, wholesale requirements, methods of payment accepted, discounts, layaway, back order and return/exchange policies are also included. You will find information about samples and catalogs for each business, as well as instructions for phone, fax and mail orders. ❧

Choosing the Supplier that Best Suits Your Needs

BY MARNIE PANEK

Marnie Panek is a self-taught doll artist. She has won several Best of Show awards and has been featured in many doll magazines. After qualifying for a juried position in the "Uniquely B.C." section of the Vancouver (British Columbia) Trade Show, Marnie was selected to represent "Made in B.C. Products" in the B.C. International Showcase. As a guest speaker for various organizations, Marnie shares her vast knowledge of both making and collecting dolls. She has been interviewed about her dollmaking for a feature segment on television.

Marnie Panek

*W*hether you slowly slipped into doll artistry or dove in with both feet, you require supplies and accessories to make and dress your dolls. Getting started by choosing a medium was the easy part. Now we move on to choosing a supplier for everything from porcelain to eyes, and making decisions on how to keep your treasures from being a room full of "naked" characters.

This Indian maiden of Cernit by Kathy Wormhood is an example of a well-developed concept.

Choosing a Concept

No matter what your choices are, you must decide on a concept or theme for the doll. Keep in mind that your skill level, as well as the supplies accessible to you, will determine the type of doll you can make. Perhaps the most important element in choosing a concept is your taste. Does it lean toward old-fashioned or modern, or do you just take artistic license and combine an assortment of styles?

You can design your doll to fit a theme, such as a fairy tale, a book or movie character, a historic figure or even an ultramodern fantasy figure. Or, if you decide to go with the unconventional, your imagination can be your guide. If you are aiming for authenticity, then you'll need to research your subject, either by purchasing reference books or by using the library. Your research should also include checking the copyright of the subject you wish to portray through your work so as not to violate any laws. For instance, most cartoon characters are copyrighted, meaning that you need permission to create a doll that portrays them. Each copyright holder has different requirements, so it is best to write or phone the registered copyright holder, tell them what you wish to do and ask for their permission. They will advise you of any restrictions. Your local phone company or library will have phone books for other areas of the country so you can obtain both a phone number and an address.

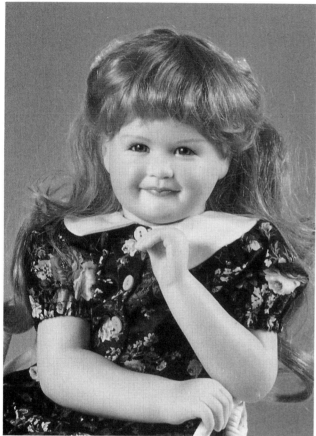

"Ricci," a classic little girl porcelain doll with synthetic hair and glass eyes, wears a floral jumpsuit. Mavis Snyder made a limited edition of 100 Ricci dolls.

Deciding on the Edition Size

Whether you decide on a one-of-a-kind doll, a small limited edition or an open edition, the quantity of supplies available could determine the success of your edition. That single family heirloom can be used to costume or accessorize a one-of-a-kind doll, but it will not provide materials for a larger edition. It can, of course, serve as an inspirational guide for you or someone else to make something similar in a larger volume. You must set the quantity of an edition at a workable number, or the project is doomed to failure. A small, handmade edition allows a more personal touch, and such dolls are usually considered superior in quality and will sell at a premium. A large edition, on the other hand, can be duplicated more consistently and cost-effectively if you use manufactured supplies to meet your requirements for a greater number of costumes or accessories. Quality can suffer when you try to be a machine and overextend yourself.

Some of the work can be contracted out to other artisans, but remember that their ability to produce in volume can affect the quality and edition size also. As an artist, you must also consider that taking the mass production route—with more machine involvement and others helping with your work—takes your dolls out of the small world of doll artistry and into the larger realm of doll production. While this is not necessarily a bad choice, you must weigh carefully the pros and cons of giving up some control over your dolls.

Determining Your Needs

When you are deciding on a supplier for your basics, remember that the supplier's job is to serve you, the customer. With so many options available, you must carefully evaluate your own requirements and determine which type of supplier best meets your needs. Even experienced artists who work in a particular style do not always use the same suppliers.

Some parts or accessories can be best furnished by a large supplier. The larger companies may have distributors in your area. These suppliers may have minimum dollar amounts or quantities which you will have to meet.

The wholesale choice may be best if you will need a large quantity for an edition, or if you will use the same material for several different dolls. The wholesale market will usually require your business letterhead and your license and taxation numbers. Wholesalers may also require references. Often a retail store having a super discount sale or inventory reduction sale can net you a price close to wholesale. If the quantities you require are small, a retail outlet can substitute for the wholesaler, provided they have sufficient items in stock for your needs. But remember, reordering would most likely be impossible.

Many home-based businesses are also available. These businesses may be preferable if you are making a doll with more exacting workmanship or special requirements. Keep in mind that home-based businesses do not have the ability to fill large orders. Often their prices and personal service make them a good choice, however.

More than 90 suppliers are listed in this chapter, along with information on their products and business practices. This will give you a place to start your search, but do not limit yourself. Some operators of small home-based businesses may not be listed here, either because we missed them or because they felt that a listing would open them up to more business than they could handle. Ask a friend or another artist for recommendations. If this is not an option, try visiting a doll-related store or attending doll shows.

An advantage to visiting a store in person is that your senses of touch and sight can aid you with your selection. The availability of a sales assistant who can answer questions is also an asset. You can judge the quality, rather than leaving the evaluation to another person for your later acceptance or disappointment. Another advantage to shopping in person is that you can take home the product you have selected and start using it immediately.

Shopping by Mail

When there are no stores or shows close to you, try ordering by mail or telephone. The listings in this chapter will tell you which businesses sell through the mail and whether they accept phone and fax orders. You can ask for free samples, if available, or purchase small amounts from various suppliers so that you can be the final judge of product quality before you place a large order.

If you are connected to the Internet, keep in mind that this technology is in its infancy as a shopping medium. Laws protect you when you make purchases in stores, by mail or on the telephone, but not all those laws have caught up with the Internet. If you are giving a credit card number or other personal information on-line, make sure the supplier offers secure transmission. Always check with the Better Business Bureau in the city in which your supplier is registered, whether you are buying over the Internet or through more traditional methods.

When ordering by mail, phone or the Internet, don't be afraid to ask questions. You cannot ask too many questions, and remember that no question is dumb if it can help you avoid a misunderstanding and a hassle. Be specific. Make sure that you explain exactly what you want. Be clear and precise in your descriptions. If you are ordering by mail, make sure you fill in all the information that is required. Omissions cause delays or errors. Always ask to be informed about new products and price changes.

Understanding Business Policies

Once you have chosen a supplier, make sure you understand the company's business practices, including method of payment, shipping methods, and return and back-order policies. Most of this information is provided in the listings in this chapter.

When dealing by mail or phone, don't forget to ask about deposit requirements, payment plans and discounts. Ask if the supplier takes credit cards, checks or cash only. If you request a catalog (most are either free or refundable with your first order), it will most likely answer these questions and provide order blanks for your convenience. Read the information and ask questions about anything that is not clear. Be sure you understand how long it will take for the company to fill your order, as this will determine when you can start producing.

When deciding on an edition size or choosing whether or not to accept a back order, consider all the potential problems that could affect your schedule. Include time to cover unexpected and annoying delays and even have some contingency plans to keep you on schedule so you do not have to keep postponing a delivery date—and potentially lose an order—for reasons you cannot control. The supplier's back order policy is an integral part of your planning.

You should also be aware of the supplier's return policy in case of damaged or defective products. If the damage occurs in transit or the package has been opened and the defect renders the product useless, then you'll need a replacement or refund to recover your losses. But what if you chose an inappropriate item or color, or if you authorized substitutes and the substitute is of inferior quality? What happens? The return policy then becomes a very important part of your decision. Make sure you have a clear understanding of it.

Assuming you are not taking your purchase with you, the terms of delivery should now be established. Has the shipping cost been included? Does the supplier require prepayment or allow for COD? Now inquire as to the time of expected arrival and method of shipment. Does the supplier use US mail or another carrier? Is delivery by air or ground? Is the delivery schedule next-day air, which is more costly, or regular, a slower but more economical method? Can you choose the shipment method you need each time you place an order? You may have to place a rush order, and a quicker delivery may be required. The different options can make the shipping price vary. Insuring the shipment may cost extra and is usually well worth the added fee for peace of mind.

This Native American doll by Jack Johnston is elaborately costumed and accessorized.

"Nosalie," a 22″ cloth doll by Carol-Lynn Rössel Waugh, is dressed in a dress and headband and accessorized with two artist-made bears.

Dressing and Accessorizing Your Doll

You must recognize your own skill level, strengths and weaknesses when deciding how to dress and accessorize a doll. Ask yourself whether you want to make the accessories and costume yourself, or whether you would feel more comfortable buying the components and assembling. If you want to challenge yourself and make the costume and accessories from scratch, first judge your skill level from beginner to advanced and remember that the quality of your finished piece will depend on how honest you are with yourself. If you overestimate your abilities, then you might be unhappy with the product or quit in despair. Do your skills cover everything from designing and making patterns through fitting and machine sewing and then on to hand-stitching the finishing touches? If so, many suppliers listed in this chapter provide fabrics, laces, ribbons, buttons and other materials you can use in making costumes. The same standards should apply to the accessorizing, including hats, wigs, shoes and props. If you plan to make your own wig, you have the luxury of both choosing the material (mohair, human hair, synthetic fiber) and creating a style and color that is as yet unseen. The time spent making a handmade wig will be a factor in your

schedule, price and edition size. Using a commercially available wig is equally acceptable, and the shorter, more convenient time frame is a bonus. However, you are limited in the styles and colors available.

If you prefer to purchase and then assemble, you will have to decide whether to hire dressmakers to make costumes for you or to do it yourself. Some costume designers and makers specializing in doll costumes are listed in this chapter. Choose a costume designer and maker whose work complements your style.

There is a third option, and that is collaboration—combining your abilities with those of others by making the items you do best and delegating the rest to others who are more skilled at their particular crafts. Collaboration offers a much broader scope of possibilities to achieve your goal.

Once you have evaluated the information provided in these listings and considered suppliers beyond the scope of this book, you can make an informed decision and choose a supplier that suits your needs. Place an order for a sufficient quantity to complete your edition. When your supplies arrive, you can begin the fun part—making your treasure! &

Supplies, Clothing and Accessories

ALICE'S DOLL WORKSHOP

Alice L. Johnson
2200 Charleston Dr.
Aurora, IL 60506
Phone: (708)892-3081 CST
In business since: 1989

SUPPLIES:

Armatures: Plastic pre-assembled armatures in 4 sizes; wire armatures in 7 sizes

Bodies: Leatherette, porcelain, pre-sewn cloth (mainly muslin); Seeley's composition (includes baby, toddler, French, German, and the new mechanical and walking bodies)

Eyes: Kemper flat oval acrylic, round acrylic, acrylic paperweight, bright eyes (Glastics), Glastic Realistics, oval glass, paperweight, round glass; Seeley's—very small glass eyes on a wire; Global—flat glass eyes; Karl doll eyes—German round glass eyes

Fabrics for hair: Seeley's mohair, wefted, undyed and dyed—2 yard package. Wig dyes also available. Jean Nordquist unwefted, undyed and dyed—1 yard package

Lashes: Kemper 17mm baby, 20mm baby and thick, 20mm double lashes, 24mm very thick, 32mm thin and very thick, 32mm wispy double lashes

Molds: Seeley's, Doll Artworks, Jean Nordquist doll molds, Bell and Byron doll and ceramic molds, and many others

Paints: Seeley's, Jean Nordquist, Willoughby Colors china

Slips: Seeley's porcelain

Tools: Seeley's, Marx Scharff brushes, Orton Cones, Prop (both blanket and fluffy), stilts, hydrated alumina and firing sand; Seeley's, Kemper, Master Eye Bevelers, National Artcraft and Treebite

Wigs: Kemper modacrylic and Global modacrylic, mohair, human hair

Other supplies: Doll teeth (plastic and porcelain); brush cases; doll joints; mold bands and mold straps, optivisors, pates, shoulder plate connectors and screwgles; stringing elastic; soft-fired greenware for antique and modern dolls

CLOTHING:

Clothing (ready-made): Vee's Victorian panties, bloomers, dresses, headbands; Kemper socks, tights, shoes, cowboy hat; Talina's shoes, underwear sets, slips

Fabrics for doll clothing: Capitol Imports, Swiss batiste, poly/cotton batiste

Lace: Capitol Imports cotton laces (beading, edging, insertion), Entredeauxs, Swiss Embroideries (edgings and insertions)

Patterns for doll clothing: Connie Lee Finchum, Granny's Crocheted Heirlooms, Maimie Doll, Paule Fox Pattern Co., Seeley's

Ribbons: Silk ribbon in 2mm, 4mm, 7mm

Trimmings: Silk ribbon, silk ribbon roses

Other clothing supplies: Sewing machine needles, extra fine thread, pin-tuck feet, sewing books about doll clothes, silk ribbon embroidery

ACCESSORIES:

Scaled props/accessories: Kathy's Kreations for Dolls, doll jewelry, hat—cowboy (felt) and straw. Doll stands, including cradle type, metal, wood, sadle type.

BUSINESS INFORMATION:

Type of business: Wholesale and retail, from home

Wholesale requirements: Minimum dollar amount of $25

Home appointments: M, T, F, Sat, 10-2. W, Th, 10-8 (and by appointment).

Accepts: Check, money order

Discounts: Quantity discounts on brushes, china paints, laces, porcelain slip, wigs. Wholesale buyers and dealers receive discounts on most of their purchases.

Return/exchange policy: Returns and exchanges allowed with sales receipt and merchandise in original packaging.

Samples: Sample book of all cotton laces, $10.50, available by mail.

Mailing list: Write or call to be included.

Phone orders: Orders can be left on voice mail at any time.

Mail orders: Will ship to US. Include name, address, phone number. Customer will be billed.

Shipping information: Shipping is included in the price of the order. Shipped via UPS or US Mail. Allow 2 days to 2 weeks.

ADDITIONAL INFORMATION:

Alice's Doll Workshop is a Seeley Super Doll Center. Also carries decorations, jewelry, ornaments, carousel horses, chess sets, doll books, doll workbooks, doll magazines, Seeley's worksheets.

ALL FOR A DOLL

Mary Barrette
735 Pomeroy
Nipomo, CA 93444
Phone: (805)929-4079 PST
In business since: 1989

SUPPLIES:

Armatures: Locline

Bodies: Composition and fabric for porcelain dolls

Clays: Porcelain slip, Seeley's

Eyes: Glastic, Glastic realistic, Karl's glass eyes, puppen naugen flat, oval and round glass eyes

Fabrics for cloth dolls: Swiss batiste and trims

Lashes: All colors and sizes.

Paints: Virginia La Voryna

Patterns for cloth dolls: Connie Lee Finchum and Brown House

Slips: Seeley

Tools: Jean Nordquist brushes and Playhouse tools

Wigs: Global, Playhouse, Monique

CLOTHING:

Clothing (ready-made): Vee's Victorian

Lace: Swiss batiste

Patterns for doll clothing: Brown House and Connee Lee Finchum.

ACCESSORIES:

Scaled props/accessories: Playhouse

BUSINESS INFORMATION:

Type of business: Wholesale and retail, by mail only.

Home appointments: Please schedule 1 day in advance.

Accepts: Check, money order, Visa, MC

Layaway: Negotiable

Back order policy: Negotiable

Return/exchange policy: 10% restocking on special orders. No fee otherwise.

Catalog: Color, $2. Price list, free.

Mailing list: Write to be included.

Phone orders: M-Sat, 10-5.

Mail orders: Will ship to US. Include name, address, phone and credit card number.

Shipping information: Shipping included in the price of order. Shipped via UPS. Allow 1 week for delivery.

ALL THAT GLISSONS

Theresa A. Glisson
154 West Hill St.
Goldsboro, NC 27534
Phone: (919)778-6921 EST

SUPPLIES:

Clays: All types of polymer

Fabrics for cloth dolls: Sold at shows only.

Tools: Kemper sculpting tools

CLOTHING:

Lace: Sold at shows only.

Trimmings: Sold at shows only.

BUSINESS INFORMATION:

Type of business: Retail only, from studio, by mail and at shows

Wholesale requirements: Please schedule 1 day in advance.

Price list: LSASE

"IF YOU WANT TO KEEP YOUR DOLL AS A COLLECTIBLE, HAVE ANOTHER OUTFIT MADE FOR IT. ALSO, NEVER COVER A DOLL WITH PLASTIC AND STORE IT IN THE ATTIC. THIS IS EXPERIENCE SPEAKING!"

Kate Fillman, Kathryn Productions, Brookfield, IL

ANDACO

Box 43
Amsterdam, NY 12010
Phone: (518)295-8517 EST
Fax: (518)295-8517

ACCESSORIES:

Furniture: Heirloom wicker cradles, carriages and basinets for baby dolls; trunks, baby rockers and high chairs. All products are hand woven in America using authentic 1900-era designs, and have a glossy, washable white finish.

BUSINESS INFORMATION:

Type of business: Wholesale and retail, by mail

Wholesale requirements: A five piece minimum on each model. Mimimum dollar amount $250

Discounts: About 40% for wholesale; please call for quote.

Return/exchange policy: Prior written authorization needed. 15% restocking fee.

Catalog: Color

Mail orders: Prepayment required.

ANGIE'S DOLL BOUTIQUE, INC.

Lynne Reid and Frankie Lyles
1114 King St.
Alexandria, VA 22314
Phone: (703)683-2807 EST
Hours: T-Sat, 11-5:30.
In business since: 1976

SUPPLIES:

Armatures: Plastic, assorted sizes

Bodies: Composition, cloth

Clays: Cernit

Eyes: Assorted sizes/colors; Glastic realistic and glass

Fabrics for hair: Mohair—wefted

Lashes: Assorted colors by Monique.

Molds: Seeley's antique and modern reproduction molds

Paints: Seeley's china dry.

Patterns for cloth dolls: Brown House, Easy Sew and Seeley's

Slips: Porcelain slip by Seeley's

Tools: Seeley's supplies

Wigs: Ready-made Monique wigs and Seeley's mohair wigs

Other supplies: Greenware, doll kits

CLOTHING:

Clothing (ready-made): Available

Patterns for doll clothing: Brown House, Seeley's

ACCESSORIES:

Furniture: 18″ chairs, brass bed, wooden tables

Scaled props/accessories: Jewelry by Kate Webster

Doll-related collectibles: Shoes, socks

BUSINESS INFORMATION:

Type of business: Retail only, at store location and by mail

Accepts: Check, money order, Visa, MC, DC, AE

Discounts: Six items and over on wigs, eyes, slip

Price list: SASE for greenware and doll kits

Mailing list: Write to be included.

Phone orders: T-Sat, 11-5:30.

Shipping information: Will ship to US. Prepayment required. COD. Shipped via UPS. Allow 4 to 6 weeks for delivery.

ANN'S DOLLS

Ann Graham
3000 Gateway St., Gateway Mall #614
Springfield, OR 97477
Phone: (541)747-3369 PST
Hours: M-Sat, 10-9. Sun, 11-6.
In business since: 1988

SUPPLIES:

Armatures: Locline, ¼″ and ³/₁₆″

Bodies: Most brands are available. Custom doll bodies available.

Eyes: Complete lines of Playhouse, Global. Glass, plastic and flat.

Lashes: Complete Playhouse line

Slips: Many Seeley

Stuffing: Plastic beads, Polyfil—sold by the bag and in bulk.

Tools: Brushes, masks

Wigs: Global, Playhouse and Monique.

More about supplies: Playhouse and Global Distributors. Most items in stock. Can fill special orders in about 2 days.

CLOTHING:

Clothing (ready-made): Custom-made and commercial line Vee's Victorians.

Patterns for doll clothing: Fancy Frocks line

Ribbons: All colors and varieties available.

ACCESSORIES:

Furniture: Doll case, table, chairs, cradles, beds. More available on order.

Scaled props/accessories: Pianos, instruments, trunks, tricycles, dish sets and more.

BUSINESS INFORMATION:

Type of business: Wholesale and retail, at store location and by mail.

Accepts: Check, money order, Visa, MC, DC

Discounts: 40% to shops

Layaway: 30% down, 90 days. No refunds; exchange available until item is delivered.

Back order policy: Will notify customer.

Return/exchange policy: Exchange only, unless item is damaged.

Catalog: For Playhouse and Global, $5.

Phone orders: During business hours or on answering machine. Will return calls.

Mail orders: Will ship to US. Include item number from catalog. Prepayment required.

Shipping information: Customer may choose COD or prepayment for cost of shipping. Shipped via UPS or method preferred by customer. Allow two weeks for delivery.

ADDITIONAL INFORMATION:

Shop stocks all types of dolls, supplies and accessories. Offers wholesale to other shops and retail sales. Also hosts ongoing porcelain dollmaking classes. Call or stop by for a schedule.

ANTHONY'S OF SOLVANG

Anthony D. Bulone
P.O. Box 155
Solvang, CA 93464
Phone: (805)688-3754 PST
Fax: (805)688-3754
Hours: 8-5
In business since: 1973

SUPPLIES:

Armatures: Made of fired ceramic for doll heads of various sizes. Come in two sizes and can be used over and over.

Molds: For porcelain and composition materials. For casting complete scale human bodies with celebrity features including Elvis, Marilyn Monroe and *Gone With the Wind* characters.

Tools: Tool kits for doll sculpting and mold making

Wigs: Available

CLOTHING:

Patterns for doll clothing: Available for custom made dolls

ACCESSORIES:

Scaled props/accessories: Shoes, hats, boots, gun and gunbelt holster sets

BUSINESS INFORMATION:

Type of business: Retail only, at studio location and by mail.

Accepts: Visa, MC

Catalog/price list: b&w and color, free. Price list, free.

Phone orders: 8-6

Fax orders: Include name, address, phone number, credit card number, expiration date, product name and number.

Mail orders: Will ship to US, Canada, overseas. Prepayment required. Shipping included in the price of order.

Shipping information: Shipped via UPS or US mail. Allow 2 weeks for delivery.

ADDITIONAL INFORMATION:

Anthony designed and developed the original Barbie doll for Mattel Toys in 1957. It was released at the NY Toy Fair in 1958. The features he sculptured on the original were those of his wife Lylis.

> "ALWAYS BUY WHAT YOU LIKE. DON'T GET THE ENTIRE SERIES IF YOU DON'T LIKE ONE OF THEM."
>
> *Dolly Bodzer, Bodzer's Collectibles, Baltimore, MD*

ELINOR PEACE BAILEY

1779 East Ave.
Hayward, CA 94541
Phone: (510)582-2702

SUPPLIES:

Patterns for cloth dolls: Elinor Peace Bailey sells patterns of her original cloth doll designs. Among her 14 patterns for sale are a modern woman, a Victorian doll, a witch and St. Nick.

CLOTHING:

Patterns for doll clothing: Elinor offers a book, Pick Pockets I, of 20 wearables for cloth dolls, as well as additional patterns sold separatcly.

BUSINESS INFORMATION:

Type of business: From home, by mail

ADDITIONAL INFORMATION:

Elinor Peace Bailey is an internationally known cloth doll designer and artist. She no longer sells original dolls, but her patterns are for sale. She also teaches cloth dollmaking and lectures on related topics.

BEAR THREADS, LTD.

Sheila and James Nicol
4651 Roswell Rd., Suite D-308
Atlanta, GA 30342
Phone: (404)255-5083 EST
Fax: (404)255-4001
In business since: 1983

CLOTHING:

Buttons: mother-of-pearl

Fabrics for doll clothing: Fine Swiss, batiste, voile, dotted swiss, cotton, cotton/linen, wood challis, damask, piques, tulle, organdy, etc.

Lace: Fine Valenciene and Maline laces from France. Fine embroideries from Switzerland.

Ribbons: Distributor for Grayblock Ribbon Mills.

Trimmings: Fine French and Swiss

BUSINESS INFORMATION:

Type of business: Wholesale only

Wholesale requirements: Fabrics 10/13 yards; laces/trims 20-30 yards. Must have vendor's license.

Samples: Fabrics, $4.

Catalog/Price list: Color, $4. Price list, free.

Phone orders: Anytime

Fax orders: Name, address, phone number and fax number

Mail orders: Will ship to US, Canada, overseas. Include name, address, phone and fax numbers. New orders COD: overseas orders are pre-pay only.

Shipping information: Shipped via UPS. Overseas—freight fowarder. In US, allow 1-3 days for delivery.

BEAUTY-STONE STANDS

Jean Foskey
440 Bucklen St.
Swainsboro, GA 30401
Phone: (912)237-3698 EST
In business since: 1995

CLOTHING:

Clothing (ready-made): Sugar Britches 2 piece footed outfits and christening gowns. Dresses for 20″, 25″, 26″, 27″, 28″ and 32″ dolls.

ACCESSORIES:

Scaled props/accessories: We manufacture doll stands, which we have utility patent pending on, with dura-stone bases. 5 sizes, 5 colors. Waists fit large and small dolls. Steel posts with adjustable heights; waist holders are vinyl coated.

BUSINESS INFORMATION:

Type of business: Wholesale and retail

Wholesale requirements: Wholesale prices—12 minimum. Wholesale buyers must have a vendor's license number.

Home appointments: Appointments are necessary. Please schedule M-F, 9-5.

Accepts: Check, money order, Visa, MC

Discounts: $500 orders get 10% discount off first order.

Back order policy: Allow 4-6 weeks.

Return/exchange policy: Exchange only—customer pays postage.

Samples: 1 of each size—minimum charge. Samples available at $10 each, stands #14; $12 each, stand #5. Available through the mail.

Catalog/Price list: Color, $2.

Phone orders: 9-5 EST.

Mail orders: Will ship to US. Include standard size, color, price, complete address and phone number. Added S&H. Prepayment required.

Shipping information: Shipping is included in the price of order. Shipped via method preferred by customer. Allow 2-4 weeks for delivery.

BEST DRESSED DOLL

Janice Newlands
385 Howell Prairie Rd. SE
Salem, OR 97301
Phone: For orders: (800)255-2313 PST
For info: (503)362-6585
Fax: (503)362-6583
Hours: By appointment
In business since: 1979

CLOTHING:

Buttons: ¼″

Clothing (ready-made): Specializes in old store stock, all factory 8″-25″ dolls.

Patterns for doll clothing: Sells patterns for replacement clothing for Toni Dolls, 8″ dolls, Cissy's, and other 40s-60s dolls. Has some antique doll clothes patterns and American Girl Dolls.

More about clothing: Specializes in old store stock for collectible dolls. Has old stock jewelry, shoes, stockings (including rayon).

ACCESSORIES:

Scaled props/accessories: Purses, flower baskets, sports equipment

BUSINESS INFORMATION:

Type of business: Wholesale and retail at store location and by mail.

Wholesale requirements: $100 at wholesale prices. Must have vendor's license.

Accepts: Check, money order, Visa, MC, DC, AE

Discounts: Volume discounts on some items.

Layaway: Available

Return/exchange policy: Returned for any reason within 5 days or exchanged for store credit.

Catalog: b&w, $3

Mailing list: Request catalog or price to be included.

Phone orders: 8-6

Fax orders: Fax completed catalog order form and credit card information.

Mail orders: Will ship to US, Canada, overseas. Mail the catalog order form. Include payment method. Prepayment required. Free shipping over $100.

Shipping information: Shipped via UPS or US mail depending on size. Allow 5-7 working days.

BROWN HOUSE DOLLS

Beverly Brown
3200 N. Sand Lake Rd.
Allen, MI 49227
Phone: For orders: (800)533-0356 EST
Fax: (517)869-2371
For info: (517)869-2833
In business since: 1981

SUPPLIES:

Patterns for cloth dolls: Available

CLOTHING:

Patterns for doll clothing: More than 300 vintage doll clothing designs. Each pattern is available in 4-6 sizes.

BUSINESS INFORMATION:

Type of business: Wholesale and retail, by mail only.

Accepts: Check, money order, Visa, MC, DC

Discounts: 10% discount for 12 patterns; 20% for 24 patterns; 30% for 48 patterns. 40-50% available to dealers on larger orders

Back order policy: No back orders. Has own print shop and publishes own patterns.

Return/exchange policy: 7 days. Returns and exchanges subject to shipping charges.

Catalog: b&w and color, $2

Mailing list: Customers receive next year's catalog if they have purchased $25 or more during current year.

Phone orders: M-F, 9-5 EST.

Fax orders: Fax catalog order form or include name, address, phone, credit card, pattern numbers

Mail orders: Will ship to US, Canada, overseas. Mail catalog order form or name, address, phone, credit card, pattern numbers. Prepayment required.

Shipping information: Shipping is included in the price of the order. Shipped via UPS or US mail. Allow 48 hours.

BUFFALO BATT & FELT

Frances Zandi, product manager
3307 Walden Ave.
Depew, NY 14043
Phone:
For orders: (716)683-4100 ext. 130/131 EST
For info: (716)683-4100
Fax: (716)683-8928
In business since: 1977

SUPPLIES:

Stuffing: Superior quality 100% virgin polyester. Brand names include Super Fluff, Ultra Fluff, Premium Slick Fiberfill and Soft-Soft.

BUSINESS INFORMATION:

Type of business: Wholesale only, by mail.

Wholesale requirements: Minimum quantity 2 cases.

Accepts: Check, money order, Visa, MC, COD

Discounts: Up to 40%

Back order policy: 24-hour turnaround

Return/exchange policy: Products are fully guaranteed.

Samples: Brochure with swatches, $1, refundable with purchase. Bag of fiberfill, $1. Pillow insert, $3. Available by mail.

Catalog/Price list: Color, $1, refundable with purchase. Price list, free.

Mailing list: Those who request information or order are included.

Phone orders: 8:30-4:45

Fax orders: Fax catalog order form.

Mail orders: Will ship to US. Prepayment required or COD. Mail the catalog order form.

Shipping information: Shipping included in the price of order. Shipped via UPS or FedEx. 24-hour turn-around.

CASCADE DOLL SHOPPE

Linda Nachbar
6290 Burton SE
Grand Rapids, MI 49546
Phone: (616)942-6786 EST
Fax: (616)942-9559
Hours: M, 10-2, and by appointment.
In business since: 1984

SUPPLIES:

Armatures: A + Connectors, Locline

Bodies: Seeley composition

Clays: Super Sculpey

Eyes: Realistic, glass, flat acrylic

Fabrics for cloth dolls: Silk metal, laces, high end fabrics for antique repro.

Fabrics for hair: Wefted mohair, English mohair

Lashes: All types.

Molds: Seeley, Bell, "Touch of Olde"

Paints: Seeley, Virginia La Varnga, CDW China Paints

Slips: Seeley porcelain

Tools: Seeley brushes, Scharft, KB-Evenheat, Cress, Olympic kilns, Rapid Fire kilns, Master Eye bevelers

Wigs: Monique, Kemper, Artworks, Mini World, human hair, mohair

CLOTHING:

Fabrics for doll clothing: Available

Lace: Available

Patterns for doll clothing: Available

Ribbons: Silk

Trimmings: Metallic trim

BUSINESS INFORMATION:

Type of business: Wholesale and retail, from home, from store location or by mail.

Wholesale requirements: $100 to open account; $25 for reorder.

Accepts: Check, money order, Visa, MC

Discounts: Varies

Return/exchange policy: No refunds.

Samples: Metal fabrics. Available by mail.

Mailing list: Write or call to be included.

Phone orders: Accepted

Fax orders: Accepted

Mail orders: Will ship to US. Prepayment required. COD.

Shipping information: Shipped via UPS or Priority Mail. Allow 2 weeks for delivery.

ADDITIONAL INFORMATION:
Also offers apprentice seminars and books related to sculpting, dollmaking and costuming.

CENTER STAGE EMPORIUM

Marilyn Prescott
172 Main St.
Kingston, NH 03848-3219
Phone: (603)642-3327 EST
E-mail: kbdx56b@prodigy.com
Hours: W-F, 10-5, Th, 10-8, Sun, 12-5.
In business since: 1994

SUPPLIES:

Armatures: Locline snapbead

Bodies: Seeley's composition bodies, including German repro, French repro, modern

Clays: Cernit, Fimo

Eyes: Glastic Realistic, Kais paperweight eyes, Karl's German Glass, Global paperweight.

Fabrics for hair: Wefted mohair, wefted human hair

Lashes: Assortment of styles

Molds: Seeley's

Paints: Seeley's and Virginia LaVorgna

Slips: Seeley's

Tools: Paragon Kilns, Bell Mini-Bars, Seeley brushes, all necessary kiln supplies and dollmaking tools

Wigs: Ready-made Global and Kemper

More about supplies: Soft-fired greenware, bisque blanks, painted bisque and kits.

CLOTHING:

Patterns for doll clothing: Brown House, Easy Sew and Connie Lee Finchum

ACCESSORIES:

Doll-related collectibles: Some artist and manufactured dolls

BUSINESS INFORMATION:

Type of business: Wholesale and retail, at store location and by mail.

Wholesale requirements: Minimum quantity varies.

Accepts: Check, money order, Visa, MC, AE

Discounts: Volume discounts

Layaway: Adjusted to suit need of the individual.

Back order policy: Ships when item is received unless instructed otherwise.

Return/exchange policy: Must be returned within 14 days for shop credit.

Catalog: Manufacturer's catalog package, $14. Price list, LSASE.

Phone orders: During shop hours

Mail orders: Will ship to US. Include name, address, phone number, check, money order or credit card info. plus specific products being ordered. Prepayment required.

Shipping information: Shipping additional. Usually shipped via US mail. Allow 3-5 weeks for delivery.

CHILDHOOD FANTASIES

Ali Hansen
P.O. Box 112275
Carrollton, TX 75011-2275
Phone: (214)323-7397 CST
Fax: (214)466-1534
Hours: By appointment only.
In business since: 1988

SUPPLIES:

Armatures: Kits assembled or by the foot. ¼", 4½" by Seton (Kemper).

Bodies: Cloth bodies, kits. Carries approximately 300 styles

Eyes: Glastic Realistic (acrylic); hand blown glass eyes; Perfect Eyes (acrylic); English paperweight (glass)

Lashes: Single and double lash sets by Playhouse.

Molds: Lady Fashion Dolls sculpted by Ali Hansen. 3 heads currently available: Savannah, Alexandra and Charmaine. More coming soon.

Wigs: Ready-made wigs by Global

CLOTHING:

Clothing (ready-made): A complete line of patterns for lady dolls. Mostly for Ali Hansen's original molds but also for dolls by other artists. (Ladies only.)

BUSINESS INFORMATION:

Type of business: Wholesale and retail, at store location and by mail. Also sell at doll and ceramic shows.

Wholesale requirements: Buyer must have a vendor's license number.

Accepts: Check, money order, Visa, MC, DC, AE

Discounts: Dealer discounts vary with items. Promotional discounts for limited time period.

Layaway: 1/3 down, 60 days

Back order policy: If an item is back ordered, will ship as soon as product is available unless customer advises us to cancel.

Return/exchange policy: Returns on incorrect or defective merchandise with advance authorization.

Catalog: b&w, $3, refundable with purchase.

Mailing list: Write or call to be included, or request catalog.

Phone orders: M-F, 8-5.

Fax orders: Include name, address, area code/phone number, credit card info, signature, items requested

Mail orders: Will ship to US, Canada, overseas. Include name, address, area code/phone number, order and amount. Prepayment required.

Shipping information: COD; shipping will be added to price of order. Shipped via UPS. Allow 1-3 weeks for delivery.

ADDITIONAL INFORMATION:

Ali Hansen has a shop (workshop is more accurate) that she uses to sculpt, design patterns, and produce kits and finished dolls.

COLLECTIBLE DOLL COMPANY

Jean Nordquist
4216-6th NW
Seattle, WA 98107
Phone:
For orders: (800)566-6646 PST
For info: (206)781-1963
Fax: (206)781-2258
Hours: M-F, 10-5. Sat, 10-2. M-Th, 6:30-9.
In business since: 1979

SUPPLIES:

Armatures: Twisted wire and popbead

Bodies: Composition antique-type and cloth body stockings

Clays: Cernit, polymer clay

Eyes: Hand Glass Craft English paperweight and crystal eyes, 8mm-32mm; Kemper oval glass paperweights, 10mm-24mm; Global oval flat back glass and round glass paperweight, 10mm-32mm; mini glass round eyes on wires, 2mm-6mm; Realistic plastic eyes, 8mm-26mm.

Fabrics for hair: Bulk continuous English mohair by the yard or pound; lambskins, Tibetan (long), Kalgon (short curl) straight or braided

Lashes: Modacrylic—all sizes and colors.

Molds: Line of 300 antique reproduction and modern and Santa Claus doll molds. Also represent Bell, Alberta and Embossart.

Paints: Jean Nordquist's Signature System China paints (dry) and glycerin medias.

Patterns for cloth dolls: Gail Wison dolls and Santa kits, primitives and Raggedys (also include accessories).

Slips: Bell porcelain

Tools: Aim kilns, Kemper tools, Jean Nordquist's Signature brushes by Global, Cornell cleaning brushes, knitting needles sizes 0-0000

Wigs: Global mohair, human hair and modacrylic, Artist Collection mohair and synthetic mohair, Bell, Playhouse and Kemper modacrylic.

Other supplies: Master eye bevelers, Jean Nordquist painting and wig-making videos, 8″ × 10″ photos with notes, painting guides, soft-fired greenware, purse frames, cork pates, Embossart

CLOTHING:

Clothing (ready-made): American Girl dresses, underwear, shoes, socks, jewelry

Patterns for doll clothing: Jean Nordquist's Collectible Doll Fashions line for antique reproduction dolls, Santas and moderns. Thurlow knits and crochets, Shirlalee crochets, designer knits for dolls—all with antique doll orientation.

Other clothing supplies: Pins, antique laces, buttons, old doll shoes, hats, parasols

ACCESSORIES:

Furniture: Antique doll furniture and child furniture, Muffy Vander Bear furniture, various wicker and hand crafted antique repro oak furniture

Scaled props/accessories: Purses, jewelry, parasol frames, trunks, suitcases

Doll-related collectibles: Glass doll dishes—repro depression glass; miniature toys for Santa pack stuffers.

BUSINESS INFORMATION:

Type of business: Wholesale and retail, at store location, by mail and at doll shows.

Wholesale requirements: Minimum quantity and dollar amounts vary by product. Net $150 opening order; reorder net $50.

Accepts: Visa, MC, check, money order

Discounts: Distributor and dealer discounts

Layaway: On finished dolls of $100 or more, 25% down and 3 equal payments over 90 days

Back order policy: Will back order items of more than $10.

Return/exchange policy: No return or exchange without authorization. Within seven days of purchase and with receipt.

Samples: Available by mail.

Catalog/Price list: b&w and color, $9 for set of 3, refundable with purchase. Price lists, free with SASE.

Mailing list: Call or request catalog to be included.

Phone orders: M-F, 9-5 PST.

Fax orders: Charge card number for Visa/MC; UPS shipping address for overseas, method of shipping (air or surface).

Mail orders: Will ship to US, Canada, overseas. Mail the catalog order form. Prepayment required. Prefer Visa/MC. COD.

Shipping information: Shipped via method preferred by customer. Delivery time depends on goods ordered and method of payment. For personal check purchases, requires 2 weeks for check to clear.

CREATE AN HEIRLOOM

Eileen Heifner
160 West St., P.O. Box 1068
Berlin, MA 01503-2068
Phone: For orders: (800)448-6173 EST
For info: (508)838-2130
In business since: 1984

SUPPLIES:

Armatures: All sizes

Eyes: German crystal, Glastic, all sizes

Lashes: All styles available.

Molds: Global

Wigs: Ready-made wigs. All style and colors from Global.

More about supplies: High quality porcelain doll kits with the supplies that go with each kit.

CLOTHING:

Patterns for doll clothing: Over 1,000 doll dressmaking patterns in all sizes and styles.

ACCESSORIES:

Furniture: Doll trunks for 18″ vinyl dolls.

BUSINESS INFORMATION:

Type of business: Retail only, by mail.

Accepts: Check, money order, Visa, MC, DC

Discounts: Quantity discounts on doll, elf, wise men and Santa heads

Back order policy: Filled as soon as possible.

Return/exchange policy: Returns must be made within 21 days of invoice. Returned items are subject to 15% restocking fee.

Catalog: b&w, $1.

Mailing list: Write to be included.

Phone orders: 9-6

Fax orders: Fax the catalog order form.

Mail orders: Will ship to US, Canada, overseas. Mail the catalog order form. Prepayment required. Shipping included in the price of order.

Shipping information: Shipped via UPS. Some items shipped same day.

"A DOLL IS MORE THAN A GIFT. IT IS AN INVESTMENT."

Marge Dowdy, Doll World & Surroundings, Columbus, GA

CR'S CRAFTS

Susan Krein
Box 8-SD96
Leland, IA 50453
Phone: (515)567-3652 CST
Fax: (515)567-3071
Hours: M-F, 8:30-3:30.
In business since: 1981

SUPPLIES:

Armatures: Locline plastic armatures, La Sioux Skele-Bend Plastic armatures, wire armatures

Bodies: Cloth—stuffed and unstuffed; stuffed with wire; composition: toddler, German and modern; stuffed with porcelain hands and boots

Clays: Cernit modeling clay, Cernit doll label clay, mache clay, Fimo clay, Fimo Puppen Clay, Sculpey, Friendly Clay and Creative Paperclay

Eyes: Flat acrylic paperweight, Krystal, Glastic, flat back acrylic, Blown glass, Life-like, Glorfix

Fabrics for cloth dolls: Windsor Comfort soft sculpture fabric, Windsor Comfort Ponte Fabric, cotton muslin, weaver's cloth, poly-cotton solids (color) and Mauerhan fabric, soft-sculp skin, craft velour, Europa suede, Doe suede cloth.

Fabrics for hair: Mohair: locks, English straight, country curls, white straight. Wool: braided roving, natural popcorn, natural fleece, natural curls, folk whimsey, folk dyed sheep's natural. Other: stringlets natural, wavy locks, curly locks, dizzy frizzy, wary hair-braided, maxie and mini curly hair, curly chenille, fancy fiber. Curly ringlets, small ringlets, tangle yarn, flax fiber, pretty/hair, angel hair. Small and mini raflets.

Lashes: Stick-on eyelashes, natural, fine, whispy, angled, duo, bottom only and mini (human hair)

Molds: What a Character™ face and hand molds for clay, Glorfix head, arms and legs mold for Glorfix powder

Paints: Glorfix paint set, Mauerhan paint kits, doll face paint, Americana So-Soft paints and Deco Art paints.

Patterns for cloth dolls: CR's cloth doll patterns, Springtime cloth doll patterns, Sew Special doll patterns, Hot off the Press cloth doll books, Design Original doll books. Mimi's Universal

Toddler book, Easy-to-Make doll books, Complete Pattern Book of Soft Dolls, Dozens of Dolls book, Dream Spinners Patterns, Luv'N Stuff Patterns, Gooseberry Hill Patterns

Slips: By special order

Stuffing: Polyester fiberfill, including ultra slick, premium white, economy white and bonded; also plastic beads

Tools: Stringing tools, forceps, scissors, tweezers, eye setting tools and wax, E-Z-Lashers. Clay molding tools, brushes, sanding pads.

Wigs: Ready-made wigs. Human hair, including La Sioux newborn; mohair, including Playhouse, Synthetic Mohair; Mini World. Kemper, La Sioux, Playhouse, Mini World, Tallina's National Artcraft (Pippin's Hollow), Syndee's World of Children wigs.

More about supplies: Plastic and hard board joints, large selection of noisemakers (doll criers) and music boxes. Soft sculpture needles, extra strong thread, large selection of angel wings. Quality vinyl doll kits. Pre-painted designer procelain, pigma micron pens, numerous vinyl and porcelain head sets, Glorfix doll supplies. Mauerhan doll supplies.

CLOTHING:

Buttons: ¼″ and ⅛″ plastic buttons. Plus animals, hearts, scissors, thread, sports, train, vegetables, clocks, fancy, with rosebuds. Also button assortments (½ lb. package).

Clothing (ready-made): CR's exclusive line of designer clothing for designer porcelain dolls (14″ to 24″ dolls), including socks, tights, lace panties, pantallets, undershirt and panty sets. Also witch and Santa outfits, Syndee's 10″ doll outfits, and large selections of shoes and hats.

Fabrics for doll clothing: Border Prints, Osh Kosh Fabrics, Mission Valley Wovens, Hi-Fashion bear fabrics, Tea Dyed bear fabrics, Poly-cotton heart prints, craft velour, Europa suede, Doe suede cloth.

Fibers/threads: Polyester sewing thread, elastic thread.

Lace: Flat laces, gathered laces, lace beading, double flat lace, gathered cluny, cluny edge, insertion lace, eyelet beading, flat eyelets, gathered eyelets, eyelet edging, battenburg edge

Leather: Pigskin suede

Patterns for doll clothing: Seeley's clothing patterns. Yesterday's children patterns. Sew-it-yourself designer clothes. Syndee's clothing patterns. CR's original clothing patterns. Large selection of sewing and crochet leaflets. Books of doll hats and bonnets, doll shoes, and heirloom doll clothes.

Ribbons: Satin ribbon (many widths), picot satin ribbon, double face satin ribbon, edged organza, organza ribbon with wired edges, silk embroidery ribbon, silken embroidery ribbon

Trimmings: Ribbon bows, grosgrain ribbon bows, ribbon roses, suede leather lacing beads, battenburg doilies and collars, buckles, appliques, seed bead appliques, pom pom and elastic, velcro nylon closure, fabric glue, wonder markers, quilting pins, sewing gauge, seam ripper, barette backs

Other clothing supplies: Disposable diapers, handbags and back packs.

ACCESSORIES:

Furniture: Wood bow swing, wood trikes, wood tractor, wood sled, wood kiddie car, wood teeter totter, rocking chairs, benches, wagons, beach chairs, wicker chairs, wicker love seat, peacock chair, twig chair, rattan cradles

Scaled props/accessories: Large selection of miniatures including mail box, phone, cookware, canning jars, cooking utensils, copper pots, garden tools, watering cans, vegetables, musical instruments, shopping bags, wicker baskets

More about accessories: Doll stands, cradle stands, musical instruments, glasses, doll crowns, hangers, umbrellas, tea sets, doll jewelry, sports, equipment, brush and mirror sets, pacifiers, rattles, doll bottles, dust covers

BUSINESS INFORMATION:

Type of business: Wholesale and retail, at store location and by mail.

Wholesale requirements: Minimum dollar amount $25 for phone orders.

Accepts: Check, money order, Visa, MC, DC, US funds only—no Canadian or foreign checks

Discounts: Large quantity discounts are available. Please put requests for price quotes in writing.

Back order policy: Will back order items expected back in stock in less than 30 days provided they amount to at least $5 and are not outside the continental US (no additional shipping and handling charged).

Return/exchange policy: Complaints about an order must be made in writing. All shortage claims and returns must be made within 30 days. Returned merchandise must be accompanied by a copy of the order and a note explaining the reason for return. Processing and handling charges for reshipment of exchanges will be charged.

Catalog/price list: Both. US, $2; Canada, $4; overseas, $7.

Mailing list: Please request catalog to be included; must order throughout year to remain on new catalog mailing list.

Phone orders: M-F, 8:30-3:30.

Fax orders: Fax the catalog order form.

Mail orders: Will ship to US, Canada, overseas. Mail the catalog order form. Prepayment required.

Shipping information: Shipping included in the price of order. Shipped via UPS or parcel post. Allow 1 week for delivery.

THE DOLL ADVENTURE

Karen Laisney
2129 S. US Hwy. 1
Jupiter, FL 33477
Phone: (407)575-4292 EST
Fax: (407)743-1978
Hours: T-Sat, 10-5.
In business since: 1991

SUPPLIES:

Armatures: La Sioux plastic

Bodies: Muslin, Kidoline, composition

Clays: Cernit

Eyes: Karl's glass eyes, glass paperweight, bright, Glastic, realistic, acrylic

Fabrics for hair: Mohair, including braided, straight, and dyed

Lashes: All sizes in light brown, medium brown, dark brown, carrot, black

Paints: Oil base and premixed powders for oil or water base

Slips: Bell ceramics

Tools: Brushes including Bell designer brushes, all tools for cleaning greenware

Wigs: Synthetic wigs by Playhouse, Kemper, Monique, Wee Three and Bell. Mohair wigs by special order.

Other supplies: Pates, neck buttons and connectors, eye wax, doll plastic joints, greenware, soft-fired greenware, bisque kits by order, magazines

CLOTHING:

Clothing (ready-made): Embroidered and hand-smocked clothes, shoes and socks, bloomers and panties, flocked velvet hats, straw hats

Patterns for doll clothing: Artist's patterns, Brown House, Connie Lee Finchum, Maime, Bell, Primrose Land and fashion doll patterns.

Other clothing supplies: Buckles

ACCESSORIES:

Furniture: Wicker and handcrafted wood.

Scaled props/accessories: Purses, baskets of flowers, book bags, books, hats, crowns, jewelry, suitcases, steamer trunks, metal and wood doll stands

BUSINESS INFORMATION:

Type of business: Wholesale and retail, at store location and by mail.

Wholesale requirements: $150 initial order. No minimum after first order.

Accepts: Check, money order, Visa, MC, DC

Discounts: Large quantity discounts

Layaway: 3 months, ⅓ each month

Back order policy: Specify preference on back orders at time of initial order. Deposit may be required on large back orders.

Return/exchange policy: No return/exchanges on clothing, custom dolls, wigs, eyes or patterns unless prior authorization is given.

Catalog/Price list: b&w and color, $5 for package (doll supplies and greenware list)

Mailing list: Write, call or request catalog or price list to be included.

Phone orders: T-Sat, 10-5.

Fax orders: Include stock number, quantity, color, size, name of item; credit card number and expiration date; address, name and phone/fax number; special shipping requests. Fax anytime.

Mail orders: Will ship to US, Canada, overseas. Include stock number, quantity, color, size, name of item; credit card number and expiration date; address, name and phone/fax number; special shipping requests. Prepayment required. Shipping included in the price of order.

Shipping information: Shipped via UPS. Allow 2-5 days for delivery.

ADDITIONAL INFORMATION:
Shop makes custom porcelain doll look alikes from photos and special theme dolls, including brides.

> "BUY THE BEST QUALITY DOLL YOU CAN AFFORD AT THE TIME."
> *Mary Ann Cook, C & W Enterprises, Salem, VA*

DOLL FASHIONS NORTHWEST

Linda Johnson
P.O. Box 12113
Portland, OR 97212
Phone:
For orders: (800)263-1544 PST
For info: (503)287-3086
Fax: (503)280-1011
In business since: 1983

CLOTHING:
Clothing (ready-made): Clothing for antiques, reproduction and collectible dolls.
More about clothing: Also do contract sewing for doll artists.

BUSINESS INFORMATION:
Type of business: From home, by mail order.
Home appointments: Please schedule 1-2 days in advance.
Accepts: Check, money order
Discounts: Volume
Return/exchange policy: Will gladly exchange or refund if returned within 10 days of receipt.
Price list: Free
Mailing list: Write to be included.
Phone orders: 8-4:30
Mail orders: Will ship to US. Mail the catalog order form. Prepayment required. Shipping included in the price of order.
Shipping information: Shipped via UPS. Allow 2-4 weeks for delivery.

THE DOLL GALLERY

Dan or Barb Giguere
P.O. Box 124
Scarborough, ME 04070-0124
Phone: (207)883-0822 EST
Fax: (207)883-0822
E-mail: bkhdgoa@prodigy.com
In business since: 1988

SUPPLIES:
Armatures: Custom-made and bead
Clays: Earth clay for sculpting, white porcelain clay, Cernit, Super Sculpey, Puppen, Fimo
Eyes: Various brands of acrylic eyes
Patterns for cloth dolls: Body patterns; custom-made original designs by special order only
Tools: Sculpting tools for use with polymer clays, earth clay and porcelain clay
Wigs: Ready-made Kemper
Other supplies: Stringing material, hooks

CLOTHING:
Patterns for doll clothing: Custom-made and custom-designed patterns by special order.

ACCESSORIES:
Doll-related collectibles: Various and changing, ranging from musical instruments to hairbrushes.

BUSINESS INFORMATION:
Type of business: Retail only, from home
Home appointments: Please schedule 1 day in advance.
Accepts: Check, money order, Visa, MC
Layaway: 25% down, 60 days, weekly payments. Layaways must be for orders over $100.
Back order policy: Customer must request.
Return/exchange policy: 10 days
Phone orders: 8 A.M.-10 P.M.
Fax orders: Include name, address, phone and fax numbers, credit card, type, number, expiration date, signature, back order request and items with sizes and color.
Mail orders: Will ship to US, Canada. Include same as fax orders, but checks also accepted. Prepayment required.
Shipping information: Charged by actual cost. Shipped via method preferred by customer. Allow 1 week for items that are in stock (usually less).

THE DOLL GALLERY

Nan Radford
675 NW Gilman Blvd.
Issaquah, WA 98027
Phone: (206)392-4684 PST
Hours: T-F, 10:30-4:30. Sat, 11-4:30.
In business since: 1989

SUPPLIES:
Bodies: Available
Eyes: Available
Wigs: Available

CLOTHING:
Lace: Available

ACCESSORIES:
Furniture: Wicker
Scaled props/accessories: Available
Doll-related collectibles: Available

BUSINESS INFORMATION:
Type of business: Wholesale and retail, at store location and by mail.
Accepts: Check, money order, Visa, MC
Discounts: To wholesale customers
Layaway: 1-3 months, depending on cost
Return/exchange policy: Accepted with customer receipt.
Mailing list: Write or call to be included.
Phone orders: During business hours
Mail orders: Will ship to US, Canada. Prepayment required. Shipping is added to cost.
Shipping information: Shipped via UPS or method preferred by customer.

DOLL HAIR ETC.

Raymond Baker
R.R. 2, Box 87
Cold Spring, NY 10516
Phone: (914)265-3490 EST
In business since: 1992

SUPPLIES:
Fabrics for hair: Mohair and wool doll hair in straight and wavy styles for all size dolls, and mini curls for small dolls. Also have a limited color selection in silk and luster fabrics.

BUSINESS INFORMATION:
Type of business: Retail only, by mail only.
Accepts: Check, money order
Layaway: 25% down, balance due when shipped.
Return/exchange policy: Full refund with cost of postage and handling.
Samples: A sample sheet with all fabrics, colors, styles, prices and shipping cost

is available. $2 per sample sheet, available through the mail.

Phone orders: Any day except holidays, 8-8.

Mail orders: Will ship to US, Canada, overseas. 25% down with balance due when shipped.

Shipping information: Shipping included in the price of order. Shipped via method preferred by customer. Allow 10 days for delivery (or sooner if requested).

THE DOLL PLACE

Geri Santoro
10324 S. Washington
Oak Lawn, IL 60453
Phone: (708)424-2767
Fax: (708)424-7644
Hours: T, Th, F, 9:30-9:30, or call for appointment.
In business since: 1986

SUPPLIES:

Bodies: Seeley
Molds: Seeley
Paints: Seeley
Slips: Seeley
Other supplies: Also sells Global, Playhouse, Monique and Kemper products

CLOTHING:

Clothing (ready-made): Vee's Victorians

ACCESSORIES:

Scaled props/accessories: Doll buggies, 1″ scale dolls

BUSINESS INFORMATION:

Type of business: Wholesale and retail, at store location and by mail.

DOLL STUDIOS

Teresa Maria
1688 NE 123rd St.
Miami, FL 33181
Phone: (305)895-0605 EST
Fax: (305)861-9848

SUPPLIES:

Eyes: Available
Paints: China
Slips: Porcelain
Tools: Brushes, sculpting tools
Wigs: Available
Other supplies: Also sells greenware; distributes for Seeley, Kemper, Kais, Bell.

CLOTHING:

Clothing (ready-made): Shoes, clothes

THE DOL-LEE SHOP

Cindra L. Lee
3160 Flying Horse Rd.
Colorado Springs, CO 80922
Phone: (719)591-5609 CST
In business since: 1977

SUPPLIES:

Armatures: Cloth, premade for current porcelain dolls.
Molds: Soft-fired greenware bisque kits, painted kits
Paints: Jean Nordquist china paint, dry for oil or water base.
Tools: Aim Kiln distributor

BUSINESS INFORMATION:

Type of business: Retail only, from home and by mail
Home appointments: Please schedule in advance.
Accepts: Check, money order, Visa, MC, AE
Discounts: On order of 4 or more dolls
Layaway: ¼ down, 3 months, ¼ each month
Back order policy: Shipped when ready.
Return/exchange policy: No questions asked unless abused.
Price list: Free with LSASE
Mailing list: Write, call or request a catalog or price list to be included.
Phone orders: 9-3
Mail orders: Will ship to US. Include name, address, payment method, items and quantity. Prepayment required. COD or shipping included in the price of order.
Shipping information: Shipped via UPS or method preferred by customer. Allow 6-8 weeks for delivery.

DOLLS BY DYAN

Dyan Lee
630 S. Loomis St.
Naperville, IL 60540
Phone: (708)420-2480 CST
Fax: (708)420-2480
In business since: 1995

SUPPLIES:

Armatures: Plastic, pop-together
Bodies: Cloth bodies for porcelain dolls
Eyes: Glass flat back paperweight, Glastic Realistic.
Fabrics for hair: Wefted mohair
Lashes: Synthetic
Molds: Seeley for porcelain dolls
Paints: Seeley China paint

Slips: Seeley porcelain
Tools: Brushes
Wigs: For porcelain dolls, synthetic

BUSINESS INFORMATION:

Type of business: Retail only, from home.
Home appointments: Appointments are necessary.
Accepts: Check, money order
Discounts: 10% to students only
Layaway: Variable
Mailing list: Write to be included.
Phone orders: M-F, 9-5.

DOLLS DELIGHT, INC.

Karen Thunberg
P.O. Box 3226
Alexandria, VA 22302-0226
Phone: For orders: (800)257-6301 EST
For information: (703)519-8845
Fax: (703)519-8847
In business since: 1991

CLOTHING:

Clothing (ready-made): American Girls Collection (18″ doll) dresses, coat, hats, shoes, boots, skates, sportswear
Patterns for doll clothing: 5 sewing patterns to fit American Girls Collection. One knitting pattern with 3 pullovers and a tam.

BUSINESS INFORMATION:

Type of business: Wholesale and retail, mail order only.
Wholesale requirements: 10 garments, any mix or $100 minimum. Buyer must have a vendor's license number.
Accepts: Check, money order, Visa, MC
Return/exchange policy: 100% refund on all items.
Catalog: Color. Retail, $2; wholesale, free.
Mailing list: Write, call, request catalog or price list to be included.
Phone orders: 10-5
Fax orders: Fax the catalog order form
Mail orders: Will ship to US, Canada, overseas. Prepayment required.
Shipping information: Added to cost of item. Shipped via UPS or Priority Mail. Allow 1-2 weeks for delivery.

> "BUY WHAT YOU LOVE."
> *Penny and Kathy, Dolls and Friends,*
> *Bellevue, WA*

DONNA LEE'S SEWING CENTER

Donna Hammons
25234 Pacific Hwy. S.
Kent, WA 98032
Phone: (206)941-9466 PST
Fax: (206)941-9486
Hours: M-Sat, 9:30-5.
In business since: 1984

CLOTHING:

Clothing (ready-made): One-of-a-kind exquisite dress, hat and pantaloons made of imported fabrics and laces to fit 26"-28" antique reproduction or modern dolls. Pictures available.

Fabrics for doll clothing: Silks, brocades, taffeta, velvets, beaded laces and embroidered organzas. Fabrics up to $200 a yard.

Fibers/threads: Cotton and Swiss Metrosene polyester.

Lace: Venice lace, some cotton lace

Patterns for doll clothing: Ribbon and Roses pattern line

Ribbons: Embroidered, sheer, wire, silk

Trimmings: Braids, French, beaded, beaded lace

Other clothing supplies: Glass cut beads used for sewing on the Venice lace, needles and thread for sewing the beads.

ACCESSORIES:

Scaled props/accessories: Silver tea sets, silver cups and saucers, spoons.

BUSINESS INFORMATION:

Type of business: Retail only, at store location or by mail.

Accepts: Check, money order, Visa, MC, DC, AE

Discounts: 20% for orders over $100 to businesses only

Back order policy: 1-2 weeks

Return/exchange policy: Exchanges only

Samples: Fabric samples by mail, $5. Pictures available of ready-made clothing.

Catalog: b&w, $4

Phone orders: M-Sat, 9:30-5

Fax orders: Fax the catalog order form.

Mail orders: Will ship to US, Canada, overseas. Mail the catalog order form. Prepayment required.

Shipping information: Shipped via US mail. Orders sent same day as received.

DONNA'S DOLL FACTORY

Donna Deiss
931 S. Casino St.
Las Vegas, NV 89101
Phone: For orders: (702)386-9148
For information: (702)243-9193
Hours: M-F, 10-2.
In business since: 1982

SUPPLIES:

Armatures: Lockline

Bodies: Cloth bodies for all doll molds carried

Clays: Seeley's porcelain, Bell porcelain

Eyes: Glass eyes, plastic eyes, Glastic eyes

Lashes: Playhouse lashes

Molds: Seeley and Bell molds

Paints: Seeley China paints

Patterns for cloth dolls: Seeley, Byron, Connie's doll patterns and more

Slips: Seeley's porcelain, Bell porcelain

Tools: Jayne Houston brushes, Seeley brushes, Seeley and Vemper tools

Wigs: Ready-made Playhouse, Monique

Other supplies: Greenware

CLOTHING:

Clothing (ready-made): For the doll molds carried

Patterns for doll clothing: Seeley, Byron, Connie's Doll Patterns and more

ACCESSORIES:

Scaled props/accessories: Shoes, socks

Doll-related collectibles: Calendars, cards

BUSINESS INFORMATION:

Type of business: Wholesale and retail, at store location and by mail.

Wholesale requirements: $80 on all Playhouse and Monique items. 40% discount. Slip is by volume. Buyer must have vendor's license.

Return/exchange policy: No returns.

Phone orders: Accepted

Mail orders: Will ship to US, Canada. COD, cash, credit cards.

Shipping information: COD; shipping included in the price of order. Shipped via UPS.

ADDITIONAL INFORMATION:

Also offers classes and repairs.

"PAPER DOLLS UNITE ART, FASHION AND NOSTALGIA IN ONE CHARMING PACKAGE."
Barb Rausch, Canoga Park, CA

DUSTMAGNET

Frances Jones
1821 Daly St.
Los Angeles, CA 91311
Phone: (213)223-5111 PST
Fax: (213)223-7250
Hours: Warehouse, 8-4:30.
In business since: 1990.

SUPPLIES:

Tools: Dustmagnet is a dry liquid for cleaning all clays. Cleans dried clays with liquid that does not melt clay or affect it in any way. It is safe and produces no silica dust.

BUSINESS INFORMATION:

Type of business: Wholesale and retail, by mail and at ceramic and doll shows.

Wholesale requirements: Minimum 3 32-oz. bottles

Discounts: Quantity

Price list: Free

Mailing list: Write or call to be included

Phone orders: M-F, 8-4:30

Fax orders: Include name, address, phone, MC or Visa number, expiration date, quantity

Mail orders: Shipped to US. Include same info as fax orders. Prepayment required.

Shipping information: Shipped via UPS. Allow 7-10 days for delivery.

ADDITIONAL INFORMATION:

Dustmagnet is a patented product meeting all government standards. It cuts time for greenware cleaning in half and, by eliminating silica dust, prevents silicosis.

DWAINE E. GIPE

1406 Sycamore Rd.
Montoursville, PA 17754
Phone: (717)323-9604 EST

SUPPLIES:

Paints: Water based acrylic

Tools: Airbrush equipment, parts and service

BUSINESS INFORMATION:

Type of business: Wholesale and retail, by mail only.

DYNASTY DOLL COLLECTION

Donna R. Rovner
1 Newbold Rd., P.O. Box 36
Fairless Hills, PA 19030

Phone: For orders: (800)736-GIFT
(4438) EST
For information: (215)428-9100
Fax: (215)428-9200
In business since: 1977

CLOTHING:

Clothing (ready-made): A variety of
styles designed to fit 15″, 16″, 18″ and
20″ dolls. Wedding dresses, ball
gowns, pinafore dresses, baby
dresses, school jumpers. All clothing
comes with a slip and pantalettes.

ACCESSORIES:

Furniture: Green wire and rattan doll
furniture for 16″-22″ dolls. Loveseat
and coffee table; 2 chairs with a table.
Doll-related collectibles: Doll giftware
items

BUSINESS INFORMATION:

Type of business: Wholesale and retail
manufacturer, importer, wholesaler.
Wholesale requirements: No minimum
quantity. Mimimum dollar amount
$150. Buyer must have tax resale
number.
Mail orders: Will ship to US, Canada.
Include item number, name of item
and payment. Prepayment required.
Shipping information: $5 per doll.
Shipped via UPS or RPS. Allow 4-6
weeks for delivery.

EAGER PLASTICS INC.
Peter Cumerford
3350 W. 48th Place
Chicago, IL 60632-3000
Phone: (312)927-3484 or (312)650-
5850.
Fax: (312)650-5853
In business since: 1975

SUPPLIES:

Tools: Liquid plastic, rubber and foam
applications of all kinds, including silicone rubber to make molds and cast-
able liquid plastics for making reproductions. Hundreds of formulas
available in small quantities with instructions. RTV 1000, the most popular silicone rubber, is a tough tear-
resistant rubber which is true to size
and accurate. EP7509 is the most popular casting media. It is an easy-to-use
50/50 mix that is demoldable in 10-15
minutes. Parts have a pleasing ivory
color.

BUSINESS INFORMATION:

Type of business: Wholesale and retail,
by mail.
Accepts: COD or cash in advance
Phone orders: Accepted
Fax orders: Accepted
Mail orders: Prepayment required or
COD.
Shipping information: COD. Shipped
via UPS. Next day delivery for orders
in stock.

> "BUY ONLY WHAT YOU LIKE, AND DON'T WORRY
> ABOUT HOW MUCH IT WILL BE WORTH."
> *Linda Kemp, Linda's Lov-Lez House of Dolls*
> *& Bears, Mentor, OH*

FANCYWORK AND FASHION
Jean Becker and Joan Hinds
4728 Dodge St.
Duluth, MN 55804
Phone: For orders: (800)365-5257 CST
For information: (218)525-5811
Fax: (218)525-5811
In business since: 1989

CLOTHING:

Patterns for doll clothing: Have self-
published 4 books for Doll Costuming. Two books are patterns for
clothes to fit 18″ vinyl dolls such as
Pleasant Co., Götz, Lissi, etc. One
book is smocking patterns and designs
for dolls. The fourth book is a description of children's clothing from the
1930s to present and includes twenty-
five patterns for outfits from these
eras to fit 16 different popular vinyl
and porcelain doll bodies.

BUSINESS INFORMATION:

Type of business: Wholesale and retail,
by mail only.
Wholesale requirements: 3 books or pat-
terns. Buyers from MN must have a
vendor's license number.
Accepts: Check, money order, Visa, MC
Return/exchange policy: Money re-
funded with receipt.
Catalog: b&w, free with LSASE
Mailing list: Write, request catalog to be
included.
Phone orders: Available
Fax orders: Fax the catalog order form
Mail orders: Will ship to US, Canada,
overseas. Mail the catalog order form.
Prepayment required.

Shipping information: Shipping included in the price of order. Priority
mail; UPS for more than 10 books.
Allow 1-2 weeks for delivery.

GABRIELE'S INC.
Gabriele Cardy
Box 880-91
Blaine, WA 98231
Phone: (604)534-4762
Fax: (360)332-5511
In business since: 1983

SUPPLIES:

Fabrics for cloth dolls: Cotton, muslin
Fabrics for hair: Wool roving, braided
Patterns for cloth dolls: Available
Tools: Professional stuffing tools,
needles
Wigs: Synthetic in several styles
Other supplies: Custom hand silk-
screened/airbrushed doll faces with
body and clothing patterns; identity
labels

CLOTHING:

Patterns for doll clothing: Available
Other clothing supplies: Extra silk-
screened faces

BUSINESS INFORMATION:

Type of business: Wholesale and retail,
by mail
Wholesale requirements: Custom silkscreening wholesale orders require a
quote. Doll kits/faces, mimimum 3 per
order number. Buyer must have tax ID
number.
Accepts: Check, money order, Visa, MC
Discounts: 10% coupon with orders
Samples: Samples of custom-screened,
natural fiber identity labels, $3, avail-
able by mail.
Catalog/Price list: b&w and color, $3.
Price list, $3.
Mailing list: Write or request catalog or
price list to be included.
Phone orders: M-F, 9-5.
Fax orders: Fax items requested plus
credit card number.
Mail orders: Will ship to US, Canada,
overseas. Include items requested plus
card number. Prepayment required.
Shipping information: Shipping in-
cluded in the price of order. Shipped
via method preferred by customer.
Allow 1-3 weeks for delivery.

> "DOLLS AS AN ART FORM COMBINE THE QUALITIES OF TWO-DIMENSIONAL AND THREE-DIMENSIONAL WORK—BOTH PAINTING AND SCULPTURE, WITH THE ADDED TEXTURAL QUALITIES OF FABRICS AND OTHER MATERIALS."
>
> *Maggie Finch and Martha Finch-Kozlosky, Bennington, VT*

GALLERY COLLECTION MOLDS

Jessica M. Heberle
1817 Hawkins Rd.
St. Louis, MO 63026
Phone:
For orders: (800)831-2280 CST
For info: (314)861-0055
Hours: To visit the factory and show-room an appointment is needed.
In business since: 1992

SUPPLIES:

Bodies: Pre-sewn for bodies to fit animal molds.
Molds: Doll molds, animal molds, ornament molds, figurines
Paints: China paint, own line of colors called Gallery Collection Molds Colours Collection.
Patterns for cloth dolls: Body patterns for all our molds, plus dress outfits
Tools: Distributor for Even Heat Kiln, Inc.

CLOTHING:

Patterns for doll clothing: Various sizes and styles to fit all molds.

ACCESSORIES:

Doll-related collectibles: Currently starting a new line. The first is a 3 layer throw. All pieces will be sold for a limited time.

BUSINESS INFORMATION:

Type of business: Wholesale only, by mail or at shows.
Accepts: Check, money order, Visa, MC, DC
Discounts: Join club on an annual basis and receive the lowest discounts and freight free shipping in the continental US—assistance with freight to other areas.
Back order policy: As much of the order as possible is shipped out ASAP. The back order is filled when the product arrives.
Price list: SASE
Mailing list: Join the club. Call for information.

Phone orders: M-F, 8:30-5
Mail orders: Will ship to US, Canada, overseas. Include phone number, name, address, tax number, payment method. Prepayment required. COD. Members of club—free or assisted if not in the continental US.
Shipping information: Shipped via UPS. Allow 2 weeks on average for delivery.

GEORGIE'S CERAMICS AND CLAY ART PAK

Jamie Englert
756 NE Lombard
Portland, OR 97211
Phone:
For orders: (800)999-2529 PST
For info: (503)283-1353
Fax: (503)283-1387
Hours: M-Sat, 9-5.
In business since: 1965

SUPPLIES:

Armatures: Plastic pop and snap style
Bodies: Composition-latex; cloth fabric stretch
Clays: Cernit, Sculpey, Roma Plastaline (manufactured on site)
Eyes: Glass oval paperweights, real life acrylics, realistic acrylic
Fabrics for hair: Mohair (wefted), lambskin
Lashes: Large selection of assorted styles and colors
Molds: 36 lines, including Georgie's own designs, Seberta, Seeley, Bell, Byron, Dona.
Paints: Seeley, Bell, Willoughby china
Patterns for cloth dolls: Seeley, Bell and Connie Lee Finchum
Slips: Seeley, Bell, Colonfee
Tools: Skutt, Duncan kilns
Wigs: Global (human, mohair and synthetic), Playhouse

CLOTHING:

Buttons: Tiny and small available
Lace: By special order
Leather: By special order
Patterns for doll clothing: Antique and modern
Ribbons: By special order
Trimmings: Small antique beads. Other items by special order.
Other clothing supplies: Parasols and parasol frames

ACCESSORIES:

Scaled props/accessories: Pianos, doll cases, shopping carts, baseballs, mitts

BUSINESS INFORMATION:

Type of business: Wholesale and retail, at store location and by mail.
Accepts: Check, money order, Visa, MC, DC, AE
Catalog: b&w, $5
Mailing list: Write or call to be included.
Fax orders: Fax the catalog order form
Mail orders: Will ship to US, Canada, overseas. Prepayment required.
Shipping information: Shipped via UPS, US mail or method preferred by customer.

GRANDMA'S DOLLINGS

Mary Ann Bowman
3400 Westminster Rd.
Oceanside, NY 11572
Phone: (516)766-4172 EST

SUPPLIES:

Armatures: Available
Bodies: Composition
Clays: Water-based clays
Eyes: Glastic Realistic, Karls' glass eyes
Lashes: Available
Paints: Seeley's China paint
Slips: Seeley's
Tools: All tools and brushes for doll sculpting and dollmaking
Wigs: Playhouse, Tallinas, Monique, Global
Other supplies: Stands

CLOTHING:

Clothing (ready-made): Vee's Victorian, Minnie's Doll Clothing

ACCESSORIES:

Furniture: Handcrafted wood
Scaled props/accessories: Available

BUSINESS INFORMATION:

Type of business: Wholesale and retail, from home.
Wholesale requirements: Must have a vendor's license.
Home appointments: Please schedule in advance.
Accepts: Check, money order, AE
Layaway: 20% plus 4 payments, not to exceed 4 months.
Return/exchange policy: No return on special orders.
Mailing list: Write to be included.
Phone orders: 9-5

ADDITIONAL INFORMATION:

Offers doll-sculpting and dollmaking classes. Finished original and reproduction dolls, costumed and undressed also available.

HAMILTON EYE WAREHOUSE

Carol Hamilton
Box 450-BB
Moorpark, CA 93021
Phone: (805)529-5900 PST
In business since: 1986

SUPPLIES:

Eyes: Imported solid glass paperweight, best quality eyes, hollow blown glass and 8 different styles and qualities of acrylic eyes in different shades, 8mm-30mm. Large stock.

CLOTHING:

Ribbons: High-quality silk ribbon
Trimmings: Imported high-quality cotton lace, silk lace, white and ecru, at reasonable prices.

ACCESSORIES:

Scaled props/accessories: Adult size, battenburg lace, parasols for lady dolls. Some plain; some have flowers attached.

BUSINESS INFORMATION:

Type of business: Wholesale and retail, by mail order and trade shows.
Wholesale requirements: Minimum dollar amount $100. Buyer must have a vendor's license number (CA only).
Accepts: Check, money order, Visa, MC
Discounts: On more than 12 pairs of eyes
Return/exchange policy: Return within 14 days, no alterations.
Catalog/Price list: Color, $1. Price list, free.
Mailing list: Request catalog to be included.
Phone orders: 8-6
Mail orders: Will ship to US, Canada, overseas. Mail the catalog order form. Prepayment required.
Shipping information: Shipping included in the price of order. Shipped the same day via method preferred by customer.

ADDITIONAL INFORMATION:

Also sells doll books, doll jewelry.

HANDCRAFT DESIGNS, INC.

Tony Kohn and Liane Kohn
63 E. Broad St.
Hatfield, PA 19440
Phone: For orders: (800)523-2430 EST
For information: (215)855-3022
Fax: (215)855-0184
In business since: 1972

SUPPLIES:

Armatures: Hand armatures for polymer and air-dry clays
Clays: Cernit, Premier, La Doll and Crafty Air Dry
Fabrics for hair: Natural mohair, combed wool in various colors
Tools: Eyewax for temporary setting of eyes (Mini Hold) for porcelain
Other supplies: Matte, ultra glaze

ACCESSORIES:

Scaled props/accessories: Musical instruments: sax, trumpet, clarinet, flute, violin, in ⅙+ scale.

BUSINESS INFORMATION:

Type of business: Wholesale and retail, by mail only. Sells mostly to stores and professional dollmakers, but will sell to retail consumers when products are not readily available.
Wholesale requirements: Minimum dollar amount $50; distributor pricing has different requirements.
Accepts: Check, money order, Visa, MC, open credit to storefront accounts with references.
Discounts: Available
Back order policy: Items shipped as available, unless customer cannot wait.
Return/exchange policy: Please send a written request or call before return.
Samples: Will send small orders so customers can sample products they haven't used before. Retail cost.
Catalog: Color, SASE with 55¢ postage.
Phone orders: 9-5.
Fax orders: Fax the catalog order form or address, items ordered and payment, Visa/MC if not a open account customer.
Mail orders: Will ship to US, Canada, overseas. Include all necessary information and method of shipment. Prepayment required; customer will be billed if credit has been established. Actual cost added to merchandise cost for open account and credit card or-

ders. Prepaid orders, add $5 for up to $99 orders; add $7.50 for $100-199 orders.
Shipping information: Shipped via UPS or method preferred by customer. Ships within 48 hours 90% of the time.

HEARTWARMERS

117 Main St., P.O. Box 517
Lennox, SD 57039-0517
Fax: (605)647-5047 CST
Hours: Appointment only, 9-5
In business since: 1977

SUPPLIES:

Armatures: ¼″ to ½″ (heavy)
Bodies: Will make for each doll kit purchasing
Eyes: Flat or Glastic rounds
Lashes: Variety of colors and sizes
Paints: Seeley, Byron, Bell
Slips: Seeley and Bell
Stuffing: Factory outlets—light golden color
Tools: Brushes, cleaning cubes, pink sanders, sponge sander, palettes, knife, cleaning scalpels, etc.
Wigs: Variety of sizes, colors, and makes

CLOTHING:

Clothing (ready-made): Variety of sizes, styles, colors

BUSINESS INFORMATION:

Type of business: Wholesale and retail, at store location and by mail.
Wholesale requirements: Minimum dollar amount $100. Must have vendor's license, federal ID number or sales tax number, business card; separate order blank available for wholesale.
Accepts: Check, money order
Discounts: 10% discount on 3 doll kits; wholesale separate
Layaway: 20% down, 3 equal payments, 90 days
Back order policy: If doll isn't in, will check on waiting period, let customers decide if they can wait.
Return/exchange policy: 7 days return policy if not satisfied with quality.
Catalog/Price list: b&w, $7, with bimonthly updates free. Price list included with catalog.
Mailing list: Automatically included with $7 catalog fee
Fax orders: Check or money order to follow within 5 days.

Mail orders: Will ship to US, Canada, overseas. Mail the catalog order form. Prepayment required.

Shipping information: Shipping is $6.50 per doll. Shipped via UPS or method preferred by customer. Parcel Post to Canada, Alaska, Hawaii and overseas. Allow 2-4 weeks, soft-fire; 4-6 weeks, unpainted bisque; 6-8 weeks, painted kits.

HEAVENLY DOLLS

Yvonne Moslar
404 W. Meeker St.
Kent, WA 98032
Phone: (206)852-5643 PST
Fax: (206)852-1435
Hours: T-Sat, 9:30-4.

SUPPLIES:

Armatures: Locline
Bodies: Handmade cloth and composition bodies
Clays: Porcelain—Seeley, Bell, Colorific
Eyes: Plastic, glass
Fabrics for hair: Mohair—loose, dyed, wefted and braided
Lashes: Playhouse and Kemper lashes, human lashes
Molds: Mystic
Paints: Nordquist, La Vorgna, Seeley's
Stuffing: Fiberfill, pellets
Tools: Kemper tools, Skutt and Aim Kilns, Nordquist, Jayne Houston and Seeley's brushes
Wigs: Ready-made modacrylic, mohair

CLOTHING:

Clothing (ready-made): Handmade clothes in stock or through custom orders. Has several talented women making clothes for the shop.
Patterns for doll clothing: Nordquist and Connie Lee Finchum

ACCESSORIES:

Furniture: Chairs, buggies, horses, etc.
Scaled props/accessories: Wings, musical instruments, wagons, etc.

BUSINESS INFORMATION:

Type of business: Wholesale and retail, at store location and by mail.
Wholesale requirements: Buyer must have vendor's license.
Accepts: Check, money order, Visa, MC, DC
Discounts: 40% on Kemper and Playhouse

Return/exchange policy: Up to 10 days to exchange for other items.
Catalog: b&w and color, $5
Mailing list: Write, call, request catalog to be included.
Phone orders: T-Sat, 9:30-4.
Fax orders: Fax catalog order form. Include name, address, phone number, method of payment.
Mail orders: Will ship to US, Canada, overseas. Include name, address, phone number, method of payment. Prepayment required.
Shipping information: Paid at time of shipment. Allow 1-6 weeks for delivery.

HEDY KATIN CLOTH DOLL PATTERNS

Hedy Katin
572 Edelweiss Dr.
San Jose, CA 95136
Phone: (408)265-1839 PST
In business since: 1991

SUPPLIES:

Patterns for cloth dolls: Patterns for a teenager, three tiny babies, a large country girl and a wig pattern.

BUSINESS INFORMATION:

Type of business: Retail only, by mail.

IRONSTONE YARNS

Jack Emmott
P.O. Box 365
Uxbridge, MA 01569
Phone: For orders: (800)343-4914 EST
For information: (508)278-5838
Fax: (508)278-7433
In business since: 1972

SUPPLIES:

Fabrics for hair: Yarns, mohair, wool, cotton, synthetic, looped yarns, brushed yarns, novelty effect yarns, metallic yarns

BUSINESS INFORMATION:

Type of business: Wholesale only
Wholesale requirements: Minimum dollar amount $50
Accepts: Check, money order, Visa, MC
Samples: Yarn book $20. Available by mail.
Catalog/Price list: Color, $20. Price list, free.
Mailing list: Request catalog to be included.

Phone orders: 8-5 EST. 24-hour answering machine.
Fax orders: Include name, address, telephone number (to confirm).
Mail orders: Will ship to US, Canada, overseas. Customer will be billed with approved credit.
Shipping information: Shipped via method preferred by customer. Allow 4 days for delivery.

> "DOLLS ARE SCULPTURES OF MUSEUM QUALITY PRODUCED BY THE GREAT TALENTS OF THIS TIME PERIOD AND NEED TO BE CARED FOR AT LEAST AS CAREFULLY."
>
> *Toni Volk, Zip's Toys To Go, Ardmore, PA*

J. SCHOEPFER, INC.

Jim Schoepfer
460 Cook Hill Rd.
Cheshire, CT 06410
Phone: For orders: (800)875-6939 EST
For information: (203)250-7794.
Fax: (203)250-7796
Hours: 8-4:30.
In business since: 1907

SUPPLIES:

Eyes: 28 different styles of glass and plastic eyes for dolls. Besides own production eyes carries brand names like Karl, Glastic and Glastic Realistic.

BUSINESS INFORMATION:

Type of business: Wholesale and retail, at store location and by mail.
Wholesale requirements: Minimum dollar amount $25. Discounts are according to quantity purchased.
Accepts: Check, money order, Visa, MC, AE, COD (cash or certified check)
Discounts: Based on volume
Back order policy: No charge until sent; no shipping charge.
Return/exchange policy: No-questions-asked exchange policy; call prior to exchange for instruction.
Catalog/Price list: Color, free. Price list, free.
Phone orders: 8-4:30
Fax orders: Fax catalog order form or name, address, phone number, means of charge.
Mail orders: Will ship to US, Canada, overseas. Prepayment required.

Shipping information: Shipped via method preferred by customer. Allow 7-10 working days or by special delivery (next day, second day, etc.).

ADDITIONAL INFORMATION:

"We have manufactured and sold only eyes since 1907. We sell the best quality at the lowest prices and have the largest selection available in the industry today," Jim says.

JACKSON RANCH

Pat and Denise Jackson
HC-63 Box 44
Christoval, TX 76935
Phone: (915)651-7875 CST
In business since: 1979

SUPPLIES:

Fabrics for hair: Raw mohair—loose, various lengths and styles

BUSINESS INFORMATION:

Type of business: Wholesale and retail, by mail only.
Accepts: Check, money order
Discounts: Volume discounts
Return/exchange policy: Guaranteed satisfaction or your money back.
Samples: Mohair, $3, available by mail.
Price list: $1, or free with sample.
Phone orders: 7 A.M.-8 P.M.
Mail orders: Will ship to US, Canada, overseas. Prepayment required. Purchaser pays the freight charge.
Shipping information: Shipped via UPS, US mail or method preferred by customer. Allow 3-7 days after order received.

JANE'S ORIGINAL ART DOLL SUPPLIES

Jane Poole and Bob Poole
6003 S. 1300E
Salt Lake City, UT 84121
Phone: For orders: (800)560-4958 MST
For information: (801)272-4958
In business since: 1990

SUPPLIES:

Armatures: Manufactures steel wire body armatures and hand armatures. We sell these 10″, 12″, 14″, 16″, 18″, 20″, 24″ and 24″ double strength. The armatures are sold in pairs.
Bodies: Body stockings to stuff for soft sculpting in different sizes and colors
Clays: Cernit
Eyes: Acrylic round eyes, Glastic paper-weight eyes, Judith Howe (porcelain) eyes. All colors and sizes.
Fabrics for hair: Mohair, braided and wavy
Tools: Sculpting tools, including some manufactured by company

ACCESSORIES:

Scaled props/accessories: Jack Johnston books and videos, eyeglasses, doll jewelry, buckles, hair combs, park bench, bicycles, fire engine, pursuit plane, little purses, money, coins.

BUSINESS INFORMATION:

Type of business: Wholesale and retail
Wholesale requirements: 12 or more for wholesale; 100 or more for distributor.
Home appointments: Appointments are necessary. Please schedule same day.
Accepts: Check, money order, Visa, MC
Back order policy: No charge until mailed
Catalog/Price list: b&w, free
Mailing list: Request catalog to be included.
Phone orders: 8-6
Mail orders: Will ship to US, Canada.
Shipping information: Shipped via method preferred by customer. Most orders are mailed the day after ordering, except weekends.

ADDITIONAL INFORMATION:

Jane is Jack Johnston's mother. All of her supplies to make one-of-a-kind dolls are to Jack's specifications. Also holds seminars taught by Jack.

JEAN DIXON

Box 46, Hwy. 287
Masterson, TX 79058
Phone: (806)935-7478 CST
In business since: 1982

CLOTHING:

Ribbons: Narrow, old ribbon made of silk, rayon or blends.

BUSINESS INFORMATION:

Type of business: Retail only, by mail.
Samples: 6 yards of fabric. Please specify color. Please send SASE and $1.

JONES MOLD CO. INC.

Melissa Jones
919 4th Ave. S.
Nashville, TN 37210
Phone: (615)251-8989 CST
Fax: (615)251-8738

Hours: M-F, 8-4, and by appointment on weekends.
In business since: 1980

SUPPLIES:

Molds: Doll molds, ceramic molds
Patterns for cloth dolls: Available
Slips: Ceramic slip
Patterns for doll clothing: For clothes to fit Jones molds.

BUSINESS INFORMATION:

Type of business: Wholesale and retail, at store location and by mail.
Wholesale requirements: Minimum dollar amount $65.
Catalog/Price list: Color, $6.75. Price list, $1, refundable with purchase.
Mailing list: Write, call or request catalog to be included.
Phone orders: 8-5 CST.
Fax orders: Available
Mail orders: Will ship to US, Canada, overseas. Include tax number. Prepayment required.
Shipping information: Shipped via UPS or method preferred by customer. Allow 2 weeks for delivery.

JUDITH HOWE INC.

Judith Howe
1240-D N. Jefferson
Anaheim, CA 92807
Phone: (714)630-4677 PST
Fax: (714)630-6938
In business since: 1980

SUPPLIES:

Armatures: Armature kits for use with Romex wire; animal armatures, also made from Romex wire
Eyes: Porcelain eyes in sizes from 10-30mm; 17 different colors including pink (for bunnies) and slit pupils (for cats and goats)
Tools: Universal stem to be siliconed to the back of flat-backed eyes so that the regular eye-setting tool can be used.

ACCESSORIES:

Scaled props/accessories: Doll stands, 2 types. One is a saddle stand that works very well on lady or fashion dolls as it doesn't interfere with costume. Priced from $6.95. The second is a "cinch" kit for 98¢—customer provides a wood base and a length of ¼″ dowel; the cinch strap slips over the dowel.

BUSINESS INFORMATION:

Type of business: Wholesale and retail, at store location and by mail.

Wholesale requirements: There is no minimum, but the larger the order, the larger the discount. Buyer must have vendor's number.

Accepts: Check, money order, Visa, MC

Discounts: Discounts to business only. Starts at 20% and goes to 55% depending on amount of purchase.

Back order policy: If there is a back order, tries to ship in 1-2 weeks.

Return/exchange policy: Products are guaranteed for 30 days and can be returned for any reason.

Catalog/Price list: b&w, free. Price list, free.

Mailing list: Write or call to be included.

Phone orders: M-F, 7-7. Sat-Sun, 9-3.

Fax orders: Fax the catalog order form.

Mail orders: Will ship to US, Canada, overseas. Prepayment required for about 90% of customers; net 30 for about 10% of customers.

Shipping information: Shipping included in the price of order. Shipped via UPS. Allow 1-2 weeks for delivery.

JUDY'S DOLL SHOP

Judy George
1201A Hwy. 70 E.
New Bern, NC 28560
Phone: (919)637-7933 EST
Hours: M, T, TH, F, Sat, 9:30-5.
In business since: 1984

SUPPLIES:

Armatures: Handmade wire or snap plastic links for 12"-30" dolls

Bodies: Handmade bisque, handmade cloth, Seeley composition

Clays: Cernit

Eyes: Kemper eyes from 3mm-30mm

Lashes: Available

Paints: Seeley china

Slips: Seeley

Tools: Kemper dollmaking tools

Wigs: Kemper modacrylic

CLOTHING:

Clothing (ready-made): Available

Patterns for doll clothing: Connie Lee Finchum and Dell patterns

ACCESSORIES:

Furniture: Chairs, baskets, stroller, beds, etc.

BUSINESS INFORMATION:

Type of business: Wholsale and retail, at store location.

Wholesale requirements: Must have vendor's license.

Accepts: Check, money order, Visa, MC, DC

Layaway: 30% down, 60 days

Return/exchange policy: Returns must be in same condition as when bought

Phone orders: 9:30-5

Mail orders: Will ship to US. Prepayment required.

Shipping information: Shipping is included in the price of the order. Shipped via UPS.

JUST HER STYLE

Jonell Belke
445 Dillard Lane
Coppell, TX 75019
Phone: (214)462-8669 CST
In business since: 1993

CLOTHING:

Clothing (ready-made): Barbie fashions for vintage and contemporary Barbies—haute couture, suits, formals.

More about clothing: Makes designer 11½" dolls and their clothing with all handmade accessories.

ACCESSORIES:

Scaled props/accessories: Barbie gloves, hose, poodles, magazines, hats, purses, etc.

Doll-related collectibles: Custom designed one-of-a-kind 11½" dolls, Barbies.

More about accessories: Custom designs, reproductions

BUSINESS INFORMATION:

Type of business: Retail only, by mail

Home appointments: Sells through mail only and prefers not to have customers visit at home.

Accepts: Check, money order

Discounts: Coupons, first-time customer discounts, show specials, fashion-of-the-month club

Layaway: ¼ to ⅓ down—minimum order $100 for layaways. 3-4 payments.

Back order policy: Notification of delay, approximate time, etc.

Return/exchange policy: Return for defective merchandise within days; 10% restocking fee; postage not refunded; credit only on return special orders.

Samples: Fabric samples, $1, available by mail.

Catalog/price list: b&w, $1; color, $6; each refundable with purchase. Price list, $1; accessories list, refundable with purchase.

Mailing list: Request a catalog to be included.

Phone orders: 5-10

Mail orders: Will ship to US, Canada, overseas. Mail the catalog form. Prepayment required.

Shipping information: Shipped via US mail. Add $5-6 for shipping. Allow 4-6 weeks on fashions, 2-4 weeks on designer dolls.

ADDITIONAL INFORMATION:

Design recreation (900-1600 Series), Barbie fashions, original designs, designer dolls also available.

KATE WEBSTER COMPANY

Kate Webster
83 Granite St.
Rockport, MA 01966-1315
Phone: (508)546-6462 EST
Fax: (508)546-6466
In business since: 1985

SUPPLIES:

Other supplies: Nylon fairy wings (wire armature) in 5 sizes and small metal fairy wings

CLOTHING:

Buttons: Miniature mother-of-pearl, glass, metal, plastic, antiqued, plus tiny snaps.

Fabrics for doll clothing: Cottons: Swiss batiste, lawn, organdy, dotted Swiss, fusible cotton, muslin, all-over tulle. Silks: taffeta, gauze, chiffon, Dupionni, China silk, charmeuse, velvet, Krinkle metallic, organza.

Fibers/threads: Fine, 100% cotton sewing thread for hand or machine sewing.

Lace: English cotton, French cotton, Valenciences, re-embroidered tulle, cotton tulle, silk tulle, vintage laces, Swiss embroideries

Patterns for doll clothing: A small selection of fine patterns for antique reproductions designed by Karin Buttigieg.

Ribbons: Plain and fancy 100% silk ribbons, French rayon jacquards, antique reproductions, vintage ribbons

Trimmings: Miniature rayon braids and

trims in over 50 colors including picot trims and fringes, plus some reproduction French silk trims.

Other clothing supplies: Hat-making supplies: hat wire, buckram, crinoline, wet-n-set, straw braid. Fairy wings: 3 styles; 8 sizes.

More about clothing: Also carry old beads, tiny buckles, pailettes (old-style sequins), sewing needles, dyes, metal parasol frames, metal purse frames

ACCESSORIES:

Scaled props/accessories: Doll jewelry, purses and parasol frames. *Jewelry Division:* The world's largest manufacturer of jewelry for dolls and teddy bears. 95% made entirely in the US and include: hinged eyeglasses, tiaras, brooches, necklaces, earrings, kilt pins, bracelets, pearls, beads, cameos, lockets, timepieces, keys, hair combs, whistles, coins, fans, harmonicas. Hundreds of styles.

Doll-related collectibles: Gold-plated and silver-plated watchcases for people who like to decorate them with miniature dolls and doll-related objects.

BUSINESS INFORMATION:

Type of business: Wholesale and retail, by mail or at a few, select doll shows.

Wholesale requirements: Minimum quantity textile orders, 5-30 yards depending on item. Jewelry orders under $50 incur a $5 handling fee.

Accepts: Check, money order, Visa, MC, DC.

Return/exchange policy: 5 days to return

Samples: Fabric, trim, ribbon, vintage ribbon and hat-making supply samples. Full set, $12.50; individually, $2-4. Single swatches are 25¢ with SASE. Available by mail.

Catalog/Price list: b&w and color, $3

Mailing list: Request a catalog to be included.

Phone orders: M-F, 9-5 EST.

Fax orders: Name, address, phone, credit card info, quantity and description of item ordered.

Mail orders: Will ship to US, Canada, overseas. Mail the catalog order form or name, address, phone, credit card info, quantity and description of item ordered. Prepayment required or COD; open accounts available to

businesses with established credit.

Shipping information: Shipping charges are detailed on order form and in catalog. Shipped via method preferred by customer. COD. Allow 5-10 days for delivery.

ADDITIONAL INFORMATION:

Customers receive a newsletter several times a year with a schedule of shows, plus information regarding new and special purchase items, sales, etc.

KATHRYN'S PRODUCTIONS

Kate Fillman
4521 Elm Ave.
Brookfield, IL 60513
Phone: (708)485-5811 CST
In business since: 1984

ACCESSORIES:

Furniture: Wood tables and chairs, high chairs by special order only.

BUSINESS INFORMATION:

Type of business: Wholesale only to doll artists, by mail only.

Home appointments: Please schedule 1 week in advance.

Accepts: Check, money order, Visa

Mail orders: Will ship to US. Customer pays ⅓ of cost with order, COD at delivery

Shipping information: Shipped via method preferred by customer. Allow 4-6 weeks total for delivery.

LINDA J. KAYS

42 Mitchell St.
Norwich, NY 13815
Phone: (607)334-8375 EST
Fax: (607)334-8375
E-mail: kayslj@norwich.net
In business since: 1994

SUPPLIES:

Fabrics for hair: Human hair wefts, sold in 2 yard packages. 8 different styles, 9 colors.

Tools: Sculpting tools

BUSINESS INFORMATION:

Type of business: Wholesale and retail, by mail.

Samples: $5

Price list: SASE

K.C. DOLLS

Kristie McKnight
45 Industrial Park Rd. W.
Tolland, CT 06084

Phone: (860)872-8838 EST
Fax: (860)872-1836
Hours: M, W, F, 10-3; T-Th, 10-5; Sat, 9-1.
In business since: 1990

SUPPLIES:

Armatures: Locline available pre-made, or by the foot

Eyes: Plastic flat-backed oval, Glastic Realistic, glass

Lashes: Bell Ceramics, Monique and Playhouse

Molds: Bell Ceramics

Paints: China paints by Bell Ceramics; Kesting and Spanish Colores by Victory Molds

Tools: Kemper, Bell Ceramics, Playhouse

Wigs: Playhouse, Kemper, Bell Ceramics and Monique

Other supplies: Teddy Bear joints, greenware and doll kits

CLOTHING:

Buttons: Neck buttons

Patterns for doll clothing: Selection corresponds with the greenware list; also the Elegant Needle; Ribbons and Roses; Bell Ceramics.

ACCESSORIES:

Scaled props/accessories: Shoes, socks

BUSINESS INFORMATION:

Type of business: Wholesale and retail, at store location and by mail.

Accepts: Check, money order, Visa, MC, DC, AE

Discounts: To dealers with a valid tax ID number.

Layaway: 25% down, 90 days. Layaway on finished products only.

Back order policy: Back orders are cancelled unless otherwise advised by purchaser.

Return/exchange policy: Full refund or exchange on supplies. Greenware that has been broken is inspected for pouring flaws; if no flaw is found, will charge for replacement parts.

Catalog/Price list: b&w, $5, refundable with purchase. Price list, free.

Mailing list: Write, call or request catalog to be included.

Phone orders: Regular business hours

Fax orders: Include shipping address, method of payment

Mail orders: Will ship to US. Include

items ordered, shipping address, method of payment and phone number. Prepayment required. Shipping included in the price of order.

Shipping information: UPS. Allow 4-6 weeks for delivery.

KEMPER DOLL SUPPLIES

Jane Stack
13595 12th St.
Chino, CA 91710
Phone: For orders: (800)388-5367 PST
For info: (909)627-6191
Fax: (909)627-4008
Hours: 8-4:30
In business since: 1947

SUPPLIES:

Armatures: Plastic

Bodies: Pre-sewn unstuffed body for 18″ dolls

Clays: Cernit polymer clay—all colors. Darwi air-drying clay.

Eyes: Glass eyes (paperweight and oval). Bright eyes and realistic eyes, acrylic eyes (round and paperweight) and oval flatback eyes.

Lashes: Single lashes, double lashes, baby lashes, etc. 8 different styles.

Tools: Cleanup brushes, sanders, eye sizers, cleaners

Wigs: 40 different styles, 16 colors, mod-acrylic, mohair and synthetic mohair.

ACCESSORIES:

More about accessories: Sells vinyl doll kits with body pattern or pre-sewn body.

BUSINESS INFORMATION:

Type of business: Wholesale and retail at store location and by mail.

Wholesale requirements: $200 minimum for dealer, with a 40% discount; $3,300 minimum for distributor with a 60% discount.

Accepts: Check, money order, Visa, MC, DC

Back order policy: Will back-order at customer's request.

Return/exchange policy: Will accept returns made within 7 days of receipt of order if there is a problem with the product.

Catalog/Price list: Color catalog, free. Price list, free.

Mailing list: Please write or call to be included.

Phone orders: 8-4:30

Fax orders: 24 hours. Include where to ship, phone and fax number, method of shipment, method of payment, contact person.

Mail orders: Will ship to US, Canada, overseas. Include where to ship, phone and fax number, method of shipment, method of payment, contact person. Prepayment required. COD or credit card.

Shipping information: UPS or method preferred by customer. Most orders shipped in 24 to 72 hours.

KEZI'S PREMIER CLOTH DOLL PATTERNS

P.O. Box 17631
Portland, OR 97217
Phone: (503)286-9385 PST
Fax: (503)285-6303
In business since: 1979

SUPPLIES:

Patterns for cloth dolls: Beautifully-crafted patterns from one of America's most popular cloth doll designers. Kezi's clear, easy-to-follow instructions encourage you to express your own creativity.

BUSINESS INFORMATION:

Type of business: Wholesale and retail by mail.

Catalog: Color, $2

MASTER EYE BEVELER

Jackie Kemp
P.O. Box 924
Enfield, CT 06082
Phone: (860)749-0465 EST
Fax: (860)749272
In business since: 1990

SUPPLIES:

Tools: Eye bevelers and cleaning tools. Tools are used to cut and bevel around doll eyes in greenware stage so that you can achieve a great fit. If the doll eyes do not fit properly, your doll will not look good or sell for a good price. Other tools include extra fine stylus, no-chip ear piercing tool, detail tool, mini tool kit, mini cone shape, eye setter, master diamond perfecter, little eye setter, master mixer.

BUSINESS INFORMATION:

Type of business: Wholesale and retail from home.

Wholesale requirements: 150 tools,

20%; 300 tools, 40%. Must have vendor's license.

Home appointments: Sells through the mail only and prefers not to be called upon at home.

Accepts: Check, money order, Visa, MC

Discounts: At shows

Return/exchange policy: Business stands behind all of their eye bevelers.

Samples: Master mixer sample used to stir slip is offered at a reduced rate of $10 plus $2.50 shipping (by mail).

Catalog/Price list: b&w. Free with LSASE. Price list free.

Mailing list: Request catalog to be included.

Phone orders: Any time. Leave a message on machine, will return call if not available.

Fax orders: Include name, address, phone, fax number and order.

Mail orders: Will ship to US, Canada, overseas. Include items wanted, complete address clearly written, telephone and fax number, tax number. Prepayment required. COD.

Shipping information: Shipped via UPS or US mail. Allow 1 week for delivery.

> "BUY WHAT YOU LIKE. YOU ARE GOING TO LIVE WITH YOUR DOLL FOR A LONG TIME. DO NOT BUY FOR FUTURE VALUE ONLY!"
> *Nancy Pritchard, Wild Spirit Doll Studio, E. Providence, RI*

MASTERPIECE EYE CO.

3603 Johnston St., Suite Q
Lafayette, LA 70503
Phone: For orders: (800)256-3937 CST
For info: (318)988-9881
Fax: (318)988-9884
Hours: M-F, 10-5.
In business since: 1984

SUPPLIES:

Eyes: Company sells the only soft, contourable eye available in the world today. Eyes look like glass but fit the doll's skin. Made from a material used for human eye replacements.

BUSINESS INFORMATION:

Type of business: Wholesale and retail at store location and by mail.

Wholesale requirements: Initial order

must be 50 pairs of eyes in any color or size. Following orders must be 5 pairs per month.

Discounts: 40% to dealers. 25% for those who buy 25 pairs and 2 pairs per month afterwards. Buy 6, get 7th free.

Layaway: ⅓ down, 3 months

Return/exchange policy: No refunds. Will exchange.

Samples: Single eye samples in any size.

Catalog/Price list: Color, $5. Price list, SASE.

Mailing list: Write or call to be included.

Phone orders: Available

MATERIAL THINGS

J. Dianne Ridgley
P.O. Box 25291
Fresno, CA 93720
Phone: (209)434-0231 PST

SUPPLIES:

Tools: The Ultimate Stuffer, designed for fast, efficient stuffing of dolls or any other fabric creation. Its patented brass tip is specially designed to grab fiber and pull it into the object. The heavy brass shaft absorbs the pressure needed for packing fibers without bending, and the hand finished wooden handle is sculpted for comfort. Each tool is individually hand crafted.

BUSINESS INFORMATION:

Type of business: Wholesale and retail by mail and at selected quilt shops.

> "IF A DOLL MAKES YOU SMILE, THAT'S
> ALL THAT MATTERS."
> *Nancy Farley, Auctions by Nancy, Apex, NC*

MIMI'S BOOKS AND PATTERNS FOR THE SERIOUS DOLLMAKER

Gloria J. "Mimi" Winer
300 Nancy Dr.
Point Pleasant, NJ 08742
Phone: (908)899-6687 EST
Fax: (908)714-9306
E-mail: firebird@exit109.com
In business since: 1985

SUPPLIES:

Molds: Polysilicon molds for casting polyurethane and polyvinyl resins or push molding polymer clays and paper clays

Patterns for cloth dolls: Step-by-step teaching patterns for many dolls in knit fabric on muslin. All dolls have needle modeled faces and bodies. Some dolls have optional new clay or resin faces. These are exceptional patterns for techniques, self-study or teaching.

Other supplies: Books on dollmaking techniques; dollmaker's sourcebook.

BUSINESS INFORMATION:

Type of business: Wholesale and retail by mail only.

Wholesale requirements: Ten titles, may be mixed; magazine and add-on patterns not included. Sales tax certificate required only in NJ to avoid sales tax.

Accepts: Check, money order, Visa, MC

Discounts: Wholesale to anyone who orders in quantity, including clubs.

Back order policy: Business prints its own books and patterns. Will ship as soon as items are reprinted.

Return/exchange policy: 100% satisfied or credit/money back.

Samples: To wholesale accounts or editorial review only. Free.

Catalog/Price list: b&w, free. Price list, free.

Mailing list: Request catalog to be included.

Phone orders: 9-8

Fax orders: Include Visa or MC number, expiration date, signature, name, address, telephone, items and quantities wanted.

Mail orders: Will ship to US, Canada, overseas. For overseas only, specify air or surface. Prepayment required. Wholesale accounts will be billed, net 30. Shipping included in the price of order. Wholesale and overseas orders, customer must pay cost of shipping.

Shipping information: Shipped via US mail. Allow 2-3 weeks for delivery, US.

MONIQUE TRADING CORP.

Sales Dept.
270 Oyster Point Blvd., Suite 100
South San Francisco, CA 94080-1911
Phone: For orders: (800)621-4338 PST
For info: (415)266-6863
Fax: (800)FAX-WIGS, (415)266-6860
E-mail: monique@wavi.com

Website: http://www.wavi.com/monique/
In business since: 1985

SUPPLIES:

Armatures: Joints

Eyes: Glastic, Glastic Realistic, British paperweight glass; crystal glass, Crystal Pupperauger, acrylic, Far East crystal glass, flat-back acrylic, Glamourous Glass, oval Glass, Karl Eyes. Also sells eye wax.

Fabrics for hair: Mohair braid and mohair curly imported from England

Lashes: 15 styles in various popular colors

Tools: Eye sizers, spring connectors

Wigs: Ready-made wigs make up 95% of their business. Customers must see catalog of contemporary and classic wig styles. Also sells wig caps. See Internet online catalog.

CLOTHING:

Clothing (ready-made): Tights, stockings, underwear, knee-highs, anklets, booties.

Other clothing supplies: Elastic cord

ACCESSORIES:

Scaled props/accessories: Doll stands (metal and wooden)

BUSINESS INFORMATION:

Type of business: Wholesale only

Wholesale requirements: $3000 initial order and maintain $1000/month for distributors (60% discount). Minimum dollar amount of $200 per order for dealers to receive 40% discount.

Accepts: Check, money order, Visa, MC, AE

Discounts: Only to dealers and distributors

Back order policy: Customers will be contacted prior to sending.

Return/exchange policy: Accepted within 15 days of invoice date if there is a manufacturer's defect or related problems. Returns subjected to a 20% restocking fee.

Samples: Wigs to artists and manufacturers. Negotiable. Available through the mail.

Catalog: Color, $2

Price list: Free

Phone orders: 7-4

Fax orders: Fax customer's form letter

Mail orders: Will ship to US, Canada, overseas. Prepayment required; net 30 with good credit report.

Shipping information: Shipping included in the price of order. Shipped via UPS, FedEx or RPS. Allow 7-10 days for delivery.

NANA'S DOLLS

Geneva Cornelius
2207 Cardinal Lane
Garland, TX 75042
Phone: (214)276-0229 CST
In business since: 1990

CLOTHING:

Clothing (ready-made): Modern and some antique

BUSINESS INFORMATION:

Type of business: Retail only, with discount for quantity; operated from home.
Home appointments: Please schedule in advance.
Accepts: Check, money order, Visa, MC
Discounts: 10%, 6 items; 20%, 12 items
Layaway: ⅓ down, 2 months
Back order policy: Most clothes are made to order.
Return/exchange policy: Call within 3 days for return instructions.
Catalog/Price list: b&w, $3, refundable with purchase.
Mailing list: Request catalog or price list to be included.
Phone orders: 9-8
Fax orders: Name of doll, size, color, style and second choice of color and style.
Mail orders: Will ship to US. Send catalog order form. Prepayment required. COD, shipping included in the price of order or added in prepayment.
Shipping information: Allow 3-4 weeks for special orders, 1-2 weeks for merchandise on hand.

NATIONAL NONWOVENS

Janet Bunce
P.O. Box 150
Easthampton, MA 01027
Phone: (800)333-3469 EST
Fax: (413)527-0456
In business since: 1905

SUPPLIES:

Fabrics for cloth dolls: Heirloom quality wool blend felts, washable acrylic colored felts   .

CLOTHING:

Fabrics for doll clothing: Quality wool blend felts, economic acrylic color felts
Trimmings: Colored felts

BUSINESS INFORMATION:

Type of business: Wholesale only. Wool and acrylic felt manufacturing.
Wholesale requirements: Minimum dollar amount $200.
Accepts: Check, money order
Fax orders: Available

NEWARK DRESSMAKER SUPPLY INC.

Lucy W. Perusse
6473 Ruch Rd.,
P.O. Box Box 20730
Lehigh Valley, PA 18002
Phone:
For orders: (610)837-7500 EST
For info: (610)837-0198 or call (800)736-6783
Fax: (610)837-9115
Hours: M-F, 8-4:30.
In business since: 1956

SUPPLIES:

Bodies: Muslin
Eyes: Wiggle, solid black, animals, sew-on
Fabrics for cloth dolls: Skin, cotton prints, soft sculpture, soft sculpture fabric, knit, velour, felt
Fabrics for hair: Curly, acrylic fiber, wool, wavy
Lashes: Novelty, brown and black
Molds: Lisbeth Kate mold
Paints: Fabric, acrylic
Stuffing: Stuf and Fluf

CLOTHING:

Buttons: Available
Clothing (ready-made): Hats, collars, cowboy hats, straw hats
Fabrics for doll clothing: Available
Fibers/threads: Available
Lace: Available
Patterns for doll clothing: Red Riding Hood, Cinderella
Trimmings: Available

ACCESSORIES:

Scaled props/accessories: Hats, glasses, stands, shoes, wooden doll heads

BUSINESS INFORMATION:

Type of business: Wholesale and retail by mail.
Wholesale requirements: Minimum dollar amount $125.

Accepts: Check, money order, Visa, MC, DC
Discounts: 10% off orders $50 to $99.99. 20% off orders over $100.
Back order policy: Will not back order if order is under $4.
Return/exchange policy: Replacement, credit or refund available.
Samples: Available
Catalog/Price list: b&w and color, free.
Mailing list: Call or request a catalog to be included.
Phone orders: Available
Fax orders: Fax the catalog order form
Mail orders: Will ship to US, Canada, overseas. Mail the catalog order form. Prepayment required. Shipping included in the price of order.
Shipping information: Shipped via UPS or US mail. Orders processed within 24 hours.

ORIGINALS BY ELAINE/PARKER-LEVI

Bobby Campbell
901 Oak Hollow Pl.
Brandon, FL 33510
Phone: For orders: (813)654-0335 EST
For info: (813)685-8790
Fax: (813)654-8490
In business since: 1988

SUPPLIES:

Fabrics for hair: Silk, mohair and every hair fabric for miniatures.
Molds: Full line of original miniature molds; full line of molds for 8″ to 28″ original dolls
Other supplies: Brushes for miniature painting, "Little Doll Artist" (how-to book on making miniature dolls), "Crowning Glory" (how-to wig book for miniature dolls).

CLOTHING:

Patterns for doll clothing: Patterns for 8″-28″ original dolls. Only sells patterns for their own dolls.

BUSINESS INFORMATION:

Type of business: Retail only, by mail or phone
Home appointments: Please schedule 24 hours in advance.
Accepts: Check, money order, Visa, MC
Discounts: Quantity discounts
Return/exchange policy: Satisfaction guaranteed
Catalog/Price list: Large doll, color, $7 plus $2.50 shipping. Miniature doll,

color, $6 plus $1.25 shipping.

Phone orders: 9-8

Fax orders: Include product, name, address, phone, card number and expiration date.

Mail orders: Will ship to US, Canada, overseas. Send product, name, address, phone, card number and expiration date. Prepayment required. COD in US only; shipping added on other orders.

Shipping information: Shipped via UPS or US mail. Orders go out immediately.

OSAGE COUNTY QUILT FACTORY

Virginia Robertson
400 Walnut Box 490
Overbrook, KS 66525
Phone: (913)665-7500 CST
Fax: (913)665-7148
In business since: 1979

SUPPLIES:

Fabrics for cloth dolls: 100% cotton flesh tones in eight shades, designed by Virginia Robertson

Fabrics for hair: Wool roving, braided roping

Patterns for cloth dolls: Large selection available

Tools: Stuffing tools, pens and pencils for cloth doll face painting, needles, thread, dye, etc.

CLOTHING:

Fabrics for doll clothing: Huge selection available

Patterns for doll clothing: Large selection available

BUSINESS INFORMATION:

Type of business: Wholesale and retail by mail

Wholesale requirements: Minimum quantity 6 per title. Minimum dollar amount is $35. Photocopy of state resale number.

Accepts: Check, money order, Visa, MC, COD

Discounts: Wholesale

Back order policy: Returns money and lets the customer know when to reorder.

Return/exchange policy: No returns or exchanges unless product is defective. Must have pre-authorization.

Samples: Free doll body swatches upon

request with catalog purchase or SASE

Catalog/Price list: b&w and color, $2. Price list, free upon request.

Mailing list: Write to be included.

Phone orders: M-F, 9-5. Answering machine always on.

Fax orders: Fax the catalog order form

Mail orders: Will ship to US, Canada, overseas. US retail customers pay $3.25 per order, Canadian and overseas customers add 15% for surface shipping, 40% for air. Wholesale customers pay actual shipping expense.

Shipping information: Shipped via UPS. Allow 7-10 days for delivery.

PAGE'S DOLLS

Lillian Page
6969 L. 5 Lane
Escanaba, MI 79829
Phone: (906)786-6565 CST
In business since: 1991

SUPPLIES:

Bodies: Composition

Eyes: Available

Fabrics for cloth dolls: Available

Molds: Seeley

Paints: China

Slips: Seeley porcelain

Tools: Brushes, sculpting tools

Wigs: Kemper

Other supplies: Distributes Seeley and Kemper supplies. Also sells soft-fired greenware (porcelain).

CLOTHING:

Clothing (ready-made): Shoes, stockings

Fabrics for doll clothing: Available

Patterns for doll clothing: Available

ACCESSORIES:

Furniture: Stands

PARAGON INDUSTRIES, INC.

2011 South Town E. Blvd.
Mesquite, TX 75149-1122
Phone:
For orders: (800)876-4328 CST
For info: (214)288-7557
Fax: (214)222-0646
Hours: M-Th, 7-5:30.
In business since: 1948

SUPPLIES:

Tools: Kilns, kiln furniture, portable electronic temperature controllers, pyro-

metric cones, kiln wash, stilts, Orton kiln vents, kiln repair cement, instructional videos

BUSINESS INFORMATION:

Type of business: Wholesale and retail. Sells through distributors and dealers world wide.

Wholesale requirements: Minimum dollar amount $15 for retail orders, $15 for dealer orders, $25 for distributor orders (before shipping charges are added).

Accepts: Check, money order, Visa, MC, AE. For fast service, kiln parts orders can be sent COD. (COD not available for kilns.)

Discounts: To authorized distributors and dealers only. Applications welcome.

Back order policy: Kilns are the only item back-ordered. For all other merchandise, please reorder.

Return/exchange policy: Returned merchandise is subject to a 15% restocking charge if no error exists on the part of the factory.

Catalog/Price list: 2-color, free. Price list, free.

Mailing list: For authorized distributors and dealers.

Phone orders: M-Th, 7-5:30.

Fax orders: Include credit card information or establish an open account.

Mail orders: Will ship to US, Canada, overseas. Prepayment required. Shipping included in the price of order.

Shipping information: Shipped via method preferred by customer.

ADDITIONAL INFORMATION:

The company has also produced *How to Load and Fire Your Ceramic Kiln*, a 43-minute video, and *How to Make Porcelain Dolls*, a 90-minute video.

PIECEMAKERS COUNTRY STORE

Joanna Nelson
1720 Adams Ave.
Costa Mesa, CA 92626
Phone: (714)641-3122 PST
Fax: (714)641-3112
E-mail: 75552.3442@compuserve.com
In business since: 1977

SUPPLIES:

Tools: Doll needles in 3 sizes—3½", 5⅛", 7". Needles have clean eyes and are known for their sharpness, sturdiness, strength and ease in threading.

BUSINESS INFORMATION:

Type of business: Wholesale and retail. Wholesale inquiries should be made to Piecemakers Warehouse, 1281 Logan Ave., Suite A, Costa Mesa CA 92626. Phone: (714)641-9663. Fax: (714)641-2883. Store location and mail order.

PLUM CREEK DOLLMAKERS

Helen Schaeffer
647 Plum Creek Rd.
Bernville, PA 19506-9007
Phone: (610)488-6568 EST
Fax: (610)488-6568
Hours: M, T, Th, 10-4. W, 7 P.M.-10 P.M. Sat, 10-2.
In business since: 1972

SUPPLIES:

Armatures: Preassembled body skeletons in sizes to fit 16″-18″, 20″-22″, 24″-26″ and 28″-30″ dolls

Bodies: Complete in-stock inventory of Seeley composition bodies and mechanical bodies, prestuffed muslin baby bodies, ready to stuff leatherette bodies in sizes from 12″ to 28″ Mod Bod™

Clays: Earthenware and porcelain, available in 25 lb. blocks

Eyes: Karl's German Glass, French paperweight, Glastic Realistic, acrylic eyes. All sizes and colors manufactured.

Fabrics for hair: Wefted and dyed mohair locks by Seeley in undyed/white, pale blonde, chestnut, classic brown, Spanish black, golden blonde, golden red and ash blonde

Lashes: 17mm baby eyelashes, 20mm thicker eyelashes, 24mm eyelashes, double eyelashes in 20mm and 30mm

Molds: Seeley, Modern Doll Art Co., Byron, Doll Artworks

Paints: Complete line of Seeley China paints and media

Patterns for cloth dolls: Available

Slips: Seeley French bisque available in 2½-gallon boxes. Gallons of Seeley Porcelain: French Bisque, Dresden Flesh, Naturelle, American Bisque. Lady White, Pure White, Mordic White, Pearl White, Terra Cotta, Aztec Tan, French Chocolate. Brown Velvet, Oriental Flesh and Ebony. Quarts of: Wedgewood Blue, Green, Pink, Citrus Yellow.

Stuffing: Fiberfill, plastic pellets or "baby beans" for making weighted, poseable dolls.

Tools: Cress kilns—3 sizes always in stock. Firing cones, firing sand, hydrated alumina, fiberprop, kiln furniture. Kemper Tools—all tools in stock from Stilts eyesizers to eyesetters. Seeley brushes—complete line of specialty brushes. Optivisor by Donegan

Wigs: Complete line Kemper synthetic and mohair wigs. Seeley mohair—fairy and puppet wigs.

Other supplies: Greenware and bisque of hundreds of molds. Full line of head connectors, shoulder plate connectors, eye wax, eye setting compound, plasticizer, Nichrome wire, stilts and mold straps, rubber bands, fiber prop, stringing elastic, composition body stains, mold soap, grit scrubbers, doll stands

CLOTHING:

Buttons: JHB mini buttons for doll clothes.

Clothing (ready-made): Gabriella Wilke, German silk dresses for antiques and reproductions, Minnie's Dollhouse Clothes, Sand Castle Creations, Doll Fashions Unlimited, Performance Design, and some one-of-a-kind creations.

Fabrics for doll clothing: Swiss batiste in three grades: "Nelo," "Nelona," and "Christening Gown Quality." Also Swiss lawn, some silk taffeta.

Fibers/threads: Silk ribbon for dress embellishment/silk ribbon embroidery.

Lace: Large assortment French laces and Swiss embroideries sold by the yard.

Leather: Garment leather for shoemaking.

Patterns for doll clothing: Full selections of Byron For Antiques, Doll Emporium, Seeley, Doll Artworks, Dolls Delight, Inc.

Ribbons: Wired, variegated color ribbon and silk ribbon in assorted colors

Trimmings: Large selection of jewelry by Kathy's Creations, pins, earrings, necklaces, crowns.

Other clothing supplies: Large selection of sewing books, June Taylor's Heir-loom Shape and Press Lace Shaping Boards, Heat and Bond, Perfect Pleaters®, fabric stabilizer, doll needles. Full line of Kemper and Byron doll shoes. Large selection doll tights, socks, stockings, underwear sets, bloomers, hats, parasols, etc.

ACCESSORIES:

Furniture: Fine wood cradles, beds, poster beds, reproduction doll carriages, rocking horses, Chippendale chairs, wicker carriages, beds, table and chair sets, sleighs, leather and fabric trunks, wardrobes

Scaled props/accessories: Full line of musical instruments, large selection china tea sets, miniature cutlery sets, pressed glass punch bowl sets and glasses and pitcher sets.

Doll-related collectibles: Exclusive, copyrighted heirloom doll treasures. Afghan—50″ × 65″ cotton throw featuring pictures of eleven dolls.

More about accessories: Has many one-of-a-kind furniture pieces which are not pictured in catalog.

BUSINESS INFORMATION:

Type of business: Wholesale and retail, at store location and by mail.

Wholesale requirements: Usually 12 dozen lots minimum, some exceptions apply. Must have a vendor's license.

Accepts: Check, money order, Visa, MC, DC

Discounts: Catalog offers quantity discounts. Examples: 20% off 3 or more yards of lace of Swiss batiste; 20% off 3 or more brushes, tools or bodies.

Back order policy: Cancels back orders after 30 days and requests that customer reorder at later date.

Return/exchange policy: Returns accepted within 10 days providing item is in salable condition in original packaging. No returns on books, patterns or cut yardage of fabric or lace. Exchanges permitted within reasonable length of time.

Catalog: b&w and color, $5

Mailing list: Write or call to be included.

Phone orders: M-Th 10-5 EST.

Fax orders: Include name, address, telephone number, charge card number with expiration date, signature. Itemized list of merchandise desired.

Mail orders: Send name, address, telephone number, charge card number with expiration date, signature, itemized list of merchandise desired. Prepayment required. Shipping included in the price of order.

Shipping information: Shipped via UPS or method preferred by customer. Orders received before noon EST will be shipped that day.

ADDITIONAL INFORMATION:
Carries a large inventory of books on doll collecting, doll research, dollmaking, sculpting and mold making, dress and pattern making, knitting and crocheting for dolls and more. Books from Hobby House, Dover Publishing, Seeley and Scott Publishing. Also carries Doll Lover tee shirts, sweatshirts and aprons. Has a line of Kemper vinyl doll kits in three complexion colors, ready to assemble and dress.

POLYFORM PRODUCTS COMPANY

Wayne Marsh, marketing manager
1901 Estes Ave.
Elk Grove Village, IL 60007
Phone: (708)417-0020 CST
Fax: (708)427-0426
Hours: 9-4:30
In business since: 1967

SUPPLIES:
Clays: Manufactures oven-bake polymer clays. One of the company's six clays, Super Sculpey, is widely used by doll artists. It is beige in color and has a ceramic-like, translucent, matte finish. It takes tooling beautifully. It can be carved, drilled and sanded after baking and smoothed to a satiny finish before baking. It can be painted with waterbase acrylic, if desired, and is also compatible with certain cosmetics that may be used for adding natural highlights for emphasis. Available in 1 lb., 8 lb. and 24 lb. bulk sizes.

"LOVE WHAT YOU DO AND DO WHAT YOU LOVE, AND IT WILL ALWAYS BE EVIDENT IN YOUR FINISHED WORK!"

Patricia Ryan Brooks, Summerton, SC

THE PORCELAIN ROSE

Glennis Dolce
P.O. Box 7545
Long Beach, CA 90807

Phone: (310)424-9728 PST
Fax: (310)424-9728
E-mail: porcrose@aol.com
In business since: 1980

CLOTHING:
Buttons: Hundreds of styles of hand painted porcelain buttons. Many reproduction picture buttons and vintage designs.
Other clothing supplies: Porcelain flowers used as an embellishments in dollmaking. Lace draping for clothing, jewelry, etc.

BUSINESS INFORMATION:
Type of business: Wholesale and retail, by mail only.
Wholesale requirements: 6 pieces per design—buttons; 1 dozen per design—flowers. Minimum dollar amount of $50. Must have vendor's license.
Accepts: Check
Discounts: Quantity
Back order policy: Back orders shipped on prepaid orders. All back orders under $25 cancelled.
Return/exchange policy: Requires immediate notification (upon receipt) of any problems.
Samples: Buttons, flowers. Offered at cost on a per request basis.
Catalog: Color, free. Price list, free.
Phone orders: 8-5 PST; answering machine on 24 hours
Fax orders: Fax customer info, including phone number and order.
Mail orders: Will ship to US, Canada, overseas. Mail customer info and list of items.
Shipping information: COD. Shipping included in the price of order. Will ship via UPS. Allow 2 weeks for delivery.

PORTLAND PO HENRY SUPPLY

Chris Brunoi
8 Fox St.
Portland, ME 04101
Phone: (207)772-3273 EST
Fax: (207)780-6451
E-mail: bruni@delphi.com
Hours: M, T, Th, F, 9-5. W, 8-8. Sat, 9-12.
In business since: 1992

SUPPLIES:
Clays: Available

Paints: Available
Slips: Available
Tools: Available

BUSINESS INFORMATION:
Type of business: Wholesale and retail, at store location and by mail.
Accepts: Check, money order, Visa, MC, AE
Discounts: Volume
Catalog: b&w, free
Price list: Free
Mailing list: Write to be included.
Phone orders: Available
Fax orders: Available
Mail orders: Will ship to US, Canada, overseas.
Shipping information: COD. Shipped via UPS.

RITA'S CHILDREN

Rita Harth
461 North Service Rd., W. B10
Oakville, Ontario L6M 2V5
CANADA
Phone: (905)825-2927 EST
Fax: (905)825-2980
Hours: M-F, 5-10 and by appointment.
In business since: 1993

SUPPLIES:
Armatures: Locline and custom-made wire armatures
Bodies: Custom-made cloth bodies for all doll types, by special order only
Clays: Cernit, water-based modeling clay
Eyes: Real Eyes™
Lashes: Human hair eyelashes, various styles and colors
Molds: By special order only
Paints: Seeley china paints; other brands by special order
Slips: Seeley, porcelain slip
Stuffing: Polyester fiberfill by the pound
Tools: Brushes, other tools
Wigs: Full line of Monique wigs, other brands by special order.
Other supplies: Soft-fired greenware

CLOTHING:
Clothing (Ready-made): Custom-made
Leather: Pig or lamb skins

ACCESSORIES:
Furniture: Antique reproduction chairs and sofas

BUSINESS INFORMATION:
Type of business: Wholesale and retail, at store location and by mail.

Wholesale requirements: Minimum $200 (Canadian). Must have vendor's license.

Accepts: Check, money order, Visa, MC, AE

Discounts: Quantity discounts on orders of $200 and up.

Layaway: 3-6 months; no fee

Return/exchange policy: Satisfaction guaranteed on all mail orders. For other sales, exchanges must be made within 30 days of purchase.

Catalog/Price list: $10 (Canadian), refundable with purchase. Price list, free.

Phone orders: Anytime.

Fax orders: Detailed order

Mail orders: Will ship to US Canada, overseas. Detailed order. Prepayment required. Shipping included in the price of order.

Shipping information: Shipped via method preferred by customer. Allow 10 days for delivery.

S & S DOLL HOSPITAL

Susan Schroeder
3100 Harvest Lane
Kissimmee, FL 34744
Phone: (407)957-6392 EST
Fax: (407)957-9427
In business since: 1981

SUPPLIES:

Wigs: Monique and Mini World modacrylic

CLOTHING:

Clothing (ready-made): Susan handmakes doll dresses designed using antique laces. They are simple in style but artfully composed.

ACCESSORIES:

Scaled props/accessories: Doll shoes in various colors and sizes, ice skates, hats with flowers.

BUSINESS INFORMATION:

Type of business: Retail only from home, by mail and at doll shows.

Home appointments: Please schedule 1 day in advance.

Accepts: Check, money order

Discounts: 10% for dealers or shops buying 4 or more dresses

Layaway: ⅓ down, 3 months

Price list: Free

Phone orders: 8 A.M.-9 P.M.

Fax orders: Available

Mail orders: Will ship to US, Canada, overseas.

Shipping information: Shipped via UPS or US mail. Allow 1-2 weeks for delivery.

SARA BERNSTEIN DOLLS AND BEARS

Sara B. Bernstein
10 Sami Ct.
Englishtown, NJ 07726
Phone: (908)536-4101 EST

SUPPLIES:

Patterns for cloth dolls: Designed by Sara. Include complete instructions.

BUSINESS INFORMATION:

Type of business: Retail only, by mail.

Catalog: $1 and SASE

SEELEY'S

Joanne Tobey
P.O. Box 669
Oneonta, NY 13820
Phone: (800)433-1191 EST
Fax: (607)432-2042
Hours: M-F, 8-5.
In business since: 1946

SUPPLIES:

Bodies: Authentic reproductions of composition bodies, ModBods™

Fabrics for hair: Mohair Locks™ in a variety of colors, also undyed

Molds: Hundreds of molds for authentic reproductions of German and French antiques, and molds for modern dolls.

Paints: China paints

Slips: Seeley's Porcelain Slip, including the industry standard for dolls, Seeley's French Bisque®

Tools: Brushes and cleaning tools, scrubbers, tiles, etc.

CLOTHING:

Patterns for doll clothing: Hundreds of unique patterns for antique reproductions, plus outfits for modern dolls.

BUSINESS INFORMATION:

Type of business: Wholesale and retail at store, by mail, and through a worldwide distribution network.

Accepts: Check, money order, Visa, MC, DC

Catalog: Color, $8.50. Refundable with purchase.

Price list: Free

Mailing list: Call or write to be included.

Phone orders: 8-5.

Fax orders: Include item, quantity, payment information, shipping/ordered by information.

Mail orders: Will ship to US, Canada, overseas. Send item, quantity, payment information, ship to/ordered by. Prepayment required.

Shipping information: COD. Shipped via method preferred by customer. Allow 4 weeks for delivery.

SIMPSON'S LIBERTY DOLL SUPPLY

Judy Simpson
6189 US 68 N.
Wilmington, OH 45177
Phone: For orders: (800)317-3170 EST
For info: (513)382-4546
In business since: 1993

SUPPLIES:

Armatures: Locline

Eyes: Acrylic, flat acrylic, German crystal, glass oval, Glastic Realistic

Fabrics for hair: Modacrylic, mohair, mohair supplies for making wigs

Lashes: Human eyelashes—hand tied, full, wispy, slanted, tapered double, straight double, strip

Tools: Sanding pads, brushes, stringing kits, eye sizers, diamond wheels, plastic tie wrap connectors, pliers, casting kits, eartherim stylus, wipeout, laces, cleanup tools

Wigs: Modacrylic and mohair wigs by Playhouse

CLOTHING:

Buttons: Small black jet type and pastel baby buttons

Clothing (ready-made): Custom-sewn clothing from old patterns for antiques and modern dolls.

More about clothing: All clothing is custom-sewn to customer specifications.

ACCESSORIES:

Scaled props/accessories: Gold clubs, soccer ball, baseball bat, gloves and balls, catchers mask, tennis bag and racket, football, skateboard, luggage, purses, musical instruments

BUSINESS INFORMATION:

Type of business: Wholesale and retail, by mail only.

Wholesale requirements: Minimum dollar amount $10 for non-credit card orders; $20 for credit card orders. If a dealer, buyer must have a vendor's license number.

Accepts: Check, money order, Visa, MC

Discounts: 20% to retail customers; 40% to dealers

Back order policy: Offers option to keep back order, choose different style or receive refund.

Return/exchange policy: Will accept any return or exchange if returned in same condition as when shipped and within 30 days.

Catalog/Price list: Color, $2. Refundable with purchase. Price list, free.

Mailing list: Request catalog to be included.

Phone orders: M-F, 8-4.

Mail orders: Will ship to US, Canada, overseas. Prepayment required. Shipping included in the price of order.

Shipping information: Shipped via parcel post; UPS when necessary or requested. Allow 5 days to 1 week for credit card, 7 to 12 days for personal check.

ADDITIONAL INFORMATION:

Carries Playhouse products plus various items from other manufacturers. All clothing is custom sewn in shop.

> "FALL IN LOVE WITH YOUR DOLLS, AND HOPEFULLY
> OTHERS WILL LOVE THEM, TOO!"
> *Joan Ibarolle, Walnut Creek, CA*

SOUTH FORTY FARMS

Georgia G. Thomas
1272 16½ Rd.
Fruita, CO 81521
Phone: (970)858-3687 MST
Hours: M-F, 8-4.
In business since: 1991

SUPPLIES:

Fabrics for hair: Mohair: available in all stages of preparation (bred specifically for doll market), including "in the grease," combed curls wefted, dyed (including custom colors). All hair hand combed, no harsh chemicals or large machinery. Tibetan lamb available for skin, wigs, etc.

CLOTHING:

Fabrics for doll clothing: Garment quality furs and leathers.

Leather: Garment quality leather. Lambskins in glove or suede finishes, wide range of colors—by order.

Other clothing supplies: Furs for trim, or cradle based "guardians."

ACCESSORIES:

Scaled props/accessories: Often have unique items such as bark wigwams and other Native American handmade items.

BUSINESS INFORMATION:

Type of business: Wholesale and retail by mail.

Wholesale requirements: Minimum dollar amount $30. Must have vendor's license.

Accepts: Check, money order

Back order policy: As a large portion of this business is custom orders, has a 4-6 week policy.

Return/exchange policy: Ten days to return or exchange. Items must not be used.

Samples: Hairstyle types and colors. Individual requests are free; sample card is $5; available by mail.

Price list: Free

Mailing list: Write, call or request catalog to be included.

Phone orders: M-F, 8-4 MST.

Mail orders: Will ship to US, Canada, overseas. Prepayment required. Customer will be billed after credit has been established. Shipping included in the price of order.

Shipping information: Shipped via method preferred by customer. Allow 2-3 days from sending date.

SOUTHERN OREGON POTTERY SUPPLY

Bill Morgan
111 Talent Ave., P.O. Box 158
Talent, OR 97540
Phone: (541)535-6700 PST
Fax: (541)535-5929
Hours: T-Sat, 10-5.
In business since: 1978

SUPPLIES:

Clays: Water based modeling clays (approximately 30), oil based plasticines, air drying clays, Cernit.

Paints: Sonie Ames china paints; Laguna glazes, underglazes

Slips: Full line of Smooth and Silky doll porcelain slips in gallons and dry 50 lb. bags

Tools: Skutt, Paragon, Cress, Aim and Olympic kilns, brushes, kiln venting equipment, mixing equipment, cermicron and Clean Stream ceramic and porcelain dust filters, respirators, Kemper and Pierce tools, porcelain prop, doll sand

More about supplies: Offers kiln repairs and parts; Scott Publishing dollmaking books; plaster mold-making supplies, books and cones; kiln furniture pyrometers, etc.

BUSINESS INFORMATION:

Type of business: Wholesale and retail, at store location and by mail.

Accepts: Check, money order, Visa, MC, DC

Discounts: Dependent on items purchased. Please inquire. Kilns are normally a minimum of 15% off list price.

Layaway: ⅓ down, 60 days

Back order policy: Back orders shipped ASAP or cancelled on buyer's request.

Return/exchange policy: Returns accepted only on prior approval on unused, unopened items. Return shipping must be prepaid. 10% restocking fee on orders filled properly.

Catalog: Kiln brochure, free; full supply catalog, $5. Refundable with purchase.

Mailing list: Write or call to be included.

Phone orders: T-Sat, 10-5.

Fax orders: Include the completed order form available in the catalog or include name, address, daytime phone, shipping address if different, items ordered, method of payment, credit card number and expiration date.

Mail orders: Mail the order form or include information above. Prepayment required.

Shipping information: COD or prepaid at customer's request. Shipped via method preferred by customer. Allow 1-4 weeks for delivery.

ADDITIONAL INFORMATION:

Offers advice and suggestions on kiln sizes, features, electrical requirements, etc. Please call.

SWEET DREAMS

Lee Klimas
9 S. 674 Highland Rd.
Hinsdale, IL 60521
Phone: (708)325-8180 CST
In business since: 1994

SUPPLIES:

Armatures: Locline ½″, ⅜″, ¼″
Bodies: Cloth bodies
Clays: Cernit
Eyes: Karl's German glass eyes, bright eyes, Realistic eyes, plastic eyes, all in sizes 8mm-26mm. All colors.
Fabrics for hair: Mohair, in bulk or braided; caps for wigs
Lashes: Full upper and lower lashes for all size dolls.
Paints: Distributor for Virginia La Vorgna paints. Paints are water based or oil-based, specifically formulated for today's artist.
Patterns for cloth dolls: Available
Stuffing: Fiberfill (cotton)
Tools: Tools for lace draping, pottery, ceramics; Scharff brushes
Wigs: Playhouse, Kemper

CLOTHING:

Patterns for doll clothing: Brown House doll patterns

ACCESSORIES:

Scaled props/accessories: Ice skates, bats, balls, baseball gloves, violins

BUSINESS INFORMATION:

Type of business: Wholesale and retail, at store location and by mail.
Home appointments: Please schedule 1 day in advance.
Accepts: Check, money order
Discounts: Dealer discounts are available to businesses with a tax number.
Back order policy: Will call to make sure order is still needed.
Return/exchange policy: Special orders are returned with a 15% charge.
Catalog/Price list: Color, $2, refundable with purchase. Price list, free.
Mailing list: Write, call or request catalog to be included.
Phone orders: 9-5, or leave message on answering machine
Mail orders: Will ship to US. Send name, phone, address. Shipping included in the price of order if retail.
Shipping information: Shipped via UPS. Allow 10-14 days for delivery.

TREFFEISEN U.S.A.

Carolina Barksdale
4172 Corporate Square, Unit A
Naples, FL 33942
Phone: (941)643-9702 EST
Fax: (941)643-1798
In business since: 1984

CLOTHING:

Clothing (ready-made): Dresses, suits, coats, underwear, machine and hand knitted socks, leather shoes and purses, hats
More about clothing: High quality clothing and accessories. Only cotton, silk and wool fabrics are used. Shoes and purses are real leather. All clothing items are made by seamstresses. Hats are made from felt or straw, sizes available for dolls from 15″-29″.

ACCESSORIES:

Furniture: Wooden dress stands, hat stands, clothes racks
Scaled props/accessories: Hangers for doll clothing
Doll-related collectibles: Yearly calendar

BUSINESS INFORMATION:

Type of business: Wholesale only, by mail
Wholesale requirements: First order of the year minimum required. Must have vendor's license.
Back order policy: Ship when item comes in.
Return/exchange policy: 3 days for damages, no returns.
Catalog/price list: Color, $4.50. Price list, free.
Mailing list: Write or request a catalog or price list to be included.
Phone orders: 9-5
Fax orders: Include name, phone number, address.
Mail orders: Will ship to US, Canada, overseas. Include name, phone number, address. Prepayment required Canada and overseas. COD or prepay.
Shipping information: Shipped via UPS, FedEx or method preferred by customer.

"START CATALOGUING DOLLS FROM DOLL #1—IT IS ALMOST IMPOSSIBLE TO CATCH UP LATER!"
Gladys Brown, Holt, MI

TRUEBITE INC.

Ed Calafut
2590 Glenwood Rd.
Vestal, NY 13850
Phone: For orders: (800)676-8907 EST
For info: (607)785-7664
Fax: (607)785-2405
In business since: 1983

SUPPLIES:

Armatures: Plastic, moveable
Eyes: Flirty eye ASM kits
Tools: Cutting, grinding, drilling and cleaning tools for porcelain ceramic glass; doll wire twisting pliers, Sand-O-Flex cleaning wheels, 3M abrasives, Dremel motion tools; non-staining hand cream, tools to make doll furniture
Other supplies: Needles

BUSINESS INFORMATION:

Type of business: Wholesale and retail at factory location. Do not have show room but can view product in front office. Call first.
Wholesale requirements: $10 minimum dollar amount
Accepts: Check, money order, Visa, MC, COD
Discounts: By quantity and dollar amount
Back order policy: We ship within 48 hours. Any back orders are usually filled within 2 weeks.
Return/exchange policy: 15% restocking change on returns and exchanges.
Samples: Sample cleaning kit $19.95 by mail.
Catalog/Price list: b&w, free. Price list, free.
Mailing list: Write, call or request catalog to be included.
Phone orders: 9-5.
Fax orders: Available
Mail orders: Will ship to US, Canada, overseas. Prepayment required. Shipping included in the price of order.
Shipping information: Shipped via method preferred by customer. Allow 7-10 days.

TWIN PINES OF MAINE, INC.

Nicholas J. Hill
P.O. Box 1178
Scarborough, ME 04070-1178
Phone: For orders: (800)770-DOLL EST
For info: (207)883-5541

Fax: (207)883-1239
E-mail: nick@twinpines.com
Website: http://www.twinpines.com
In business since: 1976

SUPPLIES:

Tools: For cleaning dolls (Formula 9-1-1); for removing stains like ink, dye, food, mildew, fungus and metal (Remove-Zit); for cleaning all fabrics, including silk, taffeta, organdy, cotton, rayon, nylon, polyolefin, in cold water (PERK!)

BUSINESS INFORMATION:

Type of business: Wholesale and retail, by mail and at shows.
Accepts: Check, money order, Visa, MC
Catalog/Price list: b&w, free
Phone orders: 7 days, 24 hours
Fax orders: Name, address, credit card information, products
Mail orders: Will ship to US, Canada, overseas. Prepayment required.

2 JP RANCH

Polly Holmes
4735 W. Quince Ave.
Silver Springs, NV 89429
Phone: (702)577-2100 PST
In business since: 1976

SUPPLIES:

Fabrics for hair: Loose, white, dyed, washed naturally colored, grey and black mohair; roving mohair; loose and roving wool.
Other supplies: Goats wear coats to keep mohair clean. Long mohair, 8″-10″, available in spring.

BUSINESS INFORMATION:

Type of business: Wholesale and retail, by mail only.
Wholesale requirements: Minimum dollar amount of $75. Buyer must have a vendor's license.
Accepts: Check, money order
Price list: Free
Mailing list: Write to be included.
Phone orders: Available
Mail orders: Will ship to US, Canada, overseas. Mail the catalog order form. Prepayment required.
Shipping information: Shipped via method preferred by customer.

UNIQUE PRODUCTS

Joan P. Schwartz
6510 Newman Circle E.
Lakeland, FL 33811
In business since: 1992

ACCESSORIES:

Furniture: All wood, available unfinished or in oak or walnut finish. Furniture is for doll 22″ and under. Each piece is handcrafted. Special orders are also available.

BUSINESS INFORMATION:

Type of business: By mail
Accepts: Check or money order
Catalog/Price list: b&w, free with SASE. Price list, free with SASE
Mail orders: Will ship to US. Prepayment required. Shipping included in the price of order.
Shipping information: Shipped via UPS. Allow 2 weeks for delivery.

VICTORIAN REPLICAS

David Newton
P.O. Box 866
Menlo Park, CA 94026
Phone: (415)552-6367 PST
Fax: (415)552-4253
Hours: 10-5
In business since: 1990

ACCESSORIES:

Furniture: Beautiful handcarved mahogany chairs to display your treasure. Chippendale armchair and sofa, Victorian deep-buttoned cotton velvet grandfather chair and sumptuous chaise lounge.

BUSINESS INFORMATION:

Type of business: Wholesale and retail, at store location and by mail.
Wholesale requirements: Minimum quantity, 2 chairs.
Accepts: Check, money order, Visa, MC, AE
Return/exchange policy: Guaranteed satisfaction.
Catalog/Price list: Color photos, free
Phone orders: Available
Fax orders: Available
Mail orders: Will ship to US, Canada. Prepayment required for retail; wholesale is COD. Shipping included in the price of order.
Shipping information: Shipped via UPS. Allow 10 days for delivery.

WEE THREE, INC.

Airport Business Park
130 Doolittle Dr., Unit #4
San Leandro, CA 94577
Phone: For orders: (800)624-4759 PST
For info: (510)632-1101
Fax: (510)632-5859
In business since: 1986

SUPPLIES:

Lashes: Individual pack, 100 pair/box. Econo-pack, 10 pairs/card. Colors include black, dark brown, brown, neutral, blonde.
Wigs: 100% modacrylic synthetic fiber; 100% mohair wig, 100% human hair wigs

BUSINESS INFORMATION:

Type of business: Wholesale only. Sell to distributor and dollmaking institutions only.
Wholesale requirements: Minimum 1 dozen per color, per size. Minimum dollar amount of $200 or more per order or per shipment. Must have vendor's license.
Accepts: Check, money order
Discounts: For distributors
Catalog: Color
Price list: Free
Phone orders: Available
Fax orders: Include the completed order form available in the catalog
Mail orders: Will ship to US, Canada, overseas. Prepayment required.
Shipping information: COD. Shipped via UPS.

WESTSIDE PRINTING

Karen Bea Chambers
7521 Hwy. 80 W.
Fort Worth, TX 76116
Phone: (817)244-5454 CST
In business since: 1990

SUPPLIES:

Patterns for cloth dolls: Westside Printing will print artist's doll patterns for sale.

CLOTHING:

Patterns for doll clothing: Westside Printing will print patterns for doll clothing.

BUSINESS INFORMATION:

Type of business: Printing work for the dollmakers only.
Wholesale requirements: 250 patterns

minimum. Buyer must have a vendor's license.

WHIMSICAL CLOTH DOLL CREATIONS

Bonnie Hoover
26889 Lakewood Way
Hayward, CA 94844
Phone: (510)887-4250 PST
In business since: 1990

SUPPLIES:

Patterns for cloth dolls: Bonnie designs the patterns she sells. They include Agnes The Flag Keeper and Blynkum-Santa's helper.

BUSINESS INFORMATION:

Type of business: Wholesale and retail, by mail.

WILD SPIRIT DOLL STUDIO

1235 Wampanoag Trail
Barrington, RI 02915
Phone: (401)245-5013 EST (weekends, evenings)
(401)433-1235 (T-Sat, 10-5)
In business since: 1994

SUPPLIES:

Armatures: Available
Bodies: Available
Clays: Fimo, Super Sculpey, Promat, Cernit
Eyes: Available
Fabrics for hair: Mohair
Lashes: Available

BUSINESS INFORMATION:
Type of business: At store location.

WILDER'S DOLL CENTER

Rusty Wilder
350 E. Walton Blvd.
Pontiac, MI 48340
Phone: (810)334-1177 EST
Hours: M, F, Sat, 10-4. T, W, Th, 9-9.
In business since: 1980

SUPPLIES:

Armatures: Beaded wire
Bodies: Porcelain and cloth
Clays: Porcelain, air-dry and oil-based
Eyes: Available
Fabrics for cloth dolls: Muslin, Wamsutta
Fabrics for hair: Mohair, wefted, braided
Lashes: Available
Molds: Original
Paints: China and glazes
Slips: Available
Stuffing: Polyester
Tools: Available
Wigs: Synthetic and mohair
Other supplies: Manufactures mold boards—inner body, stands, neck supports, etc.

CLOTHING:

Buttons: Doll size and charm.
Clothing (ready-made): Available
Fabrics for doll clothing: Suede, fur, velvet
Lace: White, black, beige

Patterns for doll clothing: Brown House and several others plus own originals
Ribbons: Available
More about clothing: Custom-made clothing a specialty.

ACCESSORIES:

Furniture: Available

BUSINESS INFORMATION:

Type of business: Wholesale and retail, at store location, by mail or shows.
Wholesale requirements: Minimum dollar amount $50. Must have vendor's license.
Accepts: Check, money order, Visa, MC, DC
Discounts: 40% on most items to dealers, 10% on most items to students
Layaway: 20% down, balance by month. No time limit.
Back order policy: Available.
Catalog/Price list: b&w and color, $6.50, refundable with purchase. Price list, comes with catalogue.
Mailing list: Write, call or request a catalog or price list to be included.
Phone orders: During store hours
Mail orders: Will ship to US and Canada. Send complete order form. Prepayment required. Shipping included in the price of order.
Shipping information: Shipped via UPS, method preferred by customer or US mail.

4

Doll Artists

A Guide to Chapter Four

There is nothing more precious than an artist-made doll. If you have ever tried to make a doll, or even watched someone else do it, you know how much time, effort and attention to detail are involved, from the designing stage to the finishing touches. No matter how many dolls you own or how long you have been a collector, the magic of this birthing process never escapes you. (Look an artist doll in the face, and you see the hours of work that went into finishing her.)

This chapter includes listings of doll artists who sell their original dolls. These listings can be used by doll collectors looking for new dolls, by stores looking for dolls to sell, and by fellow artists looking for networking opportunities. If you are an artist, be sure to read the article by Barb Giguere following this guide.

The listings include the same kind of detailed information found in other chapters, as well as a photograph of the artist's work when one was provided. Each artist was asked to send one photo along with his or her questionnaire for inclusion in the book. Many of the dolls shown are one-of-a-kind or limited editions that have already been sold out, so you may not be able to order a particular doll that is pictured in this book. Rather, these photos are provided as a sample of the artist's work.

Requirements for Inclusion

Due to the number of people making dolls today in the US and Canada, we were forced to limit this chapter to those who design and make original dolls. We used the definition of "doll artist" described in Carol-Lynn Rössel Waugh's Introduction for Doll Artists at the beginning of this book.

These artists had to sign a statement which indicated that they understood the definition we were using. I feel that this statement is important and should be included here, as it is the best way to explain the content of this chapter and the reasons we decided to define the term "doll artist" as we did. The statement read as follows:

"In *The Doll Sourcebook,* the term 'doll artist' will mean anyone who designs and makes his or her own dolls. This includes only those who design the concept, make a mold of the doll or have a mold made for them, and then make the actual doll with their own hands from start to finish. It also includes those who hand-sculpt all their dolls. Finally, the definition includes cloth doll makers who design and create the entire cloth doll from start to finish. In order to be listed as a doll artist in *The Doll Sourcebook,* the artist must design and make at least some of their original dolls from start to finish, except for the molds, the eyes and the wigs. Costumes and accessories may also be made by someone else.

"Due to the large number of people making dolls in the US and Canada, we had to limit the definition of doll artist to include only those who are designing and making their own dolls at the present time. We are not able to include those who design for manufacturers only, although those who design for manufacturers and also design and make original dolls may be included. We also are not able to include those who make dolls using others' molds or others' designs, or those who make antique or modern reproduction dolls. While we think these craftspeople are talented and provide an important service, we do not have the space to include them in this book.

"The practice of 'tweaking'—changing a mold slightly in order to create a doll which is then sold as an original—is considered by artists and collectors to be an unacceptable practice, and the editor of this book agrees with this standard. If the editor finds that someone listed in this book has participated in this practice, she will remove that listing from the book."

In addition to signing the statement above, the artists were asked to indicate whether they make all, most or some of the following for their dolls: heads, bodies, wigs, shoes and accessories/props. Also, they were asked to indicate whether they design or make their dolls' clothing. This information is included in each listing.

We realize that some of the most popular names in the industry are actually designers and not artists. For this reason, the manufacturer listings include the names of designers who work for them. Also, artists who now have cottage industries—those who design and have a team of people make the dolls under their direct supervision—are included in the chapter on manufacturers as well. The only people intentionally left out of the book, then, are reproduction artists, and this is simply because there are so many repro artists out there that we could not fit them all in the book.

The Listings

The listings include the name, company name and contact information for each artist. Remember that the address is a mailing address only and not a store location. The listing will tell you how long the artist has been making or selling dolls, the mediums he or she uses, and the scope of his or her work. Price ranges, descriptions of the dolls (provided by the artists themselves, like all the information), and special-order policies are also included. If the artist's work is manufactured or is available in mold form, the listing will tell you the names of companies offering the artist's work in these forms. Information on artists' catalogs and price lists and where they sell their dolls (including shops, shows, computer sales, home/studio visits and phone, fax or mail orders) is included, as are layaway policies, discounts and return/exchange policies. ❧

Marketing Yourself as Well as Your Dolls

BY BARB GIGUERE

Barb Giguere left a twenty-year engineering and management consulting career to follow her heart. She has been a sculptor and serious doll artist since 1985. Barb is charter member and Executive Director of the Maine Society of Doll and Bear Artists, a nonprofit educational organization with a worldwide juried membership.

Barb Giguere

You're making dolls. You've researched the best ways to display them. You're using lighting that accents your display nicely. Everyone thinks your work is wonderful, and your presentation brings ooohs and aaahs. Your dolls are within the price range of dolls that are selling. Show attendance is good. And people *are* spending money. But other artists' original dolls are selling, and yours are not. What's wrong?

You're not marketing yourself.

Yes, it's as simple as that. Relax. It's much easier than you think. You already have one thing unique to your dolls—*you*. Like your dolls, your persona can and must be your own creation. No one else can be you. An artist puts a part of himself or herself into each creation. Ask a dozen artists to make a doll of a blue-eyed, tousle-haired blonde four-year-old seeing her new kitten for the first time. Each doll will be different. Some may have similar characteristics, but what makes each doll different is the artistic interpretation that comes from within the maker. It's often called the doll's soul.

There are many, many doll artists out there; only a handful are well known. Why? Those who endure, those who succeed, know they must promote themselves as much as their work. Collectors buy into success, into a mystique that surrounds an artist. It's like the aura surrounding some actors, making them more successful than others. The acting community's business is promoting images. You must work as hard as an actor at building an image of yourself and your work.

As you attend doll shows, open your eyes and really see what others are doing. Why are some really great dolls not selling while some not-so-great dolls are instant hits? What makes the difference? What is the suc-

cessful artist doing that others are not? Watch. Listen. Take notes. Do you see an image, a personality who's alive, happy, customer-oriented and knowledgeable, well-dressed and successful? As you observe others, see how many different ways people do this. You, too, can learn to market yourself, your work and your look. Here are some ground rules to follow.

Step One: Become Your Own Best Resource

Your studio and product are part of a vast industry. To succeed in the business, you need to know the products and the players—both the dolls and the humans! Study doll magazines and read books about other artists. Learn who is doing what and for whom. Which artists are teaching classes and seminars? Which are attending signings at shops? Which are attending certain shows? Which artists work in which media?

Make time to study old magazines. You will be

amazed at how quickly names come and go. It takes hard work and determination to succeed in the doll world, just as in every other field. When you're working alone, you wear all the hats—all the jobs are your responsibility. How can you possibly do all this research and make dolls, too?

Time Management

Incorporate time management skills into each day. You know by now that dollmaking is an obsessive, all-consuming activity. You won't want to do or talk about anything else. But every so often, you will need to take a break from your creative work. Use this time for research. Photocopy articles you'll want to read again later, and place these in file folders or in a three-ring binder as soon as you find them. You'll save a lot of time you'd be spending later searching for those elusive pages. Keep information about retailers on index cards, in a rotary card file, or in a computer database. Begin now. Backtracking to find old information and old contacts becomes a chore. Anything that keeps you from your dollmaking will soon become annoying, especially when you're getting ready for a show or trying to fill an order.

Learn From Other Artists

Share your knowledge as freely as you ask questions. You will quickly learn that you have entered a wonderfully "giving" world of artists, show promoters, shop owners, suppliers and others. The success of each depends on the others. Most will be eager to find another soul to talk with about dolls. Artists tend to be hermits, yet they crave input from others. Learn about other artists' work, and share yours with them. Some of the best critiquing you'll get will be from other artists. Most of us have experienced the same problems. There's nothing more rewarding than having another artist praise your work. Network, network, network.

Step Two: Develop Your Public Image

You are now an ambassador for yourself, for your dolls, every day. People see you at shows and remember you. Someone approaches you in the grocery store or at the corner gas station and asks, "Aren't you the doll lady?" Now it's happened. *You* are what they remember. Your image is building. Let's make it a good one!

Consider Your Look

First, let's work on your "looks." Remember Cinderella! Take the time and spend the money for a makeup and hair make-over. Have your colors done and your hair styled. Learn which clothing styles flatter your body shape. If it isn't in its best shape, work to fix it. Make phone calls and ask others for references to find the very best make-over specialist in your area. You'll be amazed at how much better you feel about yourself. Can you imagine the time you'll save shopping for clothes when you look only at clothes in the colors and styles that are right for you? This leaves more time for the important things. Don't think of it as an extravagance; it's an investment, one you'll also be able to use when selecting colors and styles for your dolls' costumes. Are there certain outfits or colors that bring you compliments? It's probably because you're wearing *your* colors. Just think of the reaction your dolls will get when they wear *their* colors!

Practice Your Act

Do you remember watching successful artists at shows? What were they doing that was different? Are you afraid you won't act right? Do what actors do—practice before getting on stage. You'll need a table where you can set up a display of your work, someone to act as a customer, and a video camera. If you can't find someone to operate the camera, put it on a tripod. Now, tape yourself interacting with your "customer." Have the customer play different roles: a "browser" who knows nothing about dolls; an avid collector who is skeptically examining your work for flaws; a collector trying to get a good deal. When you watch the video, you will see how you look to others and what your body language says. Ask someone who will give you honest input to watch the video. Learn what you need to change. Do the role-playing again and again until you are happy.

Step Three: Build a Following

Now you're ready to really put your best foot (and those of your dolls) forward to the world. Shows are only a small part of presenting yourself and your dolls. One of the greatest rewards comes from public service presentations. Everyone is familiar with "play dolls" and antique dolls. Few realize artist-made dolls are among the top collectibles in today's market. Contact schools, libraries, nursing homes, museums, civic groups, church groups and local clubs. These groups are always looking for someone to present a program for their meetings. By doing this, you will be providing a great service to doll artists everywhere—educating the public about artist-made dolls. Everyone knows someone who is a doll collector. This will be time well spent.

Become an Authority

Select one doll-related area or topic in which you are especially interested, and learn all you can about it. Push yourself to become an authority. Give presentations. Write articles for newspapers, collectible magazines and doll magazines. Do you know a lot about dolls from a certain locale, manufacturer or era? Are you a chemist who can educate collectors about the various materials used to manufacture dolls? Do you have knowledge about costuming of past eras? Have you developed new or different methods of using a material or paint? Do you make wigs or shoes? Share your expertise in articles and presentations. People will begin to learn about you—and you will be building name recognition that can translate into sales.

Write a Press Release

Don't let the momentum stop now. You have only started building a local following. Your most difficult task probably will be writing a press release about yourself. An artist friend of mine who is basically very shy asked me to review a press release she'd prepared about herself. It was amazing. How did she do such a wonderful job? She studied articles about different artists in the magazines, studied press releases about people in other industries, and used them as a format to create her own press release. I changed only two lines, and those were about her dolls.

Create a press release for publication before your next show. Include information about yourself and your work. Keep in mind that *you* should be the central theme. Your dolls will change as they are sold and you make new ones, but you are the constant factor. So make the press release about you! It is far better to prepare a press release yourself than to let others write things with which you won't be happy. In most cases, publications will use whatever you send them. Only a few will edit the release.

Send press releases to area newspapers before each show you do, even if the show is in another city or state. Have you created a new line of dolls? Are you donating a doll to raise money for a charitable organization? Have you created a portrait doll? Every one of these is a good reason for a press release. Successful artists

seem to somehow get their names in every issue of every doll magazine. Look at local papers and notice how many of the articles are non-news, "human interest" stories. If you continue to present newspapers with press releases, they will realize that you are doing something, that you are newsworthy. Wouldn't you like a feature article about you and your dolls? It can and does happen.

"Freeing the Spirit," one of a Cernit limited edition of 5, is a hand-sculpted doll dressed in hand-painted fabrics by Barb.

"When should I do this?" you ask. Whenever your work will be included in a gallery showing. Whenever you're exhibiting at a show that may draw attendance from the area where the newspaper is circulated (remember, collectors will travel for shows and even plan vacations around them). Whenever you've created a new line. Whenever you make a special edition for a shop. Send out those press releases! Newspapers always need "fillers," and fillers can lead to an article about you.

Shown on page 101 is a press release that was published by over thirty East Coast newspapers. Several newspapers contacted me for further information and a photo for a longer article. These articles certainly drew the attention of those who would not have read anything

PRESS RELEASE

The Maine Society of Doll and Bear Artists
P.O. Box 124, Scarborough, ME 04070-0124
Telephone: (207)883-3771

Scarborough, ME—August 8, 1995

Local sculptor and internationally known doll artist Barb Giguere of Scarborough, Maine, has sculpted a pair of dolls depicting events and people who have impacted her life. One represents a disabled veteran, a double amputee sitting in a wheelchair, obviously suffering from post-traumatic stress disorder. The other doll represents a U.S. Army nurse returning to the states with the young veteran.

Barb visited Washington, DC following the unveiling of the Vietnam Veterans' War Memorial. The memory of the young veteran she saw has remained with her for over twelve years, inspiring her to memorialize him as a doll. Her mother, a World War II Army nurse serving in Europe, was the inspiration for the other doll.

Many local people helped to make these sculptures a reality. Whity Beairsto of Mark it With a "B" in Stratham, New Hampshire, made the wheelchair. Jerry Thomas supplied the desk-sized POW-MIA flag that is displayed on the back of the wheelchair and the U.S. flag, folded as is proper following a funeral, that the veteran is holding in his lap. The dog tags worn by both dolls are engraved by Classic Impressions of Portland.

These dolls are posed in front of a large photo of the statue in Washington, DC representing three U.S. soldiers in Vietnam (the photograph was donated by another Vietnam veteran). The nurse's pin and Lieutenant's bars were worn during WWII by the artist's mother, who was a resident of the Maine Veterans Home in Scarborough until her death last month.

These dolls will be exhibited at the Doll and Teddy Bear Expo '95 in Washington, DC, August 26 and 27. Barb has donated these dolls to raise money for establishing a Stress Management program for the staff of the Maine Veterans Home here in Scarborough. She hopes that every veterans' organization in southern Maine will participate in the fund-raising endeavor.

Here is a press release that was published by over 30 East Coast newspapers.

about dolls but who were interested in veterans' affairs, nursing homes, fund-raising and the arts.

Press releases are free advertisements. You have nothing to lose by sending them to local media as well as to doll-related publications. By contrast, paid advertising in local media is usually not a good investment. You are far better off spending your advertising dollars in publications for collectors. Another good place to advertise is in the programs of shows in which you're participating. Many show promoters solicit ads only from businesses, but will accept ads from artists as well. If a show program contains information collectors want to retain, the program is a good place for your ad. Contact show promoters about advertising in their show programs and tell them, "I'm an original artist and I'll be doing your show." They will often include your name in their ads for the show. Voilà! Free advertising.

Photos: Your Own or Professional?
As a professional doll artist, you will want to have photographs of every doll you create. Photographs can ac-

"Kira," this one-of-a-kind Cernit portrait doll by Barb Giguere, is photographed before a plain background so her features and clothing stand out. This is an example of a good photograph that the artist shot at home.

company press releases and magazine advertisements. Few people know how to take quality photos that will transfer well to magazine pages. Just as some people are more photogenic than others, so are some dolls. If you want to try taking your own photos, take many photos of the same doll from many angles to get one really good shot. Use a solid-color, uncomplicated background. Beware of harsh lighting and shadows. Some of my best photographs were taken on our screened-in porch during a downpour.

You will want to experiment with film, as different brands of film react differently to color. One-hour film processing or labs processing large volumes of film each day may not be your best choice when it's time to have your photos developed. You'll do a lot better at small facilities where humans do the work.

The cost of film and processing and the time involved often make a professional photographer the right decision. Photographers have different rate schedules. Some charge per hour and per print or slide. Some charge per sitting, providing proofs only. Others charge per hour using your film, and you pay for the processing. Some come to your home or studio; others have you bring your dolls to their studio. Learn what you will get for your time and money. A poor-quality photo is a poor representation of both doll and artist.

Many professionals specialize in photographing dolls and bears. You will find some listed in this book. Other good choices are photographers specializing in photographing high-end craft work for magazines, advertisements or flyers. Portrait photographers can also serve you well. A good "doll shot" is a combination of portrait shot and a product or advertising shot. You might get lucky and find a photographer who collects dolls and will barter photography expertise for a doll. Look around.

Exposure in Doll-Related Publications
If you are ready to reach a larger audience but find that it is too expensive and time-consuming to travel to shows beyond a certain distance, it is time to consider advertising in the doll and collectible magazines. Begin by identifying your market. Are your collectors traditional doll collectors, or do they think of themselves as art collectors? If they are primarily doll collectors, doll magazines are the place for your advertising dollars. If your customers are gallery collectors who don't consider themselves doll collectors, place your advertisements in collectible art magazines.

Barb's "Phyllis-Jeanne" is a limited edition porcelain doll of 25.

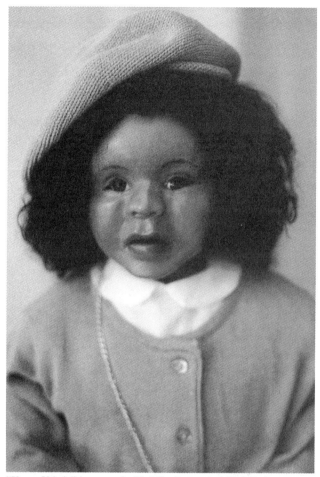

"Young Valerie" is a one-of-a-kind Cernit portrait doll by Barb.

Think about what times of year bring the most sales. Magazines distributed just prior to these periods are the issues that should bring the greatest response to your advertisements. Contact each magazine for their ad copy deadlines; the deadlines are usually several months prior to publication of each issue.

At least one doll magazine publishes small articles about news from artists' studios. If you want information about you and your work to appear in the magazines, you have to let them know what you're doing. One artist who has had wonderful coverage in all the doll magazines said he made appointments to visit their offices. Although this isn't practical for everyone, it has certainly been a successful plan for him. More than ten articles have been published about his dolls in two years. And yes, you should create press releases for doll magazines as well. Magazines won't go to you until you let them know you're there. Like collectors and shop owners, they follow familiar names.

Most doll magazines accept photos of new work. The magazines, however, often have a backlog of these shots. Sometimes photos are not published for up to eighteen months. Is your work evolving and developing? Only send magazines photos of work you think will still represent your work a year from now. If you're secure in your work and the quality of the photograph, send one to each magazine. Include a self-addressed stamped envelope for return of the photograph.

A lot to digest? Perhaps. Remember, you eat an elephant one bite at a time. Others have succeeded using these methods. You can, too.

Doing What You Love

Remember, you're in this business because you want to be. You are lucky to be able to do what you love. Show everyone you meet how much you enjoy your job!

Always remember the special bond between artist and collector. You are providing collectors with special treasures they will have for years to come, and you want them to remember *you* as well as your dolls. You have the key to success in this industry . . . your own aura, your own mystique. Now you're marketing *you!*

Artists

MONIE ABEL
MONIE ABEL'S DOLLS
1624 17th Ave. S.
Escanaba, MI 49829
Phone: (906)786-6069 EST
Making dolls since: 1986
Selling dolls since: 1990

PRODUCT INFORMATION:
Mediums: Clay, porcelain
Scope of work: Monie makes limited edition dolls. Artist makes all heads, bodies, accessories and molds, and makes shoes and props for most dolls. She also makes some wigs. She designs and sews all dolls' clothing.
Price range: $100-800
Description of dolls: Most of Monie's dolls are showcase size dolls ranging from 4½″ to 20″ in size. Antique flowers, ribbon and lace are used when possible. Smaller dolls are trimmed in miniature laces and silk ribbon. The dolls show expression and emotion, making them seem almost alive.
Price list: Send SASE
Mailing list: Write to be included.
Dolls sold: In retail doll shops, at shows, by mail, from artist's home/studio.
Shops: Send SASE for list.
Shows: Send SASE for list.
Mail orders: Will ship to US, Canada. Down payment with order.
Shipping information: Shipped via UPS. COD.
Layaway: ⅓ down, 3 months.
Discounts: Wholesale for retailers at 50%
Return/exchange policy: Returns must

be made within 10 days of receiving doll.

ADDITIONAL INFORMATION:
Monie's work received Judges' Choice award from Ashton-Drake in 1990; 1st place at the Michigan Dollmakers show in Detroit, 1991; 2nd and 3rd place in professional division at Dollmakers Challenge in Branson, Missouri, 1991; and 1st place in original category at the International Dollmakers Association in Detroit, 1991. Her work has appeared in *Contemporary Doll Collector* magazine. Abel is a member of the International Dollmakers Association.

MELISSA ADAMS
ZAKLIN DOLLS
50 Cleaves St.
Auburn, ME 04210
Phone: (207)784-4855 EST
Making dolls since: 1992
Selling dolls since: 1995

PRODUCT INFORMATION:
Mediums: Porcelain, Cernit, Fimo, Washi paper
Scope of work: Artist makes one-of-a-kind direct sculptures and limited editions of 10-50 dolls. Artist makes all heads and bodies and most shoes and accessories/props. She designs and sews all clothing.
Price range: $100-2,500
Description of dolls: All of Melissa's dolls are original. The heads and limbs are made of porcelain or polymer clays. The bodies are cloth, leather or polymer clay. The artist uses glass or high-quality acrylic eyes, and in some cases the eyes are Cernit or Fimo, which she models and paints. Wigs and lashes are made of synthetic fibers or human hair. Antique fabrics are often used. All dolls are signed and numbered by the artist.
Special orders: Artist models portrait dolls from photographs. Any special requests will be considered on an individual basis. This includes cost and

time allotted for completion.
Dolls sold: At shows, by mail
Shows: Send SASE for list.
Phone orders: Accepted
Mail orders: Will ship to US, Canada, overseas. Prepayment is required.
Shipping information: Shipped via UPS, FedEx, air mail (overseas). COD. The buyer may call the artist with location and preferred method of shipping. The artist will then determine shipping cost and add to the price of the doll.
Layaway: 25% nonrefundable deposit. Regular monthly payments.
Return/exchange policy: Enclosed with doll

ADDITIONAL INFORMATION:
Melissa is a member of MSDBA. She is also a portrait artist.

CLARA M. ALLEN
51-5455 Borden Place
Powell River, British Columbia
V8A 3W1
CANADA
Phone: (604)483-4800 PST
Making dolls since: 1989
Selling dolls since: 1989

PRODUCT INFORMATION:
Mediums: Cernit with cloth
Scope of work: Dolls are one-of-a-kind direct sculptures. Artist designs the patterns for all her cloth dolls. She makes all heads and bodies and some wigs, shoes and accessories/props. She either designs the clothing and hires a seamstress to sew them, or buys clothing ready-made.

Price range: $200-900

Description of dolls: Clara's dolls are one-of-a-kind with Cernit heads, hands and feet and cloth (weighted) bodies. They are 19"-24" long and designed to wear baby clothes. Artist's newborn and young babies are meant to portray the cherished memories of babyhood.

Dolls sold: In retail doll shops, by mail or from artist's home/studio.

Shops: Call or send SASE for list.

Home/studio visits: Please schedule in advance.

Phone orders: M-F, 9-5.

Mail orders: Will ship to US, Canada, overseas. Prepayment required. Allow 3 weeks for delivery.

Shipping information: Shipped via postal system. Shipping is included in the price of the doll.

Layaway: 1/3 down, to be paid in 3 months

ADDITIONAL INFORMATION:
Clara's work has been featured in *Contemporary Doll Collector.*

S. CATHERINE ANDERSON
ANDERSON CREATIONS
208 Ridge Dr.
Sikeston, MO 63801
Phone: (314)471-0521 CST
Fax: (314)471-3285
Making dolls since: 1993
Selling dolls since: 1993

PRODUCT INFORMATION:
Mediums: Cernit, soft sculpture

Scope of work: Dolls are one-of-a-kind direct sculptures. Artist makes all heads, bodies and shoes and most accessories/props. No wigs are used. Hair is attached directly to scalp one strand at a time. All clothing is designed and custom made by the artist.

Price range: $2,000-3,000

Description of dolls: Catherine's dolls are hand-sculpted Cernit children with very detailed soft sculpture bodies. Eyes are hand-sculpted and hand-painted for maximum expression. Each piece has special armature that allows independence from doll stand.

Special orders: Artist accepts 1 or 2 portrait orders per year. Waiting list for portraits varies. Customers should allow 6-12 months for order's completion.

Mailing list: Write or call to be included.

Dolls sold: In retail doll shops, at occasional shows

Shops: Send SASE for list.

Shows: Artist United, February show in New York for one-of-a-kind artists.

Phone orders: M-F, 8-5.

ADDITIONAL INFORMATION:
Anderson received 2 nominations in 1993 for a *Dolls* Award of Excellence. Her work has been featured in *Toy Box* and *Dolls—The Collector's Magazine.*

SUNNIE ANDRESS
SUNNIE ANDRESS DESIGNS
Pinebank Cottage R.R. 1, Box 407A
Newport, VT 05855
Phone: (802)766-5156 EST
Making dolls since: 1991

PRODUCT INFORMATION:
Mediums: Cloth, wood, papier mâché

Scope of work: Artist makes one-of-a-kind direct sculptures. She makes all heads, bodies, wigs and shoes and some accessories/props. She designs and makes most dolls' clothing.

Price range: $100-250

Description of dolls: Sunnie's Santas and folk art figures are built on wood and wire "skeletons" attached to wooden bases. Ranging in height from approximately 18"-30", the figures are padded and stitched from the inside out, using layers of fabrics and trims to make a vertical "collage." New and old fabrics, found objects, Sunnie's own handmade accessories and some purchased items are combined. Faces are either needle-sculpted cloth or papier mâché. Santas and folk dolls are not literal representations of the human face and figure, but are intended to create the illusion of a living "personality" which interacts with each person differently.

Dolls sold: At shows, from artist's studio, in retail gift shops.

Shops: Send SASE for list.

Shows: Send SASE for list.

Home/studio visits: Please schedule 1-2 days in advance.

Return/exchange policy: All sales final

ADDITIONAL INFORMATION:
Andress is a member of MSDBA. Because she completes a limited number of Santas each year, Sunnie encourages calls from collectors who would like to see photographs and/or visit her studio before they order.

LAWAN ANGÉLIQUE
2458 W. Bayshore Rd. #7
Palo Alto, CA 94303
Phone: (415)494-8830 PST
Fax: (415)852-3908
E-Mail: jack@batnet.com
Making dolls since: 1989
Selling dolls since: 1990

PRODUCT INFORMATION:
Mediums: Cloth, wire, Paperclay

Scope of work: Artist's dolls are one-of-a-kind direct sculptures. Cloth dolls are designed and made by the artist. Artist makes all heads, bodies and wigs and most accessories/props and shoes. Artist designs and makes all clothing.

Price range: $150 and up

Description of dolls: Lawan's cloth dolls are needle sculpted in the West German tradition. Hers dolls are bold, colorful, whimsical, avant-garde, historic, literary and sacred, evoking movement and emotion.

Special orders: A deposit of 1/2 of approximate price is required. Payments are determined before doll is made. Allow 6 weeks or more.

Mailing list: Write to be included.

Dolls sold: At shows or by mail

Shows: Call or send SASE to request list.

Phone orders: Accepted

Mail orders: Will ship to US, Canada, overseas. Prepayment required.

Shipping information: Shipped via UPS. Shipping is included in the price of the doll.

Layaway: 1/2 down, 3 months

Return/exchange policy: All sales are final.

ADDITIONAL INFORMATION:
Lawan's work has been featured in *Contemporary Doll Collector* and *The Doll By Contemporary Artists*. She is involved in design and theatre arts, and frequently speaks to doll groups and teaches about her craft. She participates in many cloth doll gallery shows.

ARDIS
ARDIS OF STARCROSS
123 Shalako
Kerrville, TX 78028
Phone: (210)895-5469 CST
Making dolls since: 1992
Selling dolls since: 1992

PRODUCT INFORMATION:
Mediums: Porcelain with partial cloth body
Scope of work: Artist makes limited editions of 6-20 dolls. She designs all cloth doll patterns and makes all heads, bodies, wigs, accessories/props (except chairs) and molds. The artist also designs and sews all clothing.
Price range: $900-1,500
Description of dolls: Ardis' dolls are painted and fired five times, then waxed. Her family raises champion angora goats, and she uses the hair to make dolls' wigs.
Special orders: Customer may pick a head in stock, choose eye and hair color and type of outfit. Allow artist two months to complete a special order.
Designs manufactured by: House of Hatten (resin dolls)
Mailing list: Write to be included.
Dolls sold: In retail doll shops, at shows, by mail, from the artist's home/studio.
Shops: Call or send SASE for list.
Shows: Send SASE for list.
Home/studio visits: Please schedule in advance.
Phone orders: M-F, 9-5.

Mail orders: Prepayment required, except for established accounts. Always allow 5 days for delivery.
Shipping information: Shipped via UPS. New accounts COD or prepaid.
Layaway: 20% down. Will work terms with each person.
Discounts: Doll shops 50% off
Return/exchange policy: If not satisfied with work, exchange can be arranged.

ADDITIONAL INFORMATION:
Ardis was nominated for a *Dolls* Award of Excellence in 1995. She has been featured in *Contemporary Doll Collector* and *Dolls—The Collector's Magazine*.

JANIE ASHCRAFT
UNIQUELY YOURS
Rt. 1, Box 1429
Qulin, MO 63961
Phone: (314)328-4846 CST
Making dolls since: 1989
Selling dolls since: 1989

PRODUCT INFORMATION:
Mediums: Polymer clays mixture, Cernit, Super Sculpey
Scope of work: Dolls are one-of-a-kind direct sculptures. Artist makes all heads and bodies and some wigs, shoes and accessories/props. She designs all clothing.
Price range: $350-2,000
Description of dolls: Janie's dolls are all one-of-a-kinds sculpted in Cernit/Sculpey. She uses angora, mohair or human hair for wigs. Vintage accessories are carefully selected and used whenever possible.
Special orders: Artist makes portrait dolls. She requires very clear photographs, front and side views. Allow 2-3 months to complete a portrait doll.
Designs manufactured by: Tom Banwell Design (one limited edition piece, limited to 25).

Dolls sold: In retail doll shops, at shows, by mail, from artist's home/studio.
Shops: Call for list.
Phone orders: M-Sat, 9-6.
Mail orders: Will ship to US, Canada, overseas. Customer will be billed or will ship COD.
Shipping information: Shipped via UPS.
Layaway: Available
Return/exchange policy: All sales are final.

ADDITIONAL INFORMATION:
Janie has been featured in *The Art of the Doll* (Abbeville Press, 1995), *Contemporary Doll Collector* and *Doll Design*.

SANDRA F. BABIN
RIBBONS AND RINGLETS
515 W. Main St.
Houma, LA 70360
Phone: (504)876-1637 CST
Making dolls since: 1985
Selling dolls since: 1985

PRODUCT INFORMATION:
Mediums: Porcelain
Scope of work: Dolls are one-of-a-kind direct sculptures. The artist makes most heads, bodies, shoes and accessories/props and makes wigs for some dolls. She designs and sews all clothing.
Price range: $600-3,000
Description of dolls: Sandra's dolls are one-of-a-kind, hand-sculpted with wire armature, wrapped bodies. Finished doll is completely waxed over, giving it an antique look. Her pieces include babies, toddlers, young girls, young ladies, angels and cherubs with vintage fabrics and flowers.
Special orders: Artist does special orders for angels. Allow 2-4 months to complete a special order.
Designs manufactured by: Franklin, Ashton-Drake.
Dolls sold: In retail doll shops, at shows, by mail, from artist's home/studio.
Shops: Call for list.
Shows: Call for list.
Home/studio visits: Please schedule in advance.
Phone orders: M-Sat, 9-5.
Shipping information: Shipped via UPS, FedEx. Shipping is included in the price of the doll.

Layaway: $300 down, balance in 12 months

Return/exchange policy: If not completely satisfied, return for refund within 1 week.

ADDITIONAL INFORMATION:
Sandra has been featured in *Dolls—The Collector's Magazine* and *Contemporary Doll Collector*. She is a member of UFDC and ODACA.

KIM DIANE BAIERL
W13261 Scandi St., P.O. Box 395
Ripon, WI 54971
Phone: (414)748-3990 CST
Making dolls since: 1984
Selling dolls since: 1984

PRODUCT INFORMATION:
Mediums: Cernit, Paperclay, porcelain, resin
Scope of work: Dolls are one-of-a-kind direct sculptures (Cernit/Paperclay) or limited editions of 10-50 dolls (resin/porcelain). Artist makes all heads, bodies and molds and most wigs, shoes and accessories/props. She designs and sews all clothing.
Price range: $95-1,050
Description of dolls: All Kim's dolls feature hand-painted eyes, and most have handmade mohair wigs. They frequently have modeled shoes, and clothing made from hand-painted silk or antique fabrics. Sizes range from 7"-30".
Catalog/price list: Photos and prices, $2.
Mailing list: Write to be included.
Dolls sold: At shows, by mail, from artist's home/studio.
Shows: Send SASE for list.
Home/studio visits: Please schedule 1 week in advance.
Phone orders: Leave message with phone number and best time to return your call.

Mail orders: Will ship to US. Prepayment required, or COD.
Shipping information: Shipped via UPS. Shipping is included in the price of the doll. Allow 3-4 weeks for porcelain or resin dolls; immediate shipment available for one-of-a-kinds.
Layaway: 25% down, term not to exceed 6 months
Discounts: Wholesale to legitimate retail doll shops; copy of resale certificate and photograph of storefront required.

ADDITIONAL INFORMATION:
Kim has been featured in *Contemporary Doll Collector*. She is a member of UFDC and ODACA. She also has written an article for *Dollmaking Crafts and Designs*.

S. KAYE BANKS
KATIE-DID ORIGINALS
16009 Northlake Village Dr.
Odessa, FL 33556
Phone: (813)920-3269 EST
Making dolls since: 1994
Selling dolls since: 1994

PRODUCT INFORMATION:
Mediums: Cloth, porcelain
Scope of work: Dolls are one-of-a-kind or limited editions of up to 6. Artist designs patterns for all cloth dolls. Artist makes all heads, bodies and molds and most wigs and accessories/props. Artist designs and sews clothes for one-of-a-kind dolls and designs clothing for limited editions.
Price range: $300-3,000
Description of dolls: Kaye's 18" cloth dolls are made of muslin and have oil painted faces. Porcelain dolls are 25". Features include special children's faces with unusual skin tones and beautiful eyes.
Special orders: Artist makes miniature portrait dolls, 3"-6", from good photos

and color descriptions. Allow 3-6 months.
Designs manufactured by: Duck House, for home shopping.
Catalog/price list: Pictures available. Price list, free.
Mailing list: Write or call to be included.
Dolls sold: In retail doll shops, at shows, by mail, from artist's studio.
Shops: Call or send SASE for list.
Shows: Call or send SASE for list.
Home/studio visits: Available
Phone orders: Available
Mail orders: Will ship to US, Canada, overseas. Prepayment required.
Shipping information: Shipped via UPS. Shipping is included in the price of the doll.
Layaway: 20% down, 6-8 months
Return/exchange policy: Satisfaction guaranteed. Damaged dolls will be exchanged or repaired.

BETSEY BAKER
BETSEY BAKER DOLLS
R.R. 2, Box 87
Cold Spring, NY 10516
Phone: (914)265-3490 EST
Making dolls since: 1970
Selling dolls since: 1972

PRODUCT INFORMATION:
Mediums: Paperclay, wire armature, Super Sculpey
Scope of work: Dolls are one-of-a-kind direct sculptures. Artist makes all heads, bodies, wigs, shoes and accessories/props. Artist designs and sews all dolls' clothing.
Price range: $275 and up
Description of dolls: Each doll or setting is carefully planned before the work is started. Whether it is a single figure or a setting, the accessories usually have to be made just after the armature so a natural position will be attained. Heads are sculpted of Paperclay,

hands and feet are Super Sculpey. Bodies are wire armature padded and covered with jersey type material, needle-sculpted into correct proportions. Faces and eyes are painted with acrylic paints as you would paint a portrait. Eyes are painted to get good expression. Careful attention is paid to costuming using fabrics in scale, sometimes dyeing to get the right color. Old lace and trims are used when possible. Hair is mohair or wool glued to the heads. Animals are sculpted from Super Sculpey or Paperclay. Furniture is basswood.

Price list: $1 and SASE

Dolls sold: At shows, by mail or from artist's home/studio.

Shows: Send SASE

Home/studio visits: Please schedule 1 week in advance.

Mail orders: Will ship to US, Canada and overseas. Prepayment required. Allow 4 weeks for delivery.

Shipping information: Will ship via UPS. Shipping is included in the price of the doll.

Layaway: 20% down, 4 months

Return/exchange policy: Doll may be returned within 2 weeks for refund of purchase price minus shipping and handling expenses.

ADDITIONAL INFORMATION:

Baker's work has appeared in *Contemporary Doll Collector, Dolls—The Collector's Magazine*, and *Fantastic Figures* by Susanna Oroyan. She is a member of UFDC, ODACA and AADA.

SHIRLEY BARAN
FRIENDS FOREVER™
P.O. Box 691
Windsor, CA 95492
Phone: For orders: (707)837-8512 or (916)939-1826 PST
Fax: (707)837-8512

Represented by: Thomas Boland Company, 15-125 Merchandise Mart, Chicago, IL 60654. Phone: (312)822-0697 or (800)555-5120 for orders. Fax: (312)822-7228

Making dolls since: 1986
Selling dolls since: 1987

PRODUCT INFORMATION:

Mediums: Porcelain

Scope of work: Artist makes original one-of-a-kind dolls and limited editions of 5-30. She makes the heads, bodies and molds for all her dolls. She designs and sews all clothing.

Price range: $700-1,800 (retail)

Description of dolls: Shirley's illustrator's art background allows her to create well-proportioned dolls. They are girls and boys in the 3-8 year age group. Their costumes are representative of a specific period. Some are all porcelain, including head, body, arms and legs. Dolls are very expressive and meticulously finished.

Special orders: For portrait dolls, Shirley requires several good color photos of subject, front and side views. Allow 3-6 months.

Designs manufactured by: The Franklin Mint, Hamilton Collection.

Catalog/price list: Send SASE for color catalog or price list.

Mailing list: Write or call to be included.

Dolls sold: In retail shops, at shows, by mail, from artist's studio.

Shops: Send SASE for list.

Shows: Send SASE for list.

Home/studio visits: Please schedule 2 weeks in advance.

Phone orders: M-F, 9-5 PST.

Fax orders: Accepted

Mail orders: Will ship to US. Prepayment required. Allow 6-8 weeks for delivery.

Shipping information: Will ship via UPS or FedEx. Shipping is added to price.

Layaway: 20% down, 5 months

Discounts: 50% to qualified store owners

Return/exchange policy: Customer satisfaction guaranteed.

ADDITIONAL INFORMATION:

Shirley won an award for most popular doll at IDEX, 1995; 2 best in category awards and 2 blue ribbons at the San Mateo China Doll Show, 1987 and 1989. Her bronze and terra-cotta sculptures are

shown in art galleries in the San Francisco Bay area.

MIRREN BARRIE
R.R. 1, Box 9640
Waterbury Center, VT 05677
Phone: (802)244-6995 EST
Making dolls since: 1967
Selling dolls since: 1967

PRODUCT INFORMATION:

Mediums: Cloth, paper

Scope of work: Artist designs patterns for all cloth dolls, which are created in limited editions of up to 10. Artist makes all heads, bodies, wigs, shoes, and accessories/props; also designs and sews all dolls' clothing.

Price range: Cloth, $120-800; paper, $70-200

Description of dolls: Mirren's cloth dolls are mainly historical and ethnic men, women and children, featuring hand embroidery and hand weaving when required. Paper dolls are 3-dimensional people made with an unlimited range of paper. Dolls are carefully researched for authenticity of detail and stand 8"-12".

Dolls sold: By mail and at annual NIADA conference

Phone orders: M-F, 9-5.

Mail orders: Will ship to US, Canada, overseas. Customer will be billed when doll sufficiently advances to set a mailing date. The customer must then send check in full plus mailing fee. The doll will be sent 5 days after receipt of check.

Shipping information: Shipped via UPS or Priority Mail

Return/exchange policy: Each situation is judged separately. If doll is returned within 6 weeks, undamaged, full money will be refunded. No exchanges.

ADDITIONAL INFORMATION:

Barrie's work has been featured in *Dolls—The Collector's Magazine, Doll Reader*, and *Needle Arts—Magazine of the Embroiders' Guild of America, Inc.*, in addition to a number of local publications. She is a member of the Green Mountain Doll Club of Vermont, NIADA and UFDC.

KATHY BARRY-HIPPENSTEEL
HIPPENSTEEL DOLLS, INC.
1522 Miner St.
Des Plaines, IL 60016
Phone: (708)298-2001 CST
Fax: (708)390-0780
E-Mail: hipdolmkr@aol.com
Making dolls since: 1982
Selling dolls since: 1982

PRODUCT INFORMATION:

Mediums: Porcelain, vinyl, resin

Scope of work: Dolls are created in limited editions of 10. Artist makes some heads, bodies, wigs, accessories/props and molds. Artist designs all dolls' clothing.

Price range: $75-250

Description of dolls: Dolls are mostly babies and toddlers, however some little girl dolls. Most have cloth bodies.

Molds: Directly from artist.

Designs manufactured by: Ashton-Drake Galleries

Mailing list: Write to be included.

Dolls sold: In retail doll shops, by mail or via computer

Shops: Send SASE for list.

Computer sales: E-mail: hipdolmkr@aol.com

Home/studio visits: Artist owns a retail doll store, Maggie's Toybox (e-mail: maggietoy@aol.com). Hours are M-F, 10-7, and Sat, 10-4 CST.

Phone orders: Call during above business hours.

Fax orders: Include your name, address, phone number, item to purchase, Visa/MC number, expiration date.

Mail orders: Will ship to US, Canada, overseas. Prepayment required.

Shipping information: Shipped via UPS or US mail.

Layaway: 20% down, 30-60 days.

Discounts: Quantity discounts available.

Return/exchange policy: No refunds unless product is damaged. Must have prior notification to return.

ADDITIONAL INFORMATION:

Kathy is a two-time DOTY and *Dolls* Award of Excellence Nominee. She has received one IDEX award and a Canadian Collectible of the Year Award. Her work has appeared in *Dolls—The Collectors Magazine*, *Doll Artists at Work* and *Doll Reader*.

JEANIE BATES
PRESENT IDEA
21978 SW Creek Dr.
Tualatin, OR 97062
Phone: (503)692-1371 PST
Making dolls since: 1993
Selling dolls since: 1994

PRODUCT INFORMATION:

Mediums: Cloth

Scope of work: Dolls are one-of-a-kind direct sculptures. Artist designs the patterns for all dolls. She makes all heads, bodies, wigs and shoes and most accessories/props. She also designs and sews all clothing.

Price range: $500-2,500

Description of dolls: Dolls have a carved foam-core skull with batting and copper wire supporting the facial features. A wire armature supports the body which is shaped with sewn batting.

Catalog/price list: Color, $5-10, refundable with purchase. Price list, free.

Mailing list: Write or call to be included.

Dolls sold: In retail doll shops, at shows and by mail.

Shops: Call or send SASE for list.

Shows: Send SASE for list. Everyone on mailing list will be notified.

Home/studio visits: Please schedule 1 week in advance.

Phone orders: M-F, 9-5.

Mail orders: Will ship to US. Prepayment required. Allow 7-10 days for delivery.

Shipping information: Shipped via UPS. Shipping included at full retail, $10 charge to wholesale.

Discounts: Wholesale prices offered to retail stores.

ADDITIONAL INFORMATION:

Jeanie has been featured in *Contemporary Doll Collector*. She has won Best of Show and 1st Place awards at several shows. She is a member of AADA.

JOAN BENZELL
JOAN'S BISQUE BE'BE'S
8 Secluded Lane
Rio Grande, NJ 08242
Phone: (609)886-4552 EST
Fax: (609)889-1758
Making dolls since: 1986
Selling dolls since: 1986

PRODUCT INFORMATION:

Mediums: Porcelain

Scope of work: Artist makes special and limited edition dolls. She makes all heads, bodies, wigs and molds and designs and sews all clothing.

Price range: $85-185

Description of dolls: Joan's dolls are small scale and have swivel heads on torsos with arms and legs made of porcelain. They are assembled on wire armatures.

Special orders: Available. Allow up to 6 months.

Mailing list: Write to be included.

Dolls sold: At shows and by mail

Shops: Send SASE for list.

Shows: Send SASE for list.

Phone orders: Accepted

Fax orders: Include name, address, phone number and description of doll, including hair color, style and fabric color.

Mail orders: Will ship to US and Canada. Prepayment required.

Shipping information: Shipped via UPS. COD or shipping added to price of doll.

ADDITIONAL INFORMATION:

Joan was elected to the NAME Academy of Honor in 1974. Her work has been featured in *Small Dolls*, *Contemporary Doll Collector*, *Nutshell News*, *Miniature Collector* and *Miniature Gazette*. She is a member of ODACA, UFDC, Fellow/International Guild of Miniature Artisans and NAME.

> "To create dolls is to be spiritually uplifted. My wish is to uplift those who collect my dolls with that same joy."
> *Shirley Hunter Peck, Simi Valley, CA*

SUZANNE BERG
SUZANNE BERG, DOLLMAKER
1264 Estate Dr.
West Chester, PA 19380
Phone: (610)696-8873 EST
Making dolls since: 1980
Selling dolls since: 1980

PRODUCT INFORMATION:

Mediums: Cloth

Scope of work: Artist designs patterns for all cloth dolls. Artist makes some heads, bodies, wigs, shoes and accessories/props. Artist designs and sews all dolls' clothing.

Price range: $30-185

Description of dolls: Suzanne's dolls have stuffed, muslin bodies, hand-embroidered faces and hand-applied yarn wigs. Many are story characters, dressed in period clothing. Artist does smocking (hand) and topsy turvy dolls (such as Red Riding Hood, Grandmother and the Wolf).

Price list: Send SASE for list.

Mailing list: Write or call to be included.

Dolls sold: At shows, by mail, from artist's home/studio.

Shows: Call or send SASE for list.

Home/studio visits: Please schedule 1-2 weeks in advance.

Phone orders: 9-9 EST.

Mail orders: Will ship to US. Prepayment is required. Allow 1 week-1 month for delivery.

Shipping information: Shipped via UPS. Shipping is included in the price of the doll.

ADDITIONAL INFORMATION:

Suzanne's work has appeared in *Dolls—The Collector's Magazine* and her local newspaper. She is a member of the Pennsylvania Guild of Craftsmen and won a 2nd place award at Needleworks '95.

AMY ALBERT BLOOM
31 Philadelphia Ave.
Shillington, PA 19607
Phone: (610)775-8993 EST
Making dolls since: 1975
Selling dolls since: 1994

PRODUCT INFORMATION:

Mediums: Cloth, Sculpey, wood

Scope of work: Artist designs patterns for all cloth dolls. Artist makes all heads, bodies, wigs and shoes and some accessories/props. Artist designs and sews all dolls' clothing.

Price range: $8-35

Description of dolls: Most dolls are made of fabric with wool, fake fur or mohair yarn for hair. Faces are stitched or painted, and some have a wooden bead for a head and wooden bead hands. Some tiny dolls are made of Sculpey, with wool hair and cloth skirts. These are not articulated. Recent designs include a 5″ bendable felt doll with mohair yarn hair, dolls made from old camel's hair coats with fake fur hair and dressed in peasant-style clothes, and a doll with a felt head shaped like a cherry pie.

Catalog: b&w, free

Mailing list: Write or call to be included.

Dolls sold: At shows, by mail, from artist's home/studio.

Shows: Everyone on mailing list will be notified.

Home/studio visits: Please schedule in advance.

Phone orders: 9-10 EST.

Mail orders: Will ship to US, Canada, overseas. Prepayment required. Allow 2-4 weeks for delivery.

Shipping information: Shipped via UPS and US mail. Postage is charged for foreign orders.

Return/exchange policy: If a doll is returned within 1-2 weeks in new condition, will refund price minus postage for US orders or complete price for foreign orders.

ADDITIONAL INFORMATION:

Over the years, Amy has designed many dolls, paper dolls, toys, doll clothes and stuffed animals as well as other craft and sewing projects for magazines including *Better Homes and Gardens, Family Circle, Woman's Day, Craftworks for the Home* and *Doll Reader*; and for craft leaflets such as *McCall's Creates*.

BLU FROGG GARDENS
1155 Llagas Rd.
Morgan Hill, CA 95037
Phone: (408)779-2719 PST
Fax: (408)779-2719
E-Mail: rdzek@garlic.com
Making dolls since: 1982
Selling dolls since: 1983

PRODUCT INFORMATION:

Mediums: Porcelain, cloth, poured latex, faustonielle, high-fire terra-cotta

Scope of work: Makes dolls in limited editions and designs all cloth doll patterns. They make all heads, bodies, wigs, accessories/props and molds. They also design and sew all clothing.

Price range: $100-1,000

Description of dolls: Dolls include Rumplefolk™, poured latex with illustrated backdrops and individual stories; Essence of Ivory, figures with enhanced sculptural qualities, usually adult female dancers; and Renaissance at noon, high-fire terra-cotta in the Italian style.

Catalog/price list: Color brochure, free

Mailing list: Write or call to be included.

Dolls sold: At shows, by mail, from artist's home/studio (in 1998)

Shows: Send SASE for list.

Home/studio visits: In 1998, by appointment only

Phone orders: M-F, daytime and early evening.

Fax orders: Available

Mail orders: Will ship to US, Canada, overseas. Prepayment required. Allow 3 weeks for Rumplefolk™, possibly longer for other dolls.

Shipping information: Shipped via UPS and US mail

Layaway: Regular payments, 6 months is ideal.

Return/exchange policy: Call first; 30-day limit

ADDITIONAL INFORMATION:

Blu Frogg Gardens dolls have been featured in *Doll Crafter* and *Contemporary Doll Collector*. The artists are members of MSDBA. They have 2 books: *Sculpting the Original Doll—The Blu Frogg Method* and *Mold-Making for the Original Doll—The Blu Frogg Method*, both published by Pollywogg Publications. They also teach sculpting and mold making seminars.

MARTHA BOERS AND MARIANNE REITSMA
1890 Parkside Dr.
Pickering, Ontario L1V 3S4
CANADA
Phone: (905)831-1183
Making dolls since: 1982
Selling dolls since: 1992

PRODUCT INFORMATION:

Mediums: Head, hands and feet sculpted from Super Sculpey with wire armature and cloth body.

Scope of work: Artists' dolls are one-of-a-kind direct sculptures. Artists make most heads, bodies, wigs and shoes and some accessories/props. They design and sew all clothing.

Price range: $1,000 and up

Description of dolls: Martha and Marianne's highly realistic dolls are inspired by moments in history, literary characters and sometimes outright fantasy. Marianne creates a wire armature for a figure about 17″ tall, decides on an interesting pose, and builds the figure with foil. She then sculpts the head, hands and feet out of Super Sculpey. Marianne is an expert at capturing wonderful expressive lifelike faces. After painting, the doll goes to Martha, who finishes the body, sews the clothes and adds hair and accessories. Martha creates intricate costumes with much attention to details. The fabrics are stressed, "aged," stained and carefully painted to give that "lived in" look.

Dolls sold: In retail doll shops, at shows, by mail and from artist's home/studio.

Shops: Call to request list.

Shows: Call to request list.

Home/studio visits: Please schedule in advance.

Phone orders: 9-8.

Mail orders: Will ship to US, Canada, overseas. Prepayment required. Order shipped immediately after payment.

Shipping information: Shipped via UPS. Shipping is included in the price of the doll.

Return/exchange policy: Each case is treated individually.

ADDITIONAL INFORMATION:
Martha and Marianne won 1st prize at the First Canadian Doll Convention in 1993. Their work has been featured in *Canadian Doll Journal* and *Contemporary Doll Collector*.

DEB BONHAM ART DOLLS
REPRESENTED BY: DOLLCO
22248 Cohasset St.
Canoga Park, CA 91303
Phone: (818)702-0315 PST
Fax: (818)702-9275
E-Mail: debbonham@aol.com
Making dolls since: 1991
Selling dolls since: 1992

PRODUCT INFORMATION:

Mediums: Cernit

Scope of work: Dolls are one-of-a-kind direct sculptures. Artist makes all heads, bodies, wigs and shoes and some accessories/props. She also designs and sews all clothing.

Price range: $700-1,500

Description of dolls: Deb's dolls are one-of-a-kind original sculptures. Each head, hand and foot (or shoe) is individually sculpted, by hand, in Cernit. No molds are used to aid in the sculpting process. Heads are designed so that they may be moved from side to side, as well as up and down. Wire armatures enable the hand-stitched cloth bodies to be posed. The ethnic

and historical costumes are handcrafted after carefully researching for authenticity.

Catalog/price list: Color photos, $5. Price list, free.

Mailing list: Write to be included.

Dolls sold: In retail doll shops, at shows.

Shops: Call for list.

Shows: Call for list.

Home/studio visits: Please call to arrange in advance.

ADDITIONAL INFORMATION:
Deb has been featured in *Dolls—The Collector's Magazine*, *Contemporary Doll Collector* and *Doll Designs*. She is a member of The Professional Doll Makers Art Guild.

CAROLE BOWLING
CAROLE BOWLING DOLLS
P.O. Box 116
West Roxbury, MA 02132
Phone: (617)327-5094 EST
Fax: (617)323-7547
E-Mail: ejbell@aol.com
Making dolls since: 1974
Selling dolls since: 1974

PRODUCT INFORMATION:

Mediums: Fimo, Lumicast resin, cloth

Scope of work: Artist makes limited edition and one-of-a-kind dolls. She makes all heads and bodies, most wigs and some shoes and accessories/props. Artist designs all clothing and hires a seamstress to sew for edition work; she designs and sews all clothing for one-of-a-kinds.

Price range: $600-4,500

Description of dolls: Carole's dolls are produced as small, high-quality, limited editions in a fine quality resin called Lumicast. Each doll is hand-painted in a fine art style, including the eyes. A new collection is created each year in time for Toy Fair, and typically includes 3 or 4 unique dolls limited to about 20 pieces each. She also sculpts several one-of-a-kind dolls per year.

Catalog/price list: Color catalog and price list, free.

Mailing list: Write or call to be included.

Dolls sold: In retail doll shops, at shows, by mail.

Shops: Send SASE for list.

Shows: Send SASE for list.

Fax orders: Fax catalog order form.

Mail orders: Will ship to US, Canada, overseas. Prepayment is required before delivery. Allow 6 weeks for delivery.

Shipping information: Shipped via UPS. Shipping fee is charged with final payment.

Discounts: Quantity discounts are available. Contact artist for details.

Return/exchange policy: All sales are final.

ADDITIONAL INFORMATION:
Carole was the 1992 DOTY winner in the cloth category and has been featured in *Contemporary Doll Collector* and *Dolls—The Collector's Magazine.* She is a member of NIADA.

ELIZABETH BRANDON
ELIZABETH BRANDON PORCELAIN ORIGINALS
5916 W. 53rd
Mission, KS 66202
Phone: (913)722-0140 CST
Making dolls since: 1970
Selling dolls since: 1979

PRODUCT INFORMATION:
Mediums: Porcelain

Scope of work: Artist creates limited edition dolls. Artist makes all heads, bodies, wigs, shoes, molds and most accessories/props and designs all clothing.

Price range: Up to $5,000

Description of dolls: Dolls are realistic figures of all ages, some in fixed poses and some completely jointed.

Dolls sold: At shows, by mail.

Shows: Artist attends annual NIADA conference.

Return/exchange policy: 10 days after delivery, dolls may be returned.

ADDITIONAL INFORMATION:
Brandon's work has been featured in

Dolls—The Collector's Magazine. She is a member of NIADA.

LOIS B. BRO
LBRO ORIGINAL DESIGNS
1312 Summers Dr.
Pendleton, SC 29670-9663
Phone: (864)646-8900 EST
Making dolls since: 1980
Selling dolls since: 1980

PRODUCT INFORMATION:
Mediums: PVC clays, porcelain, fabric

Scope of work: Artist's dolls are all one-of-a-kinds. She makes the heads, bodies, wigs, shoes, accessories and molds for all her dolls, and designs and sews all dolls' clothing.

Price range: $50-800

Description of dolls: Lois' dolls usually represent an era or concept of design. She designs original portrait dolls of children and adults on a commission basis.

Special orders: Photographs required. $100 nonrefundable deposit with commission. Client is not required to take finished piece if not satisfied. Allow 6 months.

Molds: Sometimes available directly from artist.

Price list: Free

Mailing list: Write or call to be included.

Dolls sold: From artist's home/studio.

Home/studio visits: Please schedule 1 week in advance.

Phone orders: M-F, 9-4.

Mail orders: Will ship to US, Canada, overseas. Prepayment required.

Shipping information: Shipped via UPS or US mail.

Layaway: 20% down

Return/exchange policy: Customer may return within 10 days for refund, minus shipping, no questions.

ADDITIONAL INFORMATION:
Lois has received several awards. Her dolls have been shown in Dollmaker's Magic and Celebration of the Doll since 1992. Her work has been featured in *Doll Life* and *Contemporary Doll Collector.* She is a member of UFDC Carolina Foothills Doll Club, UFDC Greenville Doll and Toy Collectors Club, Association of People Who Play With Dolls and Take This Doll and Stuff It (a cloth doll group). Lois has experience in teaching doll

sculpting and mold making seminars and has a video available. She creates historically correct clothing "from the skin out," and does antique doll restorations.

JOAN L. BROCHU
ALL HEARTS COME HOME FOR CHRISTMAS
Box 855, Center Rd.
Hardwick, VT 05843
Phone: (802)472-6839 EST
Making dolls since: 1992
Selling dolls since: 1994

PRODUCT INFORMATION:
Mediums: Cernit heads, hands, and feet or boots. Cloth stuffed body with a wire armature.

Scope of work: Artist makes one-of-a-kind direct sculptures. She makes the heads, bodies, hair and boots for all her dolls, and designs and makes most clothing.

Price range: $198 and up

Description of dolls: Joan's one-of-a-kind Santas have hand sculpted heads, hands and boots. Those with mittens have a mitten armature made by Joan. Some have cloth or fur boots. Many come with a quilt, tree wreath, collectible teddy, rabbit or toy bag.

Special orders: Will make a Santa in customer's choice of colors and materials, size, theme. Allow 6 weeks.

Catalog/price list: $3 for pictures. SASE for price list.

Mailing list: Write or call to be included.

Dolls sold: In retail doll shops, at shows, by mail, from artist's home/studio.

Shops: Call to request or send SASE for list.

Shows: Call to request or send SASE for list.

Home/studio visits: Please schedule in advance.

Phone orders: Anytime

Mail orders: Will ship to US, Canada,

overseas. Prepayment required, or COD.

Shipping information: Shipped via UPS.

ADDITIONAL INFORMATION:

Joan's work has been featured in *Santas Across America*, a video by Gaietto Production Co., *1994 Christmas Book of Early American Life*, *Golden Glo of Christmas Past*, *Contemporary Doll Collector* and *Snowbound Farms Collectibles*. She is a member of AADA, NECDAN and MSDBA.

EARLINE MAPLES BROHMER
CREATIONS BY EARLINE
4045A Transport St.
Palo Alto, CA 94303
Phone: For orders: (800)711-3590 PST
For information: (510)830-0381
Fax: (415)494-6235
Making dolls since: 1991
Selling dolls since: 1993

PRODUCT INFORMATION:

Mediums: Cernit

Scope of work: Dolls are one-of-a-kind direct sculptures. Artist makes all heads, bodies, wigs, shoes and most accessories/props. All clothing is designed by the artist and sewn by a seamstress.

Price range: $400-2,000

Description of dolls: Earline makes baby dolls, pretty women, and old people with character. She describes her dolls as having lots of feeling and emotion—happy and fun.

Special orders: Artist makes portrait dolls from photographs (all sides of head and hands and full shot of figure); also include height. Allow 6 weeks.

Catalog/price list: b&w and color brochure, pictures and price list, free.

Mailing list: Write or call to be included.

Dolls sold: In retail doll shops, at shows, from artist's home/studio.

Shops: Send SASE for list.

Shows: Send SASE for list.

Home/studio visits: Please schedule 2 weeks in advance.

Phone orders: M-F, 7-2.

Fax orders: Include name of doll.

Mail orders: Will ship to US, Canada, overseas. Prepayment is required. ½ down and ½ on receipt. Allow 3 weeks for delivery.

Shipping information: Shipped via UPS. Shipping is included in the price of the doll.

Layaway: 30% down, 90 days

Discounts: 2 or more dolls, 20% off listed price

Return/exchange policy: Refunds and exchanges available

ADDITIONAL INFORMATION:

Earline was awarded a Blue Ribbon for 1st place in Professional Class for Sculpting at Bohler Show, Anaheim, CA. She has been featured in *Contemporary Doll Collector* and *Doll Crafter*. She is a member of Professional Doll Makers Art Guild and ADAMA.

PATRICIA RYAN BROOKS
P.O. Box 1290
229 E. Main St.
Summerton, SC 29148
Phone: (803)485-4202 EST
Making dolls since: 1977
Selling dolls since: 1978

PRODUCT INFORMATION:

Mediums: Hand carved basswood, poly resin clay, porcelain

Scope of work: Dolls are one-of-a-kind direct sculptures. Artist makes all heads, bodies, wigs, and shoes and most accessories/props. She designs and sews all clothing.

Price range: $1,000-3,500

Description of dolls: Patricia's highly realistic likenesses of contemporary children are captured in one-of-a-kind, diminutive "clothed figurative sculptures." She also specializes in characters from children's literature, including both male and female adult figures, multi-figure vignettes, mother and child themes, and Father Christmas figures.

Special orders: Artist makes portrait dolls. She requires several photographs and 25% deposit when she is ready to begin the doll. Allow 4-6 weeks.

Molds: Artist sells molds through doll suppliers. Commercial molds are available from Bell Ceramics.

Designs manufactured by: Hamilton Collection (wood) and Danbury Mint (porcelain). Manufactured dolls are designed exclusively for these companies and are not duplicates of one-of-a-kind dolls made for collectors.

Mailing list: Write or call to be included.

Dolls sold: In retail doll shops (only occasionally), at the annual NIADA conference and occasionally other shows.

Shops: Call for list.

Shows: Call for list. Everyone on mailing list will be notified of upcoming show dates.

Home/studio visits: Please schedule 1 day in advance.

Phone orders: The artist will discuss orders over the phone, but all particulars must be in writing.

Mail orders: Will ship to US, Canada, overseas. Prepayment required. Allow 3-4 weeks for delivery.

Shipping information: Shipped via UPS, FedEx or method preferred by customer. Shipping is included in the price of the doll (unless customer requests special overnight delivery).

Discounts: Available for multi-doll orders, like portrait dolls of 2 or more children from the same family.

Return/exchange policy: Satisfaction guaranteed

ADDITIONAL INFORMATION:

Patricia has been featured in *Doll Reader*, *Dolls—The Collector's Magazine*, *Contemporary Doll Collector*, *Doll Castle News* and *Augusta Magazine*. She is a member of NIADA. She also does illustration, writing, public speaking and doll-making classes, and is the author of *Babes In Wood: An Introduction to Doll Carving* (©1980 Patricia Ryan Brooks).

DOC AND TASI BROWN
NATIVE SUN STUDIOS

Rt. 1, Box 528-J
Sylva, NC 28779
Phone: (704)586-9580 EST
Making dolls since: 1994
Selling dolls since: 1994

PRODUCT INFORMATION:

Mediums: Porcelain, cloth, polymer clays

Scope of work: Artists' dolls are one-of-a-kind direct sculptures or limited editions. Artists make all dolls' heads, bodies and molds and most wigs, shoes and accessories.

Price range: $40-800

Description of dolls: Doc and Tasi's dolls have extremely expressive faces which the artists achieve by carving the greenware. The dolls come in a variety of sizes, ages and cultures. Doc and Tasi work as a husband and wife team, with the Native American dolls coming from Tasi.

Special orders: A clear photo and description of subject are required for portrait dolls. Any special clothing requirements must be included with photo. Allow 8-12 weeks.

Price list: SASE

Dolls sold: At shows, by mail, and through agent

Shows: Send SASE for list.

Home/studio visits: Please schedule in advance.

Phone orders: M-Sun, after 7 P.M. EST.

Mail orders: Will ship to US, Canada, overseas. Customer will be billed. Allow 8-10 weeks for delivery.

Shipping information: Shipped via UPS. Shipping is included in the price of the doll.

Return/exchange policy: Call for arrangements.

ADDITIONAL INFORMATION:

Native Sun Studio dolls have been featured in *Contemporary Doll Collector.* The artists are IFDM members.

GLADYS BROWN

1916 Chestnut
Holt, MI 48842
Phone: (517)694-8380 EST
Making dolls since: 1959
Selling dolls since: 1959

PRODUCT INFORMATION:

Mediums: Wood

Scope of work: Dolls are one-of-a-kind direct sculptures. Artist makes all heads, bodies, wigs, shoes and accessories/props. Artist designs and sews all dolls' clothing.

Price range: $500 and up

Description of dolls: Dolls are all hand carved of basswood and tupelo. They are in the 12"-14" size range. The dolls are made completely of wood and are jointed at shoulders, hips and, if the costume allows, at the neck. The dolls are mounted on a base, but may be removed and will stand alone. The artist works from folk art pictures and photographs and especially enjoys doing children from early studio portraits. Antique materials are used wherever possible. Accessories complete the "scene," including pets, toys, etc. Each outfit is thoroughly researched.

Special orders: Artist creates portrait dolls from photos. Project requires photographs or copies of folk art paintings.

Dolls sold: By mail

Phone orders: Accepted

Mail orders: Will ship to US, Canada, overseas. Customer will be billed.

Shipping information: Shipped via UPS. Postage and handling extra.

ADDITIONAL INFORMATION:

Artist has won many blue ribbons at national and regional UFDC events. She is a member of UFDC, Greater Lansing Doll Collectors Club, ODACA, Schoenhut Collectors Club and Friends of Hitty.

JEAN BROWN
"THE BROWN BRATS"

P.O. Box 65 307 Mill St.
Sheridan, MT 59747
Phone: (406)842-5158 MST
Fax: (406)842-5158
Making dolls since: 1993
Selling dolls since: 1994

PRODUCT INFORMATION:

Mediums: Cernit and Fimo clays

Scope of work: Dolls are one-of-a-kind direct sculptures. Artist designs all cloth doll patterns. She makes all heads and most bodies. She also makes some accessories/props; wigs and shoes are bought ready-made. Artist designs and sews all clothing.

Price range: $250-650

Description of dolls: Artist makes both boy and girl dolls, mostly of children 5-12 years old. Larger dolls sizes are 12" to 30" and can wear children's clothing and shoes, sizes 0 and 1. Most have their own sweater. Clothing is one-of-a-kind.

Special Orders: Artist makes some portrait dolls from photographs, both front and side views. She does not do babies. She requires at least half payment with order. Must give her 6 weeks for portrait dolls.

Catalog/price list: b&w catalog with price list, free

Dolls sold: In retail shops, at shows, by mail or from artist's home/studio

Home/studio visits: Please schedule a few days in advance.

Phone orders: M-F, 7-1:30 and 6-9.

Mail orders: Will ship to US. Prepayment required. Allow 2 weeks for delivery.

Shipping information: Shipped via UPS. Payment method decided at time of sale.

Layaway: 30% down unless other arrangements are made.

ADDITIONAL INFORMATION:
Jean's dolls have been featured in *Montana Standard* newspaper and in *Contemporary Doll Collector*. She also makes figurines.

LAUREL BROWN
LAUREL BROWN ORIGINALS
R. 2, Box 116A
St. James, MN 56081
Phone: (507)375-5524 CST
Making dolls since: 1992
Selling dolls since: 1995

PRODUCT INFORMATION:
Mediums: Cernit and resin (Lumicast)
Scope of work: The artist makes one-of-a-kind direct sculptures and limited editions of 35 dolls. She makes all heads, bodies, wigs, shoes and accessories/props. She also designs and sews all clothing.
Price range: Limited editions, $395; one-of-a-kinds, $300-1,000
Description of dolls: Laurel has been creating one-of-a-kind hand-sculpted dolls since 1993. Each setting is carefully constructed first on paper and then in the 3-dimensional scene that is necessary to "capture one moment of time" in a doll. She prefers real-life scenarios rather than fantasy scenes. She has recently added small limited editions that are cast in resin.
Mailing list: Write or call to be included.
Dolls sold: In retail doll shops, at shows, by mail, from artist's home/studio
Shops: Send SASE for list.
Shows: Send SASE for list. Everyone on mailing list will be notified of upcoming show dates.
Home/studio visits: Please schedule 2 days in advance.
Phone orders: Accepted
Mail orders: Will ship to US, Canada, overseas. 25% payment upon placing order, balance due COD.

Shipping information: Artist ships ground UPS unless otherwise requested; delivery is usually within 10 days.
Layaway: 25% down, 6 months. Delivery of doll will follow receipt of last payment.
Discounts: Quantity discounts and seasonal sales. Call for more details.
Return/exchange policy: Returns and/or exchanges will be handled with expediency if there is a flaw in the workmanship.

ADDITIONAL INFORMATION:
Laurel received a nomination for *Dolls* Award of Excellence 1995. She also has been featured in *Dolls—The Collector's Magazine*. She is a member of Professional Dollmakers Art Guild.

RUTH ALDEN BROWN
1606 SW Heather Dr.
Grants Pass, OR 97526-5830
Phone: (541)471-1750 PST
Making dolls since: 1976
Selling dolls since: 1978

PRODUCT INFORMATION:
Mediums: Wood
Scope of work: Artist's dolls are one-of-a-kind direct sculptures made entirely of wood. Artist makes all heads, bodies and wigs and some shoes. She designs and makes all clothing.
Price range: $700
Description of dolls: Ruth's dolls are made of basswood, and each is hand carved. The bodies are one design, but because of the hand carving vary a little. The heads are usually portraits. Ruth only sculpts children. Dolls are dressed to match the picture of the person. The wigs are human hair. Dolls are spring jointed (neck, shoulders, elbows, hips and knees).
Special orders: Artist makes portrait

dolls from photos. Job requires $4 \times 5''$ or larger full-face portrait of a child age 2-6, including eye color, hair color and clothing color. Allow 6-12 months for job's completion (uusually less than 6 months, depending on the amount of orders).
Price list: Color pictures available on request.
Dolls sold: At shows and by mail
Shows: Send SASE for list.
Mail orders: Will ship to US, Canada. When doll is finished, customer is sent picture, and if they like it, then they send payment. Doll is shipped as soon as payment is received.
Shipping information: Shipped via UPS, $7-10 depending on where shipped.
Layaway: 25% down, 6 months after doll is finished
Return/exchange policy: Since dolls are sold on pre-approval, there are no returns.

ADDITIONAL INFORMATION:
Artist has won 1st, 2nd and 3rd place awards in UFDC Conferences from 1990 to 1994 (Regions 1 and 25). Brown is a member of ODACA, Dolls of the Attic of Southern Oregon, and Grants Pass Doll Collectors.

SONJA BRYER
PORCELAIN BY SONJA BRYER
4108 Beechwood Dr.
Bellbrook, OH 45305
Phone: (513)848-4828 EST
Making dolls since: 1978
Selling dolls since: 1980

PRODUCT INFORMATION:
Mediums: Porcelain, wax
Scope of work: Dolls are created in limited editions of 25. Artist makes all heads, some bodies, wigs, shoes, accessories/props, molds. Artist designs all dolls' clothing.

Price range: $500-1,800

Special orders: Artist makes portrait dolls from photos. Starting price is $4,000. Customer may submit pictures. If the child is especially cute or beautiful the artist may work a special deal. Allow 6 months, depending on artist's work load at the time.

Designs manufactured by: Ashton-Drake

Price list: Free with large SASE.

Mailing list: Write or call to be included.

Dolls sold: In retail shops, at shows

Shops: Send SASE for list.

Shows: Send SASE for list.

Phone orders: Accepted

Mail orders: Will ship to US, Canada, overseas. Prepayment required. Allow 4-6 weeks for delivery.

Shipping information: Shipped via UPS, FedEx.

Layaway: Call for terms

Return/exchange policy: Call first before returning.

ADDITIONAL INFORMATION:

Sonja was nominated for DOTY awards in 1990, 1992 and 1996. Her work has appeared in *Dolls—The Collector's Magazine*, *Contemporary Doll Collector* and *Doll Reader*. She is a member of UFDC and ODACA. She is also a fashion illustrator, paper doll artist and figurine sculptor.

KAT BUNKER
P.O. Box 593
North Reading, MA 01864
Phone: (508)664-3571 EST
Making dolls since: 1988
Selling dolls since: 1988

PRODUCT INFORMATION:

Mediums: Polymer clays, Paperclay

Scope of work: Dolls are one-of-a-kind direct sculptures. Artist makes all heads, bodies, wigs, shoes and accessories/props. Artist designs and sews all dolls' clothing.

Price range: $400-1,500

Description of dolls: Kat's pieces have ranged from realistic portrait work to fantasy figures, from Native American and other tribal figures to characters from other countries.

Special orders: Artist does special orders for special characters or ideas, as well as for portrait dolls. Portrait dolls are worked from a variety of photographs, including at least one very clear front view and profile view. All details are discussed before work begins. Allow 2-3 months.

Mailing list: To advertise classes held in artist's home/studio. Write or call to be included.

Dolls sold: By mail or from artist's home/studio.

Home/studio visits: Please schedule 1 week-1 month in advance.

Phone orders: Leave message on answering machine. Artist will call back.

Mail orders: Will ship to US, Canada, overseas. Prepayment required. Customer will be billed for shipping.

Shipping information: Shipped via UPS. Shipping is included in the price of the doll.

ADDITIONAL INFORMATION:

Kat's work has appeared in a series of 6 articles on portrait sculpture in *Doll Crafter*.

MARY ALICE BYERLY
MARY BYERLY ORIGINALS
1497 Roslyn Rd.
Grosse Point Woods, MI 48236
Phone: (313)881-7467 EST
Fax: (313)881-7607
Making dolls since: 1989
Selling dolls since: 1989

PRODUCT INFORMATION:

Mediums: Porcelain

Scope of work: Artist makes one-of-a-kind and limited editions of 5-10 dolls. She makes all heads, bodies, shoes, accessories/props and molds and most wigs. She also designs and sews all clothing.

Price range: $600-4,000

Description of dolls: Creates character dolls and one-of-a-kind vignettes, including Santas, elves and whimsical characters.

Molds: Directly from artist.

Dolls sold: In retail doll shops, at shows, from artist's home/studio.

Shops: Send SASE for list.

Home/studio visits: Please schedule in advance.

Phone orders: Accepted

Mail orders: Will ship to US, Canada, overseas. Allow 6 weeks for delivery.

Shipping information: Shipped via UPS. Shipping is included in the price of the doll.

Layaway: ½ down, 1 year

Return/exchange policy: Return as shipped within 10 days of receipt. Doll must be in same condition as shipped.

ADDITIONAL INFORMATION:

Mary Alice has been featured in *Dolls— the Collector's Magazine*; *Contemporary Doll Collector*; *Santa Dolls—Historical to Contemporary*, by Ann Bahar (Hobby House Press); *The Doll by Contemporary Artists*, by Wendy Lavitte and Kristina Goddu (Abbeville Press); and *Black Dolls II*, by Mita Perkins.

CHERI CALVERT
ANTELOPE MOUNTAIN DESIGNS
906 Coeur d'Alene Ave.
Coeur d'Alene, ID 83814
Phone: (208)765-7754 PST
Making dolls since: 1985
Selling dolls since: 1985

PRODUCT INFORMATION:

Mediums: Leather

Scope of work: Dolls are created in limited editions of 10-25. Artist makes all heads, bodies, shoes, molds and some accessories/props. Artist designs and sews all dolls' clothing.

Price range: $300-1,000

Description of dolls: Cheri's leather sculptures carry with them a breath of fresh mountain air, a feeling of rich earthiness, and a simple country charm, all representative of the love that goes into the meticulous hand stitching of each limited edition and one-of-a-kind piece. Cheri began working in leather in 1973. The influence of Native American culture and her time spent living in Alaska and the Northern Rockies is evident in her designs and her desires to preserve an ancient craft. She created her first mountain man doll in the spring of 1985. Faces were crude back then, produced by stretching deerskin over a Styrofoam ball and using bead headed pins for the eyes. The ensuing years and the development of sculpting and mold-making skills have refined this unique deerskin face to capture the hearts of many.

Special orders: Artist makes special order dolls. Requires 20% deposit. Allow 6-8 weeks.

Catalog price list: Color brochure and price list, $2.

Mailing list: Write or call to be included.

Dolls sold: In retail doll shops, at shows, by mail, from artist's home/studio.

Shows: Call or send SASE for list.

Home/studio visits: Please schedule in advance.

Phone orders: T-Sat, 9-5.

Mail orders: Will ship to US, Canada, overseas. Prepayment required. Allow 6-8 weeks for delivery.

Shipping information: Shipped via UPS. Shipping is included in the price of the doll.

Layaway: Flexible terms

Return/exchange policy: 100% satisfaction guaranteed. Full refund or exchange within 30 days of receipt.

ADDITIONAL INFORMATION:
Calvert received blue ribbons at the Dollmaker's Challenge sponsored by *Doll Reader* and Silver Dollar City in Branson, Missouri, in 1990 and 1991. Calvert's work has appeared in *Doll Artistry* and *Early American Life*. She is a member of ODACA amd UFDC.

MARGERY CANNON
MARGERY CANNON ORIGINALS
985 Vista View Dr.
Salt Lake City, UT 84108
Phone: (801)583-0118 MST
Making dolls since: 1987
Selling dolls since: 1987

PRODUCT INFORMATION:
Mediums: Cloth

Scope of work: Dolls are one-of-a-kind direct sculptures. Artist designs patterns for all cloth dolls. Artist makes all heads, bodies, wigs and shoes and most accessories/props. Artist designs and sews all dolls' clothing.

Price range: $600-1,000

Description of dolls: Margery's dolls are cut from her own patterns, sewn together, and then stuffed around a wire armature. Teeth are of Cernit. Inset glass eyes are fringed with eyelashes made from silk chiffon threads.

Dolls sold: In retail doll shops, at shows, by mail, from artist's home/studio.

Shops: Call for list.

Shows: Call for list.

Home/studio visits: Please schedule 1 day in advance.

Phone orders: Call anytime

Mail orders: Will ship to US, Canada, overseas. Prepayment is required. Allow 1 week for delivery.

Shipping information: Shipped via US mail. Shipping is included in the price of the doll.

Layaway: Flexible terms

Return/exchange policy: Returns accepted if not satisfied.

ADDITIONAL INFORMATION:
Margery has received 3 DOTY nominations; 2nd place in Global Doll Society competition; 2 awards at the 3rd (juried) International Art Competition for the Museum of Church History and Art; and a nomination for the 1995 One-of-a-Kind

Dolls Classic Award. In four regional cloth doll shows, Margery's dolls won 4 1st places in class; 4 1st places in division; 4 Judge's Choice; and 4 Viewer's Choice awards. Her work has been featured in *Contemporary Doll Collector*, *Doll Life*, *The Cloth Doll*, *Doll Reader*, *Dolls*, *Doll Artistry* and *Sew News*.

JENNIFER CANTON
11192 Olde Town Place
Smithfield, VA 23430
Phone: (804)357-9656 EST
E-Mail: jcanton619@aol.com
Making dolls since: 1993
Selling dolls since: 1993

PRODUCT INFORMATION:
Mediums: Polymer clays (Fimo, Cernit, Super Sculpey)

Scope of work: Dolls are one-of-a-kind direct sculptures. Artist makes all heads, bodies, wigs and shoes. She also designs and sews all clothing.

Price range: $95-2,400

Description of dolls: Jennifer works exclusively with polymer clays, antique and modern fabrics, trims and natural fibers. She strives to impart the essence of life's experiences to her one-of-a-kind figures.

Special orders: Contact artist about special requests. Photographs required for portrait dolls. 50% deposit required, balance due on completion. Allow 6-8 weeks for delivery.

Price list: Free

Mailing list: Write to be included.

Dolls sold: At shows, by mail, from artist's home/studio.

Shows: Everyone on mailing list will be notified of upcoming show dates.

Home/studio visits: Please schedule 24 hours in advance.

Phone orders: M-F, 9-6.

Mail orders: Will ship to US, Canada.

Prepayment is required. Allow 6-8 weeks for delivery.

Shipping information: Shipped via UPS. Shipping is included in the price of the doll.

Layaway: ½ down, balance within 4 months

Return/exchange policy: All sales final

ADDITIONAL INFORMATION:

Jennifer is a winner of the Thelma Akers Memorial Award—Peninsula Fine Arts Center, and the 1994 Juried Exhibition—Newport News, VA. Jennifer has been featured twice in *Contemporary Doll Collector.* She is a member of AADA and Original Doll Artists Association, Longwood, FL.

DIANNE CARTER AND MOLLY KENNEY FANTASY DOLL WORKS

2845 Lakeview Dr.
Santa Cruz, CA 95062
Phone: For orders: (408)475-3443 PST
For info: (510)339-9091
Fax: (408)475-3443
Making dolls since: 13 years (Molly) and 7 years (Dianne)
Selling dolls since: 13 years (Molly) and 7 years (Dianne)

PRODUCT INFORMATION:

Mediums: Dianne: polymer clays. Molly: Fabrics, feathers, furs.

Scope of work: Dolls are one-of-a-kind direct sculptures or limited editions of up to 20. Artists make all heads, bodies and shoes, most wigs and accessories/props, some molds. Molly designs and sews all dolls' clothing.

Price range: $150-1,100 (wholesale)

Description of dolls: Fantasy Doll Works is a collaboration of the talents of Molly Kenney and Dianne Carter. Each piece is carefully and individually created. Dianne sculpts heads and feet and uses fine quality blown glass eyes. Molly fashions cloth bodies on wire armatures and designs and sews costumes using both vintage and new fabrics, feathers, furs and skins. The images are both fantasy and realistic and reflect a wide variety of topics and moods.

Special orders: Artists make portrait dolls from photos and other custom dolls. Artists will work individually with the buyer to arrive at a design.

Allow 8-12 weeks for project's completion.

Mailing list: Write or call to be included.

Dolls sold: In retail doll shops, at shows, by mail and from artist's home/studio.

Shops: Call for list.

Shows: Call for list.

Phone orders: Anytime

Fax orders: Fax order along with name, address, phone. Send deposit of 25%.

Mail orders: Will ship to US, Canada, overseas. Prepayment is required or will COD. Allow 8-12 weeks for delivery.

Shipping information: Shipped via UPS. Shipping is added to price which is prepaid, sent COD or billed.

Layaway: Terms negotiable

Return/exchange policy: Return only if broken in shipment. Exchange only with artists' approval.

ADDITIONAL INFORMATION:

Dianne and Molly were nominated for a *Dolls* Award of Excellence in 1995. They are members of the AADA and the Professional Doll Makers Art Guild. Dianne makes figurines—a line of 20 called "Ondine Figures." Dianne has been a newspaper illustrator for 10 years.

GENNIE CARTMILL
GENNIE CARTMILL CREATIONS
1864 W. 190 South
Rexburg, ID 83440
Phone: (208)356-4359 EST
Making dolls since: 1994
Selling dolls since: 1994

PRODUCT INFORMATION:

Mediums: Cernit

Scope of work: Dolls are one-of-a-kind direct sculptures. Artist makes all heads, bodies and shoes; some wigs and accessories/props. Artist designs and sews all doll's clothing.

Price range: $800-5,000

Description of dolls: Gennie Cartmill creations are hand-sculpted individually with meticulous care by the artist in Cernit clay (bodies are soft sculptured). The costumes have been designed, created, sewn and hand-detailed by the artist. Additional touches and accessories (most made by the artist) complete the unique heirloom treasure.

Special orders: Artist creates portrait dolls from photos. Project requires good, clear close-up photographs, including profile and/or ¾ shots of face. Each doll takes from 100-150 hours. Allow 1-3 months for project's completion.

Dolls sold: At shows, by mail, from artist's home/studio.

Shows: Call for list.

Home/studio visits: Please schedule 1 day in advance.

Phone orders: Evenings (after 6)

Mail orders: Will ship to US, Canada, overseas. Prepayment is required or COD. Allow 1 week at the latest for delivery.

Shipping information: 2 day air. Cost is added to price of doll (average is $25).

Layaway: $100 minimum monthly until paid

Discounts: Discounts are given ($100 off) for 2 dolls purchased

Return/exchange policy: Doll can be returned up to 30 days (negotiable) after receipt of doll if unhappy with doll for *any reason* (workmanship, quality, etc.). If part of doll is broken, that section will be resculpted.

ADDITIONAL INFORMATION:

Gennie's work was nominated for a 1995 *Dolls* Award of Excellence. Her work has appeared in *Contemporary Doll Collector* and *Dolls—The Collector's Magazine.* She is a member of the Professional Dollmakers Guild and the AADA. She is also an oil painter, illustrator, watercolorist, potter, sculptor, pen and ink and pencil artist.

> "IMAGINATION IS THE ARTIST'S TENDER, TO BE FREELY SHARED WITH OTHERS."
> *Glennis Dolce, The Porcelain Rose, Long Beach, CA*

MICHAEL CARTMILL
MICHAEL CARTMILL ORIGINALS
530 S. Dobson #259
Mesa, AZ 85202
Phone: (602)649-2911
Making dolls since: 1994
Selling dolls since: 1994

PRODUCT INFORMATION:
Mediums: Cernit, clay
Scope of work: Dolls are one-of-a-kind direct sculptures. Artist makes all heads, bodies, wigs and shoes and most accessories/props. Artist designs and sews all dolls and clothing.
Price range: $300-800
Description of dolls: All dolls are individually sculpted by the artist, including heads, hands and feet (or shoes). Soft body sculpturing with wire armatures are also used. The costumes have been created, sewn and hand detailed by the artist. Additional touches and accessories complete these heirloom treasures.
Special orders: Artist makes portrait and special order dolls from photographs, with a specialization in North and South American Natives. Allow 2 months for project's completion.
Dolls sold: By mail, from artist's home/studio.
Home/studio visits: Please schedule in advance.
Mail orders: Will ship to US, Canada. Prepayment is required. Other arrangements can be made. Allow 1 week for delivery.
Shipping information: Shipped via UPS. Shipping is included in the price of the doll.
Layaway: $100/month until paid, or other arrangements can be made.
Discounts: If 2 or more dolls are bought at once
Return/exchange policy: Within 30 days

for reasons of workmanship, quality or damage from shipment.

ANTONETTE CELY
3592 Cherokee Rd.
Atlanta, GA 30340-2749
Phone: (770)936-9851 EST
E-Mail: donnybob@netdepot.com
Making dolls since: 1982

PRODUCT INFORMATION:
Mediums: Cloth. Faces are cloth over molded Fimo or Sculpey.
Scope of work: Dolls are one-of-a-kind direct sculptures, or artist designs patterns for cloth dolls. Artist makes all heads, bodies, wigs, shoes, accessories/props and molds. Artist designs and sews all dolls' clothing.
Price range: $1,000
Description of dolls: Dolls are one-of-a-kind cloth ¼ scale. Dolls average 16″ in height. Artist specializes in nudes and historically costumed women dolls and works mainly on commission.
Special orders: Artist makes portrait dolls from photos. Details for commissions are worked out between artist and client. All specifics are put in writing and signed by both parties before any money changes hands. Allow 1 year for project's completion.
Mailing list: Write to be included.
Dolls sold: By mail
Phone orders: M-F, 9-5
Mail orders: Will ship to US, Canada, overseas. ½ down payment when ordering. Allow up to 12 months for delivery.
Shipping information: Shipped via UPS. Customer is billed for shipping.
Return/exchange policy: Client has to examine doll and decide whether to accept it. If unsatisfied, it may be returned or exchanged.

ADDITIONAL INFORMATION:
Antonette's work has appeared in the periodicals *Doll Reader*, *Dolls—The Collector's Magazine*, *Contemporary Doll Collector*, *The Cloth Doll*, *Doll Life*, and also in *The Art of The Doll*, *Mother Plays With Dolls*, *The World's Most Beautiful Dolls*, and *A Crafter's Book of Angels* doll books. She is a member of NIADA and the Southern Highland Craft Guild. Antonette also writes a column titled

"Costume Construction" for *The Cloth Doll* magazine. She is the author of the series *Dollmaking: Theory and Practice* (Volume One—Creating Your Own Fabric; Volume Two—Cloth Dollmaking).

KATHI CLARKE
KATHI CLARKE ORIGINALS
140 Jackson
Oconto, WI 54153
Phone: (414)834-2968 CST
Making dolls since: 1980
Selling dolls since: 1982

PRODUCT INFORMATION:
Mediums: Cloth, needle sculpture
Scope of work: Artist designs all patterns for cloth dolls. Artist makes all heads, bodies, wigs, shoes and some accessories/props. Artist designs and sews all doll's clothing.
Price range: $175-200
Description of dolls: Dolls are about 6″ tall on wire armatures, including fingers to make them more poseable.
Special orders: Artist makes "similar, but not exact" portrait dolls from photographs. She requires pictures and description of hair color, eye color and any special features. Allow 1 month for completion of order.
Designs manufactured by: L.L. Knickerbocker Co., Inc., Ashton-Drake.
Price list: Send SASE for list.
Dolls sold: In retail doll shops, at shows, by mail, from artist's home/studio, doll conventions.
Shows: Send SASE for list.
Home/studio visits: Please schedule 2 days in advance.
Phone orders: M-F, 9-5
Mail orders: Will ship to US, Canada, overseas. Prepayment is required. Allow 2 weeks for delivery.
Shipping information: Shipped via UPS. Shipping is added to price of doll.

Layaway: 25% down with monthly payments.

Discounts: Multiple orders

Return/exchange policy: Layaway return—down payment of 20% kept for storage.

ADDITIONAL INFORMATION:
Clarke has won blue ribbons at doll conventions, and her work has been featured in *Dolls—The Collector's Magazine.* Clarke is a member of ODACA, AADA and UFDC. She also makes teddy bears, bunnies and kitties.

MARCI COHEN
MARCI COHEN STUDIO
267 Concord Dr.
Freehold NJ 07728
Phone: (908)462-4033 EST
Making dolls since: 1985
Selling dolls since: 1989

PRODUCT INFORMATION:
Mediums: Porcelain, wax-over-porcelain, Cernit

Scope of work: Dolls are created in limited editions. Artist makes all heads, bodies and molds, some wigs and shoes. Artist designs and sews some dolls' clothing.

Price range: $50-2,000

Description of dolls: Dolls are all ages, from babies to adults.

Special orders: Requires full face and profile photo, 8 × 10 desirable. Allow 3 months for completion.

Designs manufactured by: Lloyd Middleton's Royal Vienna Collection, Effanbee Doll Company

Dolls sold: In retail doll shops, by mail.

Shops: Call for list.

Home/studio visits: Please schedule in advance.

Phone orders: M-F, 9-5.

Mail orders: Will ship to US. Allow 3 months for delivery.

Shipping information: Shipped via UPS, FedEx. Shipping is included in the price of the doll.

Layaway: 50% down at time of order, balance when doll is completed and ready to be shipped.

ADDITIONAL INFORMATION:
Cohen's work was nominated for the *Dolls* Award for Excellence for 3 years. Her work has appeared in *Doll Reader* and *Dolls—The Collector's Magazine.*

DEBORAH COLSTON
R.R.#2, 7 Riverview Rd.
Seagrave, Ontario L0C 1G0 CANADA
Phone: (905)985-8919 EST
Fax: (905)985-3537
Making dolls since: 1993
Selling dolls since: 1993

PRODUCT INFORMATION:
Mediums: Cernit

Scope of work: Dolls are one-of-a-kind direct sculptures. Artist makes all heads, bodies, wigs and shoes and most accessories/props. She also designs and sews all clothing.

Price range: $550-1,500

Description of dolls: Dolls bodies are cloth with a wire armature. The head, hands, feet, lower limbs and chest (depending on the figure) are hand sculpted. Fabric for costumes are often hand painted, beaded or embroidered. The artist uses purchased eyes, and mohair or human hair for the handmade wigs. Inspired by Indonesian puppets, she also creates exotic rod puppets.

Dolls sold: In retail doll shops, at shows, by mail, from artist's home/studio by appointment.

Shops: Call or send SASE for list.

Shows: Call or send SASE for list.

Home/studio visits: Please schedule 1 week in advance.

Phone orders: M-F, 9-3:30.

Mail orders: Will ship to US, Canada, overseas. Prepayment required. Allow 2 weeks if dolls are already made.

Shipping information: Priority US mail. Mail check to artist; when received and cleared doll will be sent. Shipping paid by customer.

Layaway: 25% deposit, 90 days; payment in full before shipping.

Return/exchange policy: Will repair dolls if damaged in shipping.

ADDITIONAL INFORMATION:
Deborah is a member of AADA.

JUDITH L. CONDON
WEHRLY DOLLS
3226 Mayflower St.
Jacksonville, FL 32205
Phone: (904)389-8075 EST
Making dolls since: 1972
Selling dolls since: 1972

PRODUCT INFORMATION:
Mediums: Porcelain

Scope of work: Dolls are created in limited editions of 10-25. Artist designs patterns for all cloth dolls. Artist makes all heads, bodies, wigs, shoes, accessories/props and molds. Artist designs and sews all dolls' clothing.

Price range: $300-900

Description of dolls: Judith's dolls are all porcelain and jointed usually at the neck, shoulders, elbows, wrists, waist, hips, knees and ankles. They range in size from 7" to 22".

Special orders: Artist makes portrait dolls from photographs. Requirements vary, but good photos and measurements are necessary. Allow 6 months.

Mailing list: Write to be included.

Dolls sold: By mail, from artist's home/studio.

Home/studio visits: Please schedule 1-3 days in advance.

Phone orders: Accepted

Mail orders: Will ship to US, Canada, overseas. Prepayment is required. Delivery time depends on the order.

Shipping information: Shipped via UPS, FedEx. In US, cost of shipping is included in price of doll. In Canada and overseas, shipping is added to price.

Layaway: Flexible

Return/exchange policy: Artist sends

photo of the completed doll before mailing. If customer is not happy with the doll, exchange or return available (if doll is in good condition).

ADDITIONAL INFORMATION:
Artist is an NIADA member.

CHRISTIE CUMMINS
CHRISTIE CUMMINS DOLLS

5901 Warner Ave., Suite 389
Huntington Beach, CA 92649
Phone: (714)843-6734 PST
Fax: (714)841-8934
Making dolls since: 1990
Selling dolls since: 1993

PRODUCT INFORMATION:

Mediums: Porcelain direct sculpture in clay, porcelain slip cast, resin

Scope of work: Artist makes one-of-a-kind direct sculptures and limited editions of 20-30 porcelain dolls and 50 resin dolls. She makes heads, bodies and molds for all dolls and wigs for most dolls. Shoes are bought ready-made. She also designs and sews clothing or buys antiques.

Price range: $700-3,000

Description of dolls: Artist's one-of-a-kinds are limited to 12 dolls in original sculpture form. Her molded porcelain slip cast dolls are in small limited editions. A new medium for 1996 is resin.

Special orders: Artist makes portrait dolls. Child must be at least 6 years of age. Allow 3-6 months to complete a portrait doll.

Mailing list: Write or call to be included.

Dolls sold: In retail shops and by mail.

Shops: Call for list.

Phone orders: M, T, Th, F, 5-9. W, Sat, 9-5.

Fax orders: Must have doll name and the collector or store name; a signed contract with a deposit is a must for processing.

Mail orders: Will ship to US, Canada, overseas. Prepayment required.

Shipping information: Shipped via FedEx.

Layaway: 6 months. 20% down, 5 months. Signed contract required.

Return/exchange policy: All sales final.

ADDITIONAL INFORMATION:
Christie has been featured in *Dolls—The Collector's Magazine, Contemporary Doll Collector* and *Doll Reader.* She is a member of MSDBA.

NORMA CUNNINGHAM

2110 Royal Blvd.
Elgin, IL 60123
Phone: (708)695-7371 CST
Making dolls since: 1990
Selling dolls since: 1991

PRODUCT INFORMATION:

Mediums: Sculpey, Fimo, Cernit

Scope of work: Artist makes one-of-a-kind direct sculptures and designs all cloth doll patterns. She makes all heads, bodies, wigs and shoes and some accessories/props. She also designs and sews clothing.

Price range: $100-600

Description of dolls: Norma makes all types of dolls from children to Santas. Most have clay head, hands and feet with cloth bodies.

Mailing list: Write or call to be included.

Dolls sold: In retail doll shops, at shows, by mail, from artist's home/studio.

Shops: Send SASE for list.

Shows: Send SASE for list.

Home/studio visits: Please schedule 1 week in advance.

Phone orders: Accepted

Mail orders: Will ship to US. Deposit required. Allow 4 weeks for delivery.

Shipping information: Shipped via UPS, FedEx. Payment discussed individually.

ADDITIONAL INFORMATION:
Norma is a member of AADA.

PEGGY DEY
TIMELESS TREASURES

2909 Oxford Rd.
Lawrence, KS 66049-2828
Phone: (913)842-6416 CST
Fax: (913)841-0591
Making dolls since: 1989
Selling dolls since: 1991

PRODUCT INFORMATION:

Mediums: Porcelain, vinyl limited editions of 500 pieces

Scope of work: Dolls are created in limited editions of 10-25. Artist makes most heads, bodies and molds; some shoes and accessories/props. Artist designs and sews all dolls' clothing.

Price range: $900-4,000

Description of dolls: Peggy's dolls are primarily toddlers ranging from 2-6 years old. Many dolls come with various props that further define their individuality. They consist of a porcelain head, shoulderplate, arms and legs on a cloth body. Each body incorporates a full-bodied armature for maximum poseability.

Special orders: Photos suggested for portrait dolls. If a child's face has special appeal, artist will agree to do a limited edition that can be marketed. She will also do special costume requests. Allow 3-6 months minimum.

Molds: Directly from artist and through doll suppliers. Send SASE for list of suppliers or call.

Designs manufactured by: Effanbee, Hamilton Collection, Dynamic Group for HSC.

Catalog/price list: Color, $7. Price list, free.

Mailing list: Write or call to be included.

Dolls sold: In retail doll shops.

Shops: Send SASE for list.

Home/studio visits: Please schedule 1 week in advance.

Phone orders: M-Sat, 9-5.

Fax orders: Include name of doll, quantity, shop address, etc.

Return/exchange policy: Contact within 30 days of delivery. Every effort will be made to correct problem. If not resolved, the customer will be given a credit.

ADDITIONAL INFORMATION:
Peggy's dolls have been nominated for DOTY Awards in 1992 and 1993 and the *Dolls* Award of Excellence in 1994. Her work has appeared in *Dolls—The Collectors Magazine*, *The World's Most Beautiful Dolls* and *Contemporary Doll Collector*.

> "ANYONE INTERESTED IN BUYING REPRODUCTION DOLLS SHOULD TAKE A CLASS TO MAKE AT LEAST ONE DOLL TO LEARN WHAT MAKES A REPRODUCTION DOLL A COLLECTIBLE DOLL."
> *Elna Meagher, Fantasia Dolls, Sparks, NV*

JACQUES DORIER WASHI DOLLS
Jacques Dorier
93 Shirley St.
Winthrop, MA 02152
Phone: (617)846-6582 EST
Fax: (617)846-4285
E-mail: washij@aol.com
Making dolls since: 1986
Selling dolls since: 1986

SHIRLEY TOWNSEND DOLAN
31 Lisa Lane
Bristol, RI 02809
Making dolls since: 1995
Selling dolls since: 1995

PRODUCT INFORMATION:
Mediums: Super Sculpey, Cernit, Fimo
Scope of work: All dolls are one-of-a-kind direct sculptures. Artist makes most heads, bodies, wigs, shoes and accessories/props. Artist designs and sews all doll's clothing.
Price range: $300-1,000 and up
Description of dolls: Doll sculptures include child and adult characters in creative vignettes. They are anatomically detailed, full body sculptured caricatures.
Dolls sold: From artist's home/studio

ADDITIONAL INFORMATION:
Dolan's work has been featured in *The Bristol Phoenix* of Bristol, Rhode Island. Dolan is a registered nurse and hobbyist doll artist. She advocates and promotes doll sculpting for therapeutic stress reduction and creative expression.

> "NEVER UNDERESTIMATE A DOLLMAKER!"
> *Pam Fitzpatrick and Jennifer Ranger,*
> *The Dollmakers, Monrovia, CA*

DOINA DONEAUD ("NINI")
"NINI DOLLS"
507 E. Chicago St.
Rapid City, SD 57701
Phone: (605)343-0380 MST
Making dolls since: 1980
Selling dolls since: 1980

PRODUCT INFORMATION:
Mediums: Cloth (felt)
Price range: $400-500
Description of dolls: Nini's character dolls imitate true portraits of children. Dolls have attached eyes, made with artist's original design. Bodies are molded in felt using original body and limb molds; no seams in the front of arms and legs. Size of dolls ranges from 10"-16". The dress is ethnic Romanian.
Special orders: Call or write to request special orders. Allow 6 weeks.
Dolls sold: In retail doll shops, at shows, by mail and from artist's home/studio
Phone orders: Accepted
Mail orders: Will ship to US, Canada, overseas. Customer will be billed.
Shipping information: Shipped via UPS. Shipping is included in the price of the doll.
Return/exchange policy: Call to discuss if doll is not acceptable.

ADDITIONAL INFORMATION:
Doina is a member of ODACA.

PRODUCT INFORMATION:
Mediums: Japanese Washi handmade paper
Scope of work: Average edition size is 25. Artist makes heads, bodies, wigs, shoes, accessories/props and molds for all dolls. Artist designs and produces all dolls' clothing.
Price range: $20-$2,000
Description of dolls: These Washi (Japanese handmade paper) dolls are made by folding or shaping by hand. No part of the doll is molded. They are slim figures, inspired by scenes or characters depicted in the Kabuki Theater and the Japanese prints Ukiyo-e.
Special orders: Allow 1-3 months
Catalog: b&w and color catalogs, free. Price list, free.
Mailing list: Write or call to be included.
Dolls sold: In retail dolls shops, at shows, by mail
Shops: Send SASE for list
Shows: Everyone on mailing list will be notified, or send SASE for list.
Home/studio visits: Please schedule 1 week in advance.
Phone orders: M-Sat, 10-6.
Fax orders: Fax catalog order form.
Mail orders: Will ship to US. Prepayment required. Allow 3-6 weeks for delivery.
Shipping information: UPS, COD. Shipping is added to cost of doll.
Layaway: Up to 5 months with credit card automatic billing. Deposit varies.

Discounts: 40% discount on wholesale orders

Return/exchange policy: Satisfaction guaranteed. Refund or credit available. Shipping and handling is non-refundable.

ADDITIONAL INFORMATION:
Jacques has been featured in *Contemporary Doll Collector* and *Dolls—The Collector's Magazine*. He is a member of APWPD and OPDAG. Jacques also teaches Washi doll making workshops and hat making for dolls, bears and humans. He has self-published a book called *Washi Doll Making*.

DOTTIE DUNSMORE
DOTTIE DUNSMORE ORIGINALS
6515 Mount Vista Rd.
Kingsville, MD 21087
Phone: (410)592-2228
Making dolls since: 1993
Selling dolls since: 1993

PRODUCT INFORMATION:

Mediums: Porcelain, Cernit, Sculpey, Fimo, Paperclay, plastilina

Scope of work: Most dolls are one-of-a-kind direct sculptures; porcelain dolls are made from original molds in limited editions of 5-30. Artist makes all heads and bodies, most shoes, and some wigs and accessories/props. Artist designs and sews all dolls' clothing.

Price range: $300-1,300

Description of dolls: Dottie tries to "capture the beauty of all generations. From the innocence of a child to the knowing look of an elder, my desire is to have my dolls express a mood, tell a story or generate a feeling."

Special orders: Requires photos of subject from all angles and complete information as to clothing and materials in writing. Artist makes portrait dolls from photos. Turnaround time depends on the order and current work load.

Catalog/price list: Single page color flyer, free

Mailing list: Write or call to be included.

Dolls sold: In retail doll shops, at shows, by mail, from artist's home/studio.

Shops: Call for list.

Shows: Call. Everyone on mailing list will be notified of upcoming shop dates.

Home/studio visits: Please schedule in advance.

Phone orders: Orders accepted anytime. Artist will return messages.

Mail orders: Will ship to US, Canada, overseas. Prepayment is required. Time allowed for delivery depends on availability of doll.

Shipping information: Shipped via UPS. Shipping is included in the price of the doll.

Layaway: Minimum 20% down. Balance due before delivery. Layaway not to exceed 90 days.

Return/exchange policy: No returns will be accepted without prior authorization. If box is damaged in shipping, do not accept delivery. If there is hidden damage, contact shipper immediately. For UPS claims, you must save all original cartons and packing material.

LEE DUNSMORE
LEE DUNSMORE ORIGINALS
255 W. 88th St. #3B
New York, NY 10024
Phone: (212)874-2259 EST
Fax: (212)579-9403
Making dolls since: 1993
Selling dolls since: 1993

PRODUCT INFORMATION:

Mediums: Cernit, Paperclay, cloth bodies

Scope of work: All the artist's dolls are one-of-a-kind direct sculptures. The artist makes all heads, bodies, shoes and accessories/props. The artist also makes some of the wigs. All clothing is designed by the artist.

Price range: $1,000-3,000

Description of dolls: Lee makes dolls that are realistic in appearance, covering a wide range of subject matter from young girls and boys to older men and women, including ethnic groups. Fantasy dolls are also included.

Designs manufactured by: Ashton-Drake Galleries

Dolls sold: In retail doll shops, at shows, by mail.

Shows: Call for list.

Shipping information: Shipped via UPS. Shipping is included in the price of the doll.

Return/exchange policy: All sales are final.

ADDITIONAL INFORMATION:
The artist won a *Dolls* Award of Excellence in 1994.

ROBBIE F. FAIR
SUNDAY'S CHILD
178 S. Quinsigamond Ave.
Shrewsbury, MA 01545
Phone: (508)798-3174 EST
Making dolls since: 1989
Selling dolls since: 1990

PRODUCT INFORMATION:

Mediums: Porcelain

Scope of work: Robbie makes one-of-a-kind dolls and limited editions of 3. All heads, bodies and molds and some wigs and shoes are artist-made. Clothing is sometimes purchased ready-made, and sometimes designed and made by artist.

Price range: $895-2,600

Description of dolls: Robbie's original sculptures depict children and teens. Their porcelain heads, arms and legs are attached to cloth bodies. Each child may be posed in multiple positions. Sizes range from 18″-36″.

Special orders: Portrait dolls and custom clothing available. Artist tries to honor all customer's special requests. Allow 18 months for delivery. Add 4-6 weeks for custom clothing.

Dolls sold: In retail doll shops, at shows, by mail.

Shops: Call or send SASE for list.

Phone orders: M-F, after 5.

Mail orders: Will ship to US, Canada, overseas. Prepayment required.

Shipping information: Shipped via UPS. Shipping is included in the price of the doll.

ADDITIONAL INFORMATION:

Robbie's work has appeared in *Contemporary Doll Collector, Dolls—The Collector's Magazine* and *Doll Reader.* Robbie is a member of the Global Doll Society.

DONNA FAVILLE
FAVILLE ORIGINAL DOLLS
15129 SE 184th St.
Renton, WA 98058
Phone: (206)226-9227 PST
Making dolls since: 1992
Selling dolls since: 1993

PRODUCT INFORMATION:

Mediums: Porcelain

Scope of work: Dolls are created in limited editions of up to 25. Artist makes all heads, bodies, wigs, shoes and molds; designs and sews all doll's clothing.

Price range: $500-1,200

Description of dolls: Donna creates elegant lady dolls in sizes 22"-39" with mohair and human hair wigs and glass paperweight eyes. Dolls are costumed in rich silks and brocades, some with hand embroidery and beaded work. Each series includes exotic ethnic dolls in African and Asian costumes.

Special orders: Artist accepts special orders for portrait dolls. Requires full front view photo no smaller than

3" × 3" of face. Allow 8-12 weeks.

Price list: Free

Mailing list: Write or call to be included.

Dolls sold: In retail shops, at shows, by mail

Shops: Call for list.

Shows: Call for list.

Home/studio visits: Please schedule in advance.

Phone orders: M-Sat, 8-8 PST.

Mail orders: Will ship to US, Canada, overseas. Customer will be billed. Allow 4-6 weeks for delivery.

Shipping information: Shipped via UPS. COD available.

Layaway: 25% down; 3 payments. (Longer term layaway also available through Regina's Doll Heaven in Seattle.)

Discounts: Wholesale buyers can receive 40% discount; retail buyers can receive a 20% discount for cash prepayment.

Return/exchange policy: May return within 30 days if doll is in good condition. Dolls damaged in shipping replaced promptly.

ADDITIONAL INFORMATION:

Donna received a nomination for a 1995 DOTY award. Her work has been featured in *Contemporary Doll Collector.*

MARGARET FINCH
106 Liberty Ave.
New Rochelle, NY 10805
Phone: For information: (914)633-3004 EST
Making dolls since: 1949
Selling dolls since: 1952

PRODUCT INFORMATION:

Mediums: Carved wood and needle-modeled cloth

Scope of work: The artist makes one-of-a-kind direct sculptures and designs all cloth doll patterns. She makes all

heads, bodies, wigs, shoes and accessories/props. She also designs and sews all clothing.

Price range: $500-4,000

Description of dolls: Margaret has been making dolls and collecting materials for 45 years and has a huge store of varied and beautiful fabrics, ribbons, laces, etc. In order to get correct colors and patterns, she sometimes dyes, paints or weaves. Her work includes nonhistorical dream-figures and her series, Images of the Goddess.

Special orders: Artist does special orders. She says that special orders must be a subject she can feel excited about doing. Piece may be refused at completion, but a 5% deposit at time of order is nonrefundable. Must give her at least a month to complete doll, but it depends on current work schedule, time required for research and difficulty of costume.

Mailing list: Write or call to be included.

Dolls sold: At shows, by mail, from artist's home/studio.

Shows: Everyone on mailing list will be notified. Call or send SASE for list.

Home/studio visits: Please schedule several weeks in advance.

Phone orders: Accepted

Mail orders: Will ship to US, Canada, overseas. Prepayment required.

Shipping information: Shipped via UPS. Shipping is included in the price of the doll.

Layaway: 20% down, 1 year.

Return/exchange policy: Doll delivered upon full payment. Piece may be refused and returned in mint condition, but 5% will be withheld from refund.

ADDITIONAL INFORMATION:

Margaret is featured in *The Doll by Contemporary Artists,* by Goddu and Lavitte, 1995; and has been featured in *Dolls—The Collector's Magazine.* She is a member of NIADA and National Doll and Toy Collectors Club. She also has written sev-

> "DOLLMAKERS SHOULD CREATE THEIR OWN STYLES. THIS GIVES EACH DOLL A SPECIAL INDIVIDUALITY AND KEEPS US ALL INTERESTED IN NEW TECHNIQUES AND IDEAS."
> *Ali Hansen, Childhood Fantasies, Carrollton, TX*

eral articles for souvenir journals and co-edited 2 issues of the NIADA souvenir journal.

MARGARET ("MAGGIE") FINCH AND MARTA FINCH-KOZLOSKY
TRANSCENDENCE
9 Catamount Lane
Bennington, VT 05201
Phone: (802)442-5520 EST (Marta), (914)633-3004 (Maggie)
Making dolls since: 1950 (Maggie); 1978 (Marta).
Selling dolls since: 1950 (Maggie); 1978 (Marta).

PRODUCT INFORMATION:
Mediums: Wood, cloth, modern low-fired synthetic clays
Scope of work: The artists make one-of-a-kind direct sculptures and design all cloth doll patterns. They make all heads, bodies, wigs, shoes and accessories/props. They also design and sew all clothing.
Price range: $2,000-5,000
Description of dolls: Dolls are made by a mother/daughter team, currently working together under the name Transcendence. (Maggie also works alone.) Dolls are usually historical figures, inspired by great literature or paintings—especially medieval or Renaissance. All sculpting is done by Marta. The eyes are either hand-painted or antique glass. The historical research and costuming for all Transcendence dolls is done by Maggie.
Special orders: The artists accept commissions, particularly for historical figures or dolls inspired by medieval or Renaissance paintings. A commissioned work may be refused upon completion, but a 3-5% deposit at time of order is nonrefundable. Allow

6 months to a year for completion of order.
Price list: Available with SASE. Photos are available at $1 each.
Mailing list: Write or call to be included.
Dolls sold: At shows (where one-of-a-kind dolls are featured), by mail, at NIADA annual conference.
Home/studio visits: Please schedule several weeks in advance.
Phone orders: Accepted
Layaway: 20-33⅓% down, payments up to about a year. Doll delivered when paid in full. If payments not completed, money refunded when doll sells to another buyer.

ADDITIONAL INFORMATION:
The artists have been featured in *Dolls— The Collector's Magazine*. They are members of NIADA.

CAROLYN FOLSOM
CAROLYN'S CREATIONS
164 DeWitt Ave.
Bangor, ME 04401
Phone: (207)945-3324 EST
Making dolls since: 1993
Selling dolls since: 1994

PRODUCT INFORMATION:
Mediums: Cernit with cloth bodies and Cernit shoes or bare feet
Scope of work: Dolls are one-of-a-kind direct sculptures. Artists makes most heads, bodies, wigs and shoes. For character dolls, she uses a body designed by Jack Johnston, then stuffs the body and soft sculptures. She designs and sews all clothing.
Price range: $200-275
Description of dolls: Carolyn's original character dolls have wire armature bodies, soft sculptured for a realistic shape. Their hands are sculptured to hold something such as a violin or fishing pole. Clothes are made espe-

cially for the occasion they represent. Baby dolls have sitting cloth bodies stuffed with fiberfill. Their heads, hands and feet are of sculptured Cernit; eyes are plastic. Heads turn from side to side to pose; arms and hands hold blankets or toys; feet are bare.
Price list: $1, refundable with purchase.
Dolls sold: At shows, by mail, from artist's home/studio
Shows: Call or send SASE for list.
Home/studio visits: Please schedule 1 day in advance.
Phone orders: Accepted
Mail orders: Will ship to US. Prepayment required.
Shipping information: Shipped via UPS. Shipping and handling prepaid.

ADDITIONAL INFORMATION:
Carolyn is a member of Maine-ly Doll Club and MSDBA.

MARY ELLEN FRANK
P.O. Box 021137
Juneau, AK 99802-1137
Phone: (907)364-2294 AST
Making dolls since: 1988
Selling dolls since: 1989

PRODUCT INFORMATION:
Mediums: Wood, Polyform with fabric bodies.
Scope of work: Artist's dolls are one-of-a-kind direct sculptures. Artist makes all heads, bodies, wigs and shoes and some accessories/props. She designs and sews all clothing.
Price range: $700-2,500
Description of dolls: Mary Ellen carves portraits of native American elders of the Canadian and Alaskan North using woods found in their homelands. She generally finds her subjects in historical photograph collections. The people are clad in garments based on tra-

ditional designs. Furs and leathers are those found where the people live. The artist sometimes tans these herself.

Special orders: Artist makes portrait dolls and prefers elderly people with character. She uses good b&w photographs, preferably profile, ¾ and full face. Must give her 1 year to complete a portrait doll.

Price list: Free

Mailing list: Write or call to be included.

Dolls sold: In retail doll shops, at shows, by mail, at fine art galleries.

Shops: Call or send SASE for list.

Shows: Call or send SASE for list.

Home/studio visits: Please schedule a week in advance.

Phone orders: M-F, 10-4.

Mail orders: Will ship to US, Canada, overseas. 25% deposit, then bill the rest. Allow 2-3 weeks for delivery.

Shipping information: Registered mail. Shipping is included in doll price.

Layaway: 25% down, 1 year

Discounts: Available to dealers purchasing 3 or more. Please contact to discuss.

Return/exchange policy: Allowed within 1 month.

ADDITIONAL INFORMATION:
Mary Ellen won the Juneau Arts and Humanities Council grant award in 1994 and an award of excellence at the Pacific NW Arts & Crafts Fair, Bellevue, WA, 1992. She has been featured in *Contemporary Doll Collector, Folk Art Magazine* and *NW Travel Magazine* and in *The Doll by Contemporary Artists* (Goddu and Lavitt, 1995). The artist's dolls are in permanent collections at the Rosalie Whyel Museum Of Doll Art, Bellevue, WA, and the Musee Des Poupées, Josselin, France. Her work is included in the 1996 exhibit "The Doll By Contemporary Artists" at the Museum of American Folk Art, New York City.

ELENA GEORGE/ELENA COLLECTIBLES
REPRESENTED BY: DOLLCO
22248 Cohasset St.
Canoga Park, CA 91303
Phone: (818)702-0315
Fax: (818)702-9275
Making dolls since: 1994

Selling dolls since: 1994

PRODUCT INFORMATION:

Mediums: Wax-over-porcelain, ceramic, Fimo, Sculpey, resin

Scope of work: Artist makes limited editions of 3-5 dolls and one-of-a-kind. She makes all heads, bodies, wigs, shoes, accessories/props and molds. She also designs and sews all clothing.

Price range: $800-8,000

Description of dolls: Elena's dolls are handcrafted and fashioned with carefully selected materials. Rare old pieces as well as new are combined and used to embellish the dolls. Artist is inspired by literary, folk, fantasy and southern characters. Each doll is researched and created in its entirety by the artist.

Catalog/price list: Color photos, $5. Price list, free.

Mailing list: Write to be included.

Dolls sold: In retail doll shops, at shows, from artist's home/studio, directly from DOLLCO

Shops: Call for list.

Shows: Call for list.

Home/studio visits: Please schedule 2 weeks in advance.

ADDITIONAL INFORMATION:
Creator of the tableau, "Dreams of Children," acquired by Demi Moore to be exhibited at the Doll Gallery and Museum.

JANET GERVAIS
J. GERVAIS PORTRAIT HEIRLOOM DOLLS
P.O. Box 474
Old Orchard Beach, ME 04064
Phone: (207)934-5011 EST
Making dolls since: 1992
Selling dolls since: 1992

PRODUCT INFORMATION:

Mediums: Wood, muslin, fiberfill

Scope of work: All dolls are one-of-a-kind direct sculptures. Artist makes most heads, bodies, shoes, accessories/props and molds. Artist designs and sews all dolls' clothing.

Description of dolls: J. Gervais Portrait Heirloom Dolls are created from photos. Each doll is made from clear pine, upon which the portrait is rendered in acrylic paints and then signed and dated. Head and body are wood; arms and legs are muslin and fiberfil. Soft arms and legs are attached and clothing is sewn in colors of customer's choice. All orders are special orders—specify dress/slacks for girls, women. Gervais has also created an 8-piece, limited edition series (of 50 each) called "Portraits of Antiquity." These are portrait dolls from selected antique photos, costumed in 1800s dress.

Special orders: Artist creates portrait dolls from photos. Send SASE for order form. There may be an extra charge for clothing such as a wedding dress or to recreate clothing as in photograph. Allow 8-10 weeks from receipt of order for delivery.

Price list: Send SASE for list.

Mailing list: Write to be included.

Dolls sold: At shows, by mail, samples in retail doll and gift shops

Shops: Send SASE for list.

Shows: Send SASE for list.

Home/studio visits: Please schedule in advance.

Phone orders: After 6 EST

Mail orders: Will ship to US, Canada, overseas. Prepayment is required. Allow 10 weeks for delivery.

Shipping information: Shipped via UPS, US mail

Return/exchange policy: If the customer is not satisfied with the portrait doll, artist will repaint the portrait at no additional charge. Customer must send clearer, additional photos.

ADDITIONAL INFORMATION:
Janet is a member of MSDBA. She also sculpts 10″-12″ figurines in fabric and clay. She is also a graphic artist who has illustrated children's books.

BARB GIGUERE
MEMORIES AND SMILES. . .
P.O. Box 124
Scarborough, ME 04070-0124
Phone: (207)883-0822 EST
E-Mail: bkhd60a@prodigy.com
Making dolls since: 1985
Selling dolls since: 1989

PRODUCT INFORMATION:
Mediums: Cernit, direct sculpt porcelain
Scope of work: Dolls are one-of-a-kind direct sculptures. Artist makes all heads and bodies, most wigs and shoes and some accessories/props. Artist designs and sews all doll's clothing.
Price range: $500-4,000
Description of dolls: Dolls reflect real people of all ages and range from 10½"-48". Each doll accurately portrays a real person. Each captures a memory—a moment in time.
Special orders: Artist makes portrait dolls from photos. Requires 6 to 12 photos of the person, including portrait and profile shots of the head. Allow 6 to 12 months for job's completion (depending on schedule at time of order and the doll itself).
Catalog/price list: b&w, $2; color, $4. Price list, send #10 SASE.
Mailing list: Write, call or e-mail to be included.
Dolls sold: In retail doll shops, at shows, by mail, from artist's home/studio or via computer.
Shops: Send SASE for list.
Shows: Send SASE for list. Everyone on mailing list will be notified.
Computer sales: Through Prodigy's online Original Artist Collectors Club
Home/studio visits: Please schedule 3 days in advance.
Phone orders: M-Sun, 10-8.
Fax orders: Include name of doll, your name, shipping address, phone number, fax number, Visa or MC number, expiration date and signature preferred. Specify preferred method of shipping—next day or 2-3 day.
Mail orders: Will ship to US, Canada, overseas. Prepayment required. Allow 1 week (if doll is ready for shipping when order is placed).
Shipping information: Shipped via UPS, FedEx, Priority Mail, Express Mail. Actual cost added to cost of doll.
Layaway: 25% nonrefundable deposit. Monthly payments thereafter not to exceed 4 months.
Discounts: MSDBA Collectors Club members
Return/exchange policy: Must notify within 48 hours of receipt—contact artist for arrangements.

ADDITIONAL INFORMATION:
Barb was named 1996 Doll Artist of the Year for "Dolls Along the Mohawk." She also received an Alumni Recognition Award for achievement—Maine College of Art and in 1994, and was appointed Executive Director of MSDBA by unanimous vote of membership. Barb's work has appeared in *Contemporary Doll Collector* and *Dolls—The Collectors Magazine.* She has written for numerous magazines, contributed to Betterway Books, and served as editor for the monthly publication *Networking News For Artists.*

KAREN GLEASON
THE VICTORIAN TRADITION
P.O. Box 673
Biggs, CA 95917
Phone: (916)868-1180 or (916)674-9940 PST
Making dolls since: 1992
Selling dolls since: 1993

PRODUCT INFORMATION:
Mediums: Porcelain

Scope of work: Karen makes limited editions of 5-50 dolls. She makes all heads, bodies and accessories/props, and some shoes and molds. She designs and sews all clothing.
Price range: $795-1,295
Description of dolls: Karen creates original limited edition and one-of-a-kind porcelain art dolls. Each one of these collectible characters is handmade by the artist. All feature human or mohair wigs and beautiful glass eyes. Costumes are artist-designed and made of natural fabrics.
Special orders: Artist will work with customer on a special theme doll. Allow 6-8 months.
Price list: Free
Mailing list: Write or call to be included.
Dolls sold: In retail doll shops, at shows, by mail or from artist's home/studio
Shops: Send SASE for list.
Shows: Send SASE for list.
Phone orders: Between August 30 and June 15 at (916)868-1180. Anytime at (916)674-9940.
Mail orders: Will ship to US, Canada, overseas. Prepayment required. Allow 2-4 months for delivery.
Shipping information: Shipped via UPS, FedEx
Layaway: 20% down, 4 months
Discounts: Quantity

ADDITIONAL INFORMATION:
Karen is a member of the Doll Artisan Guild.

THERESA A. GLISSON
ALL THAT GLISSONS
154 W. Hill St.
Goldsboro, NC 27534
Phone: (919)778-6921 EST
Making dolls since: 1988
Selling dolls since: 1988

PRODUCT INFORMATION:

Mediums: Porcelain, polymer clay

Scope of work: Artist makes one-of-a-kind direct sculptured dolls and vignettes and limited editions of 5 dolls. She makes all heads and bodies and most wigs, shoes, accessories/props and molds. She also designs and sews all clothing.

Price range: $60-400; teacup fairies in antique cup, $150. Molds: $80-100

Description of dolls: Theresa makes 1″-1′ scale doll molds, some of which include her "Gone With The Wind" series. She also makes teacup fairy and mermaid molds. Her dolls are realistic looking, with lifelike hands.

Molds: Available directly from the artist and through doll suppliers.

Catalog/price list: b&w and color catalog with separate snapshots for $5, nonrefundable. Price list available for large SASE.

Mailing list: Write or call to be included.

Dolls sold: In retail doll shops, at shows, by mail, from artist's home/studio

Shops: Send SASE for list.

Shows: Call or send SASE for list.

Home/studio visits: Please schedule 1 day in advance.

Phone orders: For molds only

Mail orders: Will ship to US, Canada. Unless customer is on artist's mailing list, prepayment is required. Allow 3-4 weeks for molds; original dolls 2-3 months.

Shipping information: Shipped via UPS. Small orders shipped via mail. $3.50 shipping and handling for doll; call for quote on molds.

Discounts: 40% on 6 or more original molds to retailers; 25% on 4 or more Teacup Fairies

Return/exchange policy: No returns or exchanges unless damaged in shipping.

ADDITIONAL INFORMATION:

Theresa has been featured in *Dolls In Miniature* magazine, *The Sparkling Star* newspaper, and *The Enchanted Doll House Collectors Club* newsletter. She also sculpts figurines and sells sculpting tools, instruction books and clays.

KRISTIN GLOWACKI
P.O. Box 231
Silver Spring, PA 17575
Phone: (717)285-2392 EST
Making dolls since: 1991
Selling dolls since: 1993

PRODUCT INFORMATION:

Mediums: Polymer clays

Scope of work: Dolls are one-of-a-kind direct sculptures. Artist makes all heads, bodies, wigs, shoes, and accessories/props. Artist designs and sews all dolls' clothing.

Price range: $200-800

Description of dolls: All dolls are completely original in concept as well as construction. No molds are used. Heads and extremities are polymer clays, bodies are cloth over wire. The artist uses Cernit and Sculpey III, and all dolls are in the 12″-17″ range. Previous works have depicted humor, fantasy and every day life. The artist is now working on Civil War soldiers and their families.

Special orders: "Likenesses" can be arranged, i.e., hair color, eye color, general description and type of uniform, etc.

Dolls sold: In retail doll shops, by mail.

Shops: Send SASE for list.

Phone orders: M-Sat, 6-8.

ADDITIONAL INFORMATION:

Glowacki's work has appeared in *Doll Life* and *Contemporary Doll Collector.*

RALPH AND MARY L. GONZALES
BLU FROGG GARDENS
1155 Llagas Rd.
Morgan Hill, CA 95037
Phone: (408)779-2719 PST
Fax: (408)779-2719
E-Mail: rdzek@garlic.com
Making dolls since: 1982
Selling dolls since: 1983

PRODUCT INFORMATION:

Mediums: Porcelain, latex, terra-cotta

Scope of work: The couple make original artist dolls in limited editions; edition size varies. Ralph sculpts all parts of the doll and paints the features. Mary designs and sews all clothing.

Price range: $100-1,000

Description of dolls: Dolls include Rumplefolk™, Dotty Dollmaker, Harmony Healer, Gretta Gossip, Gerald Guardian and more. Dolls come with story, backdrop, beanbag. Other doll lines are "Essence of Ivory," female dancers with enhanced sculptural effects, and "Renaissance at Noon," in high fired Italian terra-cotta.

Catalog: Color brochure available. Call or send LSASE.

Mailing list: Write or call to be included.

Dolls sold: At shows or by mail.

Shows: Call or send SASE for list.

Phone orders: Accepted

Mail orders: Will ship to US, Canada, overseas. Prepayment required. Allow 3 weeks. Call first.

Shipping information: Shipped via UPS or US mail.

Layaway: Regular payments, ideally 6 months

Return/exchange policy: Call first.

ADDITIONAL INFORMATION:

Mary and Ralph are members of MSDBA. They are authors of *Soulstring The Original Doll—The Blu Frogg Method* and *Mold Making for the Original Doll—The Blu Frogg Method* (Pollywogg Press).

JULIE GOOD-KRÜGER
GOOD-KRÜGER DOLLS, INC.
1842 William Penn Way, Suite A
Lancaster, PA 17601
Phone: For orders: (800)426-2794 EST
For information: (717)399-3602
Fax: (717)399-3021
Making dolls since: 1977

Selling dolls since: 1980

PRODUCT INFORMATION:

Mediums: Porcelain, vinyl. Also Cernit, Sculpy, wax-over-porcelain

Scope of work: Artist creates limited editions of up to 5,000. Artist makes most heads and bodies and some wigs, shoes and accessories/props. Artist designs all doll's clothing and hires a seamstress to sew.

Price range: $75-750

Description of dolls: In 1977, Julie sculpted her first 10 dolls, inspired by stories her parents told her about their childhoods. She remembers "wanting each doll to be evocative of a mood, with expressions and gestures carefully illustrating a vignette. Future subjects I chose for my dolls were personal recollections or observations. I still want the faces and gestures of my dolls to illustrate a story or a thought." She also loves to design hand-embellished costumes.

Molds: Available directly from artist.

Designs manufactured by: Ashton-Drake

Catalog/price list: Color, free. Price list, free.

Mailing list: Write, call, sign up at shows to be included

Dolls sold: In retail doll shops

Shops: Call for list

Home/studio visits: Please schedule 1 day in advance.

Phone orders: M-F, 8-4:30 EST.

Fax orders: Include name, address, item desired, date, method of payment

Mail orders: Will ship to US, Canada, overseas. Prepayment is required.

Shipping information: COD. Delivery time depends on item ordered, if it is in production. Shipped via UPS, FedEx

Return/exchange policy: Refund or exchange if not satisfied.

ADDITIONAL INFORMATION:

Julie's work has been featured in *Doll Reader, Contemporary Doll Collector, Dolls—The Collector's Magazine, Doll World, Doll Crafter*, local tourist publications and newspapers. She belongs to UFDC. Julie has written "how-tos" for magazines, given talks to local groups and at shows, and created figurines. She also does some painting and some non-doll portrait sculpture.

SCOTT R. GRAY
NOT JUST ANOTHER PRETTY FACE
1101 17th Ave. #308
Seattle, WA 98122-4653
Phone: (206)328-4075 PST
Making dolls since: 1987
Selling dolls since: 1994

PRODUCT INFORMATION:

Mediums: Paperclay, resin crystal, porcelain, terra-cotta

Scope of work: Artist makes heads, bodies, wigs, shoes and accessories/props for all dolls. He also designs and sews all clothing.

Price range: $2,500-6,500

Description of dolls: Artist says his dolls are not "pretty." They are usually humanoid, but oftentimes they combine human and animal or human and object form, e.g., cookware or machinery. He adds that he is not averse to adding an extra arm or leg if it seems appropriate.

Price list: SASE

Mailing list: Write to be included.

Dolls sold: At shows or by mail

Shows: Send SASE for list.

Phone orders: M-F, 10-4.

Mail orders: Will ship to US, Canada, overseas. Prepayment required.

Shipping information: Shipped via UPS. Added to invoice.

ADDITIONAL INFORMATION:

Scott has been featured in *Contemporary Doll Collector* and *Dolls—The Collector's Magazine*, and in *The Doll By Contemporary Artists*, by Goddu and Laviti, (Abbeville Press). He is a member of NIADA.

DESSA RAE GREENWOOD
"D" ORIGINALS
3030 W. 5600 S.
Roy, UT 84067
Phone: (801)773-6492 MST
Making dolls since: 1978

Selling dolls since: 1978

PRODUCT INFORMATION:

Mediums: Cernit, Sculpey, Fimo, cloth

Scope of work: The artist makes one-of-a-kind direct sculptures and designs all cloth doll patterns. She makes all heads, bodies, wigs, shoes, accessories/props and eyes. She also designs and sews clothing.

Price range: $35-1,200

Description of dolls: Dessa Rae hand sculpts one-of-a-kind Cernit dolls. They range from miniature to lifesize babies. She hand-rolls Cernit eyes and paints them. She uses human hair or mohair. All bodies are ultrasuede and are fully poseable.

Mailing list: Write to be included.

Dolls sold: In retail doll shops, at shows, by mail, from artist's home/studio

Phone orders: Accepted

Mail orders: Will ship to US, Canada. Prepayment is required. Allow 4 weeks for delivery.

Shipping information: Shipped via UPS. Shipping is included in the price of the doll.

Return/exchange policy: Doll may be returned within 30 days of receipt for repair, or exchange for a doll of similar value.

ADDITIONAL INFORMATION:

Dessa Rae was nominated for a *Dolls— The Collector's Magazine* Award of Excellence and has been featured in *Contemporary Doll Collector*. She is a member of the Professional Doll Makers Art Guild. She also makes Cernit figurines.

JUDITH GRIFFIN
MAPLE NOOK DESIGNS
Rt. 3, Box 4850
Maple Nook Shores
Oakland, ME 04963
Phone: (207)465-7290 EST
Making dolls since: 1989
Selling dolls since: 1989

PRODUCT INFORMATION:

Mediums: Polymer clay

Scope of work: Dolls are one-of-a-kind direct sculptures. Artist makes all heads, bodies, wigs and shoes, some accessories/props. Artist designs and sews all dolls' clothing.

Price range: $60-250

Description of dolls: Judith makes

Santas, Belsnickles and other folk characters with hand sculpted polymer clay faces and hands, fabric clothing, and mohair and natural fiber beards and hair.

Special orders: Artist makes portrait dolls from photos. Requirements vary.

Price list: SASE

Mailing list: Write or call to be included.

Dolls sold: At shows, by mail, from artist's home/studio and at galleries.

Shows: Call or send SASE for list.

Phone orders: 3 P.M.-9 P.M.

Mail orders: Will ship to US, Canada. COD. Allow 2 weeks for delivery of in-stock items.

Shipping information: Shipped first class US mail. COD.

Layaway: Available

Return/exchange policy: Returns or exchanges only in rare instances. (Shipping damage excluded.)

ADDITIONAL INFORMATION:
Griffin is a member of the MSDBA.

DEANNA GULLETT
SISSY AND ME
2566 Cross Country Dr.
Beavercreek, OH 45324
Phone: (513)429-3303
Fax: (513)429-3303
E-Mail: ag081@dayton.wright.edu
Making dolls since: 1992
Selling dolls since: 1993

PRODUCT INFORMATION:
Mediums: Porcelain, Fimo, Cernit, Super Sculpey, resin

Scope of work: Dolls are one-of-a-kind direct sculptures, or created in limited editions. Artist makes some heads, bodies, wigs, shoes, accessories/props and molds. Artist designs all dolls' clothing.

Price range: $100-up

Description of dolls: Deanna's dolls and collectibles are marketed under the tradename of Sissy and Me. Many are character dolls that possess a rustic, homely quality, with touches of humor, while the porcelain dolls tend to be more contemporary and doll-like. The artist paints all dolls' faces, hands, and feet; hand-sets their eyes and lashes; and styles their wigs. Some have hand-painted eyes, but most have either hand-set glass or acrylic eyes. Their eyelashes are either hand-painted or hand-glued hair, while their eyebrows, mouths and blush are hand painted. The dolls' bodies are usually cloth and filled with new and/or clean, recycled materials. Limited edition dolls are currently done in porcelain or resin from molds.

Special orders: Artist makes portrait dolls from photos. Requires 50% down payment to start project, balance due upon completion. Requires three photos of the subject for portrait dolls, front view, three-quarters view and side view (profile). Allow 6-8 weeks minimum.

Catalog/price list: Color, $2, refundable with purchase. Price list, send SASE.

Mailing list: Write, call, attend shows, e-mail or fax to be included.

Dolls sold: In retail doll shops, at shows, by mail, by e-mail.

Shops: Call or send SASE for list.

Shows: Call or send SASE for list.

Home/studio visits: Please schedule 2 weeks in advance.

Phone orders: 9-6 EST.

Fax orders: Include name of doll; hair or eye color if there is a choice; price; customer's name, address, phone number; preferred method of shipment; method of payment

Mail orders: Will ship to US, Canada, overseas. Prepayment is required. Allow 6-8 weeks minimum for delivery.

Shipping information: Shipped via UPS, FedEx (customer's preference). Shipping is included in the price of the doll.

Layaway: 25% down; 3 months (90 days) at 25% payment per month. Dolls will be shipped within 10 days of final payment.

Discounts: Wholesale prices are available to dealers

Return/exchange policy: 30 days from shipping date for returns, replacements or repairs. Special orders—no returns or exchanges.

ADDITIONAL INFORMATION:
Deanna is a member of AADA and UFDC. She also sculpts collectibles, teaches art and sculpting classes to adults and children and gives lectures and presentations on dolls and/or sculpting to organizations.

RETÄGENE HANSLÏK
RETÄGENE HANSLÏK DOLLS
533 Fairview Ave.
Arcadia, CA 91007
Phone: (818)447-4228 PST
Making dolls since: 1990
Selling dolls since: 1991

PRODUCT INFORMATION:
Mediums: Cernit

Scope of work: Dolls are one-of-a-kind direct sculptures. Artist makes all heads, bodies, wigs, shoes and accessories/props. Artist designs and sews all doll's clothing.

Price range: $1,000-3,000

Description of dolls: "Alternative Doll Art" portrays contemporary men and women, often in scenes depicting alternative lifestyles. The artist uses Cernit because of its translucent beauty and tensile strength. Particular care is given to details such as linings in pants pockets and vests, sculpting tiny buttons, constructing leather shoes, and even building an occasional chair.

Special orders: Artist does a very limited number of portrait dolls from photos subject to time available and degree of difficulty, and priced accordingly.

Dolls sold: In retail doll shops, at shows,

by mail, from artist's home/studio and directly from DOLLCO at (818)702-9275.

Shops: Send SASE for list.

Shows: Send SASE for list.

Home/studio visits: Please call in advance.

Phone orders: 9-5 PST. Please leave message; artist will call back.

Mail orders: Will ship to US, Canada, overseas. Prepayment required. Allow one to two weeks domestic.

Shipping information: Shipped via UPS. Shipping is paid in advance with doll price.

Layaway: ⅓ down, 90 days (3 equal payments and shipping). Deposit nonrefundable

Return/exchange policy: Full refund if damaged in shipping or if returned in same condition as shipped (within 10 days).

ADDITIONAL INFORMATION:
Hanslik's work has been featured in *Dolls—The Collector's Magazine* and shown in all major doll magazines over the past 5 years. She is a member of AADA.

GISELE HANSON
662 Ashley Rd.
West Chazy, NY 12992
Phone: (518)493-7150 EST
Making dolls since: 1985
Selling dolls since: 1993

PRODUCT INFORMATION:
Mediums: Porcelain, cloth bodies

Scope of work: Artist makes only one doll from a mold or makes limited editions of 5-20 dolls. She makes heads, bodies, wigs, shoes, accessories/props and molds for all dolls. She also designs and sews all clothing.

Price range: $350-700

Description of dolls: Gisele's dolls have

porcelain heads, hands and legs with cloth bodies, and mohair or sheepskin wigs. They are usually under 15″ tall. They are dressed simply in natural fiber material. Her intent is to portray children and sometimes adults in everyday situations with a natural and unpretentious look.

Dolls sold: In retail doll shops, by mail and from artist's home/studio.

Home/studio visits: Please schedule in advance.

Phone orders: M-F, after 5 P.M.

Mail orders: Will ship to US, Canada, overseas. Customer will be billed. Allow 6 weeks for delivery.

Shipping information: Shipped via UPS. Shipping is included in the price of the doll.

Layaway: Available

Return/exchange policy: Full satisfaction guaranteed or full refund.

JEANNINE HAPPE
JEANNINE HAPPE ORIGINALS
3 Jones Lane
Blairstown, NJ 07825
Phone: (908)362-7801 EST
Making dolls since: 1994
Selling dolls since: 1995

PRODUCT INFORMATION:
Mediums: Cernit, Super Sculpey

Scope of work: Dolls are one-of-a-kind direct sculptures. The artist makes all heads, bodies, wigs and shoes and most accessories/props. She designs and sews all clothing.

Price range: $500-1,000

Description of dolls: Jeannine's dolls are sculpted from Cernit. Their bodies are cloth with a wire armature. Most dolls are clothed in vintage fabrics or furs or are trimmed in vintage laces. Although the artist has done several types of dolls ranging from Santa Claus to Snake Charmers, her specialty is children ranging in ages 2-10.

Special orders: Artist does not do portrait dolls, but will make dolls with requested specifications such as hair and eye color, approximate age, mood, etc. Completion time varies depending on artist's schedule at time of order.

Mailing list: Write or call to be included.

Dolls sold: In retail doll shops, at shows,

by mail, from artist's home/studio.

Shops: Call or send SASE for list.

Shows: Call or send SASE for list.

Home/studio visits: Please schedule in advance.

Phone orders: M-Sun, 9-8.

Mail orders: Will ship to US, Canada. Prepayment is required.

Shipping information: Shipped via UPS. Shipping is added to price of doll and must be prepaid.

Layaway: 25% down, 2 months

Discounts: On wholesale orders only

Return/exchange policy: Dolls are not returnable.

ADDITIONAL INFORMATION:
Jeannine is a member of AADA.

TRISH HARDING
OAK, THORN AND ASH COLLECTION
2323 Lynn St.
Bellingham, WA 98225
Phone: (360)671-8682 PST
Making dolls since: 1986
Selling dolls since: 1986

PRODUCT INFORMATION:
Mediums: Porcelain, Cernit, Super Sculpey, cloth

Scope of work: Artist creates dolls in limited editions. Artist creates some heads, bodies, wigs, shoes, accessories/props and molds. Artist designs all dolls' clothing.

Price range: $250 and up

Special orders: Artist creates portrait dolls from photos. Allow 90 days for project's completion.

Molds: Directly from artist

Catalog/price list: Free price list

Mailing list: Write to be included.

Dolls sold: In retail doll shops, by mail, from artist's studio, galleries

Home/studio visits: Please schedule 1 week in advance.

Phone orders: Th-F, 8-5.

Mail orders: Will ship to US, Canada, overseas. Prepayment required. Allow 10 days for delivery.

Shipping information: Shipped via UPS or US mail. COD.

ADDITIONAL INFORMATION:
Trish's work has appeared *in Contemporary Doll Collector.* She has also created Chrismas ornaments, a card line, figurines, illustrations and prints.

SONJA HARTMANN
SONJA HARTMANN ORIGINALS
100 Linda Circle
Downingtown, PA 19335
Phone: (610)269-8513 EST
Fax: (610)269-9914
Making dolls since: 1981

PRODUCT INFORMATION:
Mediums: Porcelain, vinyl
Price range: $395-1,500 (retail prices)
Description of dolls: Dolls have jointed
    bodies, which makes them very
    poseable. Dolls are created com-
    pletely in Hartmann's studio.
Catalog/price list: Color, free, for dealers
    only. Price list also available.
Mailing list: Write to be included.
Dolls sold: In retail doll shops, at shows
Shops: Call for list.
Shows: Call for list.
Phone orders: Accepted
Fax orders: Accepted

ADDITIONAL INFORMATION:
Sonja received the *Dolls* Award of Excellence in 1991 and 1994, and Doll of the
Year, 1992. Her work has appeared in
*Doll Reader, Contemporary Doll Collec-
tor* and *Dolls—The Collector's Magazine.* She also served as organizer and
host of the annual doll exhibition "Mas-
terpieces of the World" in New York
City.

HEI MANA CREATIONS
14649 McCormick
Van Nuys, CA 91411
Phone: (818)789-7206
Making dolls since: 1991
Selling dolls since: 1991

PRODUCT INFORMATION:
Mediums: Resin cloth
Scope of work: Artist makes only one
    doll from each mold, or dolls are cre-
    ated in limited editions of up to 500.
    Artist makes all heads, bodies, wigs,
    accessories/props and molds. Artist
    designs and sews all dolls' clothes, or
    hires a seamstress to make it.
Price range: $150-$500
Catalog/price list: Color, $3, refundable
    with purchase. Price list.
Mailing list: Write or call to be included.
Dolls sold: In retail doll shops
Shops: Send SASE for list.
Home/studio visits: Please schedule 3
    weeks in advance.

Phone: M-F, 9-4.
Mail orders: Prepayment required.
    Allow 6 weeks for delivery.
Shipping information: Shipped via
    FedEx
Discounts: We sell wholesale—mini-
    mum of 3 dolls.

ADDITIONAL INFORMATION:
Hei Mana Creations have appeared in
Contemporary Doll Collector and
Dolls—The Collector's Magazine.

LINDA HENRY
LINDA HENRY ORIGINALS
230 Kramer St.
Canal Winchester, OH 43110
Phone: (614)837-5383 EST
Fax: (614)837-4799 or (614)837-8011
E-Mail: bearlooms@aol.com
Making dolls since: 1980
Selling dolls since: 1990

PRODUCT INFORMATION:
Mediums: Predominately porcelain, also
    Super Sculpey, Cernit
Scope of work: Artist makes limited edi-
    tions of 5-50 dolls. She makes heads
    and molds for all dolls. She also
    makes most bodies and accessories/
    props and some shoes. Wigs all
    bought ready-made. She designs and
    sews all clothing.
Price range: $495-695
Description of dolls: The artist designs
    dolls ranging in ages from toddlers to
    young women. The vast majority have
    been girl dolls. She is currently work-
    ing on a series of biblical angels.
Designs manufactured by: L.L. Knick-
    erbocker for the Marie Osmond Col-
    lection (since 1990)
Mailing list: Write, call or e-mail request
    to be included
Dolls sold: At shows, by mail or by
    e-mail for web page address on the
    Internet

Shows: Send SASE for list.
Computer sales: E-mail should be sent
    to address above for more informa-
    tion.
Phone orders: M-F, 9-7.
Fax orders: Include name, address,
    phone, fax, e-mail, credit card number
    (Visa/MC accepted)
Mail orders: Will ship to US, Canada,
    overseas. 50% deposit, balance due at
    shipping. Allow 4-6 months for deliv-
    ery.
Shipping information: Shipped via UPS
    or FedEx. Shipping is included in the
    price of the doll.
Layaway: 20% down with order, 20% per
    month until balance is paid in full.
Return/exchange policy: 30-day return
    or exchange policy

ADDITIONAL INFORMATION:
Linda is a member of MSDBA. She also
designs plush animals, her specialty being plush with porcelain faces. She is a
freelance writer, speaker, and host for
porcelain dollmaker chats on America
Online.

EDNA HIBEL
EDNA HIBEL GALLERY
311 Royal Poinciana Plaza
Palm Beach, FL 33480
Phone: (407)655-2410 EST
Fax: (407)848-9633
E-Mail:
    p007345b@pbfreenet.seflin.lib.fl.us
Making dolls since: 1985
Selling dolls since: 1985

PRODUCT INFORMATION:
Mediums: Porcelain, wax, wood, cloth
Scope of work: Dolls are created in
    limited editions of 6. Artist makes all
    heads and some accessories/props.
    Artist purchases ready-made or an-
    tique clothing, and sometimes designs
    clothing.
Price range: $400-4,000
Designs manufactured by: Everyest,
    Fithin
Catalog/price list: Color, free. Price list
    free.
Mailing list: Write, call, fax or e-mail to
    be included.
Dolls sold: In retail doll shops, at shows,
    Edna Hibel Gallery and Hibel
    Museum of Art, via e-mail.

Shops: Call, fax, e-mail or send SASE for list.

Shows: Call, fax, e-mail or send SASE for list.

Computer sales: E-mail to address above.

Phone orders: M-S, 10-5.

Fax orders: Fax catalog order form. Include doll name, stock identification number, retail price.

Mail orders: Will ship to US, Canada, overseas. Prepayment is required. Allow 2 weeks for delivery.

Shipping information: Shipped via UPS, FedEx, US mail. COD, prepaid.

Layaway: Layaway offered only on unique dolls. 20% down, balance monthly up to 3 months.

Return/exchange policy: Exchanges granted for obvious damage in shipping.

ADDITIONAL INFORMATION:

Hibel has received a commission by the National Archives; an Honorary Doctorate from Eureka College (alma mater of President Ronald Reagan); a tribute in US Congressional Record; and an International Humanitarian Award from Boys' Towns of Italy, Rome. Hibel's work has been featured in *Collectors Mart*; the *Chicago Tribune*; *Collector Edition*; *Art Business News*; the *Palm Beach Post*; and *Collector News*. She is a member of the Night Owl Doll Club, Palm Beach County, Florida. Hibel is also a painter, lithographer, serigrapher, sculptor and porcelain artist. She has published *A Big Day for Betsy at the Wenham Museum* (JAR Publishers, 1977).

KATE HIDDLESTON
60375 Arnold Market Rd.
Bend, OR 97702
Phone: (541)388-0106 PST
Making dolls since: 1993
Selling dolls since: 1993

PRODUCT INFORMATION:

Mediums: Polymer.

Price range: $500-2,400

Description of dolls: Photographs of Kate's dolls are often mistaken for real children. Each one-of-a-kind doll, sculpted in polymer clay with meticulous attention to detail, is a mixed media, fine art sculpture.

Mailing list: Write or call to be included.

Dolls sold: At shows, by mail, from artist's home/studio or via computer

Shows: Call or send SASE for list.

Computer sales: See my web page at http://www.transport.com/~newsom/kih/home.html

Home/studio visits: Please schedule 1 day in advance.

Phone orders: Any time

Mail orders: Will ship to US, Canada, overseas. Prepayment required. Allow 2 weeks for delivery.

Shipping information: Shipped via UPS. Shipping price is added to the price of the doll and included in prepayment.

Layaway: 3 months for dolls of up to $1,500; longer for more expensive dolls

Discounts: Multiple purchases, collector discounts

Return/exchange policy: Will refund or exchange if doll is returned undamaged within 2 weeks of shipping date. Customer pays all shipping costs.

ADDITIONAL INFORMATION

Kate is also a nationally known and collected professional bronze sculptor. She has been sculpting miniature to life-size bronze work for 20 years.

YOSHIKO HORNICK
REPRESENTED BY DOLLCO
22248 Cohasset St.
Canoga Park, CA 91303
Phone: (818)702-0315 PST
Fax: (818)702-9275

E-Mail: 71174.3224@compuserve.com
Making dolls since: 1987
Selling dolls since: 1994

PRODUCT INFORMATION:

Mediums: Porcelain, Cernit, Super Sculpey

Scope of work: Artist makes mainly one-of-a-kind and very limited edition dolls. She makes all heads, bodies and molds, most wigs, and some shoes and accessories/props. She designs and sews all clothing.

Price range: $130-1,800

Description of dolls: One-of-a-kind dolls are comprised of mostly young adults and children and have individually attached eyelashes and small attached hairs over painted eyebrows for more realism.

Catalog/price list: Color photo, $5, refundable with purchase. Price list free.

Mailing list: Write to be included.

Dolls sold: In retail doll shops, at shows

Shops: Call for list.

Shows: Call for list.

ADDITIONAL INFORMATION:

Yoshiko has been featured in *Contemporary Doll Collector* and *Dolls—The Collector's Magazine*.

DOROTHY ALLISON HOSKINS
DOROTHY ALLISON HOSKINS ORIGINAL DOLLS
7411 Mary Ann St.
Fairbanks, AK 99701
Phone: (907)452-2688 AST.
Making dolls since: 1984
Selling dolls since: 1985

PRODUCT INFORMATION:

Mediums: Porcelain

Scope of work: Dolls are one-of-a-kind direct sculptures. The artist makes all heads, bodies, wigs and shoes. Some accessories/props are designed and made by other artists. The artist also designs and sews all clothing.

Price range: $1,000 and up

Description of dolls: Dorothy's dolls are all one-of-a-kind sculptured directly from porcelain. Most are adult females, sometimes accompanied by babies. She makes larger dolls (19″-21″) as well as 1″ = 12″ scale miniatures. Both sizes of dolls are ethnic, historical, contemporary or fantasy.

Dolls sold: In retail doll shops, by mail,

from artists' home/studio and at NIADA Conference

Shops: Send SASE for list.

Shows: Send SASE for list.

Home/studio visits: Please schedule 2 days in advance.

Phone orders: M-F, 9-5.

Mail orders: Will ship to US, Canada, overseas. Payment at time of purchase. Shipped immediately if finished; arrangement made with buyer for specific dates.

Shipping information: Shipped via UPS or registered mail. Shipping is included in the price of the doll.

Layaway: Arranged with buyer

Return/exchange policy: Accepted for any reason within 2 weeks as long as doll is in perfect condition.

ADDITIONAL INFORMATION:

Dorothy has been featured in *Contemporary Doll Collector*, *Dolls—The Collector's Magazine* and *Doll Reader*, and in the book *Most Beautiful Dolls in the World*. She is a member of NIADA, ODACA, IDMA and Arctic Doll Makers. She also makes 2 figurines cast in epoxy depicting Alaskan Eskimos.

SHERRY HOUSLEY
REPRESENTED BY DOLLCO
22248 Cohasset St.
Canoga Park, CA 91303
Phone: (818)702-0315 PST
Fax: (818)702-9275
E-Mail: thomreneei@aol.com
Making dolls since: 1989
Selling dolls since: 1989

PRODUCT INFORMATION:

Mediums: Synthetic clay (Super Sculpey), occasionally resin

Scope of work: Most dolls are one-of-a-kind direct sculptures. Artist also makes limited editions of 35 dolls. She makes all heads, bodies, wigs,

shoes and accessories/props. She also designs and sews all clothing.

Price range: $800-1,800

Description of dolls: Sherry specializes in very realistic ethnic and unusual characters. She creates mostly one-of-a-kinds but also produces some limited editions in resin.

Special orders: No portrait dolls. Occasionally does special request if the theme appeals to her. Allow 8-10 weeks average for completion.

Designs manufactured by: Ashton-Drake

Catalog/price list: Color photos, $5, refundable with purchase. Price list, free.

Mailing list: Write to be included.

Dolls sold: In retail doll shops, at shows

Shops: Call for list.

Shows: Call for list.

ADDITIONAL INFORMATION:

Sherry has been featured in *Contemporary Doll Collector*, *Doll Life* and the *Tampa Tribune*.

JOAN IBAROLLE
414 Blackstone Court
Walnut Creek, CA 94598
Phone: (510)932-2138 PST
Making dolls since: 1985
Selling dolls since: 1987

PRODUCT INFORMATION:

Mediums: Porcelain

Scope of work: Artist makes limited editions of 5-10 dolls. She makes some heads, bodies, wigs, shoes, accessories/props and molds. She also designs and sews most clothing.

Price range: $1,000-1,500

Description of dolls: Joan uses pictures for inspiration. Her dolls' costumes are made from fine fabric. They have handmade shoes and English glass eyes.

Designs manufactured by: Ashton-Drake

Dolls sold: In retail doll shops, by mail, from artist's home/studio

Home/studio visits: Call for appointment in advance.

Phone orders: M-F, 9-5.

Mail orders: Will ship to US. Delivery time depends on doll.

Shipping information: Shipped via UPS. Shipping is included in the price of the doll.

Layaway: By arrangement with customer

Return/exchange policy: Must return within 30 days.

ADDITIONAL INFORMATION:

Joan has won 2 awards from the Doll Artisan Guild: 1990, Blue Ribbon, Professional; 1993, Best in Category, Original Doll, Professional. She also has been featured in *Contemporary Doll Collector*. The artist is a member of UFDC and Walnut Creek Valley Doll Club. She also makes pottery.

THOM AND RENÉE IVERSON OF IVERSON DESIGN
REPRESENTED BY DOLLCO
11134 127th Place NE
Kirlkand, WA 98033
Phone: For orders: (818)702-0315 PST (DOLLCO)
For info: (206)827-2638 (Iverson Design)
Fax: (818)702-9275 (DOLLCO), (206)827-2638 (Iverson Design)
E-Mail: thomreneei@aol.com
Making dolls since: 1990
Selling dolls since: 1994

PRODUCT INFORMATION:

Mediums: Cernit, porcelain

Scope of work: Dolls are one-of-a-kind Cernit and porcelain dolls in limited editions. Artists make all heads, bodies, wigs, shoes and molds and most accessories/props. Artist designs and sews all clothing.

Price range: Porcelain $400-500; Cernit $1,000

Description of dolls: Iverson Design makes one-of-a-kind art dolls sculpted in Cernit and porcelain limited editions. Dolls tend to be influenced by historical people and themes. One-of-a-kind Cernit dolls range from fantasy figures such as angels and elves to realistic portraits of jazz and blues musicians. Their first porcelain doll, limited to 20 pieces, portrays a young lady; each individually painted and dressed so that no 2 are alike. All the costumes in the edition are historically based.

Special orders: Accepted. Allow 3 months.

Catalog/price list: Color photos, $5, refundable with purchase. Price list, send SASE.

Mailing list: Write to be included.

Dolls sold: In retail doll shops, at shows and directly from DOLLCO

Shops: Call for list.

Shows: Call for list.

Home/studio visits: Please call in advance.

Phone orders: M-F, 9-5, through Iverson Design or DOLLCO

Fax orders: Include your phone number.

ADDITIONAL INFORMATION:
Iverson Design was nominated for a 1994 Award of Excellence and won an IDEX award for Best Ethnic Doll 1995. Their work has been featured in *Contemporary Doll Collector.* They also have written articles for *Doll Crafter* on doll costuming.

ANN JACKSON
P.O. Box 1335
Addison, IL 60101-8335
Phone: (630)543-8832 CST
Making dolls since: 1988

Selling dolls since: 1988

PRODUCT INFORMATION:
Mediums: Porcelain, wax, cloth

Scope of work: Dolls are created in limited editions of 1-50. Artist makes all heads, some bodies, wigs, shoes and accessories/props. If an edition is small, the artist designs and sews the clothes. If the edition includes 25 or more, the artist hires a seamstress.

Price range: $85-4,500

Description of dolls: Ann's dolls are beautifully sculpted, detailed Victorian to modern dolls in wax and porcelain. Great ladies, enchanting children, angels, mermaids and Santas in all original costumes are available. Custom orders accepted. Dolls include museum-quality china, painted porcelain, poured wax and wax-over porcelain, one-of-a-kinds and small editions.

Special orders: Artist makes portrait dolls from photos. Special orders require extra time and money. Allow 3-12 months for project's completion, depending on difficulty.

Molds: Small number available directly from artist

Designs manufactured by: The Franklin Mint

Price list: $1, refundable with purchase

Mailing list: Write to be included.

Dolls sold: In retail doll shops, by mail

Shops: Send SASE for list.

Phone orders: 7 days, 2-10. Phone messages will be returned.

Mail orders: Will ship to US, Canada, overseas. Prepayment required. Allow 6 weeks for delivery.

Shipping information: Shipped via UPS. Shipping is included in the price of the doll.

Layaway: Available

Return/exchange policy: Dolls may be exchanged up to 3 days after receipt with authorization.

JOHNI JACOBSEN
JOHNI JACOBSEN STUDIO
105 Harding Ave.
Fox River Grove, IL 60021
Phone: For information: (708)639-7259 CST
Making dolls since: 1993
Selling dolls since: 1993

PRODUCT INFORMATION:
Mediums: Polymer clays

Scope of work: Dolls are one-of-a-kind direct sculptures. Artist makes all heads and bodies, most wigs and some shoes and accessories/props. Artist designs and sews all dolls' clothing.

Price range: $795-1,500

Description of dolls: John's dolls are mostly contemporary children with painted eyes and expressive faces. The hair is either mohair or human hair, and most dolls stand on their own.

Dolls sold: In retail doll shops, at shows, by mail

Shops: Call for list.

Phone orders: M-F, 10-5.

Mail orders: Will ship to US

Shipping information: Shipped via FedEx. Shipping is included in the price of the doll.

Discounts: To dealers only

ADDITIONAL INFORMATION:
Jacobsen's work was awarded Best of Show in Zion, Illinois, 1993 and 1994; Best Of Division in Racine, Wisconsin, in 1993; and 1st place in Great Lake Doll Artist Show, Michigan, 1993. Jacobsen's work has appeared in *Contemporary Doll Collector.* Jacobsen is a member of AADA.

BARBARA JENKINS
26 San Rafael Ave.
San Anselmo, CA 94960
Phone: (415)456-6019 PST
Making dolls since: 1980
Selling dolls since: 1980

PRODUCT INFORMATION:
Mediums: Porcelain (with cloth bodies and wire armature)

Scope of work: Artist makes limited editions of 30-40 dolls. She makes all heads, bodies, wigs, shoes and molds and some accessories/props. Artist also designs and sews all clothing.

Price range: $50-150

Description of dolls: Barbara makes her dolls of porcelain bisque from her own original molds. They are scaled 1" = 1' (for doll houses). The women are usually 5¼"-5½" tall, the men usually 6" tall, the young children 4", and the small children 3". Each head is signed and dated. The dolls are dressed in period costume (various periods) in appropriate fabrics, usually silk and fine cotton.

Special orders: The artist welcomes special requests but doesn't do portrait dolls. Allow 2-3 months.

Price list: Free

Dolls sold: In retail doll shops, miniature shows

Shops: Call for list.

Shows: Call for list.

Phone orders: Any day, evenings

Mail orders: Will ship to US, Canada, overseas. Prepayment is required.

Shipping information: Shipped via UPS or insured mail. Shipping is included in the price of the doll.

Return/exchange policy: Satisfaction is guaranteed. Returns and exchanges can be arranged with the customer.

ADDITIONAL INFORMATION:
Barbara has been featured in *Miniatures Showcase* and *Nutshell News*. She is a member of ODACA and NAME.

PATTI JOHNSON
STUDIO 206
625 Main St.
Columbus, MS 39701
Phone: (601)327-5040 CST
Making dolls since: 1991
Selling dolls since: 1991

PRODUCT INFORMATION:

Mediums: Low-fire clay, plastic clay, wire on wood/plastic armature

Scope of work: Dolls are one-of-a-kind direct sculptures. Artist designs patterns for all cloth dolls. Artist makes all heads, bodies, wigs, shoes and most accessories/props. Artist designs and sews all dolls' clothing.

Price range: $45-900

Description of dolls: Patti's pieces are presented in a theme setting. Smaller pieces are freestanding. Sizes range from miniature to life size. Some themes revolve around 18th century nursery rhymes. They are called creative characters and vary in size and dimension. Some are one-character pieces, and others are multiple characters.

Special orders: Artist makes portrait dolls from photos. Required ½ deposit before starting, balance upon completion. Allow 3 months.

Dolls sold: At shows, from artist's studio, galleries

Shops: Call or send SASE for list.

Shows: Call or send SASE for list.

Home/studio visits: Please schedule 1 week in advance.

Phone orders: T-Th, 1-6.

Mail orders: Will ship to US, Canada. Prepayment required. Allow 2 weeks for delivery.

Shipping information: Shipped via UPS. COD.

Discounts: Discounts are negotiable

Return/exchange policy: No exchanges or returns on commissioned pieces

ADDITIONAL INFORMATION:
Johnson's work received the Best in Show award at the 1994 Columbus Arts Festival, 1st place in the 3-dimensional category at the 1993 Columbus Arts Festival, and was 1 of 60 pieces accepted to the Meridian Museum of Art Annual Juried Show. Johnson's work has appeared in the Debut section of *Contemporary Doll Collector*. Johnson has also been an oil painter and watercolorist for the past 25 years.

JACK JOHNSTON
JOHNSTON ORIGINAL ART DOLLS
1447 N. Carrington Lane
Centerville, UT 84014
Phone: (800)560-4958 or (801)299-9908 MST
Fax: (801)299-9088
Making dolls since: 1990
Selling dolls since: 1990

PRODUCT INFORMATION:

Mediums: Cernit, resin, polymer clay, porcelain

Scope of work: Dolls are one-of-a-kind direct sculptures. Artist makes most heads, bodies, wigs, shoes and accessories/props. Artist designs all dolls' clothing.

Price range: $1,500-30,000

Description of dolls: Jack Johnston dolls are one-of-a-kind dolls representing characters, historical and realistic persons. Each doll tells a story. In many cases, the dolls describe the artist's life or fantasies. Most of the dolls are kept in museums and private collections; however, many are sold to manufacturers for reproduction.

Special orders: Artist makes portrait dolls from photographs. Requires photos of full face, top side of hands, side view, back view and top view. Allow 3 months for project's completion.

Molds: Through doll suppliers

Designs manufactured by: Franklin Mint, Ashton-Drake, L.L. Knickerbocker, Bell Ceramics

Catalog/price list: b&w, free. Price list free.

Mailing list: Write to be included.

Dolls sold: In retail doll shops, at shows, by mail, from artist's home/studio, directly from the artist through an online computer system, museums, magazines, major trade shows

Shops: Call or send SASE for list.

Shows: Call or send SASE for list.

Home/studio visits: Please schedule 1 day in advance.

Phone orders: M-W.

Fax orders: Accepted

Mail orders: Will ship to US, Canada, overseas. Prepayment is required. 50% down, balance upon receipt. Allow 1 week for delivery after doll is completed.

Shipping information: Shipped via UPS. COD.

Layaway: 30% down, 10% per month (no interest)

Discounts: 20% off on multiple orders up to 6, 30% off up to 12, 50% off 13 or more

Return/exchange policy: Guarantees against poor workmanship.

ADDITIONAL INFORMATION:
Johnston's work has been nominated for a *Dolls* Award of Excellence in 1992, 1993 and 1994, and was nominated for *Dolls* One-of-a-Kind Classic, 1994. Johnston's work has been featured in *Dolls—The Collector's Magazine, Doll World, Doll Crafter, Contemporary Doll Collector, Doll Reader, Dollmakers*

Workshop, Orlando Magazine, Deseret News and *Orlando Sentinel*. He is a member of the Professional Doll Makers Art Guild. He has had published *Johnston Original Art Dolls* (self-published, 1991-94), *The Art of Making and Marketing Art Dolls* (Scott Publications, 1994) and *The Advanced Art of Making and Marketing Art Dolls* (Scott Publications, 1996). Johnston teaches dollmaking seminars each week in 50 different locations internationally. A brochure and calendar are available. Please send SASE to the address above or call (800)560-4958.

SANDRA WRIGHT JUSTISS
DOLLS OF ORIGINAL DESIGN
720 Maplewood Ave.
Ambridge, PA 15003
Phone: (412)266-1492 EST
Making dolls since: 1983
Selling dolls since: 1983

PRODUCT INFORMATION:

Mediums: Porcelain, Paperclay, wax, Super Sculpey, Cernit, Fimo, terra-cotta

Scope of work: Dolls are one-of-a-kind direct sculptures and limited editions of up to 10. Artist designs patterns for all cloth dolls. Artist makes all heads, bodies, wigs, shoes, accessories/props and molds. Artist designs and sews all dolls' clothing.

Price range: $150-2,000

Description of dolls: Sandra's dolls are mostly classical in feeling. Often they are illustrated characters from literature and opera, legends and classical paintings.

Special orders: Artist makes portrait dolls from photos (discussed on an individual basis). Allow 1 year for delivery.

Price list: Send SASE for list.

Mailing list: Write or call to be included.

Dolls sold: In retail doll shops, at shows,

directly from the artist by mail, from artist's home/studio.

Shops: Call to list.

Shows: Call or send SASE for list.

Home/studio visits: Please schedule 2 days in advance.

Phone orders: Yes

Mail orders: Will ship to US, Canada, overseas. Prepayment is required. Delivery time depends on order.

Shipping information: Shipped via UPS. Shipping is included in the price of the doll.

Layaway: ⅓ down, ⅓ each month for 3 months. Extended time available for expensive pieces.

Discounts: Members of Aux-ODACA; dealer with a tax number (for resale)

Return/exchange policy: Seldom needed. Will discuss on an individual basis.

ADDITIONAL INFORMATION:

Justiss has won blue ribbons at many shows, including UFDC, Doll Artisan Guild and Art Galleries. Justiss' work has appeared in *Doll Reader, Contemporary Doll Collector, Dolls—The Collector's Magazine* and *Doll News*. She is a member of UFDC and ODACA. The artist writes for doll magazines and souvenir journals and creates paper dolls for same.

MR. ADNAN SAMI KARABAY
1414 N. Fairfax Ave. #204
Los Angeles, CA 90046
Phone: (213)882-6255 PST
Making dolls since: 1989
Selling dolls since: 1989

PRODUCT INFORMATION:

Mediums: Polyform clay, Paperclay

Scope of work: All dolls are one-of-a-kind direct sculptures.

Price range: $700-6,000

Description of dolls: Dolls are all hand sculpted and painted. Artist uses 18th

and 19th century fabrics, trims and beads whenever possible. Artist also uses hand-dyed fabrics to achieve the balanced harmony of textiles and doll. Miniature room settings are also created using antiques to scale.

Special orders: Artist makes portrait dolls from photos. He prefers working from life, not from photos. 16″ tall is the best size for portraits. Non-portraits are also available. The size and type of human or animal face and the size and color range must be provided. Allow 2-4 weeks for projects completion.

Mailing list: Write or call to be included.

Dolls sold: In retail doll shops, at shows, by mail, museums, and fine art galleries

Shops: Send SASE for list.

Shows: Send SASE for list.

Home/studio visits: Please schedule 1 week in advance.

Phone orders: Anytime

Mail orders: Will ship to US, Canada, overseas. Prepayment is required.

Shipping information: Shipped via FedEx. Prepaid by collector prior to shipping.

ADDITIONAL INFORMATION:

Karabay's work has appeared in *Contemporary Doll Collector; Doll Reader; Nutshell News; Le Magazine de la Maison de Poupée et de la poupée d'Artiste.*

HEDY KATIN
572 Edelweiss Dr.
San Jose, CA 95136
Phone: (408)265-1839 PST
Making dolls since: 1982
Selling dolls since: 1982

PRODUCT INFORMATION:

Mediums: Cloth and porcelain

Scope of work: The artist makes one-of-a-kind sculptures and limited editions of 5-6 dolls. She also designs all cloth doll patterns. The artist makes all heads, bodies, wigs, shoes, accessories/props and molds. She designs and sews all clothing.

Price range: $600-1,000

Description of dolls: Hedy's cloth dolls have a papier mâché face mask that she sculpts and covers with fabric. They are realistic little children of different nationalities.

Price list: Free

Mailing list: Write to be included.

Dolls sold: In retail doll shops, at shows, by mail

Shops: Send SASE for list.

Phone orders: M-F, 10-5.

Mail orders: Will ship to US. Prepayment is required. Allow 2 weeks for delivery.

Shipping information: Shipped via UPS; regular US mail to Alaska. Shipping is included in the price of the doll.

Return/exchange policy: No returns, exchanges only.

ADDITIONAL INFORMATION:
Hedy is a member of NCDMA (a cloth doll making organization) and ODACA. She also designs doll patterns for many doll magazines and teaches dollmaking at seminars and for private doll clubs.

LINDA J. KAYS
42 Mitchell St.
Norwich, NY 13815
Phone: (607)334-8375 EST
Fax: (607)334-8375
Making dolls since: 1989
Selling dolls since: 1990

PRODUCT INFORMATION:
Mediums: Polymer clay
Scope of work: Dolls are one-of-a-kind direct sculptures. Artist makes all heads, bodies, wigs, shoes. Artist designs and sews all dolls' clothing.

Price range: Approximately $500

Description of dolls: Dolls are hand-sculpted characters, including elderly characters, Santas, celebrities and bag ladies. Each is sculpted individually and costumed to fit its character. The average is approximately 24″ tall, but dolls vary from 18″-36″.

Special orders: Artist makes portrait dolls from photos. Call for quote. Requires 3 close-up, clear facial photographs. Allow 8 weeks for project's completion.

Catalog/price list: b&w, $1. Price list comes with brochure.

Mailing list: Write to be included.

Dolls sold: In retail doll shops, at shows, by mail

Shops: Call or send SASE for list.

Shows: Call or send SASE for list.

Phone orders: M-S, 9-8 EST.

Fax orders: Fax description of doll wanted.

Mail orders: Will ship to US, Canada, overseas. Prepayment required. COD with a previous deposit. Allow 8 weeks for delivery.

Shipping information: Shipped via UPS. Shipping is added to invoice.

Layaway: A $50 deposit, 6 month holding time

Return/exchange policy: Will exchange for a character of equal value

ADDITIONAL INFORMATION:
Linda has won 1st prize in the Philadelphia Black Doll Convention (1991), 1st prize in the Delaware Doll Show (1992), and 1st prize in the Patchoque Doll Show (1993-94). Her work has appeared in *Doll Life*, *Contemporary Doll Collector* and *Folkart Treasures*. She also teaches sculpting classes for dollmaking.

SHARLEEN KELSEY
REPRESENTED BY: DOLLCO
22248 Cohasset St.
Canoga Park, CA 91303

Phone: (818)702-0315 PST
Fax: (818)702-9275
Making dolls since: 1988
Selling dolls since: 1989

PRODUCT INFORMATION:
Mediums: Porcelain
Price range: $300-1,000
Description of dolls: Sharleen specializes in lifelike dolls and makes expressive children, ethnic dolls and lady dolls. She has also made fantasy mermaid dolls. She uses models for all her dolls, and often models them after her children and grandchildren.

Special orders: Good photos, including profile photos and 3-4 views with the same expression, are required. Allow 3 months.

Molds: Through doll suppliers

Designs manufactured by: The Jones Mold Company

Catalog/price list: Color photos available, $5, refundable with purchase. Price list free.

Mailing list: Write to be included.

Dolls sold: In retail doll shops and at shows

Shops: Call for list.

Shows: Call for list.

Home/studio visits: Please schedule in advance.

Mail orders: Will ship to US. Prepayment required. Allow 1 month for delivery.

ADDITIONAL INFORMATION:
Sharleen's work has been featured in *Doll Crafter* and *Contemporary Doll Collector*. She also creates oil paintings and portraits.

PENNY MCINTIRE KENDALL
7312 S. Lowden Rd.
Oregon, IL 61021-9737
Phone/fax: (815)652-4237 CST
Making dolls since: 1991

Selling dolls since: 1992

PRODUCT INFORMATION:

Mediums: Polymer clays

Scope of work: Dolls are one-of-a-kinds or limited editions of up to 20. Artist makes all heads, bodies, wigs and shoes, most accessories/props and some molds. Artist designs and sews all dolls' clothing.

Price range: $400-2,000

Description of dolls: Penny's current doll series, *Ladies of Style*, focuses on fashionable older women with amusing or poignant stories to tell. These women exhibit chutzpah, character and flair. Dolls range from 13″ to 18″ tall. Unless otherwise noted, all dolls are hand sculpted in polyform clay. Only the finest fabrics and fibers are used.

Mailing list: Write or call to be included.

Dolls sold: At shows, by mail, from artist's home/studio

Shows: Send SASE for list. Everyone on mailing list will be notified.

Home/studio visits: Please schedule 1 week in advance.

Phone orders: Accepted

Mail orders: Will ship to US, Canada, overseas. Prepayment required. Allow 1-2 weeks usually for delivery.

Shipping information: Shipped via UPS, Express Mail. Shipping added to cost of doll.

Layaway: Will negotiate with buyer.

Discounts: Wholesale discount varies, depending upon doll.

Return/exchange policy: Depends upon circumstances, but artist will do her best to see that the buyer is satisfied.

ADDITIONAL INFORMATION

Penny was a 1994 nominee for a *Dolls* Award of Excellence. Her work has been featured in *Dolls—The Collector's Magazine*. Kendall belongs to the Professional Doll Makers Art Guild, AADA and MSDBA.

LINDA S. KERTZMAN
THE LINDENFOLK
37 W. Main St., Box 98
Morris, NY 13808
Phone: (607)263-5988 EST
Making dolls since: 1966
Selling dolls since: 1968

PRODUCT INFORMATION:

Mediums: Mixture of Cernit and Super Sculpey

Scope of work: Dolls are one-of-a-kind direct sculptures. She makes all heads, bodies, wigs and shoes and some accessories/props. She also designs and sews all clothing.

Price range: $200-4,000 (for a scene)

Description of dolls: Linda wants her creations to bring a feeling of peace— an escape from the hectic world.

Special orders: Artist will do special pieces if she likes the idea. No portrait dolls. Allow 1 year.

Price list: Free

Mailing list: Write or call to be included.

Dolls sold: In retail doll shops, at shows, by mail or from artist's home/studio

Shops: Call for list.

Shows: Call for list.

Phone orders: M-Th, 7-noon, 7-9 (evenings). $25 down and letter of confirmation required.

Mail orders: Will ship to US, Canada, overseas. Prepayment required. Allow less than 1 week for delivery.

Shipping information: Shipped via UPS or FedEx. Shipping is included in the price of the doll.

ADDITIONAL INFORMATION:

Linda has won a 1st place *Dolls* Award of Excellence, and three 1st place Ashton-Drake awards, and has been a DOTY nominee. Her work has been featured in *Fantastic Figures* by Susanna Oroyan; *Angels from the Heart* by Ho Phi Le; *The Doll by Contemporary Artists*, by Kristina Goddu and Wendy Lavitt; and in *Doll Reader, Dolls—The Collector's Magazine, Doll Designs, Doll Castle, Catskill Life, Florida Quarterly* and *The Fairy Book*. She is a member of UFDC.

VIRGINIA KILLMORE
VIRGINIA KILLMORE DOLLS
4168 Bussey Rd.
Syracuse, NY 13215
Phone: (315)492-4576 EST
Fax: (315)492-3792
Making dolls since: 1970
Selling dolls since: 1985

PRODUCT INFORMATION:

Mediums: Cloth

Scope of work: Some of Virginia's dolls are one-of-a-kind direct sculptures.

She makes all heads, bodies, hair, shoes and accessories for these dolls. She designs and sews all dolls' clothing.

Price range: $9-1,200

Description of dolls: All Virginia's cloth dolls are one-of-a-kinds and have armature, including hands and fingers. Hand-painted faces create a 3-dimensional effect.

Special orders: Will work with customer to create the doll. Allow 2 months.

Price list: SASE

Mailing list: Write or call to be included.

Dolls sold: In retail doll shops, at shows, galleries and museum shops

Shops: Send SASE for list.

Shows: Send SASE for list.

Home/studio visits: Please schedule 2 weeks in advance.

Phone orders: T-Th, 9-3.

Fax orders: Fax description of dolls, address and when they are needed.

Mail orders: Will ship to US, Canada, overseas. Prepayment required. Allow 2-3 weeks for delivery.

Shipping information: Shipped via UPS

Layaway: $50-100 down. Regular withdrawals from Visa available.

Discounts: After first purchase, any doll $25 or more is 15% off.

Return/exchange policy: Dolls can be returned within 10 days of receipt. Call first to make arrangements.

ADDITIONAL INFORMATION:

Virginia's work has been featured *The Doll by Contemporary Artists* by Lavitt and Dodder.

ROSEMARY KING
ROMINĀ CREATIONS
3996 Forsythe Dr.
Lexington, KY 40514
Phone: (606)224-8135 EST
Making dolls since: 1994
Selling dolls since: 1994

PRODUCT INFORMATION:

Mediums: Polymer clay (Cernit, Super Sculpey)

Scope of work: Dolls are one of-a-kind direct sculptures. Artist designs all patterns for cloth dolls. Artist makes all heads, bodies, wigs and shoes and some accessories/props. Artist designs and sews all dolls' clothing.

Price range: $250-1,000

Description of dolls: All Rominā dolls are original. Head, hands, feet and most of the shoes are sculpted in polymer clay. They have soft bodies with wire armatures. The clothing is designed and made by the artist.

Special orders: Makes dolls that bear likeness to a person, but are not direct portraits. Specify hair and color, clothing, shoes, mannerisms. Allow 2-3 months, depending on the complexity of the order.

Mailing list: Write to be included.

Dolls sold: At shows

Shows: Call or send SASE for list.

Phone orders: M-F, 9-5. Artist will return messages.

Shipping information: Shipped via UPS. COD.

Return/exchange policy: Only if broken during shipping

ADDITIONAL INFORMATION:
Rosemary's work has been featured in the *Lexington Herald Leader* and *Jet* magazine.

MARILYN KLOSKO
MAGUSTINE ARTS AND
COLLECTIBLES, INC.
9437 Kilimanjaro
Columbia, MD 21045
Phone: (301)596-6156 EST
Making dolls since: 1990
Selling dolls since: 1991

PRODUCT INFORMATION:

Mediums: Porcelain

Scope of work: Dolls are created in limited editions. Artist makes all heads, bodies, wigs, shoes and molds. Artist designs all dolls' clothing.

Price range: $700-1,400

Description of dolls: All Marilyn's studio editions are created, in their entirety, by the artist, including sculpture, mold making, all aspects of the

production process, human hair wigs, clothing, hats and shoes.

Catalog: Color photo brochure, $5, refundable with purchase.

Price list: Free

Mailing list: Write to be included.

Dolls sold: In retail doll shops, at shows, by mail

Shows: Everyone on mailing list will be notified.

Phone orders: M-F, 10-3.

Mail orders: Will ship to US, Canada, overseas. Prepayment required. Allow 8-10 weeks for delivery.

Shipping information: Shipped via UPS. Shipping included in price of doll in continental US or Canada. International shipping costs must be prepaid.

Layaway: 20% deposit, 20% per month

Return/exchange policy: No returns or exchanges

ADDITIONAL INFORMATION:
Klosko is a member of the MSDBA.

FAYETTE KNOOP
FAYETTE KNOOP/ORIGINAL CHARACTER DOLLS
P.O. Box 237
North Freedom, WI 53951
Phone: (608)522-3606 CST
Making dolls since: 1990
Selling dolls since: 1990

PRODUCT INFORMATION:

Mediums: Cernit, some cloth

Scope of work: Dolls are one-of-a-kind direct sculptures. Artist makes all heads and some bodies, wigs, shoes and accessories/props. She designs and sews all clothing.

Price range: $40-400

Description of dolls: Each doll is an original creation, from the smaller beanbag dolls to the life-size characters. Most are elderly grannies and grandpas of various ethnic groups.

Special orders: Artist will try to do special requests, such as dolls related to a profession or a hobby. Must give her 3-4 months to complete special order.

Dolls sold: In retail shops, at shows and by mail

Phone orders: M-Sat, 10-10.

Mail orders: Will ship to US, Canada. Prepayment required.

Shipping information: Shipped via UPS or US mail. Shipping is included in the price of the doll.

Layaway: ½ payment down, 3 months

ADDITIONAL INFORMATION:
Fayette has been featured in *Contemporary Doll Collector*. For the past 3 years she has been invited to submit a cloth doll to Doll Makers Magic, The Figure in Cloth Tours.

ANGELIKA LA HAISE
DOLL MAKER
R.R.#3
Lanark, Ontario K0G 1K0
CANADA
Phone: (613)278-2115 EST
Making dolls since: 1986
Selling dolls since: 1986

PRODUCT INFORMATION:

Mediums: Wood (hand carved) and porcelain (very limited editions)

Scope of work: Dolls are one-of-a-kind hand carved wood and very limited editions of 3-12 porcelain dolls. Artist makes all heads, bodies and molds when applicable. She also makes most wigs and shoes and some accessories/props. She designs and sews all clothing.

Price range: $300-2,000

Description of dolls: Some of Angelika's dolls are a combination of wood and cloth while others are entirely wood. Clothes for both wood and porcelain dolls are made with the finest materials. Some dolls wear hand-knit sweaters.

Special orders: Artist does portrait dolls very rarely and only with a great deal of negotiation and meeting. Allow 2-8 months depending on other orders.

Designs manufactured by: Carousel Canada Inc., Hamilton Collection

Dolls sold: In retail doll shops, at shows and by mail

Shops: Send SASE for list.

Home/studio visits: Please schedule in advance.

Phone orders: Accepted M-F

Return/exchange policy: Return within 10 days of receipt; mailing cost and customs tax will be deducted.

ADDITIONAL INFORMATION:
Angelika was winner of a 1992 DOTY in the Wooden Doll Category. She has been featured in *Dolls of Canada* by Evelyn Rolson Strahlendorf and in *Contemporary Doll Collector* and various newspapers in Canada. She also gives talks and demonstrations on dolls.

BARBARA J. LADY
OCHOCO ORIGINALS
325 Quarry Rd.
Albany, OR 97321
Phone: (503)928-4085 PST
Making dolls since: 1989
Selling dolls since: 1989

PRODUCT INFORMATION:

Mediums: Synthetic clay

Scope of work: Barbara's dolls are all one-of-a-kind. Artist makes all heads and bodies; most shoes and accessories/props and some wigs.

Price range: $150-5,000

Description of dolls: Barbara's direct sculpture dolls are representative of a variety of ethnic, gender, age and size subjects.

Special Orders: Artist makes portrait

dolls from photographs. Front and profile photos are helpful. Prearrangements for costs and conditions for purchase approval are required. Allow about 2 months.

Price list: Available

Dolls sold: In retail doll shops, at shows, by mail, from artist's home/studio

Shop: Call or send SASE for list.

Shows: Call or send SASE for list.

Home/studio visits: Please schedule a day in advance.

Phone orders: Any day

Mail orders: Will ship to US, Canada, overseas. Prepayment required. Layaway may be arranged. Shipping within 48 hours.

Shipping information: Shipped via UPS. Shipping is included in the price of the doll.

Layaway: ⅓ down, 6 months

ADDITIONAL INFORMATION
Barbara's work has been featured in *Doll Reader*, *Contemporary Doll Collector* and *Fantastic Figures* by Susanna Oroyan. Barbara belongs to the UFDC affiliated Doll and Toy Craftsmen of Oregon, and teaches sculpting at doll shops and doll shows.

JAINE LAMB
34 Queen St.
Orillia, Ontario L3V 1B7
CANADA
Phone: (705)325-2044 EST
Making dolls since: 1992
Selling dolls since: 1992

PRODUCT INFORMATION:

Mediums: Cernit, Super Sculpey, Paperclay, Porcelain

Scope of work: Dolls are one-of-a-kind direct sculptures. The artist makes all heads, bodies and wigs, and some shoes and accessories/props. She designs and sews all clothing.

Price range: $450-2,000

Description of dolls: The artist's dolls range from Santas and Christmas themes to children and old folk, and many fantasy pieces. All are hand sculpted, assembled, painted and dressed in many different fabrics, modern to antique.

Special orders: The artist makes portrait dolls from photographs (front, both sides, back and ¾ profiles). Must give her approximately 6 months to complete a doll.

Price list: Free

Mailing list: Write or call to be included.

Dolls sold: In retail doll shops, at shows, by mail, from artist's home/studio

Shows: Call or send SASE for list.

Home/studio visits: Please schedule by phone in advance.

Phone orders: Available

Layaway: Prefers 30% down. Balance can be equalized over 6 months or a year.

Return/exchange policy: Will repair or replace damaged goods (if customer receives them damaged).

ADDITIONAL INFORMATION:
Jaine won an award at the The International Doll Expo, Gallery of Dolls '95, and the Quinte Hastings Doll Club Best of Show and 1st Prize ribbon in 1993. She also has been featured in *Contemporary Doll Collector*. She is a member of the Canadian Doll Co-op.

DEBRA LAMKIN
DEBRA'S DARLING DOLLS
701 Matthews-Pineville Rd.
Matthews, NC 28105
Phone: (704)847-7733 EST
Making dolls since: 1986
Selling dolls since: 1994

PRODUCT INFORMATION:

Mediums: Porcelain with cloth armature bodies

Scope of work: Artist makes limited editions of 25-50 dolls. She makes some heads, bodies, wigs and accessories/props; shoes are bought ready-made. She designs all clothing and either sews it herself or hires a seamstress to sew.

Price range: $995-2,000

Description of dolls: Debra's dolls are portraits of childhood.

Price list: SASE

Mailing list: Write or call to be included.

Dolls sold: In retail doll shops, at shows, by mail, from artist's home/studio. Artist is represented by Thomas Boland and Company.

Shops: Call or send SASE for list.

Phone orders: M-F, 9-9. Sat, 9-1.

Mail orders: Will ship to US, Canada, overseas. Prepayment is required from new accounts; established accounts will be billed. Allow 4-6 weeks.

Shipping information: Shipped UPS, FedEx. COD or added to invoice (established accounts).

Layaway: 20% down; remainder divided into 6 equal monthly payments.

Discounts: Wholesale to licensed shops only

Return/exchange policy: 15-day return with original packing

ADDITIONAL INFORMATION:
Debra has been featured in *Dolls—The Collectors Magazine*, *Doll Reader* and *Contemporary Doll Collector*.

DEBORAH A. LAW
DOLLS BY DAL
P.O. 190 Belgrade Rd.
Mt. Vernon, ME 04352
Phone: (207)293-2401 EST
Fax: (207)293-2991
Making dolls since: 1991
Selling dolls since: 1991

PRODUCT INFORMATION:

Mediums: Sculpey, Fimo, Cernit

Scope of work: Dolls are all one-of-a-kind direct sculptures with soft bodies. Artist makes all heads, bodies, shoes and accessories/props, most wigs. Artist designs and sews all doll clothing.

Price range: $90-900

Description of dolls: Dolls are original, with finely hand-tailored clothing, and include subjects ranging from

elves, mermaids, witches and Santas to dolls a child would love.

Special orders: Artist will fill special orders. Her specialty is making an outfit to customer's specifications from an article of clothing (such as grandma's wedding dress). Allow 6-8 weeks.

Dolls sold: At shows, from artist's studio

Shows: Send SASE for list.

Home/studio visits: Please schedule 2 days in advance.

Layaway: 25% down, 3 months

ADDITIONAL INFORMATION:
Law is a member of MSDBA. She has been a professional tailor for 28 years.

JILANE LEGUS
JILANE ORIGINALS
4472 Smith Lake Rd. SE
Osakis, MN 56360
Phone: (612)859-2083 CST
Making dolls since: 1992
Selling dolls since: 1992

PRODUCT INFORMATION:

Mediums: Super Sculpey, Cernit

Scope of work: Dolls are one-of-a-kind direct sculptures. Artist makes all heads, bodies, shoes and some wigs and accessories/props. Artist designs and sews all dolls' clothes.

Price range: $200-1,500

Description of dolls: Jilane's dolls include clothing, shoes, and headgear that have been carefully designed and hand crafted.

Special orders: Artist makes portrait dolls from photos. Project requires $150 deposit and clear close-up front, back, side and ¾ front photos. Allow 3-6 months for portrait dolls, others 1-2 months.

Dolls sold: In retail shops and by mail

Shops: Send SASE for list.

Home/studio visits: Please schedule a day in advance.

Phone orders: M-F, 7-7.

Mail orders: Will ship to US, Canada, overseas. Prepayment required.

Shipping information: Shipped via UPS. Shipping cost is added to the price of doll.

Layaway: 20% down, payments by arrangement

Return/exchange policy: If customer is not happy with the doll, may return it within 30 days for a full refund—not to include shipping cost.

DENISE LEMMON
MOUNTAIN BABIES DOLL FACTORY
6713 296th St. E.
Graham, WA 98338
Phone: (206)847-6479 PST
Making dolls since: 1979
Selling dolls since: 1979

PRODUCT INFORMATION:

Mediums: Porcelain, wood

Scope of work: Dolls are created in limited editions of 10-20. Artist designs patterns for all cloth dolls. Artist makes all heads, wigs and shoes, most accessories/props, some bodies. Artist designs and sews most dolls' clothing.

Price range: $1,800-6,000

Description of dolls: The "Mountain Babies" are dolls made for the discerning collector. Most are made from porcelain and wood and are known for their high quality, detail and expert craftsmanship. Denise's dolls are often representative of current events, and contain many layers of detail that are carefully brought together to form a true work of art. An example of this interesting technique would be "Sarah, Child of the Northwest." This doll was made to represent the spirit of living in the Pacific Northwest. She was created originally in commemoration of the 1989 Washington State Centennial. Denise also made a series of one-of-a-kind dolls to represent various environmental issues. The dolls' costumes are intricate with animals and plants painted and appliqued on them. Denise Lemmon makes nearly every part of her dolls herself, from the soft mohair eyelashes to the beautifully finished leather shoes. Her one-of-a-kinds in costume are both elaborate and exclusive. She makes a total of about 30 dolls per year.

Designs manufactured by: Solo Industries, Bill Lamborn

Price list: $1, refundable with purchase

Mailing list: Write or call to be included.

Dolls sold: In retail shops, at shows and by mail

Shops: Call for list.

Home/studio visits: Please schedule 1 week in advance.

Phone orders: M-F, 9-7.

Mail orders: Will ship to US, Canada, overseas. Prepayment required. $100 nonrefundable deposit when ordering. Allow 6 months-1 year for delivery.

Shipping information: Shipped via UPS. Shipping is included in the price of the doll.

Layaway: 3 months same as cash

Discounts: To wholesalers—about 40%

ADDITIONAL INFORMATION:
Lemmon received a 1st place IDEX one-of-a-kind award. Lemmon's work has appeared in *Dolls—The Collector's Magazine* magazine. She is a graphic artist and illustrator, fine arts educator and painter.

HELGA WALKER LONG
YESTERDAY'S MEMORIES
928 Shunpike Rd.
Cape May, NJ 08204
Phone: (609)884-3953 EST
Making dolls since: 1984
Selling dolls since: 1987

PRODUCT INFORMATION:
Mediums: Cernit, porcelain

Scope of work: Dolls are one-of-a-kind direct sculptures. Artist makes all heads, bodies, wigs, shoes and accessories/props. Artist designs and sews all dolls' clothing.

Price range: $250-875

Description of dolls: Helga creates primarily children (humorous and lifelike). She also makes fairytale and other characters.

Mailing list: Write or call to be included.

Dolls sold: In retail shops, at shows and from artist's home/studio

Shows: Call for list.

Home/studio visits: Please schedule 2 days in advance

Mail orders: Will ship to US, Canada. Prepayment required.

Shipping information: Shipped via UPS. Shipping is included in the price of the doll.

ADDITIONAL INFORMATION:
Walker Long's work has appeared in *Contemporary Doll Collector.* She is a member of the Professional Doll Makers Art Guild.

SYLVIA LYONS
PORCELAIN PEOPLE
8280 Wild Horse Valley Rd.
Napa, CA 94558
Phone: (707)224-8280
Fax: (707)224-1016
Making dolls since: 1975
Selling dolls since: 1975

PRODUCT INFORMATION:
Mediums: Porcelain, porcelain and cloth, Paperclay

Scope of work: Artist makes limited editions of 10-35 dolls. She makes all heads, bodies, shoes, accessories and molds, and most wigs and eyes. She designs and sews all clothing.

Price range: $75-1,200

Description of dolls: Sylvia's originals are created with an emphasis on multi-jointed swivel head animals, dolls, historical and bridal figures. The majority measure 1″ or 1½″ to 1 foot. Larger pieces up to 36″ tall are generally made of Paperclay with wired, bendable armatures. Fairytale and storybook characters are well represented. Commissions and portraits are accepted.

Special orders: Provide photographs in

color clearly depicting posture, head and hands. 20% deposit is required; remainder must be paid when order is completed. Allow 3 months.

Catalog/price list: b&w, send large SASE. Price list, send large SASE.

Mailing list: Write, call or fax request to be included.

Dolls sold: In retail shops, at shows or from artist's home/studio

Shops: Call for list.

Shows: Call for list or send SASE.

Home/studio visits: Please schedule 1 week in advance.

Phone orders: 8-6 PST.

Fax orders: Include name, address and phone number of buyer, name and price of the item plus color (if optional).

Mail orders: Will ship to US, Canada, overseas.

Shipping information: Shipped UPS, FedEx or US mail for overseas orders or at customer's request. Shipped COD, or shipping is added as a separate item on the bill.

Layaway: 20% down, minimum of $25 per month.

Return/exchange policy: Damaged or flawed pieces may be exchanged. Portrait dolls may be returned if customer is not pleased. 20% deposit is forfeited for all other returns.

ADDITIONAL INFORMATION:
Sylvia's work has been featured in *Dolls—The Collector's Magazine, Contemporary Doll Collector, Nutshell News, Maison de Poupie* (France) and *Dolls in Miniature.* She is a member of ODACA, IGMA, UFDC, and NAME. She also makes portrait bridal figurines.

LOIS K. MCAULIFFE
58 Spring St. #8
Medfield, MA 02052-2423
Phone: (508)359-5053 EST

Fax: (508)785-0138
Making dolls since: 1994
Selling dolls since: 1995

PRODUCT INFORMATION:

Mediums: Heads, hands and feet sculpted of polymer clay (Super Sculpey and Super Sculpey/Fimo mix); cloth bodies

Scope of work: Dolls are one-of-a-kind direct sculptures. Artist makes all heads and bodies, some accessories/props. Artist designs and sews all dolls' clothing.

Price range: $200-600

Description of dolls: Lois creates lady dolls dressed in beautiful period costumes. The 22″ dolls have heads, hands and feet made of polymer clay, over which 5 layers of acrylic paint are applied. They have hand-painted eyes, applied eyelashes, cloth bodies and modacrylic fiber wigs. Her elegantly costumed characters have stepped right off the pages of a storybook. In addition to the dolls, her imaginative props help to bring the stories to life. "The Princess and the Frog" catches the princess mid-gasp and includes the golden ball and a grassy base where the frog sits next to a wishing well. "The Scullery Maid" is singing as she scrubs a blackened pot complete with soap suds. Her dolls have expressive faces and graceful hands, with each tiny fingernail individually attached.

Price list: Free with SASE.

Mailing list: Write or call to be included.

Dolls sold: At shows, by mail

Shows: Send SASE for list.

Home/studio visits: Please schedule 3 weeks in advance.

Mail orders: Will ship to US, Canada. Prepayment is required. Allow 4 weeks for delivery.

Shipping information: Shipped via UPS. Shipping is included in the price of the doll.

Layaway: 20% down—nonrefundable. Dolls may be on layaway for up to one year. If order is cancelled before doll is shipped, money will be refunded less the nonrefundable 20% deposit.

ADDITIONAL INFORMATION:

Lois is a member of MSDBA and AADA. She has a small, home-based business making cloth dolls and stuffed animals which she sells through local gift shops.

CINDY M. MCCLURE
CINDY M. MCCLURE ENT. LTD.
13215 C. SE Mill Plain, Suite 472
Vancouver, WA 98684
Phone/fax: (360)834-1411
Making dolls since: 1982
Selling dolls since: 1983

PRODUCT INFORMATION:

Mediums: Porcelain and wax-over-porcelain, Sculpey, Cernit and ceramic clay

Scope of work: Artist makes limited editions of 10-250 dolls. She makes all heads and bodies, most accessories/props and molds, and some wigs. All shoes and some wigs and accessories/props are bought ready-made. Artist designs all clothing; she sews some clothing.

Price range: $800-5,000

Description of dolls: Cindy sculpts from live models (anyone's children).

Special orders: Artist makes portrait dolls from photographs. She needs several photographs, most importantly the profile and head circumference measurements. Allow 1 year for portrait doll.

Designs manufactured by: Ashton-Drake

Catalog: Color brochures, photos and price list, free.

Mailing list: Write or call to be included.

Dolls sold: In retail doll shops, at shows, by mail, from artist's home/studio

Shops: Call or send SASE for list.

Shows: Call or send SASE for list.

Phone orders: 9-5.

Fax orders: Fax brochure order form.

Mail orders: Will ship to US, Canada, overseas. Prepayment is required. Allow 6-12 weeks for delivery.

Shipping information: Shipped via UPS. Shipping is included in the price of the doll.

Layaway: 25% down—payments according to your budget (within reason). No refunds.

Return/exchange policy: No cash refunds. All money will be credited toward another doll.

ADDITIONAL INFORMATION:

Cindy won the 1994 *Dolls* Award of Excellence for "Cross Stitch," seen on this book's cover. She was a winner of the 1995 *Dolls* Dolls of Excellence and was also nominated for the 1995 DOTY award. She has been featured in *Dolls—The Collector's Magazine* and *Collectors Mart Magazine*.

MELISSA A. MCCRORY
MELISSA ORIGINALS
2309 Wildwood Ave.
Jackson, MI 49202
Phone: (517)784-4591 EST
Making dolls since: 1978
Selling dolls since: 1978

PRODUCT INFORMATION:

Mediums: Porcelain

Scope of work: Artist makes limited editions of 25 dolls. She makes heads, bodies, wigs, shoes, accessories/props and molds for some dolls. She also designs and sews all clothing.

Price range: $200-2,500

Description of dolls: Artist's subjects are real children with many expressions and motion.

Special orders: Artist makes portrait dolls. Allow 1 year.

Designs manufactured by: HSN or Kaies Parc

Mailing list: Write or call to be included.

Dolls sold: In retail shops, at shows, by mail, from artist's home/studio

Shops: Send SASE for list.

Shows: Call or send SASE for list.

Home/studio visits: Please schedule 1 week in advance.

Phone orders: M-Th, 9-5.

Mail orders: Will ship to US, Canada, overseas. Prepayment required. Allow 8-10 weeks for delivery.

Shipping information: Shipped via UPS, US mail. Shipping cost is added to price of doll.

Discounts: Dealer discount

ADDITIONAL INFORMATION:

Melissa's work has been featured in *Contemporary Doll Collector, Dolls—The Collector's Magazine* and *Doll Reader.* She also has writen articles for *Doll Crafter.*

SARA MCGOODWIN-YOUNG
REPRESENTED BY: DOLLCO

22248 Cohasset St.
Canoga Park, CA 91303
Phone: (818)702-0315 PST
Fax: (818)702-9275
E-Mail: thomreneei@aol.com
Making dolls since: 1991
Selling dolls since: 1991

PRODUCT INFORMATION:

Mediums: Porcelain, polymer clays, mixed medium, cloth and resin

Scope of work: Some dolls are one-of-a-kind direct sculptures. Artist sometimes makes one doll from each mold or makes limited editions of 10-500 dolls. She designs most cloth doll patterns. She makes all heads, bodies, wigs, shoes, accessories and molds. She designs and sews most clothing.

Price range: $25-2,000

Description of dolls: Sara's dolls range from small, simple Native American "Spirit Dolls," inexpensive unlimited editions and delicate faerie and guardian angels to larger editions of historically accurate dolls such as Native Americans or Native Africans, to elaborate one-of-a-kind "captured moments." Sara sometimes makes more than one doll with a complete set and a story. Dolls are detailed and colorful with exotic fabrics of silk and wool, feathers and intricate beadwork. Artist also incorporates "found treasures" of antique or imported quality.

Special orders: Artist will work from a description, photos and drawings.

Completion time depends on project.

Catalog/price list: Color photos, $5, refundable with purchase. Price list free.

Mailing list: Write to be included.

Dolls sold: In retail doll shops and at shows

Shops: Call for list

Shows: Call for list

Mail orders: Will ship to US, Canada, overseas. Prepayment generally is required. Customer pays ½ down, balance due before shipping. Allow 4-6 weeks or as arranged.

Shipping information: Shipped via UPS.

ADDITIONAL INFORMATION:

Sara has been featured twice in the Debut section of *Contemporary Doll Collector.*

HEATHER BROWNING MACIAK

387 Glamorgan Cr. SW
Calgary, Alberta T3E 5B7
CANADA
Phone: (403)246-0790 MST
Making dolls since: 1989
Selling dolls since: 1990

PRODUCT INFORMATION:

Mediums: Porcelain

Scope of work: Dolls are created in limited editions of 5-10. Artist makes all heads, bodies, wigs, shoes, accessories/props and molds. Artist designs and sews all dolls' clothing.

Price range: $500-750

Description of dolls: All Heather's dolls are artist's signature editions, designed and created top-to-toe by the artist. The eyes are hand-painted and go through several firings to achieve a soft, natural look. Wigs are of various natural fibers and furs and are hand dyed. Editions are small, and no face will ever be used again once the edition is sold out, guaranteeing the collector a rare treasure.

Catalog/price list: Color, $5. Price list, included with catalog.

Mailing list: Write to be included. Automatic inclusion with purchase.

Dolls sold: In retail doll shops, at shows, by mail, from artist's home/studio

Shops: Please write to request—no SASE required.

Shows: Everyone on mailing list will be notified.

Home/studio visits: Please schedule 1 or 2 days in advance.

Phone orders: Accepted

Mail orders: Will ship to US, Canada, overseas. Prepayment required. Allow 1 week after doll is ready.

Shipping information: Will ship Canada Post. Shipping is included in the price of the doll.

Layaway: ⅓ downpayment, then 2 payments over the next 2 months. Doll is shipped upon receipt of last payment.

Return/exchange policy: Customer must call first; doll must be returned within 7 days, in same condition in which it left artist's studio.

ADDITIONAL INFORMATION:

Heather was nominated for *Doll Reader*'s DOTY awards in 1992 and 1993; 1st place in artist doll category UFDC National 1992; 1st place in category Calgary Exhibition and Stampede, 1991 and 1992; 1st place overall at Calgary Exhibition and Stampede, 1995; and an award of merit for exceptional work. Her work has appeared in *Doll Reader, Contemporary Doll Collector, Canadian Doll Journal* and *Charlton's Price Guide to Canadian Dolls.* Maciak is a member of the Calgary Doll Club, Foothills Doll Club (NFDC) and APWPWD. She has also done some paper doll work, written for *Doll Reader, Doll World, Doll News* (UFDC), and offered slide presentations for UFDC.

CHRISTINE MACINNIS
LITTLE PEOPLE

R.R.#1 Site 50, Compartment 50
Denman Island, British Columbia
V0R 1T0
CANADA
Phone: (604)335-2958 PST
Making dolls since: 1985
Selling dolls since: 1988

PRODUCT INFORMATION:

Mediums: Cloth, wire, yarn, leather

Scope of work: Dolls are one-of-a-kind direct sculptures or artist-designed patterns for cloth dolls. Artist makes all heads, bodies, wigs, accessories/props. Artist designs and sews all dolls' clothing.

Price range: $4-10

Description of dolls: Christine's durable, bendable dolls are the perfect size for doll houses. They are handcrafted with a strong copper wire frame and tightly wrapped with yarn. The heads are cotton with sewn-on yarn hair and stitched features. Their clothing is removable. You may choose from mouse, bear or people dolls of all ages. The mouse and bear dolls have hand-stitched leather heads.

Special orders: Artist makes special order dolls. Hair, eye and skin color may be requested on order form.

Catalog/price list: b&w, send SASE

Mailing list: Write or call to be included.

Dolls sold: By mail, from artist's home/ studio, local craft shops.

Home/studio visits: Please schedule 1 week in advance.

Phone orders: Anytime

Mail orders: Will ship to Canada. Prepayment is required. Allow 4-6 weeks for delivery.

Shipping information: Regular mail. Shipping charge added on order form, $3.50 on all orders.

Discounts: If 5 or more items are ordered, take 10% off

Return/exchange policy: Will exchange or refund if customer is not happy.

ADDITIONAL INFORMATION:
MacInnis is a member of the Local Arts Alliance.

DEBORAH KEYES MCKENZIE
GRAMPA'S GIRL ORIGINALS
31 Schoolhouse Rd.
Amherst, NH 03031-1602
Phone: (603)673-3679 EST
Fax: (603)673-3945
E-Mail: qabf27b@prodigy.com
Making dolls since: 1993
Selling dolls since: 1995

PRODUCT INFORMATION:
Mediums: Cernit, polymer
Scope of work: Dolls are one-of-a-kind direct sculptures. She makes all heads, bodies, wigs, shoes and some accessories/props. The artist also designs and sews all dolls' clothing.
Price range: $150-800
Description of dolls: Deborah's doll designs include adult men and women, fantasy women, storybook characters, clowns and some children. Wigs are handcrafted of mohair or Cotswold wool; shoes are either sculpted or handmade of leather or cloth by the artist.

Mailing list: Write or call to be included.

Dolls sold: At shows, by mail, from artist's home/studio, on American Academy of Doll Artists Fall Tour

Shows: Everyone on mailing list will be notified.

Home/studio visits: Please schedule 1-2 days in advance.

Phone orders: Accepted.

Mail orders: Will ship to US, Canada, overseas. Prepayment is required. Add $15 shipping and handling charge; overseas shipping charge may be higher. Allow 1-2 weeks for delivery.

Shipping information: Shipped via UPS; additional charge $15.

Layaway: Nonrefundable deposit of 20% down, with balance to be paid in full within 90 days; doll will be shipped upon receipt of final payment. Does not include shipping and handling charges.

Return/exchange policy: Returns accepted within 10 days with a 20% handling fee. Doll must be in original condition/packaging. No exchanges.

ADDITIONAL INFORMATION:
Deborah's work has been featured in *Contemporary Doll Collector.* She is a member of AADA and MSDBA.

ANN MCNICHOLS
MCNICHOLS DOLLS AND GALLERY
4280 Pearl Harbor Dr.
Naples, FL 33962
Phone: (941)261-7891 EST
Making dolls since: 1979
Selling dolls since: 1980

PRODUCT INFORMATION:
Mediums: Porcelain
Scope of work: Artist makes limited editions of 10-15 dolls. She makes all heads, bodies and molds most wigs, and shoes and accessories/props. She

also designs and sews all clothing.

Price range: $100-1,000

Description of dolls: Many of Ann's dolls are ethnic or historical in subject.

Special orders: Artist makes portrait dolls. She needs very good photographs to work from. Allow 2-3 months for a portrait doll.

Catalog: Color brochure, free

Mailing list: Write to be included.

Dolls sold: In retail doll shops, at shows, by mail, from artist's home/studio

Shops: Call for list.

Shows: Call for list.

Home/studio visits: Visit M-F, 10-5, but a phone call is advised before visit.

Phone orders: M-F, 10-5.

Mail orders: Will ship to US, Canada, overseas. Payment can be arranged to suit the buyer. Allow 6-8 weeks for delivery.

Shipping information: Shipped via UPS or FedEx. COD or other arrangement.

Layaway: Can be arranged to suit the buyer.

Discounts: On purchases of more than 1 doll or to repeat customers.

ADDITIONAL INFORMATION:
Ann received the Best of Original *Dolls* award in 1992 from IDMA, West Palm Beach, Florida, and has been featured in *Contemporary Doll Collector.* She is a member of IDMA, Original Doll Maker Association and UFDC. She also sculpts museum replicas.

CAROLE MADDOCKS
CAROLE ANN CREATIONS
5 Crestview Dr.
N. Scituate, RI 02857
Phone: (401)934-1924
Making dolls since: 1993
Selling dolls since: 1994

PRODUCT INFORMATION:
Mediums: Soft sculpture

Scope of work: Dolls are one-of-a-kind direct sculptures. Artist designs patterns for all cloth dolls. Artist makes all heads, bodies, wigs and shoes and most accessories/props. Artist designs and sews all dolls' clothing.

Price range: $200-250

Description of dolls: 19″-21″ soft sculpture men, women and babies with wire armatures and detailed Victorian costumes. Faces wear various expressions, including smiling, talking, etc. Dolls wear embroidered jewelry, and fingers are wired for individual finger poses. Hairstyles and hats are designed for each doll. Each doll is different. No molds are used.

Special orders: Artist makes portrait dolls from photos. Project requires photo of subject with facial expressions as wished in sculpture. Color photos. Allow 4-6 weeks.

Catalog/price list: Color, $6, refunded with purchase. Price list included in catalog.

Dolls sold: By mail or from artist's home/studio

Home/studio visits: Please schedule 1 week in advance.

Phone orders: Weekdays, 5:30-7.

Mail orders: Will ship to US, Canada, overseas. Prepayment required. Allow 2-4 weeks for delivery.

Shipping information: Shipped via UPS. Shipping will be added to price of doll.

Layaway: 20% down and rest worked out with purchaser.

Discounts: 30% discount for purchase by store for resale.

ADDITIONAL INFORMATION:
Carole has received a 2nd place Ida Lewis Doll Club Award. Her work has appeared in *Contemporary Doll Collector.* She is a member of the 1770 Doll Club.

NORMA J. MALERICH
May thru October:
526 Sarah Ln. #24
St. Louis, MO 63141
November thru April:
2200 S. Ocean Blvd. #902
Delray Beach, FL 33483
Phone: (314)432-0966 CST (MO),
(407)274-0708 EST (FL)

Selling dolls since: 1985

PRODUCT INFORMATION:
Mediums: Cloth
Scope of work: Artist designs patterns for all cloth dolls.
Price range: $100-200
Description of dolls: Norma's dolls are stuffed and sewn with multi-fabrics. They are painted and embellished with sequins, "jewels" and glitters. Current size is 33″ tall. Each doll is named and signed by artist on back.
Mailing list: Write to be included.
Dolls sold: By mail, from artist's home/studio, art galleries throughout the US and Canada.
Shops: Send SASE for list.
Home/studio visits: Please schedule in advance.
Phone orders: Any day
Mail orders: Will ship to US. Allow 2 months for delivery.
Shipping information: Shipped via UPS. COD.
Return/exchange policy: If not happy, send back within 10 days of receipt of doll.

ADDITIONAL INFORMATION:
Norma's work has appeared in *Contemporary Doll Collector, Dollmaker's Journal, Sun Sentinal Newspaper,* and *Suburban Journal-St. Louis, Missouri.*

EMILY T. MANNING
STARCHILD TOY CO.
4809 Ravenswood Rd.
Riverdale, MD 20737
Phone: (301)864-5561 EST
Making dolls since: 1993
Selling dolls since: 1995

PRODUCT INFORMATION:
Mediums: Cloth
Scope of work: Dolls are one-of-a-kind direct sculptures. Artist designs patterns for all cloth dolls. Artist makes all heads and bodies. Artist designs and makes some dolls' clothing, and sometimes uses ready-made or antique clothing.

Price range: $65-250

Description of dolls: Emily's 18″-36″ soft huggable dolls sit on your hip and use real baby clothes, made from heavy duty double knit cotton/polyester. Limbs are stitched with upholstery thread for easy repair. Wigs are sewn on, and faces are sculpted and painted. Dolls are signed and dated with birth certificates and spiritual messages (not religious).

Special orders: Artist will create special order dolls. Allow 2-4 months.

Catalog/price list: Color, $2, refundable with purchase.

Price list: Free

Mailing list: Write or call to be included.

Dolls sold: At shows, by mail, from artist's home/studio

Home/studio visits: T-Sun, 12:30-5 (but call first if you are not local to our area).

Phone orders: Accepted

Mail orders: Will ship to US, Canada. Prepayment required. If doll is already made, allow 1 week delivery.

Shipping information: Will ship via UPS. Shipping is added to doll price and varies depending on doll and customer location.

Layaway: ⅓ down, 2 additional payments of ⅓

Discounts: Artist has 10% sales.

Return/exchange policy: Returns within a week in original condition only.

MARY LOU MANNING
MARY LOU MANNING STUDIO
4942 Bel Pre Rd.
Rockville MD 20853
Phone: (301)460-5992 EST
Fax: (301)460-5992

Making dolls since: 1992
Selling dolls since: 1993

PRODUCT INFORMATION:

Mediums: Hydrostone, Paperclay, Super Sculpey, LA Doll, Premiere

Scope of work: Dolls are one of a kind direct sculptures. Artist makes all heads, bodies, wigs, shoes and accessories/props. Artist designs and sews all dolls' clothing.

Price range: $300-500

Description of dolls: Mary Lou's dolls are mostly older, famous figures such as Dolly Levi and Katherine Hepburn, or modeled after figures from paintings, such as Mary Cassatt's Mother (from Le Figaro), and Young Woman from Manet's "Behind Bar at Folies Bergere."

Special orders: Artist creates special order dolls. Allow 3 months.

Dolls sold: At shows, from artist's home/studio

Shows: Send SASE for list.

Home/studio visits: Please schedule appointment in advance.

Phone orders: 9-5 (discussion must be in-depth)

Mail orders: Will ship to US. Prepayment required. Allow 3 months on order; dolls already made will be shipped immediately.

Shipping information: Shipped via UPS. Shipping is included in the price of the doll.

Layaway: Terms discussed on an individual basis.

Return/exchange policy: Dolls paid for fully in advance will be completely refunded on return of doll within 3 weeks at purchaser's expense.

ADDITIONAL INFORMATION:

Mary Lou is an apprentice in PDA. She also makes figures and plaques from completely original clay, molded in rubber and usually cast in Hydrostone.

"AS LONG AS THERE ARE LITTLE GIRLS, THERE WILL
BE DOLL ARTISTS."

Melissa A. McCrory, Jackson, MI

DIANA MARTINDALE
MARTINDALE ORIGINALS
4942 Ponderosa Dr.
Park City, UT 84098
Phone: (801)649-6151 MST
Making dolls since: 1978
Selling dolls since: 1978

PRODUCT INFORMATION:

Mediums: Super Sculpey, Cernit

Scope of work: Artist's dolls are one-of-a-kind direct sculptures. Artist makes all heads, bodies and shoes and some wigs and accessories/props. She designs and sews all clothing.

Price range: $100-5,000 (portrait dolls may be higher)

Description of dolls: Diana's dolls range from small, inexpensive character dolls (8″) to larger, more complex dolls (15″). Many are done in a setting with handmade accessories, and most are mounted on bases. Her most intricate dolls are done as fine art pieces—a pastel painting of a subject with a doll to complement the painting. They are displayed together in a specially designed frame that can be hung on the wall and viewed as a total art piece. Price depends on the complexity and size of the pieces. She does not take orders for her regular dolls.

Special orders: Artist will make special order combination doll/painting art pieces or portrait dolls without the painting. She requires half down to start and the balance on completion. Details negotiated by phone. Allow 6 months or longer for completion, depending on the complexity of the piece.

Dolls sold: At shows, from artist's home/studio

Shows: Call for list.

Home/studio visits: Please schedule 2-3 days in advance.

ADDITIONAL INFORMATION:

Diana is a member of UFDC and ODAC. She also creates pastel portraits and paintings (usually of people) and custom pewter casting (pins, medallions, etc.).

JOEL M. MARTÓNE
JOEL'S CREATIONS
1327 W. Colorado Ave.
Colorado Springs, CO 80904
Phone: (719)636-9032 MST
Making dolls since: 1966
Selling dolls since: 1966

PRODUCT INFORMATION:

Mediums: Cloth, antique fabrics, Sculpey, plastic, wood, fur

Scope of work: Dolls are one-of-a-kind direct sculptures. Patterns for cloth dolls are all self-designed. Artist makes some heads, bodies, wigs, shoes and accessories/props. Artist designs and sews all dolls' clothing.

Price range: $50-200

Description of dolls: Joel's creations are all one-of-a-kind with no molds. He creates bears of vintage fabric, hedgehogs, mice, rabbits, cloth dolls and Sculpey dolls and figures (2″-5′ tall).

Dolls sold: At artist's gallery and antique shop

Home/studio visits: Visit Joel's shop, Rhyme and Reason, in Colorado Springs.

Shipping information: Shipped via UPS. COD. Shipping is included in the price of the doll.

Discounts: Offers 20% off, in-shop discounts to regular customers.

ADDITIONAL INFORMATION:

Joel was chosen to show at the National Doll Federation Conferences in Atlanta and Philadelphia, and has been an ODACA member since 1980.

KEZI MATTHEWS
THE KEZI WORKS
P.O. Box 17631
Portland, OR 97217
Phone: (503)286-9385 PST
Fax: (503)285-6303
Making dolls since: 1979
Selling dolls since: 1980

PRODUCT INFORMATION:

Mediums: Cloth

Scope of work: Artist designs patterns for all cloth dolls. Artist makes all heads, bodies, wigs, shoes and accessories/props. Artist designs and sews all dolls' clothing.

Price range: $600 and up

Patterns: Directly from artist

Catalog/price list: 2-color, $2. Price list also available.

Mailing list: Write to be included.

Dolls sold: By mail

Phone orders: T-F, 10-4:30.

Fax orders: Fax catalog order form.

Mail orders: Will ship to US, Canada, overseas. Prepayment is required. Allow 4 weeks for delivery.

Shipping information: US mail. Shipping is included in the price of the doll or postage and handling added (for patterns) by customer.

Discounts: Artist will occasionally offer discounts on patterns (specifically postage) when orders top a certain price.

Return/exchange policy: Unconditional—no questions asked.

ADDITIONAL INFORMATION:
Kezi's work has been featured in *The Cloth Doll Magazine* and *Dolls—The Collector's Magazine.* Her illustrations and articles have appeared in *Dollmaking, Doll Castle News, Doll World* and *Collector Editions.*

LORRIE MESSINA
UNIQUE DOLL ARTISTRY BY LORRIE
35416 Shook Lane
Clinton Township, MI 48035
Phone: (810)792-0969 EST
Making dolls since: 1992
Selling dolls since: 1995

PRODUCT INFORMATION:

Mediums: Porcelain, Super Sculpey, Fimo, Cernit, clay

Scope of work: Some dolls are one-of-a-kind direct sculptures. Artist sometimes makes only one doll from a mold, and also makes limited editions of 10-20 dolls. She makes some heads, bodies, wigs, shoes, accessories/props and molds. She designs and sews all clothing.

Price range: $2,500-4,000

Description of dolls: Lorrie's dolls are specialty character representations of men, women and children, designed with a fine arts approach, with detail in clothing and props. All dolls have painted eyes, real hair added to lashes, brows, moustaches, etc. They are authentic in scale, but interpreted and vignetted in artist's own style, often using antique fabric, trims and props.

Special orders: Artist makes portrait dolls. She requires good photographs from all angles and a 50% nonrefundable deposit. Allow approximately 8 weeks; time varies depending on work demands of the project.

Molds: Directly from artist or through doll suppliers. Send SASE for list of suppliers or call.

Designs manufactured by: Seeley

Catalog/price list: Color photographs, $5, refundable with purchase. Price list available.

Mailing list: Write or call to be included.

Dolls sold: By mail, from artist's home/studio

Shows: Call or send SASE for list.

Home/studio visits: Please schedule 2 weeks in advance.

Phone orders: M-F, 10-4.

Mail orders: Will ship to US, Canada, overseas. Prepayment required.

Shipping information: Shipped via UPS. Shipping is included in the price of the doll.

Layaway: 50% nonrefundable down payment. Balance due prior to shipping; 1 year paid in full

Return/exchange policy: Within 10 days of receipt. Return in same condition as received.

ADDITIONAL INFORMATION:
Lorrie received the 1995 Rolf Ericson Award for Excellence in Doll Sculpting. Her work has been featured in *Doll Crafter* and *Doll Pro Magazine.* She is a member of The Doll Artisans Guild. She also has written articles for *Doll Crafter* and *Doll Pro.* She teaches porcelain doll classes, does seminars on sculpting, and guest-lectures on creativity and art.

KAREN A. MORLEY
FANTASY AT YOUR FINGERTIPS
913 East Grant Ave.
Eau Claire, WI 54701
Phone: (715)835-8877 CST
Making dolls since: 1991
Selling dolls since: 1991

PRODUCT INFORMATION:

Mediums: Fimo/polymer clay

Scope of work: Dolls are one-of-a-kind direct sculptures. Artist makes all heads, bodies, wigs and shoes and some accessories/props. Artist designs and sews all dolls' clothing.

Price range: $900-2,000

Description of dolls: Karen makes dolls directly sculpted in Fimo. Her specialty is laughing children or child-faeries with beautifully sculpted teeth. She uses difficult-to-find antique fabrics, laces and trim to create their clothing (which is not usually removable). Their shoes are sculpted. Their bodies are poseable. She also does other dolls such as trolls, monsters, angels, faeries, ladies and a few Santas.

Dolls sold: In retail doll shops, at shows, by mail, out of the artist's studio

Shops: Send SASE for list.

Shows: Send SASE for list.

Home/studio visits: Please schedule 2 days in advance.

Phone orders: Accepted

Shipping information: Will ship to US, Canada, overseas. Prepayment is required. Allow 2 weeks for delivery. Shipped via UPS. Shipping is extra, pre-paid with cost of doll.

Layaway: For dolls under $1,000, ⅓ down, 3 month. For dolls over $1,000, 1 year. No refunds on cancelled layaways.

Discounts: Offers a discount to retail shops only. Call or send SASE for prices.

Return/exchange policy: Dolls may be returned within 10 days. If doll is broken in shipping, customer can have it repaired (by artist), exchange or return for a refund.

ADDITIONAL INFORMATION:

Karen's dolls have been in *Contemporary Doll Collector.* They have also been featured in *Dolls—The Collector's Magazine.* Morley is an associate member in Stone Soup Dollmaker's Group, a Minneapolis-based group. She is also a part-time watercolor artist, with experience painting glass shades to match the bases of antique Gone With the Wind lamps. Morley was one of the few artists in the midwest to actually fire the paint on the glass, which makes the painting permanent. Before Morley started creating dolls, she was a dealer in antique dolls. She also bought and sold other antiques for 12 years.

"MAKING DOLLS IS LIKE PLAYING AND GETTING PAID FOR IT!"

Cindy McClure, Vancouver, WA

BILL NELSON
CHARACTERS BY BILL NELSON
107 E. Cary St.
Richmond, VA 23219
Phone: (804)783-2602 EST
Fax: (804)783-2602
E-Mail: bndollart@aol.com
Making dolls since: 1984
Selling dolls since: 1985

PRODUCT INFORMATION:

Mediums: Oven-baked polymer clay, mixed media

Scope of work: Artist's dolls are one-of-a-kind direct sculptures. Artist makes all heads, bodies, wigs and shoes and some accessories/props. He designs all clothing and makes some clothing.

Price range: $2,000-5,000

Description of dolls: Dolls are fantasy creations, including elves, dwarfs and gnomes. All are happy or inquiring or curious, loaded with personality and appearing as if they have something to say and are about to say it. Faces with charm and warmth and wit that evoke an emotional response from the viewer are the artist's specialty.

Dolls sold: In retail doll shops, at shows, by mail, from artist's home/studio

Shops: Call or send SASE for list or video.

Shows: Call or send SASE for list or video.

Home/studio visits: Please schedule in advance.

Phone orders: M-F, 10-4 EST

Mail orders: Will ship to US, Canada, overseas. Prepayment required. Allow 2 weeks for delivery.

Shipping information: Shipped via UPS, FedEx. Shipping is not included in the price of the doll.

Layaway: 50% up front. The remainder due within 6 months of purchase, or doll is for sale again. Nonrefundable deposit. Artist retains possession of the doll until all payments are made.

Discounts: On older dolls

Return/exchange policy: No policy for returns or exchanges

ADDITIONAL INFORMATION:

Bill's work has appeared in *Contemporary Doll Collector, Dolls—The Collector's Magazine,* and *Doll Reader.* He is a member of NIADA and is also a professional illustrator.

JILL NEMIROW-NELSON
JILL'S MICROCOSMOS
24 Orange Ave.
Clifton, NJ 07013
Phone: (201)916-1634 EST
Fax: (201)916-1634
Making dolls since: 1992
Selling dolls since: 1993

PRODUCT INFORMATION:

Mediums: Porcelain, polymer clay

Scope of work: Miniature dolls are created in limited editions of up to 100 pieces. Artist makes all heads, bodies, wigs, shoes, accessories/props and molds. Larger, non-miniature dolls sometimes have commercially made wigs, shoes and eyes. Artist designs and sews all dolls' clothing.

Price range: $125-600

Description of dolls: Jill sculpts miniature children, adult ladies, faeries, angels and more. Many dolls are fantasy-oriented. Also included in the collection are modern (doll house-sized) ladies, Renaissance gals and a few "period" women dressed in silks, crystals and real fur trim.

Special orders: Artist makes portrait dolls from photos. Must have detailed photos of the subject, including front and side views, and detailed description of eye and hair color, outfits, expression, etc. 50% nonrefundable deposit required. Allow 1-3 months.

Catalog/price list: Color, $6, refundable with purchase. Price list included with catalog.

Mailing list: Only for those who sign up at shows. Updates of my color "portfolio" are sent to anyone who purchases my work.

Dolls sold: In retail doll shops, at shows, by mail, from artist's home/studio

Shops: Send SASE or call for list.

Shows: Send SASE or call for list. Everyone on mailing list will be notified (local only).

Home/studio visits: Please schedule by phone in advance.

Mail orders: Will ship to US. Prepayment required. Artist ships *everything*, including catalogs, via UPS. Delivery is usually 5 days from the time the doll is completed.

Shipping information: Shipped via UPS. Prices for shipping included in catalog.

Layaway: 50% payment (not refundable) is due at time of order, and 2 more payments over 2-month period for the remaining balance is required.

Discounts: Wholesale—please inquire. Regular customers are offered a variety of "specials."

Return/exchange policy: Only within 10 days of purchase. Must call first. Shipping damage will be repaired after UPS insurance settlement.

ADDITIONAL INFORMATION:

Jill's work has appeared in *Doll Life, Dateline Journal, Doll Crafter, Dolls in Miniature, Miniature Showcase* and *Dollmaking Crafts and Designs.* She is the "Small Talk" columnist for *Doll Making Crafts and Designs.*

BILL O'CONNOR
575 Lujo Circle
Palm Springs, CA 92262
Phone: (619)323-3897 PST

> "THE LOVE OF DOLLS IS A COMMON LANGUAGE
> THAT SPANS NATIONAL BARRIERS."
> *Carol-Lynn Rössel Waugh, Winthrop, ME*

Making dolls since: 1948
Selling dolls since: 1948

PRODUCT INFORMATION:

Mediums: Porcelain, cloth, papier mâché, chicken wire and found materials

Scope of work: Artist makes limited edition dolls and designs all cloth doll patterns. He makes most heads and bodies and some wigs, shoes and accessories/props. He also designs and sews all clothing.

Price range: $285-1,500

Description of dolls: The doll's neck is sunk into the head to enhance the neckline of the costume. Arms and legs are moveable, eyes are glass or painted. A brass plaque with doll's name, number in series, date and artist's name is included with each doll, as well as the customer's name on the doll, date, and artist's name for insurance identification.

Designs manufactured by: Duck House Inc. for QVC

Price list: SASE

Mailing list: Write or call to be included.

Dolls sold: In retail doll shops, at shows, by mail, from artist's home/studio

Shops: Call or send SASE for list.

Shows: Call or send SASE for list. Everyone on mailing list will be notified.

Home/studio visits: Please schedule date and time in advance.

Phone orders: Accepted

Mail orders: Will ship to US, Canada, overseas. Prepayment required. Deposit of $100, balance on completion. Allow 3-4 months for delivery.

Shipping information: Shipped via UPS. Shipping is included in the price of the doll.

Layaway: $100 deposit, balance on completion of doll. Call about shipping date as dolls are insured and must be signed for.

Return/exchange policy: 30 days for returns

ADDITIONAL INFORMATION:

Bill has been featured in *Contemporary Doll Collector.* He is a member of AADA.

BARBARA I. OGDEN
DOLLS, DOLLS, DOLLS
1925 Nipmuck Path
Hanover, MD 21076
Phone: (410)551-6356 EST
Fax: (410)551-6356
E-Mail: mnsu01a@prodigy.com
Making dolls since: 1992
Selling dolls since: 1992

PRODUCT INFORMATION:

Mediums: Cotton Stockinet Fabric

Scope of work: All artist's dolls are one-of-a-kind direct hand painted cloth dolls. She designs the patterns for all her cloth dolls. She makes all heads and bodies, most accessories and some shoes. She designs and sews all clothing.

Price range: $150-200

Description of dolls: Barbara's molded-face cloth doll, called the Oggie Doll®, is 20″ tall, made of 100% stockinet material, and stuffed with 100% polyester filling. Each seam is individually double-sewn. The head consists of a hard mask covered with cotton stockinet fabric. The fabric is stretched over the mask, glued on and finger-pressed in order to reveal each delicate facial feature. Then the eyes are painted the appropriate color. The eyelids, eyelashes, eyebrows, nostrils, lips and cheeks are hand-painted. Finally the eyes are given a touch of gloss to give them "sparkle." For her higher priced dolls, Barbara also uses realistic glass eyes. She then paints the brows and lips and applies eyeliner as well as eye lashes to complement the facial features. Barbara designs and sews the clothing worn by each Oggie Doll® using quality materials, and knits the sweaters and cardigans.

Special orders: Please provide color photographs with written explanations for size and special instructions (if applicable). Allow 1 extra week plus shipping time.

Catalog/price list: b&w and color, $5, refundable with purchase. Price list free.

Mailing list: Write to be included.

Dolls sold: At shows, by mail, from artist's home/studio or via computer

Shops: Call or send SASE for list.

Shows: Call or send SASE for list. Every

previous doll customer will receive a schedule.

Computer sales: mnsu01a@prodigy.com

Home/studio visits: Please schedule 1 day in advance.

Phone orders: 7 days, 9-5.

Fax orders: Fax catalog order form, or the doll number or doll name.

Mail orders: Will ship to US, Canada. 50% down; customer will be billed for remainder. Allow 1 week plus shipping time for delivery.

Shipping information: Shipped via UPS or US mail. Shipping and handling is extra ($6/doll).

Layaway: ⅓ down, 60 days

Return/exchange policy: 100% satisfaction guaranteed. If unhappy with doll, full refund minus shipping and handling.

ADDITIONAL INFORMATION:
Barbara has won a few 1st prize awards for display and merchandise at doll shows. Her work has appeared in *Doll Reader* and the *Washington Post*. She is a member of MSDBA, UFDC, IDMC and Snip-Snap Sewing Club.

SANDRA THOMAS OGLESBY
400 W. French Ave.
Orange City, FL 32763
Phone: (904)775-0942 EST
Making dolls since: 1992
Selling dolls since: 1992

PRODUCT INFORMATION:

Mediums: Super Sculpey, clays and Paperclay

Scope of work: Most dolls are one-of-a-kind direct sculptures. Artist makes all heads, bodies, wigs, shoes and molds, and most accessories/props. She designs and sews all dolls' clothing.

Price range: $300-800

Description of dolls: Sandra's sculptures are animals, angels, sprites and young

girls. The work ranges from 12"-16" tall.

Price list: Photos with price list available on request. Photos must be returned if a purchase is not made.

Dolls sold: In retail doll shops, at shows, by mail, from artist's home/studio

Shops: Send SASE for list.

Shows: Send SASE for list.

Home/studio visits: Please schedule 1 week in advance.

Phone orders: M-Sat, 12-7. The doll is started only when a deposit is received.

Mail orders: Will ship to US, Canada, overseas. Prepayment is required. Allow approximately 3 weeks if the doll is in stock.

Shipping information: Shipped via UPS or US mail for lighter boxes. Shipping is included in the price of the doll within the continental US. Currently, customer will be billed for shipping anywhere else; payment expected before doll is mailed.

Layaway: 25% down; 6 months. Doll stays with artist until payments completed.

Discounts: Wholesale prices available to retail outlets

Return/exchange policy: Exchanges for construction defects only.

ADDITIONAL INFORMATION:
Oglesby's work has appeared in *Contemporary Doll Collector*, *Dolls—The Collector's Magazine*, and *Doll Life*. She is a member of the Original Doll Artists Association.

SUSANNA OROYAN
FABRICAT DESIGN
3270 Whitbeck Blvd.
Eugene, OR 97405
Phone: (503)345-0242 PST
Making dolls since: 1964
Selling dolls since: 1970

PRODUCT INFORMATION:

Mediums: Paperclay, polymer clay, cloth

Scope of work: Dolls are one-of-a-kind direct sculptures. Artist designs patterns for all cloth dolls. Artist makes most heads, bodies, wigs, shoes, accessories/props and molds. Artist designs and sews all dolls' clothing.

Price range: $250-2,250

Special orders: Artist makes special or-

der dolls. Conditions vary. Call to discuss project. Allow 3-6 months for project's completion.

Price list: SASE

Dolls sold: By mail and at NIADA and other doll conferences

Phone orders: Accepted

Mail orders: Will ship to US, Canada, overseas. Prepayment required. Allow 30 days for delivery.

Shipping information: Shipping included in the price of the doll.

Discounts: May be available on multiple orders/purchases.

Return/exchange policy: 90% refund if returned within 10 days of receipt.

ADDITIONAL INFORMATION:
Susanna's work has appeared in *Doll Reader*, *Doll World* and *Contemporary Doll Collector*. She is a member of NIADA and UFDC. Oroyan is also an author and regular contributor to doll publications. Her titles include *Contemporary Artist Dolls* (Hobby House, 1986) and *Fantastic Figures* (C&T Publishing, 1994). She is also owner/publisher of Fabricat Design (10 titles in print on doll-making subjects).

MARNIE PANEK
MARNIE'S WORLD OF DOLLS INC.
P.O. Box 685
Port Coquitlam, British Columbia
V3B 6H9
CANADA
Phone: (604)942-6941 PST
Fax: (604)942-9641
Making dolls since: 1986
Selling dolls since: 1987

PRODUCT INFORMATION:

Mediums: Porcelain, Cernit, Super Sculpey

Scope of work: Artist makes only 1 doll from each mold, or dolls are created in limited editions of 5-25. Artist makes all heads, bodies, molds, and most shoes and accessories/props and some wigs. Artist designs and sews all dolls' clothing.

Price range: $199.99-1,999.99

Description of dolls: Marnie's award-winning quality porcelain dolls are totally made by artist and include hand-painted eyelashes (no false lashes). Signed, numbered certificate and box are included. Special orders upon request.

Special orders: Available

Catalog/price list: b&w and color, $2, refundable with purchase. Price list free.

Mailing list: Write or call to be included.

Dolls sold: In retail shops, at shows, by mail, from artist's home/studio

Shops: Call for list.

Home/studio visits: Please schedule 1 hour in advance.

Phone orders: 7 days, 9-9 PST.

Fax orders: Accepted

Mail orders: Will ship to US, Canada, overseas. Prepayment required. Allow 1-2 weeks in US and Canada; 2-4 weeks overseas.

Shipping information: Shipped via UPS, FedEx, mail, Loomis, Can Par, Purolator, Bus. Shipping included in the price of the doll.

Layaway: Flexible—6 equal payments.

Return/exchange policy: Will replace defects.

ADDITIONAL INFORMATION:
Marnie received "The Norma" in 1990. Her work has appeared in *Victorian Harvester, Canadian Doll Journal, Collectibles Canada Dolls, Doll Reader* and *Contemporary Doll Collector.* She is a member of MSDBA.

MAZIE PANNELL
ANASTASIA'S PORCELAIN DOLLS
6717 Brants Lane
Fort Worth, TX 76116
Phone: (817)738-7800 CST
Making dolls since: 1993
Selling dolls since: 1993

PRODUCT INFORMATION:
Mediums: Porcelain
Scope of work: Artist makes limited editions of 100-250 dolls. She makes heads, bodies, wigs, shoes and accessories/props for some dolls. She designs and sews all clothing.

Price range: $495-975

Description of dolls: Mazie's original limited edition porcelain dolls are 25"-40", dressed in velvets, silks and moires. All dolls are sculpted, painted, dressed and decorated by artist. Each doll has glass eyes, pierced ears, necklace or other jewelry, real children's shoes, tights and pretty underwear.

Special orders: Dolls may be ordered with special coloring (eyes and hair) and clothing. Allow 6-8 weeks for completion of a special order.

Catalog: Color photos, $3, refundable. Price list, free.

Dolls sold: In retail shops, at shows, by mail, from artist's home/studio, antique stores

Shops: Call for list.

Shows: Call for list.

Home/studio visits: Please schedule in advance.

Phone orders: M-Sat, 9-6.

Mail orders: Will ship to US. Prepayment required. Allow 6-8 weeks for delivery.

Shipping information: Shipped via UPS. COD.

Layaway: ½ down, 3-4 months. Will work with customer.

ADDITIONAL INFORMATION:
Mazie's work was featured in *Doll Crafter.*

JIM AND SUE PARKER
PARKER PEOPLE
2247 Shadowood Dr.
Ann Arbor, MI 48108
Phone: (313)973-2840 EST
Making dolls since: 1979
Selling dolls since: 1980

PRODUCT INFORMATION:
Mediums: Latex composition, Fimo, Cernit, cloth
Scope of work: Dolls are one-of-a-kind

direct sculptures, or created in limited editions of 20-50. Artist designs patterns for all cloth dolls. Artist makes some heads, bodies, wigs, shoes, accessories/props and molds. Artist designs and sews all dolls' clothing.

Price range: $500-5,000

Description of dolls: Parker People dolls are made with as many vintage fabrics, laces, and trims as possible. Mohair and wool pelts are used to make wigs. The latex is given a rich classic patina that resembles early painted wood dolls. Many of Jim and Sue's dolls have painted, intaglio eyes.

Price list: Only on current dolls. Free with LSASE. $2 for color photos.

Mailing list: Write or call to be included.

Dolls sold: In retail doll shops, by mail, from artist's home/studio

Shops: Call or send SASE for list.

Home/studio visits: Please schedule 2 weeks in advance.

Phone orders: 7 days a week, 9-9.

Mail orders: Will ship to US, Canada, overseas. Prepayment is required. Layaway is available. Allow 4-6 weeks usually for delivery.

Shipping information: Shipped via UPS. Overseas—US postal service. $10 if within continental US, extra for COD and outside continental US.

Layaway: 25% nonrefundable down payment with up to 12 equal monthly payments.

Discounts: Wholesale prices are available to shops and dealers. Longtime customers also receive a discount.

Return/exchange policy: With a direct purchase, artists honor returns and exchanges if available. Layaways are more difficult, due to the long time frame.

ADDITIONAL INFORMATION:
The Parkers have received nominations for *Dolls* Awards of Excellence (1990, 1991, 1995) and a *Doll Reader* DOTY nomination (1995). Their work has appeared in *Contemporary Doll Collector, Dolls—The Collector's Magazine* and *Doll Reader.* The Parkers have taught various seminars on sculpting, wig making, pattern making, etc.

JOYCE PATTERSON
FABRICIMAGES
P.O. Box 1599, 239 Magnolia
Brazoria, TX 77422
Phone: (409)798-8183 CST
Making dolls since: 1990
Selling dolls since: 1990

PRODUCT INFORMATION:
Mediums: Cloth
Scope of work: Cloth dolls, original, one-of-a-kind, made entirely by artist. She makes all heads, bodies and wigs and some shoes and accessories/props. She designs and sews all clothing.
Price range: $150-600
Description of dolls: Joyce's cloth character dolls have hand-painted faces, and each doll is signed and dated. The original designs portray everyday activities in the lives of real or imagined characters. Accessories and props provide the appropriate environment, especially with custom-order dolls, that can depict one's profession, favorite activities or hobbies.
Special orders: Request type of character or special theme. Include any specific characteristics such as eye and hair color, approximate age, size, hairstyle, glasses or not, specific style of clothes, shoes. List special interests or hobbies, occupation, recreational activities, pets or specific accessories to consider. Send a photo if available. Allow a minimum of 4-6 weeks; time depends on backlog. 20% deposit required.
Mailing list: Write to be included.
Dolls sold: At shows and by mail
Shows: Everyone on mailing list will be notified.
Phone orders: M-F, after 7 P.M. Sat-Sun, 9-5.
Mail orders: Will ship to US and Canada. Customer will be billed. Allow minimum 4-6 weeks for custom order. 6-10 days for available pieces.
Shipping information: Shipped via UPS. Shipping is included in the price of the doll.
Return/exchange policy: None on commissioned pieces. 30 days from purchase date on noncommissioned dolls.

ADDITIONAL INFORMATION:
Joyce has won numerous awards at shows and fairs in Texas and Montana, including awards from World Wide Dollmakers. Joyce has been featured in *Dollmaker's Journal* and *Contemporary Doll Collector.* She is a member of UFDC, World Wide Dollmakers and an associate member of Original Doll Artists Association.

SHIRLEY HUNTER PECK
AMERICAN BEAUTY DOLLS
2492 Hansen Court
Simi Valley, CA 93065
Phone: (805)522-3410 PST
Making dolls since: 1984
Selling dolls since: 1985

PRODUCT INFORMATION:
Mediums: Cloth (felt) and porcelain
Scope of work: Artist makes limited editions of 10-20 porcelain dolls and 20-100 felt dolls. She makes all heads, most bodies, and some accessories/props. Wigs, shoes and some accessories/props are bought ready-made. Artist designs all clothing.
Price range: $200-400 felt dolls, $350-800 porcelain
Description of dolls: Shirley's felt dolls have sweet, hand-painted faces and fully jointed felt bodies. The felt is imported from England. She dresses them as storybook characters, such as Cinderella, Snow White and Hansel and Gretel. She does all the sculpting, molding and painting of the felt dolls. She also does sweet and pensive porcelain faces. These dolls are dressed in silks and velvets. She has a musician series and a 14″ all-porcelain Mother Goose series.
Catalog: Color catalog available, free
Mailing list: Write or call to be included.
Dolls sold: In retail doll shops, at shows, by mail
Shops: Call or send SASE for list.
Shows: Call or send SASE for list.
Phone orders: M-F, 10-7; call anytime and leave message.

ADDITIONAL INFORMATION:
Shirley's cloth dolls have been nominated for *Doll Reader*'s DOTY Award in the Cloth Category in 1990-1991, 1993-95, and *Dolls* Award of Excellence in 1993, 1991, 1990. She has been featured in *Dolls—The Collector's Magazine, Doll Reader* and *Contemporary Doll Collector.* She is a member of UFDC.

PENNY PENDLEBURY
PENNYDOLL CREATIONS
1650 Wisteria Glen
Escondido, CA 92026
Phone: (619)745-4185 PST
Making dolls since: 1978
Selling dolls since: 1978

PRODUCT INFORMATION:
Mediums: Cloth, wax, papier mâché
Scope of work: Dolls are one-of-a-kind papier mâché and Paperclay or unlimited editions; artist designs patterns for all cloth dolls. Artist makes all heads, bodies and accessories/props, most wigs and some shoes. Artist designs and sews all dolls' clothing.
Price range: $225-750
Description of dolls: Penny is creating a "Little Women" series in poured wax plus an Amy in Paris and Laurie. The dolls are all papier mâché and Paperclay. The American Heritage Series consists of cloth torsos, hands and feet with latex base stockinette heads.
Price list: Color photos and price list, $1 plus SASE
Mailing list: Write to be included.
Dolls sold: At shows, by mail or from artist's home/studio
Shows: Send SASE for list.
Home/studio visits: Please schedule 3 days in advance.
Phone orders: 4-6 P.M. PST.
Mail orders: Call for production date and instructions on layaway or payments. Allow 10 days if production is complete and 6 months if doll has to be produced.
Shipping information: Shipped via UPS. Shipping price quoted when doll is ordered.
Layaway: Minimum 10% down, 6 months
Return/exchange policy: Refunds or exchanges available on dolls returned

within 30 days undamaged. Satisfaction guaranteed.

ADDITIONAL INFORMATION:
Pendlebury has won 1st place and honorable mention ribbons at local and regional conventions. Her work has appeared in local newspapers and *Antique and Collectibles* (published in El Cajon, CA). Pendlebury is a member of UFDC, the Cameo Doll Club of Southern California and ODACA. Pendlebury has published *New Reflections*, a how-to book on making a stockinette-covered head and cloth body that is constructed in the manner of the Alabama Baby. Book and precast head—$25 plus $3 package and postage.

W. HARRY PERZYK
2860 Chiplay St.
Sacramento, CA 95826
Phone: (916)383-1532 PST
Making dolls since: 1960
Selling dolls since: 1984

PRODUCT INFORMATION:
Mediums: Wood, porcelain
Scope of work: Dolls are one-of-a-kind direct sculptures. Artist makes all heads, bodies, wigs and shoes and some accessories/props. Artist designs and sews all dolls' clothing.
Price range: $598-30,000
Description of dolls: All dolls are both wood and porcelain, lifelike sculptures and are international in scope. They feature actual persons of historical importance. Every doll is original.
Special orders: Artist makes special order and portrait dolls, including historical figures. Portrait dolls demand sittings and not photographs for quality work. Allow 3-6 months.
Catalog/price list: Photos and price list, free.
Mailing list: Write or call to be included.
Dolls sold: At shows, by mail, from artist's home/studio

Shows: Call or send SASE for list. Everyone on mailing list will be notified.
Home/studio visits: Please schedule 3 days in advance.
Phone orders: Anytime
Mail orders: Will ship to US, Canada, overseas. Prepayment required. 90 days same as cash. Allow 1-2 weeks for delivery.
Shipping information: Shipped via UPS, FedEx. Shipping is added to cost of doll.
Layaway: 20% down, 90-180 days same as cash
Return/exchange policy: All shipped dolls are insured with safe delivery guaranteed.

ADDITIONAL INFORMATION:
Perzyk's work has appeared in *Doll Crafter, Contemporary Doll Collector, Doll Reader, Doll Artistry, Sacramento Bee, Sacramento Union* and the book *Dolls By Contemporary Artists.* Perzyk is a well-known author and lecturer on doll topics.

ELLEN L. PETERSON
PETERSON ORIGINAL ART DOLLS
996 Main St.
Norwell, MA 02061
Phone: (617)659-7645 or (508)945-5865 EST
Fax: (617)659-7645 or (508)945-5865 EST
Making dolls since: 1992
Selling dolls since: 1993

PRODUCT INFORMATION:
Mediums: Cernit
Scope of work: Dolls are one-of-a-kind direct sculptures. Artist makes heads, bodies, wigs, shoes and accessories/props. Artist designs and sews all dolls' clothing.
Price range: $800-1,000
Description of dolls: Ellen's dolls are 16″

Cernit children with expression.
Mailing list: Write or call to be included.
Dolls sold: In retail doll shops, at shows, by mail, from artist's home/studio, galleries
Shops: Call for list.
Shows: Call for list. Everyone on mailing list will be notified.
Phone orders: Anytime
Fax orders: Fax the doll's name and shipping address.
Mail orders: Will ship to US, Canada, overseas. Prepayment is required or COD. Allow 2 weeks for delivery.
Shipping information: Shipped via UPS, FedEx. Shipping is included in the price of the doll.
Layaway: ⅓ down, ⅓ within 30 days and balance within next 30 days—will ship when paid in full.
Return/exchange policy: Money back within 30 days if not satisfied.

ADDITIONAL INFORMATION:
Ellen won a 1993 Great Lakes Doll Artists Award and a 1995 Global Award. Her work has appeared in *Dolls—The Collector's Magazine, Contemporary Doll Collector* and *Doll Crafter.* She is a member of the Professional Dollmakers Art Guild, AADA and MSDBA.

DEBORAH PFEIFER
PFEIFER PEOPLE
P.O. Box 167
Girdwood, AK 99587
Phone: (907)783-2734 APT
Making dolls since: 1980
Selling dolls since: 1981

PRODUCT INFORMATION:
Mediums: Nylon and various fabrics and leathers
Scope of work: Dolls are one-of-a-kind direct sculptures. Artist designs all cloth doll patterns. She makes heads, bodies, wigs, shoes and accessories/

props for all dolls. She also designs and sews all clothing.

Price range: $100-500

Description of dolls: Pfeifer People are one-of-a-kind needle sculptures. They average about 9″ tall. Deborah specializes in portraiture dolls that are completely handmade.

Special orders: Artist makes portrait dolls. All special orders require a 50% deposit and complete description of person, hair color, eye color, style of clothing and any accessories. Give her 1 month to complete a portrait doll.

Price list: Free

Mailing list: Write to be included.

Dolls sold: At shows, by mail or from artist's home/studio

Home/studio visits: Please schedule 1 week in advance.

Phone orders: M-F, 6-9 P.M., Sat-Sun, 10-6.

Mail orders: Will ship to US, Canada, overseas. Prepayment required. Allow 4-6 weeks for delivery.

Shipping information: Shipped via US mail. Shipping charges are extra.

Layaway: 50% down, 10% per month, up to 1 year.

Return/exchange policy: Dolls can be returned for full refund of purchase price within 30 days of purchase. No return on postage paid.

ADDITIONAL INFORMATION:
Deborah has been featured in *Contemporary Doll Collector*.

NANCY L. PRITCHARD
WILD SPIRIT SCULPTURE STUDIO
3 Sullivan Terrace
Barrington, RI 02806
Phone: (401)245-5013 or (401)433-1235 EST
Making dolls since: 1994
Selling dolls since: 1994

PRODUCT INFORMATION:

Mediums: Polymer clays, Super Sculpey, Fimo, Cernit

Scope of work: Dolls are one-of-a-kind direct sculptures. The artist makes all heads, bodies, wigs and accessories/ props. Shoes and some clothing are bought ready-made. She designs some clothing.

Price range: $295-595

Description of dolls: Nancy creates one-of-a-kind dolls, usually fantasy figures out of nature.

Special orders: The artist makes portrait dolls that are caricatures of real people. Allow 2 weeks.

Mailing list: Write or call to be included.

Dolls sold: In retail doll shops, at shows, by mail, from artist's home/studio

Shops: Call or send SASE for list.

Shows: Call or send SASE for list.

Home/studio visits: Please schedule 24 hours in advance.

Phone orders: M-F, 10-5.

Mail orders: Will ship to US, Canada, overseas. Prepayment is required. Allow 2 weeks for delivery.

Shipping information: Shipped via UPS or RPS. Free shipping in US.

Layaway: 25% down, 25% per month, 4 months

Discounts: Reorders receive 10% off

Return/exchange policy: Report damage on arrival. If customer is unhappy, artist will replace.

ADDITIONAL INFORMATION:
Nancy has been featured in *Dolls—The Collector's Magazine*. She is a member of MSDBA and AADA.

ROBERT RAIKES
RAIKES ORIGINALS
P.O. Box 8428
Catalina, AZ 85738
Phone: (520)825-5788 MST
Fax: (520)825-5789

Making dolls since: 1976
Selling dolls since: 1976

PRODUCT INFORMATION:

Mediums: Wood, cloth

Scope of work: Dolls are all one-of-a-kind, direct sculptures. Artist makes all heads for dolls. Artist designs all dolls' clothing.

Price range: $1,200-5,000

Description of dolls: Robert Raikes creates a wide range of art dolls that encompass everything from traditional, contemporary, and historical dolls to fantasy and character dolls. One of the most recognizable features of all Raikes dolls is the use of wood in their construction. Currently, Robert is working on a fairly elaborate collection of fantasy figures. They go from elves, gnomes, fairies and pixies that are all wood and completely poseable to elaborate woodland creatures with human and elfish characteristics. Some of these more elaborate pieces are in the 24″-27″ range. The fantasy dolls are costumed in a large range of natural materials, including leathers, feathers and stones. In some of the more traditional dolls Robert even goes so far as to hand-print his fabric.

Special orders: Artist makes special order portrait dolls. Allow up to 6 months. Down payment of ⅓ is required. Balance due when doll is ready to be shipped.

Mailing list: Write, call, or fax number to be included.

Dolls sold: At shows, by mail, from artist's home/studio, directly from artist through an online computer system, Ravenwood Gallery in Catalina, AZ

Shows: Call or send SASE for list.

Computer sales: Raikes advertises on the Internet; the ad contains information on how to order.

Home/studio visits: M-F, 8-4. Weekends by appointment.

Phone orders: M-F, 8-3.

Fax orders: Include completed and detailed description of doll, name, address and phone number, Visa or Mastercard account number

Mail orders: Will ship to US, Canada, overseas. Allow 2 weeks.

Shipping information: Shipped via UPS.

Shipping cost will be quoted to customer when order is taken.

Layaway: ⅓ down payment and monthly payments. No interest added, and the customer can take as long as is needed to purchase the piece.

Discounts: Wholesale prices for stores

Return/exchange policy: Artist has a liberal policy and believes collectors should be 100% satisfied with his work.

ADDITIONAL INFORMATION:
Robert's work has been featured in *The Raikes Bear and Doll Story*, by Linda Mullins. Through the auction at the Robert Raikes Annual Convention, he has contributed to National Institute of Youth Ministries, Salvation Army, Children's Burn Center, Good Bears of the World and the earthquake victims in Kobi, Japan.

JEANETTE RAMBERG
KUSKOKWIM TRADITIONAL DOLLS
P.O. Box 1985
Homer, AK 99603
Phone: (907)235-2752 AST
Fax: (907)235-6250
Making dolls since: 1988
Selling dolls since: 1989

PRODUCT INFORMATION:
Mediums: Polyclay, fur, leather
Scope of work: Dolls are one-of-a-kind direct sculptures. The artist makes most heads, bodies, wigs, and accessories/props. Shoes are bought ready-made. Artist designs and sews all clothing.
Price range: $850-950
Description of dolls: Kuskokwim traditional dolls are one-of-a-kind dolls portraying Alaska's Yūpik Eskimo culture. These are activity dolls depicting traditional native practices. All are hand-sculptured and hand-sewn, with hand-carved implements. The dolls are approximately 12″ tall and are poseable. The artist mounts each doll on a piece of driftwood found along the beach in her home-town of Homer, Alaska.
Special orders: Payment in advance. Allow 2 months.
Price list: Free
Dolls sold: In retail shops, at shows, by

mail, from artist's home/studio, in museums and art galleries
Shows: Call or send SASE for list.
Home/studio visits: An appointment is necessary.
Phone orders: Accepted
Fax orders: Include name, address, phone, style of doll requested (shaman, storyteller, fishing lady, hunter, mother with baby)
Mail orders: Will ship to US, Canada, overseas. Prepayment is required or COD. Allow 6 weeks for delivery.
Shipping information: Shipped via UPS, FedEx, mail, air freight. Shipping added to purchase price.
Discounts: 10-15% discount for 2 or more dolls ordered
Return/exchange policy: All dolls subject to approval by customer.

ADDITIONAL INFORMATION:
Jeanette has won several People's Choice and Division and Fair Champ awards at the Alaska State Fair and the Jurors' Choice Award at the Pratt Museum Spring Juried Art Show 1993. She has been featured in *Craftworks For the Home*.

REAL PEOPLE DOLLS
MARLENA H. NIELSEN
1217 S.E. 52nd
Portland, OR 97215
Phone: (503)239-0465 PST
Making dolls since: 1991
Selling dolls since: 1992

PRODUCT INFORMATION:
Mediums: Porcelain, cloth
Scope of work: Dolls are created in limited editions of 10-25. Artist designs patterns for all cloth dolls. Artist makes all heads, bodies and molds, most wigs and some accessories/props. Artist designs all dolls' clothing.
Price range: $1,200-1,800
Description of dolls: The most common comment about Marlena's dolls is "they look like real people." Marlena says, "When I hear this, I know I am achieving one of my valued goals. The next most common comment is 'they all look so different' and again I know I'm on track. I enjoy celebrating people of all cultures and ethnic origins through my dolls, but most im-

portantly, I create a person with a personality, a story to share or just someone to talk to or be with."
Special orders: Artist makes special order dolls in very limited numbers. She is willing to consider children, especially ethnic children, possibly with their parents; however, she must be very inspired to accept a request. Allow 1 year.
Molds: Directly from the artist. For international distributors please send SASE.
Designs manufactured by: The Danbury Mint, The Dynamic Group for Home Shopping Network, Kais for Home Shopping Network
Catalog/price list: Color photos, free. Price list, free.
Mailing list: Write or call to be included.
Dolls sold: In retail doll shops, at shows or by mail
Shops: Call for list.
Shows: Everyone on mailing list will be notified.
Phone orders: Accepted
Fax orders: Please call first
Mail orders: Will ship to US, Canada, overseas. Customer/collector will pay the shipping unless otherwise arranged. Prepayment required.
Shipping information: Shipped via UPS, usually 3 days. Shipping is paid by collector/customer.
Layaway: Arrangements can be flexible based on customers needs; however, a general guideline would keep payments no longer than 6 months.
Return/exchange policy: Always guaranteed return within 7 days of receipt. Refund will be made immediately upon receipt of doll.

ADDITIONAL INFORMATION:
Nielsen's work has appeared in *Dollmaking Craft and Design* and *Contemporary Doll Collector*.

"... THE TREASURE SECRETLY GATHERED IN YOUR HEART WILL BECOME EVIDENT THROUGH YOUR CREATIVE WORK."
a quote from Albrecht Dürer,
submitted by Deborah Colston,
Seagrave, Ontario, Canada

MONICA REO
CREATIONS IN PORCELAIN
16077 Hauss
East Pointe, MI 48021
Phone: (810)774-1566 EST
Making dolls since: 1993
Selling dolls since: 1990

PRODUCT INFORMATION:
Mediums: Porcelain, cloth
Scope of work: Dolls are created in limited editions. Artist designs all patterns for cloth dolls. Artist makes some heads, bodies, wigs, accessories/props and molds. Artist designs all dolls' clothing.
Price range: $1,000-3,500
Description of dolls: All of Monica's dolls have painted eyes, mohair handmade wigs, costumes of fine fabrics, and handmade leather shoes or boots.
Special orders: Portrait dolls available. Allow 12-20 weeks for completion.
Catalog/price list: Color photos available at no cost
Mailing list: Write to be included.
Dolls sold: At shows, from artist's home/studio or art gallery
Shops: Call for list.
Shows: Call for list.
Home/studio visits: Please schedule in advance.
Phone orders: After 6 P.M.
Mail orders: Will ship to US, Canada, overseas. Prepayment required.
Layaway: ½ down, 90 days. Must be paid in full before delivery.
Return/exchange policy: All sales final.

ADDITIONAL INFORMATION:
Monica has won 7 People's Choice awards, 4 Judge's Choice and 5 Best of Show awards. She has over 50 awards, blue ribbons and rosettes for her work. Her work has appeared in *Doll Crafter* and *Contemporary Doll Collector*. She is a member of Doll Artisan Guild and the Michigan Doll Artisan Society.

ROSEMARY RHODES
A CLASSIC IMAGE
615 W. Cota St.
Shelton, WA 98584
Phone: (360)426-5447 PST
Making dolls since: 1984
Selling dolls since: 1985

PRODUCT INFORMATION:
Mediums: Porcelain
Scope of work: Artist makes limited editions of 25 dolls. She makes heads and molds for all dolls and most bodies. Wigs, shoes and accessories/props are bought ready-made. She designs all clothing.
Price range: $450-2,200
Description of dolls: Original porcelain dolls reflect children ages 1-7 years. The dolls range from 25"-45" true-to-life size. Most dolls have open mouths with set-in tongues and teeth for realism. They have synthetic or human hair wigs, armatured.
Catalog/price list: Color catalog, $10, b&w catalog, $3, refundable with purchase. Price list, available with SASE.
Mailing list: Write or call to be included.
Dolls sold: At shows, by mail, from artist's home/studio
Shows: Call or send SASE for list.
Home/studio visits: Please schedule 2 days in advance.
Phone orders: M-F, 9 A.M.-10 P.M.
Mail orders: Will ship to US, Canada, overseas. Prepayment required. Established customers may make payments after receiving doll. Allow 6-8 weeks for delivery.
Shipping information: Shipped via UPS. Shipping is included in the price of the doll.
Layaway: 30% deposit, 12 months
Discounts: 50% on purchase of 3 or more dolls at same time
Return/exchange policy: Return for

refund within 10 days, exchanges within 30 days.

ADDITIONAL INFORMATION:
Rosemary has been featured in *Doll Crafter* and *Contemporary Doll Collector*.

HOPE ROBBINS
REPRESENTED BY: DOLLCO
22248 Cohasset St.
Canoga Park, CA 91303
Phone: (818)702-0315 PST
Fax: (818)702-9275
Making dolls since: 1990
Selling dolls since: 1993

PRODUCT INFORMATION:
Mediums: Paperclay, Cernit with wired cloth bodies
Scope of work: Dolls are one-of-a-kind direct sculptures. Artist makes all heads, bodies, wigs, shoes and accessories/props. She also designs and sews all clothing.
Price range: $700-2,000
Description of dolls: Hope's dolls are realistic adult dolls. Each has a story from a book, a play, an opera or other idea. Artist tries to achieve a speaking gesture or pose which embodies the idea.
Special orders: Artist makes portrait dolls. She needs good photographs, front and side. Giver her 1 month to complete a special order.
Catalog/price list: Color photos, $5, refundable with purchase. Price list, free.
Mailing list: Write to be included.
Dolls sold: In retail doll shops and at shows
Shops: Call for list.
Shows: Call for list.
Home/studio visits: Please schedule 1 week in advance
Mail orders: Will ship to US, Canada, overseas. Allow 2 weeks-1 month for overseas delivery.
Shipping information: Shipped via UPS.

ADDITIONAL INFORMATION:
Hope has been featured in *Contemporary Doll Collector*.

> "DILIGENCE AND LONG HOURS ARE A NECESSITY."
> *Jim & Sue Parker, Ann Arbor, MI*

MICHELLE ROBISON
ROBISON'S FAIRY FOLK
16-316 Co. Rd. N
Napoleon, OH 43545
Phone/fax: (419)758-3286 EST
Making dolls since: 1989
Selling dolls since: 1990

PRODUCT INFORMATION:

Mediums: Hand-mixed porcelain (own recipe, not commercial)

Scope of work: Artist makes heads, bodies, wigs, shoes and molds for all dolls and accessories/props for most dolls. Artist designs and sews all clothing.

Price range: $600-2,000

Description of dolls: Some of Hope's figures are 1-piece porcelain, anatomically correct. Sizes range from 2½"-13". Clothing is made from vintage laces and fabrics accented with Swarovski crystals. Real feathers on wire amatures are used to imitate bird wings. Real butterfly or cicada wings are also used and are treated to extend the durability. She makes some props, and nature provides the rest. Sometimes she makes wings in glass. She also uses semi-precious stones and sterling silver.

Special orders: 20% nonrefundable deposits are required for all pieces. Requires pictures of individuals to be rendered, from all angles. If the person is famous, must have permission. Allow 2-4 months for completion.

Catalog/price list: Will send color photo upon request. Cost depends on number of photos and is refundable with purchase. Price list available; cost refundable with purchase.

Dolls sold: In retail doll shops, at shows, by mail, out of the artist's studio

Shops: Call or send SASE for list.

Shows: Call or send SASE for list.

Home/studio visits: Please schedule 2 days in advance.

Phone orders: Anytime

Fax orders: Shop or individual info. and credit card info. She accepts Visa, MC or certified check.

Mail orders: Will ship to US, Canada, overseas. Payment required. Allow 2-7 days for delivery.

Shipping information: Insured first class mail. Shipping is included in the price of the doll (retail). Added to cost if wholesale.

Layaway: 30-90 days depending on price. Terms negotiable. 30% down, nonrefundable (restocking fee).

Discounts: Multi-order discounts. Call for terms.

Return/exchange policy: Returns must be within 10 days in original condition or exchange 10 days equal or greater value.

ADDITIONAL INFORMATION:
Michelle was a presidential scholar, Defiance College, 1992. Her work has appeared in *Dolls in Miniature* and *Dolls—The Collector's Magazine*. She has a BS in Fine Arts and minor in Criminal Justice from Defiance College. She studied under master potter Steve Smith, who taught her to mix glazes and porcelain, jewelry casting and glassworking skills. She also offers classes on an individual basis upon request.

ALEXANDER AND MARINA ROYZMAN
MAR CREATIONS
570 Fort Washington Ave., Suite #2B
New York, NY 10033
Phone/fax: (212)927-9548
Making dolls since: 1990
Selling dolls since: 1990

PRODUCT INFORMATION:

Mediums: Cloth, porcelain, Fimo, Super Sculpey, La Doll

Scope of work: Dolls are one-of-a-kind, direct sculptures or limited editions of up to 35. Artists design patterns for all cloth dolls, make all heads, bodies, wigs, shoes and accessories/props and design and sew all dolls' clothing.

Price range: $1,000-12,000

Description of dolls: Alexander and Marina make hand-sculpted portrait dolls and doll compositions which include 2 or more dolls sculpted out of Fimo or La Doll or made in cloth. Many dolls represent portraits of great ballet performers of past and present. Sometimes they create porcelain dolls limited to editions of 3 or 5 pieces.

Special orders: Artists make portrait dolls from photos. 30% deposit required. Allow 3 months.

Mailing list: Write or call to be included.

Dolls sold: In retail doll shops, at shows, by mail, from artists' home/studio

Shops: Call for list.

Home/studio visits: Please schedule appointment in advance.

Phone orders: Evenings, 7-10.

Fax orders: Fax address, name and method of payment.

Mail orders: Will ship to US, Canada, overseas. Prepayment is required. Allow 1 week for delivery.

Shipping information: Shipped via UPS. Shipping is included in the price of the doll.

Layaway: 30% down payment. Time will depend on the price of the doll.

Return/exchange policy: No returns or exchanges, but artist gives warranty to repair any damage during delivery.

ADDITIONAL INFORMATION:
The artists' work has appeared in *Dolls—The Collector's Magazine* and *The Doll by Contemporary Artists* (Abbeville Press, 1995). They also create figurines, illustrations, photographs for doll publications and video filmings of doll shows and sculptures.

JULIA RUEGER
JULIA RUEGER, LTD.
P.O. Box 3282
Crestline, CA 92325
Phone: For orders: (909)338-2133 PST
Fax: (909)338-8138 or (800)DOLLS2U
Making dolls since: 1986
Selling dolls since: 1987

PRODUCT INFORMATION:

Mediums: Porcelain, resin

Scope of work: Dolls are created in limited editions of 25-35. Artist makes some heads, bodies, wigs, shoes, accessories/props and molds. Artist designs all dolls' clothing, and hires a seamstress to make it.

Price range: $250-1,250

Description of dolls: Julia's dolls are famous for their freckled faces, bright costumes and original concepts.

Special orders: Artist makes special order dolls. Allow 6-8 weeks.

Molds: Directly from artist

Designs manufactured by: Artist has done work for Schmid Bros. and Hamilton Collection and is working with Ashton-Drake.

Catalog/price list: Color, $4.50, refundable with purchase. Price list free.

Mailing list: Write or call to be included.

Dolls sold: In retail doll shops, at shows.

Shops: Call or send SASE for list.

Shows: Call or send SASE for list.

Home/studio visits: Please schedule 7 days in advance.

Phone orders: 9-5.

Fax orders: Fax product desired, complete shipping address, credit card information.

Mail orders: Will ship to US, Canada, overseas. Prepayment is required or COD. Allow 4-6 weeks for delivery.

Shipping information: Shipped via UPS. COD or prepayment.

Discounts: Wholesale to stores

Return/exchange policy: Will take back dolls that have been broken or damaged in transit. Claims must be made within 10 days.

ADDITIONAL INFORMATION:

Julia's work won an IDEX award in 1994 and was nominated for a *Dolls* Award of Excellence. Her work has appeared in the periodicals *Contemporary Doll Collector*, *Dolls—The Collector's Magazine*, *Doll Reader*, *Doll Life* and *Doll Crafter*; and the books *The World's Most Beautiful Dolls* and *Doll Artists at Work*. She also sculpts figurines and has a plush rabbit line called "Bow Bunnies."

BOBBIE AND BILL SCHLEGEL
RAINBOWS AND THINGS
18 Hope Place
Ringwood, NJ 07456
Phone: (201)962-7690
Fax: (201)962-6716
Making dolls since: 1991
Selling dolls since: 1994

PRODUCT INFORMATION:

Mediums: Porcelain

Scope of work: Dolls are created in limited editions of 5-25. Artist makes all heads, bodies, accessories/props, molds, and some shoes. Artist designs and sews all dolls' clothing.

Price range: $200-950

Description of dolls: Lifelike children in porcelain

Catalog/price list: Artist will send colored pictures on request. Send SASE for price list.

Dolls sold: In retail doll shops, at shows, by mail, from artist's home/studio, by fax

Shops: Call or send SASE for list.

Shows: Call or send SASE for list.

Home/studio visits: Please schedule 2 days in advance.

Phone orders: 8-7.

Fax orders: Accepted

Mail orders: Will ship to US. Prepayment is required. Cash, COD, UPS. Allow 6-8 weeks for delivery.

Shipping information: UPS. Cost of shipping added to price of doll.

Layaway: ⅓ down, 60 days

Discounts: Wholesale

ADDITIONAL INFORMATION:

The Schlegels displayed dolls on request by the governor of New Jersey at the governor's mansion in 1994. They were also commissioned to create a special Victorian doll in the likeness of Eleanor G. Hewitt for the New Jersey state park, Ringwood Manor, and a special doll in

the likeness of Edwina Mueller on display in Doll Castle Museum, Washington, New Jersey. The Schlegels' work has appeared in *Doll Castle News*, *Doll Reader*, *Dolls—The Collector's Magazine*, *Contemporary Doll Collector*, and northern New Jersey newspapers. They are members of MSDBA.

JENNIFER SCHMIDT
JENNIFER SCHMIDT DOLLS
25 Castle Rock Dr.
Mill Valley, CA 94941
Phone: (415)381-2432 PST
Fax: (415)381-6508
Making dolls since: 1989
Selling dolls since: 1992

PRODUCT INFORMATION:

Mediums: Porcelain, Cernit/resin

Scope of work: Dolls are created in limited editions of 5-35. Artist makes all heads, bodies and some wigs. Artist designs all dolls' clothing.

Price range: $795 and up

Description of dolls: Highly expressive and softly refined, Jennifer's dolls exude life. Every detail plays a role in the composition as a whole. The artist's sculpting communicates the mood, character and race of each small person. Her layered painting accentuates these aspects and works along with the natural fabrics, textures, colors and designs to complete the work of art. The delicate handmade clothes worn by the dolls are often knit or crocheted for texture. Many outfits are fully lined, and careful attention is payed to the overall scale of the piece. At 14″ tall, Jennifer's limited edition porcelain toddlers are small yet poseable. The artist is currently creating larger scale dolls, as well as one-of-a-kinds.

Designs manufactured by: The Hamilton Collection, Fisher-Price

Catalog/price list: b&w individual color photographs are available upon request. SASE. Price list, available.

Mailing list: Write or call to be included.

Dolls sold: By mail. May sell in select shops and shows in the future.

Phone orders: Leave a message, and your call will be returned.

Fax orders: Include name, address, phone number, name of doll/dolls of interest.

Mail orders: Will ship to US, Canada, overseas. A deposit of $100 is required to hold the order, then full payment of balance is due before shipping. Allow 6 months-1 year for completion time. Then, after full payment is received, allow 3-4 weeks (usually less) for delivery.

Shipping information: Shipped via FedEx. Shipping is included in the price of the doll—except overseas.

Layaway: A $100 deposit, then whatever is comfortable for the customer to pay until full payment of balance is due when doll is ready.

Discounts: If buying more than 2 dolls, remaining purchases are 10% discounted.

Return/exchange policy: Every doll is fully refundable within 2 weeks after it is received, if returned in same condition as shipped.

ADDITIONAL INFORMATION:
Jennifer also has been steadily creating wildlife sculpture and design, toy sculpture and design and crystal sculpture and design for several leading manufacturers in the industry since 1989.

D. SCHWELLENBACH
D. SCHWELLENBACH—ARTIST'S DOLLS
1703 Burton St.
Beloit, WI 53511-2841

Phone: (608)365-7997 CST
Making dolls since: 1987
Selling dolls since: 1994

PRODUCT INFORMATION:

Mediums: Cloth, wire and wood combinations with polyester fiberfill

Scope of work: Dolls are one-of-a-kind direct sculptures. Artist designs patterns for all cloth dolls. Artist makes all heads, bodies, wigs and shoes; most accessories/props. Artist designs and sews all dolls' clothing.

Price range: $500-2,000

Description of dolls: D. Schwellenbach's dolls are about 14″ high with wooden heads secured to a wire reinforced cloth and fiberfill body, intricate crocheted yarn coiffures, delicate hand-drawn and tinted facial features and lavish hand-detailed original gowns. Each one is individually copyrighted and signed by the artist.

Catalog/price list: Color, $3. Price list comes with catalog.

Mailing list: Write or call to be included.

Dolls sold: At shows, by mail, from artist's home/studio

Shows: Call or send SASE for list. Everyone on mailing list will be notified of upcoming show dates.

Home/studio visits: Please schedule 3 days in advance.

Mail orders: Will ship to US, Canada, overseas. Prepayment is required. Allow 8 weeks maximum for delivery.

Shipping information: Shipped via UPS. Shipping is included in the price of the doll.

Discounts: Sales are offered at regular intervals to highlight new lines of dolls. The artist usually advertises and sends notices to mailing list.

Return/exchange policy: If you are not 100% satisfied with your purchase, you may return it within 10 days for a full refund.

ADDITIONAL INFORMATION:
Schwellenbach's work appeared in *Doll Reader*.

SUSAN SCOGIN
SUSAN SCOGIN EDITIONS LTD.
57755 Martin Lane
Slidell, LA 70460
Phone: For orders: (504)649-3468 CST

For info: (504)641-7788
Making dolls since: 1985
Selling dolls since: 1985

PRODUCT INFORMATION:

Mediums: Porcelain and epoxy resin

Scope of work: Artist makes limited editions of 250 average. Dolls for 1996 are 100 or less. She designs the patterns for all cloth dolls. Artist makes all heads, bodies, wigs, shoes, and molds. She also makes some accessories/props. She designs all clothing.

Price range: $140-375 limited editions, $750-1,500 one-of-a-kinds.

Description of dolls: Susan's dolls are miniature $\frac{1}{12}$ scale figures, realistically sculpted, dressed and wigged in contemporary styles. Limited edition dolls are cast in a natural-looking resin.

Designs manufactured by: Concord Miniatures, "Little Miracles" series.

Catalog/price list: Color catalog and price list free.

Mailing list: Write or call to be included.

Dolls sold: In retail doll shops, at shows, by mail

Shops: Call or send SASE for list.

Shows: Call or send SASE for list.

Phone orders: M-Sat, 10-6.

Mail orders: Will ship to US, Canada, overseas. Prepayment is required. Visa, MC. Allow 3-6 weeks for delivery.

Shipping information: Shipped via UPS or US mail. Shipping is included in the price of the doll.

Layaway: Arrangements made on individual basis.

Return/exchange policy: Return for refund within 2 weeks if not satisfied.

ADDITIONAL INFORMATION:
Susan has been featured in *Contempo-*

> "TRY TO DISTANCE YOURSELF FROM YOUR WORK SO YOU CAN KEEP A CRITIC'S EYE ON YOUR DOLLS. DON'T HESITATE TO REJECT WHAT YOU DON'T LIKE. ALLOW ENOUGH TIME FOR OBJECTIVITY, AND BE VERY SURE YOU LIKE THE DOLL EVEN WHEN SHE HAS BEEN OUT OF YOUR HANDS FOR A MONTH. TIME IS A GREAT EYE-OPENER."
> *Doina Doneaud, Rapid City, SD*

rary Doll Collector, Nutshell News and *Miniature Collector.* She is a member of NIADA.

MYRA SHERROD
BORN YESTERDAY DOLLS
11 Cherrywood Court
St. Peters, MO 63376
Phone: (314)928-1368 CST
Making dolls since: 1980
Selling dolls since: 1980

PRODUCT INFORMATION:
Mediums: Polymer clays.
Scope of work: Artist's dolls are one-of-a-kind direct sculptures. Artist makes all heads and bodies and most wigs, shoes and accessories/props. She designs and sews all dolls' clothing.
Price range: $600-1,500
Description of dolls: Myra's dolls are original pieces sculpted of polymer clays with wire armatured bodies. Artist's specialty is portrait work, as well as historical figures. All facets of work are individualized, custom-designed and created by hand.
Special orders: Artist makes portrait dolls from photographs. 50% deposit required with balance due upon completion. Price includes shipping. Allow 6-8 weeks for project's completion, depending upon artist's prior commitments.
Dolls sold: In retail doll shops, at shows, by mail
Shops: Call for list.
Home/studio visits: Please schedule in advance.
Phone orders: Daily, 8-8.
Mail orders: Will ship overseas. Deposit with balance paid at time of shipment.
Shipping information: Shipped via UPS. Shipping is included in the price of the doll.
Return/exchange policy: Satisfaction guarantee offered on quality of work-

manship. Repair/replacement guarantee offered on breakage which might occur during shipping.

ADDITIONAL INFORMATION:
Sherrod's work has appeared in *Polyinformer* (National Polymer Clay Guild Newsletter), *Contemporary Doll Collector, Dolls—The Collector's Magazine* and *Doll Reader.* She is a member of UFDC, AADA, ODACA and the National Polymer Clay Guild.

GAIL J. SHUMAKER
GAIL J. SHUMAKER ORIGINALS
3999 Brush Rd.
Richfield, OH 44286
Phone: For orders: (800)578-4991 EST
For information: (216)659-0670
Fax: (216)659-0670. Call first.
Making dolls since: 1985
Selling dolls since: 1985

PRODUCT INFORMATION:
Mediums: Cernit, porcelain, very limited edition vinyl
Scope of work: Dolls are one-of-a-kind, direct sculptures (Cernit). Artist makes most heads and bodies and some wigs. Artist designs all doll's clothing.
Price range: $89-4,500
Description of dolls: Gail's vinyl dolls range in size from 13″-35″ life size. The life-size dolls can wear size 2T clothing and most are on floppy bodies for poseability. The Cernit and porcelain dolls are on armatures so that they can stand or sit and hold objects. All of the one-of-a-kind and very limited edition life-size vinyl dolls are hand painted, signed, lashed and wigged by the artist.
Special orders: Artist makes portrait dolls in Cernit or porcelain from photographs. She requires 8″×10″ color photos of front and sides. There is a deposit necessary. There is a waiting list for orders at this time. Allow at least 6 months.
Price list: Free
Mailing list: Write or call to be included.
Dolls sold: In retail doll shops, at shows, from artist's home/studio
Shops: Call for list.
Shows: Send SASE for list.
Home/studio visits: Please schedule 1 week in advance.

Phone orders: T and Th only.
Fax orders: Include name of doll, name of purchaser, Visa or MC number with expiration date.
Mail orders: Prepayment is required. Allow 2 weeks for delivery.
Shipping information: Shipped via UPS, FedEx or US mail at customer's request. Shipping is included in the price of the doll. COD used for all costs—doll and shipping and handling.
Layaway: ⅓ down, payments to fit the individual
Return/exchange policy: Accepts returns with a 10% restocking fee. Doll must be returned in original condition—wrapped as received—no damage, or buyer will be charged.

ADDITIONAL INFORMATION:
Gail received a 1994 IDEX award. She was a 1994 DOTY nominee; 1994, 1995 *Dolls* Award of Excellence nominee. Gail's dolls have been shown in *Doll Reader, Dolls—The Collector's Magazine* and *Contempory Doll Collector.* She also does pen and ink drawings, oils and sculpts horses.

JEANNE SINGER
JEANNE SINGER DOLLS
Box 98
Bloomfield, NY 14469
Phone: (716)657-6257 EST
Fax: (716)657-4881
Making dolls since: 1979
Selling dolls since: 1979

PRODUCT INFORMATION:
Mediums: Porcelain
Price range: $400-4,000
Description of dolls: Jeanne's dolls are fully porcelain. They are jointed at the head, shoulder, wrist and ankle, or, if made with a soft body and armature, at the head, wrist and ankle.
Special orders: Please provide three clear photos of subject—full, ⅓ and ¾. Artist requires 50% commission fee and 50% on approval. Allow 6 weeks-6 months.
Designs manufactured by: Danbury Mint, Ashton-Drake
Mailing list: Write or call to be included.
Dolls sold: In retail doll shops, at shows, by mail, from artist's home/studio
Shops: Send SASE for list.

Shows: Send SASE for list.

Home/studio visits: Please schedule in advance.

Phone orders: M-F, 8 A.M.-9 P.M.

Mail orders: Will ship to US, Canada, overseas. Prepayment required. Allow 3-6 weeks for delivery.

Shipping information: Shipped via UPS or Parcel Post for overseas. For Canadian or overseas purchases, shipping is added to the price of the doll.

Layaway: 10% down, 6 monthly payments

Return/exchange policy: Exchanges for damage in shipping only.

ADDITIONAL INFORMATION:

Jeanne was nominated for the *Dolls* Award of Excellence. Her work has been featured in *Dolls—The Collector's Magazine.* She is a member of ODACA and UFDC. She also makes figurines.

LOUISE SPELL

Rt. 4, Box 289
Collins, MS 39428
Phone: (601)797-4224 CST
Making dolls since: 1988
Selling dolls since: 1990

PRODUCT INFORMATION:

Mediums: Cernit, Sculpey

Scope of work: Dolls are one-of-a-kind direct sculptures. Artist designs all patterns for cloth dolls. Artist makes some heads, bodies, shoes, wigs, molds and accessories/props. Artist designs and sews all dolls' clothing.

Price range: $100-150

Description of dolls: Cernit and Sculpey dolls are of young people ages 7-20, and stand about 8″ high. Their clothes are made primarily from cotton knit. Old World Santas, made of Cernit, stand 15″-18″ tall and have wool hair and beards. Their coats are brocade, fur, velvet and quilted materials. All dolls and Santas have painted eyes.

Dolls sold: From artist's home/studio

Home/studio visits: Available

Phone orders: Anytime

Layaway: Requires 50% down

Discounts: Offers discounts for older dolls.

ADDITIONAL INFORMATION:

Louise's work has been featured in *Contemporary Doll Collector* and in local papers.

BARB SPENCER
THE ENCHANTED ATTIC

Oakview Addition
Route 5, Box 165AAA
El Dorado Springs, MO 64744
Phone: (417)876-5131 CST
Fax: (417)876-3671
Making dolls since: 1990
Selling dolls since: 1990

PRODUCT INFORMATION:

Mediums: Cloth (frequently adorned with antique lace/trims), wool hair

Scope of work: Artist designs patterns for all cloth dolls. Artist makes all heads, bodies and wigs, most shoes and some accessories/props. Artist designs and sews all doll's clothing.

Price range: $50-500

Description of dolls: Most of Barb's original doll bodies are made from flesh-tone dyed unbleached muslin, and doll heads are attached to a tab neck, which gives the dolls a defined chin. Some dolls have seamed foreheads and noses; others have flat faces. The faces are applied with permanent-ink micron fabric pens, acrylic paint and colored pencils. Dolls' limbs are jointed in various ways. Some are constructed with wire armatures. Clothing is constructed from mostly new fabric, which generally gives the appearance of antique fabric. Often the clothing is adorned with antique lace, trims and hand beading. Most dolls have sewn-on footwear such as laced boots, heels and slippers. Some have purchased shoes. Barb designs dolls to match interior home designs, using customers' fabric of choice, designing to customers' specifications.

Special orders: Dolls are priced the same when artist uses a customer's fabric as when using her own fabric. Allow 2-3 weeks.

Molds: Artist sells original patterns for dolls, but not for one-of-a-kind pieces.

Catalog/price list: Color pattern catalog, $2. (refunded with order of 2 or more patterns). The catalog does not show artist's one-of-a-kind dolls. Must write for pictures or see advertisements in doll magazines. Price list included with fold-out color brochure.

Mailing list: Write or call to be included. Automatically put on the list with purchase of first doll.

Dolls sold: By mail, from artist's home/studio

Home/studio visits: Please schedule in advance.

Mail orders: Will ship to US, Canada, overseas. Prepayment is required. Allow 2-3 weeks to make the doll, plus UPS or other delivery (overseas customers).

Shipping information: Shipped via UPS. Shipping is included in the price of the doll.

Layaway: $25 deposit, 6 months. No finance charge. No returns.

Return/exchange policy: Return undamaged within 10 days for full refund.

ADDITIONAL INFORMATION:

One of Barb's original dolls was selected to travel to many states in the "Dollmakers Magic" Show. Spencer's work has appeared in *Dollmaking Crafts and Designs, Doll World, Doll Life, Doll Designs, Sunbonnet Crafts, Crafts 'N Things, Dolls—The Collector's Magazine, Contemporary Doll Collector, Victorian Sampler, Doll Castle News, Dollmakers Journal, Creative Product News* and *Craft and Needlework.* She is a member of the National Cloth Doll Makers Association, UFDC, Dollabilities (a doll club in Kimberling City, Missouri) and the Association of People Who Play With Dolls. Spencer has a regular column, "Hints From The Attic," in *Dollmaking Crafts and Designs.* She has published *Impressions With Expressions,* a book of traceable faces and information (self-published) and *Traceable Faces For Cloth Dolls* (the Jones Publishing Co.). In 1992-1993, Spencer was selected to enter an original doll design in *Dollmakers Magic,* a traveling exhibit in which only 35 designers are selected each year. Her dolls have also been exhibited with *In Celebration of the Doll: The Figure in Cloth*. She has exhibited her dolls at international markets, conferences and museums, has had dolls in international challenges, and has designed dolls for fabric companies and a lace company.

PAUL SPENCER
SPENCER WOODEN ORIGINALS
1414 Cloverleaf
Waco, TX 76705
Phone: (817)867-1012 CST
Making dolls since: 1985
Selling dolls since: 1985

PRODUCT INFORMATION:
Mediums: Wood (basswood, oak)
Scope of work: Artist makes one-of-a-kind, hand-carved wooden dolls. He makes heads for all dolls and some bodies, shoes and accessories/props.
Price range: $100-1,500 and up
Description of dolls: All wooden parts of dolls are hand-carved from solid wood. Paul's dolls have either hand-carved, wooden bodies or cloth bodies with hand-carved head and limbs. Each doll comes with a certificate of authenticity, signed and dated.
Special orders: Artist makes portrait dolls from photographs. He needs profile, full-face and ¾ face photographs, color if possible. Allow 2 months.
Price list: Free
Mailing list: Write or call to be included.
Dolls sold: At shows, by mail, from artist's home/studio or from U.K. representative
Home/studio visits: Please schedule 1 week in advance.
Phone orders: M-F, 9-5, some evenings
Mail orders: Will ship to US, Canada, overseas. Prepayment required. Allow 3 weeks for delivery if dolls are in stock.
Shipping information: Shipped via UPS.

COD. Shipping and handling fee charged.
Layaway: 20% down, monthly payments
Discounts: 30% discount to dealers

ADDITIONAL INFORMATION:
Paul has received 5 DOTY nominations. He has been featured in *Doll Reader* and in Patricia Smith's *Doll Values and Modern Collector's Dolls*. He also makes figurines and angels.

JOYCE R. STAFFORD
JOYCE STAFFORD ORIGINAL DOLLS
26W 126 Mohican Dr.
Wheaton, IL 60187
Phone: (708)653-8146 CST
Making dolls since: 1966
Selling dolls since: 1968

PRODUCT INFORMATION:
Mediums: Porcelain
Scope of work: Artist makes limited editions of 10-25 dolls. She makes all heads, bodies, wigs, shoes, accessories/props and molds. She also designs and sews all clothing.
Price range: $300-700
Description of dolls: Most of Joyce's dolls are children and babies. She occasionally makes adult lady dolls.
Special orders: Artist occasionally makes a one-of-a-kind portrait dolls, direct sculpture. Allow 3 months.
Dolls sold: At shows, by mail, from artist's home/studio
Home/studio visits: An appointment is necessary.
Phone orders: Accepted
Mail orders: Will ship to US. Prepayment is required. Allow 7-10 days for delivery.
Shipping information: Shipped via UPS. Shipping is included in the price of the doll.
Return/exchange policy: Varies depending on situation.

ADDITIONAL INFORMATION:
Joyce is a member of NIADA and ODACA. She also makes paper dolls.

LINDA L. STELLWAGON
CHESAPEAKE BAY DOLLS
219 W. Miner St.
West Chester, PA 19382
Phone: (610)430-0229 EST
Making dolls since: 1994
Selling dolls since: 1995

PRODUCT INFORMATION:
Mediums: Molded felt faces (hand-painted) with felt bodies
Scope of work: Dolls are created in limited editions of 10-75. Artist designs patterns for all cloth dolls. Artist makes most heads, bodies and shoes and some accessories/props. Artist designs and sews all dolls' clothing.
Price range: $349-649
Description of dolls: Linda's goal is to create lifelike children with a warm feeling. Just as much care goes into the choice of fabrics as the designs of the outfits. "Most of my dolls have accessories of action. As we know, children are seldom not in motion," Linda says. "I want people to experience my dolls, bringing them joy if only for a moment, in this fast-paced world. If I can bring a smile to just one face, all of my time and effort has truly been rewarded."
Price list: Call for quote on specific doll.
Mailing list: Write or call to be included.
Dolls sold: In retail doll shops, at shows, by mail
Shops: Call or send SASE for list.
Shows: Call for list. Everyone on mailing list will be notified of upcoming show dates.
Phone orders: Call anytime. If unavailable, leave a message.
Mail orders: Will ship to US, Canada, overseas. Prepayment is required. Call for information on delivery time.
Shipping information: Shipped via UPS. Shipping is included in the price of the

doll (Canada and overseas additional rate).

Layaway: $150 down/doll and balance for up to 6 months unless otherwise approved.

Discounts: Sometimes offers discounts on dolls purchased or orders taken at shows.

Return/exchange policy: Returns or exchanges within 10 days as long as doll is in perfect condition. Repairs available at any time. Fee and shipping depend on repair.

ADDITIONAL INFORMATION:
Linda's work was featured in *Contemporary Doll Artist.* She is a member of AADA.

BRENDA STEWART
PEDDLER'S WORKSHOP
1562 Rooker Rd.
Mooresville, IN 46158
Phone: (317)831-1566
Making dolls since: 1982
Selling dolls since: 1982

PRODUCT INFORMATION:
Mediums: Porcelain, wax, cloth, polyform

Scope of work: Dolls are one-of-a-kind direct sculptures, or created in limited editions. Artist designs patterns for all cloth dolls. Artist makes all heads, bodies, wigs, shoes, accessories/props and molds. Artist designs and sews all dolls' clothing.

Price range: $50-1,500

Description of dolls: Brenda specializes in ethnic dolls, particularly American Indians.

Special orders: Artist creates portrait dolls from photos. Orders for portrait dolls require pictures showing the person to be portrayed—face view, profile, etc., plus the actual measurements of the person involved if possible. Allow at least 6 months for project's completion.

Price list: Free

Mailing list: Write or call to be included.

Dolls sold: In retail doll shops, at shows, by mail, from artist's home/studio

Shops: Call or send SASE for list.

Shows: Call or send SASE for list.

Home/studio visits: Please schedule 2 days in advance.

Phone orders: Anytime is fine.

Mail orders: Will ship to US, Canada, overseas. Prepayment is required.

Shipping information: Shipped via UPS. A shipping charge is added.

Layaway: ¼ down. Artist will work with the customer to determine payment schedule and time allotted.

Discounts: Offers ODACA patrons a discount.

Return/exchange policy: All dolls must meet the satisfaction of the customer or they may be returned or exchanged.

ADDITIONAL INFORMATION:
Stewart's work has appeared in *Dolls— The Collector's Magazine, Doll Designs, Western Doll Collector* and *UFDC Souvenir Journal.* She is a member of ODACA, UFDC and the Global Doll Society. She also sculpts figurines and busts.

MARY LEE SUNDSTROM
CLASSICS IN WOOD
825 Loma Vista Place
Santa Paula, CA 93060
Phone: (805)525-0409 PST
Making dolls since: 1938
Selling dolls since: 1984

PRODUCT INFORMATION:
Mediums: Wood

Price range: $395 and up

Description of dolls: Mary Lee makes dolls in conjunction with Sandy and Don Reinke, who have their own line of wooden dolls copied from classics. The artist creates an original in wood and then makes a rough copy for reproduction. The dolls are then carved and painted and wigs are created. Most dolls are from the artist's books.

Price list: Free

Mailing list: Write or call to be included.

Dolls sold: At shows, by mail, from artist's home/studio, at The Rosalie Whyel Museum of Doll Art, Bellevue, Washington

Shows: Call or send SASE for list.

Home/studio visits: Please schedule 2 weeks in advance.

Phone orders: 8-8 PST.

Mail orders: Will ship to US, Canada, overseas. Prepayment required. Delivery time varies with the length of the waiting list.

Shipping information: Shipped via FedEx. A flat fee of $9.50 for shipping is charged for each doll.

Layaway: $50 down, 9 months maximum

Return/exchange policy: Artist asks for a $50 nonrefundable deposit, but will refund the remainder for any or no reason and is willing to make exchanges.

ADDITIONAL INFORMATION:
Mary Lee's work has appeared in *Doll Reader, Dolls—The Collector's Magazine* and *The Los Angeles Times.* She is a member of UFDC.

CARLA THOMPSON
CARLA THOMPSON ART DOLLS
2002 Roundleaf Green
Huntsville, AL 35803
Phone: For orders: (800)326-0276 CST
For information: (205)533-0923
Fax: (205)534-3537
Making dolls since: 1980
Selling dolls since: 1982

PRODUCT INFORMATION:
Mediums: Cloth, porcelain

Scope of work: Artist makes one-of-a-kinds and limited editions of 10-75, and designs patterns for all cloth dolls. Artist makes all heads, bodies, molds, some wigs and accessories/props. Artist designs and sews all dolls' clothing.

Price range: $500-2,500

Description of dolls: Carla's dolls resemble one another because they come from the same source and reflect the same philosophy—that the face of the doll should convey a sense of real emotion, not just an "expression." Dolls are always either jointed or wired so that collectors can pose the pieces as they wish. The artist creates fabric dolls done in small editions and one-of-a-kind porcelain dolls.

Special orders: Artist makes special order dolls. Allow 4-6 weeks.

Price list: $2, refundable with purchase

Mailing list: Write to be included.

Dolls sold: In retail doll shops, at shows, by mail

Home/studio visits: Current dolls are on display at artist's retail store—The 9th Ave. Gallery, 3502 9th Ave., Huntsville, AL 35805.

Phone orders: M-F, 8-4.

Fax orders: Include name, address, name of doll, and charge card number (Visa/MC). Fax charge orders only.

Mail orders: Will ship to US, Canada, overseas. Prepayment is required. Allow 2 weeks to US, Canada. Delivery time for overseas depends on method of delivery.

Shipping information: Shipped via UPS. Shipping is included in the price of the doll. Overseas shipping extra.

Layaway: 10% down, 6 months; also Visa/MC.

Discounts: Wholesale to stores—rates available to verified retail stores

Return/exchange policy: 30 day return

ADDITIONAL INFORMATION:
Thompson's work has been nominated for and won *Dolls* Awards of Excellence and *Doll Reader*'s DOTY awards. Thompson's work has appeared in *Doll Reader*, *Dolls—The Collector's Magazine* and *Contemporary Doll Collector*. She is a member of UFDC and NIADA.

"THE COLLECTOR IS ALWAYS THE INDIVIDUAL VIOLATED WHEN AN ARTIST COMPROMISES HER WORK FOR THE SAKE OF MONEY. ALTHOUGH WE ENJOY EARNING A LIVING AT WHAT WE LOVE TO DO, IT SHOULD BE AN ARTIST'S SOLE GOAL TO CREATE PART OF HERSELF THAT CAN BE GIVEN AWAY TO SHARE THE EXPERIENCES OF HER LIFE AND LOVES."
Christie Cummins, Huntington Beach, CA

ANN TIMMERMAN
4934 Altadena South
Birmingham, AL 35244
Phone: (205)991-8436 CST
Fax: (205)995-5657 or (205)991-8436
Making dolls since: 1991
Selling dolls since: 1992

PRODUCT INFORMATION:

Mediums: Porcelain, Lumicast, resin

Price range: $900-2,300

Designs manufactured by: Georgetown Collection, Inc.

Price list: Free

Dolls sold: In retail doll shops, at shows

Shops: Call or send SASE for list.

Shows: Call or send SASE for list.

Phone orders: Accepted

Fax orders: Include name of doll, quantity

Mail orders: Will ship to US. Prepay or ship COD. Allow 6 months-1½ years.

Shipping information: Shipped via UPS. COD.

ADDITIONAL INFORMATION:
Timmerman had a doll voted show favorite at IDEX in 1994; 12 other dolls have received *Doll Reader*'s DOTY and *Dolls* Awards of Excellence nominations. Timmerman's work has been featured in *Dolls—The Collector's Magazine*, *Doll Reader*, *McCalls*, *Ladies Home Journal* and *Contemporary Doll Collector*. Timmerman is also active in drawing, painting, related arts and sewing.

INGEBORG TINIUS
ORIGINAL WOOD-DOLL WORKSHOP
7699 Blazing Saddle Dr.
Santa Maria, CA 93454
Phone: (805)937-3820 PST
Making dolls since: 1985
Selling dolls since: 1985

PRODUCT INFORMATION:

Mediums: Bisque, wood

Scope of work: Artist's dolls are one-of-

a-kind direct sculptures. Artist makes all heads, bodies, wigs, shoes and accessories/props. She designs and sews all dolls' clothing.

Price range: $38-125

Description of dolls: Ingeborg's dolls are original and wood carved, with carved hair or wigs. They are dressed in old-fashioned dresses, bonnets or hats with painted shoes and socks or bare feet and plain shaped or jointed legs. They stand 7"-22".

Special orders: Artist requires photo of child's face, front and side and age of child. Allow 3 weeks.

Catalog: b&w, free

Mailing list: Write to be included.

Dolls sold: At shows, by mail

Shows: Send SASE for list.

Home/studio visits: Please schedule in advance.

Mail orders: Will ship to US, Canada. Prepayment is required. COD.

Shipping information: Shipped via UPS. Shipping is included in the price of the doll.

Return/exchange policy: Money back guarantee for doll only, not shipping.

ADDITIONAL INFORMATION:
Ingeborg's work has been featured in *Doll Reader* magazine. She is also a member of the Los Padres Artist Guild.

RUTH TREFFEISEN
TREFFEISEN USA
4172 Corporate Square, Unit A
Naples, FL 33942
Phone: (941)643-9702 EST
Fax: (941)643-1798
Making dolls since: 1970s
Selling dolls since: 1970s

PRODUCT INFORMATION:

Mediums: Porcelain and vinyl

Scope of work: Artist makes limited editions of 10-30 dolls in porcelain, and 1,000 in vinyl. She designs all cloth doll patterns. Artist makes heads, bodies and molds for all dolls and designs all shoes and accessories/props. Wigs are bought ready-made. She designs all clothing.

Price range: Vinyl dolls $300-700; porcelain $2,700-7,000

Description of dolls: Ruth's vinyl dolls are available in limited editions of 1,000 worldwide. All have human hair wigs and cloth bodies and are stuffed with sheep wool and hand-crafted with real eyelashes. They are hand-painted and dressed with leather shoes, socks, underwear and dresses of high-quality fabrics such as cotton, silk or flannel. Porcelain dolls are made by the artist herself with glass eyes, human hair or mohair wigs and cloth bodies.

Catalog/price list: Color, $4.50, nonrefundable

Mailing list: Write to be included.

Dolls sold: In retail doll shops

Shops: Send SASE for list.

Home/studio visits: Please schedule 2 months in advance for visit of studio in Germany.

Phone orders: M-F, 9-5.

Fax orders: Accepted

Mail orders: Will ship to US, Canada, overseas. Prepayment is required for Canada and overseas orders.

Shipping information: Shipped via UPS. COD.

NANCY VAN CLEVE
STONEY POINT CREATIONS
412 Stoney Point Rd.
Hutchinson, MN 55350
Phone: (612)587-7474 CST
Making dolls since: 1990
Selling dolls since: 1990

PRODUCT INFORMATION:

Mediums: Cernit

Scope of work: Dolls are one-of-a-kind direct sculptures. Artist makes some heads, bodies, wigs and accessories/props. Artist designs all dolls' clothing.

Price range: $800-1,200

Description of dolls: Dolls have Cernit heads, hands and feet, with cloth and wire bodies. Child dolls are dressed in casual contemporary clothes.

Dolls sold: In retail doll shops, at shows

Shops: Call for list.

Shows: Call for list.

Home/studio visits: Please schedule 1 month in advance.

Phone orders: 7 days, 9-5.

Mail orders: Will ship to US, Canada, overseas. Prepayment is required. Allow 2 weeks for delivery.

Shipping information: Shipped via UPS. Shipping is usually included in price.

Return/exchange policy: Return within 2 weeks of receipt for exchange of new doll.

ADDITIONAL INFORMATION:

Van Cleve's work has appeared in *Contemporary Doll Collector, Doll Reader,* and *Dolls—The Collector's Magazine.*

ANNIE WAHL
THE ART ROOM
10330 Upper 196 St. Way W
Lakeville, MN 55044
Phone: (612)469-5327 CST
Making dolls since: 1986
Selling dolls since: 1986

PRODUCT INFORMATION:

Mediums: Super Sculpey, polymer clays

Scope of work: Dolls are one-of-a-kind direct sculptures. Artist makes all heads, bodies, wigs, shoes and accessories/props. Artist designs and sews all dolls' clothing.

Price range: $400-1,400

Description of dolls: Annie's clay dolls are lifelike replicas of kindly old people, including Old World Santas, Victorian peddlers and other such characters. Each is individually researched, sculpted, hand-painted, signed, dated and registered by the artist.

Special orders: Artist makes special order dolls, but not exact portraits. She asks for descriptions and photos for general idea. Allow 1-2 years.

Dolls sold: In retail doll shops, at shows, by mail, galleries

Home/studio visits: Please schedule days in advance.

Phone orders: M-F, 9-5.

Mail orders: Will ship to US, Canada, overseas. Prepayment is required. Allow 2-3 weeks for delivery.

Shipping information: Shipped via UPS. Shipping is included in the price of the doll.

Layaway: Negotiable

ADDITIONAL INFORMATION:

Wahl won 1st place at the 1995 Santa Fe Awards through the Global Doll Society in the one-of-a-kind category. Her work has appeared in *Doll Reader* and *Contemporary Doll Collector.* She belongs to AADA and 2 UFDC clubs. She manufactures small "snow bunting babies ornaments."

KATHRYN WALMSLEY
KATHRYN WALMSLEY DOLLS AND TOYS
8041 Shady Rd.
Oldenburg, IN 47036
Phone: (812)934-6221 EST
Making dolls since: 1980
Selling dolls since: 1984

PRODUCT INFORMATION:

Mediums: Cernit, Paperclay, cast resin

Scope of work: Kathryn makes some one-of-a-kind direct sculptures and some editions of 50 or more. She designs the patterns for all cloth dolls. She makes the heads, bodies, wigs, accessories, shoes and molds for all her dolls, and designs and sews all clothing.

Price range: $85-6,000

Description of dolls: Kathryn sculpts dolls in Cernit and Paperclay. She enjoys making mature character figures, clowns and jesters. She is often inspired by stories, illustrations and political situations.

Special orders: Available. Allow 6-12 weeks.

Catalog/price list: b&w and color, $12. Price list free.

Mailing list: Write or call to be included.

Dolls sold: In retail doll shops, at shows, by mail, from artist's studio

Shops: Send SASE for list.

Shows: Send SASE for list. Everyone on mailing list will be notified.

Home/studio visits: Please schedule 1 week in advance.

Phone orders: M-Sat, 9-2.

Mail orders: Will ship to US, Canada. Prepayment is required, or special arrangements can be made. Allow 4-6 weeks for delivery.

Shipping information: Shipped via UPS or FedEx.

Layaway: 20% down, 6-12 months

Return/exchange policy: Return and refund available on mail order or show sales. Custom orders are not returnable.

ADDITIONAL INFORMATION:
Her work has been featured in *Contemporary Doll Collector* and *Dolls—The Collector's Magazine*.

MARY WATTS
HELLO DOLLY
534 S. Bascom Ave.
San Jose, CA 95128
Phone: (408)288-7897 PST
Making dolls since: 1993
Selling dolls since: 1993

PRODUCT INFORMATION:
Mediums: Porcelain
Scope of work: Dolls are created in limited editions of 10. Artist makes all heads, bodies, wigs, shoes, accessories/props and molds. Artist designs and sews all dolls' clothing.
Price range: $1,000 and up
Dolls sold: In retail doll shops, by mail, from artist's home/studio
Shops: Call or send SASE for list.
Home/studio visits: T-F, 11-5:30, Sat, 11-5.
Phone orders: T-F, 11-5:30, Sat, 11-5.
Discounts: Wholesale

CAROL-LYNN RÖSSEL WAUGH
5 Morrill St.
Winthrop, ME 04364-1220
Phone: (207)377-6769 EST

Fax: (207)377-4158
Making dolls since: 1972
Selling dolls since: 1972

PRODUCT INFORMATION:
Mediums: Low-fire clays, cloth
Scope of work: The artist makes one-of-a-kind direct sculptures and designs all cloth doll patterns. She makes all heads, bodies and molds and some wigs, shoes and accessories/props. She designs and sews clothing or purchases antique clothing.
Price range: $200-2,000
Description of dolls: Carol-Lynn's dolls are directly sculpted children and ladies ranging in size from 6"-29" with wire armatures in their cloth bodies.
Special orders: Artist makes portrait dolls. Send photographs taken from several angles for price quote. Portraits start at $1,000. Allow 1 year.
Price list: $5, refundable with purchase
Mailing list: Write to be included.
Dolls sold: At shows, by mail, from artist's home/studio
Shows: Send SASE for list.
Home/studio visits: Please schedule 6 weeks in advance.
Phone orders: M-F, evenings only, 8-10.
Mail orders: Will ship to US, Canada, overseas. Prepayment is required.
Shipping information: Shipped via UPS. COD.
Layaway: 25% deposit (nonrefundable), 6 months
Return/exchange policy: Portraits and work done on commission may not be returned or exchanged. Other dolls have 48-hour return period after delivery.

ADDITIONAL INFORMATION:
Carol-Lynn has been featured in *Dolls—The Collector's Magazine*, *Doll Life* and *Doll Castle News*. She is a member of ODACA, UFDC, OPDAG and MSDBA. She also writes for doll publications and is the author of *Contemporary Artist Dolls* (Hobby House 1985) and co-author of *Selling Your Dolls and Teddy Bears* (Betterway Books).

CHRISTINA WEMMITT-PAUK
281 Greenbriar Rd.
Beech Mountain, NC 28604
Phone: (704)387-4755 EST
Fax: (704)387-2637
Making dolls since: 1994
Selling dolls since: 1995

PRODUCT INFORMATION:
Mediums: Cernit, stone clay, soft sculpture
Scope of work: Dolls are one-of-a-kind direct sculptures. She makes some heads, bodies, wigs, shoes and accessories/props. She designs and sews all clothing, mostly from antique fabrics and clothing.
Price range: $500 and up
Description of dolls: Christina's dolls are all one-of-a-kind. Their hair is always mohair or human and their eyes are always glass paperweight or soft glass. Special attention is given to costuming. She uses either antique fabrics or antique clothes remade to fit the special piece.
Special orders: Available. Completion time depends on the piece, up to 1 year.
Mailing list: Write or call to be included.
Dolls sold: In retail doll shops, at shows, by mail, from artist's home/studio
Shops: Call or send SASE for list.
Shows: Call or send SASE for list.
Home/studio visits: Call for appointment.
Phone orders: Accepted
Fax orders: Accepted
Mail orders: Will ship to US, Canada, overseas. Prepayment is required. Delivery time depends on piece and availability.
Shipping information: Shipped via UPS; exceptions are made. Payment depends on order.
Layaway: Available; terms depend upon

agreement with the individual and piece.

Discounts: Wholesale and retail

Return/exchange policy: All sales are final.

ADDITIONAL INFORMATION:

Christina has won an award at Strong Museum, Rochester, New York, and 1st place, ABC Productions. She has been featured in *Dolls—The Collector's Magazine, Fayetteville Observer* and in numerous other newspapers and art columns. She has also done extensive work with art galleries and museums.

LAUREN WELKER
LAUREN WELKER DOLL ARTIST
204 E. Coover St.
Mechanicsburg, PA 17055
Phone: (717)691-8110
Making dolls since: 1980
Selling dolls since: 1981

PRODUCT INFORMATION:

Mediums: Porcelain, polymer clays, wax, paper

Scope of work: Dolls are one-of-a-kind direct sculptures or limited editions of up to 50. Artist designs patterns for all cloth dolls. Artist makes all heads and bodies, most wigs and shoes, and some accessories/props. Artist designs and sews all dolls' clothing.

Price range: $45-2,000

Description of dolls: Lauren makes a complete family of doll house dolls (1″ to 1′ scale), plus larger dolls in sizes from 7″-30″. She does all the work on the dolls in her home/studio. Lauren makes both adults and children, and is interested in making life-like figures.

Special orders: Artist makes portrait dolls from photographs or live models.

Catalog/price list: b&w, LSASE. Price list, LSASE.

Dolls sold: In retail doll shops, at shows, by mail

Shows: Send SASE for list.

Home/studio visits: Please schedule 2 weeks in advance.

Phone orders: Daily, 9-9.

Mail orders: Will ship to US, Canada, overseas. Payment on completion of order. Allow 1 week.

Shipping information: Shipped via UPS. Shipping is included in the price of the doll.

Layaway: Varies with price of the doll

Return/exchange policy: If a customer breaks a doll, artist will repair it for a nominal charge.

ADDITIONAL INFORMATION:

At the UFDC's 1991 annual convention in New Orleans, Welker won 1 ribbon for doll costuming and 6 ribbons for original dolls in the mediums of wax, porcelain and paper. Welker's work has appeared in *Dolls—The Collector's Magazine, The Sentinel* (Carlisle, Pennsylvania), *Doll Life, Miniature Showcase* and *Doll Reader*. She is a member of UFDC and NAME and writes articles and books about doll collecting, doll clothing and dollmaking. Welker has had published *Fashions to Fit Ginny and Jill* (Hobby House Press, 1982), *Fabulous Fifties Fashions* (Hobby House Press, 1984) and *Six Famous American Women, A Doll Maker's Workbook* (Hobby House Press, 1987).

"LOLO" WESTRICH
P.O. Box 785
Middletown, CA 95461
Phone: (707)987-3279
Making dolls since: 1991
Selling dolls since: 1991

PRODUCT INFORMATION:

Mediums: Cloth, Cernit, Super Sculpey; also mixed-medium dolls

Scope of work: Dolls are one-of-a-kind direct sculptures or one-of-a-kind molded. Artist designs patterns for all cloth dolls. Artist makes all heads, bodies, wigs, shoes and accessories/props. Artist designs and makes all dolls' clothing.

Price range: $200 and up

Description of dolls: Lolo's Cernit dolls are generally about 16″ tall. Although some portray infants or toddlers, most

are "lady dolls," many of which are authentically dressed American Indians. Artist specializes in cloth dolls that are permanently dressed in handwork (needle lace, crocheting, weaving etc.) for which the bodies themselves serve as base.

Dolls sold: In retail doll shops "on a small scale only."

Return/exchange policy: All sales final.

ADDITIONAL INFORMATION:

Lolo's work has appeared in *Dollmaking Crafts & Designs* and *Contemporary Doll Collector*. She is a member of UFDC, Lake County, California chapter. Westrich is also a professional illustrator, poet, article and story writer and portrait sculptor. Her scratchboard and pastel art work, as well as scrimshaw, have been featured in several California galleries. Artist's designs appear in the how-to articles which she writes for doll magazines and will appear in herforthcoming book, *Sewing Basket Dolls, Dress Them in Handwork*, published by Jones Publishing Co.

JUDI WILFERT
CALIFORNIA DOLLS
3100 Dutton Ave., Suite 114
Santa Rosa, CA 95407
Phone: (707)527-6548 PST
Making dolls since: 1990
Selling dolls since: 1995

PRODUCT INFORMATION:

Mediums: Super Sculpey, resin

Scope of work: Dolls are one-of-a-kind direct sculptures. Artist makes all heads and bodies, most wigs, and some accessories/props. Artist designs and sews all doll's clothing.

Price range: $495-995

Description of dolls: Judi says, "My dolls are an eclectic group of people who develop and grow completely out of my imagination. My inspirations come from the art deco period, from people I have known and from movies that grab me."

Special orders: Artist creates portrait dolls. Customers can request hair and eye color. Otherwise, they must leave the contour of the doll up to the artist. Allow 3 months.

Mailing list: Write to be included.

Dolls sold: At shows, from artist's home/ studio

Shops: Call or send SASE for list.

Shows: Everyone on my mailing list will be notified of upcoming show dates.

Home/studio visits: T-F, 10-3. Sat, 10-1.

Phone orders: T-F, 10-3. Sat, 10-1.

Mail orders: Will ship to US, Canada, overseas. Prepayment is required. Allow 12 weeks US and Canada; 14 weeks overseas.

Shipping information: Shipped via UPS. Shipping is included in the price of the doll.

Layaway: ⅓ down (nonrefundable). For $500-1,000 priced dolls, ⅓ down and time is negotiable.

Discounts: Offers wholesale discount

Return/exchange policy: Artist will repair, return or exchange, at no charge.

ADDITIONAL INFORMATION:
Wilfert is a member of UFDC. She also teaches reproduction dollmaking and sculpting, wig making, mold making and casting.

JAN WILENSKY
WILENSKY ONE OF A KIND
2011 Long Leaf Court #G
Santa Rosa, CA 95403
Phone: (707)577-0434 PST
Fax: (707)577-0434
Making dolls since: 1991
Selling dolls since: 1992

PRODUCT INFORMATION:

Mediums: Copper, bronze, sterling, gold, fine silver, porcelain, polymer clays

Scope of work: Artist makes only 1 doll from each mold. Artist makes all heads, bodies, wigs, shoes, accessories/props, molds. Artist designs and sews all dolls' clothing.

Price range: $500-1,000

Description of dolls: Jan's dolls are indestructible heirlooms. Head and hands are cast in hollow semi-precious metal. The dolls' costumes, wigs and accessories are all handmade. Dolls in other mediums are also available.

Special orders: Artist creates portrait dolls from photos. Job requires ⅓ deposit up front (nonrefundable). Allow 3 months.

Mailing list: Write or call to be included.

Dolls sold: In retail doll shops, at shows, by mail, from artist's home/studio

Shops: Send SASE for list.

Shows: Everyone on mailing list will be notified of upcoming show dates.

Home/studio visits: Please schedule 1 day in advance.

Phone orders: 7 days, anytime. Artist will return messages ASAP.

Fax orders: Fax name, number, what you are looking for. Artist will return calls and faxes ASAP.

Mail orders: Will ship to US, Canada, overseas. COD. Allow 2 weeks for delivery.

Shipping information: Shipped via UPS, FedEx, Airborne Express. COD, or shipping is charged at the time of the sale.

Layaway: ⅓ down. Artist is very flexible and willing to meet customer's needs.

Discounts: Established collectors of artist's work (owners of 2 or more dolls) receive $50 off.

Return/exchange policy: Returns and exchanges available. Refunds are minus shipping costs.

ADDITIONAL INFORMATION:
Jan has won 1st and 2nd place awards in Seeley's Doll Show, and been named Artist of the Year at Stuart School. Her work has appeared in *Contemporary Doll Collector* and *Dolls—The Collector's Magazine*. She is a member of The Good Enough Group, AADA, The Professional Doll Makers Guild, MSDBA and The Redwood Empire Doll Club. Wilensky also sculpts figurines and modern sculptures, makes jewelry and pottery, and teaches art at a local school.

BARBARA WILSON
409 Commercial St.
Hanceville, AL 35077
Phone: (205)352-4024 CST
Making dolls since: early 1970s
Selling dolls since: 1986

PRODUCT INFORMATION:

Mediums: Porcelain

Scope of work: Dolls are created in limited editions. Artist makes most heads, bodies, wigs, shoes, accessories/props and molds. Artist designs and sews all dolls' clothing.

Price range: $250-450

Description of dolls: Barbara's dolls have an ethereal quality. Historical fashions have one-of-a-kind heads—pieces built by hand in porcelain clay. This work is similar to work done by Martha Thompson. Clothing is historically accurate using unique trims and natural fibers.

Special orders: Allow 6-8 weeks.

Price list: Send SASE for list.

Mailing list: Write to be included.

Dolls sold: At shows, by mail, from artist's home/studio

Shows: Send SASE for list.

Home/studio visits: Please schedule 1 day in advance.

Phone orders: Anytime

Mail orders: Will ship to US, Canada. Prepayment is required. Allow 6-8 weeks for delivery.

Shipping information: Shipped via UPS. Shipping is included in the price of the doll.

Layaway: ⅓ down, regular payments, no time requirement

Return/exchange policy: Notify artist by mail.

ADDITIONAL INFORMATION:
Artist won 1st place for artist original in Pensacola (1992); 1st, 2nd, and 3rd place awards at the 1995 UFDC Conference in Memphis. Barbara's work has appeared in *Contemporary Doll Collector*. She is a member of UFDC, NAME and the Birmingham Doll Club.

PATRICIA WIMPORY
CELTIC IMAGES
271 Matchedash St. N.
Orillia, Ontario L3V 4V8
CANADA
Phone: (705)326-9719 EST
Making dolls since: 1993
Selling dolls since: 1993

PRODUCT INFORMATION:

Mediums: Cernit

Scope of work: Dolls are one-of-a-kind direct sculptures. Artist makes all heads, bodies, wigs, shoes and accessories/props. Artist designs and sews all dolls' clothing.

Price range: $350-3,000 Canadian

Special orders: Artist makes portrait dolls from photos. Project requires color photo—full front, side and ¾ views. She usually makes head and shoulders portraits only; full length costs about twice as much. Allow at least 3 months.

Catalog/price list: Color, $10 (CAN), refundable with purchase. Price list included with catalog, refundable with purchase.

Dolls sold: By mail and from artist's home/studio

Home/studio visits: Please schedule 1 month in advance.

Phone orders: By chance, days, weekends and evenings after 7

Mail orders: Will ship to US, Canada, overseas. Prepayment required for finished pieces. At least 50% nonrefundable down payment for new orders. Delivery time depends on size and complexity of sculpture required.

Shipping information: Customer pays for shipping and handling.

Return/exchange policy: No returns or exchanges after sale and delivery are finalized.

ADDITIONAL INFORMATION:
Patricia received 1st, 2nd and 3rd award ribbons at the First Annual Canadian Doll Convention in Hamilton. Her work has appeared in *Contemporary Doll Collector.* She is also a painter.

GUSTAVE "FRITZ" WOLFF
WIMBLEDON COLLECTION
P.O. Box 21948
Lexington, KY 40522-1948
Phone: For orders: (606)277-8531 EST
For info: (606)277-9231
Making dolls since: 1970
Selling dolls since: 1970

PRODUCT INFORMATION:
Mediums: Porcelain
Scope of work: Dolls are created in limited editions of up to 600. Artist designs patterns for all cloth dolls. Artist makes all heads and molds. Artist designs dolls' clothing.
Price range: $60-500
Catalog/price list: Color, $5, refundable

with purchase. Price list included in catalog.

Mailing list: Write to be included.
Dolls sold: In retail doll shops.
Shops: Call for nearest dealer.
Home/studio visits: Show room, M-F, 8-5 EST.
Phone orders: M-F, 8-5 EST.
Fax orders: Fax catalog order form.
Mail orders: Will ship to US, Canada, overseas. Prepayment required for all retail orders. Customer will be billed, or doll will be shipped COD for wholesale orders. If item is in stock, it normally ships 2-3 days after receiving order.
Shipping information: Shipped via UPS, RPS
Layaway: 4 equal payments, 4 months
Return/exchange policy: 30 day full replacement or refund

ADDITIONAL INFORMATION:
Fritz's work has appeared in *Contemporary Doll Collector, Giftware News, Dolls—The Collector Magazine, Collector's Mart Magazine* and *Doll Reader.*

MARCIA DUNDORE WOLTER
DUNDORE DOLLS
3740 N. Primrose Lane
Morris, IL 60450
Phone: (815)942-6985 CST
Making dolls since: 1990
Selling dolls since: 1991

PRODUCT INFORMATION:
Mediums: Porcelain
Scope of work: Dolls are created in limited editions of 35. Artist designs patterns for all cloth dolls. Artist makes all heads, bodies and molds and some accessories/props. Artist designs and sews all dolls' clothing.
Price range: $395
Description of dolls: Dundore Dolls have porcelain heads, shoulder plates, hands and feet attached to a cloth body. They range in size from 22″-32″. Most move from side to side. All of the dolls have wire or plastic armatures or a combination of both to aid in the poseability of the doll. A complex cloth body is designed specifically for each doll to complete the total sculptural effect from head to toe. The infants' cloth upper arms and legs are "hinged" and wired to allow for

complete motion. Each doll has hands and feet sculpted specifically for that doll to fit its original concept.

Catalog/price list: Color, $5, refundable with purchase. Price list, $2, refundable with purchase.

Mailing list: Write or call to be included.

Dolls sold: In retail doll shops, at shows, by mail, from artist's home/studio

Shops: Call for list.

Shows: Send SASE for list.

Home/studio visits: Please schedule several days in advance.

Phone orders: Accepted

Mail orders: Will ship to US, Canada, overseas. Prepayment is required. Allow 1-4 weeks for delivery.

Shipping information: Shipped via UPS or FedEx.

Layaway: $100 down and $50/month. 50% down to reserve a particular number in the edition. Doll will be shipped after last payment is made.

Discounts: 5% discount on 2nd doll if two dolls are ordered together.

Return/exchange policy: The cost of the doll will be refunded if the customer returns the doll in 15 days.

ADDITIONAL INFORMATION:
Marcia is a member of AADA.

MELISSA WYATT
812 Midland Ave.
York, PA 17403
Phone: (717)846-9537 EST
Making dolls since: 1986
Selling dolls since: 1986

PRODUCT INFORMATION:
Mediums: Fimo, Cernit
Scope of work: Dolls are all one-of-a-kind direct sculptures. Artist makes most heads, bodies, wigs, shoes and accessories/props.
Price range: $1,000-1,500
Description of dolls: Melissa's dolls are

ladies, children and some men, usually 18″ in height, inspired by paintings, music, literature and faces she finds beautiful or appealing.

Dolls sold: In retail doll shops, at shows.

Shops: Call for list.

Shows: Call for list.

ADDITIONAL INFORMATION:

Wyatt's work has appeared in *Doll Reader, Contemporary Doll Collector* and *Nutshell News.* Wyatt is a member of AADA, and has written how-to articles for *Nutshell News.* She started by making miniature dolls (1″-1′ scale).

ZOFIA AND HENRY ZAWIERUSZYNSKI ZAWIERUSZYNSKI ORIGINALS

2610 37th Ave. NE

St. Anthony, MN 55421

Phone: (612)789-0034

Fax: (612)782-2135

Making dolls since: 1986

Selling dolls since: 1994

PRODUCT INFORMATION:

Mediums: Porcelain

Scope of work: Dolls are created in limited editions of 35-75 and one-of-a-kind. Artists make most heads, bodies, wigs, shoes, accessories/props and molds. Artists design and sew most dolls' clothing.

Price range: $895-3,500

Description of dolls: Zofia and Henry's dolls are 26″-32″ originals in porcelain with poseable bodies and glass eyes.

Each one is individually molded, painted, coiffed and dressed, making it truly unique.

Catalog/price list: Color, $10, refundable with purchase.

Dolls sold: In retail doll shops, at shows.

Shops: Call or send SASE for list.

Shows: Call or send SASE for list.

Home/studio visits: Please schedule in advance.

Phone orders: Anytime

Fax orders: Fax catalog order form.

Mail orders: Will ship to US, Canada, overseas. Prepayment is required.

Shipping information: Shipped via UPS. COD.

Discounts: Periodic discounts of 10%-20% at shows

Return/exchange policy: Exchange only, 7 days

ADDITIONAL INFORMATION:

Honors won include Miss USA Doll Pageant, best of porcelain, 1993; The Greater Midwest Show, 1st, 1994; JDEX 1995, 1996; DOTY nomination 1996, *Dolls* Award of Excellence nomination, 1996. The Zawieruszynski's work has appeared in the *Pioneer Journal.* They are members of JCA and the Global Doll Society. The Zawieruszynskis are natives of Poland where they completed their education, studying drawing, painting, sculpture and ceramics. In 1988, they moved to America and settled in Minnesota, where they now focus on sculpting and creating beautiful, limited edition and one-of-a-kind porcelain dolls.

FAWN ZELLER

8825 E. Ren Place

Inverness, FL 34450

Phone: (904)726-2851

Making dolls since: 1945

Selling dolls since: 1950

PRODUCT INFORMATION:

Mediums: Porcelain

Scope of work: Dolls are one-of-a-kind direct sculptures. Artist makes all

heads, bodies, wigs, shoes and accessories/props. Artist designs patterns for all cloth dolls. Artist designs and sews all dolls' clothing.

Price range: $100-3,000

Description of dolls: Fawn has completed more than 100 portraits of famous people. She has been featured on several national television shows, including the Today Show. She was commissioned to do a life-size sculpture of Jackie Kennedy before the watching public.

Special orders: Artist makes portrait dolls from photos. Project requires 5 views (close-up, different angles, all same expression). Allow 3 months.

Mailing list: Available

Dolls sold: At shows, by mail.

Home/studio visits: Available

Shipping information: Shipped via UPS.

Layaway: $100 a month

Return/exchange policy: Dolls are unconditionally guaranteed.

ADDITIONAL INFORMATION:

Fawn was a featured artist at the UFDC Convention in 1991 in New Orleans and a featured artist in the Nashville Tennessee 1993 Rebels Club. Her work has appeared in NIADA's *Art of the Doll* and *Front Page Chronicles.* She is a member of the Orange Blossom Doll Club, and an honorary member of Florida West Coast Doll Club, Belles and Beaux, Sugar Babes of Florida and Pioneer Doll Club of Tampa. A book was written by Sybill McFadden, published by Hobby House Press, 1984, about Fawn's life and work. She was among the 4 founders of NIADA.

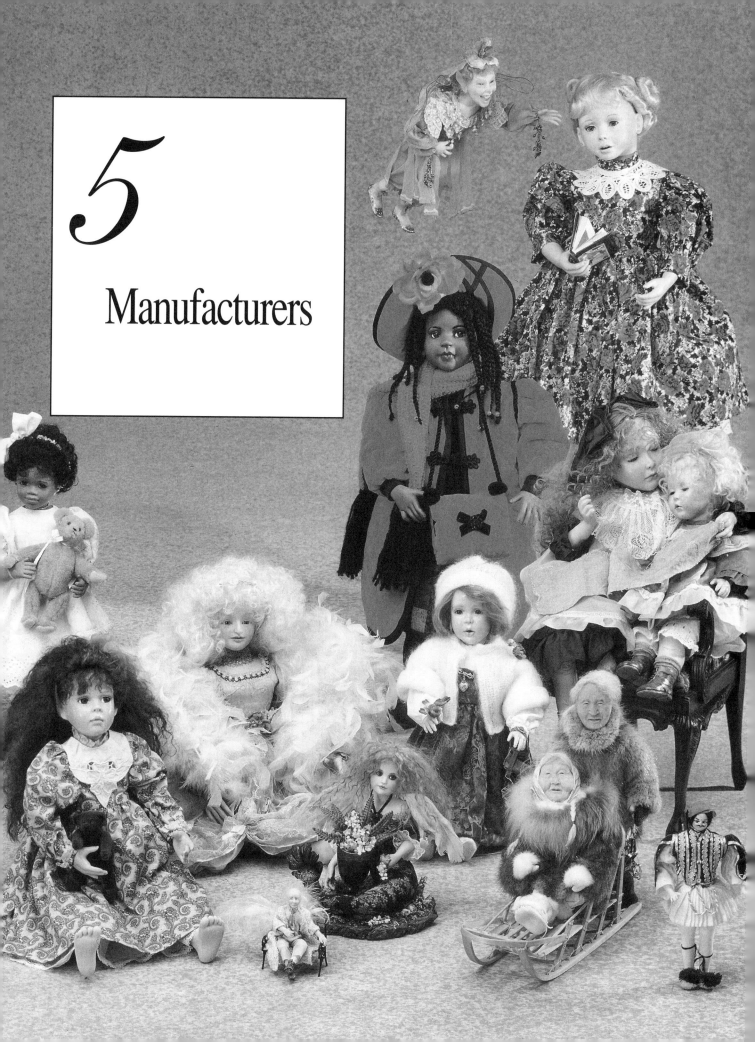

5
Manufacturers

A Guide to Chapter Five

oday's collectibles will become pieces of history. This makes doll collectors historians of sorts, saving today's history for coming generations. No sourcebook would be complete without mention of the manufacturers that make history and provide pleasure to doll collectors everywhere.

These listings can be used in several ways. First, they are meant to acquaint new collectors with some of the major doll manufacturers, and give them a company history and product description. Second, retail store owners can use these listings to get in touch with manufacturers whose products they want to carry. Third, artists who are interested in designing for manufacturers can learn about their guidelines in this chapter. Artists should also read the article by Linda Henry following this introduction.

It is always best to support your local doll shop, but if you are unable to find a manufactured doll through a shop, other available sales outlets are listed here. In addition, if a manufacturer's club is available, information is included in these listings.

Manufactured dolls are constantly changing, so the product descriptions and names of designers may not be completely accurate. To stay abreast of the many changes in the doll world, be sure to read one or more of the periodicals available to doll collectors.

The Listings

The listings in this chapter include the company's address and contact numbers, as well as the year in which the company was founded. If the company offers a catalog, the listing will tell you whether it is for retailers, collectors or both, and how much it costs.

Companies have provided product descriptions. This information was provided in late 1995 or early 1996 and may not be completely up-to-date due to continually changing selections. It will, however, give you an idea of the types of products available. The description often includes names of designers whose work was available at the time of publication.

Business information includes how retailers can purchase the company's products (listed under "Wholesale") and how collectors can purchase the company's products (listed under "Retail"). In addition, information about inquiries from artists who would like to have their designs mass-manufactured are also included. If unsolicited inquiries are not accepted, the listing will say so. Otherwise, information is provided on what to send, what the company is looking for, and any additional guidelines, as long as the company provided this information.

Information on a manufacturer's club, if one exists, is also included. Finally, if the company chose to include company history, it is added under the "Additional Information" heading.

From Artist to Designer: Working With Manufacturers

BY LINDA HENRY

Linda Henry has been designing original porcelain dolls and collectible bears for manufacturers since 1990. During that time she has designed for L.L. Knickerbocker Creations, The Annette Funicello Bear Collection, The Marie Osmond Doll Collection, Silent Sentiments and The Georgetown Collection. She lives in Canal Winchester, Ohio.

Linda Henry

*F*or many artists, the idea of designing for a manufacturer is very appealing. While it's true that there are many benefits, care should be taken to explore disadvantages which could lead to future disappointment. If you are hoping to become an overnight celebrity, you may want to look into another field. It takes hard work, time, and lots of determination to make it in the commercial doll industry. Depending upon your contract, designing dolls may bring you considerable name recognition in the doll world, but it won't happen overnight.

The Pros and Cons

Don't consider a career as a designer if you don't like working under the pressure of deadlines, or if you have a hard time taking criticism of your work. Also, if you are the type of artist who insists on using the finest materials for your dolls, ask yourself if you will you be satisfied with a manufacturer using materials of a lesser quality on a doll with your name on it. Keep in mind that in many cases, the manufactured piece loses something in translation from the artist's original.

When designing for a manufacturer, you may find that your work must go through several different levels of approval before an order is placed. That could mean that you are responsible for making changes to the doll at each level. Most artists are unaware that from the time a contract is signed, it may be up to two years before their manufactured doll makes it into the market. If you have an exclusive contract without a retainer, you may also find yourself "on the shelf" for extended periods of time without an income.

The advantages of having your designs manufactured are obvious. You are released from the stress of daily production. The costs of advertising, processing orders, and shipping are no longer your responsibility. If your dolls are sold overseas, the manufacturer deals with distribution, customs costs, freight and taxes. If you like working with a definite production schedule and deadlines and you enjoy the challenge of constantly creating new pieces, then designing for a manufacturer may be perfect for you.

How to Be Discovered

The best way to begin a career as a designer is to promote yourself as an artist so that a manufacturer interested in your work will come to you. You could be on your way to being discovered without even realizing it!

The Show Circuit

If you have been on the show circuit for a while, chances are that manufacturer's reps have already seen your work. They scout for new talent at shows all over the world. You say you haven't seen any? They don't always wear three-piece suits and hand out business cards. Often they are wearing casual clothes and might even appear to be doll collectors. Occasionally they will pick up one of your business cards and call you sometime after the show. In most cases, if they are interested in your work, they will introduce themselves and make an appointment to talk to you privately.

Magazine Exposure

Several artists have told me that they were discovered by manufacturers due to publicity they received in the trade magazines. About a year ago I was approached by a manufacturer who saw my work featured in a magazine article. I did some prototype work, but it did not lead to a contract. You must be prepared for disappointment. Many times these encounters seem glamorous at first but, for one reason or another, fall through.

Shop Exposure

Some manufacturers send scouts to shops to get an idea of the work doll artists are doing. If you are selling your work in several shops, you may be discovered this way. If a scout likes your work, she may purchase one of your dolls and contact you later.

Portfolio Submission

Sometimes you will have to take the first step and submit your portfolio to a manufacturer. The listings in this chapter include contact information and guidelines for artist's submissions. Most companies employ a staff of designers to develop new products for them, but many are receptive to offers of rights to new ideas from sources outside the company. They receive numerous unsolicited ideas, many of which are not new or are already in the public domain.

If you are interested in submitting your portfolio for consideration, call the manufacturer and ask for their Product Development Manager or Outside Submissions Department to obtain the necessary forms. You'll usually be asked to sign a disclosure statement, which releases the manufacturer from any obligation unless a formal written contract is signed. I began my doll career in 1986, when I wrote a children's book and designed a line of characters for it. My goal was to have the book

published and to have the characters available in the toy market. My lawyer made sure that my copyrights were all in order and put together a disclosure statement for me. I approached several large manufacturers and found that most of them had a disclosure or submission statement of their own that they wanted me to complete prior to receiving samples.

Keep one copy of the agreement for your records and send one signed and dated copy, together with the materials you wish to have considered, to the manufacturer. Make sure you enclose a detailed packing list. You might also consider asking for an "acknowledgment of receipt" form from your shipper. You will probably hear within four to six weeks whether they are interested in your submission. Even if they are not interested, they will usually keep a copy or description of your disclosure for their records.

Network Referrals

Despite the large number of doll artists working today, we all know that at its heart the doll world is really a very small place. It is not uncommon for doll artists to help each other whenever possible, and this includes referring each other to manufacturers looking for fresh ideas. My first contract with a manufacturer came to me in this way. A friend of mine in the doll industry recommended me when the doll company for which he worked needed someone to design plush accessories for their dolls.

It's always a good idea to stay in touch with people you know in the industry, including the contacts you have made at various companies—even if such contacts never resulted in a contract. Companies are restructured periodically. A contact you had at one company may have moved to another company in the industry. You may want to resubmit your portfolio to the new company and see what develops. The best way to keep up with what is going on in the doll world is to read the magazines and talk to fellow artists regularly. The more you know, the better your chances of finding a place for your designs.

Researching the Company

Before approaching a company or entering into an agreement with a company that has approached you, it is always a good policy to ask for referrals from other artists whom the company has had under contract. If you have been referred to a manufacturer by another artist whom you trust, this may not be necessary. In most cases, however, make sure that other artists have been satisfied with the company's work, and that the company has a good reputation for how they treat their designers. It would also be to your advantage to see samples of some of the advertising and marketing brochures the company has produced.

One advantage to joining a group such as the Maine Society of Doll and Bear Artists is that they offer a "better business bureau" of sorts where artists can exchange information about manufacturers and reps. Such groups will also refer one person to another to get professional input and can direct artists to places that can solve business problems. Some groups even offer a newsletter containing interviews with manufacturers and tips on what to look for in contracts. Again, keeping in touch with what is going on in the doll industry and making and maintaining contacts with other artists is very important if you want to be successful in this business.

Finding a Lawyer

Before entering into any written agreement, I highly recommend that you consult a lawyer. If possible, contact one who has had experience in the doll or collectible industry. Ask friends or business acquaintances whom they have found to be satisfactory. The local bar association may be able to recommend someone if you require specialized legal experience.

If your resources are very limited, the Legal Aid Society may be of help. For information and possibly free legal services related specifically to your work as a designer, contact Volunteer Lawyers for the Arts, which has chapters in many states. If you cannot find them in your phone book or through your local bar association, writer to Volunteer Lawyers for the Arts, One East 53rd Street, Sixth Floor, New York, NY 10022, or call (212) 319-2787.

Negotiating a Contract

Fairness and honesty should be your main concern when negotiating a contract. Look for clear, precise wording that leaves very little that can be interpreted in different ways. The written contract is far more important than any verbal "implication" you think you hear. There are no hard-and-fast rules when it comes to negotiating contracts, but below are some contract terms that should be red flags to every artist.

Exclusive vs. Nonexclusive Contracts

"Exclusive" means that you may not design for other companies while still working under contract for the company with which you signed. You will have to decide if this will work for you. In most cases, a contract will not permit the artist to reproduce or provide any of the works or derivatives of the works to any company or person other than the manufacturer. Make sure that you will still be able to sell your own original creations at shows and to shops. The manufacturer may also restrict the size of any limited edition you may produce on your own.

Length of Contract

Also called "the term of the agreement," the length of contract can vary greatly. Most of the contracts I have seen have been for three, five or ten years. Many contracts also have a renewal period at the manufacturer's option. Some artists may feel more comfortable writing contracts on a "work-by-work" basis.

Final Approval

It is to the artist's advantage to reserve the right of final approval. Ask to see a factory sample of the manufacturer's interpretation of your doll before it goes into production. After all, your name will be associated with this product, and you want to be proud of the final outcome.

First Refusal

Be cautious of the phrase "right of first refusal." Under this clause, the purchaser has the right to consider any other designs you create for mass production. In other words, you may take your design to another company only if the manufacturer with which you are currently working has seen the design and decided not to mass-produce it. Make sure that you understand what that means and that you are willing to accept those terms.

Payment Terms

The terms related to payment may be confusing. Before you sign a contract, be sure you understand exactly when and how you will be paid.

Development Fees

If you successfully negotiate for development fees, the manufacturer will pay you a predetermined amount to cover the direct development costs of an approved work. In return, you may be asked to submit one or more samples of the doll, patterns, instructions and samples of materials used.

Flat Fee

Occasionally an artist will prefer to work for a flat fee. This means that the artist receives a one-time, predetermined amount for the development of the doll. Normally this works out to less than if the artist had opted for royalties, a percentage of the revenue for each doll sold.

Royalties

Several factors need to be considered when discussing royalties. To some degree, royalty percentages depend on your status in the industry. If you are a newcomer, you may not be able to command as high a royalty as someone who is considered an icon in the business. An agent or rep can sometimes help you negotiate for better percentages, but you must remember that you will be sharing the percentage with the agent. Make sure you know how much of your royalties the rep is asking for before she begins negotiating with the manufacturer.

You may be offered straight royalties or given an advance against future royalties. Consider the size of the edition as well as the royalty percentage: an offer of 5 percent on a limited edition of 500 pieces is much different from 1 percent on 500,000 pieces! Just as important is understanding the difference between percentages based on the retail, wholesale or factory cost. For example, a doll that sells retail for $100 probably had a wholesale cost of $50. The factory cost of that same doll may be less than $20. Make sure you understand whether your royalty is based on the retail, wholesale or factory cost.

Payment of royalties can vary depending on the manner in which the product is distributed. Some manufacturers pay quarterly. Others pay within a predetermined length of time after they have received payment from their customers. The artist should receive a royalty statement showing shipments, revenues and paid sales for each of the works designed for the company. Some companies may even guarantee the artist a minimum annual amount to maintain the contract.

What If You Don't Get Paid?

If you do not get paid, consider the following suggestions. Begin by refusing to do further work if asked. Send copies of your invoice to the buyer (manufacturer). If you do not receive a response after sending invoice copies, warn the buyer that you will take further legal action. If the amount is small, file a complaint in small claims court. If the amount is substantial, consult a lawyer.

Important Production Questions

Below are some important questions to ask about the production process. Answers to these questions should be explicit in your contract.

- Which of the following will you be responsible for supplying: the original doll, costuming, accessories, plaster molds, patterns for bodies and clothing, finished wax (from which production molds can be made)?
- Who insures these materials during transit to and from the factories, or for that matter anytime they are out of your possession?
- Will your original doll and patterns or molds be returned to you if the project fails to proceed?
- What happens if a factory sample has already been made and then the project is rejected? Who owns that sample?
- How much will you be paid if your prototype or molds are damaged or lost?
- Will you receive factory samples at no cost?
- Once the dolls are in production, will you be able to purchase them at a reduced cost if you choose? If so, how many will they allow you to buy, and can you resell them at shows or shops here and abroad?
- Can the factory elect to produce dolls from rejected designs later on? If so, how much will you be paid?
- What proof of sales will the manufacturer give you?

Test Periods

Some large manufacturers may conduct extensive test marketing on your design before going into full production. In many cases they spend thousands of dollars researching through consumer surveys or measuring the results of selective advertising. You may be asked to create several different dolls for each one that actually goes into full production. Again, I want to stress that designing is a hard job, and that very few artists have gained the fame and fortune they originally anticipated.

Copyright and Copyright Licensing

Whenever you allow your work to be reproduced, make sure that you are credited and that the copyright notice

When designing for a manufacturer, you must expect your doll to undergo several major changes between the time the concept is accepted and the time the doll goes into production. Linda Henry's 10″ "Kelly" (© 1995) is pictured here as it was originally submitted for the Marie Osmond Doll Collection.

After Marie Osmond's input and several changes in costuming, accessories and concept, "Kelly" is ready for production.

symbol, ©, appears with it. Never let your work be reproduced without copyright notice.

When you license the rights to reproduce your dolls, you reserve all other reproduction rights for a particular creation. The right to reproduce your work is one of the most valuable rights you have. Licensing gives others limited rights to your work without forcing you to give up your copyright. Examine carefully what rights you are selling, and how you will be paid for each type of reproduction.

A license agreement should specify how long the license will last and whether the user may market the reproductions throughout the world or only in specific locations. It should also state whether or not you are

giving permission for the copyrighted image of your work to be used on, say, figurines, greeting cards, calendars, plates, or in any other way.

There are two types of licensing, exclusive and non-exclusive. The person granting the license, usually the owner, is considered the licenser, and the person receiving the license is the licensee. Under an exclusive license, a piece of the copyright is given away, perhaps only for a brief time, in a restricted territory, or for a restricted medium. No other person, not even the copyright owner, can exercise the rights that have been licensed. The non-exclusive license permits the copyright owner to give more than one person the same rights. Even the copyright owner can exercise the granted rights.

A prospective licensee will probably pay a lot more for an exclusive license than for a non-exclusive one, since exclusivity gives the licensee a monopoly in the area the license covers. Another advantage for the exclusive licensee is that he becomes the owner of the licensed rights and can bring a copyright infringement action on his own.

Do you want an advance against royalties? An advance is an up-front, lump sum payment to be applied against future royalties in order to encourage the licensee to make sales and make up for the advance. In other words, you will be paid a certain amount, and when the doll begins to sell on the market, you will receive no royalties until the royalty percentage of profits equals the amount of your advance.

You also may want the licensee to pay you a minimum guaranteed royalty in order to keep the license in effect. If you don't require this, the licensee can keep the license going without making substantial payments.

Before you grant a license, carefully consider its scope. If you want to continue exercising rights yourself or license others to do so, you must carefully limit the rights granted. Remember that if you grant a non-exclusive license for certain rights, you can't grant an exclusive license to someone else for those rights.

Work Made for Hire Contracts

Be cautious of contracts that contain the words "work made for hire" or "all rights purchased." In the situation of a work made for hire, you are considered an employee of the company. By definition, under such a contract, the employer is granted the copyright for works created by its employee. The rationale for this is that the employee has already been rewarded for creating the copyrightable material by a salary from the employer. Under these circumstances the other party will be able to use your creation in any way they wish without paying you, consulting you or, depending on the terms of the contract, crediting you.

There are other ways to tell if you are being contracted for a work made for hire. Check for language that states (usually at the beginning of the contract) that you are assigning all rights and interest in your work, including the copyright, to the manufacturer. Is payment a flat fee or an advance against royalties? A flat fee may indicate that you have been paid in full. Is the copyright in your name or the manufacturer's?

Distribution and Promotion

Make sure you know how and where the product will be distributed. This will vary greatly among manufacturers and may include any of the following: retail sales, wholesale, direct mail, magazines, television, newspapers, catalogs and the World Wide Web (the Internet). Also, does the contract include worldwide rights? Where are the dolls going to be made? In what factories and in what countries? Do these countries abide by the international copyright agreement? Beware of the words "marketed in [the United States]." This may indicate that the company intends to market the dolls elsewhere and not pay you royalties.

Finally, make sure you are clear on how your dolls will be promoted. How will your name be used in conjunction with the doll? Will it be used in their advertising, on the sewn-in tag and on the box? Will the doll come with a certificate identifying you as the designer? What kind of promotional campaign does the manufacturer have planned? Will you be asked to make personal appearances at shops and shows? Will the manufacturer cover all your expenses to do so? Make sure all of this is covered in your contract.

Termination and Cancellation

Often, contracts will provide for termination by the other party but not by you. The contract should provide for termination by *both* parties. If the contract asks you to do a lot of work on speculation before getting paid, be sure there is some kind of cancellation or "kill" fee, so that if the contract is canceled, you are compensated for the work you have done.

A Difficult Endeavor

Again, if you want to design for a manufacturer, keep in mind that it is not an easy endeavor. You may be surprised at how much time and work is involved between the initial conversations with a manufacturer and the time the actual manufactured dolls you designed make it on the shelf. If you decide to try your hand at designing, you will be successful if you proceed with caution and carefully consider each clause in your contract, with a lawyer's help. Remember that you know what is best for your business and yourself!

Manufacturers

ANNALEE MOBILITEE DOLLS INC.

Box 708, Reservoir Rd.
Meredith, NH 03253-0708
Phone: Orders from retailers: (800)258-4647
For info: (603)279-3333 EST
Founded in: 1954

PRODUCT INFORMATION:

Catalog: Available to retailers, collectors and wholesalers. Color, free. Request by mail.
Description: Annalee Mobilitee Dolls Inc. is a manufacturer of soft-sculptured dolls that can be repositioned. Chief artist is Annalee Thorndike. Dolls are all handcrafted and all made in the US.

BUSINESS INFORMATION:

Wholesale: Retail businesses should call to order dolls.
Retail: Collectors may call to order dolls or join the company's collector's club.

MANUFACTURER'S CLUB:

Name: The Annalee Doll Society
Membership fee: $29.95/year
Membership includes: Member doll, collectible enameled lapel pin dated with year of membership and special edition Annalee felt pen.
Advantages: Quarterly edition of magazine for 1 year, allowed to attend members-only events and to purchase members-only dolls.

ASHTON-DRAKE GALLERIES

9200 N. Maryland Ave.
Niles, IL 60714
Phone: Orders from retailers: (800)323-8140 CST
Orders from individuals: (800)634-5164
For info: (800)634-5164
Fax: (708)966-3026
Founded in: 1985

PRODUCT INFORMATION:

Catalog: Available to retailers or collectors. Color, free. Request by phone, mail or fax.
Description: Among collectors world-wide, the Ashton-Drake Galleries is known for offering premiere-quality dolls and other fine collectibles at prices that are consistently the best in the market. The company's value-priced collector dolls are crafted to their own exceptional standards, known as the Uniform Grading Standards for Dolls, and then designated "Premiere Quality." Ashton-Drake dolls are designed by leading artists from all over the world. They are crafted in bisque porcelain, hand-painted, and costumed with exceptional skill and attention to detail. Virtually every doll is hand numbered, comes with its own matching numbered Certificate of Authenticity, and is fully guaranteed. The company also offers a variety of doll-related collectibles, such as miniature dolls and ornaments, all hand-painted and beautifully crafted in fine porcelain and other materials. Designs by Yolanda Bello, Kathy Barry-Hippensteel, Titus Tomescu, Julie Good-Krüger, Mary Tretter, Dianna Effner, Cindy Mc-Clure, Gaby Rademann, Corinne Layton, Joan Ibarolle, Michele Girard-Kassis.

BUSINESS INFORMATION:

Wholesale: Retail businesses may purchase dolls in retail outlets. Call the retail 800 number for information.
Retail: Collectors may purchase products directly. Collectors may send SASE for retail catalog. Call to order dolls or order through direct mail ads.
Artists' inquiries: No unsolicited inquiries accepted.

ADDITIONAL INFORMATION:

Company history: The Ashton-Drake Galleries offered its first porcelain collectible doll to the public in 1985. This doll—a lovable baby boy clown called "Jason," designed by doll artist Yolanda Bello—has become a legend among collectors. Originally issued for just $48.00, the edition of "Jason" has been sold out for many years, and the doll now appears on the secondary market for prices well in excess of $500. "Jason" was the first issue in the Yolanda's Picture-Perfect Babies® collection, which has become one of the best-known modern doll collections worldwide (the entire collection of eleven dolls is completely sold out). Since the mid-1980s, Ashton-Drake has issued hundreds of different collector dolls in exclusive editions by dozens of leading doll artists. Doll themes range from endearing, realistic baby portraits to the most elegant bride, fashion and celebrity dolls. Over the years, several of these dolls have won prestigious industry-wide awards, including *Doll Reader's* DOTY Award, the *Dolls* Award of Excellence and the top doll award from the National Association of Limited Edition Dealers.

AVONLEA TRADITIONS INC.

#1-9030 Leslie St.
Richmond Hill, Ontario L4B 1G2
CANADA
Phone: (905)886-7651 EST
Fax: (905)886-7653
Founded in: 1988

PRODUCT INFORMATION:

Catalog: Available to retailers or collectors. Color, $3. Request by phone, mail or fax.
Description: Avonlea Traditions manufactures and distributes a comprehensive line of products related to the ever-popular classic story, Anne of Green Gables. The company has porcelain dolls, vinyl dolls, soft dolls, paper dolls, doll accessory kits, doll-making kits and a pop-up doll house book along with other Anne of Green Gables merchandise such as collectible figurines, activity sets, stationery, clothing, books, music, a quarterly newsletter and much more. The com-

pany won "Canadian Collectible Doll of the Year" in 1992.

BUSINESS INFORMATION:

Wholesale: Retail businesses may purchase dolls in retail outlets, call to order, order dolls through catalog or ask for a sales rep to call.

Retail: Collectors may purchase products directly, order a retail catalog or call.

Artists' inquiries: No unsolicited inquiries accepted.

ADDITIONAL INFORMATION:

Company history: Avonlea Traditions was formed in 1988 for the purpose of manufacturing and distributing products based on the Anne of Green Gables story. Dolls and other items are made by artisans, cottage industries and factories in Canada and abroad. The company sells to specialty shops and by mail order to Canada, the US and overseas. A quarterly newsletter is available, *The Avonlea Traditions Chronicle.* Subscription is $14/4 issues (one year); $24/8 issues (2 years); $33/12 issues (3 years). The fee includes newsletters and complimentary catalogs. The publication will keep collectors up-to-date on everything happening in the world of Anne of Green Gables, including new product introductions.

CAMP VENTURE INC.

100 Convent Rd.
P.O. Box 402
Nanuet, NY 10954
Phone: Orders from retailers: (800)682-3714 EST
For info: (914)624-3860
Fax: (914)624-7065 or (914)624-7064
Founded in: 1969

PRODUCT INFORMATION:

Catalog: Available to retailers or collectors. Free. Request by phone, mail or fax.

Description: Dolly Downs Dolls are high quality 14″ soft dolls made by people with disabilities. The dolls come fully clothed and wear a backpack which contains an audio tape and a story book. Dolly is an excellent way to introduce children to diversity, inclusion, and a value orientation based on caring and sharing. The dolls come in male and female versions of Caucasian blond, African-American, and European/Latino (olive skin—dark hair).

ADDITIONAL INFORMATION:

Company history: Camp Venture, Inc. is a not for profit provider of habilitative services and family-like care to people with developmental disabilities in Rockland County, New York. It was started 26 years ago by a group of families who had children with various disabilities for which little or no services and facilities were available.

CAROUSEL CANADA INC.

129 Rowntree Dairy Rd. #20
Woodbridge, Ontario L4L 6E1
CANADA
Phone: Orders from retailers: (800)387-0338 EST
For info: (905)851-3192
Fax: (905)851-3238
Founded in: 1985

PRODUCT INFORMATION:

Catalog: Available to retailers or collectors. Color. Request by mail or fax.

Description: Carousel Canada distributes a unique selection of fine-quality porcelain collector dolls and jesters. Featuring the "Renaissance Collection®," "The B.B. Doll Collection" and in Canada only, "The Doll Maker" and "Effanbee Doll" lines. Designs by Angelika LaHaise, Rita Harth, Sharon Rae, Brenda Brink.

BUSINESS INFORMATION:

Wholesale: Retail businesses may call to order dolls or order dolls through catalog.

Retail: Collectors may order a retail catalog and complete the enclosed order form or call to order.

Artists' inquiries: Send photos of current work, production schedule capabilities and limitations. (For artists interested in doing their own small signature series editions).

ADDITIONAL INFORMATION:

Company history: Carousel Canada Inc. was established in 1985 as an importer and distributor of giftware, specializing in collectible dolls. To date, the company has dolls being produced in South Africa, China, Canada and Taiwan, with additional imports from the US.

DADDY'S LONG LEGS

300 Banks St.
Southlake, TX 76092
Phone: (817)481-4800 MST
Fax: (817)488-8876
Founded in: 1989

PRODUCT INFORMATION:

Catalog: Color, free. Request by mail.

Description: Daddy's Long Legs are realistic African-American characters from an era long ago. The company is family owned and operated. Karen Germany's award-winning designs have assisted in bridging gaps between cultures and generations, making Daddy's Long Legs one of the newest but most popular American-made collectibles.

BUSINESS INFORMATION:

Wholesale: Retail businesses should call to order dolls.

Retail: Collectors may call for a location near them carrying Daddy's Long Legs.

Artists' inquiries: Artists wishing to present their designs should call for specific information.

MANUFACTURER'S CLUB:

Name: Daddy's Long Legs Collectors Club

Membership fee: $25/year or $40/2 years

Membership includes: Free figurine, subscription to *Star News* newsletter, and annual convention.

Advantages: Opportunity to purchase members-only dolls and invitations to signings featuring Karen Germany.

THE DOLL FACTORY, INC.

260-B Business Pwky.
Royal Palm Beach, FL 33411
Phone: Orders from retailers: (407)795-8777 (EST)
Fax: (407)795-3450
Founded in: 1971

PRODUCT INFORMATION:

Catalog: Available to retailers or collectors. Color. Retailers, free; collectors, $3. Request by mail.

Description: Diana Dolls, Rottenkids, German Doll Carriages, Artisan Porcelain Dolls, Zapf Collector Dolls. Designs by Brigitte Leman, Christine Kleinert, Bettina Feigenspan-Hirsch, Barbara Prusseit, Heidi Plusczok.

BUSINESS INFORMATION:

Wholesale: Retail businesses should call to order dolls or order dolls through catalog.

Retail: Collectors may order a retail catalog and complete the enclosed order form or call to order dolls.

Artists' inquiries: Artists wishing to present their designs should send photos of the product. According to quantity requirements and ultimate price, will produce products in US, Spain, Germany or Mexico.

ADDITIONAL INFORMATION:

Company history: Founded in 1971, The Doll Factory originated as a manufacturer of dolls and expanded to retail in 1974, opening a mail order department in 1980. Today, 95% of sales are wholesale to other retailers of manufactured products or distributed exclusively for other manufacturers in Europe and Asia.

DYNASTY DOLL COLLECTION, INC.

1 Newbold Rd.
P.O. Box 36
Fairless Hills, PA 19030
Phone: Orders from retailers: (800)736-GIFT (4438) EST
Orders from individuals: (800)736-GIFT (4438)
For info: (215)428-9100
Fax: (215)428-9200
Founded in: 1977

PRODUCT INFORMATION:

Catalog: Available to retailers or collectors. Color, $7.50. Request by phone, mail, fax or contact Dynasty Representative.

Description: The Dynasty Doll Collection is created under the direction of Anne L. Dolan and Donna R. Rovner. Anne and Donna work with many doll artists from around the world who sculpt dolls that will augment the current line. Some artists will design costumes for the dolls they sculpt while others prefer Anne and Donna to design them. Dynasty Dolls are made of the finest porcelain bisque and all costumes are copyrighted. All Dynasty Dolls have porcelain heads, arms and legs with a cloth stuffed body. The authentic period costumes are researched to ensure that every detail is

as it should be. Dynasty has produced some of the finest Victorian dolls on the market today. Dynasty offers the collector a quality doll at an affordable price. In addition to period dolls, Dynasty offers contemporary dolls, baby dolls, Indians, brides and clown dolls. Designs by Hazel Tertsakian, Gail Hoyt, Teena Halbig, Ron Lee, Bongkoj Lee. Dynasty also produces many private label dolls for individual clients.

BUSINESS INFORMATION:

Wholesale: Retail businesses may purchase dolls in retail outlets. Call to order dolls, order dolls through catalog, set up appointment with Dynasty Representative, or attend a trade gift show or Toy Fair and place an order at our booth.

Retail: Collectors may purchase products directly "if there is no doll shop near their home. We prefer collectors to contact a doll shop directly." Collectors may order a retail catalog, join the company's collector's club "coming soon," or order through direct mail advertisements in doll publications.

Artists' inquiries: Artists wishing to present their designs should send photos, résumé letter of introduction. The process to reproduce an artist's work can take up to a year or more.

ADDITIONAL INFORMATION:

Company history: The world-renowned Dynasty Doll Collection has been producing collectible dolls for over 15 years. The line is one of the finest collections available in North America. Dynasty's promise of value and quality is evident in their attention to details. Until May 31, 1995, Dynasty was a division of Cardinal, Inc., a family owned and operated giftware business founded in 1946. As of June 1, 1995, the Dynasty Doll Collection became incorporated under the direction of her new owner, James T. Sheridan. Now located in Fairless Hills, Pennsylvania, the Dynasty Doll Collection continues to grow and provide collectors with quality dolls at an affordable price. The Dynasty Doll Collection has plans to expand the number of artists that sculpt dolls for the line. A collectors' club is planned for

the near future with lots of exciting dolls and accessories for the doll collector.

EFFANBEE DOLL CO.

1026 W. Elizabeth Ave.
Linden, NJ 07036
Phone: (908)474-8000 EST
Fax: (908)474-8001
Founded in: 1910

PRODUCT INFORMATION:

Catalog: Color, $5 to consumers. Free to dealers. Request by phone, mail or fax.

Description: One of the oldest trade names in doll collecting, Effanbee is still recognized as a leader in collectible dolls. Effanbee's mission is to bring quality dolls to the market at affordable prices. They work in vinyl and porcelain, producing artist designed dolls and dolls from their archives.

BUSINESS INFORMATION:

Wholesale: Retail businesses may purchase dolls in retail outlets or call to order.

Retail: Collectors may purchase directly or order through direct mail advertisements in doll publications.

Artists' inquiries: Contact the company by letter with photograph of doll or photographs of work. If interested, company will contact artist. Be realistic about your work and desires.

ADDITIONAL INFORMATION:

Company history: Founded in 1910 as a toy doll company, Effanbee dolls have been played with from generation to generation. In 1995, a private investor group purchased Effanbee. The company's mission is to restore the image of a quality doll company to the doll collector.

FPC INTERNATIONAL, INC.

P.O. Box 650038
Fresh Meadows, NY 11365
Phone: (718)463-5151 EST
Fax: (718)886-7749
Founded in: 1990

PRODUCT INFORMATION:

Catalog: Available to retailers only. Color, free. Request by phone, mail or fax.

Description: FPC International Inc. offers exquisite doll and teddy bear fashions and fine porcelain artist dolls in editions limited to ten pieces and one-of-a-kind, for the discriminating collector. The exclusive doll fashions from Germany's foremost designer STURM are executed in fine silks, linens, cottons and leather for the shoes, in styles to suit a fine artist. Sizes for dolls are from 7″ to 30″ and teddy bears from 8″ to 16″. The porcelain artist dolls are designed and hand-made by Germany's Uta Flegel. The dolls have porcelain heads, breast-plates, arms and legs and soft bodies with wire armatures. Natural hair and hand-painted eyes and clothes of her own design distinguish Uta Flegel's children.

BUSINESS INFORMATION:

Wholesale: Retail businesses may call to order.

Artists' inquiries: No unsolicited inquiries accepted.

ADDITIONAL INFORMATION:

Company history: Growing out of a passion for dolls and years of collecting, FPC International, Inc. (Fine Porcelain Creations International, Inc.) was founded in 1990 for the purpose of bringing to the American market the creations and workshops of German artists. The company searched Thuringia and Saxony, the traditional German toy centers, where fine artisans still handcraft dolls and doll accessories with great care and pride in their tradition. Until the fall of the Berlin wall, these artists and workshops had been unknown or forgotten for decades. The company is proud to offer these exquisite porcelain children and doll fashions. It has been a pleasure to see them regain recognition among American collectors.

"TAKE YOUR TIME, SHOP AROUND, ENJOY THE HUNT, AND YOUR HEART'S DESIRE WILL COME TRUE!"

Patricia Allgeirer, Barbie Dolls & Collectibles, Hawley, PA

GAMBINA DOLLS

2005 Gentilly Blvd.
New Orleans, LA 70119
Phone: Orders from retailers: (800)426-2462 CST
For info: (504)947-0626
Fax: (504)947-7542
Founded in: 1973

PRODUCT INFORMATION:

Catalog: Available to retailers or collectors. Color, $5, with credit toward first purchase. Request by phone, mail or fax.

Description: Gambina Dolls include limited edition porcelain dolls, ethnic dolls, Native American dolls, embroidered face rag dolls, heritage dolls, historical dolls and vinyl dolls. Designs by Curtis Giarrusso, Joel Eguigure, Charles Gambina.

BUSINESS INFORMATION:

Wholesale: Retail businesses may purchase dolls by phone, order catalog.

Retail: Collectors may order a retail catalog and complete the enclosed order form, call to order, join the company's collector's club or order through direct mail advertisements in doll publications.

Artists' inquiries: No unsolicited inquiries accepted.

MANUFACTURER'S CLUB:

Name: Gambina Doll Collectors Club
Membership fee: $10 first year; $2 per year.
Membership includes: Certificate, newsletter, discounts.
Advantages: First shot at new editions/limited editions.

ADDITIONAL INFORMATION:

Company history: Gambina Dolls was started in 1973 by Charles and Beverly Gambina after they fell in love with a handmade doll sold by an elderly woman in New Orleans' French Quarter. Since then Gambina Dolls has made every imaginable kind of doll from soft cuddly rag dolls to fine porcelain dolls such as the official Christopher Columbus limited edition doll in 1993. Ever since its earliest days, Gambina Dolls has featured African American dolls which are meant to capture the dignity, legends, experience and humor of a noble cul-

ture forever intertwined in the story of America. In 1995, Gambina Dolls introduced a Native American and Southwest porcelain doll collectible line.

GREAT AMERICAN DOLL COMPANY

1050 North Batavia, Building B
Orange, CA 92667
Phone: For orders: (800)847-3655 PST
For info: (714)744-5440
Fax: (714)744-9896
Founded in: 1980

PRODUCT INFORMATION:

Catalog: Available to retailers or collectors. Color, free. Request by mail.

Description: The Great American Doll Company offers fine quality porcelain dolls priced from $99 and up. The company also offers fine quality vinyl dolls made in America. The dolls are sold throughout the world and feature beautiful packaging and exquisite designs. The company has won many prestigious magazine awards. Designers include Rotraut Schrott from Germany and Bruno Rossellini from Italy.

BUSINESS INFORMATION:

Wholesale: Retail businesses may purchase dolls by phone by calling (800)VIP-DOLL, or by completing a catalog order form.

Retail: Collectors may purchase dolls directly from company by phone, through the company's collector's club, or through direct mail advertisements in doll publications.

Artists' inquiries: No unsolicited inquiries accepted.

MANUFACTURER'S CLUB:

Name: Rotraut Schrott Collector's Club
Membership fee: Free
Advantages: Collectors in the club will receive mailings about new dolls and will be the first to see them. They are also entitled to a monthly newsletter keeping them abreast of new happenings in the company and with the artists.

ADDITIONAL INFORMATION:

Company history: The Great American Doll Company was founded in 1980 by Michael Lam.

JOHANNES ZOOK ORIGINALS

1519 Badour Rd.

P.O. Box 256

Midland, MI 48640

Phone: (517)835-9388 EST

Fax: (517)835-6689

E-mail: secrist1@chris.com

Founded in: 1983

PRODUCT INFORMATION:

Catalog: Available to retailers or collectors. Color, $3. Request by phone, mail or fax.

Description: Johannes Zook Originals are American-made vinyl collectibles that are near life-size. They are designed after contemporary children. Designs by Pat Secrist, Joanna Secrist.

BUSINESS INFORMATION:

Wholesale: Retail businesses may call to order dolls or order dolls through catalog.

Artists' inquiries: Inquiries should include a sample of the doll design in a sculpture, preferably finished in porcelain, with the proposed cost. No drawings will be accepted. Call to receive price quote. If price is accepted by customer, production will start on the agreed upon date.

ADDITIONAL INFORMATION:

Company history: Apple Valley Doll Works began when Pat sculpted his first original doll face and Joanna designed and made clothing for the doll. They spent a few months learning and creating in their kitchen. By the end of 1983, they had produced 30 porcelain dolls. Over the next three years, they expanded into vinyl dolls, and began to create their first 22″ porcelain dolls and limited edition dolls. Currently, a 7,500 square foot factory has been established in Midland, Michigan, complete with a rotational molding oven. This makes them one of only a small handful of doll companies in the world where the artist/ sculptor designs and actually produces the dolls on site. Within the factory, they plan to continue the company's tradition of creating high-quality products in vinyl for the discriminating collector.

KÄTHE KRUSE PUPPEN GMBH

Alte Augsburger Str. 9

Donauwörth 86609

GERMANY

Phone: (01149)906-706780

   6 hours ahead of EST

Fax: (01149)906-7067870

US address: Käthe Kruse Doll Co.

122 Westover Rd.

Troy, NY 12180

Phone: (518)273-0726

Fax: (518)273-0754

Founded in: 1911

PRODUCT INFORMATION:

Catalog: Available in color, $7 for German catalog; $2 for American catalog.

Description: Käthe Kruse Puppen manufactures quality dolls, plush toys, terry toys and wooden toys. All Käthe Kruse dolls are handmade.

BUSINESS INFORMATION:

Wholesale: Retail businesses may notify the US office. They should call to order dolls, and must show proof they are retailers with photo of store with clear signage. Must have tax number and credit references.

KISH AND COMPANY

11632 Busy St.

Richmond, VA 23236

Phone: (804)379-4362 EST

Fax: (804)379-2780

Founded in: 1992

PRODUCT INFORMATION:

Catalog: Available to retailers or collectors. Color, free. Request by phone, mail or fax.

Description: Kish and Company dolls are vinyl dolls from 10½″ to 16″ tall, including "Childhood Favorite" characters from children's classic stories and nursery rhymes. Other dolls available reflect the essence of childhood in different time periods. Dolls in the 12½″ range are fully jointed. Each doll has human hair wigs and clothing made of the finest natural fabrics. Designs by Helen Kish.

BUSINESS INFORMATION:

Wholesale: Retail businesses may purchase dolls by phone.

LEE MIDDLETON ORIGINAL DOLLS

1301 Washington Blvd.

Belpre, OH 45714

Phone: Orders from retailers: (800)242-3285 EST

Orders from individuals: (614)423-3121

Fax: (614)423-5983

Founded in: 1980

PRODUCT INFORMATION:

Catalog: Available to retailers or collectors. Color, $3. Free to retailers. Request by phone, mail or fax.

Description: Original vinyl and porcelain dolls by doll artist and sculptor Lee Middleton. They are handcrafted in Belpre, Ohio. All designs are by Lee Middleton.

BUSINESS INFORMATION:

Wholesale: Available.

Retail: Collectors may order through direct mail dealer, advertisements in doll publications or call for nearest dealer.

Artists' inquiries: Unsolicited inquiries accepted.

> "CREATING ONE ORIGINAL DOLL DOES NOT MAKE ONE AN ARTIST. THE ARTIST IS SEEN THROUGH A BODY OF WORK MARKING DEDICATION TO AND LOVE OF THE ART FORM."
> *Ann McNichols, Naples, FL*

LLOYD MIDDLETON'S ROYAL VIENNA COLLECTION

R.R. #2, Box 333, P.O. Box 367

Little Hocking, OH 45742

Phone: Orders from retailers: (800)845-1845

For info: (614)989-2082 EST

PRODUCT INFORMATION:

Catalog: Available to collectors. Free. Request by mail.

Description: Manufacturer of vinyl dolls for 1,300 dealers all over the country.

BUSINESS INFORMATION:

Wholesale: Retail businesses should call to order dolls.

MATTEL, INC.

Phone: 1-800-524-8697

PRODUCT INFORMATION:

Description: Mattel, Inc. is best known for Barbie, the doll that has remained a favorite among little girls and collectors alike. Timeless Creations, the collectible/specialty doll division of Mattel, Inc., offers Barbie and other dolls especially for doll collectors. Look for their advertisements in collectible doll magazines, or call the number above for the dealer nearest you.

MCASLAN DOLL COMPANY

159 Gracey Rd.
Canton, CT 06019
Phone: (860)693-6765 EST
Founded in: 1991

PRODUCT INFORMATION:
Catalog: Available to retailers or collectors. Color and b&w, free. Request by phone or mail.
Description: Artist Sandi McAslan does original sculptures of character children dolls in both porcelain and vinyl limited editions. All aspects of the dolls are designed by Sandi and created by the company's artisans, including the wigs and costumes. The company's primary goal is to produce high-quality, unique collectible dolls which are affordably priced for collectors. Designs by Sandi McAslan.

BUSINESS INFORMATION:
Wholesale: Call to order.
Artists' inquiries: No unsolicited inquiries accepted.

MANUFACTURER'S CLUB:
Name: McAslan Doll Collectors Club
Membership fee: Free
Advantages: Advance mailing of new dolls, doll clothes and furniture; a "Club Members Only" doll available.

ADDITIONAL INFORMATION:
Company history: Sandi McAslan was an abstract painter before turning to dollmaking. Sandi and husband Jim own and operate their business from a studio at home while raising 3 young children. They began in 1991 and have grown to be a popular and widely known company. Their dolls are available in 43 states and Canada. Sandi has been honored with *Doll Reader's* DOTY and *Dolls* Award of Excellence nominations for many years.

MUSCOVY COMPANY INC.

870 Research Dr. #12
Palm Springs, CA 92262
Phone: (619)323-7575 PST
Fax: (619)323-8887
Founded in: 1990

PRODUCT INFORMATION:
Catalog: Available to retailers or collectors. Color. Request by phone, mail or fax.
Description: Designs by Alexandra Kukinova. Muscovy Company Inc. makes handmade porcelain, ceramic and cloth dolls depicting festive clothing primarily from the late 18th and early 19th centuries of specific provinces of Russia. Alexandra Kukinova, the creator of these dolls, spares no detail. Each doll is exquisitely designed and produced to perfect scale and, where possible, with the exact technique used at that time. Each embellishment is handcrafted. The lace is hand-crocheted, the boots are handmade by cobblers, and the pearls and ribbons are hand-applied. Even the copper shields, helmets, and swords are handcrafted by talented artisans. The intricate patterns of embroidery require hand guidance in the embroidery machine. The dolls have realistic eyes, real eyelashes and hand-painted faces. Editions are limited.

BUSINESS INFORMATION:
Wholesale: Retail businesses should call to order dolls or order dolls through catalog.
Retail: Collectors may purchase products directly. Available only if there is no dealer in their area.

ADDITIONAL INFORMATION:
Company history: Muscovy Company, Inc., a trading company, discovered Alexandra Kukinova on a business trip to Moscow. After many conversations, it was decided that Muscovy Company, Inc. would provide exclusive representation of the ALEXANDRA+MOSCOW doll collection. The new editions with flesh-toned porcelain and realistic eyes were introduced in limited quantities at the International Doll Expo in Arlington, Texas in January 1995. ALEXANDRA will be introducing 3 additional dolls in 1996.

PITTSBURGH ORIGINALS

150 Gamma Dr. #3
Pittsburgh, PA 15238
Phone: (412)963-9050 EST
Fax: (412)963-9491
Founded in: 1986

PRODUCT INFORMATION:
Catalog: Available to retailers or collectors. Color. Request by phone or mail.
Description: Chris Miller is the only designer of these rag dolls. Some types are: 14″ vinyl, 8″ vinyl cloth, porcelain limited edition dolls. The company's motto is "Playmate today—treasure tomorrow."

BUSINESS INFORMATION:
Wholesale: Retail businesses should call to order dolls or order dolls through catalog.

RUSSIAN COLLECTION

R.R. 1, Box 5
Intervale, NH 03845
Phone: (603)356-7832 EST
Fax: (603)356-5540
Founded in: 1993

PRODUCT INFORMATION:
Catalog: Photographs available to collectors only. Free. Request by phone, mail or fax.
Description: Sells one-of-a-kind, hand painted nesting dolls from Russia. Sets range from 5 to 30 pieces.

BUSINESS INFORMATION:
Retail: Collectors may call to order.

SANDY DOLLS, INC.

P.O. Box 3222
3389-A S. Scenic
Springfield, MO 65808
Phone: Orders from retailers: (800)607-2639 CST
For info: (417)887-7255
Fax: (417)887-7327
Founded in: 1993

PRODUCT INFORMATION:
Catalog: Available to retailers only. Color, free. Request by phone, mail, fax or receive one at trade show booths.
Description: Sandy Dolls, Inc. is a wholesale distributor of quality ethnic dolls and seasonal decorations. Historically researched and authentically designed and costumed Native Ameri-

can dolls are available in three different series with the Traditions and the Warrior and Princess series each as limited editions. The quality vinyl dolls are tribal and Nation specific with representation primarily from the period 1860-1890. Each hang tag provides information on the specific tribe which is represented. The Sandy Dolls seasonal decorations are angels, Santas and ornaments, made with high quality velvets and satins—exquisitely sculpted in vinyl. Gorgeous trims and adornments set the decorations apart from all others. Sandy Dolls, Inc. backs its quality products with quality service and on-demand shipping. In 1996, African-American dolls and African-American seasonal decorations will be introduced. Designs by Ruben Tejada, Stella Dy and Gigi Dy.

BUSINESS INFORMATION:

Wholesale: Retail businesses may call to order, order dolls through catalog, or place order at trade shows. For all initial orders, credit references are required.

Artists' inquiries: No unsolicited inquiries accepted.

> "INVENT YOUR OWN STYLE. DO NOT TRY TO COPY YOUR FAVORITE ARTISTS. TRY, TRY AGAIN!"
> *Nancy Pritchard, Wild Spirit Doll Studio, E. Providence, RI*

SEYMOUR MANN, INC.

230 Fifth Ave., Suite 1500
New York, NY 10001
Phone: Orders from retailers: (212)683-8175 EST
Orders from individuals: (212)683-5229
For info: (212)683-7262
Fax: (212)213-4920
Founded in: 1968

PRODUCT INFORMATION:

Catalog: Available to retailers or collectors. Color, $7.50. Mail a request with address and enclose a check, cash or money order.

Description: These dolls feature fine craftsmanship and exceptional artistry and have won numerous awards and praise among collectors. Designs by Eda Mann, Pamela Phillips, Edna

Dali, Margie Costa, Paulette Aprille, June Amos Grammer, Gwen McNeil, Lynne Randolph, Hannah K. Hyland.

BUSINESS INFORMATION:

Wholesale: Retail businesses should order a catalog and complete the enclosed order form, or contact one of the company's salespeople in New York, Atlanta, Chicago, Dallas or Los Angeles.

Retail: Collectors may order a retail catalog and complete the enclosed order form.

Artists' inquiries: Artists wishing to present their designs should send photographs of work, list of prices, résumé, and cover letter introducing themselves and their work.

MANUFACTURER'S CLUB:

Name: Seymour Mann Collectible Doll Club.

Membership fee: $5

Membership includes: Mailings, announcements and flyers enabling members to purchase upcoming dolls before other collectors.

Advantages: Members hear about new dolls and awards.

ADDITIONAL INFORMATION:

Company history: Originally founded as an art studio, Seymour Mann, Inc. has grown to include many award-winning doll artists and designers. Every year, the artists are recognized and have been awarded either *Doll Reader's* DOTY, *Dolls* Award of Excellence or Collectible of the Year. After their retirement, many Seymour Mann dolls have appreciated in value. Edition sizes vary from 2,500-7,500, and each doll has a hang tag that states edition size of the series and description of the artist. Most dolls have the "Seymour Mann, Inc." name on the back of the neck.

SIGIKID

21-11 24th Dr.
Astoria, NY 11102
Phone: (718)274-8249 EST
Fax: (718)274-8834
Founded in: 1856

PRODUCT INFORMATION:

Catalog: Available to retailers. Color, free. Available to collectors for $10.

Request by phone, mail or fax.

Description: sigikid manufactures high quality collectibles, including mohair bears, plush animals, dolls, marionettes, textile gifts and wooden toys. Dolls are limited editions with human hair wigs and hand painted eyes. Designs by Ilse Wippler, Angelika Mannersdorfer, Ute Kase Lepp, Martha Armstrong Hand, Brigitte Deval, Barbara Frebel, Gisela Hoffmann, Antoinette Froschmayer Gaerny.

BUSINESS INFORMATION:

Wholesale: Retail businesses may call to order.

Artists' inquiries: Include photos, press kit and résumé.

MANUFACTURER'S CLUB:

Name: Sigikid Club (Club is only available in Europe as of this date)

Membership fee: 20 DM

ADDITIONAL INFORMATION:

Company history: In 1856, H. Scharrer and Koch GMBH—the parent company of sigikid—founded a trading company and sold glass beads, marbles and wooden toys. In 1968, the present owners renamed the company sigikid and began to develop a new line of toys and collectibles to compliment the new name. Today, an assortment of more than 3,500 products make up the sigikid line of high design, high quality goods.

THOMAS BOLAND AND CO., INC.

15-125 Merchandise Mart
Chicago, IL 60654
Phone: For orders: (800)555-5120 CST
For info: (312)822-0697
Fax: (312)822-7228
Founded in: 1969

PRODUCT INFORMATION:

Catalog: Available to retailers or collectors. Color and b&w, $5, refundable against first order. Request by phone, mail or fax.

Description: Thomas Boland and Co. offers art dolls, limited edition and one-of-a-kind doll art, collectible plush characters, teddy bears and doll-related collectible accessories. Designs by Linda Mason, Pam Phillips, Pat Thompson, Pat Kolesar, Nancy Wiley O'Brien, Terry Stone, Ed

Mackert/Regina Saunders, Bill Nelson, Jackie Austin, George Berger.

BUSINESS INFORMATION:

Wholesale: Retail businesses may call to order or see displays at trade shows in all major gift/doll/art markets, including Atlanta, IDEX, New York, Chicago, Denver, Florida, Washington DC, Los Angeles, Santa Fe.

Retail: Collectors may call to order or order through direct mail advertisements in doll publications or trade show booth sales.

Artists' inquiries: Include pictures of work, biographical information, list of major awards, educational training, shops that do or have carried their dolls.

ADDITIONAL INFORMATION:

Company history: The Thomas Boland Co., founded in 1969, is dedicated to the development, presentations and display of doll art. The company has represented many of the major doll artists and promoted their work. Thomas P. Boland, president and industry maven, has a worldwide reputation for the development of doll artists and their work in the marketplace.

TREFFEISEN USA

4172 Corporate Square, Unit A
Naples, FL 33942
Phone: (941)643-9702 EST
Fax: (941)643-1798
E-mail: 102105,1220@compuserve.com or ancamay@aol.com
Founded in: 1993

PRODUCT INFORMATION:

Catalog: Available to retailers or collectors. Color, $4.50. Catalog of smaller dolls only, free. Request by mail, fax or e-mail.

Description: Treffeisen USA offers limited edition artist dolls in vinyl and porcelain, a complete line of exclusive

doll clothes and accessories, and a doll calendar. Designs by Ruth Treffeisen, Germany.

BUSINESS INFORMATION:

Wholesale: Retail businesses may call to order or order dolls through catalog.

Artists' inquiries: Unsolicited inquiries accepted.

MANUFACTURER'S CLUB:

Name: Ruth Treffeisen Collector's Club
Membership fee: $49.95 per year
Membership includes: Collector's kit with information about vinyl and porcelain dolls, accessories catalog, calendar and magazine.
Advantages: Club members can purchase club doll and be part of doll raffles. Firsthand information about the artist and her work.

ADDITIONAL INFORMATION:

Company history: Ruth Treffeisen has been creating limited edition dolls for over a decade. She has an international reputation and has won many nominations and awards with her dolls over the years. She has been featured in many doll books in Germany and the US.

WIMBLEDON COLLECTION

P.O. Box 21948
Lexington, KY 40522-1948
Phone: (606)277-8531 EST
Fax: (606)277-9231
Founded in: 1970

PRODUCT INFORMATION:

Catalog: Available to retailers only. Color, free. Please supply resale tax ID number. Mail or fax a request.

Description: Wimbledon Collection features a full line of porcelain dolls along with the Gustave and Gretchen Wolff Designer Series. All dolls feature porcelain heads, arms and legs. Each one is unique in its own individ-

ual way. Designs by Gustave and Gretchen Wolff.

BUSINESS INFORMATION:

Wholesale: Retail businesses should order a catalog and complete the enclosed order form. Send via mail or fax and state resale tax ID number.

ADDITIONAL INFORMATION:

Company history: Gustave (Fritz) Wolff was educated at Northland College and the University of Wisconsin. He was the apprentice of world famous ceramicist Robert Eckels. Fritz taught art at a number of institutions before beginning his doll business in 1970. He moved his operation to Lexington, KY in 1974, and the Wimbledon Collection of fine porcelain dolls soon became known internationally. Unique design along with special attention to detail and value have been the hallmark of the artist since the beginning.

WINDSOR HEIRLOOM COLLECTION

300 Carlsbad Village Dr.
Suite 108A-351
Carlsbad, CA 92008-2999
Phone: (619)929-1055 PST
Fax: (619)929-1069 or (619)929-9131
Founded in: 1993

PRODUCT INFORMATION:

Catalog: Flyers on individual dolls are available to retailers or to collectors. Color.

Description: Windsor Heirloom Collection provides high quality production dolls expertly sculpted from artists' original pieces to the general public at affordable prices.

BUSINESS INFORMATION:

Retail: Collectors may order a flyer and complete the enclosed order form, call to order or order through direct mail ads in doll publications.

Artists' inquiries: Artists wishing to present their designs should send photographs of their work.

6

Shows

A Guide to Chapter Six

The sense of excitement in the air, the sheer number and variety of dolls and the personal contact with artists and manufacturers all make shows one of the best places to experience the doll world. Because there are a vast number and variety of shows available, we decided to split the show listings into two major categories. "Show Promoters" includes organizations or businesses that produce two or more doll shows per year, and "Single Shows" includes those shows that are produced independently of any other doll show. The doll show listings also give information about exhibits or competitions associated with the show. Also included in this chapter are listings of exhibits, including traveling and other exhibits that are not part of a show, as well as competitions that are run independently of a show. The article by Christina Wemmitt-Pauk and Anna Mae Walsh Burke that follows this guide will give you a wealth of insider's information on how to successfully sell at a show.

The listings in this chapter cannot substitute for the month-by-month listings of shows provided in most doll magazines. However, if you are a collector, the listings will give you some idea of which shows you should attend. If you are an artist, the detailed information will help you target the shows that will be best for your work. Please contact show organizers for more information, as dates and locations are subject to change.

The Listings

There are three categories of listings in this chapter: show promoters, single events and exhibits.

The listings include the name of the show, the contact person's name and contact information. Following this general information is the year in which the first event was held; when, where and how long the event lasts; and what types of products are sold at the show. In addition, the admission cost, the average attendance, and dealer information, such as type and cost of space, how space is distributed and how to apply are included. Finally, services, educational opportunities, special exhibits, door prizes and drawings, competitions and auctions held in conjunction with the show are listed.

Success on the Show Circuit

BY CHRISTINA WEMMITT-PAUK AND ANNA MAE WALSH BURKE

Christina Wemmitt-Pauk, a well-known doll and teddy bear artist, has coordinated several museum and gallery shows, including "Fantasy Forest," a show organized by the Arts Center in Fayetteville, North Carolina. She lives in Beech Mountain, North Carolina, with her husband and youngest son.

Anna Mae Walsh Burke has been collecting and making dolls since childhood. In addition to her extensive collection of antique and "special" dolls, she also sculpts one-of-a-kind dolls in Sculpey and Cernit. She is the author of ten books and more than one hundred articles in a variety of fields and is a practicing attorney in Fort Lauderdale, Florida, where she lives with her husband, son, daughter and mother, all of whom are in support of her "doll habit."

*D*oing a show can be hard work—expensive, time-consuming and tiring. It can also be very rewarding, both financially and psychologically. If you approach it with the right attitude, it can even be fun. There are many types of shows, each with their own opportunities. Learning how to use these opportunities to your advantage is the key to success.

Why Do a Show?

If you are an artist, being willing and able to show your dolls distinguishes you from the person who makes dolls as a hobby. Doing a show takes you from the

Christina Wemmitt-Pauk

Anna Mae Walsh Burke

isolated world of making dolls that you, your family and friends think are wonderful to the critical reality of the doll-loving public.

Whether you are an artist or a dealer in dolls old or new, shows will provide you with an audience that is already interested in your product. Shows give you the opportunity to meet potential customers who, with continued exposure to your dolls and your name, may select your dolls for future purchases. If you are a doll artist, shows give you the opportunity to meet doll dealers who may want to sell your dolls in their stores, and manufacturers who may select an original doll you have made to be part of their product line. (See the article accompanying chapter one for more information on wholesale shows, and the article accompanying chapter

What You Should Know About a Show

The listings is this chapter give basic information on each promoter or show, but before deciding on a show, get answers to the following questions:

- How many doll shows has this promoter done? Where were they located?
- Was the show well attended?
- Was the show successful in terms of the number of dolls sold? Some shows may have a smaller attendance, but larger sales, so attendance figures can be deceiving.
- Were those in attendance buying dolls that are comparable to yours in price and style?
- Were the attendees mostly high-end or low-end collectors?
- Were attendees buying mostly antique and old dolls, manufactured dolls or art dolls?
- Will the show be advertised in the media? At other doll shows the promoter runs?
- Will advertisements include the names of artists and dealers who will be exhibiting?
- Does the promoter or organizer offer notices or postcards that you can send to those on your mailing list? Will those who present the notice receive a discount? If so, be sure to include your name, return address and booth number on the card.

five for more information about selling your designs to wholesalers.)

Doing a show puts you in touch with new buyers and potential buyers. Keep careful records of your buyers, and include them in all mailings. Be certain to include those who have expressed an interest in your dolls but have not yet bought anything. To collect names and addresses, you might try having a drawing for a small prize so that people who visit your booth leave their names and addresses, which you can then add to your mailing list.

For the dollmaker, though, there are other advantages to doing shows that go beyond sales. Doll shows give you the chance to get feedback on your work from both other artists and potential customers. You have the chance to shop for supplies in person and meet new suppliers. Perhaps most importantly, you have the opportunity to network with other artists. Shows give you

the opportunity to renew acquaintances, make new friends, and experience the camaraderie and the competition that exist among creative people. You may get some ideas as to what is selling this year, but don't let that shape your work. Continue to make what your creative instincts tell you is your best work. What appears to be selling may be only a short-lived trend.

If you are a beginner, ask for suggestions. Walk around, introduce yourself, and talk to other artists about what works for them. While some artists are reluctant to reveal their techniques and sources for materials, others are open and helpful. Don't be disappointed if one of your favorite doll artists does not share all of his or her secrets. You must remember that you are competitors, both for sales and for admiration from the doll-buying public.

Many shows offer workshops and lectures in which you can learn new techniques or find out about new materials. At the same time, shows give you the opportunity to share your own knowledge. Analyze your work. What could you teach beginning dollmakers? Do you have a special skill or technique, or expertise in marketing or designing? If you have the opportunity to conduct a workshop, you will be promoting yourself and your work. Put together the foundation for a workshop that you can offer at different shows.

The Promoter or Organizer

When deciding which shows to attend, one of your most important considerations should be the reputation and experience of the promoter or organizer. Some promoters do several shows each year in various locations. In this book, anyone who produces two or more shows a year is called a "promoter," and anyone who does only one show per year is called an "organizer." The promoter or organizer may be an individual, a charitable organization, a civic organization, a doll club or a magazine.

If you are considering a particular show, your first step is to get the exhibitor package from the promoter. It will give you information about past shows and the show you are considering. Next, talk to previous exhibitors. If you don't know any, ask the promoter for names, addresses and phone numbers. Contact some past exhibitors whose work is similar to your own to see how they viewed the past show. Will they participate in the upcoming show? If not, why not? Was their work received well at previous shows? What can they tell you about the people who came to the show? Asking the questions in the sidebar at left will also be helpful.

The relationship between the promoter and the artists or dealers is very important. If the promoter speaks negatively about the other artists in your presence, you may be certain that you will be a topic for some other conversation. Are the artists treated with respect and dignity or just as sources of income for the promoter? Other artists will be able to tell you.

Types of Shows

There are several types of shows to consider, depending on the kinds of dolls you make or sell, your financial constraints, and the level of your work.

Don't Go to a Show Alone

If at all possible, take someone with you to the show. You'll need a break from your own booth for food, to see other exhibits, to compare your work with other work being displayed, to talk to other doll artists, and to learn new techniques. It's difficult to talk without distraction to potential customers if you also have to watch your booth yourself. It is always when you take five minutes to find the restroom that six customers come up with cash in their hands, but are lost because the person in the next booth who was watching yours for you couldn't make the sale.

Small Shows

If you are a new artist, a small show is a good place to begin building a following. Everyone at the show will see your booth. If you charge high prices, however, there may not be many buyers willing to pay your price at a small show. On the positive side, smaller shows will be less expensive to enter and usually include dolls only, so you can be sure the visitors will be interested in your product.

Large Shows

It is easy to get lost among the hundreds of booths at a large show. Competition is stiffer, but there are many advantages as well. Obviously, more people attend, so your dolls have more exposure to the public. A collector who attends only one show per year will usually try to attend a large show, so this may your only chance to impress many collectors, especially those who are venturing out of their local area. Also, shop owners and manufacturer's reps are more likely to attend a large show, even if it is not designated as a wholesale show. (For tips on doing wholesale shows, see the article opening chapter one.)

Dolls-Only vs. Mixed Shows

Dolls-only shows will attract only one type of person—doll collectors. Everyone attending the show wants to buy a doll, and this can be an advantage. At the same time, when everyone is selling dolls, and everyone is buying dolls, competition tends to increase.

At a mixed show of any sort, be it art, craft or antique, you may attract customers who would never see your product otherwise. This too can be an advantage. Sometimes, even a doll artist or dealer of antique dolls is better off at another type of show. If you sell high-end dolls, perhaps your work would sell better at a fine art show. If you are an antique doll dealer and find that doll show visitors are mostly interested in art dolls, you may be better off at an antique show. Again, only through experience will you learn who your buyers are.

Be realistic about your skill level and reputation. What quality level does the show represent? Regular craft shows probably do not attract people who will spend the money that your dolls demand. You are selling a work of art and must recognize it as such.

If you also make or sell other items, such as bears or antiques, should you bring them to a show, or should you limit your display to dolls? There are two schools of thought on the matter. One says that if it can attract someone into your booth and you can sell it, bring it. The other school says that you should try to build your reputation in one area, and that other items might distract the potential buyer from purchasing. Trial and error will tell. If it is a product of your creativity, it may well enhance your reputation, and in that case bring it if you can.

Due to space constraints, we have only listed shows that include only or mostly doll artists and dealers. To learn about fine art shows, read the magazine *Sunshine Artist* or a similar publication that lists fine art and craft shows. Antique doll dealers may find general antique shows listed in one of the many antique and collectible magazines on the market.

Museum and Gallery Exhibits

Museum and gallery exhibits are unique in that a great amount of prestige accompanies them. The public recognizes that the museum or gallery has placed its stamp

Considering Costs

Doing a show is an investment of time, money and energy. Will you get a good return on your investment? Here is a checklist of the costs to consider when deciding whether to do a show.

Costs for every show:

- The exhibit fee (cost of a table or booth, or percentage of sales)
- The cost of getting your exhibit and dolls from a delivery point (possibly your car or the shipping area) to your exhibit space
- Union fees for assembling your booth and unpacking your dolls
- Fees for electricity and lighting equipment, if not included, and for installing fixtures
- Fees for equipment rental, such as tables and chairs, if not provided
- Parking, if not free
- Food
- The cost of extension cords, tape, and display equipment and decorations you supply
- The cost of business services and supplies, including credit card services, receipt books, order forms, etc.
- The cost of insuring your dolls

For out-of-town shows:

- Travel costs, including plane fare, taxi fare, or gas and mileage (if you are driving)
- The cost of shipping your dolls to the show location if necessary, including insurance to cover damage or loss
- Hotel lodging if not within local distance
- Tips for bellmen

Once you've considered all the items on this checklist, ask yourself if it will be financially worthwhile to do the show. Remember that the rewards associated with attending a specific show may not be immediate. Are you willing to invest in the future of your business by building a following through exposure at this show? Weigh all the pros and cons before making a final decision.

of approval on your work. While you may not need this stamp of approval, art collectors who do not usually buy dolls will see your work as art, and this can be a great advantage to you. Art collectors are accustomed to spending substantial sums of money on artwork. Some gallery patrons buy because they like to support art, as much as because they like the object they purchased. You can benefit from this attitude. At an exhibit, your work will be sold by people who are skilled at selling artwork.

Museums and galleries are not listed in this chapter, although some of the doll museums in the museum chapter may have special juried exhibits. In addition, you can find listings of art galleries, as well as tips on marketing fine art, in *Artist's and Graphic Designer's Market,* published annually by Writer's Digest Books.

Juried Shows

Gallery and museum exhibits are examples of juried shows. There are also some juried shows that include dolls only. Juried shows require that you submit examples of your work, usually five slides. The jury will decide whether to extend an invitation to you. It is always difficult to determine if you have a good chance at being invited. If you have previously attended the show, you may have some idea of the quality of the work of the previous participants, but the jury may change with each show, presenting you with an unknown factor. Listings of juried shows in this chapter include the items you will need to send as well as the deadline dates, but it is a good idea to contact the promoter or organizer well in advance, as these requirements may change.

Show Location

The show's location is very important. Is the location convenient for you? If you have to travel a considerable distance, stay in a hotel, take vacation time from your regular job or ship your work, consider whether the added costs and time will be worthwhile. Don't forget about costs like food, taxi fare (to get from the airport to the hotel or from the hotel to the convention center or display area), parking fees at the hotel and tips for bellmen.

Ask for specific information about the location. Is parking readily available? Is there a fee for parking or is it free? Can you get in and out of the show easily? Can potential customers get in and out of the show easily? Is it an indoor or outdoor show? You should also ask about dining and restroom facilities.

Booth Space

Consider also the space available to you for showing your dolls. You must first select the type of space you want from those available and pay the promoter's fee. Sometimes there will be different fees for different booth and table sizes.

It may also cost you money to set up your booth. Some locations require that you hire union labor to set up your booth, limiting what you are allowed to do yourself. In these locations, you cannot even use a screwdriver to turn a screw to assemble your booth. One of us has designed a booth that can be assembled without using a single tool in order to avoid the extra hassle and expense in locations that require union help.

You must also determine exactly what you get for your fee. In some cases it is just a single table in a booth. Make certain you are clear on all requirements. You may be charged a very large fee for an additional table even though you have already paid for the booth. At some shows, you may be able to bring your own additional tables, but this is not usually the case. Will you have to rent chairs or will they be provided? Does the promoter or hotel restrict you from bringing your own? You certainly will not want to stand for all of the long hours of the show.

Electricity is another consideration. Many halls are dark, and shadows do nothing for your work. People like to come into a booth that is brightly lit. Do all booths come with electricity? Do you have to make advance arrangements to have electricity available? The electricity may be there, but you may have to make arrangements to turn it on, and arrangements usually mean money. Bring several heavy outdoor UL-approved cords, as flimsy ones would not be allowed. Bring tape to make certain the cords stay flat and out of the way, and clamps to hang any spotlights you may have. You may be able to bring your own lighting, or you may be restricted to renting from the promoter or the convention host. Be certain you know what you are getting and what you will have to pay for.

Advance Planning

You must have dolls if you are going to do a show. This may seem obvious, but at times you could find yourself almost out of work to show because of a prior show, or because of something in your life that kept you from working. It is best to schedule your shows well ahead of time so that you can make certain you will have work to show. Most show promoters prefer that exhibitors apply months in advance, and doing so has many advantages. Popular shows are filled quickly, and waiting lists are common. Sometimes the early bird gets first choice

of space, although many promoters distribute space according to previous participation or according to who they think will draw a crowd.

If you've planned well, you should have several dolls to show. Bring all of your work that is presentable. If you have a doll that is not for sale, bring it for display so that people can see the kind of work you do. If you are trying something new, bring it along. Get feedback on it. How do people respond to it? What do the other doll artists think of it?

Bring a photo album of dolls you have already sold. Make sure you have already taken photos of the dolls you will be selling at the show, especially if buyers will be taking the dolls home with them. You will want to have a photo of every doll you sell. Your portfolio should also include any articles written about you and your dolls.

Christina finishes decorating a booth she is sharing with another artist at the Doll & Teddy Bear Expo in Arlington, Virginia.

An Attractive Display

Having an attractive display is second in importance only to the dolls themselves. Begin by selecting the best booth you can afford. If you are going to be successful, it is important that you look successful. You could just set your work on the table and hope people stop and look, but your sales potential is much increased if you provide an attractive and exciting display, perhaps with a theme that fits the dolls you make. Does the show have a theme? Is it a seasonal show? Does your work fit into the show's theme? Can you find some variation on the theme that will work for your dolls? At the 1995 show in Schaumburg, Illinois, the theme was "Hooray for Hollywood," and one of us displayed and sold almost life-size figures of Dorothy, the Cowardly Lion, the Tin Man and the Scarecrow.

Again, learn from others. Ask yourself how your work compares with the work of the other artists who will show there. What themes and displays can you remember from other shows that you have attended? What drew you into a booth to look at work you later bought?

Put together a display that can be used many times with slight variations. This will allow you to establish a presentation that your customers will come to look for. Remember that you may have to ship and install your exhibit, so make it of components you can handle with your "team," with a minimum of hired personnel, or even by yourself. If you establish a backdrop area, you should plan to have some shelves on it. Depending on the number you are able to install, shelves will double or triple your display area. Shelves also bring your dolls to the customers' eye level, where they are much more likely to catch their attention.

Make your booth tasteful, charming or elegant according to the dolls you are going to show. Try setting up your booth ahead of time at home and make certain all of the pieces work together. Ask the advice of your friends. Take some pictures at home and think about how you could improve your booth. Be sure to bring material to drape the tables. The promoter may give you a white drape, but it would be nice to have something different to complement your work.

Christina and her son, John Paul III, who frequently accompanies her to shows, are showing off one of Christina's creations.

Selling Yourself

You have done your best to draw potential customers into your booth. Now that you have them in your space, you have thirty to ninety seconds to catch the potential doll buyer. What do you say? Everyone has a different approach. Some people are shy about talking to custom-

ers, but you will not make as many sales that way. People like to meet the artist. If you make a good impression, they will be more likely to tell their friends about you.

Talk about your dolls. If they are looking at a particular piece, tell them what inspired you to make it. If it won an award at a previous show, have the award on display and point it out. If it is available in another costume, tell them. If it does something interesting, like ride a bicycle, show them. If there is something special or unique about the piece, talk about it. If you have nothing to say, at least introduce yourself and ask if they have any questions. Don't get between people and your work, but do interact with them.

Protecting Yourself and Your Dolls

Because it's your booth, you make the rules. Do whatever it takes to protect your dolls from damage. Do you want people to touch your dolls? Certainly you want them to be careful. Most people realize that dolls are delicate pieces of art, but there are always exceptions. A man who started to tap on the face of a doll made by one of the authors to see if it would mark came very close to having his finger broken by the other author! Always be courteous, but be firm about enforcing your rules.

Use fire retardant materials when you can, particularly in your display. Don't allow anyone to smoke in your booth or around your dolls. This has been getting easier to enforce in the past few years.

If you display magazines that have shown your work, make certain they are not picked up by visitors who think they are for the taking. It might be difficult to replace them.

Take all precautions to protect yourself from theft. Have a method of holding onto checks and cash—don't just leave them lying around. You should at least have a cash box you can keep an eye on or a purse that stays on you into which you put money, checks and signed charge receipts. Keep an eye on your purse and your dolls as well. There are thieves who make a practice of picking pockets and taking wallets at crowded shows. Others steal dolls. Don't give them the opportunity, especially when you are feeling tired at the end of the show. Your regular homeowner's insurance probably will not cover your dolls and may not cover your money because it was part of a business transaction. Be careful even as you leave the show. Don't become a statistic just because "all doll people are nice."

Money Matters

Selling dolls is a business like any other. You will usually have to collect sales tax if you are going to deliver the dolls at the time of sale. If the show is out-of-state for you, the promoter will be able to help you with this. If you take an order and ship the doll later, as is often done, you will have to collect the sales tax and pay it to your home state. You should have an arrangement to pay sales tax for your business. You may want to incorporate your business or you may just want to be the sole proprietor. Talk to your accountant or attorney about the difference.

Keep every receipt for everything you spend on your business. This includes the costs of materials, doing the show, advertising, shipping, and long distance telephone calls to customers, promoters, dealers and suppliers. Always record the buyer's name, address and phone number.

You may be able to make arrangements with your bank to accept charge cards. This will cost you a little money, but it may be the only way to make a sale in this age of plastic. There are ways of checking to see if the credit card is "good." Your bank will provide you with a toll-free number to do this. This is a good task for that other person who is with you if you don't have a portable phone. You may be able to get a credit card machine so that you can imprint the customer's card on the slip, or you may have to just write the number in by hand.

There are check approval services to which you can subscribe. Taking a check is always a gamble, but you may be able to "read" your customers pretty well. For all of the dolls we have bought and sold over the years, we have never given a bad check nor have we received one. The risk, however, is always there. It is especially difficult to collect on a bad check that is from out of town. Write the customer's driver's license number and social security number on the check for extra security. Most people will readily give at least their driver's license number.

Business Policies

You may want to take a partial payment up front and hold the doll, delivering the doll when full payment has been made. Be certain to set out terms, such as how long you will hold the doll and whether the deposit is refundable if the customer does not make the additional payments. Have a firm return policy, such as "No returns for any reason," which is clearly written on the receipt and explained to the customer. If you are going to ship a doll, know in advance what the shipping costs are going to be, including the cost of the box and insurance, and include them in the price of the doll. Shipping always costs more than you think it will. You may want to determine an average amount to charge per doll, as most of your dolls will probably cost approximately the same to ship.

If you are willing to take orders for your dolls, make that clear. Don't take so many orders that you can never fill all the requests. Let the buyer know approximately how long it will take for you to fill an order. They may be willing to wait, especially if it is a one-of-a-kind doll. It is better to tell the buyer it will be three months before the doll is shipped than to underestimate the time it will take and then get an irate letter in two months demanding the doll.

Remember, it is the promoter's job to get people to the show, but it is your job to attract customers to your display! Make your booth and dolls look their best. Even if you aren't successful, look successful and look like you are enjoying yourself. After all, everybody loves dolls. Dollmakers should be happy people! ❧

Shows

SHOW PROMOTERS

AUDREY WILLMANN SHOWS
Audrey Willmann
P.O. Box 814
Sugar Creek, IL 60554
Phone: (708)264-0004
Fax: (708)264-2737
First event: 1980

BASIC INFORMATION:
Events per year: 4
Times of year: March, August, September, November

BARBARA PETERSON'S SHOW AND SALE FEATURING BARBIE
Barbara Peterson
P.O. Box 5329
Fullerton, CA 92635-0329
Phone: (714)525-8420 PST
Fax: (714)447-8466
First event: 1989
Mailing list: Write or call to be included.

BASIC INFORMATION:
Events per year: 12
Times of year: 1 per month
Locations: Disneyland Hotel, 1150 W. Cerritos Ave., Anaheim, CA
Duration: 1 day
Types of events: These events include dolls and related items only.
Doll-related products sold: Retired manufactured dolls; modern manufactured dolls; doll clothing and accessories; vintage, hard to find and new Barbies and related dolls.
Admission: $5; $2 for children 5 years and under.

DEALER INFORMATION:
Dealers: Over 100
Space available for: Retail businesses selling dolls and related items, collectible and modern doll dealers, sellers of dollmaking supplies, sellers of doll clothing and accessories, doll artists, doll clubs/organizations, restoration experts, doll fashion designers
Space distributed: First-come, first-serve basis

Application process: Apply 2 months in advance: last minute cancellations happen, so feel free to apply closer to the show date if you wish.
Average cost of booth/table: $85

SPECIAL FEATURES:
Services for collectors: Mattel doll designers are on hand to sign dolls. Ruth Handler, the creator of Barbie, has been a repeated guest signer.
Door prizes/drawings: Door prizes and $1 raffle

BARBIE GOES TO SHOWS
Marl Davidson
10301 Braden Run
Bradenton, FL 34202
Phone: (813)751-6275
Fax: (941)751-5463
First event: 1991

BASIC INFORMATION:
Events per year: 11
Times of year: Year-round
Locations: Nationwide
Duration: 1 day, 10-4
Doll-related products sold: Barbies and Barbie items
Average Attendance: 1,500
Admission: $5

DEALER INFORMATION:
Dealers: 50
Space distributed: To participants from the previous year first; remaining spaces on first-come, first-serve basis.
Average cost of booth/table: $95-125 and up

BELLMAN CORP.
Stephanie Bellman
11959 Philadelphia Rd.
Bradshaw, MD 21021
Phone: (410)329-2188
Fax: (410)679-6919
First event: 1972

BASIC INFORMATION:
Events per year: 4
Times of year: March, June, September, December

Locations: Maryland, Gaithersburg Fairgrounds
Duration: 1 weekend
Types of events: These events include dolls and teddy bears, antiques, miniatures, doll houses, figurines and toys.
Doll-related products sold: Artist dolls, antique dolls, dollmaking supplies, doll clothing and accessories
Average Attendance: 3,000-4,000
Admission: $5 for 2 days

DEALER INFORMATION:
Dealers: 250
Average cost of booth/table: Call for information

BOHLER ENTERPRISES INC.
Virginia Bohler
P.O. Box 75001
La Puente, CA 91747
Fax: (818)810-2820
First event: 1983

BASIC INFORMATION:
Events per year: 2
Times of year: April and October
Locations: Anaheim, CA Convention Center
Duration: 3 days
Types of events: These events include dolls and crafters' ceramics.
Doll-related products sold: Doll-making supplies, doll clothing and accessories, art dolls, reproduction dolls
Admission: $6

DEALER INFORMATION:
Dealers: 400
Space distributed: First-come, first-serve basis

BRIGHT STAR PROMOTIONS, INC.
Valerie Rogers
3428 Hillvale Rd.
Louisville, KY 40241-2756
Phone: (502)423-STAR EST
Fax: (502)423-7827
E-mail: xkcb90a@prodigy.com
First event: 1982
Mailing list: Write or call to be included.

BASIC INFORMATION:

Events per year: 40

Times of year: February-July; September-November each year

Locations: OH, IN, KY, MI, GA, FL, KS, TN, NC, PA, TX

Duration: 1 day

Types of events: These events include dolls and teddy bears, miniatures, doll houses and figurines.

Doll-related products sold: Artist dolls, dollmaking supplies, doll clothing and accessories, miniature dolls

Average Attendance: 500-1,000

Admission: $4 adults, $1.50 children 12 and under

DEALER INFORMATION:

Space available for: Retail business selling dolls and related items, doll artists

Space distributed: Space is available to participants from the previous year first; remaining spaces are available on a first-come, first-serve basis. There is usually a waiting list.

Application process: Call or write a letter describing vendor products 8 months in advance. Must include photo and description of dolls.

Average cost of booth/table: $100

SPECIAL FEATURES:

Door prizes/drawings: Each dealer contributes a door prize valued over $10.

Exhibits: Club exhibits or contests in some show areas.

BRIMFIELD ASSOCIATES INC.

Norman F. Schaut

P.O. Box 1800

Ocean City, NJ 08226

Phone: (609)926-1800, (800)526-2724

Fax: (609)927-6282

First event: 1986

Mailing list: Write or call to be included.

BASIC INFORMATION:

Events per year: 2

Times of year: "Atlantique City" Spring Festival in March, "Atlantique City" Holiday Fair in October

Locations: Atlantic City Convention Center, Florida Avenue and the Boardwalk, Atlantic City, NJ

Duration: 1 weekend

Types of events: These events include dolls and teddy bears, antiques, miniatures, dollhouses, figurines and toys.

Doll-related products sold: Antique

dolls, retired manufactured dolls, artist dolls (retired editions only), doll clothing and accessories

Admission: Saturday—$15, Sunday—$10

DEALER INFORMATION:

Dealers: 1,200

Space available for: Retail businesses selling antique and collectible dolls and related items, antique doll dealers, sellers of doll clothing and accessories, doll clubs/organizations, restoration experts

Space distributed: To participants from the previous year first; remaining spaces on first-come, first-serve basis. There is usually a waiting list.

Application process: Call to receive an application form. Dealers must list categories of items which they will be selling, photos of some of the merchandise, and names of other shows in which they have participated.

Average cost of booth/table: $4.95/ square foot

SPECIAL FEATURES:

Services for collectors: Appraisals of old/antique dolls

Door prizes/drawings: Drawings for all-expense paid weekends and free tickets at each event.

Exhibits: Past exhibits have honored such events as the invention of the Monopoly game.

JEAN CANADAY

1913 Walnut St.

P.O. Box 127

Holt, MI 48842

Phone: (517)694-3663

First event: 1970

BASIC INFORMATION:

Events per year: 9

Times of year: Year-round

Locations: Lansing, MI and Kalamazoo, MI.

Duration: 1 day

Types of events: These events include dolls and teddy bears, miniatures, doll houses, figurines and toys.

Doll-related products sold: Antique dolls, retired manufactured dolls, modern manufactured dolls, artist dolls, dollmaking supplies, doll clothing and accessories

Average Attendance: 500

Admission: $3

DEALER INFORMATION:

Dealers: 70

Space available for: Retail businesses selling dolls and related items, antique doll dealers, collectible and modern doll dealers, sellers of dollmaking supplies, sellers of doll clothing and accessories, doll artists, restoration experts

Space distributed: First-come, first-serve basis. There is usually a waiting list.

Application process: Call to receive an application form.

Average cost of booth/table: $60

SPECIAL FEATURES:

Services for collectors: Appraisals of old/antique dolls

Door prizes/drawings: 25 door prizes

C.S.R. PROMOTIONS

Stan Roe

P.O. Box 1211

Skyland, NC 28776

Phone: (704)274-7732 EST

First event: 1983

Mailing list: Write, call or attend show and sign guest register to be included.

BASIC INFORMATION:

Events per year: 4

Times of year: Spring (March); Summer (July); Fall (September); Holiday (November)

Duration: 1 day

Types of events: These events include dolls, teddy bears and figurines.

Doll-related products sold: Antique dolls, retired manufactured dolls, modern manufactured dolls, artist dolls, dollmaking supplies, doll clothing and accessories

Average Attendance: 1,500

Admission: $3.50; $1 for children

DEALER INFORMATION:

Dealers: 75

Space available for: Retail businesses selling dolls and related items, antique doll dealers, collectible and modern doll dealers, sellers of dollmaking supplies, sellers of doll clothing and accessories, doll artists, doll clubs/organizations, appraisers, restoration experts

Space distributed: To participants from the previous year first; remaining spaces on first-come, first-serve basis. There is usually a waiting list.

Application process: Send SASE or call to receive an application form. Must have tax ID permit for states involved.

Average cost of booth/table: $70

SPECIAL FEATURES:

Educational opportunities: Lectures by well-known collectors/artists. Doll- and bear-making seminars.

Door prizes/drawings: Hourly door prizes. Special doll and bear drawings (raffle) at end of show.

CERAMIC ENTERPRISES—CEFI

Joan Gowell
270 W. Reading Way
Winter Park, FL 32789
Phone: (407)644-5891 EST
Fax: (407)644-5126
First event: 1969
Mailing list: Write or call to be included. Include a SASE

BASIC INFORMATION:

Events per year: 4

Times of year: February, June, October

Locations: Orlando Expo Centre, 500 W. Livingston St., Orlando, FL 32801; Kansas City Market Center, 1775 Universal Ave., Kansas City, MO 64120; Tennessee State Fairgrounds, Nashville, TN.

Duration: 2 days, Kansas City, MO. 3 days, Nashville,TN and Orlando, FL in the fall. 4 days, Orlando, FL in February.

Types of events: This event includes ceramic hobby products.

Doll-related products sold: Doll-making supplies, doll clothing and accessories, doll molds for ceramic/porcelain creations

Average Attendance: 2,500-12,000

Admission: $3-5

DEALER INFORMATION:

Space available for: Sellers of doll-making supplies, sellers of doll clothing and accessories, doll artists, doll molds

Space distributed: To participants from the previous year first; remaining spaces by waiting list and category. The February Florida Ceramic Show has a waiting list which is grouped into categories.

Application process: Send SASE to be

included. Shows are produced for ceramic hobbyists. Collectibles are discouraged, as are finished ceramic items for sale. Emphasis has always been on ceramic and ceramic related items, education in hobby ceramics and porcelain.

Average cost of booth/table: $240-450

SPECIAL FEATURES:

Educational opportunities: Dollmaking workshops, hobby ceramic techniques: glazes, stains, sculpture, mold making, china paints, brush strokes, design, claylift, embossing, etc.

Competitions: Creators of hobby ceramic/porcelain items, hobbyists, teachers/studio owners, children, professional. Categories are greenware adaptation, underglaze, glaze, stains (non-fired), hand-modeled clay, porcelain, overglaze, ceramic dolls. Prizes are ribbons, rosettes, trophies. Apply on set-up day. Submit fee and card with name, category, etc.

ADDITIONAL INFORMATION:

Ceramic Enterprises produces ceramic shows to promote the ceramic hobby industry and to encourage and educate the public in the many techniques available to them through ceramics and related items.

CEREXPO INC.

Robert C. Staib
P.O. Box 3923
Tequesta, FL 33469-9998
Phone: (407)746-4374 EST
First event: 1950
Mailing list: Write to be included.

BASIC INFORMATION:

Events per year: 4

Times of year: March, May, August, October

Locations: Pheasant Run Mega Center, St. Charles, IL; Wisconsin State Fair Park, West Allis, WI; Monmouth Park Race Track, Ocean Port, NJ

Duration: 3 days

Types of events: Ceramic supplies

Doll-related products sold: Dollmaking supplies, doll clothing and accessories

Admission: $2

DEALER INFORMATION:

Dealers: 125

Space available for: Sellers of doll-

making supplies, sellers of doll clothing and accessories, doll manufacturers

Space distributed: These events are invitation-only.

SPECIAL FEATURES:

Educational opportunities: Dollmaking workshops

Competitions: Anyone may enter. Categories are from novice to professional. Prizes are ribbons and awards. Apply 1 day in advance.

CHINA DOLL SHOWS

Lloyd Hogan
5621 Glencrest Lane
Orangevale, CA 95662
Phone: (916)989-9291 PST
First event: 1984
Mailing list: Write or call to be included.

BASIC INFORMATION:

Events per year: 16

Times of year: Year-round

Locations: San Mateo County Expo Center, San Mateo, CA; Placer County Fairgrounds, Roseville, CA; Newark/Fremont Hilton, Newark, CA; Alameda County Fairgrounds, Pleasanton, CA; El Dorado County Fairgrounds, Placerville, CA

Duration: Most are 1-day; 1 show is a 2-day.

Types of events: These events inlcude dolls and teddy bears, miniatures, doll houses, figurines and toys.

Doll-related products sold: Antique dolls, retired manufactured dolls, modern manufactured dolls, artist dolls, dollmaking supplies, doll clothing and accessories, doll books and magazines

Average Attendance: 500-2,000

Admission: $4

DEALER INFORMATION:

Dealers: 60-130

Space available for: Retail businesses selling dolls and related items, antique doll dealers, collectible and modern doll dealers, sellers of dollmaking supplies, sellers of doll clothing and accessories, doll artists, doll manufacturers, doll clubs/organizations

Space distributed: On a first-come, first-serve basis

Application process: Send SASE or call to be included at least 2 months in advance. California resale tax number required.

Average cost of booth/table: $60-270

SPECIAL FEATURES:

Educational opportunities: Dollmaking workshops, lectures by well-known collectors/artists, seminars on doll collecting (only at 2-day show).

Competitions: Members of the Doll Artisan Guild (NY). Prizes are ribbons, rosettes, cash. Apply at least one month in advance. Send for form.

THE CROSSROADS DOLL, BEAR AND TOY SHOW

Elta Lee Johnson
146 S. Sandrun Rd.
Salt Lake City, UT 84103
Phone: (801)355-3655, (801)355-3671 MST
Fax: (801)355-3672
First event: 1992
Mailing list: Write or call to be included.

BASIC INFORMATION:

Events per year: 2
Times of year: Spring and Fall
Locations: Salt Palace Convention Center
Duration: 1 day
Types of events: These events inlcude dolls and teddy bears, miniatures and toys.
Doll-related products sold: Antique dolls, retired manufactured dolls, modern manufactured dolls, artist dolls, dollmaking supplies, doll clothing and accessories
Average Attendance: 2,000
Admission: From $1 to $4

DEALER INFORMATION:

Dealers: 100
Space available for: Retail businesses selling dolls and related items, antique doll dealers, collectible and modern doll dealers, sellers of dollmaking supplies, sellers of doll clothing and accessories, doll artists, doll manufacturers
Space distributed: To participants from the previous year first; remaining spaces on first-come, first-serve basis. There is usually a waiting list.
Application process: Send SASE, call or fax to receive an application form. Dealers may apply 6 months in advance.

Average cost of booth/table: $60

SPECIAL FEATURES:

Educational opportunities: Demonstrations by dealers at their booths.
Door prizes/drawings: Grand prize is a collector doll and a young collector doll. Numerous small gifts supplied by the dealers.
Competitions: Open to doll artists, makers and collectors. Competition categories include reproduction, antique collectible, original costuming (all mediums). Rosettes are given for Best of Category and People's Choice; ribbons are given for other categories. Apply by bringing a doll or dolls to Salt Palace between 2 and 7 P.M. the day before the show.

DALLAS EXPO

Shirley Jeanson
P.O. Box 595
Harrah, OK 73045-0595
Phone: (405)739-0992
Fax: (405)739-0993
First event: 1992

BASIC INFORMATION:

Events per year: 2
Times of year: August
Locations: Plano Center, Plano, TX
Duration: Friday and Saturday
Types of events: This event includes dolls and teddy bears, miniatures, doll houses, figurines.
Doll-related products sold: Antique dolls, retired manufactured dolls, artist dolls, dollmaking supplies, doll clothing and accessories
Average Attendance: 2,500
Admission: $4

DEALER INFORMATION:

Dealers: 70-95
Space distributed: First-come, first-serve basis
Average cost of booth/table: $215 for two 8′ tables, two chairs; free electricity
Eucational opportunities: "Make and Take" seminars
Competition: Available

"SURROUND YOURSELF WITH DOLLS AND STAY YOUNG!"
Gennie Cartmill, Rexburg, ID

DOLL, BEAR AND MINIATURE SHOW AND SALE

Diana Gemmiti
14690 54th Way N.
Clearwater, FL 34620
Phone: (813)536-8857, (813)530-3801 EST
First event: 1991
Mailing list: Call to be included.

BASIC INFORMATION:

Events per year: 4
Times of year: April, June, September, December
Locations: Honeywell Minnreg Building, 6340 126th Ave. N., Largo, FL
Duration: 1 day, 10-4
Types of events: These events include teddy bears, miniatures, figurines, antiques and dolls.
Doll-related products sold: Artist dolls, doll clothing and accessories
Average Attendance: 400-500
Admission: $3 adults; $1 children 10 and under.

DEALER INFORMATION:

Dealers: 40-50
Space available for: Retail businesses selling dolls and related items, antique doll dealers, collectible and modern doll dealers, sellers of dollmaking supplies, sellers of doll clothing and accessories, doll artists, doll manufacturers, doll clubs/organizations, appraisers
Space distributed: To participants from previous year first; remaining spaces on first-come, first-serve basis. There is usually a waiting list.
Application process: Call to receive application form. Dealers may apply 4 months in advance.
Average cost of booth/table: $35

SPECIAL FEATURES:

Services for collectors: Appraisals of old/antique dolls.
Educational opportunities: Dollmaking workshops

DOLLS UNLIMITED

Carol Jensen
1315 E. 4th St.
Rochester, IN 46975
Phone: (219)6421
First event: 1980

BASIC INFORMATION:

Events per year: 4

Times of year: March, April, September, October

Locations: Holiday Inn, Logansport, IN; Holiday Inn, Plymouth, IN

Types of events: These events include dolls, teddy bears and doll houses.

Doll-related products sold: Antique dolls, retired manufactured dolls, modern manufactured dolls, artist dolls, dollmaking supplies, doll clothing and accessories

Average Attendance: 250

Admission: $2

DEALER INFORMATION:

Dealers: 20

Space distributed: First-come, first-serve basis.

Average cost of booth/table: 3 tables for $50

DORA PITTS

4697 155th St.

Clinton, IA 52732

Phone: (319)242-0139 CST

First event: 1982

Mailing list: Write to be included.

BASIC INFORMATION:

Events per year: 4

Times of year: March, April or May, September, November

Locations: March and September—Jackson County Fairgrounds, Highway 62 and 64, Maquoketa, IA; April or May—Metro Ice Sports Arena, 7201 Hickman Rd., Des Moines, IA; November—Mississippi Valley Fairgrounds, 2815 W. Locust St., Davenport, IA

Duration: 1 day

Types of events: These events include dolls, teddy bears and toys.

Doll-related products sold: Antique dolls, retired manufactured dolls, modern manufactured dolls, artist dolls, dollmaking supplies, doll clothing and accessories

Average Attendance: 1,000

Admission: $2.50; under 12 free

DEALER INFORMATION:

Dealers: 48-80

Space available for: Businesses selling dolls and related items, antique doll dealers, collectible and modern doll dealers, sellers of doll supplies, sellers of doll clothing and accessories, doll artists, bear artists, antique and collectible toys

Space distributed: To participants from the previous year first; remaining spaces are available on a first-come, first-serve basis.

Application process: Send SASE or call to be included on mailing list. Apply 5-6 months before event (new dealers). There is usually a waiting list.

Average cost of booth/table: $30 per 8-ft. table

SPECIAL FEATURES:

Door prizes/drawings: Door prizes drawn every hour. One door prize goes to a participating dealer and is two free tables for next show.

ADDITIONAL INFORMATION:

Dora says, "My shows are the largest combined doll-toy-bear shows in Iowa. Over 200 tables at Maquoketa and Des Moines shows. 145 tables at Davenport. Quality shows—worth the trip!"

GIGI'S DOLLS AND SHERRY'S TEDDY BEARS

Gigi Williams or Sherry Baloun

6029 N. Northwest Hwy.

Chicago, IL 60631

Phone: (312)594-1540 CST

Fax: (312)594-1710

First event: 1970

Mailing list: Write, call or fax to be included.

BASIC INFORMATION:

Events per year: 2

Times of year: 2nd weekend in February; 4th weekend in September.

Locations: Inland Meeting and Exposition Center, 400 E. Ogden Ave., Westmont, IL

Duration: 1 day

Types of events: These events include dolls and teddy bears, miniatures and doll houses.

Doll-related products sold: Antique dolls, retired manufactured dolls, modern manufactured dolls, artist dolls, dollmaking supplies, doll clothing and accessories, books, furniture

Average Attendance: 800-1,000

DEALER INFORMATION:

Space available for: Retail businesses selling dolls and related items, antique doll dealers, collectible and modern

doll dealers, sellers of dollmaking supplies, sellers of doll clothing and accessories, doll artists

Space distributed: To participants from previous year first; remaining spaces on first-come, first-serve basis.

Application process: Send SASE, call or fax to receive an application form. Dealers should apply 3 weeks-4 months in advance.

Average cost of booth/table:

SPECIAL FEATURES:

Services for collectors: Restringing, appraisals of old/antique dolls

Door prizes/drawings: Doll-related items

GOLDEN GATE SHOWS

Fern Loiacono

P.O. Box 1208

Ross, CA 94957-1208

Phone: (415)459-1998 PST

Fax: (415)459-0827

First event: 1984

Mailing list: Write, call or attend a show and fill out mailing list card to be included.

BASIC INFORMATION:

Events per year: 9

Times of year: January, February, March, June, August, September and November

Locations: Santa Clara Fairgrounds, 344 Tully Rd., San Jose, CA; Marin County Civic Center Exhibition Hall, San Rafael, CA; Sonoma County Fairgrounds, South E St., Santa Rosa, CA

Duration: 1 day

Types of events: These events include dolls and teddy bears, antiques, miniatures, figurines and related collectibles.

Doll-related products sold: Antique dolls, retired manufactured dolls, modern manufactured dolls, artist dolls, dollmaking supplies, doll clothing and accessories, price guides, specialty magazines and books

Average Attendance: Varies

Admission: $4 adults, $2 under age 12, under 5 free.

DEALER INFORMATION:

Dealers: 100+

Space available for: Retail businesses, antique doll dealers, collectible and modern doll dealers, sellers of dollmaking supplies, sellers of doll clothing and accessories, doll artists, restoration experts

Space distributed: Available on a first-come, first-serve basis.

Application process: Call or write for information. Apply as early as possible. Shows fill up fast. Promoter has contracts for each show that dealers must complete, stating basic information, resale number, merchandise to be sold, etc.

Average cost of booth/table: $62

SPECIAL FEATURES:

Services for collectors: Vary depending on show. Most include restorations and cleaning. All include appraisals.

Educational opportunities: Dollmaking demonstrations

Door prizes/drawings: Has hourly door prize drawings from cards filled out by attendees. Door prizes are donated by attending dealers who have their name and business announced along with the name of the prize winner.

ADDITIONAL INFORMATION:

"We promote and accept donations of toys for Toys for Tots year-round at all our shows. We donate the toys at Christmas when collections are made. We include a paragraph about donations in each press release for each show," Fern says.

MARGARET HILL

13030 Bent Pine Ct. E.
Jacksonville, FL 32246
Phone: (904)221-1235
First event: 1986

BASIC INFORMATION:

Events per year: 3

Times of year: March, August, November

Locations: Shrine Temple, 3800 St. John Bluff Rd. South, Jacksonville, FL

Types of events: These events include dolls and teddy bears, antiques, miniatures, doll houses, figurines and toys.

Doll-related products sold: Antique dolls, retired manufactured dolls, modern manufactured dolls, artist dolls, dollmaking supplies, doll clothing and accessories

Average Attendance: 700-1,300

Admission: $3.50

DEALER INFORMATION:

Dealers: 100

Space distributed: To participants from previous year first; remaining spaces on first-come, first-serve basis.

Average cost of booth/table: $50

JEAN HUFF

Rt. 1, Box 173P
Mathis, TX 78368
Fax: (512)547-3757
First event: 1980

BASIC INFORMATION:

Events per year: 5

Times of year: January, February, March, June, July

Locations: Corpus Christi, San Antonio, and Austin, TX

Types of events: These events include dolls and teddy bears, antiques, miniatures, doll houses, figurines and toys.

Doll-related products sold: Antique dolls, retired manufactured dolls, modern manufactured dolls, artist dolls, dollmaking supplies, doll clothing and accessories

Average Attendance: 700-1,000

Admission: $3 adult, $1 children under 12

DEALER INFORMATION:

Dealers: 87

Space distributed: To participants from previous year first; remaining spaces on first-come, first-serve basis.

Average cost of booth/table: $85-90 for two 8-ft. tables

INTERNATIONAL COLLECTIBLE EXPOSITION COLLECTIBLES AND PLATEMAKERS GUILD, N.A.L.E.D.

David Kissel
1 Westminster Place
Lake Forest, IL 60045
Phone: (847)295-4444 CST
Fax: (847)295-4419
First event: 1975
When: April and June
Duration: 2 public days, 2 retailer days
Mailing list: Write or call to be included.

BASIC INFORMATION:

Type of event: This event includes dolls and teddy bears, antiques, miniatures, doll houses, figurines, toys, limited edition collectibles. This is a display show; no purchasing by the public.

Dealers may place wholesale orders on retailer days.

Doll-related products sold: Modern manufactured dolls, artist dolls

Admission: $6 for 1 day; $9 for 2 days

Average Attendance: 20,000

DEALER INFORMATION:

Space available for: Doll manufacturers

Space distributed: Interested manufacturers can apply in writing.

Application process: Send SASE or call for an application form. Manufacturer must apply 1 year in advance.

Cost of booth/table: $1,290

SPECIAL FEATURES:

Educational opportunities: Seminars on limited edition collectibles.

Door prizes/drawings: Attendees have the chance to win limited edition collectibles donated by exhibitors.

Souvenirs: 2 special event pieces are sold at each show (limited edition collectibles).

Competitions: Exhibitor booth awards, including awards for single booth, double booth, 3-6 booths, over 6 booths. Prizes are plaques and ribbons. All exhibitors are eligible.

MARIAN MAAS

13 Hillview Ave.
Asheville, NC 28805
Phone: (704)298-1717
First event: 1990

BASIC INFORMATION:

Events per year: 2

Times of year: March and April

Locations: Biltmore Estate and the National Guard Armory, Asheville, NC

Types of events: These events include dolls and teddy bears, antiques, miniatures, doll houses, figurines and toys.

Doll-related products sold: Antique dolls, retired manufactured dolls, modern manufactured dolls, artist dolls, dollmaking supplies, doll clothing and accessories

Average Attendance: 140-300

Admission: From $2 to $30

DEALER INFORMATION:

Dealers: 30-40

Space distributed: First-come, first-serve basis

Average cost of booth/table: $25-30

M.A.D. SHOWS

Jerry and Diana King
50 Farmers Ave.
Ajax, Ontario L1T 3T1
CANADA
Phone: (905)427-4084, (905)427-8692
Fax: (905)427-8786
First event: 1983

BASIC INFORMATION:
Events per year: 5
Times of year: February, July, November
Locations: Markham, Toronto, Montreal
Duration: 1 weekend
Types of events: These events include antique collectible dolls and teddy bears, miniatures, dollhouses and accessories.
Doll-related products sold: Antique dolls, retired manufactured dolls, modern manufactured dolls, artist dolls, dollmaking supplies, doll clothing and accessories
Average Attendance: 600-1,000
Admission: $3.50

DEALER INFORMATION:
Dealers: 65-80
Space distributed: To participants from previous years first; remaining spaces on first-come, first-serve basis
Average cost of booth/table: $98

THE MAVEN COMPANY, INC.

Richard N. Robbins
P.O. Box 1538
Waterbury, CT 06721
Phone: (203)758-3880 EST
First event: 1972
Mailing list: Write or call to be included.

BASIC INFORMATION:
Events per year: 2
Times of year: April and November
Locations: Eastern States Exposition, 1305 Memorial Avenue, West Springfield, MA 01089 (The Better Living Center)
Duration: 2 days
Types of events: These events include dolls and teddy bears, antiques, miniatures, dollhouses and figurines.
Doll-related products sold: Antique dolls, retired manufactured dolls, modern manufactured dolls, artist dolls, dollmaking supplies, doll clothing and accessories
Average Attendance: 10,000
Admission: $4

DEALER INFORMATION:
Dealers: 215
Space available for: Retail businesses selling dolls and related items, antique doll dealers, collectible and modern doll dealers, sellers of dollmaking supplies, sellers of doll clothing and accessories, doll artists, doll manufacturers, appraisers, restoration experts
Space distributed: To participants from the previous year first; remaining spaces on first-come, first-serve basis. There is usually a waiting list.
Application process: Send SASE or call to receive an application form. Dealers may apply 1 year in advance. Must provide merchandise list, state tax and number.
Average cost of booth/table: $200

SPECIAL FEATURES:
Services for collectors: Restoration, cleaning and appraisals of old/antique dolls

NANCY JO'S DOLL SALE

Nancy Jo Schreeder
305 Robinson St.
Martinez, CA 94553
Phone: (510)229-4190 PST
Fax: (510)229-5369
First event: 1971
Mailing list: Write or call to be included.

BASIC INFORMATION:
Events per year: 4
Times of year: January, May, July, November
Locations: Fairgrounds Dr., Vallejo, CA
Duration: January, July—1 day; November, May—2 days
Types of events: These events include teddy bears, miniatures, dollhouses and toys.
Doll-related products sold: Antique dolls, retired manufactured dolls, modern manufactured dolls, artist dolls, dollmaking supplies, doll clothing and accessories
Average Attendance: Several thousand
Admission: $5.25

DEALER INFORMATION:
Dealers: 200
Space available for: Retail businesses selling dolls and related items, antique doll dealers, collectible and modern doll dealers, sellers of dollmaking supplies, sellers of doll clothing and accessories, doll artists, doll clubs/organizations, restoration experts.
Space distributed: First-come, first-serve basis
Application process: Send SASE to receive an application form. Dealers may apply 6 months in advance. Applicants must include photos of dolls.
Average cost of booth/table: $61

SPECIAL FEATURES:
Educational opportunities: Videos are shown.
Door prizes/drawings: 50-75 prizes

NEEDLEARTS ADVENTURES, L.L.C.

Sandra Sapienza
P.O. Box 331
Crownsville, MD 21032
Phone: (410)923-3415 EST
Fax: (410)923-3415
E-mail: nrtt91a@prodigy.com
First event: 1994
Mailing list: Write or call to be included.

BASIC INFORMATION:
Events per year: 2
Times of year: June; October of even-numbered years
Locations: Orlando Airport Hyatt Regency, Orlando, FL; Baltimore, MD
Duration: 3-4 days
Types of events: These events include dolls and doll related items.
Doll-related products sold: Artist dolls, doll supplies, doll clothing, doll accessories, doll-related collectibles
Admission: $350 for 3 days of workshops and special events. $5 admission to exhibits and "Bizarre Bazaar" sale event.

DEALER INFORMATION:
Dealers: 40
Space available for: Retail businesses selling dolls and related items, antique doll dealers, collectible and modern doll dealers, sellers of dollmaking supplies, sellers of doll clothing and accessories, doll artists, doll manufacturers, doll clubs/organizations
Space distributed: First-come, first-serve basis
Application process: Send SASE or call for an application form. Dealers must apply 6-12 months in advance.
Average cost of booth/table: $40

SPECIAL FEATURES:
Educational opportunities: Dollmaking

workshops, lectures by well-known collectors/artists, seminars on doll collecting, slide shows, sewing and needle arts workshops

Special exhibits: Exhibit by the doll artists who are teaching at the conference; exhibit of participant works; exhibits by doll clubs; a traveling exhibit such as the "Figure in Cloth" or the "Hoffman Challenge" dolls; exhibit of dolls made by the participants in response to a "challenge."

Door prizes/drawings: Door prizes are awarded at luncheons and other special events. There is a raffle of dolls donated by doll artists.

Souvenirs: Each conference participant receives a specially imprinted "Goody Bag" of samples and promotional material on dollmaking supplies/services. A book of original doll patterns by doll artists is sold.

OLD MOTHER'S CUPBOARD

Judi Domm
P.O. Box 4777
Fresno, CA 93477
Phone: (209)787-2208
First event: 1992
Mailing list: Available

BASIC INFORMATION:
Events per year: 8
Times of year: February, April, May, June/July, September
Locations: San Jose, CA; Modesto, CA
Duration: 1 day
Types of events: These events include dolls and teddy bears, antiques, miniatures, doll houses, figurines and toys.
Doll-related products sold: Antique dolls, retired manufactured dolls, modern manufactured dolls, artist dolls, dollmaking supplies, doll clothing and accessories
Average Attendance: 800-1,000
Admission: $4

DEALER INFORMATION:
Dealers: 350
Space distributed: To participants from previous years first; remaining spaces on first-come, first-serve basis
Average cost of booth/table: $55

ORPHANS IN THE ATTIC DOLL-BEAR-TOY SHOWS/SALES

Marge Hansen
N96W20235 County Line Rd.
Menominee Falls, WI 53051
Phone: (414)255-4465 CST
First event: 1978
Mailing list: Write or call to be included.

BASIC INFORMATION:
Events per year: 12
Times of year: Year-round
Locations: Ramada Inn I-90, Madison, WI; SERB Hall, 5101 W. Oklahoma Ave., Milwaukee, WI; Best Western, Midway Hotel, 780 Packer Dr., Green Bay, WI
Duration: Sunday, 9:30-4.
Types of events: These events include dolls, teddy bears and toys.
Doll-related products sold: Antique dolls, retired manufactured dolls, modern manufactured dolls, artist dolls, dollmaking supplies, doll clothing and accessories
Average Attendance: 800-1,000
Admission: $3; $1, 6-12 years

DEALER INFORMATION:
Dealers: 55-60
Space available for: Retail businesses selling dolls and related items, antique doll dealers, collectible and modern doll dealers, sellers of dollmaking supplies, sellers of doll clothing and accessories, doll artists, doll manufacturers, doll clubs/organizations, appraisers, restoration experts
Space distributed: To participants from the previous year first; remaining spaces are available on a first-come, first-serve basis.
Application process: Send SASE. Call up to 2 weeks before show.
Average cost of booth/table: $40-65

SPECIAL FEATURES:
Door prizes/drawings: Throughout the day.

ADDITIONAL INFORMATION:
Participants must bring their own table covers and cover all the tables to the floor.

QUALITY DOLL AND TEDDY BEAR SHOWS

Richard and Charles Schiessl
P.O. Box 2061
Portland, OR 97208

Phone: (503)284-4062 PST
First event: 1981
Mailing list: Write, call or come to a show and ask to be included.

BASIC INFORMATION:
Events per year: 6
Times of year: 4th weekend in February; 2nd or 3rd weekend in March; 4th weekend in June; 4th weekend in August; 2nd or 3rd weekend in October; 3rd weekend in November.
Locations: Portland Expo Center, 2060 N. Marine Drive, Portland, OR 97217; Puyallup Fairgrounds, Pavilion, 9th and Meridian, Puyallup, WA 98371 (P.O. Box 430).
Duration: Saturday and Sunday
Types of events: These events include teddy bears, miniatures, figurines and toys.
Doll-related products sold: Antique dolls, retired manufactured dolls, modern manufactured dolls, artist dolls, dollmaking supplies, doll clothing and accessories
Average Attendance: 3,000-4,000
Admission: $4; $3, seniors; $2, disabled and under 12

DEALER INFORMATION:
Dealers: 200 +
Space available for: Retail businesses selling dolls and related items, antique doll dealers, collectible and modern doll dealers, sellers of dollmaking supplies, sellers of doll clothing and accessories, doll artists, appraisers, restoration experts
Space distributed: Participants from the previous show in the same city first; remaining spaces are available on a first-come, first-serve basis. There is usually a waiting list.
Application process: Send SASE, call or come to a show and ask. Both days must be attended by all exhibitors.
Average cost of booth/table: $95-170

SPECIAL FEATURES:
Services for collectors: Restorations, cleaning, appraisals; services are provided by exhibitors.
Educational opportunities: Dollmaking workshops
Door prizes/drawings: Door prizes about every 20 minutes on both days. Promoter provides some; exhibitors provide most.

ADDITIONAL INFORMATION:

"This is the largest show in the Northwest. Many exhibitors have told us it is the best managed show they have seen anywhere," Richard and Charles say.

R&S ENTERPRISES

Ronald D. Funk
34 N. Vinlage Rd.
Paradise, PA 17562
Phone: (717)442-4279
Fax: (717)442-8115
First event: 1980

BASIC INFORMATION:

Events per year: 5

Times of year: March, April, June, October, November

Locations: York, PA (April and November) and Gilbertsville, PA (March, June and October)

Duration: 1 day

Types of events: These events include teddy bears and toys.

Doll-related products sold: Antique dolls, retired manufactured dolls, modern manufactured dolls, artist dolls, dollmaking supplies, doll clothing and accessories

Average Attendance: 850

Admission: $3.50

DEALER INFORMATION:

Dealers: 150-275

Space distributed: First-come, first-serve basis

Average cost of booth/table: $50

JO ANN REYNOLDS

6058 Daysville Rd.
Oregon, IL 61061
Phone: (815)732-7742 CST
First event: 1990
Mailing list: Write or call to be included.

BASIC INFORMATION:

Events per year: 3

Times of year: March, April, August

Locations: March and August: Forest Hills Lodge, 9900 Forest Hills Rd., Rockford, IL. April: Illinois Valley Banquet Center, 920 Second St., LaSalle, IL

Duration: 1 day

Types of events: These events include dolls, teddy bears and toys.

Doll-related products sold: Antique dolls, retired manufactured dolls, modern manufactured dolls, artist

dolls, dollmaking supplies, doll clothing and accessories

Average Attendance: 1,400

Admission: $2.50

DEALER INFORMATION:

Dealers: 65-70

Space available for: Retail businesses selling dolls and related items, antique doll dealers, collectible and modern doll dealers, sellers of dollmaking supplies, sellers of doll clothing and accessories, doll manufacturers, doll clubs/organizations, restoration experts

Space distributed: To participants from previous year first; remaining spaces on first-come, first-serve basis. Categories are limited. There is usually a waiting list.

Application process: Send SASE or call to receive an application form. Dealers may apply 5 months in advance.

Average cost of booth/table: $40-$120

SPECIAL FEATURES:

Services for collectors: Restoration and cleaning of old/antique dolls

Door prizes/drawings: 2 door prizes every 30 minutes

ADDITIONAL INFORMATION:

Jo Ann's shows include dealers from 9 different states.

S & S DOLL HOSPITAL

Steve Schroeder
3100 Harvest Lane
Kissimmee, FL 34744
Phone: (407)957-6392 EST
Fax: (407)957-9427
E-mail: fpqy15a@prodigy.com
First event: 1979
Mailing list: Write or call to be included.

BASIC INFORMATION:

Events per year: 8

Times of year: April, June, July, August, September, October, November

Locations: Sarasota Municipal Building, Sarasota, FL; Azan Shrine Temple, Melbourne FL; Howard Johnson's Hotel, St. Petersburg, FL; Kissimmee Agriculture Bldg., Kissimmee, FL.

Duration: 1 day or 1 weekend.

Types of events: These event includes dolls and teddy bears.

Doll-related products sold: Antique dolls, retired manufactured dolls, modern manufactured dolls, artist

dolls, dollmaking supplies, doll clothing and accessories

Average Attendance: 350-1,000

Admission: $3

DEALER INFORMATION:

Dealers: 40-90

Space available for: Retail businesses selling dolls and related items, antique doll dealers, collectible and modern doll dealers, sellers of dollmaking supplies, sellers of doll clothing and accessories, doll artists, appraisers

Space distributed: On a first-come, first-serve basis

Application process: Send SASE or call to be included. Apply 3 months to 2 weeks in advance.

Average cost of booth/table: $85

SPECIAL FEATURES:

Services for collectors: Appraisals of old/antique dolls

Door prizes/drawings: Gifts donated by dealers. One doll and one bear are raffled off for charity.

Exhibits: At the October and June shows, displays of Ginnys, GI Joes, Barbie, Alexander, and others are shown for the education of the public.

SIROCCO PRODUCTIONS, INC.

Leonard A. Swann, Jr.
5660 E. Virginia Beach Blvd. #104
Norfolk, VA 23502
Phone: (804)461-8987, (800)637-2264 EST
Fax: (804)461-4669

BASIC INFORMATION:

Events per year: 2

Times of year: May and October

Locations: Newport News, VA

Types of events: These events include dolls and related items only.

SINGLE EVENTS

"A DAY WITH . . ." (A NATIONALLY KNOWN SPEAKER) LAND O'SKY DOLL CLUB

Suzi Smith
109 Homestead Rd.
Asheville, NC 28715
Phone: (704)667-3690 or (704)298-1717 EST
E-mail: dolldr1@aol.com
First event: 1991

When: Last Saturday in March
Where: Deerpark Restaurant, Biltmore Estate, Asheville, NC
Duration: 1 day
Mailing list: Write or call to be included.

BASIC INFORMATION:

Type of event: This event includes dolls and related items only.
Doll-related products sold: Antique dolls, retired manufactured dolls
Admission: $30 (includes lunch, programs)
Average Attendance: 150

DEALER INFORMATION:

Dealers: 10 (club members only)

SPECIAL FEATURES:

Educational opportunities: Lectures by well-known collectors/artists, seminars on doll collecting.
Door prizes/drawings: Many doll-related door prizes, drawings for donated dolls, books, etc.
Souvenirs: Each attendee receives a gift souvenir from the club, and another from the table hostess.
Competitions: About 30 categories, including antique, modern, and dolls created by exhibitor. Categories change slightly each year. Prizes are ribbons and rosettes. Competitors should apply 1-3 months in advance. Request competition forms, fill them out and return with $2 for each doll entered. Bring dolls at 8:30 on the day of event.

ANTELOPE VALLEY DOLLS, BEARS AND MINIATURES SHOW

Kay Hjelm
1150 W. Ave J-8
Lancaster, CA 93534
Phone: (805)948-4460 PST
First event: 1993
When: March 9-10, 1996
Where: Antelope Valley Fairgrounds, 155 E. Ave I, Lancaster, CA
Duration: Saturday and Sunday
Mailing list: Write to be included.

BASIC INFORMATION:

Type of event: This event includes dolls, teddy bears, antiques, miniatures, doll houses, figurines and toys.
Doll-related products sold: Antique dolls, retired manufactured dolls, modern manufactured dolls, artist dolls, doll clothing, doll accessories, doll supplies, doll-related collectibles
Admission: $4; $3 for seniors and children
Average Attendance: 800

DEALER INFORMATION:

Dealers: 125 +
Space available for: Retail businesses selling dolls and related items, antique doll dealers, collectible and modern doll dealers, sellers of dollmaking supplies, sellers of doll clothing and accessories, doll artists, doll manufacturers, doll clubs/organizations, appraisers, restoration experts
Space distributed: To participants from previous year first; remaining spaces on first-come, first-serve basis.
Application process: Send SASE for an application form. Dealer must apply 3 months in advance.
Cost of booth/table: $100-225

SPECIAL FEATURES:

Services for collectors: Appraisals of old/antique dolls
Educational opportunities: Lectures by well-known collectors/artists, seminars on doll collecting, lectures on sewing (French heirloom smocking); lectures on dollmaking.
Door prizes/drawings: Tickets can be purchased for drawings held on Sunday afternoon. Door prizes are donated by vendors and drawn every hour.
Competitions: Several categories for amateur and professional porcelain dolls and cloth dolls. Prizes are ribbons and trophies. Competitors should apply at least 2 weeks before event.

BARBIE AND FRIENDS EXTRAVAGANZA

Kari Hart
1623 E. 7th St.
Duluth, MN 55812
Phone: (218)728-1593 CST
First event: 1990
When: Saturday, May 11, 1996
Where: Best Western Northwest Inn, Brooklyn Park, Minneapolis, MN
Duration: 1 day
Mailing list: Write or call to be included.

BASIC INFORMATION:

Type of event: Barbie Dolls only
Doll-related products sold: Barbies
Admission: $4

Average Attendance: 300

DEALER INFORMATION:

Dealers: 30
Space available for: Retail businesses selling dolls and related items, collectible and modern doll dealers, sellers of doll clothing and accessories (Barbie-related only)
Space distributed: First-come, first-serve basis
Application process: Send SASE for an application form. Dealer must apply 2-3 months in advance.
Cost of booth/table: $50 first table; $40 each additional

SPECIAL FEATURES:

Services for collectors: Appraisals of old/antique dolls
Door prizes/drawings: Door prizes every half hour

BELLEVILLE DOLL, TOY AND TEDDY BEAR FAIR

Kay Weber
300 Ross Lane
Belleville, IL 62220
Phone: (618)233-0940 CST
First event: 1982
When: July
Where: Belle-Clair Expo. Center, Rt. 13 and 159, Belleville, IL
Duration: 2 days
Mailing list: Write or call to be included.

BASIC INFORMATION:

Type of event: This event includes dolls and related items only.
Doll-related products sold: Antique dolls, artist dolls, doll supplies, retired manufactured dolls, doll clothing, doll-related collectibles, modern manufactured dolls, doll accessories
Admission: $3

DEALER INFORMATION:

Dealers: 120
Space available for: Retail businesses selling dolls and related items, antique doll dealers, collectible and modern doll dealers, sellers of dollmaking supplies, sellers of doll clothing and accessories, doll artists, doll manufacturers, doll clubs/organizations, appraisers, restoration experts
Space distributed: To participants from the previous year first; remaining spaces on first-come, first-serve basis.

There is usually a waiting list.
Application process: Send SASE for application form. Apply in February.
Cost of booth/table: $50

SPECIAL FEATURES:
Services for collectors: Appraisals of old/antique dolls.

BLACK DOLL ART AND COLLECTIBLE SHOW AND SALE
POD PRODUCTIONS
Pamela Turner
1525 E. 53rd St., Suite 621
Chicago, IL 60615
Phone: (312)874-8482 CST
First event: 1993
When: June
Where: Congress—Ramada, 520 S. Michigan, Chicago, IL.
Duration: 1 weekend
Mailing list: Write or call to be included.

BASIC INFORMATION:
Type of event: This event includes dolls and antiques, miniatures, figurines.
Doll-related products sold: Antique dolls, retired manufactured dolls, modern manufactured dolls, artist dolls, doll clothing, doll accessories, doll-related collectibles.
Admission: $5
Average Attendance: 1,000

DEALER INFORMATION:
Dealers: 20-25
Space available for: Retail businesses selling dolls and related items, antique doll dealers, collectible and modern doll dealers, sellers of dollmaking supplies, sellers of doll clothing and accessories, doll artists, doll manufacturers, doll clubs/organizations, appraisers, restoration experts
Space distributed: To participants from previous year first; remaining spaces on first-come, first-serve basis.
Application process: Write or call for an application form. Dealer must apply 3 months in advance.
Cost of booth/table: $300

SPECIAL FEATURES:
Services for collectors: Appraisals of old/antique dolls
Educational opportunities: Dollmaking workshops, lectures by well-known collectors/artists, seminars on doll collecting.

BLUEBONNET BEBES OF HOUSTON DOLL SHOW AND SALE
Sue Barker
2619 Charles Lane
Sugar Land, TX 77478
Phone: (713)491-4760 CST
First event: 1976
When: March
Where: Holiday Inn, I45 South, Houston, TX

BASIC INFORMATION:
Type of Event: This event includes dolls, teddy bears, antiques, miniatures, dollhouses and toys.
Doll-related products sold: Antique dolls, retired manufactured dolls, modern manufactured dolls, artist dolls, doll clothing, doll accessories, doll-related collectibles
Admission: $2.50
Average Attendance: 600

DEALER INFORMATION:
Dealers: 59
Space distributed: To participants from the previous year first; remaining spaces on first-come, first-serve basis
Cost of booth/table: $100

BROCKVILLE DOLL, MINIATURE, AND TEDDY BEAR SHOW AND SALE
BIG SISTERS ASSOCIATION OF LEEDS AND GRENVILLE
Dale Pearson
P.O. Box 791
Brockville, Ontario K6V 5W1
CANADA
Phone: (613)345-3295 EST
Fax: (613)342-8684
First event: 1995
When: 2nd weekend in June
Where: Brockville Country Club R.R. #3, Brockville, Ontario
Duration: 1 weekend
Mailing list: Write, call or fax to be included.

BASIC INFORMATION:
Type of event: This event includes dolls and teddy bears, miniatures, doll houses.
Doll-related products sold: Antique dolls, retired manufactured dolls, artist dolls, doll clothing, doll accessories, doll supplies, doll-related collectibles.
Admission: $2
Average Attendance: 600-700

DEALER INFORMATION:
Dealers: 45-50
Space available for: Retail businesses selling dolls and related items, antique doll dealers, collectible and modern doll dealers, sellers of dollmaking supplies, sellers of doll clothing and accessories, doll artists, doll clubs/organizations, appraisers
Space distributed: First-come, first-serve basis
Application process: Send SASE, call or fax for an application form. Dealer must apply in January.
Cost of booth/table: $55

SPECIAL FEATURES:
Educational opportunities: A doll contest table at which the judges of the doll contest provide feedback to participants.
Door prizes/drawings: Vendors are asked to donate a small prize for a door prize.
Competitions: Vary. Prizes are ribbons. Competitors should apply between January and May. A registration form and fee must be submitted prior to the opening of the show.

ADDITIONAL INFORMATION:
All proceeds go to the Big Sisters Association of Leeds and Grenville.

"CHILDHOOD DREAMS" DOLL SHOW AND SALE
DOLL STUDY CLUB OF JAMESTOWN, NY
Lynn Dole
Box 5
Ashville, NY 14710
Phone: (716)484-7263 or (716)763-0128 EST
First event: 1983
When: July
Where: Holiday Inn, 4th St., Jamestown, NY
Duration: 1 day

BASIC INFORMATION:
Type of event: This event includes dolls, teddy bears and miniatures.
Doll-related products sold: Antique dolls, retired manufactured dolls, modern manufactured dolls, artist dolls, doll clothing, doll accessories, doll supplies
Admission: $2
Average Attendance: 400-500

DEALER INFORMATION:

Dealers: 30

Space available for: Retail businesses selling dolls and related items, antique doll dealers, collectible and modern doll dealers, sellers of dollmaking supplies, sellers of doll clothing and accessories, doll artists

Space distributed: First-come, first-serve basis. There is usually a waiting list.

Application process: Send SASE or call for an application form. Contracts are mailed out February 1.

Cost of booth/table: $35

SPECIAL FEATURES:

Special exhibits: Dolls entered in competition are shown in the competition room.

Competitions: Anyone may enter. Categories vary from year to year. Prizes are ribbons. Applications accepted up to day of show. Competitors must complete application form.

CHRISTMAS DELIGHT
THE DOLL HOSPITAL

Jane C. Messenger
6892 Rt. 291
Marcy, NY 13403
Phone: (315)865-5463 EST
First event: 1988
When: 3rd Saturday of October
Where: First United Methodist Church, 105 Genessee St., New Hartford, NY.
Duration: 1 day
Mailing list: Write to be included.

BASIC INFORMATION:

Doll-related products sold: Antique dolls, retired manufactured dolls, modern manufactured dolls, artist dolls, doll clothing, doll accessories, doll supplies, doll-related collectibles

Admission: $3.50

Average Attendance: 500-600

DEALER INFORMATION:

Dealers: 40

Space available for: Antique doll dealers, collectible and modern doll dealers, sellers of dollmaking supplies, sellers of doll clothing and accessories, doll artists

Space distributed: First-come, first-serve basis. There is usually a waiting list. Send SASE for an application form. Dealer must apply 6 months in advance.

Cost of booth/table: $45

SPECIAL FEATURES:

Services for collectors: Appraisals of old/antique dolls; clinic for sick dolls—doctor consultation.

Door prizes/drawings: Dealers' donations and magazines

CHRISTMAS IN JULY AND
HOLIDAY DOLL SHOWS
DOLL CONNECTION NETWORK

Linda Price
P.O. Box 102
Tontitown, AR 72770
Phone: (501)361-2266 or (501)248-2386
Fax: (501)248-1967
First event: 1994
When: 3rd Saturday in July; 2nd Saturday in November
Where: Northwest Arkansas Convention Center, Holiday Inn, U.S. 71 and 412, Springdale, AR
Duration: 1 day
Mailing list: Write or call to be included.

BASIC INFORMATION:

Type of event: This event includes dolls and teddy bears, miniatures, doll houses, toys.

Doll-related products sold: Antique dolls, retired manufactured dolls, modern manufactured dolls, artist dolls, doll clothing, doll accessories, doll supplies, doll-related collectibles

Admission: $2

Average Attendance: 300

DEALER INFORMATION:

Dealers: 40-50

Space available for: Retail businesses selling dolls and related items, antique doll dealers, collectible and modern doll dealers, sellers of dollmaking supplies, sellers of doll clothing and accessories, doll artists, doll manufacturers, doll clubs/organizations, appraisers, restoration experts

Space distributed: First-come, first-serve basis

Application process: Send SASE or call for an application form.

Cost of booth/table: $30 for 1 table; $25 each for 2 or more

SPECIAL FEATURES:

Services for collectors: Restoration, cleaning or appraisals of old/antique dolls

Door prizes/drawings: Door prizes every hour with a grand prize of a doll given at the end of show.

Competitions: Open to the public. Doll collectors or artists may enter. Collector; handmade; originals; costumes. Prizes are ribbons. Apply anytime before show begins.

CLEVELAND DOLL CLUB DOLL AND BEAR
SHOW AND SALE
CLEVELAND DOLL CLUB

Deanna Pinizotto
9550 Remington Dr.
Mentor, OH 44060
Phone: (216)255-1663 EST
First event: 1982
When: 1st weekend in April (if Easter is same date, show moves to 2nd weekend).
Where: Patrician Party Center, 33150 Lakeland Blvd., Eastlake, OH
Duration: 1 day (Sunday)
Mailing list: Write to be included.

BASIC INFORMATION:

Type of event: This event includes dolls and teddy bears.

Doll-related products sold: Antique dolls, retired manufactured dolls, modern manufactured dolls, artist dolls, doll clothing, doll accessories, doll supplies, doll-related collectibles, doll books

Admission: $3; children free

Average Attendance: 500-600 people

DEALER INFORMATION:

Dealers: 50

Space available for: Retail businesses selling dolls and related items, antique doll dealers, collectible and modern doll dealers, sellers of dollmaking supplies, sellers of doll clothing and accessories, doll artists, appraisers, doll book authors

Space distributed: To participants from previous year first; remaining spaces on first-come, first-serve basis. There is usually a waiting list.

Application process: Send SASE for an application form. Dealer must apply 6-8 months in advance. 50% deposit and description of type of merchandise sold are required.

Cost of booth/table: $30-60

SPECIAL FEATURES:

Services for collectors: Appraisals of

old/antique dolls, book signings by famous authors

Special exhibits: An extensive display of dolls illustrating the year's theme

Door prizes/drawings: A doll raffle is always part of the show; 40-50 door prizes are also distributed.

ADDITIONAL INFORMATION:
Event is wheelchair accessible and located in a lovely, air conditioned party/wedding center. It includes a well-rounded offering of merchandise and ample paved parking and is located just off major expressways. Lunch is available.

COASTAL DOLL COLLECTORS' SHOW AND SALE
COASTAL DOLL COLLECTORS' CLUB OF SC

Miriam R. Little
507 Main St.
Conway, SC 29526-4337
Phone: (803)248-5643 EST
First event: 1980
When: March
Where: Myrtle Beach Convention Center, 21st Ave. and Oak St., Myrtle Beach, SC
Duration: Saturday and Sunday
Mailing list: Write or call to be included.

BASIC INFORMATION:
Type of event: This event includes dolls, teddy bears, antiques, miniatures, doll houses, figurines and toys.

Doll-related products sold: Antique dolls, retired manufactured dolls, modern manufactured dolls, artist dolls, doll clothing, doll accessories, doll supplies, doll-related collectibles

Admission: $4 for 2-day ticket; $3 per day

Average Attendance: 2,500-3,000

DEALER INFORMATION:
Dealers: 135
Space available for: Retail businesses selling dolls and related items, antique doll dealers, collectible and modern doll dealers, sellers of dollmaking supplies, sellers of doll clothing and accessories, doll artists, doll manufacturers, doll clubs/organizations, appraisers, restoration experts

Space distributed: To participants from previous year first; remaining spaces on first-come, first-serve basis. There is usually a waiting list. Send SASE

or call for an application form. Dealer must apply 6 months in advance.

Cost of booth/table: $60-75

SPECIAL FEATURES:
Services for collectors: Restoration, cleaning and appraisal of old/antique dolls

Educational opportunities: Dollmaking workshops; seminars on other doll-related subjects

Special exhibits: Educational exhibit each year

Door prizes/drawings: A door prize drawing occurs every few minutes. Show also includes a raffle, with all proceeds donated to local charities.

DOLL AND BEAR SHOW AND SALE
TIMELESS TREASURES DOLL CLUB

Norma M. Owen
859 John Adams Pkwy.
Idaho Falls, ID 83401-4024
Phone: (208)522-3410 MST
First event: 1989
When: September
Duration: 1 day
Mailing list: Write or call to be included.

BASIC INFORMATION:
Type of event: This event includes dolls and teddy bears, antiques, miniatures, doll houses, figurines, toys, doll furniture, doll cases and doll costumes.

Doll-related products sold: Antique dolls, retired manufactured dolls, modern manufactured dolls, artist dolls, doll clothing, doll accessories, doll supplies, doll-related collectibles

Admission: $2
Average Attendance: 600

DEALER INFORMATION:
Dealers: 40
Space available for: Retail businesses selling dolls and related items, antique doll dealers, collectible and modern doll dealers, sellers of dollmaking supplies, sellers of doll clothing and accessories, doll artists, doll clubs/organizations, restoration experts, doll furniture makers

Space distributed: To participants from previous year first; remaining spaces on first-come, first-serve basis. There is sometimes a waiting list.

Application process: Send SASE or call for an application form. Dealer must apply 2-7 months in advance.

Cost of booth/table: $35 for 10 × 10 booth space. Booths hold 1 small and 2 large tables. Tables $9.

SPECIAL FEATURES:
Special exhibits: Doll owned by Doll Club members have a competition table with eight categories that are judged and awarded ribbons; There is also a raffle for a charity donation.

Door prizes/drawings: All tickets are entered in a drawing. Past shows have also included a drawing for a special doll, with proceeds donated to charity.

Competitions: Only Timeless Treasures Doll Club members can enter. Categories include antique, antique reproductions modern collectibles, miniatures, original dolls, modern reproductions, collector dolls, miscellaneous. Prizes include 1st, 2nd and 3rd place ribbons and one People's Choice ribbon.

ADDITIONAL INFORMATION:
Breakfast is provided. Lunch is available for a fee.

DOLL AND BEAR SHOW AND SALE
YOUNG AT HEART DOLL CLUB

Mary Nusshoff
681 Georges Rd.
Monmouth Junction, NJ 08852
Phone: (908)329-3779 EST
First event: 1989
When: 3rd Sunday in April
Where: Holiday Inn, Jamesburg, New Jersey (at exit 8A New Jersey Turnpike)
Duration: 1 day, 10-4
Mailing list: Write or call to be included.

BASIC INFORMATION:
Type of event: This event includes dolls and teddy bears.

Doll-related products sold: Antique dolls, retired manufactured dolls, modern manufactured dolls, artist dolls, doll clothing, doll accessories, doll supplies, doll-related collectibles

Admission: $4, adults; $1.50, children
Average Attendance: 500 +

DEALER INFORMATION:
Dealers: 30-35
Space available for: Retail businesses selling dolls and related items, antique doll dealers, collectible and modern doll dealers, sellers of doll clothing and accessories, doll artists

Space distributed: To participants from previous year first; remaining spaces on first-come, first-serve basis, by category. There is usually a waiting list.

Application process: Send SASE or call for an application form. Dealers must apply 6-9 months in advance. "This is a balanced show. There must be space in your category. Dealers in antiques and collectibles should describe in general terms what they will sell (i.e. dolls from 1950s). Artists: Unless you have done our show before, please submit photos of your work."

Cost of booth/table: $50-1 table; $90-2 tables

SPECIAL FEATURES:

Services for collectors: Appraisals of old/antique dolls, $3 per doll

Door prizes/drawings: A drawing for a doll.

ADDITIONAL INFORMATION:

The Young At Heart Doll Club is a non-profit organization; part of the United Federation of Doll Clubs. Money earned goes for charitable and educational activities.

DOLL AND TEDDY BEAR
FESTIVAL AND SALE

JoAnn Gillies
4701 Fernglen Pl.
Burnaby, British Columbia V5G 3W2
CANADA

Phone: (604)433-7660 or (604)596-6935 PST

Fax: (604)276-4169

E-mail: jgillies@city.richmond.bc.ca

First event: 1993

When: October

Where: Gizek Shrine Temple, 3550 Wayburne (at Canada Way), Burnaby, B.C.

Duration: 2 days

Mailing list: Write or call to be included.

BASIC INFORMATION:

Type of event: This event includes dolls and teddy bears, miniatures and dollhouses.

Doll-related products sold: Modern manufactured dolls, artist dolls, doll clothing, doll accessories, doll supplies, doll-related collectibles

Admission: $2

Average Attendance: 1,000

DEALER INFORMATION:

Dealers: 8

Space available for: Sellers of doll-making supplies, sellers of doll clothing and accessories, doll artists, doll clubs/organizations, restoration experts

Space distributed: This is invitation-only juried event.

Application process: Dealer must provide list of items for sale, photos or slides of doll, and photos or slides of displays from other shows (optional). Return check with application by cut-off date so organizers can offer available space to newcomers.

Cost of booth/table: $100

SPECIAL FEATURES:

Services for collectors: Restoration, cleaning and appraisal of old/antique dolls

Door prizes/drawings: Offers a chance for the door prize with admission.

DOLL AND TEDDY BEAR SHOW AND SALE
HOLBROOK LIONESS CLUB

Marilyn McCarthy
10 Clair Ave.
Holbrook, NY 11741

Phone: (516)567-1618 EST

First event: 1995

When: April

Where: Knights of Columbus Hall, 9-11 Railroad Ave., Patchogue, NY

Duration: 1 day

Mailing list: Write or call to be included.

BASIC INFORMATION:

Type of event: This event includes dolls, teddy bears and antiques.

Doll-related products sold: Antique dolls, modern manufactured dolls, artist dolls, doll accessories

Admission: $3.50

Average Attendance: 500

DEALER INFORMATION:

Dealers: 48

Space available for: Retail businesses selling dolls and related items, antique doll dealers, collectible and modern doll dealers, doll artists

Space distributed: First-come, first-serve basis

Application process: Send SASE for an application form. Dealer must apply 6 months-1 year in advance.

SPECIAL FEATURES:

Door prizes/drawings: Drawing for doll-related items and teddy bears. Donations are accepted.

DOLL AND TOY SHOW
BROWARD COUNTY DOLL AND TOY
COLLECTORS CLUB

Mildred Swartzman
P.O. Box 836
Dania, FL 33004

Phone: (954)434-0818 EST

Fax: (954)739-9030

First event: 1974

When: Last Saturday in January

Where: Pompano Beach Recreation Center, 1801 N.E. 6th St., Pompano Beach, FL

Duration: 1 day, 10-5.

Mailing list: Write to be included.

BASIC INFORMATION:

Type of event: This event includes dolls and teddy bears, antiques, miniatures, toys.

Doll-related products sold: Antique dolls, retired manufactured dolls, modern manufactured dolls, artist dolls, doll clothing, doll accessories, doll supplies, doll-related collectibles

Admission: $2

Average Attendance: 450

DEALER INFORMATION:

Dealers: 35-60

Space available for: Retail businesses selling dolls and related items, antique doll dealers, collectible and modern doll dealers, sellers of dollmaking supplies, sellers of doll clothing and accessories, doll clubs/organizations

Space distributed: To participants from previous year first; remaining spaces on first-come, first-serve basis. There is usually a waiting list.

Application process: Send SASE for an application form.

Cost of booth/table: $45

SPECIAL FEATURES:

Services for collectors: Restorations, cleaning and appraisals of old/antique dolls

Souvenirs: An item related to the year's theme is made by club members and given to each person attending.

DOLL AND TOY SHOW
EVELYN MOOMAU DELMARVA
DOLL CLUB

Margaret Horn
20335 Nanticoke Dr.
Nanticoke, MD 21840
Phone: (516)873-3206, (516)896-9253
EST
First event: 1991
When: April, the Sunday after Easter
Where: Delmarva Convention Center,
Rt. 13 and Stateline Rd., Delmar MD
Duration: 1 day.
Mailing list: Call or write to be included.

BASIC INFORMATION:

Type of event: This event includes dolls
and teddy bears, antiques, miniatures,
dollhouses, toys, trains and cars.
Doll-related products sold: Antique
dolls, retired manufactured dolls,
modern manufactured dolls, artist
dolls, doll clothing, doll accessories,
doll supplies, doll-related collectibles,
doll houses, miniatures, fabrics
Admission: $3
Average Attendance: 150-300

DEALER INFORMATION:

Dealers: 35-50
Space available for: Retail business selling dolls and related items, antique
doll dealers, collectible and modern
doll dealers, sellers of dollmaking
supplies, sellers of doll clothing and
accessories, doll artists, doll clubs/or-
ganizations
Space distributed: First-come, first-serve
basis. There is usually a waiting list.
Application process: Send SASE or call
for application form. Apply 4-5
months in advance.
Cost of booth/table: $30 for a table; $90
for an 8 × 10 booth.

SPECIAL FEATURES:

Services for collectors: Varies year to
year.
Door prizes/drawings: Door prizes every
35-45 minutes. Major raffle of items
valued at $50 and over for a $1 donation.

ADDITIONAL INFORMATION:

A portion of proceeds is donated to charity and scholarship funds.

DOLL FESTIVAL AND SALE

Jo Ann Gillies or Hi Friesen
4701 Fernglen Place
Burnaby, British Columbia V5G 3W2
CANADA
Phone: (604)433-7660 or (604)596-6935
PST
Fax: (604)276-4169
E-mail: jgillies@city.richmond.bc.ca

DOLL SHOW

Peg Sours
2913 Coventry Court
Bloomington, IL 61704
Phone: (309)663-2685 CST
First event: 1982
When: 2nd Sunday of June
Where: Scottish Rite Temple, Route 51
at Mulberry St., Bloomington, IL
Duration: 1 day

BASIC INFORMATION:

Type of event: This event includes dolls
and teddy bears, antiques, miniatures,
dollhouses and toys.
Doll-related products sold: Antique
dolls, retired manufactured dolls,
modern manufactured dolls, artist
dolls, doll-clothing, doll accessories,
doll supplies, doll-related collectibles
Admission: $3 adults; $1 children 6-12

DEALER INFORMATION:

Dealers: 60
Space available for: Antique doll dealers, collectible and modern doll dealers, sellers of dollmaking supplies,
sellers of doll clothing and accessories, doll artists
Space distributed: To participants from
previous year first; remaining spaces
on first-come, first-serve basis. There
is usually a waiting list.
Application process: Send SASE for an
application form. Dealer must apply 6
months in advance.

DOLL SHOW
DOLL DREAMERS OF WNC

Alline D. Rhodes
390 Hoopers Creek Rd.
Fletcher, NC 28732
Phone: (704)684-8170 EST
First event: 1988
When: 2nd Saturday of August
Where: National Guard Armory, Brevard
Rd., Asheville, NC
Duration: 1 day

Mailing list: Write or call to be included.

BASIC INFORMATION:

Type of event: This event includes dolls
and related items only.
Doll-related products sold: Antique
dolls, retired manufactured dolls,
modern manufactured dolls, artist
dolls, doll clothing, doll accessories,
doll supplies, doll-related collectibles
Admission: $2
Average Attendance: 450-500

DEALER INFORMATION:

Dealers: 40
Space available for: Retail businesses
selling dolls and related items, antique
doll dealers, collectible and modern
doll dealers, sellers of dollmaking
supplies, sellers of doll clothing and
accessories, doll artists, doll clubs/or-
ganizations
Space distributed: First-come, first-serve
basis. There is usually a waiting list.
Application process: Send SASE or call
for an application form. Dealers must
apply 3 months in advance.
Cost of booth/table: $25

SPECIAL FEATURES:

Door prizes/drawings: Door prizes are
given every hour.

DOLL SHOW AND SALE
BORKHOLDER DUTCH VILLAGE

Patty Mast
71945 CR 101, P.O. Box 399
Nappanee, IN 46550
Phone: (219)773-2828 EST
Fax: (219)773-4828
First event: 1990
When: March, June, October
Where: Borkholder Dutch Village,
71945 CR 101, Nappanee, IN
Duration: 1 day
Mailing list: Write or call to be included.

BASIC INFORMATION:

Type of event: This event includes dolls
and teddy bears.
Doll-related products sold: Antique
dolls, retired manufactured dolls,
modern manufactured dolls, artist
dolls, doll clothing, doll accessories,
doll supplies, doll-related collectibles
Admission: $2.50 per person; 12 and un-
der free
Average Attendance: 400-600

DEALER INFORMATION:

Dealers: 30 (75-90 tables)

Space available for: Retail businesses selling dolls and related items, antique doll dealers, collectible and modern doll dealers, sellers of dollmaking supplies, sellers of doll clothing and accessories, doll artists, doll clubs/organizations

Space distributed: To participants from previous year first; remaining spaces on first-come, first-serve basis.

Application process: Send SASE or call for an application form. Dealer must apply 2-4 weeks in advance.

Cost of booth/table: $35 for 1 table, $20 per additional table

SPECIAL FEATURES:

Door prizes/drawings: Dealers donate one item. We draw a name out of a box every 15-30 min. Must be present to win.

"ALWAYS PURCHASE THE FINEST QUALITY. IF YOU CANNOT AFFORD THE FINEST QUALITY NOW, IT WOULD BE WISE TO SAVE YOUR MONEY AWHILE LONGER."

Kate Smalley, Kate Smalley's Antique Dolls, Branford, CT

DOLL SHOW AND SALE
THE CAROUSEL DOLL CLUB/USDC CLUB

Elizabeth Landis
1 Main St.
Sharon, CT 06069
Phone: (203)364-0271 EST
First event: 1974
When: Last week of April.
Where: Community Center, Kent, CT

BASIC INFORMATION:

Type of event: This event includes dolls, teddy bears, antiques, miniatures, doll houses, figurines and toys.

Doll-related products sold: Antique dolls, retired manufactured dolls, modern manufactured dolls, artist dolls, doll clothing, doll accessories, doll supplies, doll-related collectibles

Admission: $3.50

Average Attendance: 400

DEALER INFORMATION:

Dealers: 30

Space distributed: To participants from previous year first; remaining spaces

on first-come, first-serve basis

Cost of booth/table: $40 for 1 table; $70 for 2 tables.

DOLL SHOW AND SALE
THE CROOKED TREE DOLL CLUB

Lee Hoekje
6228 N. Lake Shore Dr., Box 139
Cross Village, MI 49723
Phone: (616)526-7538 EST
First event: 1994
When: Last weekend of April
Where: Stafford's Bay View Inn, Petoskey, MI
Duration: Saturday and Sunday.
Mailing list: Write to be included.

BASIC INFORMATION:

Type of event: This event includes dolls and teddy bears, miniatures, doll houses and toys.

Doll-related products sold: Antique dolls, retired manufactured dolls, artist dolls, doll clothing, doll accessories, doll supplies, doll-related collectibles

Admission: $3.50

Average Attendance: 500

DEALER INFORMATION:

Dealers: 30

Space available for: Retail businesses selling dolls and related items, antique doll dealers, collectible and modern doll dealers, sellers of dollmaking supplies, sellers of doll clothing and accessories, doll artists, appraisers

Space distributed: To participants from previous year first; remaining spaces on first-come, first-serve basis. Attempt is made to divide space by category. There is usually a waiting list.

Application process: Send SASE for an application form.

Cost of booth/table: $35

SPECIAL FEATURES:

Services for collectors: Appraisals of old/antique dolls

ADDITIONAL INFORMATION:

Part of the proceeds are donated to the Women's Resource Center in aid of the Women's Safe House in 5 counties.

DOLL SHOW AND SALE
MUSKEGON SAND DOLLERS DOLL CLUB

Sue Ritchie
2448 W. Crystal Lake Rd.
Whitehall, MI 49461

Phone: (616)894-9730 EST
First event: 1983
When: 3rd Saturday in September
Where: Walker Arena Annex, 4th and Western, Muskegon, MI
Duration: 1 day
Mailing list: Write or call to be included.

BASIC INFORMATION:

Type of event: This event includes dolls, teddy bears, antiques and miniatures.

Doll-related products sold: Antique dolls, retired manufactured dolls, modern manufactured dolls, artist dolls, doll clothing, doll accessories, doll supplies, doll-related collectibles

Admission: $2

Average Attendance: 500

DEALER INFORMATION:

Dealers: 50

Space available for: Retail businesses selling dolls and related items, antique doll dealers, collectible and modern doll dealers, sellers of dollmaking supplies, sellers of doll clothing and accessories, doll artists, doll manufacturers, doll clubs/organizations, appraisers, restoration experts

Space distributed: On first-come, first-serve basis. There is usually a waiting list. Send SASE or call for an application form. Dealer must apply 3 months in advance.

Cost of booth/table: $30

SPECIAL FEATURES:

Services for collectors: Appraisals of old/antique dolls

Door prizes/drawings: 2 door prizes are given away.

ADDITIONAL INFORMATION:

Proceeds go to buy toys for needy children and bears for kids admitted to local hospital emergency rooms.

DOLL SHOW AND SALE/SLEEPING ANGEL PRODUCTIONS

Sonja M. Barnes
441 North Bluff St.
Butler, PA 16001
Phone: (412)283-1923 EST
First event: 1991
When: March
Where: Sheraton Inn Pittsburgh North, 910 Sheraton Dr., Mars, PA
Duration: 1 day, 10-4
Mailing list: Write or call to be included.

BASIC INFORMATION:

Type of event: This event includes dolls and teddy bears, miniatures, dollhouses, figurines, toys and paper dolls.

Doll-related products sold: Antique dolls, retired manufactured dolls, modern manufactured dolls, artist dolls, doll clothing, doll accessories, doll supplies, doll-related collectibles

Admission: $3.50

Average Attendance: 500

DEALER INFORMATION:

Dealers: 40

Space available for: Retail businesses selling dolls and related items, antique doll dealers, collectible and modern doll dealers, sellers of dollmaking supplies, sellers of doll clothing and accessories, doll artists, doll clubs/organizations, appraisers, restoration experts

Space distributed: First-come, first-serve basis

Application process: Send SASE or call for an application form.

Cost of booth/table: $30

SPECIAL FEATURES:

Door prizes/drawings: Door prizes are doll related items, and a raffle for a doll.

Competitions: Dress-A-Doll Contest. First prize, $75; second, $50; third, $25. One Special Mention Award chosen by producer and staff. Pre-registration is required. $5 fee.

DOLL SHOW AND SALE
WEST VOLUSIA DOLL CLUB
Dollie Manning
3092 Grand Ave.
Delana, FL 32720
Phone: (904)734-9977
First event: 1984
When: March
Where: Volusia City Fair Grounds

BASIC INFORMATION:

Type of event: This event includes dolls and teddy bears, antiques, miniatures, doll houses, figurines and toys.

Doll-related products sold: Antique dolls, retired manufactured dolls, modern manufactured dolls, artist dolls, doll clothing, doll accessories, doll supplies, doll-related collectibles

Admission: $2

Average Attendance: 800

DEALER INFORMATION:

Dealers: 90

Space distributed: To participants from previous year first; remaining spaces on first-come, first-serve basis

Cost of booth/table: $40

DOLL STUDY CLUB OF LONG ISLAND
ANNUAL SHOW AND SALE
DOLL STUDY CLUB OF LONG ISLAND
Alyssa Greenburg
60 Richard Rd.
Pt. Washington, NY 11050
Phone: (516)883-8765
First event: 1979
When: April
Where: Sheraton Smithtown Hotel, 110 Vanderbilt Motor Pkwy., Smithtown, NY

BASIC INFORMATION:

Type of event: This event includes dolls and teddy bears, antiques and toys.

Doll-related products sold: Antique dolls, retired manufactured dolls, modern manufactured dolls, artist dolls, doll clothing, doll accessories, doll supplies, doll-related collectibles

Admission: $3.50

Average Attendance: 100

DEALER INFORMATION:

Space distributed: First-come, first-serve basis

Cost of booth/table: 1 table, $55; 2 tables, $100

DOLLS, TEDDY BEARS, TOYS AND
MINIATURES SALE
NORTHWOODS DOLL CLUB
Sharon Geisen
5817 Balsam Rd. NW
Bemidji, MN 56601
Phone: (218)751-8277 CST
Fax: (218)751-8277
When: 2nd Sunday in August
Where: Northern Inn, Hwy 2 West, Bemidji MN
Duration: 1 day
Mailing list: Write to be included.

BASIC INFORMATION:

Type of event: This event includes dolls and teddy bears, antiques, miniatures, dollhouses and toys.

Doll-related products sold: Antique dolls, retired manufactured dolls,

modern manufactured dolls, artist dolls, doll clothing, doll accessories, doll supplies, doll-related collectibles; books

Admission: $3 adults, $1.50 senior citizens

Average Attendance: 300

DEALER INFORMATION:

Dealers: 28

Space available for: Retail businesses selling dolls and related items, antique doll dealers, collectible and modern doll dealers, sellers of dollmaking supplies, sellers of doll clothing and accessories, doll artists, doll manufacturers, appraisers, restoration experts

Space distributed: First-come, first-serve basis

Application process: Send SASE for an application form. Dealer must apply 2 months in advance.

Cost of booth/table: $20

"THE DOLLMAKERS"
WHEATON VILLAGE
Doris Abeling
1501 Glasstown Rd.
Millville, NJ 08332
Phone: (800)99-VILLAGE or (609)825-6800 EST
Fax: (609)825-2410
First event: 1995
When: 3rd or 4th weekend in March
Where: Wheaton Village
Duration: 1 weekend
Mailing list: Write or call to be included.

BASIC INFORMATION:

Type of event: This event includes dolls and doll-related items only.

Doll-related products sold: Antique dolls, retired manufactured dolls, artist dolls, doll clothing, doll accessories, doll supplies, doll-related collectibles

Admission: $6 for adults, $3.50 for kids

Average Attendance: 1,000/day

DEALER INFORMATION:

Dealers: 50-60

Space available for: Retail businesses selling dolls and related items, antique doll dealers, collectible and modern doll dealers, sellers of dollmaking supplies, sellers of doll clothing and accessories, doll artists, doll clubs/organizations, appraisers, restoration experts

Space distributed: To participants from previous year first; remaining spaces on first-come, first-serve basis.

Application process: Send SASE or call for an application form. Dealers must apply in November of previous year.

Cost of booth/table: $60

SPECIAL FEATURES:

Services for collectors: Restorations or appraisals of old/antique dolls

Educational opportunities: 30 minute mini-demonstrations throughout the show

Special exhibits: Estate quality antique dolls and furniture in the Museum of American Glass during the show and folklife dolls from diverse ethnic backgrounds in The Down Jersey Folklife Center.

Door prizes/drawings: Artists and dealers are invited to supply door prizes for the show.

ADDITIONAL INFORMATION:

Wheaton Village is a unique arts institution.

ENCHANTED DOLL CLUB OF EAGLE RIVER DOLL SHOW

Barb Spiess
4971 Rummels Rd.
Conover, WI 54519
Phone: (715)547-3501 CST
Fax: (715)479-2909
First event: 1979
When: 1st Saturday in August
Where: Varies
Duration: 1 day

BASIC INFORMATION:

Type of event: This event includes dolls and teddy bears.

Doll-related products sold: Antique dolls, retired manufactured dolls, artist dolls, doll clothing, doll accessories, doll supplies, doll-related collectibles

Admission: $2

Average Attendance: 600-700

DEALER INFORMATION:

Dealers: 20 dealers and 7 or 8 club members

Space available for: Antique doll dealers, collectible and modern doll dealers, sellers of doll clothing and accessories, doll artists, appraisers, restoration experts

Space distributed: To participants from previous year first; remaining spaces on first-come, first-serve basis. There is usually a waiting list.

Application process: Send SASE for an application form. Call for application form. Dealer must apply before March 15.

Cost of booth/table: $25

SPECIAL FEATURES:

Services for collectors: Restorations, appraisals

Door prizes/drawings: 10-15 door prizes given away thoughout the day.

FALL FESTIVAL OF DOLLS SHOW
LAND O'SKY DOLL CLUB

Marian Maas
13 Hillview Rd.
Asheville, NC 28805
Phone: (704)298-1717 EST
E-mail: dolldr1@aol.com
First event: 1989
When: October
Where: National Guard Armory, Hendersonville, NC
Duration: 1 day
Mailing list: Write, call or e-mail to be included.

BASIC INFORMATION:

Type of event: This event includes dolls and teddy bears.

Doll-related products sold: Antique dolls, retired manufactured dolls, modern manufactured dolls, artist dolls, doll clothing, doll accessories, doll supplies, doll-related collectibles

Admission: $3

Average Attendance: 375-400

DEALER INFORMATION:

Dealers: 65

Space available for: Retail businesses selling dolls and related items, antique doll dealers, collectible and modern doll dealers, sellers of dollmaking supplies, sellers of doll clothing and accessories, doll artists, doll clubs/organizations, appraisers, restoration experts

Space distributed: First-come, first-serve basis. There is usually a waiting list.

Application process: Send SASE, call or e-mail for an application form.

Cost of booth/table: $25

SPECIAL FEATURES:

Services for collectors: Restorations,

cleaning and appraisal of old/antique dolls

Special exhibits: Educational exhibit with new theme each year.

Door prizes/drawings: Entry tickets are drawn for door prizes worth $5-15.

> "MOST OF ALL, CONTINUE TO GROW AND TRY NEW THINGS SO THAT DOLLMAKING WILL ALWAYS BE FUN."
> *Patricia Ryan Brooks, Summerton, SC*

FOREVER YOUNG DOLL SHOW/SALE

Bette Anderson and Darrie Dorsey
222 N. 2nd St.
Mora, MN 55051
Phone: (612)679-2961 CST
First event: 1990
When: End of July or early August
Where: Zion Lutheran Church, S. Hwy 65, Mora, MN
Duration: 1 day
Mailing list: Write or call to be included.

BASIC INFORMATION:

Type of event: This event includes dolls and teddy bears, miniatures, doll houses and toys.

Doll-related products sold: Antique dolls, retired manufactured dolls, modern manufactured dolls, artist dolls, doll clothing, doll accessories, doll supplies, doll-related collectibles

Admission: $2

Average Attendance: 215

DEALER INFORMATION:

Dealers: 16

Space available for: Retail businesses selling dolls and related items, antique doll dealers, collectible and modern doll dealers, sellers of dollmaking supplies, sellers of doll clothing and accessories, doll artists, doll manufacturers, doll clubs/organizations, appraisers, restoration experts

Space distributed: To participants from previous year first; remaining spaces on first-come, first-serve basis.

Application process: Send SASE or call for an application form. Dealer must apply 2 months in advance.

Cost of booth/table: $25

SPECIAL FEATURES:

Services for collectors: Restorations, cleaning of old/antique dolls, repair of modern and composition dolls, costuming services

Door prizes/drawings: Prizes include doll magazines subscriptions and a porcelain collector doll.

ADDITIONAL INFORMATION:
Event is handicapped accessible.

THE 4 DOLLS CO.
Shirley Arndt
2393 Teller Rd. #126
Newbury Park, CA 91322
Phone: (805)399-0136 PST
First event: 1993
When: June
Where: Pasadena Convention Center, 300 East Green St., Pasadena, CA

BASIC INFORMATION:
Type of event: This event includes dolls and teddy bears, antiques, miniatures, doll houses, figurines and toys.
Doll-related products sold: Antique dolls, retired manufactured dolls, modern manufactured dolls, doll clothing, doll accessories, doll supplies, doll-related collectibles
Admission: $5, or $4 with coupon
Average Attendance: 140

DEALER INFORMATION:
Space distributed: First-come, first-serve basis
Cost of booth/table: $120-435

FOX VALLEY AREA DOLL SHOW
Robert and Kristine Loderbauer
N121 Cty. Hwy. N.
Appleton, WI 54915
Phone: (414)730-0292 EST
First event: 1995
When: 2nd Sunday in October
Where: Apple Creek Inn, Depere, WI
Duration: 1 day
Mailing list: Write or call to be included.

BASIC INFORMATION:
Doll-related products sold: Antique dolls, retired manufactured dolls, modern manufactured dolls, doll clothing, doll accessories, doll supplies, doll-related collectibles
Admission: $1
Average Attendance: 325

DEALER INFORMATION:
Dealers: 38
Space available for: Retail businesses selling dolls and related items, antique

doll dealers, collectible and modern doll dealers, sellers of dollmaking supplies, sellers of doll clothing and accessories, restoration experts
Space distributed: To participants from previous year first; remaining spaces on first-come, first-serve basis. There is usually a waiting list.
Application process: Send SASE or call for an application form. Dealer must apply 6 months in advance.
Cost of booth/table: $12

SPECIAL FEATURES:
Souvenirs: Buttons

GOLDEN SPREAD DOLL SHOW
GOLDEN SPREAD DOLL CLUB OF AMARILLO
Jean Dixon, Secretary
Box 46, Hwy. 287
Masterson, TX 79058
Phone: (806)935-7478 or (806)352-5570 CST
First event: 1977
When: Fall
Where: Odd Fellows Hall, 7th and Monroe, Amarillo, TX
Duration: 1 day
Mailing list: Write or call to be included.

BASIC INFORMATION:
Type of event: This event includes dolls and teddy bears, antiques, miniatures, doll houses, figurines and toys.
Doll-related products sold: Antique dolls, retired manufactured dolls, modern manufactured dolls, artist dolls, doll clothing, doll accessories, doll supplies, doll-related collectibles
Admission: Free

DEALER INFORMATION:
Dealers: 25-30
Space available for: Retail businesses selling dolls and related items, antique doll dealers, collectible and modern doll dealers, sellers of dollmaking supplies, sellers of doll clothing and accessories
Space distributed: First-come, first-serve basis
Application process: Send SASE or call for an application form. Dealer must apply 3-4 months in advance.
Cost of booth/table: $20

SPECIAL FEATURES:
Door prizes/drawings: "We draw for door prizes."

Competitions: Competitions include antique, modern, bisque, cloth. Prizes are ribbons and trophies. To apply, complete index card listing category, etc., and include any pertinent information and pin to doll.

HELLO DOLLIES OF LONGMONT DOLL SALE AND SHOW
HELLO DOLLIES OF LONGMONT
Jan Rodriguez
P.O. Box 2597
Longmont, CO 80501
Phone: (303)772-3605 MST
First event: 1984
When: June
Where: Boulder, CO Fairgrounds, Hovert Nelson Rd., Longmont, CO
Duration: 1 day
Mailing list: Write or call to be included.

BASIC INFORMATION:
Type of event: This event includes dolls and teddy bears, miniatures and dollhouses.
Doll-related products sold: Antique dolls, retired manufactured dolls, modern manufactured dolls, artist dolls, doll clothing, doll accessories, doll supplies, doll-related collectibles
Admission: $2.50
Average Attendance: 1,400

DEALER INFORMATION:
Dealers: 95
Space available for: Retail businesses selling dolls and related items, antique doll dealers, collectible and modern doll dealers, sellers of dollmaking supplies, sellers of doll clothing and accessories, doll artists, doll manufacturers, doll clubs/organizations, appraisers, restoration experts
Space distributed: First-come, first-serve basis. There is usually a waiting list.
Application process: Send SASE or call for an application form. Dealer must apply 4-5 months in advance.
Cost of booth/table: $75

SPECIAL FEATURES:
Special exhibits: Competition, antique and collectible display room.
Competitions: Open to anyone. Divisions include professional, non-professional, senior (over 60 years) and junior (18 years and under). Categories include original creations (various media); costuming (various types); re-

productions (various categories). Prizes are ribbons. Competitors should apply on Friday before show. $2 entry fee; $5 for dolls 28″ or taller or 15″ or wider at the base. All dolls entered must be on sturdy bases.

HELLO DOLLIE SALE AND SHOW
HELLO DOLLIE CLUB

Florence Truedall
408 W. Walnut Rd.
Caldwell, ID 83605
Phone: (208)454-8169 MST
First event: 1980
When: October
Where: Caldwell Armory, Caldwell, ID
Duration: Saturday
Mailing list: Write or call to be included.

BASIC INFORMATION:

Type of event: This event includes dolls and dollhouses.
Doll-related products sold: Antique dolls, retired manufactured dolls, modern manufactured dolls, doll clothing, doll supplies
Admission: $2
Average Attendance: 400-500

DEALER INFORMATION:

Space available for: Retail businesses selling dolls and related items, antique doll dealers, collectible and modern doll dealers, sellers of dollmaking supplies, sellers of doll clothing and accessories, doll clubs/organizations
Space distributed: To participants from previous year first; remaining spaces on first-come, first-serve basis. There is usually a waiting list.
Application process: Send SASE for an application form. Dealer must apply 3 months in advance and provide a list of items for sale.
Cost of booth/table: $15

SPECIAL FEATURES:

Door prizes/drawings: Hourly drawings

AN INTERNATIONAL CELEBRATION OF
INNOCENCE SHOW AND SALE
CHILDREN'S MUSEUM

Colleen Sullivan
801 Camino Zozobra
Santa Fe, NM 87501
Phone: (505)982-9264 MST
When: April
Where: La Fonda Hotel, Santa Fe, NM

BASIC INFORMATION:

Type of event: This event includes dolls and teddy bears, antiques, miniatures, dollhouses, figurines and toys.
Doll-related products sold: Antique dolls, retired manufactured dolls, modern manufactured dolls, artist dolls, doll clothing, doll accessories, doll supplies, doll-related collectibles
Admission: $4

DEALER INFORMATION:

Dealers: 90
Space distributed: To participants from previous year first; remaining spaces on first-come, first-serve basis
Cost of booth/table: $45

IOWA KATE SHELLEY DOLL CLUB ANNUAL
DOLL AND TOY FAIR

Dorothy Hurst
10 Western Ave.
West Des Moines, IA 50265
First event: 1978
When: 1st Saturday in May
Where: Holiday Inn, Little Amana, I-80, Amana, IA

BASIC INFORMATION:

Type of event: This event includes dolls and teddy bears, antiques, miniatures, doll houses, figurines and toys.
Doll-related products sold: Antique dolls, retired manufactured dolls, modern manufactured dolls, artist dolls, doll clothing, doll accessories, doll supplies, doll-related collectibles
Admission: $2
Average Attendance: 500-700

DEALER INFORMATION:

Dealers: 40
Space distributed: By invitation only.

LES BOISE DOLL CLUB
UFDC

Jody Davis
8344 Partridge Dr.
Nampa, ID 83686
Phone: (208)465-5359 MST
First event: 1972
When: 1st week after Easter
Where: Nampa Civic Center

BASIC INFORMATION:

Type of event: This event includes dolls and teddy bears, antiques, miniatures, doll houses, figurines, toys.
Doll-related products sold: Antique

dolls, retired manufactured dolls, modern manufactured dolls, artist dolls, doll clothing, doll accessories, doll supplies, doll-related collectibles
Admission: $3, adults; $1, children
Average Attendance: 1,200-1,500

DEALER INFORMATION:

Dealers: 50
Space distributed: To participants from previous year first; remaining spaces on first-come, first-serve basis
Cost of booth/table: $30

LOVING MEMORIES DOLL, BEAR, TOY
AND MINIATURE SHOW
LOVING MEMORIES DOLL CLUB

Karen Falter
3090 S. River Rd. W.
S. Range, WI 54874
Phone: (715)398-7739 CST
First event: 1990
When: Last Saturday in April, last Sunday in September
Where: Superior, WI Curling Club (fairgrounds), Tower Ave., Superior, WI
Duration: 1 day
Mailing list: Write or call to be included.

BASIC INFORMATION:

Type of event: This event includes dolls and teddy bears, miniatures, doll houses, toys.
Doll-related products sold: Antique dolls, retired manufactured dolls, modern manufactured dolls, artist dolls, doll clothing, doll accessories, doll supplies, doll-related collectibles
Admission: $2, adults; $1, children under 12
Average Attendance: 280-300

DEALER INFORMATION:

Dealers: 25-30
Space available for: Retail businesses selling dolls and related items, antique doll dealers, collectible and modern doll dealers, sellers of dollmaking supplies, sellers of doll clothing and accessories, doll artists, doll clubs/organizations, restoration experts
Space distributed: To participants from previous year first; remaining spaces on first-come, first-serve basis. There is usually a waiting list.
Application process: Send SASE or call for an application form. Dealer must apply 3-4 months in advance.
Cost of booth/table: $17.50

SPECIAL FEATURES:

Services for collectors: Restorations, cleaning or appraisals of old/antique dolls available from dealers present.

Door prizes/drawings: Doll value books, doll magazine subscriptions, gift certificates

Souvenirs: Publications provided by doll related editors and fliers promoting other upcoming doll shows/sales.

THE MADISON AREA DOLL CLUB SHOW
MADISON AREA DOLL CLUB

Robbie Wahl
7102 Longmeadow Rd.
Madison, WI 53717
Phone: (608)836-6873 CST
First event: 1973
When: Last Saturday in March
Where: Madison, WI
Duration: 1 day

BASIC INFORMATION:

Type of event: This event includes dolls and teddy bears, antiques, miniatures, doll houses, figurines and toys.

Doll-related products sold: Antique dolls, retired manufactured dolls, modern manufactured dolls, artist dolls, doll clothing, doll accessories, doll supplies, doll-related collectibles

Admission: $3.50
Average Attendance: 700

DEALER INFORMATION:

Dealers: 30-40
Space distributed: First-come, first-serve basis
Cost of booth/table: $30-35

MAGIC VALLEY DOLL SHOW AND BEAR SHOW
JEROME COUNTY FAIR

Pam Kubik
P.O. Box 166, 200 N. Fir St.
Jerome, ID 83338
Phone: (208)324-7209 MST
Fax: (208)324-7059
First event: 1995
When: October
Where: Jerome County Fairgrounds, 200 N. Fir St., Jerome, Idaho
Duration: 1 day
Mailing list: Write or call to be included.

BASIC INFORMATION:

Type of event: This event includes dolls and teddy bears, miniatures and dollhouses.

Doll-related products sold: Antique dolls, retired manufactured dolls, modern manufactured dolls, artist dolls, doll clothing, doll accessories, doll supplies, doll-related collectibles

Admission: $1

DEALER INFORMATION:

Dealers: 25

Space available for: Retail businesses selling dolls and related items, antique doll dealers, collectible and modern doll dealers, sellers of dollmaking supplies, sellers of doll clothing and accessories, doll artists, doll manufacturers, doll clubs/organizations, appraisers, restoration experts

Space distributed: To participants from previous year first; remaining spaces on first-come, first-serve basis.

Application process: Call for an application form. Dealer must apply 3 weeks in advance.

Cost of booth/table: $25

SPECIAL FEATURES:

Door prizes/drawings: Dealers donate an item to be part of drawing.

"WHEN CHOOSING A DOLL, BUY WHAT YOU LIKE. IF THE VALUE DOES NOT INCREASE, AT LEAST YOU HAVE ENJOYED THE DOLL."

Sherrie McCarty, Love of Country, Urbana, OH

METRO PLEX ANNUAL DOLL SHOWS

Fred Tucker
522 Winston
Grand Prairie, TX 75052
Phone: (214)263-4577
First event: 1985
When: March
Where: Plano Convention Centre, Plano, TX

BASIC INFORMATION:

Type of event: This event includes dolls and teddy bears, antiques, miniatures, dollhouses, figures and toys.

Doll-related products sold: Antique dolls, retired manufactured dolls, modern manufactured dolls, artist dolls, doll clothing, doll accessories, doll supplies, doll-related collectibles

Admission: $3, adults; $1, children
Average Attendance: 1,000

DEALER INFORMATION:

Dealers: 79
Space distributed: First-come, first-serve basis
Cost of booth/table: $110 for booth

MICHIGAN DOLL MAKERS GUILD

Virginia B. Withers
24358 Sherbeak Dr.
Clinton Township, MI 48036
Phone: (810)469-3474 EST
When: October
Where: Northfield Hilton, Troy, MI

BASIC INFORMATION:

Admission: $3.50

DEALER INFORMATION:

Cost of booth/table: $55

MID-OHIO'S LARGEST DOLL SHOW AND SALE
MID-OHIO HISTORY MUSEUM AND MID-OHIO DOLL CLUB

Henrietta Pfeifer
700 Winchester Pike
Canal Winchester, OH 43110
Phone: (614)837-5573 EST
First event: 1986
When: April
Where: Aladdin Shrine Temple, 3850 Stelzer Rd., Columbus, OH
Duration: Sunday
Mailing list: Write to be included.

BASIC INFORMATION:

Type of event: This event includes dolls and related items only.

Doll-related products sold: Antique dolls, retired manufactured dolls, modern manufactured dolls, artist dolls, doll clothing, doll accessories, doll supplies, doll-related collectibles

Admission: $3
Average Attendance: 2,500

DEALER INFORMATION:

Dealers: 150

Space available for: Antique doll dealers, collectible and modern doll dealers, sellers of dollmaking supplies, sellers of doll clothing and accessories, doll artists, doll clubs/organizations

Space distributed: To participants from previous year first; remaining spaces on first-come, first-serve basis. There is usually a waiting list.

Application process: Send SASE for an

application form. Dealers must apply 6 months in advance.

Cost of booth/table: $50-130

SPECIAL FEATURES:

Special exhibits: Theme table

MIDWEST CERAMIC SHOW
MIDWEST CERAMIC ASSOCIATION

Joanne Cline
650 Xenia Ave.
Xenia, OH 45385
Phone: (513)372-4545 EST, (513)372-5245
Fax: (513)372-4545
When: April
Where: Hara Arena, 1001 Shiloh Rd., Dayton, OH 45010
Duration: 3 days
Mailing list: Write or call to be included.

BASIC INFORMATION:

Type of event: This event includes dolls, ceramics and supplies.

Doll-related products sold: Modern manufactured dolls, artist dolls, doll clothing, doll accessories, doll supplies

Admission: $4

Average Attendance: 10,000

DEALER INFORMATION:

Dealers: 250

Space available for: Retail business, antique doll dealers, collectible and modern doll dealers, sellers of doll-making supplies, sellers of doll clothing and accessories, doll artists, doll manufacturers

Space distributed: This is an invitation-only event. There is usually a waiting list.

Application process: Send SASE or call for an application form. There is a long waiting list. Applicants chosen from waiting list on the basis of products needed in the show and date of application. Applicants must provide list of products sold.

Cost of booth/table: $300-$325

SPECIAL FEATURES:

Educational opportunities: Dollmaking workshops (sometimes)

Door prizes/drawings: Drawing for a doll (sometimes)

Competitions: Anyone may enter. Ribbons, trophies and scholarships are among the prizes. Apply the Wednes-

day prior to the show. Write for information.

ADDITIONAL INFORMATION:

A percentage of the show profits are donated to charity.

MISS USA DOLL PAGEANT
SHOW AND SALE

Krause Drug and Gift Gallery
Vonnie Perius
Box 391, 124 S. Jefferson
Wadena, MN 56482
Phone: (218)631-2271 or (218)631-4392 CST
First event: 1986
When: August
Where: Wadena National Guard Armory Hwy. 71, North Wadena, MN
Duration: 1 day, Saturday 9-2.
Mailing list: Write or call to be included.

BASIC INFORMATION:

Type of event: This event includes dolls and related items only.

Doll-related products sold: Antique dolls, retired manufactured dolls, modern manufactured dolls, artist dolls, doll clothing, doll accessories, doll supplies, doll-related collectibles, dollhouses

Admission: $1

Average Attendance: 200

DEALER INFORMATION:

Dealers: 50 tables available

Space available for: Antique doll dealers, collectible and modern doll dealers, sellers of dollmaking supplies, sellers of doll clothing and accessories, doll artists, restoration experts

Space distributed: First-come, first-serve basis

Application process: Send SASE for an application form. Dealers must apply 7 months-1 week in advance.

Cost of booth/table: $10 for 5-foot table

SPECIAL FEATURES:

Services for collectors: Free magazines

Door prizes/drawings: Customers may register to win doll prizes when paying admission. Need not be present to win drawing at 2:00.

Competitions: Any doll that is considered pageant material. The doll must arrive on a doll stand in full length formal and be accompanied by a second favorite outfit displayed on an ea-

sel. Then she must answer 2 essay questions in 100 words each or less. Crown and Doll prizes to Queen, and 1st runner up gets a porcelain doll. Competitors should apply 7 months to day before show. Send $10 entry fee and SASE to address above for competition info.

MORRISVILLE DOLL SHOW AND SALE
MADISON HALL ASSOCIATION

Jane C. Messenger, manager
6892 Rt. 291
Marcy, NY 13403
Phone: (315)865-5463 EST
First event: 1994
When: 2nd Saturday in June
Where: SUNY Morrisville Campus, Hamilton Hall, Rte. 20, Morrisville, NY
Duration: 1 day
Mailing list: Write to be included.

BASIC INFORMATION:

Type of event: This event includes dolls and related items only.

Doll-related products sold: Antique dolls, retired manufactured dolls, modern manufactured dolls, doll clothing, doll accessories, doll supplies, doll-related collectibles

Admission: $3.50

Average Attendance: 500-600

DEALER INFORMATION:

Dealers: 55-60

Space available for: Antique doll dealers, collectible and modern doll dealers, sellers of dollmaking supplies, sellers of doll clothing and accessories, doll artists

Space distributed: First-come, first-serve basis. There is usually a waiting list.

Application process: Send SASE for an application form. Dealers must apply 4-5 months in advance.

Cost of booth/table: $40

SPECIAL FEATURES:

Services for collectors: Appraisals of old/antique dolls; clinic for sick dolls—doctor consultation.

Door prizes/drawings: Dealers donate door prizes; some doll magazines.

ADDITIONAL INFORMATION:

All proceeds are given to Madison Hall Association for restoration of courthouse, which dates back to mid-1880s.

MYRTLE BEACH SC ANNUAL DOLL SHOW AND SALE
COASTAL DOLL COLLECTORS CLUB

Mirian Little
507 Main St.
Conway, SC 29526
Phone: (803)248-5643 EST
First event: 1980
When: March
Where: Myrtle Beach Convention Center, 21st Ave. and Oak St., Myrtle Beach, SC

BASIC INFORMATION:

Type of event: This event includes dolls and teddy bears, antiques, miniatures, dollhouses, figurines, toys and jewelry.
Doll-related products sold: Antique dolls, retired manufactured dolls, modern manufactured dolls, artist dolls, doll clothing, doll accessories, doll supplies, doll-related collectibles.
Admission: $3 or $4 for 2 days
Average Attendance: 3,000

DEALER INFORMATION:

Dealers: 130
Space distributed: By invitation only.
Cost of booth/table: $55

NABER KIDS CONVENTION
NABER GESTALT CORPORATION

Janet
8915 S. Suncoast Blvd.
Homosassa, FL 94446
Phone: (904)382-1001 EST, (904)628-7076
Fax: (904)382-1002, (904)628-0611
E-mail: naberkids@aol.com
First event: 1993
When: March or April
Where: Naber Kids Doll Factory at address above

NANCY JO SCHREEDER

305 Robinson St.
Martinez, CA 94553
Phone: (510)229-4190 PST
Fax: (510)229-5369
First event: 1971

BASIC INFORMATION:

Type of event: This event includes dolls, miniatures and toys.
Doll-related products sold: Antique dolls, retired manufactured dolls, modern manufactured dolls, artist dolls, doll clothing, doll accessories,

doll supplies, doll-related collectibles

DEALER INFORMATION:

Space available for: Retail businesses selling dolls and related items, antique doll dealers, collectible and modern doll dealers, sellers of dollmaking supplies, sellers of doll clothing and accessories, doll artists, doll manufacturers, doll clubs/organizations, appraisers, restoration experts

PAYSON DOLL CLUB ANNUAL DOLL SHOW AND SALE

Phyllis Best
804 E. Phoenix St.
Payson, AZ 85541
Phone: (520)474-3107 MST
First event: 1983
When: July
Where: Payson Middle School, 304 South Meadows St., Payson, AZ

BASIC INFORMATION:

Type of event: This event includes dolls and teddy bears, antiques, miniatures, dollhouses, figurines and toys.
Doll-related products sold: Antique dolls, retired manufactured dolls, modern manufactured dolls, artist dolls, doll clothing, doll accessories, doll supplies, doll-related collectibles
Admission: $3 adults; 75¢ children
Average Attendance: 300

DEALER INFORMATION:

Dealers: 56
Space distributed: First-come, first-serve basis
Application process: All profits go to the Special Olympics.
Cost of booth/table: $35 per table

PITTSBURGH AREA DOLL SHOW AND SALES

Sonja Barnes
441 N. Bluff St.
Butler, PA 16001
Phone: (412)283-1923 EST
First event: 1992
When: March
Where: Sheraton Inn North, 910 Sheraton Dr., Mars, PA

BASIC INFORMATION:

Type of event: This event includes dolls and teddy bears, antiques, miniatures, dollhouses, figurines and toys.
Doll-related products sold: Antique

dolls, retired manufactured dolls, modern manufactured dolls, artist dolls, doll clothing, doll accessories, doll supplies, doll-related collectibles
Admission: $3.50
Average Attendance: 500

DEALER INFORMATION:

Dealers: 42
Space distributed: By invitation only.
Cost of booth/table: $30 per table

POLLYANNA DOLL SHOW AND SALE
POLLYANNA DOLL CLUB OF CA

Paula Hube
451 Donner Court
Petaluma, CA 94954
Phone: (707)763-5237
First event: 1987
When: 1st Sunday in February
Where: Petaluma Veterans Bldg., 1094 Petaluma South, Petaluma, CA

DEALER INFORMATION:

Space distributed: To participants from previous years first; remaining spaces on first-come, first-serve basis
Cost of booth/table: $45

ROANOKE VALLEY DOLL CLUB SHOW AND SALE
ROANOKE VALLEY DOLL CLUB

Judy Arrington
Rt. 2, Box 204
Scotland Neck, NC 27874
Phone: (919)826-5483 EST
First event: 1992
When: April
Where: Holiday Inn, 100 Holiday Dr., Exit 173 off I-95, Roanoke Rapids, NC 27870. (919)537-1031.
Duration: 1 day
Mailing list: Write or call to be included.

BASIC INFORMATION:

Type of event: This event includes dolls, teddy bears and toys.
Doll-related products sold: Antique dolls, retired manufactured dolls, modern manufactured dolls, artist dolls, doll clothing, doll accessories, doll supplies, doll-related collectibles
Admission: $2
Average Attendance: 250

DEALER INFORMATION:

Dealers: 20
Space available for: Retail businesses selling dolls and related items, antique

doll dealers, collectible and modern doll dealers, sellers of dollmaking supplies, sellers of doll clothing and accessories, doll artists, appraisers, restoration experts

Space distributed: First-come, first-serve basis

Application process: Send SASE or call for an application form. Dealers must apply 1-6 months in advance.

Cost of booth/table: $25

SPECIAL FEATURES:

Services for collectors: Restorations, cleaning and appraisals of old/antique dolls

ROCKFORD SPRING TOY, DOLL AND BEAR SHOW AND SALE

Jo Ann Reynolds
6058 Daysville Rd.
Oregon, IL 61061
Phone: (815)732-7742 CST
First event: 1984
When: March
Where: Forest Hills Lodge, 9900 Forest Hill Rd., Rockford IL

BASIC INFORMATION:

Type of event: This event includes dolls and teddy bears, antiques, miniatures, dollhouses and toys.

Doll-related products sold: Antique dolls, retired manufactured dolls, modern manufactured dolls, artist dolls, doll clothing, doll accessories, doll supplies, doll-related collectibles

Admission: $2.50

Average Attendance: 1,400

DEALER INFORMATION:

Dealers: 66

Space distributed: To participants from previous year first; remaining spaces on first-come, first-serve basis.

Cost of booth/table: $30 per table

SANTA FE DOLL FESTIVAL
CHILDREN'S MUSEUM

Jean Wiley
801 Camino Zozobra
Santa Fe, NM 87501
Phone: (505)820-0992 MST
When: April
Where: La Fonda Hotel, Santa Fe, NM

BASIC INFORMATION:

Type of event: This event includes dolls and teddy bears, antiques, miniatures,

dollhouses, figurines and toys.

Doll-related products sold: Antique dolls, retired manufactured dolls, modern manufactured dolls, artist dolls, doll clothing, doll accessories, doll supplies, doll-related collectibles

Admission: $4

DEALER INFORMATION:

Dealers: 90

Space distributed: To participants from previous year first; remaining spaces on first-come, first-serve basis

Cost of booth/table: $45

SEONDA'S BIRTHDAY PARTY
SEONDA DOLL CLUB

Peter Mylan
601 Bradford Pkwy.
Syracuse, NY 13224
Phone: (315)446-6246 EST
First event: 1975
When: April
Where: St. Joseph Church, Camillis, NY

BASIC INFORMATION:

Type of event: This event includes dolls and teddy bears.

Doll-related products sold: Antique dolls, retired manufactured dolls, modern manufactured dolls, doll clothing, doll accessories, doll supplies, doll-related collectibles

Admission: $3

Average Attendance: 400-500

DEALER INFORMATION:

Dealers: 40-45

Space distributed: To participants from previous year first; remaining spaces on first-come, first-serve basis.

Cost of booth/table: $35

SPRING BLOSSOMS DOLL SHOW
SOUTHERN ILLINOIS DOLL CLUB, REGION 10, UFDC

Joan Kufskie
209 Sheffield Dr.
Belleville, IL 62223-2634
Phone: (618)397-5263 or (618)234-6463 CST
First event: 1995
When: Sunday after Easter
Where: Ramada Inn, Fairview Hgts., IL 62208
Duration: 1 day
Mailing list: Write or call to be included.

BASIC INFORMATION:

Type of event: This event includes dolls

and teddy bears, miniatures, dollhouses, figurines and paper dolls.

Doll-related products sold: Antique dolls, retired manufactured dolls, modern manufactured dolls, artist dolls, doll clothing, doll accessories, doll supplies, doll-related collectibles, modern collectible dolls and accessories

Admission: $2

Average Attendance: 1,000

DEALER INFORMATION:

Dealers: 40

Space available for: Retail businesses selling dolls and related items, antique doll dealers, collectible and modern doll dealers, sellers of dollmaking supplies, sellers of doll clothing and accessories, doll artists, doll manufacturers, doll clubs/organizations, appraisers, restoration experts

Space distributed: First-come, first-serve basis

Application process: Send SASE or call for an application form. Dealers must apply 6-7 months in advance if possible.

Cost of booth/table: $35

SPECIAL FEATURES:

Services for collectors: Appraisals of old/ antique or collectible dolls

Educational opportunities: Exhibit of collectible "Ginny" dolls

SUMMERTIME WITH BARBIE
PG'S ENCHANTED DOLLS

Gloria Centi
4360 W. Oakland Pk. Blvd.
Ft. Lauderdale, FL 33313
Phone: (954)731-9192 EST
Fax: (954)739-9030
First event: 1994
When: June
Where: St. Jeromes Catholic School, 2601 S.W. 9th Ave., Ft. Lauderdale, FL
Duration: 1 day
Mailing list: Write or call to be included.

BASIC INFORMATION:

Doll-related products sold: Barbie items only

Admission: $3

Average Attendance: 400-500

DEALER INFORMATION:

Dealers: 25-35

Space available for: Retail businesses selling dolls and related items, collectible and modern doll dealers, sellers of doll clothing and accessories, doll manufacturers, doll clubs/organizations, appraisers, restoration experts, all Barbie only

Space distributed: First-come, first-serve basis

Application process: Send SASE or call for an application form.

Cost of booth/table: $50-140

TEXAS DOLL SHOW AND SALES
DOLL COLLECTORS OF IRVING TEXAS

Judy Smith
1404 Cameron
Ft. Worth, TX 76115
Phone: (817)923-5091
First event: 1972
When: April
Where: Arlington Convention Center, 1200 Ballpark Way, Arlington, TX

BASIC INFORMATION:

Type of event: This event includes dolls and teddy bears, antiques, miniatures, doll houses, figurines, toys, books and supplier.

Doll-related products sold: Antique dolls, retired manufactured dolls, modern manufactured dolls, artist dolls, doll clothing, doll accessories, doll supplies, doll-related collectibles

Admission: $4 adults; $1 for children under 12

Average Attendance: 1,000

DEALER INFORMATION:

Dealers: 125

Space distributed: First-come, first-serve basis.

Cost of booth/table: 2 8-ft. tables for $90

TIDEWATER TEDDY BEAR AND
DOLL SHOW
ABC TOYS

Nancy Walker and Edna Smith
1888 Brookwood Rd.
Norfolk, VA 23518
Phone: (804)588-6165 or (804)622-0982 EST
First event: 1991
When: 3rd Saturday in August
Where: Lake Wright Resort and Convention Center, 6280 Northampton Blvd., Norfolk, VA
Duration: 1 day

Mailing list: Write or call to be included.

BASIC INFORMATION:

Type of event: This event includes dolls and teddy bears, miniatures and dollhouses.

Doll-related products sold: Antique dolls, retired manufactured dolls, modern manufactured dolls, artist dolls, doll clothing, doll accessories, doll supplies, doll-related collectibles

Admission: $4; $3 with coupon

Average Attendance: 500

DEALER INFORMATION:

Dealers: 35-40

Space available for: Retail businesses selling dolls and related items, antique doll dealers, collectible and modern doll dealers, sellers of dollmaking supplies, sellers of doll clothing and accessories, doll artists, doll manufacturers, doll clubs/organizations, appraisers, restoration experts

Space distributed: First-come, first-serve basis

Application process: Send SASE or call for an application form.

Cost of booth/table: $150; extra tables $50

SPECIAL FEATURES:

Services for collectors: Restorations or appraisals of old/antique dolls

Educational opportunities: Videos on doll collecting shown.

Door prizes/drawings: Door prizes are given every hour.

Auction: Silent auction of dolls, bears and related items such as videos and books donated by dealers at show

TWICKENHAM DOLL CLUB ANTIQUE TO
MODERN DOLL SHOW AND SALES

Paula Van Netta
2208 Burningtree Dr. SE
Decatur AL 35603
Phone: (205)351-9269 CST
First event: 1969
When: 3rd Saturday in June
Where: Von Braun Civic Center, Huntsville, AL

BASIC INFORMATION:

Type of event: This event includes dolls and teddy bears, antiques, miniatures, dollhouses, figurines and toys.

Doll-related products sold: Antique dolls, retired manufactured dolls,

modern manufactured dolls, artist dolls, doll clothing, doll accessories, doll supplies, doll-related collectibles

Admission: $3

Average Attendance: 1,000-1,200

DEALER INFORMATION:

Dealers: 79

Space distributed: First-come, first-serve basis

Cost of booth/table: $40 per table

UPPER PENINSULA DOLL AND TEDDY
BEAR SHOW AND SALE
PAGE'S DOLLS

Lillian Page
6969 L. 5 Lane
Escanaba, MI 49829
Phone: (906)786-6565 CST
First event: 1992
When: Last Saturday of September
Where: Upper Peninsula State Fairgrounds
Duration: 1 day
Mailing list: Write or call to be included.

BASIC INFORMATION:

Type of event: This event includes dolls and teddy bears, antiques, miniatures, dollhouses, figurines and toys.

Doll-related products sold: Antique dolls, retired manufactured dolls, modern manufactured dolls, artist dolls, doll clothing, doll accessories, doll supplies, doll-related collectibles

Admission: $1

Average Attendance: 300

DEALER INFORMATION:

Dealers: 20

Space available for: Retail businesses selling dolls and related items, antique doll dealers, collectible and modern doll dealers, sellers of dollmaking supplies, sellers of doll clothing and accessories, doll artists, doll manufacturers, doll clubs/organizations, appraisers, restoration experts

Space distributed: To participants from previous year first; remaining spaces on first-come, first-serve basis.

Application process: Send SASE or call for an application form. We would appreciate a photo of display from other shows.

Cost of booth/table: $40 for 1 table; $20 each additional

SPECIAL FEATURES:

Services for collectors: Restoration or

appraisals of old/antique dolls.

Educational opportunities: Dollmaking workshops

Special exhibits: Upper Peninsula area dollmakers will have their dolls on display.

Door prizes/drawings: Porcelain doll donated by award winning artisan Lillian Page.

Souvenirs: Upper Peninsula logo and designs.

Competitions: Dolls are judged by attendees. People's choice award given for best modern/best antique. Seeley Distribution award given for best doll made from Seeley mold. This award is given by Lillian Page, Seeley distributor. Categories include baby dolls/all bisque dolls, lady dolls, French dolls/German dolls. Trophies for Best of Show—Modern and Best of Show—Classic (antique). Competitors should apply in May. Ask for competition form and we will send it to them.

WALNUT VALLEY DOLL SHOW
WINFIELD ARTS AND HUMANITIES
COUNCIL

Ruth Ann Yeary
700 Gary, Suite A
Winfield, KS 67156-3135
Phone: (316)221-2712 ext. 2 CST
First event: 1990
When: August
Where: Winfield Community Center at Baden Square, 700 Gary, Winfield, KS
Duration: 1 day, 10-4.
Mailing list: Write or call to be included.

BASIC INFORMATION:

Type of event: This event includes dolls and related items only.

Doll-related products sold: Antique dolls, retired manufactured dolls, modern manufactured dolls, artist dolls, doll clothing, doll accessories, doll supplies, doll-related collectibles

Admission: $2

Average Attendance: 750

DEALER INFORMATION:

Dealers: 16

Space available for: Retail businesses selling dolls and related items, antique doll dealers, collectible and modern doll dealers, sellers of dollmaking supplies, sellers of doll clothing and accessories, doll artists, doll clubs/organizations, appraisers

Space distributed: To participants from previous year first; remaining spaces on first-come, first-serve basis. "New vendors must be approved." There is usually a waiting list.

Application process: Send SASE or call for an application form. Dealers must apply 8-9 months in advance.

Cost of booth/table: $35

SPECIAL FEATURES:

Services for collectors: Appraisals

Educational opportunities: Workshops, videos

Special exhibits: Theme varies each year.

Door prizes/drawings: Businesses contribute items for door prizes.

Competitions: Artists and doll collectors may enter. Categories include antiques, antiques and collectibles, composition, foreign, cloth, vinyl, hard plastics, china, bisque (after 1925), miniature, paper, other, handcrafted—original sculpture, antique reproduction, modern reproduction, cloth, other media, best dressed doll. Prizes are cash and merchandise from those who donate. Competitors should apply prior to the last week before the show.

ADDITIONAL INFORMATION:

Food, beverages and lunch are served in the dining room.

EXHIBITS

IN CELEBRATION OF THE DOLL:
THE FIGURE IN CLOTH

Kathleen A. Bricker
36437 Saxony
Farmington, MI 48335
Phone: (810)471-0660 EST
Fax: (810)471-0694
E-mail: kaywozb@aol.com
When: Debuts in late October—travels throughout the year.
Where: This is a traveling exhibit that is shown in museums, doll shows and conventions, quilt shows, galleries.
Duration: Year-round

BASIC INFORMATION:

Description: Dolls must be made of cloth and should be free standing. Types of dolls range from the traditional to the contemporary and avant garde; from humorous to fanciful to contemplative. Limited to 30. The goal of In Celebration of the Doll: The Figure in Cloth is to bring to the public's attention the imaginative and skillful manipulation of cloth, the most basic of media, into exquisite, fanciful and contemplative works of art. By using the doll as the center of this collection, the exhibit also pays homage to the oldest and most revered of subjects: the human figure in its many forms and conceptualizations.

EXHIBITORS' INFORMATION:

Application process: By invitation. Artists are chosen based on submitted slides and information. Selection is dependant upon originality of design and technique and general balance of the exhibit. An attempt is made to introduce new artists yearly. Send SASE to address above in January.

Cost: Free

7
Organizations

A Guide to Chapter Seven

*S*ince I began research on this book more than a year ago, nearly everyone I've spoken with at shows, at shops and on the phone has stressed the importance of networking. Several have told me that at least for beginners, this chapter will be the most important chapter of all. After all, what fun is a hobby if you have no one to share it with—no one who can appreciate a wonderful find at a flea market, a beautiful one-of-a-kind artist doll, or the latest manufacturer's edition? What good is a career if you do not have the support of your peers, and if you in turn are not able to help out those who are just getting started in the business?

Every organization listed on these pages was born out of the need to make connections within the industry. The result is a very loving, caring community of artists and collectors who believe, for the most part, that sharing is more important than competing, and that personality is more important than value.

If you are always dying to tell somebody about the latest addition to your collection, but you can never find anyone who seems to care, this chapter is for you. Find a club or organization with regular meetings and activities in your area, and you will be lonely no longer! It is always nice to have someone to call about a particular doll, even if it's just to ask, "Do you think this is a good deal?" or "Have you ever met that artist? He's wonderful!" If there is no collector's organization available in your area, contact the United Federation of Doll Clubs to begin your own. The UFDC will have suggestions on how to get started.

If you are a doll artist, you will find that belonging to a doll artist's organization will not only provide opportunities for new friendships but will also greatly enhance your business. National doll organizations such as the Maine Society of Doll and Bear Artists will help you find answers to all kinds of business and legal questions. Such organizations also share table space at shows to make them more financially rewarding. Finally, contacts within the industry will keep you abreast of the newest doll supplies on the market and any changes in the industry. If you belong to a juried organization like the National Institute of American Doll Artists or the Original Doll Artists Council of America, you have the added benefit of prestige. Your work is taken more seriously if you are accepted into the fold of other artists.

New artists will benefit from joining groups that are less demanding in their requirements. Connecting with artists who know the ropes will help newer artists find a place in this growing industry. All of this can be accomplished with a few phone calls to the organizations on these pages.

The Listings

Presidents of local and regional organizations change annually, so the contact person listed may not be the correct contact person when you read this book. You may have to do some detective work. The UFDC will have an updated list of contact people for all its branch organizations if the address or phone number provided here is no longer correct.

We have included meeting information to give you an idea of where and when the organization meets, if at all. Meeting locations, dates and times are likely to change, however, so it is always best to contact the organization prior to attending a meeting.

The listings include contact people for each organization, as well as who the organization is for, including a statement of purpose if provided. Information about meetings, the number of members, branches, membership requirements and the application process and fees or dues is included. In addition, information about club activities and publications is listed. ❧

Organizations

ACADEMY OF AMERICAN DOLL ARTISTS

Joyce Miko
73 N. Spring St.
Concord, NH 03301
Phone: (603)226-4501 EST
Established: 1994

BASIC INFORMATION:

Type of organization: An international organization for original doll artists.
Members: 160
Branches: There are plans for 1 in Virginia and 1 in Ohio.

REQUIREMENTS:

Membership requirements: Open
Membership fees/dues: $35/year

ADDITIONAL INFORMATION:

Activities/events: Marketing program enables members to share booth space at shows throughout the country; also offers educational programs and workshops.

> "BUY WHAT YOU LOVE, NOT WHAT YOU THINK
> YOUR FAMILY AND FRIENDS WILL."
> *Retagene Hanslik, Arcadia, CA*

AFTER 5 BARBIE DOLL CLUB OF MINNESOTA

Lee Ann Peterson
2311 Humboldt Ave. S. #4
Minneapolis, MN 55405
Phone: (612)377-7633 CST
Established: 1990

BASIC INFORMATION:

Type of organization: A local organization for collectors of Barbie.
Statement of purpose: To provide information about collecting, buying or selling Barbie dolls.
Meetings: Every 6 weeks.
Members: 10

REQUIREMENTS:

Membership requirements: Juried
Application process: Collectors may attend 1 meeting as a guest. Application may be made after the meeting if openings occur. New members are chosen

by unanimous vote of members.
Membership fees/dues: $25/year

ADDITIONAL INFORMATION:

Activities/events: Meetings, projects for conventions, parties, sponsorship of a mini-convention, donations to charities.

ANNALEE DOLL SOCIETY

Sharon Eldridge, manager
P.O. Box 1137
Meredith, NH 03253-1137
Phone: (800)433-6557 EST
Fax: (603)279-6659
Established: 1983

BASIC INFORMATION:

Type of organization: A national organization for doll collectors, original doll artists, antique doll dealers, doll crafters and owners of retail businesses selling dolls.
Members: 6

REQUIREMENTS:

Membership requirements: Open
Membership fees/dues: $29.95/year

ADDITIONAL INFORMATION:

Activities/events: Members have a summer (usually June) and fall (usually end of October) auction.

ASSOCIATION OF PEOPLE WHO PLAY WITH DOLLS

Elinor Peace Bailey
1779 East Ave.
Hayward, CA 94541
Phone: (510)582-2702 PST
Established: 1992

BASIC INFORMATION:

Type of organization: An international organization for doll collectors, original doll artists, antique doll dealers, doll crafters and owners of retail businesses selling dolls.
Members: 1,200

REQUIREMENTS:

Membership requirements: Open
Membership fees/dues: $10/year

Publication: Membership includes quarterly 8-page newspaper.

BARBIE AND KEN NEW YORK DOLL COLLECTOR'S CLUB

Virginia Walker, President
523 E. 14th St. #7F
New York, NY 10009
Phone: (212)260-4439 EST
E-mail: vmwarch@aol.com
Established: 1994

BASIC INFORMATION:

Type of organization: A local organization for original doll artists, owners of retail businesses and collectors of Barbie and family.
Statement of purpose: To have fun sharing knowledge about collecting Barbie dolls.
Meetings: Monthly (2nd Wednesday). Meeting includes business portion followed by show-and-tell and/or program. A theme is set for the meeting. Dolls are brought in by members to suit the theme, then a program or guest speaker follows.
Members: 39

REQUIREMENTS:

Membership requirements: Open
Membership fees/dues: $50/year

ADDITIONAL INFORMATION:

Publication: BKNY News, free to members; 1 sample issue available to non-members, subscription $12/year. *BKNY News* is a bimonthly newsletter containing articles on upcoming dolls; doll shows in the area; Dr. Ken (restoration); feature article (usually about vintage); and BKNY Briefs (member/ meeting news).

BARBIE COLLECTOR'S CLUB OF SAN DIEGO

Cynthia Chapman, President
P.O. Box 654
Spring Valley, CA 91976
Phone: (614)660-8107 PST
E-mail: cyn4barbie@aol.com
Established: 1990

BASIC INFORMATION:

Type of organization: A local organization for collectors of Barbie and other Mattel dolls.

Statement of purpose: To encourage Barbie collecting and to educate and share information among collectors.

Meetings: Monthly

Members: 25

REQUIREMENTS:

Membership requirements: Juried

Application process: Candidate must attend three meetings and complete an application form. A sponsor is desirable. Vote is by ⅔ majority and is based on the following questions: Are the goals of the person similar to those of the club? What is the motivation for joining? Does the candidate participate and show willingness to share and contribute information?

Membership fees/dues: $20/year

ADDITIONAL INFORMATION:

Activities/events: Annual Christmas charity, club show sale, annual restoration workshop

Publication: The Barbie Beat is free to members and available to nonmembers for $6/year. It is 3-4 pages and covers the club's last 2 meetings. Also contains the latest Barbie news, released dolls, rumors of upcoming dolls; and a classified section.

BOISE TREASURE DOLL CLUB

P.O. Box 45183
Boise, ID 83711
Established: 1982

BASIC INFORMATION:

Type of organization: A local organization for doll collectors.

Statement of purpose: To share our common interest in dolls, to learn from all educational sources as well as each other, to promote doll collecting as a hobby, and to contribute to our community, as a group, whenever we are able.

Meetings: Monthly

Members: 19

REQUIREMENTS:

Membership requirements: Juried. Club limit is 25 members.

Application process: After attending 2 club meetings, applicants fill out application form for membership consideration. Current members vote, in applicant's absence, on acceptance. Applicants must be 18 years of age or older and own a small personal doll collection, any kind.

Membership fees/dues: $30/year ($23 UFDC, $7 local)

ADDITIONAL INFORMATION:

Activities/events: Annual doll show and sale which includes dolls, teddy bears, miniatures and toys (mostly related to dolls).

BRITISH DOLL ARTISTS' ASSOCIATION

June Rose Gale, chairman
49 Cromwell Rd.
Beckenham, Kent BR3 LLL
GREAT BRITAIN
Phone: (0181)658-1865
Established: 1979

BASIC INFORMATION:

Type of organization: A national organization for original doll artists.

Statement of purpose: To promote and publicize the work of original doll artists in the United Kingdom.

Meetings: Annual

Members: 45

REQUIREMENTS:

Membership requirements: Juried.

Application process: Written application may be made, at any time, to the chairman, but will only be considered at the AGM when all members present vote. Applicant must prove the originality of their work by submitting original artwork, samples and drawings and are accepted if work is of a good professional standard. Applicants are required to have a proven sales record.

Membership fees/dues: £24/year (UK members only)

ADDITIONAL INFORMATION:

Activities/events: Long-term exhibitions are held annually at venues throughout the country. One day mini-exhibitions are held at doll fairs. Two slide programs are available for presentation.

Publication: British Doll Artists Artists Directory, free to members and nonmembers. Available from Mrs. June Rose Gale, £2 or $5 (including postage). The booklet lists all current members of the association. It is illustrated and describes the members' work, etc. It is published once every two years, but is updated yearly.

The Association has recently decided to accept foreign associate members. Members keep in contact via a private newsletter that is circulated quarterly.

CHATTY CATHY COLLECTORS CLUB

Lisa Eisenstein, editor
P.O. Box 140
Readington, NJ 08870-0140
Established: 1989

BASIC INFORMATION:

Type of organization: An international organization for all types of Chatty dolls (pull-string talkers) by Mattel, 1960s.

Statement of purpose: To bring together and keep informed collectors of Mattel Chatty dolls from the 1960s.

Meetings: Annual. Luncheon is held in a different section of the United States. Past luncheons have been in MN, OH, IL, CA and NJ/PA. This gathering includes opportunities to meet other members and a sale area.

Members: 210

REQUIREMENTS:

Membership requirements: Open.

Application process: Members pay annual dues, must abide by a 7-day return policy if selling, and must be ethical in dealings with members.

Membership fees/dues: $28 by a calendar year.

ADDITIONAL INFORMATION:

Activities/events: The organization donates to a specific charity each year. Members have sent a Chatty doll to a museum in India and have donated dolls to Russian orphanages. Currently distributes sewn-to-specification dolls to AIDS children in American hospitals.

Publication: Chatty News, free to members; sample available to nonmembers for $4. Quarterly publication, approximately 40 pages. Members share photos and write about their collections, doll shows, Chatty information, history, clothing, annual luncheon, contests and fun.

COASTAL DOLL COLLECTORS CLUB OF SOUTH CAROLINA

Miriam R. Little
507 Main St.
Conway, SC 29526
Phone: (803)248-5643

BASIC INFORMATION:

Statement of purpose: The Coastal Doll Collectors Club of South Carolina is a working club interested in doll collecting, teddy bears and other related items. The club holds a monthly educational program and a monthly workshop to make and study dolls.

Meetings: Monthly. Business meetings followed by programs on doll-related subjects and refreshments.

Members: 29

REQUIREMENTS:

Membership requirements: Applicants must attend 3 meetings, have a doll collection of at least 10 dolls and be able to present a program and host a club meeting.

Membership fees/dues: $25/year

ADDITIONAL INFORMATION:

Activities/Events: Annual doll show and sale. State Day luncheon and program every 3 years.

Publication: Monthly newsletter, available free to members; includes monthly information and other related items from UFDC.

COLUMBIA DOLL CLUB

Esther Borgis
14268 Ordner Dr.
Strongsville, OH 44136
Phone: (216)238-6275 EST
Established: 1986

BASIC INFORMATION:

Type of organization: An international organization for doll collectors.
Meetings: Monthly
Members: 35

REQUIREMENTS:

Membership requirements: Open
Membership fees/dues: $6/year above Federation dues.

ADDITIONAL INFORMATION:

Activities/events: Doll show each July in conjunction with Strongsville Historic Society.

CREATIVE DOLLMAKERS SOCIETY OF NEW MEXICO

Sunny Stansbury
P.O. Box 1730
Corrales, NM 87048
Phone: (505)897-9148 MST
Established: 1993

BASIC INFORMATION:

Type of organization: A local organization for cloth doll crafters.

Statement of Purpose: To provide opportunities for people interested in dollmaking. The club holds workshops and sponsor a cloth doll category at the New Mexico State Fair.

Meetings: Monthly, 3rd Thursday, 7:00 P.M.

Members: 50

REQUIREMENTS:

Membership requirements: Open
Membership fees/dues: Free

CROOKED TREE HOLLOW RAG DOLL CLUB

Frannie Meshorer
335 Magothy Bridge Rd.
Pasadena, MD 21122
Phone: (410)360-8504 EST
Established: 1994

BASIC INFORMATION:

Type of organization: A local organization for cloth doll lovers, including doll collectors, original doll artists, antique doll dealers, doll crafters and owners of retail businesses selling dolls.

Statement of purpose: The Crooked Tree Hollow Rag Doll Club is an organization of women gathering to support and nurture their own, and each other's, creativity and to share knowledge, abilities and gifts through making cloth dolls.

Meetings: Monthly. A tea party and a tour of the "dollhouse" rooms of Crooked Tree Hollow is always held for new members.

Members: 50+

REQUIREMENTS:

Membership requirements: Open
Membership fees/dues: $2/gathering; pay only if you attend.

ADDITIONAL INFORMATION:

Activities/events: Tea parties, programs, visiting doll artists, play shops, doll shows and sales, field trips, shopping trips, charity projects, classes and presentations.

Publication: Free to members, available to nonmembers for $12/year. *Crooked Tree Hollow Rag Doll Club* includes CTH calendar of events, past and upcoming meeting information, club member biographies, listing of upcoming doll-related events, "recipe" of the month, club contest information and doll tips and ideas.

DOLL ARTISAN GUILD

Maureen Dugan
35 Main St.
Oneonta, NY 13820
Phone: (607)432-4977 EST
Fax: (607)432-2042
Established: 1977

BASIC INFORMATION:

Type of organization: An international organization for original doll artists and doll crafters.

Statement of purpose: The Doll Artisan Guild is a not-for-profit organization that sponsors a School of Dollmaking and Seminar Program.

REQUIREMENTS:

Membership requirements: Open
Membership fees/dues: $26/year

ADDITIONAL INFORMATION:

Activities/Events: The Doll Artisan Guild sponsors a School of Dollmaking and Seminar Program, competitions, and other educational programs.

Publication: *The Doll Artisan* is free to members and is a magazine for porcelain dollmakers. For more information, see the Guild's listing in chapter ten.

THE DOLL EXPRESS

Rae-Ellen Koenig
PA Tpke. Exit 21, 1 mile south on Rte. 272
Reamstown, PA 17567
Phone: (717)336-2414
Fax: (717)336-1262
Established: 1992

BASIC INFORMATION:

Type of organization: An international organization of doll collectors, original doll artists, antique dealers, doll crafters and owners of retail businesses selling dolls.

Statement of purpose: We are a 100-showcase co-operative selling dolls and bears, old and new, for collectors and dealers alike.

DOLL STUDY CLUB OF JAMESTOWN, NY

Lynn Dole, president
Box 5
Ashville, NY 14710
Phone: (716)763-0128 EST
Established: 1983

BASIC INFORMATION:

Type of organization: A local organization for doll collectors.
Meetings: Monthly.
Members: 40

REQUIREMENTS:

Membership requirements: Limited. They have a waiting list.
Application process: Membership committee goes to see doll collection of prospective member. Applicant must attend two meetings as guest and write letter requesting membership.
Membership dues/fees: $30

ADDITIONAL INFORMATION:

Activities/events: Mini regional luncheons, annual doll show.

THE DOLLY FOLLIES

Donna Bitzold
3420 Cherry Hill Dr.
Brookfield, WI 53005
Phone: (414)781-5288 CST
Established: 1990

BASIC INFORMATION:

Type of organization: A local organization for original cloth doll artists and crafters.
Meetings: Monthly
Members: 15

REQUIREMENTS:

Membership requirements: Open
Membership fees/dues: $15/year

"EDUCATE YOURSELVES SO THAT YOU NEVER HAVE CAUSE TO REGRET HAVING BOUGHT THE DOLLS YOU'VE BOUGHT."

Marilyn Prescott, Center Stage Emporium, Kingston, NH

FABULOUS FLITTERS

Joanne Jones
7107 Weldon Ave.
Bakersfield, CA 93308
Phone: (805)399-5935 PST
Established: 1988

BASIC INFORMATION:

Type of organization: A local organization for cloth doll artists.
Meetings: Weekly
Members: 12

REQUIREMENTS:

Membership requirements: Invitation only.
Membership fees/dues: Free

ADDITIONAL INFORMATION:

Activities/events: The club has sponsored shows and displays for various groups throughout the year.

FOOTHILLS RAG DOLL CLUB

Evelyn Chapman, Treasurer
36 W. Main St.
Broadalbin, NY 12025
Phone: (518)883-5328 EST
Established: 1992

BASIC INFORMATION:

Type of organization: A local organization for doll collectors, doll crafters.
Statement of purpose: To make rag dolls. The club is a spin-off of Treyon Doll Club in Gloversville, New York. Members donate their dolls to social services, including earthquake victims, hospitals, etc.
Meetings: Monthly, 2nd Monday.
Members: 15

REQUIREMENTS:

Membership requirements: Open
Membership fees/dues: Free

FRISCO FLOOZIES

Jan Cochrane, Treasurer
131 30th Ave.
San Francisco, CA 94116
Phone: (415)564-0838 PST
Established: 1993

BASIC INFORMATION:

Meetings: Monthly
Members: 12

ADDITIONAL INFORMATION:

Activities/events: The club goes on field trips and holds teaching meetings. Members make dolls, attend doll shows together and enter competitions. The club hopes to expand in the future by adding associate members.

G.I. JOE COLLECTORS' CLUB

Brian Savage, Director
12513 Birchfalls Dr.
Raleigh, NC 27614
Phone: (919)847-5263 or (800)772-6673 EST
Fax: (919)847-5132
E-mail: savagebm@aol.com
Established: 1985

BASIC INFORMATION:

Type of organization: International organization of collectors of G.I. Joe.
Statement of Purpose: The club promotes all past, present and future G.I. Joe products.
Members: 500+

REQUIREMENTS:

Membership requirements: Open
Membership fees/dues: $35

ADDITIONAL INFORMATION:

Activities/events: Custom uniform sets and special premiums are available.
Publication: Monthly newsletter includes collecting tips as well as upcoming specials and exclusives. Membership also includes a subscription to *Master Collector.*

GALS & DOLLS CLUB

Joan Ott
13740 Pierce Rd.
Saratoga, CA 95070
Phone: (408)867-0699 PST
Established: 1986

BASIC INFORMATION:

Type of organization: A local organization for original doll artists.
Statement of purpose: To make dolls. Members try to have a hands-on project each meeting and a well-known teacher. The club's aim is to expand the world of cloth dolls. Some members do sculpted dolls.
Meetings: Monthly, 3rd Tuesday.
Members: 50

REQUIREMENTS:

Membership requirements: Open
Membership fees/dues: $32/year; $20 for associates

GOLDEN SPREAD DOLL CLUB

Jean Dixon
Box 46, Hwy. 287
Masterson, TX 79058
Phone: (806)935-7478
Established: 1976

BASIC INFORMATION:

Type of organization: An international organization for doll collectors and original doll artists.
Meetings: Monthly
Members: 14

REQUIREMENTS:

Membership requirements: By invitation only.
Membership fees/dues: UFDC dues

ADDITIONAL INFORMATION:

Activities/events: Annual doll show in the fall.

THE GOODENOUGH GROUP

Penny McIntire Kendall
7312 S. Lowden Rd.
Oregon, IL 61061-9737
Phone: (815)652-4237 CST
Fax: (815)652-4237

BASIC INFORMATION:

Type of organization: An organization for original doll artists.
Statement of purpose: The Goodenough Group is an informal organization of up to 12 artists who cooperate on show exhibits and advertising.

REQUIREMENTS:

Membership requirements: By invitation only.

HAPPY HOBBY DOLL CLUB

Ruth A. Messler, Treasurer
P.O. Box 994
Alton, NH 03809-0994
Phone: (603)875-6750 EST
Established: 1984

BASIC INFORMATION:

Type of organization: A regional organization for doll collectors, especially collectors of Sasha, composition and Barbie dolls; antique doll dealers; owners of retail businesses selling dolls; original doll artists; doll crafters; paper doll artists; authors of doll books and doll costuming books.
Statement of purpose: To create, stimulate and maintain an interest in all matters pertaining to making and col-
lecting dolls and to establish and promote educational and philanthropic endeavors through dolls. The long-range goal to accomplish this objective is to establish a doll museum/educational center in the Lakes Region/Alton area of New Hampshire.
Meetings: Monthly. In addition to conducting necessary business, the club has slide programs and educational presentations, shows and shares dolls and related items and pertinent information, and holds instructional programs.
Members: 16

REQUIREMENTS:

Membership requirements: Open
Application process: Members must be 18 years or older and own at least 10 dolls (any type, or made by owner). Active members have all voting rights and must attend 5 meetings or more per year. Associate members are not required to attend meetings, have no voting privileges and must pay a postage surcharge to receive HHDC newsletter.
Membership fees/dues: $23/year

ADDITIONAL INFORMATION:

Activities/events: Regular programs include an annual doll show, participation in civic activities, regular doll donations and financial assistance to worthy community and national organizations, such as police departments and hospitals.
Publication: HHDC monthly newsletter free to members. $5 surcharge to associate members to cover postage. Presents information on local, state and national doll events, business happenings in the doll world, cartoons and other items of interest, plus a list of upcoming events. At times includes "auto-doll-ographies" of HHDC members.

> "DOLL ARTISTS WHO WANT TO GET BETTER SHOULD WORK AT IT EVERY DAY AND SEEK OUT ARTISTS THEY ADMIRE. THEY SHOULD ASK QUESTIONS AND NOT FEEL PUT DOWN BY CONSTRUCTIVE CRITICISM."
> *Patricia Ryan Brooks, Summerton, SC*

HELLO DOLLIES OF LONGMONT

Jan Rodriguez
P.O. Box 2597
Longmont, CO 80503
Phone: (303)772-3605 MST
Established: 1980

BASIC INFORMATION:

Type of organization: A local organization for doll collectors, original doll artists and doll crafters.
Statement of purpose: To create, stimulate and maintain an interest in all matters pertaining to doll collecting and to establish and promote educational endeavors through dolls.
Meetings: Monthly.
Members: 21

REQUIREMENTS:

Application process: Guests are welcome to attend meetings. After attending three meetings, prospective members may apply by written letter for membership, which will be voted upon by the club. A committee will visit to view collections, which must include a minimum of ten collectible dolls. Members must agree to hold a meeting in their home, act as co-hostess and prepare a program on some aspect of doll collecting.
Membership dues/fees: $23. Includes membership in UFDC and a subscription to Doll News.

ADDITIONAL INFORMATION:

Activities/events: The club sponsors a yearly doll show held in June. Through their philanthropic endeavors, members have donated toys to the Longmont Safehouse and Head Start for years. The club helped the Longmont Police Department establish their Teddy Bear program and the Longmont Coalition for Abused and Battered Women. Recently they donated toys and other needed items to Boulder County Social Services to be used in therapy for abused children. Many members have shared their collections with other clubs and given programs for schools, museums and nursing homes. The club also holds picnics, socials, luncheons and parties.

IMITATION OF LIFE CONSTRUCTION COMPANY, A DOLLMAKERS GUILD

Karen Wooton
P.O. Box 531
Poway, CA 92064
Phone: (619)486-0232 PST
Established: 1990

BASIC INFORMATION:

Type of organization: A local organization for doll collectors, original doll artists and doll crafters.

Statement of purpose: To share the joy and love of dollmaking and collecting, and to bring this enjoyment to the community through exhibits, workshops and programs.

Meetings: Monthly. Held at Holy Cross Lutheran Church, 3450 Clairemont Dr., San Diego. Meetings include announcements, program (speakers or hands-on activities), sharing, library, challenges and workshops.

Members: 85

REQUIREMENTS:

Membership requirements: Open.
Membership dues/fees: $25

ADDITIONAL INFORMATION:

Activities/Events: Dimensions in Dollmaking doll exhibit, an annual exhibit held in conjunction with San Diego Quilt Show. International and national dollmakers included.

Publication: Blueprints, available free to members and to nonmembers. Newsletter membership only is $12. Newsletter includes guild activities and information on doll conferences, classes and workshops, plus tips, a doll pattern, contest information and articles. They periodically arrange special exhibits in galleries to promote the public's interest in cloth and polymer dollmaking.

INTERNATIONAL DOLL DOCTOR'S CLUB

Dwaine E. Gipe
1406 Sycamore Rd.
Montoursville, PA 17754
Phone: (717)323-9604 EST
Established: 1995

BASIC INFORMATION:

Type of organization: An international organization for collectors interested in doll restoration.

Statement of purpose: To communicate ideas, methods and philosophy.

Meetings: Quarterly. Held in conjunction with the Eastern National Doll and Toy Shows, Gaithersburg, MD.

Members: 50-100

REQUIREMENTS:

Membership requirements: Open, nonprofessional and professional. Levels of proficiency indicated by awards method of recognition.

IOWA KATE SHELLEY DOLL CLUB

Dorothy Hurst
10 Western Ave.
West Des Moines, IA 50265
Phone: (515)225-7269
Established: 1969

BASIC INFORMATION:

Type of organization: A regional organization for doll collectors and original doll artists.

Meetings: 9 times/year
Members: 45-50

REQUIREMENTS:

Membership Requirements: Open
Membership Fees/Dues: UFDC dues plus $5

ADDITIONAL INFORMATION:

Activities/Events: Annual doll show in May.

JAN HAGARA COLLECTORS CLUB

Doris Priess
40114 Industrial Park N.
Georgetown, TX 78626
Phone: (512)863-9499 CST
Fax: (512)869-2093
Established: 1987

BASIC INFORMATION:

Type of organization: An international organization for doll collectors, original doll artists, antique doll dealers, doll crafters and owners of retail businesses selling dolls.

Meetings: Local chapters meet quarterly; national or regional meetings yearly.

Members: 10,000-12,000.
Branches: 18. Write or call for list.

REQUIREMENTS:

Membership Requirements: Open
Membership Fees/Dues: $44 new members, $39 to renew membership. Membership includes free figurine.

JERRI COLLECTOR'S SOCIETY

Jim McCloud
651 Anderson St.
Charlotte, NC 28205
Phone: (704)333-3211 EST
Fax: (704)333-7706
Established: 1987

BASIC INFORMATION:

Type of organization: A national organization for original doll artists.
Members: 3,000-4,000

REQUIREMENTS:

Membership Requirements: Open
Membership Fees/Dues: $10/year, includes newsletter which comes out 2 times a year.

ADDITIONAL INFORMATION:

Activities/Events: Annual convention

JUST DOLLINKS

Barbara Johnston
5713 Louis Lane
Austin, TX 78757-4418
Phone: (512)451-4820 CST
Fax: (512)451-3897
E-mail: bj@herbalgram.org
Established: 1993

BASIC INFORMATION:

Type of organization: A local organization for cloth doll artisans.

Statement of Purpose: To share skills and enthusiasm for cloth dollmaking with other artisans. The club has a charitable project each year and holds workshops with national teachers attending.

Meetings: Monthly
Members: 25-30

REQUIREMENTS:

Membership Requirements: Open
Membership Fees/Dues: $15/year

ADDITIONAL INFORMATION:

Activities/Events: Seminar held the last weekend in May sponsored by *Dollmaker's Journal* magazine. The seminar is called "Dollmaker's Magic Seminar" with top teachers from all of US.

Publication: Dollmaker's Journal, available to nonmembers. $5 per issue. Back issues only SASE. Write Dollmaker's Journal, 2900 W. Anderson Lane, #20-244, Austin, TX 78757-1124.

LAWTONS COLLECTORS GUILD

Anna Ryan
P.O. Box 969
Turlock, CA 95381
Phone: (209)632-3655 PST
Fax: (209)632-6788
Established: 1989

BASIC INFORMATION:

Type of organization: An international organization for doll collectors.
Members: 2,000

REQUIREMENTS:

Membership Requirements: Open
Membership Fees/Dues: $20 new members, $10 renewal.

ADDITIONAL INFORMATION:

Activities/Events: Has held conventions in the past.
Publication: Membership includes quarterly newsletter.

LES BEBES OF SOUTHERN NJ

Jim or Mary Calio
108 Yelka Ave.
Vineland, NJ 08360
Phone: (609)692-9260 EST
Established: 1980

BASIC INFORMATION:

Type of organization: An international organization for doll collectors, original doll artists, antique doll dealers, doll crafters, owners of retail businesses selling dolls.
Meetings: Monthly
Members: 35

REQUIREMENTS:

Membership Requirements: Invitation only. Must own 10 dolls.
Membership Fees/Dues: $8 and UFDC dues.

ADDITIONAL INFORMATION:

Activities/Events: 1 doll show and sale/year (June)

LES BOISE DOLL CLUB

Jodie Davis
8344 Partridge Dr.
Nampa, ID 83686
Established: 1970

BASIC INFORMATION:

Type of organization: An international organization for doll collectors, original doll artists, antique doll dealers,

doll crafters and owners of retail businesses selling dolls.
Meetings: Monthly
Members: 20

REQUIREMENTS:

Membership Requirements: Open
Membership Fees/Dues: UFDC dues

ADDITIONAL INFORMATION:

Activities/Events: The club holds a doll show in the spring, makes dolls for battered children, and presents seminars and slide shows when requested.

LOVING MEMORIES DOLL CLUB

Karen Falter
3090 S. River Rd. W.
South Range, WI 54874
Phone: (715)398-7739 CST
Established: 1991

BASIC INFORMATION:

Type of organization: A regional organization for doll collectors, original doll artists, antique doll dealers, doll crafters and owners of retail businesses selling dolls.
Meetings: Monthly
Members: 12

REQUIREMENTS:

Membership Requirements: Open
Membership Fees/Dues: $10/year

ADDITIONAL INFORMATION:

Activities/Events: The club holds 2 shows and sales/year (last Saturday in April and September). Profits are used to enable members to go to additional shows through year. Members also donate dolls to Salvation Army at Christmas.

THE MAD DOLLMAKERS

Diane Gloystein
6741 Crooked Creek Dr.
Lincoln, NE 68516
Phone: (402)421-3365 CST
Established: 1992

BASIC INFORMATION:

Type of organization: A local organization for doll crafters.
Meetings: Monthly. Meetings are learning sessions on every aspect of cloth dollmaking. Members share their latest creations with each other.
Members: 30

REQUIREMENTS:

Membership Requirements: Open. 30

member limit. Has a waiting list.
Membership Fees/Dues: $15/year; $8 associate

ADDITIONAL INFORMATION:

Activities/events: Annual show in September
Publication: The *Mad Dollmakers* newsletter available for free to members.

MADAME ALEXANDER DOLL CLUB

Billie Stevens, president
P.O. Box 330
Mundelein, IL 60060
Phone: (708)949-9200 CST (national office)
Fax: (708)949-9201 (national office)
Established: 1983

BASIC INFORMATION:

Type of organization: An international organization for doll collectors, original doll artists, collectors of Madame Alexander Dolls, doll crafters and owners of retail businesses.
Statement of purpose: To study, research, discuss and write about Madame Alexander Dolls, to collect and preserve them, and to conduct any and all activities that will promote collection of Madame Alexander Dolls and related items.
Meetings: Annual, all members; Board meets monthly
Members: 10,000

REQUIREMENTS:

Membership requirements: Open
Membership fees/dues: $10 introductory offer, first year; $20 renewal

ADDITIONAL INFORMATION:

Activities/Events: Annual convention (1996, Las Vegas), several premieres (1996, NY, TX, CA)
Publication: The *Review*, available to members only.

MAINE SOCIETY OF DOLL & BEAR ARTISTS, INC.

Barb Giguere, executive director/president
P.O. Box 124
Scarborough, ME 04070-0124
Phone: (207)883-0822 EST
Fax: (207)883-0822
E-mail: bkhd60a@prodigy.com
Established: 1992

BASIC INFORMATION:

Type of organization: An international organization for original doll and teddy bear artists. Associate membership includes people making fine handcrafted doll- and bear-related items, such as furniture, jewelry, etc.

Statement of purpose: To promote artist-made dolls and bears as an art form and to promote high standards of craftsmanship and quality. Priorities include educating others to appreciate artist-made dolls and bears, and continued education for members. Members work together to present artist-made pieces at trade shows throughout the world.

Meetings: Monthly. Usually the second Sunday of each month.

Members: 100

REQUIREMENTS:

Membership requirements: Juried.

Application process: To apply, request an invitation that details the application process. Quality of materials and workmanship is judged and answers to a detailed questionnaire are considered by the jury committee.

Membership dues/fees: $18, subject to change

ADDITIONAL INFORMATION:

Activities/Events: Group participation in major shows, Dolls Along the Mohawk show in October in Utica, NY area. Co-sponsors Small Wonders Show/Sale each spring with Maine Historical Society.

Publication: Networking News, free to members, available to nonmembers by subscription only ($25/year). Includes valuable business information for artists, supply sources, show information, etc.

MICHIGAN DOLL MAKERS GUILD

Virginia Withers, President
24358 Sherbeck Dr.
Clinton Township, MI 48036
Phone: (810)469-3474
Established: 1978

BASIC INFORMATION:

Type of organization: A state-wide organization for original doll artists and doll crafters working in porcelain.

Meetings: Monthly
Members: 60

REQUIREMENTS:

Membership Fees/Dues: $20

ADDITIONAL INFORMATION:

Activities/Events: Annual doll show in October, convention every 4 years.

Publication: Free to members. Includes club happenings.

MINNESOTA VALLEY DOLL CLUB

Jeanne Dorsey, secretary
Minneapolis, MN
Phone: (612)824-2357, (612)835-3958 CST
Established: 1982

BASIC INFORMATION:

Type of organization: A local organization for doll collectors.

Meetings: Monthly
Members: 12

REQUIREMENTS:

Membership Requirements: Open
Membership Fees/Dues: $20

ADDITIONAL INFORMATION:

Activities/Events: Holds show and sale in summer to benefit battered women's shelters. Participates in Jamboree Council and their benefit in the Fall.

NABER KIDS COLLECTOR'S CLUB

Wanda Naber
127 Swilgert Ave.
Lexington, KY 40505
Phone: (606)293-5209 EST
Fax: (606)293-0393
Established: 1993

BASIC INFORMATION:

Type of organization: An international organization for collectors of Naber Kids.

Statement of Purpose: To celebrate diversity, share interest in Naber Kids and have fun.

Meetings: Annually. A club doll is introduced by H.P. Naber. This doll is only available to club members.

Members: 250

REQUIREMENTS:

Membership Requirements: Open
Membership Fees/Dues: $25 to join. $15/year for renewal.

ADDITIONAL INFORMATION:

Activities/Events: Fund-raising for Save the Earth Foundation and St. Jude's Children's Hospital.

Publication: Naber Kids News Report is free to members and available to non-members for $10/year. The publication showcases new dolls and includes news, letters and articles pertaining to the history of Naber Kids.

NATIONAL CLOTH DOLL MAKERS ASSOCIATIONS (NCDMA)

Judy Waters
1601 Provincetown Dr.
San Jose, CA 95129-4742
Phone: (408)253-3656 PST
Established: 1986

BASIC INFORMATION:

Type of organization: An international organization for doll collectors, original doll artists, doll crafters (cloth dolls only).

Members: 2,000

REQUIREMENTS:

Membership Requirements: Open

ADDITIONAL INFORMATION:

Activities/Events: Biannual conference

NORTHWOODS DOLL CLUB

Sharon Geisen, Secretary/Treasurer
5827 Balsam Rd. NW
Bemidji, MN 56601
Phone: (218)751-8277 CST (home), (218)755-3750 (work)
Fax: (218)751-8277
Established: 1986

BASIC INFORMATION:

Type of organization: A local organization for doll collectors, antique doll dealers, original doll artists, doll crafters.

Meetings: Monthly
Members: 18

REQUIREMENTS:

Membership Requirements: Open. Applicant must have a doll collection of 10 or more dolls and must be 18 years or older.

Membership Fees/Dues: $25/year

ADDITIONAL INFORMATION:

Activities/Events: Annual doll show

OHIO BARBIE™ DOLL COLLECTORS CLUB

Elva Brodnick, chairman
1493 E. 361st St.
Eastlake, OH 44095
Phone: (216)942-1493 EST
Established: 1992

BASIC INFORMATION:

Type of organization: A statewide organization for doll collectors, original doll artists, collectors of Barbie dolls, doll crafters and owners of retail businesses selling dolls.

Statement of Purpose: Open to Barbie fans and friends, for sharing Barbie friendship and fun.

Meetings: Bimonthly. Meetings include programs on Barbie topics and "show and tell."

Members: 150+

REQUIREMENTS:

Membership Requirements: Open
Membership Fees/Dues: $10/year

ADDITIONAL INFORMATION:

Publication: The Barbie Beat is free to members. It includes club news, Barbie current events, news of upcoming doll shows, Club Shoppe, members' Want and Wish ads and Barbie book reviews. It usually runs 8-12 pages. Club also has members in 8-9 other states, plus Canada and Italy.

ORIGINAL DOLL ARTISTS' ASSOCIATION

Pattie Bibb, President
247 Overlook Dr.
Chuluota, FL 32766-9688
Phone: (407)365-6396 EST
Established: 1991

BASIC INFORMATION:

Type of organization: A national organization for original doll artists.

Statement of Purpose: The Original Doll Artists' Association is an educational Association dedicated to conducting educational workshops and seminars in all phases of original dollmaking and encouraging creative doll artists to display their work. ODAA shall further seek and encourage recognition of this art form by the established art and doll communities.

Meetings: 1st Tuesday of the month, September-June. There is a demonstration or a hands-on program at each meeting. Past programs have included

balancing your doll, hatmaking and eye painting.

Members: 51

REQUIREMENTS:

Membership Requirements: Open

Application process: There are 3 categories of membership: Associate (receives newsletter); Apprentice (those wishing to learn dollmaking); Artist-Active (doll artists). Apprentices may apply for Artist membership upon completion of 3 dolls (no time limit).

Membership Fees/Dues: Associate, $15/year. Apprentice and artist, $35/year.

ADDITIONAL INFORMATION:

Activities/Events: Day-long Saturday workshops for Apprentice and Artist members covering different aspects of dollmaking.

Publication: The ODAA Newsletter is free to members. It is a monthly publication which includes meeting minutes, informational handouts about programs, biographical outlines of members and many articles about all phases of dollmaking. Associate members apply from all over the US. They receive the monthly newsletter (10 per year) and other informational handouts. They may attend meetings at any time for an additional fee at the door.

ORIGINAL DOLL ARTISTS COUNCIL OF AMERICA (ODACA)

Sandra Wright Justiss, president
720 Maplewood Ave.
Ambridge, PA 15003
Phone: (412)266-1492 EST
Established: 1976

BASIC INFORMATION:

Type of organization: An international organization for original doll artists. Aux-ODACA is available for collectors and patrons.

Statement of purpose: To promote original artists and their work, to achieve and maintain a high quality of handmade doll making, and to educate collectors and the public about the field of original dolls and doll making.

Meetings: Annual.

Branches: 64

REQUIREMENTS:

Membership requirements: Juried.

Application process: Write to membership chairman for application packet. Members are chosen based on quality of work, craftsmanship and artistry.

Membership fees: $25

ADDITIONAL INFORMATION:

Activities/Events: Annual luncheon/convention, business meeting.

Publication: ODACA newsletter, free to members. Quarterly publication.

PAYSON DOLL CLUB

Phyllis Best
804 E. Phoenix St.
Payson, AZ 85541
Phone: (520)474-3107 MST
Established: 1980

BASIC INFORMATION:

Type of organization: An organization for doll collectors, original doll artists and doll crafters.

Meetings: Monthly

Members: 15

REQUIREMENTS:

Membership Requirements: Open
Membership Fees/Dues: $15/year

ADDITIONAL INFORMATION:

Activities/Events: Annual doll show in July.

PIECEMAKERS DOLL CLUB— HELLO DOLLIES

Judy Clemens, president
1720 Adams Ave.
Costa Mesa, CA 92626
Phone: (714)641-3112 PST
Fax: (714)641-2883
E-mail: 7552.3442@compuserve.com
Established: 1988

BASIC INFORMATION:

Type of organization: A local organization for doll crafters.

Statement of purpose: To provide an opportunity for dollmakers to share their talents with each other and encourage one another in new areas.

Meetings: Annual

Members: 20

REQUIREMENTS:

Membership requirements: Open
Membership dues/fees: $35/quarter

ADDITIONAL INFORMATION:

Activities/Events: Special features include friendship dolls passed along from one another for three months, each person making a different part of the doll. Once a year dolls are made and donated to a local children's hospital. An ornament exchange and pot-luck are featured in December. Doll-maker's Challenge Week is a yearly symposium with doll teachers from all over the country. A new pattern is given each month.

Publications: Hello Dollies Newsletter, available free to members.

Piecemakers Hello Dollies Doll Club is affiliated with Piecemakers Country Store, a 12,000-square-foot craft store. Piecemakers offers over 200 different classes each quarter, bringing doll teachers from all over the country.

PIN-ELLA-PS DOLL CLUB

Drusilla Esslinger, Secretary
RFD#2, Box 630
Madison, KS 66860
Phone: (316)437-2656 CST (Drusilla Esslinger) or (913)234-6677 (Beverly Radefeld)
Fax: (913)234-6678 (Beverly Radefeld)
Established: 1990

BASIC INFORMATION:

Type of organization: A regional organization for doll collectors, original doll artists, doll crafters and anyone interested in dolls.
Meetings: Monthly
Members: 40

REQUIREMENTS:

Membership Requirements: Open
Membership Fees/Dues: $20/year

ADDITIONAL INFORMATION:

Activities/Events: Doll classes, fund-raisers, doll shows and nonprofit activities, such as making dolls for a battered women's group.
Publication: Newsletter with paid membership.

> "DOLL COLLECTING IS A GAMBLE, SO BUY ONLY WHAT YOU LOVE. DON'T EXPECT BIG RETURNS IN JUST A FEW YEARS."
>
> *Emily Manning, Aunt Emily's Doll House, Riverdale, MD*

PHYLLIS' COLLECTORS CLUB

Phyllis Parkins
2301 Old Saint James Rd.
Rolla, MO 65401
Phone: (573)364-7849 CST
Fax: (573)364-2448
Established: 1989

BASIC INFORMATION:

Type of organization: A national organization for collectors of Phyllis Parkins' dolls.
Members: 1,500

REQUIREMENTS:

Membership Requirements: Open
Membership Fees/Dues: $22.50/year

ADDITIONAL INFORMATION:

Activities/Events: Conventions in even-numbered years. A special collector's doll available to members only comes out every year.
Publication: Membership includes 3 newsletters.

THE PROFESSIONAL DOLLMAKERS ART GUILD

Jack Johnston
1447 N. Carrington Lane
Centerville, UT 84104
Phone: (800)560-4958, (801)299-9908
Fax: (801)299-9088
E-mail: jjdolls@aol.com
Established: 1993

BASIC INFORMATION:

Type of organization: A national organization for original doll artists and doll crafters.

ADDITIONAL INFORMATION:

For more information, see the interview with Jack Johnston opening chapter ten.

Q.P. DOLL CLUB

Andrea Perkins
℅ Sweet P's
8459 Portland Place
McLean, VA 22102
Phone: (703)734-3251 EST
Established: 1992

BASIC INFORMATION:

Type of organization: A local organization for original cloth doll artists and doll crafters.
Meetings: Quarterly
Members: 50

REQUIREMENTS:

Membership Requirements: Open membership to Northern Virginia area.
Membership Fees/Dues: $7/year includes quarterly newsletter

ADDITIONAL INFORMATION:

Activities/Events: Monthly demo speakers and workshops. Makes dolls for children in Fairfax Hospital.

ROANOKE VALLEY DOLL CLUB

Judy Arrington, President
Rt. 2, Box 204
Scotland Neck, NC 27874
Phone: (919)826-5483 EST
Established: 1990

BASIC INFORMATION:

Type of organization: A local organization for doll collectors and doll crafters.
Meetings: Monthly
Members: 10

REQUIREMENTS:

Membership Requirements: Open
Membership Fees/Dues: $10/year

ADDITIONAL INFORMATION:

Activities/Events: Sponsors an annual doll show and sale.

ROGUE VALLEY CLOTH DOLL CLUB

Dixie Dalbec, president
350 Gibbon Rd.
Central Point, OR 97502
Phone: (503)826-4191 PST
Established: 1994

BASIC INFORMATION:

Type of organization: A local organization for doll collectors and doll crafters.
Statement of purpose: To provide an educational forum for its members through meetings, workshops, newsletters, challenge activities and an annual doll show. The club encourages dollmaking skills, creativity and collecting.
Meetings: Monthly. Club meetings are fun and educational. The highlight is the opportunity for doll club members to show and discuss newly created dolls. Also, members assist one another in the solution of doll crafting problems.
Members: 14

REQUIREMENTS:

Membership requirements: Open to anyone at least 18 years of age who is interested in making and promoting cloth dolls.

Membership fees/dues: $15/year

ADDITIONAL INFORMATION:

Activities/Events: Challenge activities, educational programs, doll show and gallery exhibits, exhibits at historical societies and participation in child-craft programs. The club members donate cloth dolls or toys to a community agency.

Publication: *Dolls "R" Us News*, free to members. Available to nonmembers. Contact Midge Van Zandt, 196 Rene Dr., Shady Cove, OR, 97539. Cost is $7/year. Monthly publication contains a President's Message, book review, doll pattern, profiles about members and story or letter by the club mascot, Dasha.

This is a busy, friendly club of people who love cloth dolls. They meet four times a year to sew on a Saturday. During these "Sewing Saturdays," they do a club project and enjoy fellowship. There is an annual club barbecue in August and a Christmas party with doll exchange among members.

RUSSIAN AND AMERICAN DOLLMAKERS ASSOCIATION (AND FRIENDS), INC. (RADA)

Lydia Aleshin
10630 Gorman Rd.
West Laurel, MD 20723-1113
Phone: (301)498-9685 EST
Russian Contact: Tania Baeva, Vavilova Str., 44-3-95, Moscow, 117333 Russia; Box Number 14047, Attn. BAEVA; Phone: (011)(7)095-135-1771; Fax: (011)(7)095-292-6511
Established: 1993

BASIC INFORMATION:

Type of organization: An international organization for doll collectors, original doll artists, antique doll dealers, doll crafters, owners of retail businesses selling dolls.

REQUIREMENTS:

Membership Requirements: Open
Membership Fees/Dues: Lifetime dues at present time $15.

ADDITIONAL INFORMATION:

Activities/Events: Shares information on starting a doll business. Promotes making dolls for orphanages. Plans a cruise conference in the future.

> "IT COSTS AS MUCH TO MAKE A GOOD DOLL AS A BAD DOLL. CONTINUE YOUR EDUCATION."
> *Linda Nachbar, Cascade Doll Shoppe, Grand Rapids, MI*

SEYMOUR MANN, INC.

Ron Webster, Vice President of Merchandising
230 Fifth Ave., Suite 1500
New York, NY 10001
Phone: (212)683-7262 EST
Fax: (212)213-4920
Established: 1944

BASIC INFORMATION:

Type of organization: An international organization for doll collectors, original doll artists and owners of retail businesses.

Statement of purpose: To recreate the original designs of doll artists at reasonable prices.

Branches: 4, in Atlanta, Chicago, Dallas and Los Angeles. Write for list or check your local telephone directory.

REQUIREMENTS:

Membership requirements: Open.
Membership dues/fees: $7.50 for a catalog.

ADDITIONAL INFORMATION:

Publication: Seymour Mann Collectible Doll catalog, available by mail. A full-color catalog illustrating available dolls for purchase.

THE SOCIETY OF THE PERMAIN BASIN DOLL ARTISANS

Elisabeth Horne, president
4209 S. County Rd. 1290
Odessa, TX 79765
Phone: (915)563-5557 or (915)563-3946 EST
Fax: (915)563-1522
Established: 1983

BASIC INFORMATION:

Type of organization: An international organization for doll collectors, original doll artists, antique doll dealers, doll crafters and owners of retail businesses.

Statement of purpose: To learn the correct way to make beautiful porcelain dolls, to learn the value of collectibles, and to learn to tell a "fake."

Meetings: Monthly. Has special teachers, speakers and projects at each meeting.

Members: 27 locally

Branches: 4: Lannon, WI; Bethalto, IL; Odessa, TX; Oneonta, NY. Write or call for list.

REQUIREMENTS:

Membership requirements: Open.
Membership dues/fees: $36/year

ADDITIONAL INFORMATION:

Activities/Events: Classes, competition and shows.

Publication: SPBDA News, available free to members and nonmembers. Publication includes list of monthly activities and projects for meetings, and information and products.

SOUTH JERSEY DOLLS AND TOYS CLUB

Jim or Mary Calio
108 Yelka Ave.
Vineland, NJ 08360
Phone: (609)692-9260 EST
Established: 1955

BASIC INFORMATION:

Type of organization: An international organization for doll collectors, original doll artists, antique doll dealers, doll crafters and owners of retail businesses selling dolls.

Meetings: Monthly
Members: 15

REQUIREMENTS:

Membership Requirements: Invitation only. Must own 10 antique dolls.
Membership Fees/Dues: UFDC dues

ADDITIONAL INFORMATION:

Activities/Events: 2 shows and sales/year (April and November).

STEILACOOM DOLL CLUB

Carole Tinsley, Founder
P.O. Box 88611
Steilacoom, WA 98388
Phone: (206)584-5131 PST (day), (206)582-0762 (evening)
Fax: (206)588-1528
Established: 1990

BASIC INFORMATION:

Type of organization: A regional organization for doll collectors, original doll artists and doll crafters. Focus is on cloth dollmaking, collecting and designing.

Statement of Purpose: To promote the enjoyment, making and history of cloth dolls, enhance dollmaking skills and share ideas and information.

Meetings: Monthly. All are welcome to attend, not just cloth dollmakers.

Members: 25

REQUIREMENTS:

Membership Requirements: Open

Membership Fees/Dues: $3/month

ADDITIONAL INFORMATION:

Activities/Events: Holds classes with professional teachers; sponsors doll show, Girl Scout tea and library displays.

Publication: Monthly newsletter. Nonmembers send SASE. Newsletter includes information on club activities, club members and doll shows, plus patterns and general information.

"AN ARTIST MUST WORK FROM THE HEART IF HER WORK IS TO BE LOVED."

Clara M. Allen, Powell River, BC, Canada

TAYO'S DOLL CLUB

Emma Allebes, Owner
10127 Fair Oaks Blvd.
Fair Oaks, CA 95628
Phone: (916)967-5479 PST
Established: 1984

BASIC INFORMATION:

Type of organization: A local organization for original cloth doll artists.

Meetings: Monthly

Members: 15

REQUIREMENTS:

Membership Requirements: Open

Membership Fees/Dues: $60/6 months

ADDITIONAL INFORMATION:

Activities/Events: $25 of the dues pays for a workshop where each member receives a total of 4 patterns and a packet of cloth. At the second meeting during the 6-month period each member is asked to bring an attached head and body that will be made into a Friendship Doll. This "head and

body" is passed from member to member. Arms, legs, clothes and other details are added. Every June and December, Emma Allebes has a tea in her home at which time the finished dolls are presented to their original owners.

TIMELESS TREASURE DOLL CLUB

Norma Owen
859 John Adams Pkwy.
Idaho Falls, ID 83401-4024
Phone: (208)522-3410 MST
Established: 1985

BASIC INFORMATION:

Type of organization: A regional organization for doll collectors, original doll artists, antique doll dealers, doll crafters and owners of retail businesses selling dolls.

Meetings: Monthly, 3rd Saturday.

Members: 85-90

REQUIREMENTS:

Membership Requirements: Open

Membership Fees/Dues: $10/year, includes monthly newsletter.

ADDITIONAL INFORMATION:

Activities/Events: Sponsors fall annual doll show (September), field trips and charity auction. Also donates Christmas gifts to women's domestic violence shelters.

TINSELTOWN BARBIE DOLL COLLECTORS CLUB

Donna Silverman
14045 Valerio St.
Van Nuys, CA 91405
Phone: (918)908-0919 PST
Fax: (818)908-9866
Established: 1989

BASIC INFORMATION:

Type of organization: A local organization for Barbie doll collectors.

Meetings: Monthly. Members discuss Barbie collecting, keep informed of what's new in the Barbie world, display recent purchases and have fun.

Members: 20

REQUIREMENTS:

Membership requirements: Open.

Membership fees/dues: none

ADDITIONAL INFORMATION:

Activities/Events: Provides workshops

and convention helpers to national Barbie Convention.

Publication: Tinseltown Barbie Doll Collectors Newsletter

TRYON TREASURES DOLL CLUB

Judy George
1201 A. Hwy. 70 E.
New Bern, NC 28560
Phone: (919)637-7933 EST
Established: 1991

BASIC INFORMATION:

Type of organization: A local organization for doll collectors, original doll artists, antique doll dealers, doll crafters and owners of retail businesses selling dolls.

Meetings: Monthly

Members: 24

REQUIREMENTS:

Membership Requirements: Open

Membership Fees/Dues: UFDC dues plus $2

ADDITIONAL INFORMATION:

Activities/Events: Sponsors doll show and sale in September. Donates to charitable organizations. Club outings to other shows.

TUCSON THREADHEADS

Lynne A. Calhoun, secretary
4430 N. Rockcliff Place
Tucson, AZ 85750
Phone: (520)749-0107 or (520)620-0555 MST
Fax: (520)792-3311
Established: 1993

BASIC INFORMATION:

Type of organization: A local organization for cloth doll crafters.

Statement of purpose: To network, to share individual talents with each other.

Meetings: Monthly, third Thursday. Members meet at each other's homes and have a program or demonstration at every meeting.

Members: 20

REQUIREMENTS:

Membership requirements: Open to those interested in cloth doll making.

Membership dues/fees: $1/month

ADDITIONAL INFORMATION:

Publication: A quarterly newsletter for members only.

TWICKENHAM DOLL CLUB

Paula Van Netta
2208 Burningtree Dr. SE
Decatur, AL 35603
Phone: (205)351-9269 CST
Established: 1970

BASIC INFORMATION:

Type of organization: A local organization for doll collectors, original doll artists.
Meetings: Monthly
Members: 40

REQUIREMENTS:

Membership Requirements: Open
Membership Fees/Dues: $5 plus UFDC dues

ADDITIONAL INFORMATION:

Activities/Events: Sponsors annual doll show, 3rd Saturday in June. Makes dolls for charitable organizations.

UNITED FEDERATION OF DOLL CLUBS, INC.

10920 N. Ambassador Dr., Suite 130
Kansas City, MO 64153
Phone: (816)891-7040 CST
Fax: (816)891-8360
Established: 1948

BASIC INFORMATION:

Type of organization: An international organization for doll collectors, original doll artists, antique doll dealers, doll crafters and owners of retail businesses selling dolls.
Meetings: Individual clubs have meetings. There are regional conferences throughout the year. There is an annual national convention held for 1 week, usually during the summer.
Members: 16,000
Branches: 871 internationally, 900 members at large. Write or call for list.

REQUIREMENTS:

Membership Requirements: Open
Membership Fees/Dues: $23/year for club members, $25/year for members at large, $433/year for international members.

ADDITIONAL INFORMATION:

Activities/Events: Has regional conferences, national convention and Research Center For Dolls located in Des Plaines, IL. Offers seminar kits. Has educational department with over 500 slides and videos for various programs.
Publication: Membership includes a subscription to quarterly magazine *Doll News.*

VINYL GODDESS CLUB OF DALLAS

Debbie Gatlin-Lelewicz
911 Wayside Way
Richardson, TX 75080
Phone: (214)238-0480 CST
Established: 1995

BASIC INFORMATION:

Type of organization: A local organization for collectors of Barbie dolls.
Statement of Purpose: To educate and preserve the history of Barbie and her fashions.
Meetings: Monthly meetings are generally held the 1st Sunday afternoon of each month. Each meeting includes a program about Barbie so that members will learn about vintage to current Barbies.
Members: 25

REQUIREMENTS:

Membership Requirements: Open
Application process: Applicant must have a collection of 10 or more Barbies or Barbie friend dolls.

WORLD WIDE DOLLMAKERS

Betty Omohundro
3364 Pine Creek Dr.
San Jose, CA 95132
Established: 1980

BASIC INFORMATION:

Type of organization: An international organization for doll collectors, original doll artists, antique doll dealers, doll crafters and owners of retail businesses selling dolls.
Members: 200
Branches: 5—Texas, Arizona and California

REQUIREMENTS:

Membership Requirements: Open
Membership Fees/Dues: $420/year

ADDITIONAL INFORMATION:

Activities/Events: Annual conference every summer.
Publication: Membership includes a periodical that comes out every 3 months.

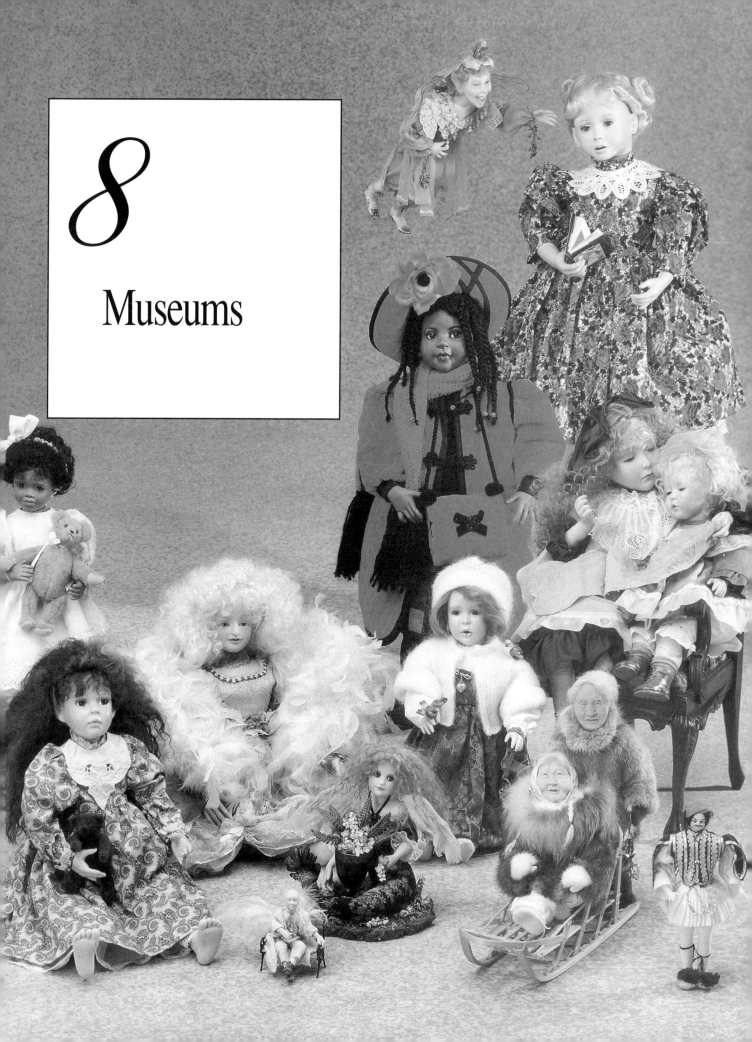

8

Museums

A Guide to Chapter Eight

$\mathcal{M}$useums bring to life the historical significance of dolls. The museums listed on these pages are exclusively for dolls, or include several doll exhibits. The interviews on the following pages give the reader some idea of the various types of museums of interest to doll collectors. Museums are also great places to locate experts, and many offer appraisal and restoration services and wonderful gift shops as well. All doll collectors and artists will enjoy visiting these unique collections and learning more about their hobby and the role it plays in the history of the world. Why not visit one of these museums during a vacation? If you are planning a visit, be sure to call first to verify that the hours listed here are still correct.

The Listings

The museum listings include the hours and admission cost of the museum, the year in which it was founded and what the collection includes. A description of the museum and its exhibits is sometimes provided. In addition, special features, such as tours, educational programs, gift shops and other information are also listed. If provided, the museum's history is included under "Additional Information."

Dorothy Tancraitor of the Yellow Brick Road Doll and Toy Museum

BY ALICE P. BUENING

Alice P. Buening is editor of *Children's Writer's and Illustrator's Market,* published by Writer's Digest Books. She is also a lifelong fan of *The Wizard of Oz* (it's her very favorite movie).

Most everyone has seen the classic film *The Wizard of Oz* at least a half dozen times. And anyone who's watched it knows how difficult it is to get to "somewhere over the rainbow." First you need a cyclone. Then you must get bonked on the head and travel with your dog through dreamland in a spinning, flying house, finally crash-landing on top of a ruby-slippers-clad wicked witch in a land of little people. And getting back home is even tougher!

Well, that was 1939—a lot has changed since then. These days you can get to Munchkinland from the New Jersey Turnpike. Okay, it's not the "real" Munchkinland, but The Yellow Brick Road Doll and Toy Museum in Mullica Hill, New Jersey, is as close as you can get (outside of Hollywood). Dorothy Tancraitor and her husband Steve have been running the museum, which houses a collection of thousands of dolls for show and sale, since 1987.

Follow the Yellow Brick Road

To reach the museum from the street, patrons follow a real yellow brick road leading to the back-door entrance. But the golden path doesn't stop there. Just as in MGM's Oz, it's lengthy and filled with interesting, albeit odd, sights.

"The first thing you see is a fountain. You circle it and shoot through the backyard past a sign that says Munchkinland," Dorothy Tancraitor says. "Then there's Glinda [the Good Witch of the North]—she's made from a department store dummy. Glinda is enclosed in a glass case with a little dancing girl. Kids can press a button and make her dance. Around back there is a little house. The wicked witch's feet are sticking out from underneath, and Dorothy is peeking out

Dorothy stands beside the sign at the entrance of the museum to welcome its many visitors.

the back window. She has just landed in Munchkinland. It's a fascinating place."

The yellow brick road winds through Dorothy and Steve's acre and a half of ground. On the way, visitors find a man of straw standing near a fence flanked by black crows. He's life-size and has footprints painted next to him where patrons stand to have their photos taken with the Scarecrow. A bicycle-riding Wicked Witch of the West flies above a tree.

And just as in the movie, there's a talking tree, with eyes that open and close with the push of a button. When large groups of kids visit, Steve converses with them through the tree from an out-of-the-way barn. (The tree, however, does not throw its apples.) There are even lunch box trees under which visitors can picnic.

"Although we're only open Friday, Saturday and Sunday, people can come in our backyard anytime and have lunch. Not a weekend goes by that we don't have fifty, sixty, a hundred people in the backyard," Dorothy says.

A castle also stands along the yellow brick road. It houses some of Dorothy's treasures—very collectible

Oz pieces. The castle is also home to the Wizard of Oz himself (made from a department store Santa mannequin). Wearing a top hat and striped vest, he stands over a badge of honor for the Cowardly Lion, a diploma for the Scarecrow, and a heart for the Tin Man—gifts the great and powerful wizard bestowed upon Dorothy Gale's traveling companions.

Visitors leaving the castle walk into the fictional Dorothy's yard back in Kansas, featuring a pigpen filled with concrete pigs, a cellar door, and items such as old washing machines and feeders for pigs. It's part of a replica of an entire antique Kansas town.

The Tin Man is in the middle of chopping wood, wearing his heart and grinning from ear to ear.

The Museum's Beginnings

The Tancraitors opened the free museum after they retired from more than twenty-five years of running their own flower shop. Operating the shop, in fact, helped Dorothy get her collection of dolls going. "I always bought china and glass," she explains. "Then dolls and toys started to crop up at auctions and I started buying dolls. The first doll I bought was for my granddaughter who is now eighteen. It was for her first birthday. My doll collection was the result of not resisting a bargain. My business was in a nice area in Pittsburgh, and the customers started bringing me dolls, so I accumulated a tremendous amount in a very short period of time. And of course the question was, 'What am I ever going to do with all this?' "

The Tancraitors had purchased property in Florida before Disney World was built, planning to retire there. Instead, they sold it for a nice profit to a Days Inn.

"We decided that it was too hot in Florida, and we had always gone to the shore here in Jersey, so we looked for a location where we could live and have a small business. That's how we found Mullica Hill," Dorothy says. Mullica Hill is an antique town with about a hundred active dealers, as well as several restaurants and shops.

During their flower-shop days, the Tancraitors always closed in January and February to vacation (which they still do), and Dorothy had seen a number of doll shops in her travels. Opening a doll museum seemed like the perfect thing to do with the thousands of dolls she'd packed away for all those years. But when Dorothy and Steve moved into the town, they needed a method of bringing people to their back door. Hence, the yellow brick road was built.

"It eliminated the possibility of people going out the front door—you can only come and go in the back. It makes it a shop that can be manned by one person without worrying that there's merchandise walking out the other door," Dorothy says.

Dorothy says that she has always liked *The Wizard of Oz,* but it was not her primary collectible area. Now, she says, "I probably have every Oz item ever made. I have a huge collection," including rare older items, current merchandise, and fiftieth anniversary 1989 Oz collectibles. And since she's been listed as a source in a book on collecting Oz merchandise, Dorothy's had inquiries from other collectors worldwide—from as far away as Germany and Japan.

Thousands of Dolls for Show and Sale

But Oz memorabilia is just one small part of the collection housed in the pre-1800s building, a former funeral parlor. "In the museum area, I have eight or nine hundred dolls. I have about fifteen hundred for sale at all times here, and two thousand more that haven't even come out of the boxes."

The museum section features a great collection of older dolls and toys "that you, your mother, or even your grandmother might have had." The smallest part of the collection is dolls from the late 1800s and early

1900s. The majority of the dolls were made after the 1920s. Dorothy has a Jumeau worth about $3,000 on display, posed with an antique German tea setting. She does not sell the items found in the museum.

Both the museum and retail areas include a great variety—porcelain, bisque, composition, celluloid, plastic and wax dolls; baby dolls, elegant ladies and male dolls; movie stars, the Dionne Quintuplets and Howdy Doody; thirty years of G.I. Joe; Popeye, Dennis the Menace and Elvis; Eleanor Roosevelt and all the presidents; and anything from Frankenstein to Frank Sinatra.

The retail area features one room with items that appeal to men, such as superheroes and Star Trek figures. "I have almost as many men coming here to buy as I do women," Dorothy says. Among her other new merchandise for sale are Bugs Bunny, Disney, and Raggedy Ann and Andy items, as well as a wall of Barbie items which are "so hot it's unbelievable. I have older Barbies in my museum area, from 1959 on."

The Annual Show and Sale

Every August, Dorothy invites other retailers to her backyard for the Yellow Brick Road Annual Doll Show and Sale. Seventy sellers, dealing only in older, collectible dolls, converge in an area shaded by centuries-old trees.

"The town goes crazy—it's the biggest event of the year," Dorothy says. The show is attended by more than seven hundred buyers. "The people who sell dolls here are so successful, and sales are so good, that although they would prefer to be inside a building selling, I have a waiting list of easily twenty sellers every year. This is the best doll show in New Jersey. But once the doll show is gone, I'm still here. That's my main reason for having the show. It put us on the map. I have a very busy store."

The Patrons

The Yellow Brick Road's patrons run the gamut, from girls and boys to grandmas and grandpas. "I get a num-

The Scarecrow awaits the arrival of Dorothy on the Yellow Brick Road.

ber of kids simply because of the yellow brick road," she says. "It's not unusual to have somebody come in with their child dressed as some character from *The Wizard of Oz,* and they'll take videos of them on the yellow brick road. People can even have birthday parties in our backyard with an appointment."

Dorothy says she has as many people come to the museum to look as to buy, and nostalgia is her biggest draw. "People like to see the dolls they had when they were children, and they like to tell me what happened to their dolls. And I'm a good listener—I never cut anybody off. They stand in line, and there could be four people behind them waiting to be helped, and those people will also stand and listen to the story about the doll. After all, it's something pleasant—it's a good memory."

Sharon Smith of the Dolly Wares Doll Museum

BY KRISTIN EARHART

Kristin Earhart is a freelance writer based in Cincinnati, Ohio. She works in the production department at F&W Publications.

The Dolly Wares Doll Museum is the fulfillment of collector Dorothy Smith's dream. Dorothy founded the Florence, Oregon, museum in 1970, and today her daughter Sharon Smith builds upon the extensive collection, striving to make Dolly Wares the best doll museum on the West Coast.

Sharon says that of the more than 2,500 pieces on display, about two-thirds belonged to her mother, whose childhood interest in doll collecting was rekindled as an adult. It was through her children that Dorothy Smith rediscovered the doll world.

"In 1940, we lived in Pasadena, California, and my mother had two kids with broken dolls and nobody to fix them," Sharon remembers. In response to her children's appeals, Dorothy began mending their injured dolls and soon began her own collection as well, repairing older dolls to restore their worth and beauty.

Dorothy had moved several times as a child, and because she was forced to leave most of her belongings behind with each move, she never had the opportunity in her youth to acquire a large doll collection. By 1950, she had gathered her first small collection as an adult, but she was once again forced to abandon her dolls; this time, she sold them for extra money.

A Compulsive Habit

So, Sharon says, her mother started her collection anew, "Only this time, the disease got her bad. You see, doll collecting is like alcohol and drugs. It's compulsive."

Dorothy acquired a large majority of her doll assortment searching through the import shops and flea markets of Los Angeles. "Being in the business," explains Sharon, "she knew all the doll people, all the dealers, all the import shops." Dorothy also belonged to four doll clubs. She had a knack for "picking things up" to add to the collection, which by the late sixties had multiplied to museum proportion.

"One day," says Sharon, "[Dorothy] decided we would move to Oregon—it was too crowded in California. We moved in 1968 and 1969 and opened the museum in May of 1970, and here I am."

Since her mother's death in 1973, Sharon has maintained the Dolly Wares Doll Museum and repair service with the same dedication as her mother. When speaking of the compulsive nature of doll collecting, Sharon explains, "I grew up around it." For her, it seems to be second nature to maintain and build the museum's collection, as well as to continue the doll repair business.

Everything in Dolls

Sharon thinks that to appreciate the expanse of the Dolly Wares collection, people need to see it for themselves. The brochure reads, "The museum that has everything in dolls," and Sharon has certainly emphasized diversity in her collecting. From a pre-Columbian figure of clay to a Lone Ranger figure, the museum is profuse in age and character. Sharon has amassed traditional baby dolls as well as ethnic dolls, giving the museum an eclectic combination of history and culture. The museum, which fills a hall 20' × 63', is arranged by category, and significant dolls have labels so that patrons can guide themselves through the museum.

The pre-Columbian figure is the oldest in Sharon's collection and is quite unique. "At one time, you could buy such pieces in import shops, and then countries passed laws prohibiting the export of artifacts," Sharon says. She is not certain if the crude clay figure was a child's toy or an instrument for religious practice. The largest piece in the museum is an elaborately carved wooden soldier from Rome that is six feet tall. He still wears his original armor of pressed leather, which was once painted silver.

Restoration Services

Another outstanding carved wood figure is a twenty-seven-inch cage doll. " 'Cage' refers to no legs and no feet," Sharon says. "The doll was built on a frame." Sharon and her mother began restoration on this doll shortly after they found her in 1960. They enlisted the

Special Displays

Sharon calls one of the theme displays in the museum "The Recreation Scene." It consists of a miniature Ferris wheel, merry-go-round, and roller coaster; each amusement ride carries little bisque dolls as passengers. Another display is exclusively wedding dolls, including everything from old china dolls to German jointed dolls, modern-day figures to ethnic brides.

Next is the section of large, old dolls including some of French origin and many German jointed dolls, the largest of which are 42″ tall and dressed in the luxurious garments of fine ladies. One unique large doll is a boy mannequin of papier-mâché created by the French manufacturer Bru Jne. and Cie. "The fact that he is a Bru makes him completely different," Sharon explains. "Bru was not known for making papier-mâché." The doll, about one hundred years old, most likely once modeled boys' fashions in a clothing store. Today, he wears high boots with a form-fitting red velvet suit fastened by brass buttons which was created by Sharon's mother.

The collection of dolls created by French firms is extensive, including works by Bru, Gaultier, Pierotti, Jumeau and Steiner. The museum also includes a rare bisque-headed doll manufactured by the china company Royal Copenhagen, dressed in plum silk in the fashion of a century ago. Sharon says this doll has an extremely sweet face and a refined elegance.

The German section is complete. "I have all the known and lesser-known manufacturers represented," says Sharon. The doll that started this collection has significant Smith family history. It is a common J.D. Kestner 154 kid body doll which belonged to Sharon's mother Dorothy when she was a child. The doll, now dressed in one of Dorothy's former thin white nightgowns, is at least eighty years old and is the only doll Dorothy was able to keep through her many migrations as a young girl.

Ethnic Dolls

Sharon's ethnic collection includes Spanish marionettes, a Brazilian cloth doll with a kerchief and real human fingernails, and American Indian tourist dolls with hand-embroidered faces and wearing dress representative of various tribe members. Other highlights include Japanese dolls adorned in kimonos, a Japanese nun, Chinese mission dolls in their originals garments reflecting the traditional styles of the early nineteenth century working class, Kenyan warriors, and a Russian

This 27″ Spanish fashion doll was made in 1630. Her torso, head and arms are carved of pear wood.

aid of Sherman Smith, a woodcarver, to replicate her arms and hands.

"When we got her, she was pretty pathetic," Sharon says. "My mother patched up her battered face and found her a wig and fitted her with period clothes. Now, she looks like an El Greco painting." The restoration of the cage doll required more than manual labor. A great deal of research was required to identify the doll. Sharon and her mother learned that the cage doll was created for Spanish royalty to send to another province or country as a presentation of the season's fashion.

Whenever Sharon is asked to complete a repair on a doll or the doll's clothing, thorough research is always involved. "I believe in trying to keep them as original as possible. I do things the old-fashioned way. I don't monkey with new plastics and epoxies—I have questions about using them with old materials."

Sharon says she learned many of her repair and sewing techniques from her mother, but she has developed several of her own because "each doll requires an individual touch. We try to keep them original."

This 16″ cloth doll from Russia is one of the many rare finds at the museum.

These 8″ composition Dionne Quintuplets by Nancy Ann are in their original box.

tea cozy. Also included are dolls of the Pacific Islands, Australia, New Zealand, Indonesia and more. The cultures represented have many delegates, giving a thorough depiction of dolls in each country.

Modern Artist Dolls

In addition to ethnic dolls, Sharon has collected the work of modern doll artists, including Hattie Spiegel's Queen Elizabeth and Philip and Pinky and Blue Boy. "I try to cover the whole bit," she says, as she lists television, cartoon, film and political personalities in the museum. She has Shirley Temple; a 1939 edition of

Scarlett O'Hara; Lindbergh; Sherlock Holmes; and John Wayne costumed in military gear. The presidents displayed include Washington, Johnson, Ike, Nixon, and a special vinyl-head figure of John F. Kennedy seated in a rocking chair that when wound up plays "Happy Days Are Here Again." Sharon thinks the museum is especially meaningful to adults who will certainly find a doll on display that was popular when they were growing up.

A Time-Consuming Job

Sharon is busy running the museum and repair shop single-handedly six days a week, but she enjoys working with dolls and doll people. "First of all, I must keep my customers happy. I need to keep up with my repairs and answer questions for people who go through the museum." When she has the time, however, she loves to choose new dolls for the museum's exhibits. When selecting exhibition dolls, Sharon says, "I don't go for worth, I go for personality. If a doll doesn't have personality, I don't want it. You choose your dolls just as you choose your friends. You prefer a friend with character over a stick-in-the-mud. If you don't like a doll, there's no use having it!"

Museums

ARIZONA DOLL AND TOY MUSEUM

Inez McCrary
602 E. Adams
Phoenix, AZ 85004
Phone: (602)253-9337 or (602)948-7973 MST
Hours: Year-round, T-Sat, 10-4; Sun, 12-4.
Admission: Adults, $2; children, 50¢
Founded in: 1987

COLLECTION:

Includes: Toys and accessories
Description: The Arizona Doll and Toy Museum located in the Stevens House at Heritage Square includes a wide variety of dolls and toys from yesterday as well as familiar modern playthings. The scenario is constantly changing as Arizona collectors share their favorites. You will love the authentic schoolroom of 1912 featuring antique dolls as the "students." A fully stocked gift shop makes available unique gift items for children and adults who are young at heart.

SPECIAL FEATURES/PROGRAMS:

Tours: Schedule in advance.
Educational Programs: Lectures by doll experts and well-known artists. Programs at local schools, luncheon groups, museums, etc. Programs include the history of dolls, with examples, doll identification, workshops.
Gift Shop: Victorian cards, scrap art, fans, stationery, patterns for making doll clothing, reference books and price guides, dolls, bears, miniatures, children's classic books, stickers and "how-to" books.
Other: The turn-of-the-century school room is everyone's favorite. Provides free school tours every Tuesday.

ADDITIONAL INFORMATION:

Museum history: The museum was started and supported by the doll clubs of Arizona. Many members share their treasured dolls and toys and serve as volunteers. The museum is nonprofit and supported by donations and gift shop proceeds.

DENVER MUSEUM OF MINIATURES, DOLLS AND TOYS

Linda Speer, Executive Director
1880 Gaylord St.
Denver, CO 80206
Phone: (303)322-1053 (office) MST, (303)322-3704 (24-hour recording)
Hours: Year-round, T-Sat, 10-4. Sun, 1-4.
Admission: Adults, $3; seniors (over 62) and children (ages 2-16), $2. (Tour groups of 10 or more receive a discounted price.)
Founded in: 1981

COLLECTION:

Includes: Doll houses, miniatures, toys, doll accessories, including buggies, clothes, paper dolls; Native American dolls and toys.
Description: The Museum has permanent exhibits of dolls, in addition to offering temporary exhibits which change on a quarterly basis. There is a large ethnic doll collection, oriental dolls, puppets, and early 1900s American manufacturers of dolls. The museum is located in a charming Dutch Colonial historic house, built in 1898, and has many antique and modern dolls on display. Special features also include doll houses, toy dishes and accessories.

SPECIAL FEATURES/PROGRAMS:

Tours: During regular business hours. Schedule in advance.
Educational Programs: Lectures by doll experts and well-known artists; doll-making workshops. Educational programs for children include corn husk dolls, Japanese paper dolls, Native American dolls, history of dolls and teddy bears, and dolls from around the world. Educational programs for adults include fashion dolls, doll collecting overview, identification of dolls, paper doll collecting and history and dollmaking.
Gift Shop: Features a wide array of gifts including dolls, handmade doll clothes, teddy bears, doll accessories and paper dolls. Many unusual and one-of-a-kind items. The shop boasts a treasure trove of gift items such as miniatures, doll house furniture, toys and games.
Other: The museum is housed in the historic Pearce-McAllister Cottage, built in 1898. Visitors travel through time from the 1800s to the present. Visitors discover the fascinating power that the cottage and artifacts possess to stir memories, fire the imagination and speak of the future.

ADDITIONAL INFORMATION:

Museum history: The museum was established in 1981 by individuals in the community interested in founding a miniature, doll and toy museum. These people included doll collectors, artists, miniaturists and business owners. It was a city-wide effort to raise funds, find a location, and renovate the historic house where the museum is now located.

THE DOLL MUSEUM

Linda Edward
520 Thames St.
Newport, RI 02840
Phone: (401)849-0405 EST
Hours: Year-round, Sun, 12-5. M, W-Sat, 10-5.
Admission: Adults, $2; age 5-11, $1; over 65, $1.50; under 5, free. A group rate of 50% off can be obtained by organizations with prior arrangement.

COLLECTION:

Description: The doll museum features a fine collection of dolls dating from the 18th century through today. Exhibits are changed seasonally, and special theme exhibits are mounted regularly.

SPECIAL FEATURES/PROGRAMS:

Tours: Not usually available, but special

arrangements can be made. Schedule in advance.

Educational programs: Museum has slide shows on the museum collection which it can present to clubs, nursing homes, church groups, etc. (Call for current availability and fees). Works with Girl Scout groups in obtaining their toymaker badges by giving a museum tour and doing a workshop where each girl makes a doll (with advance arrangements).

Gift Shop: The museum toy shop offers antique, collectible vintage, and modern artist dolls for sale as well as modern playthings, miniatures, doll accessories and reference books. Repair, restoration and appraisal services are also available.

Other: The museum has a reference library which can be used "in house" for the cost of admission.

ADDITIONAL INFORMATION:

Museum history: The Doll Museum is the result of the lifelong dream of the owner, Linda Edward. Ms. Edward's passion for dolls is evident in the diverse nature of the more than 600 dolls in the collection.

"DARE TO DREAM . . . NONE OF THE WORLD'S GREAT ARTISTS WERE BORN OVERNIGHT. THEY DEVELOPED INTO WHO THEY BECAME."

Gustave Wolff, Lexington, KY

ENCHANTED WORLD DOLL MUSEUM

Valerie LaBreche
615 N. Main
Mitchell, SD 57301
Phone: (605)996-9896 CST
Fax: (605)996-0210
Hours: March 1-December 15, M-Sat, 9-5. Sun, 1-5, off season. June-September, M-Sun, 8-8.
Admission: $3, adults; $2.50, seniors; $1, 5-17 years
Founded in: 1982

COLLECTION:

Includes: Dolls, doll accessories, furniture

Description: Over 4,000 antique and modern dolls exhibited in 400 different scenes depicting life in the early 1800s and 1900s, nursery rhymes, fairy tales and Star Trek. Also features

over 2,000 ethnic dolls from more than 125 countries. There are also doll houses, buggies, dishes, toys and miniatures and all different accessories that capture your imagination as you walk through this maze of enchantment.

SPECIAL FEATURES/PROGRAMS:

Tours: Schedule in advance. Available to motor coaches only.

Educational Programs: Seminars, contests, slide presentations. If tour groups call prior to arrival, a slide presentation and background lecture on the museum and its dolls will be arranged.

Gift Shop: Shop carries a wide assortment of antique and collectible dolls and doll-related items. A video and book on the museum are also available. Carries Department 56, Snow Babies, Dickens Village and many more unique gift items.

Other: The Building is a pink sandstone castle complete with moat, turrets and a drawbridge leading to the gift shop and into the museum. AAA Star Rated.

ADDITIONAL INFORMATION:

Museum history: The collecton was started by Sheldon Reese, a South Dakota native, who traveled extensively abroad. In 1982, the museum opened to the public as a nonprofit charitable and educational foundation governed by a seven-member board of directors. The building and its contents are now the property of the foundation, donating a percentage of any profits to charity and education.

HELEN MOE ANTIQUE DOLL MUSEUM

Helen Moe
Rt. 2, Box 332
Paso Robles, CA 93446
Phone: (805)238-2740 PST
Hours: Year-around, M-Sat, 10-5.
Admission: $3, adult; $1, child
Founded in: 1965

COLLECTION:

Includes: Dioramas, room scenes, doll houses, antique children's and doll shoes, old toys

Description: 800 dolls, including German bisque, French bisque, composition, wax and papier-mâché. Has a

doll house depicting an early 1900 home with dolls and furnishings, a Christmas scene and family gathering around a Christmas tree, a Lewis Sorenson wax Santa and more.

SPECIAL FEATURES/PROGRAMS:

Gift Shop: Books about dolls and doll supplies, good selection of Victorian paper items, gifts for all occasions.

KÄTHE KRUSE PUPPEN MUSEUM

Mrs. Tiny Riemersma
25, Bunnenhaven
Den Helder, NL, 1781 BK
THE NETHERLANDS
Phone: (*31)223-616704
Fax: (*31)223-616704
Hours: All months except November, Th-Sat, 2-5.
Admission: DFL 5.00 adults; DFL 2.50 children
Founded in: 1988

COLLECTION:

Includes: Dolls, teddy bears and other animals; dollhouse furniture.

Description: The museum displays four generations of Käthe Kruse dolls, from 1911 to today, amidst contemporary teddies and toys, three floors of nostalgia and childhood memories. The museum also houses rooms of the 1930s and 1950s, the turn of the century (1899-1901) and the 1920s.

SPECIAL FEATURES/PROGRAMS:

Gift Shop: Offers books, calendars, postcards, posters, toys, cups, nowadays dolls (Käthe Kruse), teddies, ancient doll clothing, old toys, etc.

Other: Every quarter of the year a seasonal exhibition or an exhibition about a special item, like old reading articles for education, antiques, toys, etc., is featured.

MCCURDY HISTORICAL DOLL MUSEUM

Shirley B. Paxman
246 North 100 East
Provo, UT 84606
Phone: (801)377-9935 or (801)377-5311 MST
Hours: Year-round, T-Sat, 1-5.
Admission: $2, adults; $1, children under 12.
Founded in: 1978

COLLECTION:

Includes: Paper dolls, toys, children's

books, teddy bears, puppets and marrionettes

Description: Over 3,000 antique and contemporary dolls housed in a restored carriage house on the National Register of Historic Places. Changing exhibits and activities every month, with storytelling, tea parties and other related activities.

SPECIAL FEATURES/PROGRAMS:

Tours: During regular business hours

Educational Programs: Lectures by doll experts, seminars, dollmaking workshops, storytelling, birthday parties, annual doll show and sale.

Gift Shop: Features dolls, doll clothes, doll books, animals, toys, seasonal items for the holidays throughout the year, paper dolls and children's books from great literature.

MARY METTITT DOLL MUSEUM

Marjorie Darrah
Rt. 422 W.
Douglasville, PA 19518
Phone: (610)385-3809 EST
Fax: (610)689-4538
Hours: Year-round, M-Sat, 10-4:30. Sun, 1-5
Admission: $3, adults; $1.50, children
Founded in: 1963

COLLECTION:

Includes: Dolls, toys, games

Description: This collection, started by Ms. Darrah's parents as a hobby, is an accumulation of 50 years of collecting antique dolls, toys and games. Privately owned.

SPECIAL FEATURES/PROGRAMS:

Educational Programs: Available

"DOLLS HAVE BEEN MADE IN A VARIETY OF FORMS SINCE THE BEGINNINGS OF CIVILIZATION, TAKING ON NEW CHARACTERISTICS OR BEING FASHIONED FROM DIFFERENT MATERIALS ACCORDING TO THEIR TIMES. WE ARE FORTUNATE TO BE LIVING IN A VERY EXCITING TIME, A TIME WHERE ARTISTS ARE TAKING NEW STRIDES EVERY DAY BY CREATING DOLLS THAT ARE VERY DIFFERENT THAN THOSE THAT CAME BEFORE."

Maggie Finch and Martha Finch-Kozlosky, Bennington, VT

MID-OHIO HISTORICAL MUSEUM, INC.

Henrietta Pfeifer
700 Winchester Pike
Canal Winchester, OH 43110
Phone: (614)837-5573 EST
Hours: April thru mid-December, W-Sat, 11-5.
Admission: $3
Founded in: 1982

COLLECTION:

Includes: Dolls, doll accessories and toys, including a train display, a miniature circus, tin and cast iron toys, etc.

Description: A treasury of memories best describes this outstanding collection of antique to modern dolls. Dolls date from the late 1700s through Barbie. There are thousands of dolls in settings with antique accessories, etc. There are French and German bisque dolls, papier-mâché from early 1800s, character dolls, Bye-Lo babies, Shirley Temple dolls, and other personality dolls—something from every generation from the past 200 years.

SPECIAL FEATURES/PROGRAMS:

Tours: Schedule in advance. Special rates apply for some tours.

Educational Programs: Doll programs available for organizations.

Gift Shop: Sells antique and collectible dolls, new porcelain dolls, Alexander Dolls, Barbie dolls, doll books, some accessories and custom-made clothing. Appraisals and doll repairs available.

Other: Meeting area and children's birthday party area by appointment for a fee. Research library available by appointment only.

THE NEWARK MUSEUM

43-49 Washington St.
Newark, NJ 07101
Phone: (201)596-6550 EST
Fax: (201)642-0459
Hours: Year-round, T-Sun, 12-5.
Admission: Free
Founded in: 1909

COLLECTION:

Includes: Dolls, paintings and sculptures, decorative arts and crafts

SPECIAL FEATURES/PROGRAMS:

Tours: During regular hours.

ROSALIE WHYLE DOLL MUSEUM

Rosalie Whyle
1116 108th Avenue NE
Bellevue, WA 98004
Phone: (206)455-1116 PST
Fax: (206)455-4793
Hours: Year-round, M-Sat, 10-5. Sun, 1-5.
Admission: $6, adults; $5.50, seniors; $4, children 5-17. Rates for 10 or more, less 50¢ for age category. School rate, $3 per person.
Founded in: 1992

COLLECTION:

Includes: Dolls, toys, doll houses, books, teddy bears

Description: 1,200 dolls on display. Special displays change about 4 times a year and sometimes feature an artist's work. Has private collections from dolls of the 18th century to Barbie and Ken dolls. Has hands-on treasure coves for children. The museum is dedicated to the preservation and exhibition of dolls as an art form and miniature history of humankind.

SPECIAL FEATURES/PROGRAMS:

Educational Programs: Lectures by doll experts, dollmaking workshops, lecture for schools by Rosalie Whyle. Also offers 3 informational videos.

Gift Shop: Available

SPECIAL JOYS DOLLS AND TOY MUSEUM

Joy Celleder
41 N. River Rd.
Coventry, CT 06238
Phone: (203)742-6359 EST
Hours: W-Sun, 11-5. January, February, March, Th-Sun, 11-4:30.
Admission: Free. All donations go to local fire department.
Founded in: 1989

COLLECTION:

Includes: Dolls and toys, accessories, houses, stuffed animals, German and English bears, antique adult clothing

Description: The museum is listed in AAA, and includes doll furniture, doll trunks, dolls from 1860 to Barbie dolls, paper dolls and doll dishes. The museum is also a bed and breakfast.

SPECIAL FEATURES/PROGRAMS:

Educational Programs: For elementary school children, doll groups, church

groups and historical societies
Gift Shop: Available

ADDITIONAL INFORMATION:
Museum history: The collection began as a hobby and has grown into a museum.

THE STRONG MUSEUM

Susan Trien
1 Manhattan Square
Rochester, NY 14607
Phone: (716)263-2700
Fax: (716)263-2493
Hours: Year-round, M-Sat, 10-5. Sun, 1-5.
Admission: $5, adults; $4, students and seniors; $3, 3-16; special rates for 20 or more.
Founded in: 1982

COLLECTION:
Includes: Dolls and American history. 6 changing exhibits on various topics (coldware toys, hands-on environment, kid-to-kid communications.
Description: The museum has a whimsical, hands-on small wonders miniatures exhibit, the world's largest collection of dolls, open storage cases and other toys and doll houses.

SPECIAL FEATURES/PROGRAMS:
Educational Programs: Interested large groups should contact museum.

> "EVERY TIME A DOLLMAKER CREATES A NEW DOLL, SHE ADDS SOMETHING TO HER OWN STATURE. IN SHORT, SHE HELPS CREATE HERSELF."
> *Lolo Westrich, Middletown, CA*

TOY & MINIATURE MUSEUM OF KANSAS CITY

Sandi Russell
5235 Oak St.
Kansas City, MO 64112
Phone: (816)333-9328 or (816)333-2055 CST
Fax: (816)333-2055
Hours: Year-round, W-Sat, 10-4. Sun, 1-4
Admission: $4, adults; $3.50, seniors and students; $2, 3-14 years; special rates for groups of 10 or more.
Founded in: 1982

COLLECTION:
Includes: Dolls and doll houses

Description: The museum has scaled miniatures with finely-crafted dolls in the settings and Victorian nurseries with child-sized dolls in antique brass cradle. Antique dolls include china, bisque and a selection of French fashion dolls. The museum also has contemporary dolls from the 1920s, including Patsy, Shirley Temple and Madame Alexander dolls.

VICTORIAN DOLL MUSEUM

Linda Greenfield
4332 Buffalo Rd.
North Chili, NY 14514
Phone: (716)247-0130 EST
Hours: February-December, T-Sat, 10-4:30. November and December only, Sun, 1-4.
Admission: $2, adults; $1, children
Founded in: 1970

COLLECTION:
Description: In greater Rochester, New York, in the western suburb of North Chili, lies the home of the Victorian Doll Museum and Chili Doll Hospital. A quaint two-story red building houses the unique personal collection of owner Linda Greenfield. When Linda was 8 years old, she began collecting dolls as a hobby. Since then, she has been enthusiastically collecting and perfecting her craft. This interest led to her creation of this most unique wonderland . . . family owned and self-funded. The building was one of the first commercial establishments in the town during the early 1900s. It now houses a fine doll collection, featuring over 2,000 dolls dating from the 1840s to the present. Visitors who tour the museum can view the labeled and identified dolls behind floor-to-ceiling glass cases. One can view yesteryear dolls of bisque, china, wood, wax, metal, felt, ivory and papier-mâché. There are also Kewpie dolls, paper dolls, Schoenhut dolls and Circus, Noah's Ark, toys, a small action puppet theater, Shirley Temples, the Dionne Quintuplets, Alexander and Ginny dolls, Eloise Wilkin Dolls, and a marvelous set of Betty Curtis dolls displayed in a kitchen diorama.

SPECIAL FEATURES/PROGRAMS:
Gift Shop: The Museum Gift Shop re-

flects the vintage flair of the Victorian dolls exhibited within the museum area. Although no old dolls are for sale, there is a unique blend of dolls for collectors and young beginners, including Ginny, Alexander (International and Storybook), Good-Krüger, Madeline, Raggedy Ann and Andy, porcelain and vinyl baby and lady dolls, Amish dolls and Kewpie figurines. A wonderful mix of related old-fashioned style merchandise is also offered, such as die-cut containers and reprints of old children's storybooks and posters as well as the most current doll books offering dollmaker information and price guides. Nostalgic greeting cards, calendars, post cards, paper dolls and children's coloring books are also available. There are items for every price range.

ADDITIONAL INFORMATION:
Unlimited curbside parking. Museum entrance is handicapped accessible.

> "IF A PIECE SPEAKS TO YOUR HEART, YOU WILL ALWAYS BE HAPPY WITH YOUR PURCHASE."
> *Janie Ashcraft, Qulin, MO*

WASHINGTON DOLLS' HOUSE AND TOY MUSEUM

Flora Gill Jacobs
5236 44th St. NW
Washington, DC 20015
Phone: (202)363-6400 or (202)244-0024 EST
Hours: Year-round, T-Sat, 10-5. Sun, 12-5.
Admission: $3, adults; $2, seniors; $1, children under 14 years
Founded in: 1975

COLLECTION:
Description: Has a carefully researched collection of antique doll houses, dolls, toys and games. Ms. Flora Gill Jacobs wrote the first book on doll houses as well as many other books for children and adults.

SPECIAL FEATURES/PROGRAMS:
Educational Programs: Tours through museum for birthday parties. Tours for collectors given by Flora Gill Jacobs.

WENHAM MUSEUM
Eleanor Thompson
132 Main St.
Wenham MA 01984
Phone: (508)468-2377 EST
Fax: (508)468-8004
Hours: Year-round, M-F, 10-4; Sat, 1-4.
  Sun, 2-5. Closed major holidays.
Admission: $3; $2.50, seniors; $1, 2-14
  years; group rates by reservation.
Founded in: 1953

COLLECTION:
Description: The museum includes 8 doll
  houses and a large antique toy and toy
  soldier display.

SPECIAL FEATURES/PROGRAMS:
Educational programs: Family pro-
  grams, workshops
Gift Shop: Available

ADDITIONAL INFORMATION:
Easy access, free parking. Located across
from a good restaurant and shopping.

**THE YELLOW BRICK ROAD DOLL AND TOY
MUSEUM**
Dorothy Tancraitor
P.O. Box 306
34 S. Main St.
Mullica Hill, NJ 08062
Phone: (609)478-6137 EST
Hours: March 1-December 20, F-Sun,
  12-5.
Admission: Free
Founded in: 1987

COLLECTION:
Includes: Dolls, an extensive Wizard of
  Oz collection, collectible toys, doll
  houses and doll furniture
Description: Over 100 years of hundreds
  of dolls: porcelain, bisque, composition, celluloid, wax, plastic, paper,
  wood, metal, cloth, corn husk, even
  coal. There are child dolls, characters,
  elegant ladies and male and female
  dolls. One word, "nostalgia," is syno-
  nomous with display of collectible
  dolls, whether it be a fine German or
  French creation or a famous movie
  star or comic strip character.

SPECIAL FEATURES/PROGRAMS:
Tours: Schedule in advance.
Gift Shop: Gift shop offers dolls, toys
  and other items that are unusual, old
  or hard to find.
Other: Dolls and small antiques may be
  brought in for appraisal and consignment. Also buys individual items and
  complete collections. Doll repair is
  available.

ADDITIONAL INFORMATION:
Museum history: See the interview that
  opens this chapter.

> "MAKE YOUR PAST PART OF YOUR PRESENT
> WITH DOLLS!"
> *Gennie Cartmill, Rexburg, ID*

251

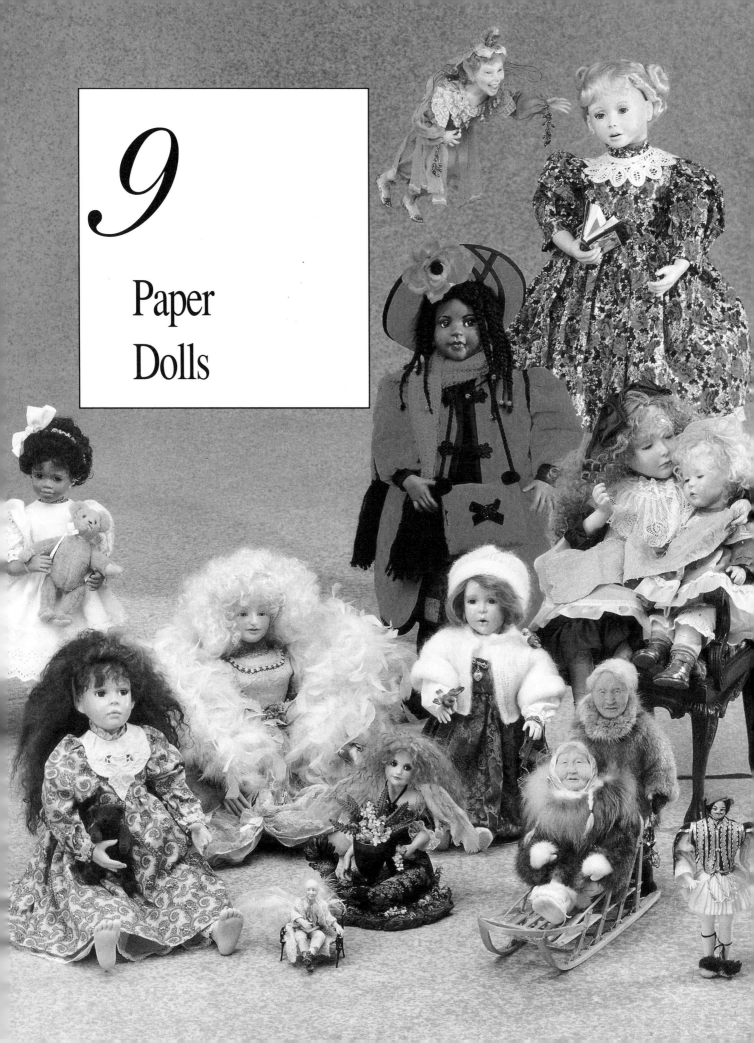

9

Paper
Dolls

A Guide to Chapter Nine

*P*aper dolls are so connected to the world of dolls that to leave them out of this book would have been to ignore a major portion of the industry. Collectors of paper dolls are usually doll collectors, and vice versa. As children, we had few toys as inexpensive or as fun as paper dolls. As adults, we treasure the memories of these dolls, pieces of history that so closely intertwine with our lives. Like doll artists and manufacturers, the paper doll artists and publishers listed here have provided major contributions to the worlds of art, fashion and history.

This chapter includes most of the same listings as the rest of the book, except that they are for paper dolls. Sections include dealers, artists, publishers, organizations and museums. Because they are so similar to the other listings in this book, we will not include a heading-by-heading guide to the listings in this chapter. Most

are self-explanatory. In the following pages, expert Judy Johnson shares her vast knowledge of the history of paper dolls. Her fascinating article will delight everyone, whether or not they are already collectors.

Perhaps more than in any other chapter, the businesses listed here are most often home-based. Pay careful attention to time differences (the time zone is noted in each listing), and do not stop by a business unless open hours are listed. Always be courteous, and include your first and last names, address and phone number when leaving a message.

The paper doll industry is unique in that there is a great deal of overlap among the major players. In other words, an artist is likely to be a dealer, and perhaps also an editor of a publication. Many people have been listed more than once under the various headings. ❦

A Brief History of Paper Dolls

BY JUDY M. JOHNSON

Judy M. Johnson is a leading paper doll artist and expert. Her first paper doll was published in 1984 by B. Shackman. She has also been published by Dover Publications, as well as in several national doll and teddy bear periodicals. She lives in Skandia, Michigan.

*I*t's just a flat paper object, but it has such enormous appeal that it will provide a lifetime of pleasure! For historians, paper dolls and their costumes provide a broad look at cultures around the world. Film and theater buffs will enjoy the popular figures from opera, stage, screen and even television that have appeared as paper dolls—and many have. Paper doll royalty and political figures provide opportunities for sleuths who love digging in odd places to unearth their treasures. Those who love babies, children, pretty ladies, animals or fantasy figures will find their favorite subject in paper doll form. And what woman (or man) over thirty does not remember paper dolls as the cheapest, yet most fascinating toy of childhood? It's memories like this that bring many adults back to the subject as collectors seeking the sets they played with as children.

There is nothing quite like the feeling of digging in a box of assorted papers and suddenly finding in one's hand an exact replica of a childhood toy. The years slip away with lightning speed, and such a find awakens childhood with all its simplicities and joys. If the collecting bug for paper dolls has not yet bitten you, it just may. It can be an inexpensive pastime that requires little storage space, or it can grow into a hobby as extensive as collecting antique dolls. And best of all, it is an activity you can share with children of today, teaching them manual dexterity, history, fashion and art while you have great fun together. Once you begin collecting paper dolls, they can become one of life's great passions.

Early History

Paper dolls have existed as long as there have been paper and creative people to apply images to it. Paper figures have been used in ritual ceremonies in Asian

Judy Johnson

cultures for many centuries. An ancient Japanese purification ceremony dating back to at least A.D. 900 included a paper figure and a folded paper object resembling a kimono which were put to sea in a boat. The Balinese have made shadow puppets of leather and of paper since before Christ, although we are aware of no evidence that they made separate costumes for these figures. Many dolls have been made of paper in the Orient, whether folded or otherwise constructed, but these are three-dimensional and not flat.

In France in the mid-1700s, "pantins" were all the rage in high society and royal courts. This jointed jumping-jack figure, a cross between puppet and paper doll, was made to satirize nobility. Other cultures have had special forms of paper art, including China (Hua Yang), Japan (Kirigami), Poland (Wycinanki), and Germany and Switzerland (Scherenschnitte). Many more have

"Princess Zahrina," a fantasy paper doll by Judy Johnson, comes with seven elaborate, colorful costumes. Princess Zahrina is published by B. Shackman & Co., Inc.

Paper Doll Definition

A paper doll is a two-dimensional figure drawn or printed on paper for which accompanying clothing has also been made. It may be a figure of a person, animal or inanimate object. The term may be extended to include similar items made of materials other than paper, such as plastic, cloth or wood. The term also may include three-dimensional dolls and their costumes that are made exclusively of paper. Collectors sometimes extend their collections to include other toys printed on paper, such as paper airplanes, cars and trains, animals and birds, villages, furniture and so on.

enjoyed folk art pictorial representations in cut paper, but these also do not have garments to fit the forms.

With the exception of the kimono mentioned above, these paper figures do not fit our definition of paper doll

because they do not include costumes for the figures presented. Examples of the first true paper dolls have been found in the fashion centers of Vienna, Berlin, London and Paris from as early as the mid-1700s. These are hand-painted figures and costumes created for the entertainment of wealthy adults. They may have been done by a dressmaker to show current fashions or done as satirical, sociopolitical illustrations of popular figures of the day.

A set of rare hand-painted figures dated late in the 1780s can be found in the Winterthur Museum of Winterthur, Delaware. It shows coiffures and headdresses for sale at the shop of Denis-Antoine on Rue St. Jacques, Paris. In 1791, a London advertisement proclaimed a new invention called the "English Doll." It was a young female figure, eight inches high, with a wardrobe of underclothes, headdresses, corset and six complete outfits. Dolls like these were also sold in Germany. Examples of many beautiful and extremely rare paper dolls can be seen at the John Greene Chandler Memorial Museum in South Lancaster, Massachusetts.

Mass-Produced Paper Dolls Pre-1900

McLoughlin Brothers, founded in 1828, became the largest manufacturer of paper dolls in the United States, making their dolls fairly easy to find today. They printed their paper dolls from wood blocks engraved in the same way as metal plates. Some of the most popular dolls, selling for five and ten cents a set, were Dottie Dimple, Lottie Love and Jenney June. The largest producer of paper dolls and children's books, McLoughlin Brothers was sold to Milton Bradley in 1920.

A smaller publishing company, Peter G. Thompson, published paper dolls in the 1880s. Similar to the McLoughlin style, some of their titles were Pansy Blossom, Jessie Jingle, Lillie Lane, Bessie Bright and Nellie Bly, selling for eight to fifteen cents per set. Also in the 1880s, Dennison Manufacturing Company added crepe paper to their line, starting a trend that lasted for about forty years. Crepe paper added dimension to the costumes of paper dolls and provided countless hours of fun for children at home and in schools. In the 1890s, Frederick A. Stokes and Company published several sets of paper dolls including likenesses of European royalty and America's own Martha Washington.

Imported Paper Dolls

From the 1870s to the 1890s, European manufacturers produced beautifully lithographed full-color paper

Come meet . . .
Caddie Woodlawn
. . . *a pioneer Wisconsin girl.*

inspired by the books of
Carol Ryrie Brink

illustrated by
Sue Shanahan

presented by
**The Madison Area Doll Club
of Wisconsin**

Nero

Caddie Woodlawn

"Caddie Woodlawn," by Sue Shanahan, is a pioneer Wisconsin girl inspired by the books of Carol Ryrie Brink. Caddie Woodlawn is presented by the Madison Area Doll Club of Wisconsin.

Paper Doll Milestones

First manufactured paper doll: Little Fanny, produced by S&J Fuller, London, in 1810.

First American manufactured paper doll: The History and Adventures of Little Henry, published by J. Belcher of Boston in 1812. In the 1820s, boxed paper doll sets were popularly produced in Europe and exported to America for lucky children.

First celebrity paper doll: A doll portraying the renowned ballerina Marie Taglioni, published in the 1830s. In 1840, a boxed set was done of another ballerina, Fanny Elssler, as well as of Queen Victoria.

These early paper dolls are rare and priced accordingly. It is still possible to unearth paper dolls from unexpected places, so it is imperative never to throw away old papers without thoroughly examining them for these treasures!

dolls. They often represented royalty and famous theater personalities, including the German Royal Family, the House of Windsor, and actresses Ellen Terry, Lily Langtry and Lillian Russell.

Beginning in 1866, Raphael Tuck is perhaps the best-known manufacturer of antique paper dolls. The company began "by appointment to her Majesty Queen Elizabeth II, Fine Art Publishers, London," and soon opened branch offices in New York and Paris. Their first paper doll was a baby with a nursing bottle, patented in 1893. Tuck's German manufacturing facilities were destroyed by bombing in December 1940 and all records, plates and documents were lost. Tuck dolls are easily identified by the trademark and series name and number on the back of each piece. A trademark style of this company is a set of paper dolls with many costumes and interchangeable heads. Tuck also made "regular" paper dolls. Some of their titles include Sweet Abigail, Winsome Winnie, Bridal Party, My Lady Betty, Prince Charming, the popular Fairy Tale series and many more. Tuck made paper dolls several years into the twentieth century.

Manufactured Paper Dolls Post-1900

Among the companies publishing paper dolls at the turn of the century and beyond was Selchow and Righter, who printed the famous Teddy Bear now reproduced by B. Shackman/Merrimack and Co. of New York. B. Shackman, with excellent color, die-cutting and embossing, is known for its fine-quality reproductions of dozens of antique paper dolls, making them attainable at relatively low prices.

McLoughlin and Raphael Tuck continued manufacturing paper dolls into the twentieth century. McLoughlin kept making paper dolls, along with children's story and playbooks, after its sale to Milton Bradley in 1920. Saalfield Publishing of Akron, Ohio, began making children's books, dictionaries and bibles in 1900. Their first paper dolls, done in 1918, were Dollies to Cut and Paint, combining full-color pages with black-and-white, creating further play for youngsters.

Magazine Paper Dolls

In November 1859, *Godey's Lady's Book* was the first magazine to print a paper doll in black and white followed by a page of costumes for children to color. This was the only paper doll *Godey's* ever published, but it set the trend that many women's magazines followed in years to come.

Paper Dolls in Advertising

When paper dolls surged in popularity as toys, manufacturers of all kinds of household goods took advantage of their popularity by using them to promote their wares. Paper dolls appeared in advertising, some die-cut, some as cards to cut out. A few of the products advertised with paper dolls were Lyon's coffee, Pillsbury flour, Baker's chocolate, Singer sewing machines, Clark's threads, McLaughlin coffee and Hood's sarsaparilla. These dolls were plentiful and are still fairly easy to find today, ofttimes pasted into colorful scrapbooks. Later, from the 1930s to the 1950s, companies put paper dolls into their magazine advertisements to sell such goods as nail polish, underwear, Springmaid fabrics, Quadriga Cloth, Fels Naphtha and Swan soaps, and Carter's clothing for children.

The 1900s saw an explosion of paper dolls in many lady's and children's magazines. Lettie Lane, painted by Sheila Young, made her entrance in *Ladies' Home Journal* in October 1908 and ran until July 1915. The pages included Lettie, her friends, her family, their servants and accompanying stories. The Lane family became well-known and loved all across America. *Ladies' Home Journal* continued printing paper dolls through 1948 by a variety of artists including Lucy Fitch Perkins and Gertrude Kay.

Good Housekeeping gave us Polly Pratt and her family and friends, also painted by Sheila Young, from 1919 to 1921. Grayce Drayton's immensely popular Dolly Dingle appeared in *Pictorial Review* in March 1913, then again from 1916 to 1933, interrupted in 1926 by Peggy Pryde and friends and in 1925 and 1926 by the flappers Bonnie and Betty Bobbs. After Dolly came the lovely Polly and Peter Perkins series by Gertrude Kay in 1934.

Rose O'Neill coined the word "Kewpish," meaning "cute," and created her dear little cherubs called Kewpies, first as story pages and then as paper dolls. Introduced in *Woman's Home Companion* in 1912, they enjoyed huge popularity, remaining perhaps the most widely recognized of the antique paper dolls today. Other paper dolls and toys followed in *Woman's Home Companion* throughout the 1920s: Henry Anson Bart and his paper toys, dolls by fashion illustrator Emma

Musselman, Frances Tipton Hunter's precious children, and Katherine Share's paper dolls.

The fashion magazine *The Delineator* featured Carolyn Chester's charming series of three-dimensional wraparound dolls in 1912 and 1913. Paper dolls accompanied by toys, theaters and stories remained a regular feature through 1922 with interesting paper dolls and toys to inspire patriotism during World War I. The women's magazines also had jointed dolls by Carolyn Chester, Catherine Hopkins and Alida Clement.

Good Housekeeping was a major contributor of paper dolls, showcasing the work of many artists from 1909 to the present. Sheila Young's Polly Pratt enjoyed the company of Little Louise, Thomas Lamb's Kiddyland Movies, and "walking" dolls by Elmer and Bertha Hader. *Extension* magazine, published by the Catholic Church Extension Society, presented a series by Martha Miller of Patsy, her friends and family from 1931 to 1935. They published other paper dolls off and on from 1936 through 1959.

Who doesn't know Betsy McCall, perhaps the best-known magazine paper doll in America? She came along after a long tradition of paper dolls in *McCall's* from 1904 to 1926, featuring the art of Jeremiah Crowley (animals and paper toys); Margaret Peckham, A.Z. Baker and Barbara Hale (Jack and Jill Twins); Mel Cummins (Teeny Town); Corrine Pauli; Percy Pierce (villages); the Haders (dolls and furniture); Norman Jacobsen (the Nipper series); and Nandor Hanti's McCall Family series.

A sweet-faced Betsy McCall by Kay Morrissey debuted in 1951. Morrissey was followed by an unknown artist in 1955, then by Ginnie Hoffman in 1958. Betsy McCall modeled fashions that could be made with McCall's patterns while she enjoyed travels and activities all over the United States and beyond. Betsy has come and gone over the years from the 1960s to the 1990s with various changes in style, from the 1970s "mod" look to today's attractive, modern Betsy by Sue Shanahan.

Children's Magazines

Children's magazines were the perfect place to present paper dolls for play and education. *Golden Magazine* gave us sixty pages of paper dolls by Hilda Miloche, Neva Schultz and L.M. Edens, many of ethnic style. The popular *Jack and Jill Magazine* is nearly a sure thing for finding paper dolls from 1938 to 1974. Finding those issues is exciting, but sometimes disappointing as

More Magazine Paper Dolls

Other magazines that have run paper dolls are:
The American Woman (1920s)
Butterick Fashion Magazine (1935)
Canadian Home Journal (1920s and 1930s)
Comfort (1895, 1910 to 1919)
The Designer (1917 and 1918)
The Doll's Dressmaker (1891 to 1893)
The Farm Journal (1921, 1924 and 1956)
The Farmer (1927 to 29, 1960s, 1972, 1983 and 1987)
The Housekeeper (1909 to 1911)
Judge Magazine (1925, 1937)
The Metropolitan (1924 to 1927)
Pageant (Elvis, late 1950s)
Parents' Magazine (1939 and 1940)
People's Popular Monthly (1928)
Screen Life (series of stars, 1941)
Simplicity Pattern Magazine (1934, 1949, 1950 to 1951)
Vanity Fair (1933 and 1934).

For more listings of magazine paper dolls, see Mary Young's *A Collector's Guide to Magazine Paper* (1990, Collector Books).

frequently the paper doll page has been removed. Artists who created these pages were Betsey Bates (1973); Paggy Geiszel (1940s and 1958); Tina Lee (1938 to 1951); and Irma Wilde. *Children's Playmate* printed paper dolls from 1929 to 1961 of all kinds of characters including folk characters, siblings, toys and stuffed animals.

Paper Dolls in Teachers' Magazines

Paper dolls appeared in children's activity magazines and teachers' instructional magazines such as *The Grade Teacher* (1929 to 1951); *Junior Instructor* and *Junior Home Magazine* (1919 to 1931); *Normal Instructor, Primary Plans* and *The Instructor* (1913 to 1936); and *Primary Education* and *Popular Educator* (1924, 1928 to 1929). Auctions of household goods that belonged to retired teachers are gold mines for these kinds of paper dolls.

Doll and Other Contemporary Magazines

Doll magazines, a modern phenomenon, have grown with the popularity of doll collecting and dollmaking. Virtually all of the doll and teddy bear periodicals printed in the United States today regularly print paper dolls. See the doll magazines listed in chapter ten. Other publications which frequently print paper dolls are *Better Homes and Gardens* (various craft issues), *Sew Beautiful, Barbie Bazaar* and *American Girl.* Sharp-eyed collectors watch all kinds of periodicals for the odd paper doll which may appear in the context of satire, advertising, illustration, fashion and so on.

This colonial American boy by Norma Lu Meehan comes with five distinctive outfits from the years 1620-1840. He was published in the June/July 1994 issue of *Contemporary Doll Collector.*

Newspaper Paper Dolls

The Boston Herald began printing paper dolls in the 1890s. Two lady fashion dolls were issued in the paper, and others could be ordered. Costumes in subsequent issues fit the dolls first shown. *The Boston Globe* soon followed with their own unusual paper dolls to put together. In 1907 and 1908, a Teddy Bear series was published, and in 1910, a family. After 1900, the *Boston Post* printed a series about Little Polly and Her Paper Playmates with the popular addition of Polly's older sister Prue, all in full color. The Sunshine Paper Dolls series appeared in *The Boston American* and *The Buffalo Express* in 1916.

Paper dolls enjoyed a huge resurgence in newspapers during the Great Depression, when much entertainment could be had for a nickel from the comics and the paper dolls that often appeared with them. Some paper doll characters sprang directly from the comics: the Katzenjammer Kids, Dick Tracy, Brenda Starr, Daisy Mae and Li'l Abner, Fritzy Ritz and Jane Arden. Other newspapers had their own paper doll features, such as Mopsy, Boots and Millie.

Comic Book Paper Dolls

Paper dolls arrived in comic books when comics went beyond the subjects of adventure and heroes to appeal to the female market. Little girls also loved comics, and in the 1940s and 1950s, paper doll pages included with the comics made them even more appealing. Modeling was a popular theme and a career many girls fancied themselves attaining "someday." This theme also offered a great excuse for dolls to wear lots of costumes. Publishers encouraged interest in their comics and increased sales by inviting readers to send in fashion designs.

In hundreds of comics throughout the 1950s, one will find names assigned to each costume shown. Not all issues contained paper dolls, making the collector's search more challenging. Some of these were Patsy Walker, the Patsy and Hedy series by Atlas Comics (1945 to 1967); Hedy DeVine of Hollywood (Atlas Comics, early 1950s); GAY comics with Millie, Tessie, Nellie and Hedy DeVine (Atlas, 1947 to 1952); the Millie the Model series (Atlas, 1945 to 1973); My Girl Pearl (Atlas, 1955 to 1961); A Date with Judy (National Periodical Publications, 1947 to 1960); Sugar and Spike (D.C. Comics, 1957 to 1971); Dennis the Menace (Fawcett, 1953 to the present); and the Betty and Veronica series (Archie Comics, 1950 to the present).

Bill Woggon's Katy Keene and Contemporary Fashion Model Comics

Katy Keene first appeared in Archie Comics' Suzie (1945 to 1954), Laugh (1946 to the present), Pep (1940 to the present) and Wilbur (1944 to 1946). Katy Keene, originated by Bill Woggon, is the best-loved and most well-known comic book paper doll. She appeared in her own comics—Katy Keene Charm, KK Annual, KK Glamour, KK Fashions, and others (1949 to 1961).

More Comic Book Paper Dolls

There were several short-run comic series with paper dolls. Misty (Star Comics, 1985 to 1986) was a four-issue series of comics featuring paper dolls and the art of Trina Robbins. Following in 1987 was another four-issue Renegade Press series—Trina Robbins' California Girls. Paper dolls appeared now and then in odd places like Eclipse Comics' Airboy, Fashion in Action and Portia Printz (late 1980s), Renegade's Neil the Horse (1980 to 1986), and Marvel Age #54 (1987), the "Official Marvel News Magazine."

Katy, her Sis and her friends enjoyed a revival from 1983 to 1990 with some reprints of old comics by Bill Woggon and new issues by artists Dan DeCarlo, Don Sherwood and John Lucas. A charming series by Renegade Comics, featuring the art of Bill Woggon with the aid of his protégé Barb Rausch, was Vicki Valentine (1985 to 1986). With only four issues of fun, finding Vicki is a real treat for paper doll collectors. Katy is kept alive today by Barb Rausch with the support of Bill Woggon, doing reprints and new art for Hobby House Press. Since the late 1980s, paper doll collectors have been waiting for new comic book paper dolls, and wishing especially for Katy Keene's return. With enough letters to Archie Comics, maybe it can happen.

The Golden Age of Paper Dolls

The 1930s through the 1950s can perhaps claim the title "Golden Age of Paper Dolls," as their popularity during those years has never been equaled. During the Great Depression, paper toys could be afforded by all. Despite the product shortages of World War II, paper dolls were still manufactured, though on lesser-quality papers. Parents of the 1950s revered the image of little girls lovingly playing with paper dolls, just as their mothers and grandmothers had before them.

Queen Holden

We cannot discuss paper dolls of this era without introducing artist Queen Holden, who began her career with Whitman Publishing. She painted dear babies, winsome children, families and even movie stars from 1929 to 1950. Some of her best-loved paper dolls today are Baby Patsy, Judy Garland, Baby Shower, Hair-do Dolls, Carolyn Lee, Snow White and the Dionne Quints. She created more of her sweet-faced children for Samuel Lowe Publishing from 1962 to 1971. Some believe that the Barbie doll was inspired by Queen's glamour dolls of the early 1940s. Queen Holden was and is dearly loved by her fans for her unforgettable paper dolls. When old copies of her work can be discovered, it is a joyful find. Today, B. Shackman is the authorized publisher of all her works, reprinting as many of her designs as they can find and keeping her collectors very happy indeed.

Kathy Lawrence

Queen Holden's daughter, Kathy Lawrence, often the model for her mother's lovely paper dolls, is a fine artist in her own right today, perhaps surpassing her mother's work in quality (but not in popularity, as the heyday of paper dolls had passed by the time she became a paper doll artist). Kathy's first published paper doll, done for Whitman, was her darling Beth Ann, followed by Tiny Tot Shop, similar to her mother's Tots Toggery of the 1940s. We can find Kathy's exquisite work today in the American Greetings card racks, showing her winsome children, adorable babes and cute animals. Kathy created paper dolls and other products for B. Shackman from 1980 to 1985, so the tradition goes on.

Saalfield Publishing Company

The 1940s and 1950s saw great popularity of manufactured paper dolls by many fine artists. The Saalfield Publishing Company had Maybell Mercer, Betty Bell, Ann Kovach and Jean Morse in the 1930s and 1940s, Mary Knight in the 1950s, and Irene Geiger in the 1970s. Fern Bisel Peat created many charming books from 1931 to 1937. Ruth Newton's animals in costumes are memorable. Rose O'Neill's dear Scootles and Kewpie made a delightful book in 1936. George and Nan Pollard did celebrity dolls in the 1950s and 1960s for Saalfield as well as for Samuel Lowe. Their lifelike art extended to other subjects as well. Louise Rumely is remembered for her precious babies in the early 1960s, as well for her cherub-filled Swan Soap ads of the 1940s and 1950s. Ethel Hays Simms is known for her Raggedy Ann and Andy series from the 1940s to the 1960s. Other artists can be studied in Mary Young's *Paper Dolls and Their Artists,* books I and II.

Samuel Lowe Publishing Company

A few of the popular artists of the Samuel Lowe Company are Merily Sharpe, who has been compared to

Queen Holden in style; Pelagie Doane, who was also admired as a children's book illustrator; and the Henderson sisters, Doris and Marion, who did large groups of children in play settings. Fern Bisel Peat also painted several books for this company in the 1940s, as did Queen Holden in the 1960s. Jeanne Voelz did celebrity dolls for Lowe and for Saalfield, as well as the irresistible Cuddles and Rages and other cute characters.

Whitman Publishing Companies

Besides the famed Queen Holden, in the 1940s and 1950s Whitman also published the works of Hilda Miloche, whose lifelike style is immediately recognized by collectors. (Some of her paper dolls appeared in the story pages of the popular Little Golden Books). Avis Mac (1930s) and Judy Stang (early 1970s) did sweet children dolls. Ruth Newton also did her cute animals for Whitman, and Neva Shultz was prolific in the 1960s, doing twenty-eight books. See Mary Young's books for more information on the Whitman artists.

Merrill Publishing Company

Miriam Pendleton Kimbal created books filled with children, as well as the highly-sought-after *Gone With the Wind* (1940), which sells for more than $400 today. Merrill enjoyed the popularity of Louise Rumely's sweet babes, including her Angel Babies. Florence Salter's animals are often confused with Ruth Newton's, as both artists dressed puppies and kittens in paper-doll style. E.A. Voss, noted for her children's book illustrations, did a few paper dolls for Merrill, as did the popular magazine illustrator Maud Tousy Fangel.

Western Publishing, Racine, Wisconsin

Thanks to Western Publishing of Racine, Wisconsin, many of Disney's characters became paper dolls. In addition, Doris Lane Butler did young lady dolls (1940s), and Rachel Taft Dixon was loved for her storybook and folk dolls (1930s). Ethel Bonney Taylor gave us Blondie (1941) as a paper doll. Today Western Publishing still brings us our favorite Disney characters as paper dolls, including Snow White, Pocahontas, The Little Mermaid, Beauty and the Beast and others. These books are readily found at large discount stores and newsstands.

Celebrity Paper Dolls

Celebrities and movie stars were very popular with all the major publishers. It was much simpler to portray stars in the 1930s, 1940s and 1950s, when rights were generally not secured. Studios often "owned" movie stars and their images, and the stars themselves never saw any income from their sale. With images of beloved stars and sports heroes protected today by lawyers and watchdogs all over the world, a publisher must pay for the rights to reproduce our favorite stars as paper dolls. We are fortunate that the images of royalty and politicians are generally free from these restrictions, so some contemporary figures can more readily find their way into paper doll art.

Movie Star Paper Dolls

Ladies World brought us movie stars in paper doll form from 1916 to 1918, including Mary Pickford, Billie Burke, Mary Miles Minter and Charlie Chaplin. *The Delineator* also used movie stars in a paper-doll guessing game in 1917. *Photoplay* presented Movy-Dolls in 1919 and 1920. All were ingenues of the silent screen, including the ever-charming Mary Pickford, Norma Talmadge, Charlie Chaplin and Douglas Fairbanks. In 1925, *Woman's Home Companion* did a short series of child stars as paper dolls—Jackie Coogan, Baby Peggy, and Peter Pan and Our Gang, painted by Frances Tipton Hunter. In 1925, they ran Hollywood Dollies, doing sixty-six different celebrities including Rudolph Valentino, Tom Mix, Colleen Moore, Mary Astor and Rin Tin Tin.

Barbie

Barbie may be credited or condemned for the decline in popularity of paper dolls in the late 1960s, yet in the 1990s Barbie is one of the most popular paper dolls among children and collectors alike. Paper-doll versions of Barbie and her sister, Skipper, were strong sellers in the 1970s to supplement their three-dimensional counterparts. Boyfriend Ken and girlfriend Midge were also made as paper dolls. Paper Barbies appeared in books and in boxed sets from 1962 to the present day. Little to nothing is known of the various Barbie artists until the late 1980s, when nationally known artist Tom Tierney began painting her for Western Publishing. As Tom maintains a wide network of correspondence with his fans and readers of collector publications, most were aware of his new works wherever they appeared. Another Barbie artist in the paper doll network is Barb Rausch, whose love of paper doll art started with Bill Woggon's famous Katy Keene, first done for Archie Comics.

Other Places to Find Paper Dolls

Collectors today enjoy many and varies sources of paper dolls. One may network with other collectors via paper doll newsletters and learn about the latest paper dolls published, sources for buying from catalogues and directly from artists, and news of local and regional parties and conventions. Speaking of conventions, they're the greatest place in the world to find paper dolls. First-time attendees have been heard to gush, "It's paper doll heaven in there!" upon exiting the sales floor.

Greeting card companies sometimes publish cards with paper dolls. Keep a keen eye on all the publishers' racks and review them frequently each season, and you can find paper dolls and toys on cards and even wrapping paper. "Paper dolls" may be wood, cloth, plastic or even magnetic. Fabric stores now sell dolls on yard goods. Specialty shops and catalogues carry some surprising selections.

Getting Published

Those experienced in the world of paper doll publishing know that anyone with talent can be published. Here are some tips:

1. Start with the paper doll newsletters, which like to showcase new art.

2. Join the Original Paper Doll Artists Guild (OPDAG) for ongoing information on technique and more.

3. Study the periodicals. Pick up doll and teddy bear magazines, write to the publishers for their artist guidelines, and prepare art that fits their style and themes.

4. Do your very best work on flexible (not stiff) board, and keep it clean and neat, attractively arranging the art, trims and borders to suit the dolls. Do not do lettering on the art—use an overlay to indicate where type is to be placed. Always sign and date your work with a copyright notice (©).

This "Cowgirls" paper doll by Sandra Vanderpool is pictured here along with the photos that inspired her.

5. Take good photographs of your work, or get laser copies made. Laser copies are excellent quality.

6. Send your art to a publisher, perhaps after phoning to ask which editor to direct it to. Include return postage if you want your work back, but it might be better to let them keep the art on file, so they can keep you in mind should they need a spot filled fast.

7. Repeat the process. Keep painting, study, improve, do another, send it to another publisher. Do not be discouraged by refusals. Many publishers have their schedules filled for up to two years, and simply do not have room for you, or perhaps your work does not suit their needs. If they like your work, and you can customize to their needs, they will eventually use you.

8. Be creative. Think of other areas to which paper doll art can be adapted: fashion, sports, children, satire or news, for example. Reach out to new markets. Paper dolls can appear anywhere there are images in print. 🎶

Here is a sampling of the celebrities who made their way onto paper dolls:

1930s
Sonja Henie
Princess Elizabeth
Shirley Temple
Jane Withers
Clark Gable
Vivien Leigh

1940s
Glenn Miller
Rita Hayworth
Deanna Durbin
Jeanette MacDonald
Bette Davis

1950s
Marilyn Monroe
Esther Williams
Betty Grable
Lucille Ball
Roy Rogers and Dale Evans
Ann Sothern
Doris Day
Elizabeth Taylor
Debbie Reynolds
Grace Kelly

1960s
John Lennon and Yoko Ono
Pat Boone
Annette Funicello
Dinah Shore
Natalie Wood
Rock Hudson
Kim Novak
Julie Andrews
Jackie Kennedy
Twiggy
Patty Duke
Hayley Mills
The Beverly Hillbillies
Samantha (Elizabeth Montgomery)

1970s
The Nixons
The Mouseketeers
The Brady Bunch
The Partridge Family
David Cassidy
Marie Osmond
Charlie's Angels
Gilda Radner
Amy Carter

1980s and 1990s
The Ford, Reagan, Bush and Clinton families
Miss Piggy and The Muppets
John Wayne
Prince Charles and Princess Diana
Princess Fergie

Paper Doll Artists Today

BY JUDY M. JOHNSON

elow are interviews with some of to-day's major paper doll artists.

Tom Tierney

Tom Tierney is well on his way to becoming the best-loved American paper doll artist after Queen Holden. He is the most prolific paper doll artist ever, having produced over two hundred titles for Dover Publications as well as a number of works for other publishers. Born in 1928 in Beaumont, Texas, Tom now lives and works in upstate New York. He earned a BFA in painting and sculpture from the University of Texas, studied commercial art at the University of Colorado, and has also attended Pratt Institute, the Art Students League and the High School of Visual Arts in New York City.

His first published work, a gift to his mother who was fond of paper dolls, was *Thirty from the Thirties,* featuring movie stars. It was published by Prentice Hall in 1974. Tom's primary publisher has been Dover Publications of New York. Other publishers are Western, Checkerboard, B. Shackman, and various periodicals such as *Penthouse, Contemporary Doll Magazine* and *Tennis.*

A full-time artist, Tom works on Strathmore board in India inks. He is inspired by artists G.D. Gibson, John Singer Sargent, impressionist Rene Bouche, Chuck Greenhall, paper doll artist and illustrator Frances Tipton Hunter, fashion illustrator Erte and "a host of others."

Tom says, "Through paper dolls I have met many wonderful paper doll artists and collectors, and I have come into contact with many celebrities I never dreamed of meeting. I get ideas for my art from reading or a piece on TV, or the movies or even plain conversations. When I've finished a book on real people, I feel that I know them personally. I've had to do so much research, they seem like old friends. In the future I hope my art will continue and expand."

Tom says, "Ideas can pop up anywhere! Each of my paper doll books has its own story and is unique to me." He adds, "It is sort of like having children—you don't love one more than the other, you just love them differently."

Norma Lu Meehan

Norma Lu Meehan, born in 1927 in South Bend, Indiana, lives and works in her hometown. Her children are now grown, and she and her husband Edward have six grandchildren. She began drawing paper dolls at the age of eight, then professionally in 1987, when she illustrated a cookbook with a paper doll and historical costumes. She studied fashion illustration for three years in high school, attended the Parsons School of Design for a year, and worked as a fashion illustrator for many retail accounts beginning in 1948. She attained the position of advertising director for two shops, one in South Bend and one in Chicago.

Norma Lu's first published paper doll was *Vintage Fashions* for Hobby House Press in 1991, followed by *The Victorian Paperdoll Wardrobe* in 1992. Her work has appeared in *Contemporary Doll Collector* and *Doll World* magazines. Working up to forty hours a week, Norma uses Strathmore two-ply vellum and watercolor, and does her inking with a croquille pen for black-and-white work. She has been influenced by fashion illustrators Eric Hood of Lord and Taylor and Halpern of Gimbels, by American impressionist painters, and by some contemporary paper doll artists.

"I prefer historical costume and use the collection of the North Indiana Historical Society and real people as models," Norma Lu says. "I hope people will enjoy my work and want to collect. I want to continue working with paper dolls in these golden years. I'd love to do paper dolls using the great costume collections of large urban museums. Something I found exciting in my research was learning about women who wore the gowns used in my books. I came to discover some belonged to women I know. I am thrilled to know that my books have caused people to visit our wonderful History Center in South Bend."

Sandra Vanderpool

Sandra Vanderpool, born in 1946, lives and works in Erie, Colorado, with her artist husband, John Vanderpool. She began drawing paper dolls as a child, creating more costumes for her store-bought sets. Her career as a paper doll artist began in 1987 when she was inspired to do paper dolls of people who interested her. She has a BFA in fashion illustration from Art Center College of Design in Pasadena, California. She worked full-time in the field in Los Angeles for several years, then free-lanced for a while. She returned to Colorado to teach fashion illustration and basic illustration at a local art school, where she met her husband.

Hobby House became the first publisher of Sandy's work in 1991 with *The Enchanted Realm of Fairyland*. Other works have been published in doll magazines and as convention souvenirs. In 1987, Sandy began self-publishing her sets of famous women authors, a collection which has grown to include many famous figures, telling their stories through their costumes and props. "I enjoy working on the historical sets," Sandra says. Dozens of her paper dolls are available by mail.

Working full days, five days a week, Sandy does her black-and-white sets in pen and ink using a Rotring cartridge pen and vellum paper. She prefers opaque watercolors in pans by Prang, Grumbacher and Pelikan for her full-color sets. Paper doll artists of the past, from Frances Tipton Hunter and Hilda Miloche to other artists whose names are unknown, have inspired Sandra. She also credits Toulouse-Lautrec, Degas, Aubrey Beardsley, Andrew Wyeth and John Vanderpool as influences.

"I get ideas for my art by reading lots of biographies, by listening to stories from my relatives, from fairy tales and myths and from themes suggested in OPDAG News," Sandra says. "In the course of the next ten years I want to be doing exclusive one-of-a-kind sets, hand-painted, cut and boxed, to really make it an art form, possibly exhibited in galleries. I'd like to do a portrait of myself as a four-year-old child. I want to keep challenging myself using new ideas, exploring new mediums and mastering them. I like to strike a chord with my patrons—this is the real reward—seeing their faces light up when my work speaks to them."

Sue Shanahan

Sue Shanahan, born in 1956 in Joliet, Illinois, now resides and works in nearby Mokena with her husband, Bob, and their children. Sue recalls: "When I was about ten, my sisters and neighborhood friends spent many afternoons working on paper dolls. I had a whole shoebox of clothing for mine."

Sue attended Joliet Junior College for a semester and the American Academy of Art in Chicago, but in many ways she is self-taught, having educated herself by reading books and studying other artist's work. Primarily recognized for her magazine work, Sue's first published paper doll was of her two younger children, presented in *Contemporary Doll Magazine*. Many of Sue's paper dolls are portraits of vintage and contemporary dolls, putting her work in demand by publishers of doll magazines. Her primary publisher is *Doll Reader*. Dover Publications has published her work, and she has done the famous Betsy McCall for *McCall's*.

Sue's work is unique in that she uses colored pencils as her primary medium. "I use Crescent Museum Mat Board. I first put down a layer of watercolor pencils, then work over them with Berol Prismacolor. I have been influenced by the work of paper doll artists Judy M. Johnson and Tom Tierney. Many children's book illustrators inspire me, as do the French impressionists." Considering the volume of work she has produced in the last two years, Sue must work many hours in her home studio. Look for her fine work in the pages of your favorite doll magazines.

Judy M. Johnson

Born in 1946, Judy M. Johnson has been an artist as long as she can remember. She says she was "born with a paintbrush in her mouth." From an early age, Judy took lessons in art basics from her mother's brother, John Heath. Now, living once again in her hometown of Skandia, Michigan, Judy works from her home studio. She has an artistic daughter, Jenny, who is married and owns Main Street Stamps in Kingfield, Maine. Son Ken, thirteen, lives with Judy and her life partner, Glenn.

A lifelong student of art, Judy has learned from books and from other artists, but mainly by doing, trying, creating, teaching and selling her art in one form or another all her life. As a teenager, she was a portrait artist at the New York World's Fair in 1965. Judy is a founding member of OPDAG News and a managing editor of their quarterly magazine. Her first paper doll published was in 1984, for B. Shackman of New York, on the Kitty Cucumber line of products. This led to dozens of other characters, which have been developed into hundreds of products. Dover Publishing has about sixteen of her designs either in print or on the back burner. They've also published four of Judy's pictorial archive series and an 1830s French fashion book. These products are marketed worldwide. Judy's work also appears in national doll and teddy periodicals and as souvenirs for paper doll and doll conventions.

Judy's latest news is her contribution as the major artist for a new company, Magnattraction, of Concord, Massachusetts. The owner, Stuart Bloom, has invented a revolutionary process of applying liquefied iron to cloth, upon which Judy's doll designs are printed. This "Magicloth" adheres to a magnetized doll, so the clothing holds securely with no tabs. These die-cut dolls and costumes are a new all-fun, no-frustration way of playing with paper dolls. The first lines, released in late 1995, were Judy's adaptations of Curious George, Dolly Dingle and Billy Bumps, along with a sweet baby doll, Sammy.

Judy uses whatever medium is required to get the fabric or texture effect she needs, including watercolors, markers, colored pencils or inks on bristol papers. Ideas come from everywhere—history, vintage fashion magazines and catalogs, and real dolls. "I love fabric and fashion designs. Many of the costumes I put on figures are derived from authentic sources, and many I design myself. Things like fantasy and show girls are the most fun." ❧

Paper Dolls

COMMERCIAL PUBLISHERS

B. SHACKMAN PUBLISHERS INC.

Jim Lillemoe
85 5th Ave. at 16th
New York, NY 10003
Phone: (212)989-5162 EST
Fax:(212)242-3832

PRODUCT INFORMATION:
Publishes: In-house artists' work. Also die-cut cards, tags, paper doll greeting cards.

BUSINESS INFORMATION:
Type of business: Wholesale only
Catalog: $3

LORAINE BURDICK

413 10th Ave. Court N.E.
Puyallup, WA 98372
In business since: 1956

PRODUCT INFORMATION:
Publishes: Paper-doll-related products and paper doll reference books.
Description: Publishes comic strip paper dolls by titles and years; related items from a single source such as children's magazines or a single topic including Alice in Wonderland, Snow White, movie stars; artists such as Queen Holden and Rachel Taft Dixon; and much more.

BUSINESS INFORMATION:
Type of business: Wholesale and retail
Catalog: Free
To purchase: Selected titles available from various small dealers, lists and shops.

DOVER PUBLICATIONS

Stan Applebaum
31 E. 2nd St.
Mineola, NY 11501
Phone: (516)294-7000
Fax: (516)294-4213

PRODUCT INFORMATION:
Publishes: Freelance artists' work, in-house artists' work. Also paper doll reference books, history reprints.
Description: Paper dolls are punch-outs with stickers and cutouts. Books are on such areas as reprint antique paper dolls of 1900s, Dolly Dingle dolls, presidential dolls, American family (Puritan through 1970s), entertainers, African-American, history figures, ballet, movie stars and small $1 dolls. Little Activity series includes many ethnic paper dolls. These dolls are both punch-out and stickers.

BUSINESS INFORMATION:
Type of business: Wholesale and retail
Catalog: Free

SUBMISSIONS:
Guidelines: Must write to above address for guidelines.

HOBBY HOUSE PRESS

1 Corporate Dr.
Grantsville, MD 21536
Phone: (301)895-3792
Fax: (301)895-5029

PRODUCT INFORMATION:
Publishes: Paper dolls and other doll-related books

PAM'S PAPER DOLLS AND COLLECTIBLES

Pam Boyd
P.O. Box 1054
St. Bethlehem, TN 37155
E-mail: 102662.3702@compuserve.com
In business since: 1993

PRODUCT INFORMATION:
Publishes: In-house artists' work and work that publisher solicits. Also paper doll greeting cards.
Description: Paper dolls are original artist works and prints in paper doll forms. Only a few paper dolls are published, which are exclusives for Pam's Paper Dolls and Collectibles catalog.

BUSINESS INFORMATION:
Type of business: Wholesale and retail
Catalog: $4, nonrefundable
To purchase: Available by mail, from home and at shows.

THE PAPER PALACE

Margaret and Blair Whitton
21 Pako Ave.
Keene, NH 03431
Phone: (603)352-7502 EST
In business since: 1965

PRODUCT INFORMATION:
Publishes: Paper doll reference books

BUSINESS INFORMATION:
Type of business: Wholesale and retail
Catalog: Only mailing lists on request. Send LSASE.
To purchase: Available by mail, sometimes at shows.

> "BUY PAPER DOLLS BASED ON WHAT YOU LIKE. YOU MAY WANT TO HAVE DIFFERENT CATEGORIES AND STYLES, FROM ANTIQUE TO COMICS, OR SPECIALIZE IN ONE AREA."
> *Sylvia Kleindinst, Irving, NY*

DEALERS

JANIE BARRETT

829 Kenilworth Terrace
Orlando, FL 32803
Phone: (407)898-7095 EST
In business since: 1955

PRODUCT/SERVICE INFORMATION:
Sells: Paper doll artists' work, antique and collectible paper dolls
Buys: Paper doll artists' work, paper dolls from commercial publishers, selected antique paper dolls

BUSINESS INFORMATION:
Retail: By mail, through friends and paper doll magazines.
Phone orders: Accepted
Business through the mail: Buys and sells through the mail.

LORAINE BURDICK

413 10th Ave. Court N.E.
Puyallup, WA 98372
In business since: 1956

PRODUCT/SERVICE INFORMATION:
Sells: Paper doll artists' work, antique

and collectible paper dolls, paper dolls, paper toys, children's books and related illustrators' work.

Buys: Selected antique paper dolls, entire collections.

BUSINESS INFORMATION:

Catalog: $1 semimonthly, nonrefundable, but next list free.

Mailing list: Send $1 to be included.

Wholesale: Sells to retail shops.

Retail: Sells through the mail.

Business through the mail: Buys and sells through the mail in US, Canada and overseas. Prepayment required or by arrangement. Shipping extra $4 minimum.

Shipping information: Shipped via US mail. Allow 3 weeks delivery.

Accepts: Check or money order

Layaway: Available

PAT FREY
9 Station Rd.
Cranbury, NJ 08512
Phone: (609)655-3720 EST
Fax: (609)655-3720
In business since: 1972

PRODUCT/SERVICE INFORMATION:

Sells: Paper doll artists' work, antique and collectible paper dolls

Buys: Artists' and commercial publishers' paper dolls, selected antique paper dolls, entire collections and work offered at flea markets and auctions.

Appraisals: Free

BUSINESS INFORMATION:

Retail: By mail or from home

Fax orders: Accepted

Business through the mail: Buys, sells and appraises through the mail in US, Canada, overseas. Prepayment required. Shipping included in cost of paper doll.

Shipping information: Shipped via priority mail. Allow 2 weeks for delivery.

Accepts: Cash or check

PRISCILLA JOFFEE
292 Stuart St.
Howell, NJ 07731
Phone: (908)462-6284 EST
In business since: 1961

PRODUCT/SERVICE INFORMATION:

Sells: Paper doll artists' work, antique and collectible paper dolls

Buys: Paper doll artists' work, commercial publishers' paper dolls

BUSINESS INFORMATION:

Retail: Sells at shows, at shop, by mail.

Phone orders: After 8 A.M.

Business through the mail: Buys and sells through the mail.

JUDY'S PLACE
Judy M. Johnson
P.O. Box 176
Skandia, MI 49885
Phone: (906)942-7865 EST
In business since: 1982

PRODUCT/SERVICE INFORMATION:

Sells: Paper doll artists' work and paper-doll-related goods: ornaments, stickers, notes, tags

Buys: Artists' paper dolls, commercial publishers' work and selected antique paper dolls.

BUSINESS INFORMATION:

Catalog: Send stamp

Mailing list: Write to be included.

Wholesale: Sells to retail shops, mail order houses and internationally via artist's publishers.

Retail: At shows, by mail, from home and at paper doll parties and conventions.

Phone orders: M-F, 10-10.

Fax orders: Fax order form from catalog; include list of titles, prices and shipping information.

Business through the mail: Buys, sells and appraises through the mail in US, Canada and overseas. Prepayment required. Shipping added to total.

Shipping information: Shipped via UPS or US mail. Allow 1-4 weeks for delivery.

Accepts: Check, Visa, MC, DC

ROSEMARY MCBURNETT
9878 68th Ave.
Allendale, MI 49401
Phone: (616)895-6232 EST
In business since: 1978

PRODUCT/SERVICE INFORMATION:

Buys: Paper doll artists' work, paper dolls from commercial publishers, selected antique paper dolls and entire collections

BUSINESS INFORMATION:

Retail: At shows, at shop, by mail and from home.

Home appointments: Call to arrange a time.

Phone orders: Available

Business through the mail: Buys and sells through the mail in US. Prepayment required; also trades.

Shipping information: Sometimes extra, sometimes included in cost of paper doll. Shipped via UPS or US mail. Allow 1 week for delivery.

Accepts: Check

ADDITIONAL INFORMATION:

Rosemary will travel to buy and to attend paper doll parties, auctions, shows, etc. She is very interested in Sunday Comic strips.

N.M.P.
Iva Shackelford
1734 Broken Arrow Dr.
Prescott, AZ 86303
Phone: (520)778-0823 MST
In business since: 1975

PRODUCT/SERVICE INFORMATION:

Sells: Sells own work.

Buys: Paper dolls from commercial publishers and selected antique paper dolls.

BUSINESS INFORMATION:

Wholesale: Sells to retail shops and mail order houses.

Retail: Sells at shows, by mail or out of home/studio.

Home appointments: Schedule 1 day in advance.

Phone orders: 9-5.

Business through the mail: Sells through the mail in US and Canada. Prepayment required. Shipping included in cost of paper doll.

Shipping information: Shipped via US mail. Allow 7 days for delivery.

Accepts: Cash, check

P.D. PAL
Jim Faraone
19109 Silcott Springs Rd.
Purcellville, VA 22132
Phone: (540)338-3621
In business since: 1987

PRODUCT/SERVICE INFORMATION:

Sells: Paper doll artists' work

Buys: Paper doll artists' work, paper dolls from commercial publishers, selected antique paper dolls

BUSINESS INFORMATION:

Retail: Sells at shows, by mail, from home/studio or through newsletter, *P.D. Pal.*

Phone orders: M-F, 11-11.

Business through the mail: Buys, sells and appraises through the mail in US, Canada and overseas. Prepayment required. Shipping included in cost of paper doll.

Shipping information: Shipped via US mail. Allow 10 days for delivery.

Accepts: Cash or check

Layaway: 10% down, balance by arrangement.

PAM'S PAPER DOLLS AND COLLECTIBLES

Pam Boyd
P.O. Box 1054
St. Bethlehem, TN 37155
E-mail: 102662.3702@compuserve.com
In business since: 1993

PRODUCT/SERVICE INFORMATION:

Sells: Paper doll artists' work, antique and collectible paper dolls, paper doll-related collectibles plus related books and paper doll storage supplies.

Buys: Paper doll artists' work and paper dolls from commercial publishers, selected antique paper dolls, entire collections.

BUSINESS INFORMATION:

Catalog: $4, nonrefundable

Mailing list: Write to be included or send $4 for current catalog. Automatically places name on the mailing list.

Retail: Sells at shows, by mail, from home and at paper doll parties.

Home appointments: Appointment required.

Business through the mail: Buys and sells through the mail in US, Canada and overseas. Prepayment required in US funds.

Shipping information: Shipped via UPS or US mail. Allow 1-6 weeks for delivery.

Accepts: Cash or check, US funds only.

ADDITIONAL INFORMATION:

Publishes in-house artists' work or work that is solicited. Only a few paper dolls are published which are exclusives for Pam's Paper Dolls and Collectibles catalog.

THE PAPER PALACE

Margaret and Blair Whitton
21 Pako Ave.
Keene, NH 03431
Phone: (603)352-7502 EST
In business since: 1965

PRODUCT/SERVICE INFORMATION:

Sells: Antique and collectible paper dolls, paper toys, paper theaters, children's books, advertising paper dolls.

Buys: Selected antique paper dolls, entire collections.

BUSINESS INFORMATION:

Mailing list: Write to be included.

Retail: Sells at shows and through the mail.

Phone orders: Accepted

Business through the mail: Buys and sells by mail in US. Prepayment required. Shipping included in cost of paper doll (postage listed extra on mailing list).

Shipping information: Shipped via UPS. Allow 3 weeks for delivery.

Accepts: Checks

PRINCE DOLL STUDIO

Alan or Karen Prince
P.O. Box 36607
Houston, TX 77236
Phone: (713)690-6558 CST
Fax: (713)460-4556
In business since: 1990

PRODUCT/SERVICE INFORMATION:

Sells: Original paper dolls, collectible dolls and paper doll pins, t-shirts, sweatshirts, tote bags, note cards and mugs.

Buys: Paper dolls from paper doll artists, commercial publishers, selected antique paper dolls.

BUSINESS INFORMATION:

Catalog: Free with SASE.

Mailing list: Write or call to be included.

Wholesale: Sells to retail shops.

Retail: Sells at shows, by mail and from studio.

Shop: M-F, 6:30-4:30.

Home appointments: Call first.

Phone orders: During business hours

Fax orders: Fax catalog order form.

Business through the mail: Buys and sells through the mail in US, Canada and overseas. Prepayment required.

Shipping charges are listed on order form.

Shipping information: Shipped via US mail unless otherwise requested. Allow 2-4 weeks for delivery.

Accepts: Cash, check or money order

RH STEVENS

Elsie Stevens
17838 SE Hwy. 452
Umatilla, FL 32784
Phone: (904)821-3276 EST
In business since: 1976

PRODUCT/SERVICE INFORMATION:

Sells: Antique and collectible paper dolls

Buys: Paper dolls from commercial publishers, selected antique paper dolls, entire collections

BUSINESS INFORMATION:

Price list: Monthly. First-time inquiries, $1; $10 for entire 1-year list.

Wholesale: Sells to retail shops.

Retail: Sells by mail.

Phone orders: 7 days, 9-5.

Business through the mail: Buys and sells through the mail.

SANDRA VANDERPOOL

P.O. Box 695
Erie, CO 80516
Phone: (303)828-3387 MST
In business since: 1986

PRODUCT/SERVICE INFORMATION:

Buys: Paper doll artists' work, paper dolls from commercial publishers, selected antique paper dolls and entire collections.

BUSINESS INFORMATION:

Mailing list: Write to be included.

Wholesale: Sells to retail shops and museums.

Retail: Sells at shows, by mail and from home.

Home appointments: Schedule 2 days in advance.

Phone orders: After 1 P.M.

Business through the mail: Buys and sells through the mail in US, Canada and overseas. Prepayment required. Shipping included with cost of paper doll.

Shipping information: Shipped via FedEx, UPS or US mail. Allow 2 weeks for delivery.

Accepts: Check

LORETTA WILLIS
808 Lee Ave.
Tifton, GA 31794
Phone: EST
In business since: 1980

PRODUCT/SERVICE INFORMATION:

Sells: Paper doll artists' work, antique and collectible paper dolls, t-shirts, totes, paper doll catalogs and other paper doll-related items.

Buys: Paper dolls from artists and commercial publishers' paper dolls, selected antique paper dolls, entire collections

Appraisals: $15-$100 and up for sets of highly valued paper dolls.

BUSINESS INFORMATION:

Wholesale: Sells to other paper doll dealers and collectors.

Retail: Sells at shows, by mail and from home.

Home appointments: Schedule in advance; morning or noon hours preferred.

Business through the mail: Buys, sells and appraises through the mail in US, Canada and overseas. (Please send funds in US money orders for overseas.) Prepayment required.

Shipping information: Shipped via UPS, US mail, direct mail, overseas mail. Allow 1 to 2 weeks for delivery. Shipping cost is added to merchandise cost.

Accepts: Cash, check or money orders

ARTISTS

JOHANA GAST ANDERTON
6408 North Flora Ave.
Gladstone, MO 64118-3609
Phone: (816)468-0558 CST
In business since: 1968

PRODUCT INFORMATION:

Scope of work: The artist produces some one-of-a-kind originals. She is self-published and also works for commercial publishers on a freelance basis. Her work can be found occasionally in smaller publications, such as newsletters. She works in both b&w and color.

Publishers: UFDC, Hobby House Press, Castle Press Publications

BUSINESS INFORMATION:

Price list: $3, nonrefundable

Mailing list: Send large SASE for information.

To purchase: Published work is available mainly at doll shows or craft shows, through sales list by mail and specific ads in collectors papers and magazines, and at workshops the artist conducts for various organizations.

ADDITIONAL INFORMATION:

Johana also gives lectures and slide shows upon invitation from an organization and organizes paper doll exhibits. She also conducts hands-on workshops for organizations in which participants are encouraged to create their own original paper dolls. She is a founding member of the Original Paper Doll Artists Guild (OPDAG) and is managing editor of *OPDAG News,* their quarterly publication.

"PAPER DOLLS OFFER AN OPPORTUNITY FOR
EXPRESSION THAT IS UNIQUE . . .
THERE ARE NO RESTRICTIONS."
Johanna Gast Anderton, Gladstone, MO

JOHN AXE
1637 Tanglewood
Youngstown, OH 44505
Phone: (216)759-2282 EST
In business since: 1985

PRODUCT INFORMATION:

Scope of work: The artist works for commercial publishers on a freelance basis. His work is also published occasionally by smaller publications, such as newsletters. He works in color.

Description of work: John's paper dolls are contemporary and period men, women and children. He specializes in accurate portrait subjects with authentic costumes and accessories. Some of his most successful paper dolls have been of movie stars and European royalty as children.

Publishers: Hobby House Press, Scott Publications

BUSINESS INFORMATION:

To purchase: Purchase through catalogs of Hobby House Press and Fond Memories.

ADDITIONAL INFORMATION:

John also gives lectures at UFDC doll conventions and regional conferences, at doll club meetings, and at paper doll conventions. He also gives slide shows covering historical perspective (movie star paper dolls) and organizes paper doll exhibits (the work of Queen Holden). He has done many paper dolls for UFDC and for conferences as souvenirs, and has done a souvenir paper doll for four national paper doll conventions.

MIRREN BARRIE
R.R. 1, Box 9640, Loomis Hill
Waterbury Center, VT 05677
Phone: (802)244-6995 EST
In business since: 1992

PRODUCT INFORMATION:

Scope of work: Produces handmade one-of-a-kind originals only and editions limited to 10. Works in color.

Description of work: Mirren's paper dolls are 3-dimensional, stand without support, and are completely made of paper. Costumes are also all paper, from dinner napkins to exotic Japanese papers. Subjects are mainly historical or in period dress: Queen Elizabeth I, Uncle Sam and Stuart monarchs are featured.

BUSINESS INFORMATION:

To purchase: Published work is available at the annual NIADA conference.

AMY ALBERT BLOOM
31 Philadelphia Ave.
Shillington, PA 19607
Phone: (610)775-8993 EST
In business since: 1988

PRODUCT INFORMATION:

Scope of work: The artist produces one-of-a-kind originals. She also works for magazine publishers on a freelance basis. She works in color.

Description of work: Amy makes almost all handmade paper dolls, drawn and colored in colored pencil, in very small quantities, usually under 10 of each. Sometimes she uses different papers to make dresses. She describes her work as cute, pretty and whimsical.

BUSINESS INFORMATION:

Catalog: Free. Please send large SASE.

Mailing list: Write or call to be included.

To purchase: Published work is available from the artist through the mail, at local doll/teddy/toy shows or by appointment at her home.

ADDITIONAL INFORMATION:
Amy also makes cloth dolls and designs these and other crafts for magazines, craft leaflet publishers and craft supply manufacturers. Her paper dolls have been published in *Woman's World* and *Dollmaking Crafts & Designs.*

LORAINE BURDICK
413 10th Ave. Court N.E.
Puyallup, WA 98372
In business since: 1956

PRODUCT INFORMATION:
Scope of work: Artist is self-published. She works in both b&w and color.

Description of work: Loraine's work includes some original paper dolls and reprints of antique, comic and movie paper dolls.

BUSINESS INFORMATION:
Catalog: Free

BUTTERFLY CAT STUDIOS
Charles D. Claudon
1448 North Wood, Apt. 2F
Chicago, IL 60622
Phone: (312)395-0275 CST
E-mail: videoc@aol.com
In business since: 1992

PRODUCT INFORMATION:
Scope of work: The artist produces handmade one-of-a-kind originals only and is self-published. He works in b&w and color.

Description of work: Charles started making paper dolls as a result of research on period dolls.

BUSINESS INFORMATION:
Catalog: SASE

VICTORIA CHRISTOPHERSON
Victoria's Paper Dolls
P.O. Box 84
Ridgely, MD 21660
Phone: (410)634-1953 EST
In business since: 1986

PRODUCT INFORMATION:
Scope of work: Victoria is self-published. Her work is also published occasionally by smaller publications, such as

newsletters. She works in both b&w and color.

Description of work: Victoria's catalog includes paper dolls, ornament kits and miniature kits. All are her original designs. The paper dolls are available in b&w with some available in full color. The prices range from $1.50-15. She also does small edition paper dolls from photos. Some paper dolls include historical information.

BUSINESS INFORMATION:
Catalog: LSASE

Mailing list: Write or call to be included.

To purchase: Mail order only.

ADDITIONAL INFORMATION:
Victoria presents lectures and slide shows on the history of paper dolls.

MARTHA DAVIS
13 Hillview Rd.
Asheville, NC 28805
Phone: (204)298-1717 EST
E-mail: martied@aol.com or dolldrl@aol.com
In business since: 1990

PRODUCT INFORMATION:
Scope of work: Martha produces handmade one-of-a-kind originals only. She works in color.

Description of work: Martha creates original paper dolls with 2-3 dresses and hats made of crepe paper, lace and flowers in the antique style.

BUSINESS INFORMATION:
To purchase: Contact the artist. By mail and at local shows.

DON DIFONSO
3800 Perrysville Ave.
Pittsburgh, PA 15214
Phone: (412)321-5996 EST or (412)621-4445 x4629
In business since: 1994

PRODUCT INFORMATION:
Scope of work: Artist is self-published. He works in b&w.

Description of work: Don makes original celebrity paper dolls from the Golden Age of Hollywood and Broadway. All sets are 6 sheets, 8½″ × 11″, b&w on card stock in plastic envelope. Some examples are Mae West, Ethel Merman, Bette Davis and Alice Faye.

BUSINESS INFORMATION:
Price list: Free
Mailing list: Write to be included.
To purchase: Published work is available from artist.

JUDITH DODINGTON
N. Greenlake Gallery
R.R. 1, 70 Mile House
BC V0K 2K0
CANADA
Phone: (604)456-7326 PST
In business since: 1985

PRODUCT INFORMATION:
Scope of work: Judith produces handmade one-of-a-kind originals. She is self-published. She works in b&w.

Description of work: Judith's paper dolls are usually ethnic and/or historical, heroines of science fiction novels, or outstanding women in the arts, including Natalie Cole, Georgia O'Keefe and Louise Nevelson. She also makes paper backgrounds that can be set up theatrically in a deep picture frame, plus a sheet of ideas on how to display dolls for fun.

BUSINESS INFORMATION:
Price list: Free
To purchase: Published work is available from artist.

FANCY EPHEMERA
Brenda Sneathen Mattox
615 Delray Dr.
Indianapolis, IN 46241
Phone: (317)247-4589 EST

PRODUCT INFORMATION:
Scope of work: Artist is self-published and also works for commercial publishers on a freelance basis. She is also published occasionally by smaller publications. She works in both color and b&w.

Description of work: Brenda's specialty is Victorian and vintage fashion with particular interest in brides. Occasionally she does real people, historical figures and classic movie stars. She is the author of *Victorian Bride and Her Trousseau* (Dover).

Publishers: Dover Publications Inc., Scott Publications, *OPDAG News.*

BUSINESS INFORMATION:
Price list: Free with large SASE.

Mailing list: Write to be included.

To purchase: Published work is available from Fancy Ephemera; book is available at bookstores.

ADDITIONAL INFORMATION:
Brenda also collects and trades for other artists' work. She is a longtime collector of vintage clothing and antique fashion plates which she often uses as reference material.

CAROL FAIRCHILD

364 Weaver Rd.
Myrtle Creek, OR 97457
Phone: (541)863-3994 PST

PRODUCT INFORMATION:
Scope of work: Artist produces hand-made one-of-a-kind originals. Her work is published occasionally by smaller publications, such as newsletters. She works in both color and b&w.

Description of work: Carol makes hand-made original paper dolls of women, children and animals.

BUSINESS INFORMATION:
Price list: Free with SASE.
Mailing list: Write to be included.
To purchase: Published work is available direct from artist.

"KEEP SEARCHING. YOUR PAPER DOLLS ARE OUT THERE SOMEWHERE!"

Brenda Sneathen Mattox, Fancy Ephemera, Indianapolis, IN

JIM FARAONE—P.D. PAL

Jim Faraone
19109 Silcott Springs Rd.
Purcellville, VA 22132
Phone: (540)338-3621
In business since: 1987

PRODUCT INFORMATION:
Scope of work: Jim produces handmade one-of-a-kind originals. He is self-published and also works for commercial publishers on a freelance basis. His work is published occasionally by smaller publications. He works in both color and b&w.

Description of work: Original artwork in full color and b&w. Artist's work has appeared in *Doll News* and *Contemporary Doll Collector.*

Publishers: Scott Publications (contributing writer of articles on paper dolls, Barbie dolls and collecting).

BUSINESS INFORMATION:
To purchase: Published work is available through artist's paper doll newsletter, P.D. Pal.

ADDITIONAL INFORMATION:
Jim also gives lectures at paper doll conventions. Subjects include contemporary to original artist's paper dolls. He is in charge of the paper doll artist's gallery at the national paper doll conventions.

PAT FREY

9 Station Rd.
Cranbury, NJ 08512
Phone: (609)655-3720 EST
Fax: (609)655-3720
In business since: 1972

PRODUCT INFORMATION:
Scope of work: Artist produces one-of-a-kind originals only. She is self-published and also works for commercial publishers on a freelance basis. Her work is also published occasionally by smaller publications. She works in both color and b&w.

Description of work: Pat makes movie star dolls from Shirley Temple to Marilyn Monroe. Historical figures are a specialty, ranging from B.C. to Star Trek, the Egyptians to Princess Diana. She works in all aspects of paper doll costuming, from decoupage to three-dimensional.

BUSINESS INFORMATION:
Price list: Available
To purchase: Published work is available from artist.

ADDITIONAL INFORMATION:
Pat presents lectures at doll clubs and local schools and organizes exhibits at the local library and historical museum.

EVELYN GATHINGS

4426 4th St.
Riverside, CA 92501
Phone: (909)784-0260 PST
In business since: 1982

PRODUCT INFORMATION:
Scope of work: Artist works for commercial publishers on a freelance basis. She works in color.

Description of work: Work is pets/ani-mals and children. All have turn-of-the-century clothing.

Publishers: Meresurst, Dover Publications

YUKO GREEN

P.O. Box 383182
Waikoloa, HI 96738
Phone: (808)883-9586 Hawaii time zone
In business since: 1992

PRODUCT INFORMATION:
Scope of work: Yuko works for commercial publishers on a freelance basis. Works mostly in color.

Description of work: Yuko works in soft pastel tone watercolors. All designs are of children (mostly little girls) and teddy bears. Paper dolls express happy moments of childhood and fun playful images of toys. The artist uses lots of floral images to design paper doll clothes.

Publishers: Dover Publications

BUSINESS INFORMATION:
Mailing list: Write to be included.
To purchase: Published work is available through Dover's catalog.

ADDITIONAL INFORMATION:
Yuko's work has been published in *Doll World, Dolls, Dollmaking Crafts & Designs* and *Contemporary Doll Collector.*

MARILYN HENRY

5312 Stringtown Rd.
Evansville, IN 47711
Phone: (812)423-5334 CST
In business since: 1964

PRODUCT INFORMATION:
Scope of work: Artist is self-published, and also works for commercial publishers on a freelance basis. She also is published occasionally by smaller publications. She works in both b&w and color.

Description of work: In addition to many self-published sets of paper dolls, mostly celebrities, Marilyn is working on a series of celebrities for B. Shackman and Co. The first in the series, Claudette Colbert, is completed. Future sets will include Myrna Loy, Joan Crawford and others.

Publishers: B. Shackman and Co.

BUSINESS INFORMATION:
Price list: For large SASE.

Mailing list: Write or call to be included.

To purchase: Published work is available from the artist and at various book and gift shops.

SHARON HINES-PINION

Cedar Rose Studio
1103 NE 73rd St.
Seattle, WA 98115
Phone: (206)525-9503 PST
In business since: 1992

PRODUCT INFORMATION:

Scope of work: Artist produces one-of-a-kind originals. She is self-published. She works in both color and b&w.

Description of work: Sharon's paper dolls present real historical women who led unusual and/or inspirational lives or characters from folklore and mythology. She includes a brief account of each life history or mythic story so that the paper dolls can serve an educational function in addition to being entertaining and fun. She also produces family history portraits.

BUSINESS INFORMATION:

Price list: SASE

Mailing list: Write to be included.

To purchase: Published work is available by mail order only.

ADDITIONAL INFORMATION:

Sharon was the featured artist in the Winter 1994 issue of the *OPDAG News.*

> "IF YOU BUY PAPER DOLLS FOR INVESTMENT, THE CELEBRITIES AND ANTIQUE CATEGORIES WILL BRING THE GREATEST RETURN."
>
> *Sylvia Kleindinst, Irving, NY*

JEANNE HOPF

924 Hinman Ave., Apt. 1C
Evanston, IL 60202
Phone: (708)869-7277 CST
In business since: 1934

PRODUCT INFORMATION:

Scope of work: The artist has self-published 1 set of historical paper dolls and reproduces other sets by photocopying. She works in color.

Description of work: Jeanne's work is primarily of historical periods in various countries. A few sets are fantasy subjects. She also produces Afro-American dolls. Her commercially

published set is *Jack and Jeanne's Historical Paper Dolls—Louis XVIth Period.*

BUSINESS INFORMATION:

Price list: SASE

To purchase: Published work is available by mail from the artist.

ADDITIONAL INFORMATION:

Her work has appeared in various paper doll publications.

BONNIE HOOVER

26889 Lakewood Way
Haward, CA 94544
Phone: (510)887-4250 PST
In business since: 1988

PRODUCT INFORMATION:

Scope of work: Artist produces handmade one-of-a-kind originals only and is self-published. She works in color.

Description of work: Bonnie makes fantasy paper dolls with very bright/bold colors (no pastel). She creates both cloth and paper dolls, and is known for embellished dolls, not conventional. Paper dolls have moveable joints.

Publishers: Austrialian magazine—*Dolls, Bears and Collectibles*

BUSINESS INFORMATION:

Catalog: Order forms with patterns and drawings on designs, SASE.

ILLUSTROPLAY

Erik Felker
414 E. Cedar #9
Burbank, CA 91501
Phone: (818)845-0164 PST
In business since: 1993

PRODUCT INFORMATION:

Scope of work: Artist is self-published. He works in b&w.

Description of work: Erik aims his work at children in a variety of circumstances, and he likes to explore multicultural themes in whimsical ways. His interests also include casting paper dolls in somewhat nontraditional roles, such as a uniquely mailable and portable art form/toy.

BUSINESS INFORMATION:

Catalog: Large SASE.

Mailing list: Write to be included.

To purchase: Published work is available from artist.

ADDITIONAL INFORMATION:

Erik is expanding his activity into areas related to paper dolls, such as jointed paper figures and the exploration of new materials and techniques. He is also publishing multilingual sets.

BRUCE PATRICK JONES

245 Bain Ave.
Toronto M4K 1G2
CANADA
Phone: (416)461-9894
In business since: 1974

PRODUCT INFORMATION:

Scope of work: The artist produces one-of-a-kind originals. He is self-published, and also works for commercial publishers on a freelance basis. His work can be found in smaller publications occasionally as well. He works in both color and b&w.

Description of work: Bruce enjoys creating paper dolls on a casual basis. His work has appeared in *Contemporary Doll Collector.* He particularly likes doing celebrities and real people, some of which have been in newsletters such as *P.D. Pal, Paper Doll Circle* and *Midwest P.D. and Paper Toys.*

Publishers: *Contemporary Doll Collector*

BUSINESS INFORMATION:

To purchase: By mail.

JUDY'S PLACE

Judy M. Johnson
P.O. Box 176
Skandia, MI 49885
Phone: (906)942-7865 EST
In business since: 1982

PRODUCT INFORMATION:

Scope of work: Artist is self-published and also works for commercial publishers on a freelance basis. Her work is published occasionally by smaller publications. She works in both b&w and color.

Description of work: Judy works in watercolor and various other media. She does women and children, animals and fantasy subjects in a realistic style. Her work includes Kitty Cucumber and friends, sisters, showgirls and Deva of the Universe (B. Shackman), and Francie of 50s, Georgie Giraffe, Baranaby Bunnie and Effie Elephant (Dover).

Publishers: B. Shackman Publishing Inc., Dover Publishing, Magnattraction, Scott Publications, Collector Communications, House of White Birches.

BUSINESS INFORMATION:

Catalog: For first-class stamp.

Mailing list: Write or call to be included.

To purchase: Published work is available at Judy's Place by mail order, at paper doll conventions and at gift and toy shops in US and worldwide.

ADDITIONAL INFORMATION:

Judy also presents lectures and an original artist slide show on paper dolls. She also occasionally exhibits portions of her collection.

SYLVIA KLEINDINST

12914 Ontario St.
Irving, NY 14081
Phone: (716)934-4607 EST
In business since: 1984

PRODUCT INFORMATION:

Scope of work: Artist is self-published. She also is published occasionally by smaller publications. She works in both b&w and color.

Description of work: Sylvia's paper doll subjects range from historical characters to older dolls. She likes to do stage and screen stars from the 1890s to the 1950s and costumes from the 1800s. Her color paper doll of Queen Victoria was printed in *Doll News*. She also does a doll for each issue of *Patsy and Friends* newsletter related to the theme and has created sets in watercolor to show in the Artist Gallery at national paper doll conventions.

Publishers: She has worked as an Associate Editor for *OPDAG News* for 7 years and contributes artwork and articles for each issue.

BUSINESS INFORMATION:

Price list: Large SASE.

Mailing list: Write to be included.

To purchase: Artist sells work by mail.

ADDITIONAL INFORMATION:

Sylvia has given talks on paper dolls along with her slide presentation or separately with actual work.

LINDA LAKE

Rt. 2
Marshall, IL 63441
Phone: (217)889-2265
In business since: 1978

PRODUCT INFORMATION:

Scope of work: Artist is published occasionally by smaller publications, such as newsletters. She works in b&w and color.

Description of work: Linda creates detailed historical children's paper dolls in historical clothing with detail. In 1993, she designed the "Little Orphan Annie" paper doll for region 12 at the national paper doll convention.

ADDITIONAL INFORMATION:

Linda offers lectures about older paper dolls to doll organizations, paper doll groups, community groups, libraries and YWCAs.

MARCY LEWIS

27286 Del Monte Lane
Sun City, CA 92586
Phone: (909)679-0956 PST
In business since: 1993

PRODUCT INFORMATION:

Scope of work: Artist is published occasionally by smaller publications, such as newsletters. She works in both color and b&w.

Description of work: Marcy's paper dolls include mostly children, fashion dolls, weddings, fantasy dolls and critters.

BUSINESS INFORMATION:

Mailing list: Send SASE for list and flyer.

LOU RATHJEN'S DESIGNS

Jewel L. Rathjen
1011 Benham
Richland, WA 99352-4512
Phone: (509)946-1971 PST

PRODUCT INFORMATION:

Scope of work: Artist is self-published, and also is published occasionally by smaller publications. She works in both color and b&w.

Description of work: Jewel publishes her own paper doll books and sheets. Her books are b&w English royalty, famous American women, fairies, color paper doll sheets, b&w state paper dolls and a variety of others. She is

starting to publish color royal paper doll sheets.

BUSINESS INFORMATION:

Price list: For SASE.

To purchase: Published work is available by mail. Ads are in *OPDAG News, Doll Reader, Doll World* and *Doll Castle News*.

JOHN S. LUCAS

2408 Oak St.
Michigan City, IN 46360
Phone: (219)874-6617 CST
In business since: 1979

PRODUCT INFORMATION:

Scope of work: Artist produces one-of-a-kind originals. He is self-published and also works for commercial publishers on a freelance basis. His work is also published occasionally by smaller publications. He works in both b&w and color.

Description of work: John's work is mostly fan-inspired designs in the "Katy Keene" Bill Woggon tradition, and also fantasy ideas of his own design for his characters.

Publishers: Archie Comics, Inc.; Marvel Comics, Inc.; Hobby House Press, Inc.; Colossal Studios, Inc.; McKay Press/Cala Corp., Inc.; Disney World Creative Entertainment Group, Inc.; Sterling Press, Inc.

BUSINESS INFORMATION:

Catalog/price list: $2 and large SASE, nonrefundable.

Mailing list: Write to be included.

To purchase: Ask at specialty bookstores or available from various publishers listed, or write to artist.

MRS. KNUTSEN'S VICTORIA

Vanessa L. Knutsen
11745 W. 105th Ave.
St. John, IN 46373-9113
Phone: (219)365-9809 CST
In business since: 1992

PRODUCT INFORMATION:

Scope of work: Artist produces one-of-a-kind originals. She is self-published, and her work can be found occasionally in smaller publications. She works in both color and b&w.

Description of work: Vanessa draws three main types of paper dolls: historical (*The Young Winston Churchill*), portrait (*Great-Great Aunt Emily Wissmann* with turn-of-the-century clothes), and cartoon (*T.R. Bear* based on President Theodore Roosevelt and *Mrs. K's Fat Cats*). She likes characters at least partly rooted in real life.

BUSINESS INFORMATION:

Price list: Send SASE for brochure.

Mailing list: Write or call to be included.

To purchase: Write or call artist. She ships paper dolls first-class flat unless otherwise requested. She also sells quantities at wholesale price.

NORMA LU MEEHAN

1132 Woodlawn Blvd.
South Bend, IN 46616
Phone: (219)233-8573 EST
In business since: 1989

PRODUCT INFORMATION:

Scope of work: Artist works for commercial publishers on a freelance basis and is also published occasionally by smaller publications, such as newsletters and magazines. She works in both b&w and color.

Description of work: Norma Lu is a paper doll artist and illustrator. Her work for paper doll books and magazines features historic costume collections, with a focus on authentic color. Her books include *Victorian Paper Doll Wardrobe, Edwardian Paper Doll Wardrobe, Art Deco Paper Doll Wardrobe, Nana's Trunk* and *Fashions of the 40s and 50s Paper Doll Wardrobe*.

Publishers: Hobby House Press

BUSINESS INFORMATION:

To purchase: Published work is available at Northern Indiana Center for History, Little Professor Book Center, Majareks Books, dealers, Hobby House Press and selected gift shops, doll museums and shops.

CHARLOTT NATHAN

5121 Cherbourg Dr.
Sacramento, CA 95842
Phone: (916)339-2251 PST
In business since: 1993

PRODUCT INFORMATION:

Scope of work: Artist is self-published and also works for commercial publishers on a freelance basis. She works in both b&w and color.

Description of work: Charlott makes contemporary, period and ethnic paper dolls, mostly b&w.

Publishers: She occasionally does book covers for Enslow Publishing.

BUSINESS INFORMATION:

Catalog/Price list: $1. Price list, 50¢, nonrefundable.

Mailing list: Write or call to be included.

To purchase: Published work is available from artist.

JOHN DARCY NOBLE

The Elusive Englishman
615 Hutchison St.
Vista, CA 92084
Phone: (619)945-9444, (619)945-9445 PST
Fax: (619)945-9444
In business since: 1985

PRODUCT INFORMATION:

Scope of work: Artist produces one-of-a-kind originals. He is self-published. He works in color.

Description of work: John's paper dolls are an extension of his other art forms (fantastic, decorative, benevolently surreal paintings in oil, gouache and watercolor). He believes that the paper doll is a valid art form and that there is no reason why paper dolls should not be fine art.

BUSINESS INFORMATION:

Price list: Free monthly list of available works.

To purchase: Published work available only from artist.

ADDITIONAL INFORMATION:

John is a retired museum curator. He presents slide lectures, including The Magic of Paper, Paper Dolls Through History, and The Paper Doll as a Fine Art Form. He also organizes paper doll exhibits.

> "PAPER DOLLS ARE A MARVELOUS WAY TO INTRODUCE CHILDREN TO DESIGN, TO FASHION, AND TO OLD-FASHIONED, WHOLESOME, QUIET FUN."
>
> *Carol-Lynn Rössel Waugh, Winthrop, ME*

PRINCE DOLL STUDIO

Dwayne or Karen Prince
P.O. Box 36607
Houston, TX 77236
Phone: (713)690-6558 CST
Fax: (713)460-4556
In business since: 1990

PRODUCT INFORMATION:

Scope of work: Karen is self-published, works for commercial publishers on a freelance basis and is occasionally published by smaller publications. Works in both b&w and color.

Description of work: Karen's goal when creating a paper doll is to portray an image that captures the imagination and interest of others. Dolls and children are her favorite subjects. Working in acrylics, she tries to achieve as much detail as possible, particularly enjoying the challenge of rendering intricate patterns, lace and textures. However, she says, faces are always the most fun, as they are what bring the paper doll to life. Together with her husband, Dwayne, she designs and produces gifts and accessories for doll and paper doll collectors. Recently, she has completed 2 books featuring 3-dimensional paper dolls for Hobby House Press. An active member of UFDC, she has been the artist for 2 of their national conventions and has created souvenirs and paper dolls for several other conventions, regionals and magazines.

Publishers: Hobby House Press

BUSINESS INFORMATION:

Catalog: Free with SASE.

Mailing list: Write or call to be included.

To purchase: Work is sold by mail, at shows and to various doll and gift shops throughout the country.

BARB RAUSCH

21450 Chase #212
Canoga Park, CA 91304
Phone: (818)998-0719 PST
Fax: (818)998-0719 (call first)
In business since: 1988

PRODUCT INFORMATION:

Scope of work: Artist works for commercial publishers on a freelance basis. She works in both color and b&w.

Description of work: Barb has 2 styles of paper dolls: modern high fashion glamor influenced by Katy Keene Comics and art deco fashion prints; and romantic period costume (especially male costume) influenced by Old Masters, early 20th century illustrators, and children's illustrator Sheila Beckett.

Publishers: She has drawn 2 Barbie paper doll books for Golden/Western, as well as the boxed set "Star Originals," and the dolls for 2 other boxed sets. Her Prince Charming paper doll was published by *Contemporary Doll Collector.*

BUSINESS INFORMATION:

To purchase: Barbie paper dolls are on dealers' lists, as they were widely distributed between 1989-91.

ADDITIONAL INFORMATION:

Barb also gives lectures on paper dolls. Katy Keene Comics paper dolls are her area of expertise. She has a complete collection and has done convention lectures as well as numerous paper doll fanzine articles. She has also created full-color souvenir paper dolls for several national and regional paper doll conventions, and her original art has been purchased by several California collectors.

> "A PAPER DOLL A DAY WILL CHASE
> THE BLUES AWAY."
> *Loretta Willis, Loretta's Place, Tifton, GA*

MARY REO
16097 Hauss
Eastpointe, MI 48021-1122
Phone: (810)773-2720 EST
In business since: 1991

PRODUCT INFORMATION:

Scope of work: Artist produces one-of-a-kind originals and also works for commercial publishers on a freelance basis. She works in color.

Description of work: Mary's "Giselle" character paper doll was first published in November 1993 by invitation from Scott Publications in *Contemporary Doll Collector.*

ADDITIONAL INFORMATION:

Mary gives lectures on how to design and research paper dolls, how to understand your own inspiring ideas and how to act upon them.

DAWN RILEY
1345 Candlewood Dr. NE
Keizer, OR 97303
Phone: (503)390-1752 PST

PRODUCT INFORMATION:

Scope of work: Artist produces one-of-a-kind originals. She is self-published. She works in both color and b&w.

BUSINESS INFORMATION:

To purchase: Work is available from the artist by mail or at her studio.

ADDITIONAL INFORMATION:

Dawn organizes paper doll exhibits at craft bazaars.

CHRISTINE SCARLETT
414 Montclair Dr.
Pleasantville, NJ 08232
Phone: (609)641-5322 EST
In business since: 1990

PRODUCT INFORMATION:

Scope of work: Artist produces handmade one-of-a-kind originals only. She works in b&w and color.

Description of work: Christine is a fashion designer and maker of children's paper dolls.

BUSINESS INFORMATION:

Mailing list: Send SASE.

IVA SHACKELFORD
N.M.P.
1734 Broken Arrow Dr.
Prescott, AZ 86303
Phone: (520)778-0823 MST
In business since: 1975

PRODUCT INFORMATION:

Scope of work: Iva is self-published. Work is both b&w and color.

Description of work: Iva's work includes *Fabulous Fashions of the 1930s,* an $11'' \times 17''$ book of male and female fashions; *Conestoga Kids,* an $11'' \times 17''$ book of boy and girl fashions of 1948; and *Motoring Lady Fashions,* an $8\frac{1}{2}'' \times 11''$ book of mostly female fashions from 1903-1913. All her work is comprised of original line drawing and includes coloring instructions, stands and a full color guide.

BUSINESS INFORMATION:

Catalog: $1, refundable with purchase.

To purchase: Buy directly from artist.

SUE SHANAHAN
11505 W. 193rd St.
Mokena, IL 60448
Phone: (708)479-1403 CST

PRODUCT INFORMATION:

Scope of work: Sue makes handmade one-of-a-kind originals and is self-published. She works for commercial publishers on a freelance basis and is occasionally published by smaller publications. Works in b&w and color.

Publishers: Doll Reader, Dolls, Contemporary Doll Collector, McCall's Dover Publications.

SUSAN SIRKIS
3807 Meredith Dr.
Greensboro, NC 27408
Phone: (910)282-2122 EST

PRODUCT INFORMATION:

Scope of work: Artist is self-published and also works for commercial publishers on a freelance basis. She works in b&w and color.

BUSINESS INFORMATION:

Catalog: Free

TOM TIERNEY
P.O. Drawer D
Hopewell Junction, NY 12533
Phone: (914)225-2881 EST
In business since: 1974

PRODUCT INFORMATION:

Scope of work: Artist works for commercial publishers on a freelance basis. He works in both color and b&w.

Description of work: Tom Tierney produces paper doll books which include a wide range of subjects, generally of a historic nature. They include a series of the American Presidents and their families, an American Family series and a high fashion series, as well as other subjects. He has had over 200 books published and is still in the process of producing more.

Publishers: Dover Publishing, B. Shackman and Co., Inc., and various other commercial publishers, such as magazines and specialty publishing houses on a freelance basis.

BUSINESS INFORMATION:

Price list: For SASE.

To purchase: Purchase published work from museum gift shops and boutique shops; order via Barnes and Noble or Waldenbooks; send for catalogs from Dover or B. Shackman, and order direct; or, for an autographed copy, order from Tom Tierney.

ADDITIONAL INFORMATION:
Tom occasionally gives lectures on paper dolls. He discusses his work and how he researches and creates it, backed up by original art and followed by a question-and-answer period.

SANDRA VANDERPOOL

P.O. Box 695
Erie, CO 80516
Phone: (303)828-3387 MST
In business since: 1986

PRODUCT INFORMATION:
Scope of work: Artist produces one-of-a-kind originals. She is self-published and also works for a commercial publisher on a freelance basis. Her work is published occasionally by smaller publications. She works in both color and b&w.
Description of work: Sandra creates original paper doll sets. Her target audience is primarily the paper doll collector. Her designs are original although she does enjoy replicating the format and look of vintage paper doll sets too. She has self-published over 200 sets and has commercially published *The Enchanted Realm of Fairyland* and *Forever Children*. Her work has appeared in *Doll News* and *Contemporary Doll Collector*.
Publishers: Hobby House Press, Inc.

BUSINESS INFORMATION:
Catalog/Price list: Legal size SASE.
Mailing list: Write to be included.
To purchase: Published work is available through the artist's catalog and from Hobby House Press Inc. for *The Enchanted Realm of Fairyland* and *Forever Children*.

ADDITIONAL INFORMATION:
Sandra also gives lectures on paper dolls, giving an overview of the history of paper dolls using actual items from various time periods and information on how to collect paper dolls. She also organizes paper doll exhibits on a small scale such as at a library or for interested groups.

CAROL-LYNN RÖSSEL WAUGH

5 Morrill St.
Winthrop, ME 04364-1220
Phone: (207)377-6769 EST
Fax: (207)377-4158
In business since: 1975

PRODUCT INFORMATION:
Scope of work: Artist produces one-of-a-kind originals and also works for commercial publishers on a freelance basis. She works in both color and b&w.
Description of work: Carol-Lynn's work concentrates on teddy bear and rag doll characters she has created. Her work is published in the major doll and teddy bear magazines, and she also does originals for collectors.

BUSINESS INFORMATION:
To purchase: Artist's work available on commission. She also works on assignment from magazines and publishers.

ADDITIONAL INFORMATION:
Carol-Lynn also gives lectures and slide shows on paper dolls.

"CUT SETS AND GRAB BAGS PROVIDE GREATER ENTERTAINMENT TO PAPER DOLL COLLECTORS BECAUSE IT IS FUN TO SORT THROUGH THEM AND LOOK FOR PIECES TO COMPLETE A SET."
Sylvia Kleindinst, Irving, NY

LAUREN WELKER

204 E. Coover St.
Mechanicsburg, PA 17055
Phone: (717)691-8110 EST

PRODUCT INFORMATION:
Scope of work: Artist is self-published and also works for commercial publishers on a freelance basis. She works in both color and b&w.
Description of work: Lauren designs paper dolls for doll publicatons. She also sells b&ws by mail and one-of-a-kinds and hand-colored sets at paper doll parties.
Publishers: *Dolls—The Collector's Magazine, Doll Reader, National Doll World, Doll News, Doll Life, OPDAG News,* and various convention publications.

BUSINESS INFORMATION:
Catalog: Free with LSASE.
To purchase: Work is available directly from artist.

LORAINE WELLMAN

8751 Fairdell Place
Richmond, British Columbia V7C 1W6
CANADA
Phone: (604)272-9886 PST
In business since: 1992

PRODUCT INFORMATION:
Scope of work: Artist works for commercial publishers on a freelance basis. She also is published occasionally by smaller publications. She works in both color and b&w.
Description of work: Loraine's published paper doll work consists of actual dolls drawn as paper dolls. Dolls are antique, collectible or contemporary artist's originals. Costumes include the doll's original outfit as well as imaginary clothing—sometimes contemporary, sometimes period designs—and accessories. There is usually a short write-up giving information about the doll as well as descriptions of the clothing. She contributes one paper doll (b&w) per issue to *Canadian Doll Journal*. Artist's work has also been published in *Victorian Harvester*.
Publishers: Canadian Doll Journal

BUSINESS INFORMATION:
Mailing list: Contact the publisher.
To purchase: Published work is available by subscribing to *Canadian Doll Journal*. Limited edition (100) colorized versions available from the artist (currently Susie and Doll Collector)—individually signed and numbered by the artist.

TRACY JANE WILLIAMS

10 Briarstone Ct.
Mauldin, SC 29662-2807
Phone: (803)627-0324 EST
E-mail: sew53@aol.com
In business since: 1991

PRODUCT INFORMATION:
Scope of work: Artist is self-published and is also published occasionally by smaller publications. She works in both color and b&w.
Description of work: Tracy creates paper

dolls that appeal to children, but usually with an edge that attracts an older audience. Her characters are often based on animals. Her illustration technique ranges from intricate scratchboard to open line drawings, suitable for coloring. Color work is done in either colored pencil or gouache.

BUSINESS INFORMATION:
To purchase: Write to artist.

ADDITIONAL INFORMATION:
Tracy also presents lectures on paper dolls and has used paper dolls as art projects for children in a classroom setting.

LORETTA WILLIS
808 Lee Ave.
Tifton, GA 31794
In business since: 1980

PRODUCT INFORMATION:
Scope of work: Artist produces one-of-a-kind originals and sells copies of originals. She is self-published and is published occasionally by smaller publications. She works in both color and b&w.
Description of work: Loretta creates and draws original b&w prints and sometimes uses watercolor. She has a Starr Brown character that she uses in her *Loretta's Place* paper doll newsletter.

BUSINESS INFORMATION:
Catalog/Price list: $2, refundable with purchase. Include LSASE.
Mailing list: Write to be included.
To purchase: Published work available from artist. Send for catalog/price list.

CLUBS

COLORADO PAPER DOLL COLLECTORS CLUB
Sandra Vanderpool
P.O. Box 695
Erie, CO 80516
Phone: (303)828-3387 MST
Established: 1988

BASIC INFORMATION:
Type of organization: This is a local, regional organization open to paper doll artists, collectors and dealers.
Statement of purpose: The club is for anyone from beginner to seasoned paper doll collector. The club shows what is currently available, studies a specific type of paper doll, makes paper doll items and has a sales table.
Members: 14
Meetings: Monthly. The club does not have officers is informal. Club members meet to share information and exchange ideas.

REQUIREMENTS:
Membership requirements: Open
Membership fee/dues: $5/year

ADDITIONAL INFORMATION:
Activities/Events: Hosts parties and/or shows open to anyone usually unless it is a national paper doll convention, and then only certain events are open to the public. Club sends invitations to anyone on mailing list and places notices in paper doll newsletters.

ORIGINAL PAPER DOLL ARTISTS GUILD (OPDAG)
Jenny Taliadoros
P.O. Box 14
Kingfield, ME 04947
or
Judy Johnson
P.O. Box 176
Skandia, MI 49885
Phone: (207)265-2500 (Jenny) or (906)942-7865 (Judy) EST
Established: 1984

BASIC INFORMATION:
Type of organization: This is a national organization for paper doll artists, collectors, dealers and publishers.
Statement of purpose: OPDAG is an organization of paper doll artists and enthusiasts who exchange ideas to promote the art and hobby of paper dolls.
Members: 150-200

REQUIREMENTS:
Membership requirements: Open

PAPER DOLL QUEENS AND KINGS OF METRO DETROIT
Jean Polus, President
69 Meadow Wood Dr.
Rochester Hills, MI 48307
Phone: (810)651-4629 EST
Established: 1985

BASIC INFORMATION:
Type of organization: This is a local organization for paper doll artists, collectors and dealers.
Members: 19
Meetings: Monthly. A social group presenting a featured theme each month. Club members trade paper dolls and attend paper doll parties.

SUN, SAND AND SEA
Madeline Bennett
675 Hyde Park Circle W.
Winter Garden, FL 34787
Phone: (407)656-8261 EST
Established: 1981

BASIC INFORMATION:
Type of organization: This is a local organization open to paper doll artists, collectors, dealers and publishers.
Statement of purpose: Collects paper dolls, teaches how to care for paper dolls and how to care for and preserve antique paper dolls. Does philanthropic work such as donating books of paper dolls to orphanges.
Members: 35

REQUIREMENTS:
Membership requirements: Invitation only

PUBLICATIONS

CORNERSTONES
733 de la Fuente
Monterey Park, CA 91754
Editorial: Deanna Williams and Sharon Hill
Phone: (818)284-1502 PST

BASIC INFORMATION:
Type of publication: National paper doll newsletter. Includes articles and a paper doll in each issue. Paper dolls are b&w.
Description: Cornerstones is dedicated to the study of paper dolls in their social, historic, economic, political and entertainment spheres. Each edition follows a theme.
Issues per year: 4
Specs: 20-24 pages, newsletter format, b&w
Subscription rate: $16/year

ADVERTISING INFORMATION:
Target audience: Collectors and others interested in paper dolls from an edu-

cational and intellectual point of view, as well as entertainment.

Paid circulation: 200 +

Advertising rates: 10¢/word

Demographics: Subscribers from all over the US, also in Canada, Denmark and England.

LORETTA'S PLACE PAPER DOLL NEWSLETTER

808 Lee Ave.
Tifton, GA 31794
Editorial: Loretta Willis, Editor/Publisher
In business since: 1980

BASIC INFORMATION:

Type of publication: Paper doll newsletter

Issues per year: 4

Subscription rate: $12/year. For sample, send $3.50 and LSASE. Make checks or money orders payable to Loretta Willis.

ADVERTISING INFORMATION:

Target audience: Collectors, artists, publishers, dealers, anyone interested in paper dolls.

Advertising rates: Ask for advertising information.

ADDITIONAL INFORMATION:

Send any paper doll information and b&w and color reprints of original drawings to be included in newsletter.

MRS. KNUTSEN'S VICTORIAN SAMPLER

Vanessa L. Knutsen
11745 W. 105th Ave.
St. John, IN 46373-9113
Phone: (219)365-9809 CST
In business since: 1992

BASIC INFORMATION:

Type of publication: A fanzine with theme-related paper dolls for lovers of the Victorian/Edwardian eras.

Description: *Mrs. Knutsen's Victorian Sampler* contains bits and pieces about the Victorian/Edwardian eras—news, views, history and especially people of great-grandmother's time. Each issue contains a theme-related paper doll on heavy stock and the "Victorian Fat Cats" comic strip.

Issues per year: 4

Specs: 11″ × 17″ folded to 8½″ × 11″, 4-6 pages, with separate paper dolls.

Newstand price: $2

Subscription rate: $8/year. Send 3 first-class stamps for sample issue.

ADVERTISING INFORMATION:

Target audience: The person who loves information on the Victorian era and enjoys both paper dolls and Victorian-style cat comics.

Advertising rates: Write for information on display ads. Free classified ads offered to those selling Victorian/Edwardian era paper dolls of good taste. Write for terms.

ADDITIONAL INFORMATION:

Historical and portrait paper dolls, also cartoons. Writes paper-doll-related articles for periodicals.

NORTHERN LIGHTS PAPER DOLL NEWS

Beverly Wetherington
P.O. Box 871189
Wasilla, AK 99687
Phone: (907)745-4334 Alaska time zone
In business since: 1973

BASIC INFORMATION:

Type of publication: Paper doll newsletter. Includes paper doll in each issue, b&w paper.

Description: *Northern Lights Paper Doll News* is a 32-page quarterly with a "Dress-a-Doll" in each issue. Newest paper dolls are shown plus older ones. Free ads for subscribers.

Issues per year: 4

Specs: 7″ × 8½″, 32 pages, b&w

Subscription rate: $12/year ($3.50 sample), $16 overseas

ADVERTISING INFORMATION:

Target audience: Paper doll artists and collectors

Paid circulation: 300

Advertising rates: Free to subscribers.

PAPER DOLL ART:

Guidelines: Accepts unsolicited paper doll art.

Pay: Will trade one-year subscription for paper dolls.

> "THERE IS NO AGE REQUIREMENT FOR COLLECTING, ENJOYING OR CREATING PAPER DOLLS."
> *Johanna Gast Anderton, Gladstone, MO*

OPDAG NEWS

Jenny Taliadoros or Judy M. Johnson
P.O. Box 14
Kingfield, ME 04947

BASIC INFORMATION:

Type of publication: Newsletter for the members of the Original Paper Doll Artists Guild (OPDAG). *OPDAG News* is an organization of paper doll artists and enthusiasts who exchange ideas to promote the art and hobby of paper dolls.

Issues per year: 4

Specs: 8½″ × 11″, 32-36 pages, saddle stapled, b&w with 1-color cover.

Newsstand price: $4.50

Subscription rate: $15/year US, $19 Canada, $21 overseas

ADVERTISING INFORMATION:

Target audience: Paper doll collectors and artists, dealers and publishers.

Paid circulation: 200

Advertising rates: For members: ¼ page, $18.50; ½ page $36; full page $50; classifieds 20¢/word. Double rates for nonmembers.

Demographics: US, Canada, a few European

PAPER DOLL ART:

Guidelines: Members only. Use black ink, sharp lines; sign and date; put name and address on back. No copyrighted images (stars, cartoon characters, etc.).

Pay: 4 complimentary copies of issue

SUBMISSIONS:

Guidelines: Looks for articles from members and interested parties. Send sample to *OPDAG News* at address above.

Pay: 4 complimentary copies of issue

P.D. PAL

Jim Faraone
19109 Silcott Springs Rd.
Purcellville, VA 22132
Phone: (540)338-3621
In business since: 1987

BASIC INFORMATION:

Type of publication: Paper doll newsletter

Description: *P.D. Pal* covers old, new and future paper dolls and includes articles, artist's gallery, bio on a paper doll artist, news and reviews of paper dolls and conventions, ads and pen pals.

Issues per year: 4

Specs: 30 pages minimum, corner-stapled, b&w.

Subscription rate: $14/year

ADVERTISING INFORMATION:

Target audience: All paper doll collectors.

Paid circulation: 400

Advertising rates: Free to subscribers.

PAPER DOLL ART:

Guidelines: Subscribers may submit a b&w photocopy of their work to be featured in the Artist's Gallery.

Pay: No payment.

SUBMISSIONS:

Guidelines: Subscribers volunteer to do articles.

Pay: No payment.

PAPER DOLL REVIEW

Shirley Magness Hedge and Marilyn Henry, co-editors
P.O. Box 584
Princeton, IN 47670
Phone: (812)385-4080 (Shirley Hedge)

or (812)423-5334 (Marilyn Henry) CST

In business since: 1992

BASIC INFORMATION:

Type of publication: National paper doll magazine, privately published. Includes a full-color paper doll in each issue.

Description: *PDR* includes photos, information and fun articles featuring every sort of paper doll and collection.

Issues per year: 4

Specs: 8½″ × 11″, 32 pages, stapled, b&w with full-color cover

Subscription rate: $24/year

ADVERTISING INFORMATION:

Target audience: Paper doll collectors

Paid circulation: 400+

Advertising rates: 10¢/word. Display ad rates on request.

Demographics: Persons from their early 20s to senior citizens; several are school teachers, others are artists; most all are avid paper doll collectors.

PAPER DOLL ART:

Guidelines: Welcomes collectors/writers who write well and can contribute all manner of articles and/or visual goodies. All articles must pertain to paper dolls and be clearly handwritten or

typed (double-spaced). Copies preferred.

Pay: Complimentary copies

SEW BEAUTIFUL

518 Madison St.
Huntsville, AL 35801-4286
Editorial: William Crocker
Advertising: Kathy McMakin
Phone: (205)534-8015 CST
Fax: (205)533-9630
E-mail: M,446@compuserve.com
In business since: 1987

BASIC INFORMATION:

Type of publication: National fashion magazine. Includes full-color paper dolls.

Description: Primarily covers heirloom sewing.

Issues per year: 6

PAPER DOLL ART:

Guidelines: Send sample of work and SASE if you want sample returned.

SUBMISSIONS:

Guidelines: Send sample paragraph or 2 and SASE if you want sample returned.

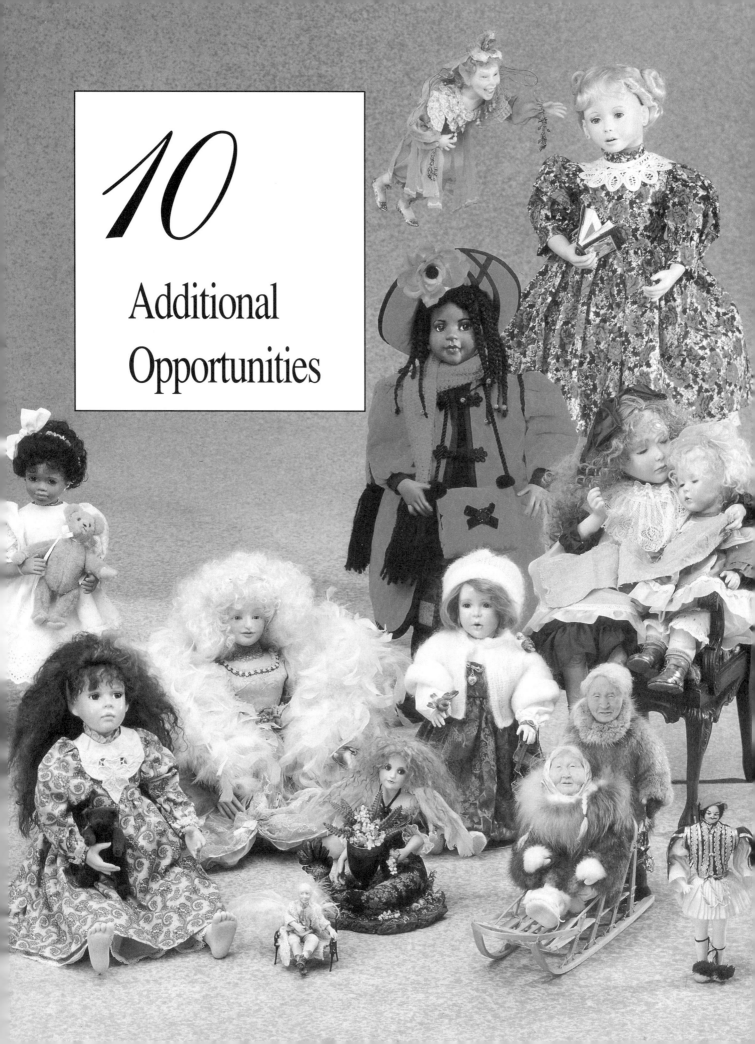

10
Additional
Opportunities

A Guide to Chapter Ten

*E*very "doll person" wears many hats in the doll world. For instance, artists often conduct workshops or produce how-to videos. Collectors may also publish newsletters or write for one of the doll magazines. An antique dealer may also offer lectures on his or her area of expertise. In this chapter, we have tried to list as many doll-related businesses that we could find that did not fit into any of the previous chapters. Any businesses that provide a sideline product or service are also listed here.

The Listings

The listings in this chapter range from a dry cleaning service for doll clothing to workshops on making original porcelain dolls. They are divided into three general sections: Educational Opportunities, Publications, and Helpful Products and Services.

It is important to note that listings are organized alphabetically within these sections. You will have to read the note following the "Type of opportunity" or "Type of product" heading to find a brief description of what a given business offers. A more thorough description, if provided, follows this heading. The listing tells you how to participate or schedule an educational opportunity, how to take advantage of a service, or how to purchase a product.

The publication listings include every type of publication, from the one-woman newsletter to the internationally distributed, glossy doll magazine. The listings describe the publications and outline advertising opportunities and submission guidelines. They also list subscription rates and other basic information.

Whatever your area of interest, you are sure to find additional opportunities, learning experiences and products of interest in this chapter!

Jack Johnston

BY CINDY LAUFENBERG

Cindy Laufenberg is editor of *Songwriter's Market,* published by Writer's Digest Books. She has also written profiles for *Writer's Market, Children's Writer's and Illustrator's Market,* and *Novel and Short Story Writer's Market.*

*I*n five short years, Jack Johnston has gone from marketing executive to master dollmaker, creating one-of-a-kind dolls and teaching others how to make their own in workshops around the world. He's also published a book on dollmaking, designed for The Franklin Mint, been nominated three times for the *Dolls* Award of Excellence, and appeared on radio and television talk shows around the country, including a thirty-minute special on PBS. Jack's rise to dollmaking fame is an inspiration to anyone thinking about entering the dollmaking business.

Jack Johnston

In 1990, Jack found himself with a lot of time on his hands after being laid off from his job as Vice President of Marketing for Dolphins Court at Sea World. As Christmas approached, Jack's wife told him she wanted a Father Christmas doll as a gift that year. Unemployed and running out of money, Jack decided to try his hand at making the doll instead of buying one.

The Father Christmas doll Jack created came out so well that he decided to try to sell it at a local craft fair. Jack rented a table for $35 and sold his doll before the show even opened! The woman at the craft table next to him loved the doll, and bought it for $129. As the day went on, Jack took orders for eight more dolls. Encouraged by his success, Jack returned to the craft show and continued selling more and more dolls, for more and more money. "I started in November," Jack recalls, "and by the end of the Christmas season I had sold about fifty dolls, and had raised my price to about $299. It's been four or five years, and I'm still making dolls. It's all working very well."

Jack's Dollmaking Classes

It's more than just working well. Jack has expanded his empire from simply creating dolls to teaching others, encouraging aspiring dollmakers from around the world to unleash their creativity to make unique dolls.

Jack began teaching the craft of dollmaking about a year after he started creating his dolls. In 1991, a doll shop in Massachusetts called Donna's Children saw Jack's work at the Toy Fair in New York, and asked if he would be interested in teaching others how to create his unique dolls. They sponsored Jack's first workshop, and it was so successful that he continued to teach. In the first year, Jack explains, "I was teaching once every two weeks, about twenty seminars. And then in the second year it had caught on so well, and was such a good source of income, that I went from doing twenty to forty-four of them. By the third year I was doing fifty workshops per year, and I still do."

Jack teaches his intensive three-day classes in twenty-two different states as well as Canada, Mexico and Australia. There are fifteen students in each class. "In the class we make the head, hands, feet and soft-

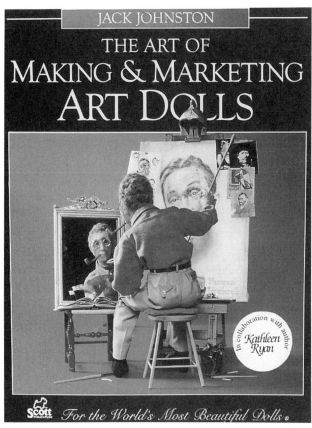

Jack Johnston has put the techniques he teaches in his workshops into book form in *The Art of Making & Marketing Art Dolls*.

sculpted body and then put it all together with its wig and paint," Jack says, "so the student leaves the class with a finished doll minus its costume. And I work with each doll as it leaves the class. So each student leaves with a very nice doll." The cost for each three-day workshop is $400, which includes all the supplies a student will need.

Jack plans to take his teaching goals even further. In the year 2000, he will open the Johnston Academy of Professional Dollmakers. "The Academy will go in a little town in Utah called Midway," Jack explains, "which is an art community in the mountains. The Academy will house artists and students to stay for a week, two weeks, or a month. They can come for one week and do a beginner's class or stay for a month and graduate with a professional certificate. The purpose of the Academy is, first, to bring education to people and to perpetuate the professionalism of dollmaking. But second," he adds with a laugh, "is to bring it to me so I can slow down my traveling!"

The Professional Dollmakers Art Guild

For those students who are serious about dollmaking as a career, Jack has founded the Professional Dollmakers

Art Guild. "The Guild is made up of the best students who have taken my classes in the last five years," he says. "We have over 120 members. We're even attracting people who aren't my students, but who want to become professionals."

The Guild is a nonprofit organization that provides a venue for artists at a very low price. Members share the booths and all costs, and "use the economies of scale for lodging, transportation and meals to offer an inexpensive method for people to market their dolls," Jack says.

As if the workshops and Guild weren't enough, Jack also started a retail and wholesale store called Jane's Original Art Doll Supplies. The retail and mail-order business is run by Jack's mother and stepfather, Jane and Bob Poole. "We not only sell, but manufacture armatures for the bodies, body stockings, and books and videos," he says. "I think they actually make more money than I do with the mail-order business!"

Five Elements of Success

Jack stresses five elements that are essential for a successful career in dollmaking. The first element is desire, which reflects the attitude a dollmaker has toward her craft. "You have to have an attitude that will allow you to work through hardships and long hours," Jack says. "You have to work through kids who are crying, 'Mommy, you don't pay attention to me anymore,' or a husband who says, 'All you do is make dolls, I never see you.' A strong desire to succeed will fuel your efforts and clear away any obstacles that may stand in your way."

The second element is time. "You must allot yourself at minimum twelve hours a day to start a business. That goes for any business, and certainly for dollmaking." Learning to make the most of your time, and being able to juggle several projects at once, is key.

The third element is support. Explains Jack, "You have to be supported by your family while you're doing this. Your family has to be tolerant and say, 'We'll help with the housework and the cooking and the kids—you just make your dolls.' "

The fourth element is talent. Jack thinks that anyone who wants to learn badly enough and has the above-mentioned elements working for them along with just a smidgen of talent can learn the art of dollmaking and be successful.

The final element is marketing. You must be able to sell your dolls if you want to make a career out of making them. Determining your market, analyzing your competition, and pricing and selling your dolls are just as important as creating the dolls themselves. "If you don't have all five of these elements," says Jack, "then your chances of becoming a professional dollmaker are limited. I believe all dollmakers are good. Some are just better than others."

This elegant elderly woman is an example of Jack Johnston's work.

The Importance of Determination

Jack tells a wonderful story about one of his students to vividly demonstrate the role that desire and determination play in the craft of dollmaking. The host of the class told Jack that one of the women taking the class, Elisse Taddie, had a handicap. 'We don't know whether or not she'll be able to sculpt, but she really wants to try,' the host told me, so I said, 'Fine, I'll be happy to help.' "

When Elisse came to the class, Jack realized the handicap was going to be a challenge for everyone. "But I was willing to help if she had the desire, and obviously she had a strong desire," Jack said. "We started sculpting and I asked Elisse, 'Do you want help?' And she said, 'No, just tell me what to do and I

will do it myself.' "

By the end of the first day, everyone in the class was finished, but Elisse was behind. She asked if she could take the work home and work into the night, and Jack gave her the supplies she would need. "The next morning, she was up to speed with everybody," Jack says. Elisse again took the supplies home with her the second night. On the third day, she finished with everyone else in the class.

"And at the end of that day, her doll was far and away the most beautiful of the class," Jack said. "She had done a beautiful lady doll and it was just wonderful. Everyone in the class had just marveled that even with her handicap she had done such great work. Now I'll tell you what her handicap was—Elisse had no hands and no arms. She sculpted with her elbows. For her, she

This little boy, created by Jack, is enjoying his new toy airplane.

had no handicap. She made up for her disability with attitude."

Just as Elisse Taddie's work is proof that desire and attitude can go a long way, so is the career of Jack Johnston. "A lot has happened in five years, and it really isn't that difficult," he says modestly. Jack has mastered that field, not only creating beautiful dolls but sharing his unique talent and vision with others. ❧

Maryanne Oldenburg

BY DAVID BORCHERDING

David H. Borcherding edits the Marketplace Series, published by Writer's Digest Books. This series includes *Mystery Writer's Sourcebook, Science Fiction Writer's Marketplace and Sourcebook,* and *Romance Writer's Sourcebook.* Dave has worked as a freelance editor and writer since 1992 and joined Writer's Digest Books full-time in 1994. He has published articles on nanotechnology in *bOING bOING* and *Utne Reader,* as well as interviews with writers and editors for *Novel and Short Story Writer's Market.*

Maryanne Oldenburg

*I*t has to come from your heart," says Maryanne Oldenburg, on the art of crafting porcelain dolls. "If it doesn't come from your heart, it's not going to come from your hands."

Maryanne speaks from experience; up to four hundred dolls come from her heart, and her studio, each year. Oldenburg Originals, her home-based company in Wisconsin, receives orders from around the world for porcelain dolls. "I did some work for a German company that put six of my dolls into vinyl production," Maryanne says. The bulk of her work, however, is filling the hundreds of individual orders that come in each year. "I'm constantly receiving requests for one-of-a-kind designs and things of that nature," she says. Most of these orders come from the New York Toy Fair and a few other doll and toy conventions around the country.

Like most doll artisans, Maryanne started out making dolls from plasticine clay, using the common brand Sculpey. Since 1976, however, she's worked exclusively in porcelain. She's become so skilled that she offers classes on porcelain doll making.

"At first I taught traveling workshops," Maryanne says. "I'd go to studios or classes where they taught the making of reproduction dolls, and I would teach sculpturing." She also attended doll conventions and conferences, where she was asked many questions. "I found myself explaining with sketches and such to many people, and eventually I was asked to teach a workshop."

That led Maryanne to teaching workshops out of her home. Once a month in her off season (May to September), students can take a five-day course while staying with Maryanne at her bed-and-breakfast/studio home. "We've got a guest bedroom that sleeps three and a guest house that sleeps four or five," she says. "So I limit attendance to between four and six people. I've had as many as eight, but I usually only take a larger group when they're all coming together, because they'll be living in closer proximity."

Learning in Style

Students come from all over the country—and even Europe—but Maryanne says that the majority live in the Midwest. "They've come from California, Florida and even Germany, but mainly they're within driving distance—Wisconsin, Michigan, Illinois, Iowa. They usually arrive late Thursday afternoon, and on Friday morning we start bright and early."

Maryanne's classes begin each day at 8:30 and go until 5:30. Students get a continental breakfast and a lunch catered by Maryanne's daughter. "Everybody's on their own for supper," she says. "We usually go to a restaurant. And after supper they have the option of working down in the studio as late as they want. Often by that time, though, they're so exhausted they all climb in bed. It's very strenuous."

The First Day

The first morning, the students pick out a subject from Maryanne's files. "I have files of children. Well, all kinds of pictures of people, but mostly children. They pick out their subject from there, and then they make a skull from Styrofoam. After finishing the skull, they start laying the clay over the skull and begin modeling." That, she says, takes the entire first day.

The Second Day

The second day, students learn the positions and proportions of the facial features. "By lunchtime, they start to get a little depressed. Everyone's doll face looks like an E.T., so they all start thinking, 'Oh, this thing is never going to come out right.' " For inspiration, Maryanne has photos of previous students with their dolls on the wall of the studio. "I show them the pictures on the wall, that rogue's gallery, and I tell them that they all felt the same way. Everyone starts joking, and by that same afternoon, as they keep working and the faces begin to form, they're ecstatic. So in a matter of an hour or two, they've changed their attitude."

The Third and Fourth Days

"They do the finishing work on the third day," Maryanne says, "and then in the afternoon of the third day, they make a shoulder plate to fit the head. It's up to them if they want to continue doing detail work on their head." On the fourth day, they switch to arms and legs. "We make a leg in the morning and an arm in the afternoon. If they're really good, they can complete one of each, but basically what they're learning is the technique of making arms and legs." This way, students can complete their dolls at home.

Throughout the process, Maryanne says, the students have to learn anatomical proportion. She has them lay out a body on paper, learning the proper sizing for the arms and legs before they even begin construction. A knowledge of anatomy, and especially studying faces, helps any doll artist, she says.

The Fifth Day

On the fifth and final day, the students take their head and learn to build up a clay bed. The clay bed is used to make a mold of the sculpted head for the porcelain casting. In the afternoon, they learn to mix and pour the molds, so that by the end of the course, they go home with a full doll head and a mold of that head.

Practice Makes Perfect

The goal of the course is to teach the students enough so that they can mix and pour their own dolls in porcelain. Maryanne says that most students have some experience with dolls, but not much with clay. "I would say that 85 to 90 percent are people who have learned to clean and paint a doll in a studio someplace, and they want to expand beyond that. Instead of making someone else's doll, they want to create their own. And 95 percent have never touched clay before. But it's in their heart and in their head to do this, and I don't think anyone has ever left disappointed with what they've accomplished."

Maryanne's advice to beginning doll artists is to read and study anatomy and faces. "Practice, practice, practice," she says. "Persistence is the only way you will accomplish anything." But above all, love what you are doing. "You have to have it in your heart. That's the only way the dolls will talk to the people." ✥

Additional Opportunities

EDUCATIONAL OPPORTUNITIES

ALL THAT GLISSONS
Theresa A. Glisson
154 West Hill St.
Goldsboro, NC 27534
Phone: (919)778-6921 EST
In business since: 1995

BASIC INFORMATION:
Type of opportunity: Dollmaking workshop
Description: Doll artist Theresa A. Glisson is now offering sculpting classes which will also include mold making. Write for more information on price, list of supplies needed and date of next class to be offered.

BUSINESS INFORMATION:
Cost: Price varies depending on what is being sculpted in the class. Call for prices.

ADDITIONAL INFORMATION:
Only 5 students per sculpting class.

ANGIE'S DOLL BOUTIQUE, INC.
Lynne Reid or Frankie Lyles
1114 King St.
Alexandria, VA 22314
Phone: (703)683-2807 EST
In business since: 1976

BASIC INFORMATION:
Type of opportunity: Dollmaking workshop
Description: Angie's Doll Boutique offers weekly classes in porcelain dollmaking.

BUSINESS INFORMATION:
To schedule: Contact Lynne Reid.
Cost: Classroom rental fee is charged according to project being offered.

"DON'T BE AFRAID TO FAIL. FAILURES ARE LESSONS ON WHAT NOT TO DO."
Bobbie and Bill Schlegel, Ringwood, NJ

ELINOR PEACE BAILY
1779 East Ave.
Hayward, CA 94542
Phone: (510)582-2702 PST
In business since: 1982

BASIC INFORMATION:
Type of opportunity: Dollmaking workshop, seminar, lecture, demonstrations
Description: The creative process is best understood in an environment of trust, where every student feels comfortable about her own preparation and equipment and where she feels confident of her teacher's preparation and skills. That is why constant experimentation and stretching on the part of both teacher and pupil brings the maximum in satisfaction in class. "The doll, to me, is a tool. I use it to introduce an element of play. My experience tells me that people connect with dolls in a way that is more direct than in any other crafting process. This connection facilitates laughter, insight, grieving and healing. I believe these to be pivotal to creative well-being, and I strive to provide a classroom environment conducive to such experiences, as well as the learning and re-enforcing of new skills," elinor writes.

BUSINESS INFORMATION:
To schedule: Phone or write to the address above.
Cost: Workshops—$300 per day; lecture—$250

BLU FROGG GARDENS
Ralph and Mary Gonzales
1155 Llagas Rd.
Morgan Hill, CA 95037
Phone: (408)779-2719 PST
Fax: (408)779-2719
E-mail: rdzek@garlic.com
In business since: 1986

BASIC INFORMATION:
Type of opportunity: Dollmaking workshop, seminar
Description: Ralph gives seminars at doll shows. Ralph and Mary also conduct 3-day workshops in sculpting and mold making.

BUSINESS INFORMATION:
To schedule: Available to doll shops or groups. Call for details.
Cost: $200 per person for the 3-day seminar. "Demonstrations are free, but should coincide with our participation in the show."

ADDITIONAL INFORMATION:
"We use a hands-on approach to sculpting, and stress the methods and mastery of materials, so that the new artist can go back home and practice what is learned," Mary writes.

CALIFORNIA DOLLS
3100 Dutton Ave., Suite 114
Santa Rosa, CA 95407
Phone: (707)527-6548 PST
In business since: 1990

BASIC INFORMATION:
Type of opportunity: Dollmaking workshop, seminar
Description: Ongoing classes and special seminars by various artists in sculpting, mold making, porcelain casting, reproduction dollmaking, wig making and heirloom sewing. They provide or have available for purchase all supplies for classes and seminars to complete the projects.

BUSINESS INFORMATION:
To schedule: Call or write with an outline of the workshop available and dates and times needed.
To participate: Workshop and seminars are held on Saturdays, Sundays and Mondays at the California Dolls shop.
Cost: Cost varies depending on activities and number of persons attending.

CASCADE DOLL SHOPPE
Linda Nachbar
6290 Burton SE
Grand Rapids, MI 49546
Phone: (616)942-6786 EST
Fax: (616)942-9559

In business since: 1986

BASIC INFORMATION:

Type of opportunity: Dollmaking workshops/supplies, silks and laces

Description: Linda offers classes in all phases of modern and reproduction dollmaking, including wig making, shoe making, hat making, eye painting and lace draping. "We invite the best dollmakers and teachers for seminars."

BUSINESS INFORMATION:

To schedule: Contact Linda.

ADDITIONAL INFORMATION:

Also sells dollmaking supplies by appointment.

CHILDHOOD TREASURES

Cynthia Musser
2081 Sandover Ct.
Upper Arlington, OH 43220
Phone: (614)457-1447
Fax: (614)457-8727
In business since: 1983

BASIC INFORMATION:

Type of opportunity: Collection management lectures

Description: Lectures to antique doll study groups and clubs about collection management, including how to evaluate and reduce collections.

CREATIVE INTEREST

Mary Reo
16097 Hauss
Eastpointe, MI 48021-1122
Phone: (810)773-2720 EST
In business since: 1993

BASIC INFORMATION:

Type of opportunity: Dollmaking workshop

Description: Workshops are conducted in Mary's home for groups of 6-8 comfortably, 10 maximum. Seminars last for 3 days, from 10-6 each day, with a lunch break of 2 hours. Offers hands-on instruction for design and assembly in 1 of 3 seminars offered: (1) Lady proportion soft bodies for porcelain dolls; (2) Wardrobe pattern drafting and clothes to fit properly; and (3) nineteenth-century lace yokes. All will work on the same project. Each participant must bring her/his own sewing machine. A list of supplies and materials to bring will be sent with the registration packet.

BUSINESS INFORMATION:

To schedule: Contact Mary by letter or phone. Mary prefers that your group have an appointed person to contact her.

Cost: Registration forms must be returned as a packet with each person's prepaid fee of $100 (subject to change) check or money order enclosed by an appointed due date. This will allow Mary to prepare your kit before seminar date.

CROOKED TREE HOLLOW RAG DOLL CLUB

Frannie Meshorer
335 Magothy Bridge Rd.
Pasadena, MD 21122
Phone: (410)360-8504 EST
In business since: 1994

BASIC INFORMATION:

Type of opportunity: Dollmaking workshop, tea party and tour of "Crooked Tree Hollow"

Description: Crooked Tree Hollow is a large country home brimming with antiques. Each floor is a scene with dolls from the 1700s, 1800s and early 1900s. Yesteryear's tea parties for children include a tour and light snacks. Children will make a special craft and enjoy playing with antique toys. Adult courses in dollmaking and various other crafts are also available.

BUSINESS INFORMATION:

To schedule: Call Frannie Meshorer.

Cost: $15-$25 per person, depending on doll or "craft" taught. Always includes complete "kit," tea party and tour. $10 per child for children's tea parties.

JUDITH DODINGTON

N. Greenlake Gallery
R.R. 1, 70 Mile House, British Columbia
V0K 2K0
CANADA
Phone: (604)456-7326 PST
In business since: 1975

BASIC INFORMATION:

Type of opportunity: Paper doll workshop

Description: Judith gives workshops in various art techniques suitable for rendering paper dolls in watercolors and/or acrylics with colored pencil or pastel pencil highlighting.

BUSINESS INFORMATION:

To schedule: Call or write.

Cost: $25 an hour

THE DOLL ADVENTURE, INC.

Karen Laisney
2129 S. US Hwy. 1
Jupiter, FL 33477
Phone: (407)575-4292 EST
Fax: (407)743-1978
In business since: 1991

BASIC INFORMATION:

Type of opportunity: Dollmaking workshop

Description: Karen teaches dollmaking from the greenware stage to the completed doll in an open workshop. Each student works at her own pace on chosen project. Classes provide step-by-step instruction on how to produce a quality heirloom doll.

BUSINESS INFORMATION:

To schedule: Call or write.

To participate: Year-round, T-Sat, 10-4. Some evenings.

DOLL ARTISAN GUILD

Maureen Dugan
35 Main St.
Oneonta, NY 13820
Phone: (607)432-4977 EST
Fax: (607)432-2042
In business since: 1977

BASIC INFORMATION:

Type of opportunity: Dollmaking workshop

Description: The Doll Artisan Guild is a not-for-profit organization that sponsors a school of dollmaking and seminar program. Members may attend educational seminars on all aspects of dollmaking and acquire titles in dollmaking.

BUSINESS INFORMATION:

To schedule: Seminars are held only by doll studios that meet certain eligibility requirements. Please contact the Doll Artisan Guild for details.

To participate: Guild seminars are held around the world at various times of the year; please call or write for a schedule.

Cost: Varies

ADDITIONAL INFORMATION:
Two programs are offered: one for modern dolls and one for the reproduction of antique dolls. Guild instructors are some of the most renowned doll artists in the world, and the Guild is known for being on the forefront of dollmaking technique.

DOLL ARTISAN GUILD
Helen Schaeffer
647 Plum Creek Rd.
Bernville, PA 19506-9007
Phone: (610)488-6568 EST, (610)488-0122
Fax: (610)488-6568
In business since: 1972

BASIC INFORMATION:
Type of opportunity: Seminar, lecture
Description: Seminar program provides continuing and higher education for dollmakers worldwide through the Doll Artisan Guild School of Dollmaking. Seminars include casting, firing a kiln, dust free cleaning, water-base china painting, doll assembly, etc. Specialty seminars available on ethnic dolls, clowns, dimensional doll painting, shoemaking, wig making or your preference. Helen Schaeffer is available to lecture to doll clubs, for doll luncheons and other events on dollmaking, collecting and various topics of historical interest.

BUSINESS INFORMATION:
To schedule: Call or write for more information. 10 student minimum; 15 maximum.
To participate: 1 or more doll artisan guild seminars are offered each month.
Cost: 3-day seminars are $265-295 per student; workshop prices vary; lectures are $75 plus expenses.

"IF YOU HAVE A GOAL, NEVER LOSE SIGHT OF IT AND ALWAYS BELIEVE IN YOURSELF. WITH THESE TWO COMPONENTS YOU CAN ACHIEVE ANYTHING. MAY THEY BE THE GUIDING FORCES IN YOUR LIFE."
Lorrie Messina, Clinton Township, MI

THE DOLL GALLERY
Nan Radford
675 NW Gilman Blvd.
Issaquah, WA 98027
Phone: (206)392-4684 PST

BASIC INFORMATION:
Type of opportunity: Dollmaking workshop

BUSINESS INFORMATION:
To participate: T, W, 6:30-9. W, 9:45-12:15. W, 1:30-4. Classes are held at shop.

DOLL SEMINARS, WORKSHOPS AND LECTURES
Dwaine E. Gipe
1406 Sycamore Rd.
Montoursville, PA 17754
Phone: (717)323-9604 EST
In business since: 1991

BASIC INFORMATION:
Type of opportunity: Seminar, lecture
Description: Hands-on doll restoration workshops are available for up to 6 students. The workshops last for 4 days. Dwaine also offers lectures to doll clubs on "things you can safely do yourself in restoration."

BUSINESS INFORMATION:
To schedule: Call or write. Time and distance determines cost. All agreements contracted promptly.
Cost: A 4-day seminar for 6 students costs $3,500 plus rental fees if applicable. $50 minimum plus travel and motel if applicable. 100% satisfaction guaranteed, or will refund all money paid.

ADDITIONAL INFORMATION:
Seminar's "hands-on" introduction to doll restoration includes papier-mâché, wood, bisque and composition; use of materials; and tools and techniques, including airbrush. Students provide dolls and finish at least 1.

DOLL STUDIOS
Teresa Maria
1688 NE 123 St.
Miami, FL 33181
Phone: (305)895-0605 EST
Fax: (305)861-9848
In business since: 1988

BASIC INFORMATION:
Type of opportunity: Dollmaking workshop
Description: Seeley workshop

BUSINESS INFORMATION:
Cost: Classes are $20/month plus supplies.

DOLLMAKER'S COMMUNITY COLLEGE
Gloria Winer (Mimi)
300 Nancy Dr.
Point Pleasant, NJ 08742
Phone: (908)899-0804 or (908)899-6687 EST
Fax: (908)714-9306
E-mail: firebird@exit109.com
In business since: 1985

BASIC INFORMATION:
Type of opportunity: Dollmaking workshop, seminar
Description: Master Dollmaker seminars and workshops by NIADA artists and other world-recognized doll artists are scheduled irregularly. They are announced in *Let's Talk About Dollmaking Magazine* as well as all doll publications. Mimi also teaches cloth and new clay techniques at Wee Folk of Cloth Dollmakers Gathering, Doll-U-San Francisco, Dollmakers Community College and G Street Fabrics and Piecemakers.

BUSINESS INFORMATION:
To schedule: Please write or call for information.
To participate: Master Dollmaker seminars are held in Point Pleasant, New Jersey. Mimi's classes are held at the locations listed above.
Cost: $45-750, depending on artist and length of class.

KAREN D'ONOFRIO
2360 Middle Country Rd.
Centereach, Long Island, NY 11720
Phone: (800)90-DOLLS or (516)981-0727 EST
Fax: (516)981-0727
In business since: 1993

BASIC INFORMATION:
Type of opportunity: Lecture
Description: Karen offers 25-35 minute presentations on the history of dolls, from the 1800s to today. This hands-on presentation is offered to small

groups of Girl Scouts, Brownies or school groups of up to 20 children, ages 6-18.

BUSINESS INFORMATION:

To schedule: Contact Karen. Program is available January-October after 4:30 on weekdays only.

Cost: Free

FANTASY AT YOUR FINGERTIPS

Karen Morley
913 E. Grant Ave.
Eau Claire, WI 54701
Phone: (715)835-8877 CST
In business since: 1995

BASIC INFORMATION:

Type of opportunity: Dollmaking workshop

Description: In a 3-day workshop, students learn how to sculpt a face, hands and feet to make a doll in polymer clay. They then paint features, add hair and create a body. Students dress dolls at home. Students learn how to work with Fimo resources for eyes, hair, etc. Classes are held in the artist's home and are limited to 10 students.

BUSINESS INFORMATION:

To schedule: Contact the artist. Times flexible for groups. Karen schedules classes 3 months in advance.

To participate: Send SASE for class schedule.

Cost: $250 per person, which includes everything to create one doll. No hotels or food included in this price.

JUNE GOODNOW

2324 Ashley Dr.
Oklahoma City, OK 73120
Phone: (405)755-2047 CST
In business since: 1990

BASIC INFORMATION:

Type of opportunity: Dollmaking workshop

Description: June's mold making and resin casting workshops teach students to sculpt the head, hands and sometimes feet to make a one-of-a-kind doll. They construct a cloth body with wire armature, then wig the doll. In a 3-day seminar, students do not dress the doll, but costume patterns are provided for students to use at home.

BUSINESS INFORMATION:

To schedule: Write or call. Dates should be planned three months in advance in order to allow "advertising time" for the event and get enough students enrolled.

Cost: A 3-day sculpting seminar fee is $400 per student. A 2½ day moldmaking and resin fee is $300 per student.

ALAN HANSLIK

533 Fairview Ave.
Arcadia, CA 91007
Phone: (818)447-4228 PST
In business since: 1995

BASIC INFORMATION:

Type of opportunity: RTV moldmaking and resin casting classes

Description: Alan offers classes on RTV moldmaking and Urithane Resin Casting for 1-5 people a session. The RTV class covers how to build mold boxes using wood or nontraditional materials, how to mount object using sprues, placement of parting lines, and methods of eliminating bubbles. The resin class covers different resin types, pigments and dyes, eliminating air bubbles, demolding and clean-up. Also included is a source list of materials and equipment.

BUSINESS INFORMATION:

To schedule: Call or write.

To participate: Classes in Alan's home are scheduled on an individual basis.

Cost: $150 per person for RTV class, $100 for resin class, or $225 for both.

HEAVENLY DOLLS

Yvonne Nosler
404 W. Meeker St.
Kent, WA 98032
Phone: (206)852-5643 PST
Fax: (206)852-1435
In business since: 1985

BASIC INFORMATION:

Type of opportunity: Dollmaking workshop

Description: Heavenly Dolls provides workshops on how to make a doll that looks like an antique or modern doll for a fraction of the cost of buying an old or artist doll.

BUSINESS INFORMATION:

To participate: Year-round. Student may begin at any time.

Cost: $5 per 3 hour class.

ADDITIONAL INFORMATION:

"A lot of my students have gone on to start or operate their own shops," Yvonne says. "Some make the dolls for their own enjoyment. Others make and sell dolls for extra income."

BONNIE HOOVER

26889 Lakewood Way
Hayward, CA 94544
Phone: (510)887-4250 PST
In business since: 1989

BASIC INFORMATION:

Type of opportunity: Dollmaking workshop

Description: Bonnie offers workshops on making cloth dolls and paper dolls, including techniques such as embellishment and wig making. Some of the classes offered are: "Embellish a Doll From Head to Toe," "Lavish Your Doll," "Big Fat Hairy Deal," "Dollmaker's Choice—Paper Dolls" and "Paper and Doll Flattery."

Cost: $5 per 3-hour class.

JACQUES DORIER WASHI DOLLS

Jacques Dorier
93 Shirley St.
Winthrop, MA 02152
Phone: (617)846-6582 EST
Fax: (617)846-4285
E-mail: washij@aol.com
In business since: 1986

BASIC INFORMATION:

Type of opportunity: Dollmaking workshop and lecture

Description: Offers a one-hour lecture demonstrating the steps involved in making a Washi doll. During the 4 or 8 hour workshops, the students make an entire Washi doll.

BUSINESS INFORMATION:

To schedule: Call for guidelines.

To participate: Call for information.

Cost: $95-$200, supplies are provided.

JEAN NORDQUIST'S COLLECTIBLE DOLL ACADEMY

Jean Nordquist
4216 6th NW
Seattle, WA 98107
Phone: (206)781-1963 PST
Fax: (206)781-2258
In business since: 1979

BASIC INFORMATION:

Type of opportunity: Dollmaking workshop, dollmaking school, seminar

Description: Jean Nordquist offers traveling seminars in the art of antique reproduction porcelain dollmaking using her premium product line. Weekly workshops are available in Seattle at her studio from both Jean and her talented staff. Jean is available to lecture on all phases of dollmaking techniques as they relate to porcelain dolls.

BUSINESS INFORMATION:

To schedule: Contact Jean by phone, fax or mail, preferably 1 year in advance of the event.

To participate: Jean offers two three-day porcelain dollmaking seminars a year in her Seattle studio—one in January and one in August.

Cost: The cost varies according to the dolls reproduced but generally in the neighborhood of $350-400.

JOHANA GAST ANDERTON LECTURES

6408 North Flora Ave.
Gladstone, MO 64118-3609
Phone: (816)468-0558 CST
In business since: 1972

BASIC INFORMATION:

Type of opportunity: Dollmaking workshop, seminar, lecture

Description: Johana tailors a seminar, lecture or workshop to the specific needs of the organization. The presentations are also keyed to the experience level of participants, beginners to advanced. Workshops are hands-on and participants will go away with finished projects for the most part. Lectures may include slide shows with commentary, exhibits with information on printed cards, and a question/answer period.

BUSINESS INFORMATION:

To schedule: Write giving as much information as possible concerning date, location, possible number of participants, level of expertise, background of the organization—its aims for members, etc., age and educational levels generally of those who will be participating. Include LSASE for preliminary information.

Cost: Cost varies according to location.

Charges are negotiable, and individual circumstances of the organization are factored in when setting fees.

JOHNSTON ORIGINAL ART DOLL SEMINARS

Jack Johnston
1447 N. Carrington Lane
Centerville, UT 84014
Phone: (801)299-9908 MST
Fax: (801)299-9088
E-mail: jjdolls@aol.com
In business since: 1989

BASIC INFORMATION:

Type of opportunity: Dollmaking workshop, seminar

Description: Jack Johnston teaches 50 seminars and workshops per year in 22 states and 3 countries. They specialize in one-of-a-kind dolls made in polymer clay. Workshops are offered to beginners, advanced, masters and professional artists. A marketing seminar is offered to serious dollmakers. Workshops last 3 days, and each student completes a head, hands, feet and body.

BUSINESS INFORMATION:

To schedule: Contact Jack Johnston. Must have a storefront or commercial studio. Requires 15 students (maximum). Students pay fee, transportation, lodging and meals. 1 year advance booking.

To participate: List of locations, addresses and phone numbers. Call toll free (800)560-4958.

Cost: $400 per student. $3,000 to schedule a 3-day workshop for 15 students.

ADDITIONAL INFORMATION:

See the interview with Jack opening this section.

JUDY'S DOLL SHOP

Judy George
1201 A Hwy. 70 East
New Bern, NC 28560
Phone: (919)637-7933 EST
In business since: 1984

BASIC INFORMATION:

Type of opportunity: Dollmaking school

Description: Classes are offered in modern and antique reproduction porcelain dolls. Classes are not structured, so you can work at your own pace to get a quality doll.

BUSINESS INFORMATION:

To participate: T, Sat, 9-12. Sat, 1-4.

Cost: $5 per class plus supplies and firing charges.

LINDA J. KAYS

42 Mitchell St.
Norwich, NY 13815
Phone: (607)334-8375 EST
Fax: (607)334-8375
In business since: 1990

BASIC INFORMATION:

Type of opportunity: Dollmaking workshop

Description: Linda's workshop teaches sculpting, designing and costuming. Students can leave with a completed hand-sculptured art doll.

BUSINESS INFORMATION:

To schedule: Call for scheduling dates if at least 5 students available.

Cost: Cost varies depending on travel expenses ($300 base per student plus expenses which are split by the students). A sculpture from the artist is given to a host having a class of 10 students.

BARBARA J. LADY

325 Quarry Rd.
Albany, OR 97321
Phone: (503)928-4085 PST
In business since: 1991

BASIC INFORMATION:

Type of opportunity: Sculpting classes

Description: Barbara teaches the art of sculpting doll-size, human-proportion figures using synthetic clay.

BUSINESS INFORMATION:

Cost: Cost is $200 per day.

JAINE LAMB

34 Queen St.
Orillia, Ontario L3V 1B7
CANADA
Phone: (705)325-2044
In business since: 1993

BASIC INFORMATION:

Type of opportunity: Dollmaking workshop

Description: Jaine provides a 2-day workshop on sculpting a one-of-a-kind doll in Cernit. "Learn the basics of how and what you can do with this fascinating clay. We sculpt a head, hands and feet on a wire armature in a soft sculpted body ready for you to take home and dress," Jaine writes.

BUSINESS INFORMATION:

To schedule: Call for information.

To participate: Call or write for information regarding dates.

LAUREN WELKER'S DOLL MAKING WORKSHOPS

Lauren Welker
204 E. Coover St.
Mechanicsburg, PA 17055
Phone: (717)691-8110 EST
In business since: 1981

BASIC INFORMATION:

Type of opportunity: Dollmaking workshop

Description: Lauren offers 1-day and half-day workshops as well as some longer ones. The most popular workshops are the dollhouse dolls workshops in which each student assembles and dresses a doll using original porcelain parts. Only basic hand sewing skills and a good pair of scissors are required. In addition to doing conventions and private workshops, she also offers a regular workshop through the York City Recreation Department (120 S. Lehman Street, York PA 17403; phone (717)854-0211).

BUSINESS INFORMATION:

To schedule: The workshop provider must have enough table space for the attendees and provide coffee and sodas if possible.

Cost: Basic workshops start at $45 per student and go up depending on what size doll is being made, the cost of accessories, etc.

LIFETIME CAREER SCHOOLS

101 Harrison St.
Archbald, PA 18403
Phone: (717)876-6340 EST
Fax: (717)876-1682
In business since: 1944

BASIC INFORMATION:

Type of opportunity: Home Study Program in Doll Repair

Description: Program teaches how to make, repair, dress, collect, restore and sell dolls of all kinds. Excellent opportunities for starting a small busi-

ness or hobby. Diploma awarded. Accredited Member, Distance Education & Training Council.

BUSINESS INFORMATION:

Cost: $649

ADDITIONAL INFORMATION:

Lifetime Career Schools has been training people in new careers and hobbies since 1944. Each program features illustrated step-by-step instruction, individual consultation service and diploma.

EMILY L. MANNING

4809 Ravenswood Rd.
Riverdale, MD 20737
Phone: (301)864-5561 EST
In business since: 1967

BASIC INFORMATION:

Type of opportunity: Dollmaking workshop, lecture

Description: Emily's "creative sox doll classes" teach students to complete a doll using freehand sewing methods. Emily also offers a slide program on "far out repairs."

BUSINESS INFORMATION:

To schedule: Call Emily.

Cost: Varies, but general cost is $55 for kit and 2 classes. Slide program fee varies but should include transportation.

NEEDLEARTS ADVENTURES, L.L.C.

Sandra Sapienza
P.O. Box 331
Crownsville, MD 21032
Phone: (410)923-3415 EST
Fax: (410)923-3415
E-mail: nrtt91a@prodigy.com
In business since: 1994

BASIC INFORMATION:

Type of opportunity: Dollmaking workshop

Description: NeedleArts Adventures, L.L.C. arranges creative workshops for sewing enthusiasts. These include 1-day and multi-day workshops and conferences on all aspects of sewing, especially wearable art and cloth dollmaking. It produces Wee Folk Of Cloth, the largest gathering in the eastern US for cloth dollmakers, featuring over 60 workshops by an international teaching staff. The emphasis is on cloth dollmaking, and there are work-

shops on related topics (surface design, marketing, etc.) and on any dollmaking medium except porcelain. NeedleArts Adventures arranges shopping expeditions in the mid-Atlantic area for dollmakers.

BUSINESS INFORMATION:

To schedule: Will arrange workshops, dollmaking retreats and shopping expeditions for groups. Call or write for more information.

Cost: Cost depends on duration and complexity.

JILL NEMIROW-NELSON

24 Orange Ave.
Clifton, NJ 07013
Phone: (201)916-1634 EST
Fax: (201)916-1634
In business since: 1994

BASIC INFORMATION:

Type of opportunity: Dollmaking workshops

Description: Jill gives lessons in the basics of doll sculpting in miniature and smaller sized dolls (under 15"). She prefers that students use oven-bake polymer clays since she does not teach mold making or painting on porcelain.

BUSINESS INFORMATION:

To schedule: Jill can only travel within a 45-minute drive from her studio, as her schedule permits.

To participate: Lessons are offered to a limited number of students in home/studio.

Cost: Cost is approximately $200 per student for 4 classes; supplies additional.

SUSANNA OROYAN

3270 Whitbeck Blvd.
Eugene, OR 97405
Phone: (541)345-0242 PST
Fax: (541)345-0242
In business since: 1980

BASIC INFORMATION:

Type of opportunity: Dollmaking workshop, seminar, lecture

Description: With 20 years experience as teacher, artist and author, Susanna Oroyan, a member of NIADA, offers lectures and classes based on her published books and patterns. Classes cover all aspects of the world of cloth and oven-cured clays.

BUSINESS INFORMATION:

To schedule: Send SASE for brochure, or call to discuss. Susanna will tailor her program to your group's needs.

To participate: Susanna usually teaches at Doll University, Dollmaker's Magic, Wee Folk of Cloth, NIADA conferences and the International Quilt Festival.

Cost: $250 plus expenses.

ADDITIONAL INFORMATION:

Classes are available in sculpture, body construction, making dolls from patterns, design critique and related dollmaking subjects.

PAGE'S DOLLS

Lillian Page
6969 L. 5 Lane
Escanaba, MI 49829
Phone: (906)786-6565 CST
In business since: 1991

BASIC INFORMATION:

Type of opportunity: Dollmaking school
Description: Page's Dolls is a Seeley Doll Making School. Regular doll classes are taught by Doll Artisan and Master of Doll Making instructors. Workshops in both modern and classic dolls are offered.

BUSINESS INFORMATION:

To schedule: Call or write.
To participate: Daily and evening doll classes are offered.
Cost: Regular doll classes are $5 per class plus supplies. Workshop costs vary, but are $279 and up.

PARAGON INDUSTRIES, INC.

2011 South Town East Blvd.
Mesquite, TX 75149-1122
Phone: (800)876-4328 or (214)288-7557 CST
Fax: (214)222-0646
In business since: 1970

BASIC INFORMATION:

Type of opportunity: Seminar
Description: The Paragon In-Plant Kiln Maintenance Seminar lasts 1½ days, usually over a Friday and Saturday. It includes electronic and manual-fire kilns. Students learn the basics of repair, maintenance and firing. Distributors, dealers and hobbyists are welcome. Includes a tour of the kiln factory.

BUSINESS INFORMATION:

To schedule: Please call for details. Twelve paying students are required. The seminar sponsor is allowed 2 students free.
Cost: Cost is $75 per student and includes a service manual in a 3-ring binder, lunch on both days and dinner the first evening.

> *"COME MAKE A BABY YOU DON'T HAVE TO SEND TO COLLEGE!"*
> *Yvonne Nosler, Heavenly Dolls, Kent, WA*

PIECEMAKERS COUNTRY STORE

Joanna Nelson
1720 Adams Ave.
Costa Mesa, CA 92626
Phone: (714)641-3112 PST
Fax: (714)641-3112
E-mail: 75552.3442@compuserve.com
In business since: 1977

BASIC INFORMATION:

Type of opportunity: Dollmaking school
Description: Piecemakers provides a unique learning situation with over 200 classes each quarter. Local teachers as well as those flown in from around the country are featured.

BUSINESS INFORMATION:

To schedule: Contact Kerry or Joanna with information regarding classes or program to be held.
To participate: A week-long symposium is held each August. Call or write to receive a quarterly schedule.

RITA'S CHILDREN

Rita Harth
461 North Service Rd. W. #B10
Oakville, Ontario L6M 2V5
CANADA
Phone: (905)825-2927 EST
Fax: (905)825-2980
In business since: 1993

BASIC INFORMATION:

Type of opportunity: Dollmaking workshop
Description: Rita teaches 1- or 2-day specialty sewing workshops, preferably on weekends.

BUSINESS INFORMATION:

To schedule: Must have 8 people per

workshop. Schedule 2 months in advance.
Cost: $95-395, depending on project.

SCULPTING AND MOLD MAKING SEMINARS

Anthony or Lylis Bulone
P.O. Box 155
Solvang, CA 93464
Phone: (805)688-3754 PST
Fax: (805)688-3754
In business since: 1981

BASIC INFORMATION:

Type of opportunity: Dollmaking workshop
Description: Workshops include 2 days of sculpting techniques and one day of mold making techniques. Each student receives the following materials: armature, tool kit, worksheets, mold book and a complete step-by-step procedure of exactly what the student does in class in print and photos. Students also receive a signed "Barbie" sheet showing Anthony, the sculptor of the original "Barbie" doll, and his wife Lylis, the model.

BUSINESS INFORMATION:

To participate: 8-10 seminars are scheduled per year. Classes consist of 8-12 students, and are conducted in your studio or doll shop. Contracts are available.
Cost: $350 per student.

SCULPTING AND MOLDMAKING SEMINARS

Marlena H. Nielsen
1217 S.E. 52nd
Portland, OR 97215
Phone: (503)239-0465 PST
Fax: (503)239-0465
In business since: 1993

BASIC INFORMATION:

Type of opportunity: Dollmaking workshop
Description: Seminars encourage students to study the human form with special emphasis on anatomical structure. Students choose their subject and bring photos to class. Students go home with their sculpture, a mold, a basic tool set and printed hand-outs.

BUSINESS INFORMATION:

To schedule: Call to make arrangements.

Cost: Student fees are $350.

SUNNY STANSBURY—HEARTCRAFT PUPPETS AND DOLLS

Sunny Stansbury
P.O. Box 1730
Corrales, NM 87048
Phone: (505)897-9148
In business since: 1989

BASIC INFORMATION:

Type of opportunity: Dollmaking workshop, seminar

Description: Topics available are: Southwestern dollmaking, dollmaking for the holiday season, hatmaking for dolls, jewelry making for dolls, costume making for dolls, animal puppets for nature storytelling.

BUSINESS INFORMATION:

To schedule: Contact Sunny for descriptions and prices.

TOM TIERNEY

P.O. Drawer D
Hopewell Junction, NY 12533
Phone: (914)225-2881 EST
In business since: 1976

BASIC INFORMATION:

Type of opportunity: Lecture

Description: Tom offers occasional lectures on his work and how he prepares and researches it, with examples of original art as illustration. He prefers to do a brief talk with an extended question-and-answer period.

BUSINESS INFORMATION:

To schedule: Write or telephone to establish dates.

Cost: $200/day, including flying time.

TRUEBITE INC.

Ed Calafut
2590 Glenwood Rd.
Vestal, NY 13850
Phone: (607)785-7664 or (800)676-8907 EST
Fax: (607)785-2405
In business since: 1995

BASIC INFORMATION:

Type of opportunity: Dollmaking workshop

Description: Ed offers workshops in cutting, grinding, engraving and cleaning porcelain, ceramic and glass. Seminars on insertion of flirty eyes and hands-on use of tools for altering and cleaning porcelain, etc. are also available.

BUSINESS INFORMATION:

To participate: Seminars are held in shops that sell Truebite products.

TWIN PINES OF MAINE, INC.

Nicholas J. Hill
P.O. Box 1118
Scarborough, ME 04070-1178
Phone: (800)770-DOLL or (207)883-5541 EST
Fax: (207)883-1239
E-mail: nick@twinpines.com

BASIC INFORMATION:

Type of opportunity: Seminar

Description: Nicholas presents seminars on doll cleaning and restoration at doll shows. He has presented seminars at the Modern Doll Convention, the Vogue Doll Convention, the Glide International Convention and the International Barbie Convention.

CAROL-LYNN RÖSSEL WAUGH

5 Morrill St.
Winthrop, ME 04364-1220
Phone: (207)377-6769 EST
Fax: (207)377-4158
In business since: 1980

BASIC INFORMATION:

Type of opportunity: Dollmaking workshop, seminar, lecture

Description: Carol-Lynn offers dollmaking seminars and hands-on workshops, as well as lectures and demonstrations on doll photography.

BUSINESS INFORMATION:

To schedule: Call or fax.

Cost: All travel expenses and lodging must be paid by the client. Fees for lectures and workshops negotiable.

CHRISTINA WEMMITT-PAUK

281 Greenbriar Rd.
Beech Mountain, NC 28604
Phone: (704)387-4755 EST
Fax: (704)387-2637
In business since: 1992

BASIC INFORMATION:

Type of opportunity: Dollmaking workshop, seminar, lecture

Description: Christina presents beginning sculpting workshops and seminars to groups and at shows. She also offers lectures on networking, professionalism and displays.

BUSINESS INFORMATION:

To schedule: Call for details.

ADDITIONAL INFORMATION:

See the article opening chapter six co-written by Christina.

WILD SPIRIT DOLL STUDIO

Nancy Pritchard
1235 Wampanoag Trail
Barrington, RI 02915
Phone: (401)245-5013 (weekends and evenings), (401)433-1235 (Tuesday-Saturday, 10-5)
In business since: 1994

BASIC INFORMATION:

Type of opportunity: Dollmaking workshop

Description: Teaches 2- and 3-day "short intensive project classes." Adult classes include Victorian and Woodland Santas and others.

BUSINESS INFORMATION:

To schedule: Call

To participate: 2- and 3-day daytime and evening workshops are held throughout the year.

Cost: 2-day workshops are $80, 3-day workshops are $120 and include all materials.

JAN WILENSKY

2011 Longleaf St.
Santa Rosa, CA 95403
Phone: (707)577-7971 or (707)577-0434 PST
Fax: (707)577-0434
In business since: 1993

BASIC INFORMATION:

Type of opportunity: Dollmaking workshop

Description: Jan teaches primarily the sculpting of the head from start to finish and will answer any and all questions related to the business and the art of dollmaking.

BUSINESS INFORMATION:

To schedule: Call or write. Limit 6-7 students per workshop.

Cost: $600 per student.

BARBARA WILSON
409 Commercial St.
Hanceville, AL 35077
Phone: (205)352-4024 CST

BASIC INFORMATION:
Type of opportunity: Dollmaking workshop
Description: Workshops available in dollmaking, costuming, French handsewing techniques, miniatures.

BUSINESS INFORMATION:
To schedule: Contact by phone or mail. Minimum of 10 students required.
Cost: Workshop costs range from $35-$75.

PUBLICATIONS

ANTIQUE DOLL WORLD
225 Main St., Suite 300
Northport, NY 11768-1737
Contacts: Donna Kaonis
Advertising: Keith Kaonis
Phone: For information: (516)261-8337
For advertising: (516)261-8337
For subscriptions: (800)828-1429
Fax: (516)261-8237

BASIC INFORMATION:
Issues per year: 7
Specs: Magazine style, color, glossy
Description: A publication for antique doll collectors. Covers antique dolls and related areas. Articles are written by leading doll experts. The publication covers shows and auctions. A calendar of events is also included with each issue.
Subscription Rate: $22.50/year

ADVERTISING INFORMATION:
Target audience: Collectors of antique dolls

SUBMISSIONS:
Submit via slides, transparencies, prints and/or negatives. Prefer copy on disk (Macintosh). Will also accept copy typed or handwritten. Include SASE.

BARBIE BAZAAR
5617 6th Ave.
Kenosha, WI 53140
Contacts: Karen Caviale
Advertising: Marlene Mura
Phone: For information: (414)658-1004
For advertising: (414)658-1881
For subscriptions: (414)658-1004

Fax: (414)658-0433

BASIC INFORMATION:
Issues per year: 6
Specs: Magazine style, color, glossy
Description: Features everything there is to know about Barbies: past, present and future. There are articles on pricing and Barbie Club news. Articles are written by people from around the world. The magazine also features Barbies from around the world.

ADVERTISING INFORMATION:
Target audience: Any Barbie doll collector

SUBMISSIONS:
Typewritten for the "Collector Profiles" and "Club News." Also will accept slides and/or 35mm prints for "Talking Barbie Talk," the question-answer section of the publication. Send SASE.

PAPER DOLLS:
Articles about Barbie paper dolls are included in occasional issues.

CANADIAN DOLL JOURNAL
1284 Adirondack Dr.
Ottawa, Ontario K2C 2V3
CANADA
Contacts: Editor: Evelyn Robson Strahlendorf
Phone: (613)727-5369 EST
Fax: (613)727-5055

BASIC INFORMATION:
Issues per year: 6
Specs: Magazine style, b&w, 8½″ × 11″
Description: Covers antique dolls described by experts, Barbie, original doll artists with photographs of their dolls. Includes doll cartoons, doll identification in the Can You Tell Me? column, stories about the quest for dolls, listings of doll shows, classified ads.
Newsstand Cost: $4.50
Subscription Rate: $21/year

ADVERTISING INFORMATION:
Target audience: The Canadian Doll Journal is a magazine for doll collectors. It covers every type of doll including chinas, piano babies, dollhouses, antiques and original artist dolls.
Rates: Full page $50. Free classified ad in each issue for subscribers.

SUBMISSIONS:
Accepts articles if they fit the focus of a doll collector's interests and are not more than 3 pages. May include photographs taken against a plain background.

PAPER DOLLS:
A paper doll is included in each issue. Articles about paper dolls are included in occasional issues. Paper dolls are b&w. Pay is $50 for doll and clothing for 2 pages.

CELEBRITY DOLL JOURNAL
Loraine Burdick
413 10th Ave. Court N.E.
Puyallup, WA 98372
Phone: PST
In business since: 1956

BASIC INFORMATION:
Issues per year: 4 subscription issues plus 4-20 "Extras."
Specs: 16 pages plus 1-page editorial. Stapled, b&w.
Subscription rate: $10/year US, $11 Canada and foreign
Description: Celebrity Doll Journal reference includes genealogy of doll, artist, and celebrity and paper doll topics. Research includes original reference and advertising, illustrations to inform, and topics to enrich cherished memories of old treasures. "Celebrity" implies someone or something well known from Shirley Temple or Dy-Dee to Santa and Tillie the Toiler. Many issues are expanded in an "Extra" for those with special interest in additional information.

ADVERTISING INFORMATION:
Target audience: Collectors interested in paper doll background.
Paid circulation: 85 by subscription; single issues sold (some in reprint).

COLLECTORS UNITED
711 S. 3rd Ave.
Chatsworth, GA 30705
Contacts: Gary Green
Phone: (706)695-8242
Fax: (706)695-0770

BASIC INFORMATION:
Issues per year: 12
Specs: Newsletter, b&w
Description: Publication highlights dolls and doll-related items. Publication is

used by its readers to buy, sell and trade dolls.

ADVERTISING INFORMATION:
Target audience: Doll collectors

CONTEMPORARY DOLL COLLECTOR

Editorial: Barbara Campbell
Advertising: Doug Kroll or Pat Brassett
30595 Eight Mile Rd.
Livonia, MI 48152
Phone: (810)477-6650 EST
Fax: (810)477-6795
Issues per year: 6
Specs: Magazine style, color, saddle-stitch binding 8½″ × 11″
Description: A color magazine devoted to doll collectors of all ages and interests. Articles are varied and comprehensive and written by well-respected authors in the doll world. Superior photography and editorial excellence have garnered this publication's numerous industry-wide awards.
Newsstand cost: $4.95
Subscription: $19.90

ADVERTISING INFORMATION:
Target audience: Collectors of all types and eras of dolls.
Paid circulation: 11,300
Rates: $1,040 for one-time, full page, b&w ad. Other rates and sizes available. Call for information.

SUBMISSIONS:
Guidelines: Accepts unsolicited manuscripts. Send query letter outlining article idea with photographic suggestions. Prefers the article and photos on spec.
Pay: varies

PAPER DOLLS:
Includes: A paper doll in each issue (a separate insert without printing on back). Article about paper dolls in occasional issues. Paper dolls are b&w and color.
PD art guidelines: Unsolicited designs accepted. Send SASE to editor for guidelines.
Pay: varies

DOLL ARTISAN

Editorial: Cheryl Berdich
Advertising: Maureen Dugan
P.O. Box 1113
Oneonta, NY 13820-5113

Phone: Editorial: (607)432-4977 EST
Advertising: (607)433-1240

BASIC INFORMATION:
Issues per year: 5
Specs: Magazine style, color
Description: A magazine for porcelain doll makers, this publication provides technical information and projects with each issue. Each issue includes projects for porcelain doll makers of various levels.
Target audience: Doll makers that specialize in reproductions of antique dolls.

SUBMISSIONS:
Guidelines: Write for guidelines.

DOLL CRAFTER

30595 Eight Mile Rd.
Livonia, MI 48152-1798
Contacts: Editor: Barbara Campbell
Editorial: Annette Malis
Advertising: Lyn Syms or Renae Stewart
Phone: For editorial information:
(810)477-6650 ext. 109 EST
For advertising: (810)477-6650 ext. 140
For subscriptions: (800)458-8237
Fax: (810)477-6795

BASIC INFORMATION:
Issues per year: 12
Specs: Magazine style, color, saddle-stitch, 7¼″ × 9¾″
Description: Doll Crafter is dedicated to creating and collecting beautiful dolls. Every month *Doll Crafter* is filled with beautiful color photographs of antique reproduction and modern dolls and informative articles by internationally recognized doll crafters and artists on how to make, collect, costume and sculpt dolls. Plus, each issue features artist profiles and much more.
Newsstand Cost: $4.95
Subscription Rate: $38.80 US; $48.80 Canada and elsewhere.

ADVERTISING INFORMATION:
Target audience: Doll crafters, collectors, doll artists and doll costumers.
Paid circulation: 66,000
Rates: Display ads available in b&w, 2-color and 4-color; Marketplace ads available to retail stores, museums, show promoters, doll artists and mail order advertisers; Doll Exchange/Classified ads also available.

Demographics: Doll Crafter readership is 99.5% female; average household income is $50,000 annually; 79.7% of readers are hobbyists; 11.7% are professional dollmakers; 8.6% are doll-making teachers.

SUBMISSIONS:
Accepts articles on how to make doll-related accessories and profiles of famous doll crafters. Also accepts stories and photos on doll museums. Payment is made upon publication, and prices vary depending upon project. Contact editorial offices.

DOLL MAGAZINE

Ashdown Publishing Limited
Avalon Court, Star Rd.,
Partridge Green
West Sussex RH13 8RY
ENGLAND
Distributed by: Heritage Press
3150 State Line Rd.
North Bend, OH 45052
Phone: (513)353-4052
Fax: (513)353-3933

BASIC INFORMATION:
Issues per year: 4
Specs: Magazine style, color
Description: This British magazine includes articles about doll collecting, reader's tales about favorite dolls, dollmaking articles and competitions, an auction showcase and much more.
Newsstand cost: $7.50
Subscription cost: $30 US; $35 Canada

DOLL NEWS

UFDC
10920 N. Ambassador Dr., Suite 130
Kansas City, MO 64153
Contacts: Janet Hallingsworth
Advertising: Shelia Needle
Phone: For information: (818)441-3330 CST
For advertising: (619)631-3768
For subscriptions: (208)344-9821
Fax: (818)441-3339 (Editorial)
(208)344-2080 (Membership)

BASIC INFORMATION:
Issues per year: 4
Specs: Magazine style, color
Description: This is the official publication of UFDC, a nonprofit publication focusing on dolls and doll research. Each issue contains 64-76 pages. The

publication is both educational and philanthropic. Each issue contains how-to articles.

ADVERTISING INFORMATION:

Target audience: Members of UFDC interested in antique and modern dolls.

SUBMISSIONS:

Send to Janet Hallingsworth. Manuscripts, photos and books should be sent first class mail needing no signature. Send SASE with return postage included.

PAPER DOLLS:

A paper doll is included in occasional issues. Articles about paper dolls are included in occasional issues. Unsolicited submissions accepted. Very selective. Send photo and copy.

ADDITIONAL INFORMATION:

Available to UFDC members only.

DOLL READER

P.O. Box 8200
Harrisburg, PA 17112
Contacts: Editor: Carolyn Cook
Editorial: Eleanor Mauch
Advertising: Jennifer Weber
Phone: For information: (717)540-6737
For advertising: (717)657-9555
For subscriptions: (800)435-9610
Fax: (717)540-6728

BASIC INFORMATION:

Issues per year: 9

Specs: Magazine style, color

Description: Appeals to all collectors and makers of antique, modern, contemporary and antique reproduction dolls or dolls as art.

ADVERTISING INFORMATION:

Target audience: Doll collectors with focus on various types of dolls.

SUBMISSIONS:

Accepts unsolicited submissions for articles. Send SASE.

PAPER DOLLS:

A paper doll is included in occasional issues. Articles about paper dolls are included in occasional issues. Unsolicited submissions accepted. Send SASE.

DOLLMAKING—PROJECTS AND PLANS

P.O. Box 5000
Iola, WI 54945
Contacts: Editor: Heidi Hermansen
Editorial: Heidi Hermansen

Advertising: Barb Lashua
Phone: For editorial info: (715)445-5000
For advertising: (715)445-5000
For subscriptions: (800)331-0038 CST
Fax: (715)445-4053
E-mail: jonespu@mail.atw.fullfeed.com

BASIC INFORMATION:

Issues per year: 6

Specs: Magazine style, color, saddle stitched, 8½″ × 11″

Description: *Dollmaking* specializes in the development and production of "hard" dolls. These include porcelain, polymer clay, composition and collector dolls (Barbie, Toni). Also includes information on costuming, accessorizing, collecting and marketing dolls.

Newsstand Cost: $3.95

Subscription Rate: 1 year, $17.95; 2 years, $32.50; 3 years, $45.95

ADVERTISING INFORMATION:

Target audience: *Dollmaking* is read by dollmakers who specialize in one-of-a-kind dolls. They consider themselves to be at the higher end of dollmaking.

Demographics: Readership is generally females in the 25-40 age group.

SUBMISSIONS:

A submission should include a clear photo of the project and a technique sheet. The author must include phone number and address with the technique sheet. Most submissions are voluntary and contributors receive subscriptions. Contract artists receive $150/project.

ADDITIONAL INFORMATION:

"We at *Dollmaking* magazine pride ourselves with being 'in-touch' with our readers. They are able to call us and talk dollmaking; in turn, we learn more about what they want from us."

DOLLS—THE COLLECTOR'S MAGAZINE

170 Fifth Ave.
New York, NY 10010
Phone: Editorial and advertising: (212)989-8700 EST
Subscriptions: (800)347-6969

> "TIME IS MEANINGLESS IN THE FACE OF
> CREATIVITY."
> *Jan Wilensky, Santa Rosa, CA*

Fax: (212)645-8976

BASIC INFORMATION:

Issues per year: 10

Specs: Magazine style, color, 8½″ × 11″

Description: A full-size glossy magazine with spectacular photography and comprehensive, exciting articles about every aspect of doll collecting, including antiques, modern, contemporary artist and contemporary manufactured dolls. Each issue includes profiles of contemporary artists, visits to public and private collections, historical stories on famous or mysterious dolls and makers of the past, identification and value information, show reports, auction reports, news from the doll world and new dolls.

Newsstand cost: $4.99

Subscription cost: $26.95

ADVERTISING INFORMATION:

Rates: Contact advertising director.

PAPER DOLLS:

Includes: A paper doll in occasional issues. Article about paper dolls in occasional issues. Paper dolls are color.

FANCYWORK'S BEST NEWS

4728 Dodge St.
Duluth, MN 55812
Contacts: Editor: Jean Becker
Phone: For editorial information: (218)525-5811 CST
For subscriptions: (218)525-5811 or (800)365-5257
Fax: (218)525-5811

BASIC INFORMATION:

Issues per year: 4

Specs: Newsletter, b&w, 12 pages 8½″ × 11″.

Description: A quarterly newsletter published by Fancywork and Fashion Press focusing on costuming 18″ vinyl dolls and modern porcelain dolls. Includes patterns, hints and accessory ideas along with supplier information.

Subscription Rate: $10/year

Target audience: Home sewers, dollmakers, and doll collectors. Especially helpful for costuming 18″ modern vinyl playable dolls and modern artist reproduction (porcelain) dolls in 16″-24″ range of sizes.

Paid circulation: 2,000

SUBMISSIONS:

One page typed, good photographs. Prefer adaptations of our original patterns. Send SASE with 55¢ postage for sample.

PAPER DOLLS:
$25 for articles; $10 for hints.

THE HIMSTEDT TIMES
3705 Hampton Lane
Cameron Park, CA 95682-8910
Contacts: Editor: Patricia Mertes
Phone: (916)677-4520 PST
Fax: (916)677-4520
E-mail: patt@msn.com or
76331.1025@compuserve.com

BASIC INFORMATION:
Issues per year: 4, plus yearly photo issue
Specs: Newsletter, color, 16 pages
Description: A source of information on Himstedt dolls as well as subscriber participation. The newsletter also has an "Ask Annette" column where Annette Himstedt answers your questions. There is also a quarterly price report on secondary market prices, interesting articles and many photos.
Subscription Rate: $24/year

ADVERTISING INFORMATION:
Target audience: Collectors of Annette Himstedt dolls
Rates: Accepts display advertising on limited space basis. Free classified ads for subscribers.

SUBMISSIONS:
Must be about Himstedt dolls or services/information useful to Himstedt collectors.

KEEPING YOU IN STITCHES NEWSLETTER
P.O. Box 85
Monterey Park, CA 91754
Contacts: Editor: Joan Jansen

BASIC INFORMATION:
Specs: Newsletter, b&w, 8½" × 11", folded
Description: *Keeping You In Stitches Newsletter* includes cloth doll patterns designed by Joan Jansen with instructions. Also included are tips on various aspects of dollmaking and clothing patterns.
Subscription Rate: $10

LAUREN WELKER'S DOLL DIARY
204 E. Coover St.
Mechanicsburg, PA 17055

Contacts: Editor: Lauren Welker
Phone: (717)691-8110 EST

BASIC INFORMATION:
Issues per year: 4
Specs: Newsletter, b&w
Description: A quarterly newsletter for doll collectors and paper doll enthusiasts. Each issue contains articles about dolls, a doll pattern and an original paper doll.
Subscription Rate: $12

PAPER DOLLS:
A paper doll is included in each issue. Paper dolls are b&w.

ADDITIONAL INFORMATION:
Please write or call to order a subscription. Send check or money order. Subscriptions may be charged by phone.

LET'S TALK ABOUT DOLLMAKING MAGAZINE
300 Nancy Dr.
Point Pleasant, NJ 08742
Contacts: Editor: Jim Winer
Editorial: Gloria Winer
Phone: (908)899-6687 EST
Fax: (908)714-9306
E-mail: firebird@exit109.com

BASIC INFORMATION:
Issues per year: 2-4
Specs: Magazine style, b&w, saddle stitch, 8½" × 11", 48 pages
Description: *Let's Talk* is a networking tool. It is full of useful technique and source information. It covers all the doll seminars and conventions in the first person from the viewpoint of a student/doll artist.
Subscription Rate: $14.95, US; $19.95 Canada; $24.95 elsewhere

ADVERTISING INFORMATION:
Target audience: For the dollmaker working in any or all media; beginner to famous artist.
Paid circulation: 2,000

SUBMISSIONS:
Articles about new techniques, experiences with a product; shows and classes.

PAPER DOLLS:
Articles about paper dolls are included in occasional issues.

MASTER COLLECTOR
12513 Birchfalls Dr.
Raleigh, NC 27614

Contacts: Editor: Brian Savage
Phone: For advertising: (800)772-6673 EST
Fax: (919)847-5132
E-mail: savagebm@aol.com

BASIC INFORMATION:
Issues per year: 12
Specs: Tabloid, b&w, saddle stitch, 11" × 13¾" trimmed.
Description: *Master Collector* contains over 2,000 ads from people buying and selling dolls and toys. All ads are indexed into classifications by type or manufacturer for easy access. Subscriptions include a free 30- word ad each month.
Newsstand Cost: $3.95
Subscription Rate: Third class, $27.95. First class, $42.

ADVERTISING INFORMATION:
Target audience: All types of doll and toy collectors. There are over 200 available indexes for ads, from Barbie to GI Joe to tin toys and everything in between.
Paid circulation: 3,700
Rates: $6.10/column inch. Discounts for camera ready ads. Call for quote.

PAPER DOLLS:
Ads for paper dolls.

ADDITIONAL INFORMATION:
Master Collector is the only indexed doll and toy trading publication on the market today.

MILLER'S BARBIE COLLECTOR
P.O. Box 8722
Spokane, WA 99203-0722
Contacts: Editor: Barbara Miller
Editorial: Dan Miller
Advertising: Barbara Miller
Phone: For information: (509)747-0139
For subscriptions: (800)874-5201
Fax: (509)455-6115

BASIC INFORMATION:
Issues per year: Quarterly
Specs: Magazine style, color

ADVERTISING INFORMATION:
Target audience: 100% Barbie collectors. This audience enjoys facts and figures about Barbie dolls with the focus exclusively on collector Barbie dolls.

SUBMISSIONS:
Submit research-oriented articles only.

The article must be written in a way that the publisher can evaluate the correctness of the facts. Information will not be returned unless prior arrangements are made.

PAPER DOLLS:

A paper doll is included in occasional issues. Articles about paper dolls are included in occasional issues.

MILLER'S MARKET REPORT FOR BARBIE COLLECTORS

Editorial: Dan Miller
Advertising: Barbara Miller
P.O. Box 8722
Spokane, WA 99203-0722
Phone: Editorial: (509)747-0139 EST
Subscriptions: (800)874-5201
Fax: (509)455-6115
Issues per year: 12
Specs: tabloid, color
Target audience: Barbie collectors. This audience enjoys facts and figures about Barbie dolls with the focus exclusively on collector Barbie dolls.

SUBMISSIONS:

Guidelines: Submit nonreturnable research oriented articles.

THE SPARKLING STAR

Bright Star Promotions, Inc.
3428 Hillvale Rd.
Louisville, KY 40241-2756
Contacts: Editor: Valerie Rogers
Phone: (502)423-STAR EST
Fax: (502)423-7827
E-mail: xkcb90a@prodigy.com

BASIC INFORMATION:

Description: The Sparkling Star newspaper has product reviews and highlights leading miniature doll artists and craftspeople. A complete show schedule from Bright Star Promotions is also included.
Subscription Rate: Free upon request.

HELPFUL PRODUCTS AND SERVICES

BLU FROGG GARDENS

Ralph and Mary Gonzales
1155 Llagas Rd.
Morgan Hill, CA 95037
Phone: (408)779-2719 PST
Fax: (408)779-2719

E-mail: rdzek@garlic.com
In business since: 1989

PRODUCT INFORMATION:

Type: Books, videos
Description: Ralph and Mary offer 2 books and 6 videos on dollmaking. Books include *Sculpting the Original Doll—The Blu Frogg Method*, and *Mold Making for the Original Doll— The Blu Frogg Method.* The 6 videos are each 1 hour long and teach various aspects of dollmaking, including sculpting the head, hands, and feet, moldmaking (basic and advanced) and costuming.

BUSINESS INFORMATION:

To purchase: Contact BluFrogg Gardens.
Cost: Each book or video is $25. Shipping is $1.74 for books and $1 for videos.

C&T PUBLISHING

Sharon Pilcher
5021 Blum, Suite #1
Martinez, CA 94553
Phone: (800)284-1114, (510)370-9600 PST
Fax: (510)370-1576
In business since: 1985

PRODUCT INFORMATION:

Description: C&T Publishing produces books to inspire creativity, including *Fantastic Figures: Ideas and Techniques Using the New Clays* by Susanna Oroyan and *The Art of Silk Ribbon Embroidery and Elegant Stitches* by Judith Baker Montano.

BUSINESS INFORMATION:

To purchase: Directly from publisher

ADDITIONAL INFORMATION

C&T Publishing's World Wide Web site can be found at: http://www.ctpub.com/~ctpub

KAREN B. CHAMBERS

7521 Hwy. 80 W.
Fort Worth, TX 76116
Phone: (817) 244-5454 CST
In business since: 1990
Offers: Karen offers pattern printing services for artists. She also offers iron-on transfers.

D & B ANTIQUES

Dwaine and Betty Gipe
1406 Sycamore Rd.
Montoursville, PA 17754
Phone: (717)323-9604 EST
In business since: 1991

PRODUCT INFORMATION:

Type: Video
Description: Video called *How To Restore Composition Dolls*

BUSINESS INFORMATION:

To purchase: Mail order
Cost: Retail: Volume and package discount. Wholesale: distributors and publishers on $39.95 video.

DOLL FASHIONS NORTHWEST

Linda Johnson
P.O. Box 12113
Portland, OR 97212
Phone: (503) 287-3086 PST
Fax: (503) 280-1011
Offers: Linda will contract with artists for her sewing services. She specializes in limited edition costuming of 250 or fewer.

THE ENCHANTED ATTIC

Barb Spencer
Rt. 5, Box 165AAA
El Dorado Springs, MO 64744
Phone: (417)876-5131 CST
Fax: (417)876-3671
In business since: 1990

PRODUCT INFORMATION:

Types: Books and patterns
Description: Traceable Faces For Cloth Dolls is published by the Jones Publishing Co. May be ordered directly from Barb Spencer at the address above. The book contains 53 8½″ × 11″ pages, 45 of which are traceable faces for cloth dolls. There are more than 300 traceable faces for pretty, whimsical, lady, children, Caucasian, non-Caucasian and bed dolls; 80 "mix and match" facial features for creating additional doll faces. Also, there are a lot of how-to's, including fabric selection and preparation, selection of tools and supplies, designing and sewing different shapes of cloth doll heads and bodies, accurate placement of facial features on the doll face, etc. The book should be an invaluable tool for cloth dollmakers.

Impressions With Expressions is a 5½" × 8½" size book, containing 31 pages of traceable faces for cloth lady and children dolls, animals, clowns and Santas. *Impressions With Expressions* also contains lots of "how-to's." This book sells for $6.50 (includes postage and handling). It is self-published.

Barb also sells 38 different patterns for cloth dolls through the mail. A fold-out color brochure is available for $2 (refundable with order of 2 or more patterns).

BUSINESS INFORMATION:

To purchase: Traceable Faces For Cloth Dolls and *Impressions With Expressions* may be purchased from Barb Spencer. Orders should be placed through the mail and accompanied by a check or money order.

Cost: Traceable Faces For Cloth Dolls sells for $11.95 (includes postage and handling). *Impressions With Expressions* sells for $6.50 (includes postage and handling). If both books are ordered together, the total cost is $18. Patterns for dolls sell for $5 or $5.50 each (most of the patterns are for more than one doll). All patterns are for doll with clothing.

ADDITIONAL INFORMATION:

The Enchanted Attic is a home-based business which sells quality one-of-a-kind dolls, pattern dolls, patterns for cloth dolls and their clothing, books and, shows, antique lace and buttons. Also sells hanging Victorian hearts and more. If you are a collector and want to purchase an original one-of-a-kind doll, contact Barb Spencer. After ordering a collectible doll, you will be kept abreast of new dolls when they become available.

FABRICAT DESIGN/BOOK AND PATTERNS

Susanna Oroyan
3270 Whitbeck Blvd.
Eugene, OR 97405
Phone: (541)345-0242 PST
Fax: (541)345-0242
In business since: 1980

PRODUCT INFORMATION:

Types: Books, patterns

Description: Books and patterns on critique, photography, dollmaking as a business, cloth doll patterns, sculpture

and body making techniques.

BUSINESS INFORMATION:

To purchase: Send SASE for brochure.

JOHNSTON ORIGINAL ART DOLLS

Jack Johnston
1447 N. Carrington Lane
Centerville, UT 84014
Phone: (801)299-9908 MST
Fax: (801)299-9088
E-mail: jjdolls@aol.com
In business since: 1989

PRODUCT INFORMATION:

Types: Books, videos

BUSINESS INFORMATION:

To purchase: Books and videos may be purchased by calling (800)560-4958

Cost: Book *The Art of Making and Marketing Art Dolls* is $29.95; videos on hands, heads, feet and bodies are $39.95 each.

MCKINLEY BOOKS AND TAPES

Bill Nelson
107 E. Cary St.
Richmond, VA 23219
Phone: (804)783-2602 EST
Fax: (804-783-2602
In business since: 1993

PRODUCT INFORMATION:

Description: McKinley books include more than 250 step-by-step photographs that reveal the award-winning doll artistry of the late Bob McKinley "as he takes you through each step of creating one of his amazing art dolls." Robert McKinley's Dollmaking Workshop videotapes include 4 videotapes with 8 hours of viewing. Bob McKinley creates a doll before your very eyes, taking you through the entire procedure step by step.

BUSINESS INFORMATION:

To purchase: From Bill Nelson at address above.

Cost: Dollmaking: One Artist's Approach is $29.95 plus $3 postage and handling. *Robert McKinley's Dollmaking Workshop* is $150 plus $5 postage and handling.

MIMI'S BOOKS AND PATTERNS FOR THE SERIOUS DOLLMAKER

Gloria Winer (Mimi)
300 Nancy Dr.
Point Pleasant, NJ 08742

Phone: (908)899-0804, (908)899-6687 EST
Fax: (908)714-9306
E-mail: firebird@exit109.com
In business since: 1985

PRODUCT INFORMATION:

Types: Books, patterns

Description: Mimi's teaching patterns and techniques books are used by many other teachers for classroom instruction.

BUSINESS INFORMATION:

To purchase: Available by mail or telephone. Wholesale in quantity. Free catalog.

NATURAL FIBER IDENTITY LABELS

Gabriele Cardy
Box 880-91
Blaine, WA 98231
Phone: (360)332-7098 PST
Fax: (360)332-5511
In business since: 1983

PRODUCT INFORMATION:

Description: Custom waterbase screening of identity labels, panels, doll faces, t-shirts, tote bags, tea towels, etc. Complete design and scan service.

BUSINESS INFORMATION:

To purchase: Send $3 for samples and price list.

Cost: Cost by quote.

ADDITIONAL INFORMATION:

Hand silkscreening on natural fibers, including cotton, hemp and silk. Waterbase inks are washable, dry cleanable, permanent, nonfading, nonstiffening and non-toxic.

ROYAL-T CLEANERS AND LAUNDRY

Michael Brief
17942 Magnolia
Fountain Valley, CA 92707
Phone: (714) 963-6110 PST
Fax: (714) 836-9239
Offers: Royal-T Cleaners and Laundry provides professional cleaning services especially for antique and collectible doll clothing. Each piece will be inspected to determine the best cleaning method. Clothing will then be professionally cleaned and wrapped in acid-free tissue paper. Doll clothing may be shipped via US mail, UPS, FedEx or any other estab-

lished carrier. The clothes will then be returned COD for shipping and cleaning charges.

Cost: Basic price starts at $5.45 for each article of clothing. Prices are based on size, material and amount of fashion detail.

ALEXANDER ROYZMAN

570 Fort Washington Ave.
New York, NY 10033
Phone: (212)927-9548 EST
Fax: (212)927-9548
In business since: 1975

PRODUCT INFORMATION:

Description: Alexander has created a series of art photos titled "Children and Dolls," as well as a series of still life photos which include dolls.

BUSINESS INFORMATION:

To purchase: Directly from artist.
Cost: Varies

"DOLLS KEEP YOU YOUNG AND HAPPY!"
Young at Heart Doll Shop, Preston, CT

SIROCCO HISTORICAL DOLL VIDEOS

Leonard A. Swann, Jr.
5660 E. Virginia Beach Blvd. #104
Norfolk, VA 23502
Phone: (804)461-8987, (800)637-2264 EST
Fax: (804)461-4669
In business since: 1991

PRODUCT INFORMATION:

Description: Covering a wide range of collector themes, Sirocco Historical Doll Videos include the following: Scarlett Dolls, Dionne Quintuplet Dolls, The Coronation Story, Dolls of the Golden Age, Shirley Temple Dolls and Memorabilia, Raggedy Ann and Andy, Johnny Gruelle's Dolls With Heart, and the Doll Makers, Women Entrepreneurs, 1865-1945.

BUSINESS INFORMATION:

To purchase: Videos can be purchased directly from Sirocco Productions for an additional $3 per video to cover shipping and handling. Please call the toll-free order number. They are also sold in museum stores, specialty doll stores and through specialty video and collector book catalogs.
Cost: $49.95

CAROL-LYNN RÖSSEL WAUGH

5 Morrill St.
Winthrop, ME 04364
Phone: (207)377-6769 EST
Fax: (207)377-4258

Offers: Carol-Lynn offers professional photographic portraits of dolls for publicity, articles and books. Her award-winning photos capture the "life" of your doll's personality. Client may ship the dolls or arrange a photo session.

Cost: $100 per sitting. $25 per slide or print. If the doll is shipped, client must pay shipping and insurance both ways. For photo sessions, client must pay travel and lodging expenses.

Additional Information: Carol-Lynn's photographs have won national awards, have been exhibited extensively in the US and Russia, and have appeared in many books and magazines, including several cover shots.

Did We Miss You?

If you would like to be in the next edition of *The Doll Sourcebook*, please type or neatly print your name and address below, and check the items that best describe your business. You will receive a questionnaire which can be completed for free inclusion in the next edition. Please be patient—there will be about two years between editions!

Name: _____

Address: _____

_____

_____

Phone: _____

I would like to be included in the following chapters of the next edition of *The Doll Sourcebook* (please circle your choices):
1. Retail businesses selling dolls
2. Antique dolls (dealers, restorations, appraisals, auctions)
3. Suppliers (sellers of dollmaking supplies, clothing and accessories)
4. Artists (you must make your own original designs as explained on pages 96-97)
5. Manufacturers
6. Show organizers (organizers of one show per year)
7. Show promoters (organizers of more than one show per year)
8. Clubs and organizations
9. Museums
10. Additional opportunities (please specify below)

_____

_____

_____

_____

Comments

We want to know what you think about *The Doll Sourcebook*! Please type or neatly print your comments in the space provided below, so we can make the next edition even better!

_____

_____

_____

_____

_____

_____

_____

_____

_____

_____

_____

_____

_____

_____

_____

_____

_____

Please send comments and requests for questionnaires to Betterway Books, *The Doll Sourcebook*, 1507 Dana Ave., Cincinnati, OH 45207, or fax to (513) 531-7107.

General Index

A

"A Day With . . ." (a nationally known speaker), 206
Abel, Monie, 104
Academy of American Doll Artists, 226
Adams, Melissa, 104
After 5 Barbie Doll Club of Minnesota, 226
Alcove, The, 21
Alice's Doll Workshop, 66
All for a Doll, 66
All Hearts Come Home For Christmas, 112
All That Glissons, 67. 127, 287
Allen, Clara M., 104
American Beauty Dolls, 154
Anastasia's Porcelain Dolls, 153
Andaco, 67
Anderson Creations, 105
Anderson, S. Catherine, 105
Anderton, Johana Gast, 269
Andress, Sunnie, 105
Angélique, Lawan, 105
Angie's Doll Boutique, Inc., 21, 67, 287
Ann Christina's Remember When Collectibles & Auctions, 58
Ann Lloyd—Antique Dolls, 48
Annalee Doll Society, 226
Annalee Mobilitee Dolls Inc., 181
Anna's Collectibles, 21
Annette's Antique Dolls, 48
Ann's Dolls, 67
Antelope Mountain Designs, 116
Antelope Valley Dolls, Bears and Miniatures Show, 207
Anthony's of Solvang, 68
Antique Doll World, 295
Antique Treasurers & Toys, 48

Ardis of Starcross, 106
Arizona Doll and Toy Museum, 247
Art Room, The, 167
Ashcraft, Janie, 106
Ashton-Drake Galleries, 181
Association of People Who Play With Dolls, 226
Auctions by Nancy, 58
Audrey Willmann Shows, 198
Aunt Emily's Doll House, 48
Avonlea Traditions Inc., 181
Axe, John, 269

B

B. Shackman Publishers Inc., 266
Babin, Sandra F., 106
Baierl, Kim Diane, 107
Bailey, Elinor Peace, 68, 287
Baker, Betsey, 107
Banks, S. Kaye, 107
Baran, Shirley, 108
Barbara Peterson's Show and Sale Featuring Barbie, 198
Barbara's Dolls, 49
Barbie and Friends Extravaganza, 207
Barbie and Ken New York Doll Collector's Club, 226
Barbie Attic, The, 49
Barbie Bazaar, 295
Barbie Collector's Club of San Diego, 226
Barbie Goes to Shows, 198
Barrett, Janie, 266
Barrie, Mirren, 108, 269
Barry-Hippensteel, Kathy, 109
Bates, Jeanie, 109
Bear Threads, Ltd., 68
Bear-A-Dise Landing, 22

Beauty-Stone Stands, 68
Belleville Doll, Toy and Teddy Bear Fair, 207
Bellman Corp., 198
Benzell, Joan, 109
Berg, Suzanne, 110
Berton Auctions, 58
Best Dressed Doll, 69
Betsey Baker Dolls, 107
Biggs Limited, 22
Billie Nelson Tyrell's Doll Emporium, 49
Black Doll Art and Collectible Show and Sale, 208
Blevins Plates 'n' Things, 22
Bloom, Amy Albert, 110, 269
Blu Frogg Gardens, 110, 128, 287, 299
Bluebonnet Bebes of Houston Doll Show and Sale, 208
Bodzer's Collectibles, 23
Boers, Martha, 111
Bohler Enterprises Inc., 198
Boise Treasure Doll Club, 227
Born Yesterday Dolls, 162
Bowling, Carole, 111
Brandon, Elizabeth, 112
Bright Star Promotions, Inc., 198
Brimfield Associates Inc., 199
British Doll Artists' Association, 227
Bro, Lois B., 112
Brochu, Joan L., 112
Brockville Doll, Miniature and Teddy Bear Show and Sale, 208
Brohmer, Earline Maples, 113
Brooks, Patricia Ryan, 113
"The Brown Brats," 114
Brown, Doc and Tasi, 114
Brown, Gladys, 114
Brown House Dolls, 69

Brown, Jean, 114
Brown, Laurel, 115
Brown, Ruth Alden, 115
Browns Gallery, 23
Bryer, Sonja, 115
Buffalo Batt & Felt, 69
Bunker, Kat, 116
Burdick, Loraine, 266, 270
Butterfly Cat Studios, 270
Byerly, Mary Alice, 116

C

C&T Publishing, 299
C&W Enterprises, 23
C.S.R. Promotions, 199
California Dolls, 169, 287
Calvert, Cheri, 116
Camp Venture Inc., 182
Canadian Doll Journal, 295
Cannon, Margery, 117
Canton, Jennifer, 117
Carla Thompson Art Dolls, 165
Carole Ann Creations, 146
Carole Bowling Dolls, 111
Carolyn's Creations, 125
Carousel Canada Inc., 182
Carriage House Collectibles, 24
Cartmill, Gennie, 118
Cartmill, Michael, 119
Cascade Doll Shoppe, 70, 287
Cat's Cradle, 50
Cedar Chest Doll Shoppe, 24
Cedar Rose Studio, 272
Celebrity Doll Journal, 295
Celia's and Susan's Dolls and Collectibles, 24
Celtic Images, 170
Cely, Antonette, 119
Center Stage Emporium, 70
Century of Dolls, A, 24, 50
Ceramic Enterprises— CEFI, 200
Cerexpo Inc., 200
Chambers, Karen B., 299

Characters by Bill Nelson, 150

Charlene's Dolls and Collectibles, 25

Chatty Cathy Collectors Club, 227

Chatty Cathy's Haven, 50

Chesapeake Bay Dolls, 164

"Childhood Dreams" Doll Show and Sale, 208

Childhood Fantasies, 70

Childhood Treasures, 288

China Doll Shows, 200

Christensen Auctions, 58

Christie Cummins Dolls, 121

Christies, 50, 58

Christmas Delight, 209

Christmas in July and Holiday Doll Shows, 209

Christopherson, Victoria, 270

Cindy M. McClure Ent. Ltd., 144

Clarke, Kathi, 119

Clark's Antique Dolls, 50

Classic Image, A, 158

Classics in Wood, 165

Cleveland Doll Club Doll and Bear Show and Sale, 209

Coastal Doll Collectors Club of South Carolina, 228

Coastal Doll Collectors' Show and Sale, 210

Cobb's Doll Auctions, 59

Cohen, Marci, 120

Collectible Doll Company, 71

Collectors United, 295

Colorado Paper Doll Collectors Club, 277

Colston, Deborah, 120

Columbia Doll Club, 228

Condon, Judith L., 120

Contempory Doll Collector, 296

Cornerstones, 277

Country Sampler, The, 25

Create an Heirloom, 72

Creations by Earline, 113

Creations in Porcelain, 158

Creative Dollmakers Society of New Mexico, 228

Creative Interest, 288

Crooked Tree Hollow Rag Doll Club, 228, 288

Crossroads Doll, Bear and Toy Show, The, 201

CR's Crafts, 72

Cummins, Christie, 121

Cunningham, Norma, 121

D

D & B Antiques, 299

"D" Originals, 129

D. Schwellenbach—Artist's Dolls, 161

Daddy's Long Legs, 182

Dallas Expo, 201

Davis, Martha, 270

Deb Bonham Art Dolls, 111

Debra's Darling Dolls, 141

Debra's Dolls, 50

Deere Crossing, 25

Demsey & Baxter, 51

Denver Museum of Miniatures, Dolls and Toys, 247

Dey, Peggy, 121

Dianne Carter and Molly Kenney Fantasy Doll Works, 118

DiFonso, Don, 270

Dixon, Jean, 81

Dodington, Judith, 270, 288

Dolan, Shirley Townsend, 122

Doll Adventure, Inc., The, 288

Doll Adventure, The, 73

Doll and Bear Show and Sale (Timeless Treasures Doll Club), 210

Doll and Bear Show and Sale (Young at Heart Doll Club), 210

Doll and Mini Nook, 26

Doll and Teddy Bear Festival and Sale (BC), 211

Doll and Teddy Bear Show and Sale (Holbrook Lioness Club), 211

Doll and Toy Show (Evelyn Moomau Delmarva Doll Club), 212

Doll and Toy Show (Broward County Doll and Toy Collectors Club), 211

Doll Artisan, 296

Doll Artisan Guild, 228, 288, 289

Doll Attic, The, 51

Doll, Bear and Miniature Show and Sale (FL), 201

Doll Crafter, 296

Doll Doctor, The, 51

Doll Express, Inc., The, 51, 59

Doll Express, The, 228

Doll Factory, Inc., The, 182

Doll Fashions Northwest, 74, 299

Doll Festival and Sale (BC), 212

Doll Gallery, The (ME), 52, 74

Doll Gallery, The (FL), 26

Doll Gallery, The (WA), 26, 52, 74, 289

Doll Hair Etc., 74

Doll Hospital, Inc., The, 26

Doll Hospital, The, 52

Doll Magazine, 296

Doll Maker, 140

Doll Museum, The, 247

Doll News, 296

Doll Place, The, 75

Doll Reader, 297

Doll Seminars, Workshops and Lectures, 289

Doll Show (Doll Dreamers of WNC), 212

Doll Show and Sale (Borkholder Dutch Village), 212, 213, 214

Doll Show and Sale (Carousel Doll Club), 213

Doll Show and Sale (Crooked Tree Doll Club), 213

Doll Show and Sale (Muskegon Sand Dollers Doll Club), 213

Doll Show and Sale/ Sleeping Angel Productions, 213

Doll Show and Sale (West Volusia Doll Club), 214

Doll Studios, 75, 289

Doll Study Club of Long Island Annual Show and Sale, 214

Doll Study Club of Jamestown, NY, 229

Doll World and Surroundings, 27

Dol-Lee Shop, The, 75

Dollmaker's Community College, 289

"Dollmakers, The" (Show), 214

Dollmakers, The (store), 28

Dollmaking—Projects and Plans, 297

Dolls and Friends, 27

Dolls by DAL, 142

Dolls by Dyan, 27, 75

Dolls by Jim, 27

Dolls Delight, Inc., 75

Dolls, Dolls, Dolls, 151

Dolls From The Heart, 28

Dolls of Original Design, 137

Dolls, Teddy Bears, Toys and Miniatures Sale (Northwoods Doll Club), 214

Dolls—The Collector's Magazine, 297

Dolls Unlimited, 28, 201

Dollsville Dolls and Bearsville Bears, 29

Doll'tor Jean's Doll Hospital, 52

Dollworks, 53

Dolly Follies, The, 229

Dolly Heaven, 53

Doneaud ("Nini"), Doina, 122

Donna Lee's Sewing Center, 76

Donna's Doll Factory, 76

D'Onofrio, Karen, 289

Dora Pitts, 202

Dorier, Jacques, 122, 290

Dorothy A. McGonagle, 55

Dorothy Allison Hoskins Original Dolls, 133

Dottie Dunsmore Originals, 123

Dover Publications, 266

Dundore Dolls, 171

Dunsmore, Dottie, 123

Dunsmore, Lee, 123

Dustmagnet, 76

Dynasty Doll Collection, 76, 183

E

Eager Plastics Inc., 77

Edna Hibel Gallery, 132
Effanbee Doll Co., 183
Elena Collectibles, 126
Elizabeth Brandon
    Porcelain Originals, 112
Empress Doll Boutique, 29
Enchanted Attic, The, 163,
    299
Enchanted Doll Club of
    Eagle River Doll Show,
    215
Enchanted World Doll
    Museum, 248

F

Fabricat Design, 152
Fabricat Design/Book and
    Patterns, 300
Fabricimages, 154
Fabulous Flitters, 229
Fair, Robbie F., 123
Fairchild, Carol, 271
Fall Festival of Dolls Show,
    215
Fancy Ephemera, 270
Fancywork and Fashion, 77
Fancywork's Best News,
    297
Fantasia Dolls, 29
Fantasy at Your Fingertips,
    149, 290
Faraone, Jim—P.D. Pal, 271
Fashion Doll, The, 53
Faville, Donna, 124
Faville Original Dolls, 124
Fayette Knoop/Original
    Character Dolls, 140
Felker, Erik, 272
Finch, Margaret, 124, 125
Finch-Kozlosky, Marta, 125
Folsom, Carolyn, 125
Foothills Rag Doll Club,
    229
For the Love of Dolls, Inc.,
    30
Forever Young Doll Show/
    Sale, 215
4 Dolls Co., The, 216
Fox Valley Area Doll Show,
    216
FPC International, Inc., 183
Frank, Mary Ellen, 125
Fraser's Doll Auction, 59
Frey, Pat, 267, 271
Friends Forever, 108
Frisco Floozies, 229

G

G.I. Joe Collectors' Club,
    229
Gabriele's Inc., 77
Gail J. Shumaker Originals,
    162
Gallery Collection Molds,
    78
Gals & Dolls Club, 229
Gambina Dolls, 184
Gathings, Evelyn, 271
Gennie Cartmill Creations,
    118
George, Elena, 126
Georgie's Ceramics and
    Clay Art Pak, 78
Gervais, Janet, 126
Gigi's Dolls and Sherry's
    Teddy Bears, 202
Giguere, Barb, 127
Gipe, Dwaine E., 76
Gleason, Karen, 127
Glisson, Theresa A., 127
Glowacki, Kristin, 128
Golden Gate Shows, 202
Golden Spread Doll Club,
    230
Golden Spread Doll Show,
    216
Gonzales, Ralph and Mary
    L., 128
Goodenough Group, The,
    230
Good-Krüger Dolls, Inc.,
    128
Good-Krüger, Julie, 128
Goodnow, June, 290
Grampa's Girl Originals,
    146
Grandma's Attic, 54
Grandma's Dollings, 78
Gray, Scott R., 129
Great American Doll
    Company, 184
Green, Yuko, 271
Greenwood, Dessa Rae, 129
Griffin, Judith, 129
Gullett, Deanna, 130

H

Hamilton Eye Warehouse,
    79
Handcraft Designs, Inc., 79
Hanslik, Alan, 290
Hanslĭk, Retägene, 130
Hanson, Gisele, 131

Happe, Jeannine, 131
Happy Hobby Doll Club,
    230
Harding, Trish, 131
Hart, Kari, 54
Hartmann, Sonja, 132
Heartwarmers, 79
Heavenly Dolls, 30, 80, 290
Hedy Katin Cloth Doll
    Patterns, 80
Hei Mana Creations, 132
Heirloom Doll, Customs
    and Restoration, 54
Helen Moe Antique Doll
    Museum, 248
Hello Dollie Sale and Show
    (ID), 217
Hello Dollies of Longmont
    Doll Sale and Show, 216
Hello Dollies of Longmont,
    230
Hello Dolly, 168
Henry, Marilyn, 271
Henry, Linda, 132
Hersh, Mary, 54
Hibel, Edna, 132
Hiddleston, Kate, 133
Hill, Margaret, 203
Himstedt Times, The, 298
Hines-Pinion, Sharon, 272
Hippensteel Dolls, Inc., 109
Hobby House Press, 266
Honeydoll's Collectibles,
    30
Hoover, Bonnie, 272, 290
Hopf, Jeanne, 272
Hornick, Yoshiko, 133
Hoskins, Dorothy Allison,
    133
Housley, Sherry, 134
Huff, Jean, 203

I

Ibarolle, Joan, 134
Illustroplay, 272
Imitation of Life
    Construction Company,
    a Dollmakers Guild, 231
In Celebration of the Doll:
    The Figure in Cloth, 223
International Celebration of
    Innocence Show and
    Sale, An, 217
International Collectible
    Exposition, 203

International Doll Doctor's
    Club, 231
Iowa Kate Shelley Doll
    Club, 231
Iowa Kate Shelley Doll
    Club Annual Doll and
    Toy Fair, 217
Ironstone Yarns, 80
Iverson Design, 134
Iverson, Thom and Renée,
    134

J

J. Gervais Portrait Heirloom
    Dolls, 126
J. Schoepfer, Inc., 80
Jackson, Ann, 135
Jackson Ranch, 81
Jacobsen, Johni, 135
Jacques Dorier Washi Dolls,
    122, 290
Jan Hagara Collectors Club,
    231
Jane's Original Art Doll
    Supplies, 81
Jean Canaday, 199
Jean Nordquist's
    Collectible Doll
    Academy, 290
Jeanne Singer Dolls, 162
Jeannine Happe Originals,
    131
Jenkins, Barbara, 135
Jennifer Schmidt Dolls, 160
Jerri Collector's Society,
    231
Jilane Originals, 142
Jill's Microcosmos, 150
Jo Ann Reynolds, 206
Joan's Bisque Be'Be's, 109
Joel's Creations, 148
Joffee, Priscilla, 267
Johana Gast Anderton
    Lectures, 291
Johannes Zook Originals,
    185
Johni Jacobsen Studio, 135
Johnson, Judy M., 272
Johnson, Patti, 136
Johnston, Jack, 136
Johnston Original Art Doll
    Seminars, 291
Johnston Original Art
    Dolls, 136, 300
Jones, Bruce Patrick, 272
Jones Mold Co. Inc., 81

Joyce Stafford Original Dolls, 164
Judith Howe Inc., 81
Judy's Doll Shop, 31, 54, 82, 291
Judy's Place, 267, 272
Julia Rueger, Ltd., 159
Julia's The Ultimate Collection, 31
Just Dollinks, 231
Just Her Style, 82
Justiss, Sandra Wright, 137

K

K.C. Dolls, 83
Karabay, Adnan Sami, 137
Kate Smalley's Antique Dolls, 54
Kate Webster Company, 82
Käthe Kruse Puppen Gmbh, 55, 185
Käthe Kruse Puppen Museum, 248
Kathi Clarke Originals, 119
Kathryn Walmsley Dolls and Toys, 167
Kathryn's Productions, 83
Katie-Did Orignals, 107
Katin, Hedy, 137
Kays, Linda J., 138
Keeping You in Stitches Newsletter, 298
Kelsey, Sharleen, 138
Kemper Doll Supplies, 84
Kendall, Penny McIntire, 138
Kertzman, Linda S., 139
Kezi Works, The, 149
Kezi's Premier Cloth Doll Patterns, 84
Killmore, Virginia, 139
Kinder Haus—Retail and Wholesale, 31
Kindler, Joan, 55
King, Rosemary, 139
Kish and Company, 185
Kleindinst, Sylvia, 273
Klosko, Marilyn, 140
Kmitsch Girls, 31
Knoop, Fayette, 140
Knutsen, Vanessa L., 273
Kuskokwim Traditional Dolls, 157

L

L.M. Crossroads, 32

La Haise, Angelika, 140
Lady, Barbara J., 141, 291
Lake, Linda, 273
Lamb, Jaine, 141, 291
Lamkin, Debra, 141
Laurel Brown Originals, 115
Lauren Welker Doll Artist, 169
Lauren Welker's Doll Diary, 298
Law, Deborah A., 142
Lawtons Collectors Guild, 232
LBro Original Designs, 112
Lee Dunsmore Originals, 123
Lee Middleton Original Dolls, 185
Legus, Jilane, 142
Lemmon, Denise, 142
Les Bebes of Southern NJ, 232
Les Boise Doll Club, 217, 232
Leslie's American Heritage, Inc., 32
Let's Talk About Dollmaking Magazine, 298
Lewis, Marcy, 273
Lifetime Career Schools, 292
Linda Henry Originals, 132
Linda J. Kays, 83, 291
Linda's Antiques, 55
Linda's Lov-Lez House of Dolls and Bears, More, 32
Lindenfolk, The, 139
Little People, 145
Little Shoppe of Dolls and Things, 32
Lloyd Middleton's Royal Vienna Collection, 185
Long, Helga Walker, 143
Loretta's Place Paper Doll Newsletter, 278
Lou Rathjen's Designs, 273
Love of Country, 33
Loving Memories Doll, Bear, Toy and Miniature Show, 217
Loving Memories Doll Club, 232
Lucas, John S., 273
Lyons, Sylvia, 143

M

MAR Creations, 159
Maas, Marian, 203
McAslan Doll Company, 186
McBurnett, Rosemary, 267
MacInnis, Christine, 145
Maciak, Heather Browning, 145
McMasters Doll Auctions, 59
Mad Dollmakers, The, 232
M.A.D. Shows, 204
Madame Alexander Doll Club, 232
Maddocks, Carole, 146
Madison Area Doll Club Show, 218
Magic Moment, 33
Magic Valley Doll Show and Bear Show, 218
Magustine Arts and Collectibles, Inc., 140
Maine Society of Doll & Bear Artists, Inc., 232
Malerich, Norma J., 147
Mann Gallery, the Art of the Doll, 34
Manning, Emily, 147, 292
Manning, Mary Lou, 147
Maple Nook Designs, 129
Marci Cohen Studio, 120
Margery Cannon Originals, 117
Marilyn's Forest of Dolls, 55
Marl and Barbie, 34
Marnie's World of Dolls Inc., 152
Martindale, Diana, 148
Martindale Originals, 148
Martóne, Joel M., 148
Mary Byerly Originals, 116
Mary Lou Manning Studio, 147
Mary Mettitt Doll Museum, 249
Master Collector, 298
Master Eye Beveler, 84
Masterpiece Eye Co., 84
Material Things, 85
Mattel, Inc., 185
Matthews, Kezi, 149
Mattox, Brenda Sneathen, 270
Maven Company, Inc., The, 204

McAuliffe, Lois K., 143
McClure, Cindy M., 144
McCrory, Melissa A., 144
McCurdy Historical Doll Museum, 248
McGoodwin-Young, Sara, 145
McKenzie, Deborah Keyes, 146
McKinley Books and Tapes, 300
McMasters, 56
McNichols, Ann, 146
McNichols Dolls and Gallery, 146
Meehan, Norma Lu, 274
Melissa Originals, 144
Melton's Antique Dolls, 56
Memories and Smiles, 127
Messier, Ruth A., 56
Messina, Lorrie, 149
Metro Plex Annual Doll Show, 218
Michael Cartmill Creations, 119
Michigan Doll Makers Guild, 218, 233
Mid-Ohio Historical Museum, 34, 249
Mid-Ohio's Largest Doll Show and Sale, 218
Midwest Ceramic Show, 219
Miller's Barbie Collector, 298
Miller's Market Report for Barbie Collectors, 299
Mimi's Books and Patterns for the Serious Dollmaker, 85, 300
Minnesota Valley Doll Club, 233
Miss USA Doll Pageant Show and Sale, 219
Monie Abel's Dolls, 104
Monique Trading Corp., 85
Montana Dolls and Collectibles, 34
Morley, Karen A., 149
Morrisville Doll Show and Sale, 219
Mountain Babies Doll Factory, 142
Mrs. Knutsen's Victoria, 273
Mrs. Knutsen's Victorian Sampler, 278

Muscovy Company Inc., 186

My Doll House of Hilltop, 35

"My Dolls" Dolls of Color, 35

Myrtle Beach SC Annual Doll Show and Sale, 220

N

N.M.P., 267, 275

Naber Kids Collector's Club, 233

Naber Kids Convention, 220

Nanalee's Dolls and Gifts, 35

Nana's Dolls, 86

Nancy Jo's Doll Sale, 204

Nathan, Charlott, 274

National Cloth Doll Makers Association (NCDMA), 233

National Nonwovens, 86

Native Sun Studios, 114

Natural Fiber Identity Labels, 300

NeedleArts Adventures, L.L.C., 204, 292

Nelson, Bill, 150

Nemirow-Nelson, Jill, 150, 292

New York Doll Hosptial Inc., 56

Newark Dressmaker Supply Inc., 86

Newark Museums, The, 249

Nielsen, Marlena H., 157

"Nini" Dolls, 122

Noble, John Darcy, 274

Northern Lights Paper Doll News, 278

Northwoods Doll Club, 233

Not Just Another Pretty Face, 129

O

Oak, Thorn and Ash Collection, 131

Ochoco Originals, 141

O'Connor, Bill, 151

Ogden, Barbara I., 151

Oglesby, Sandra Thomas, 152

Ohio Barbie™ Doll Collectors Club, 234

Old Mother's Cupboard, 205

140 Doll Works, 36

OPDAG News, 278

Orange Blossom, The, 36

Original Doll Artists' Association, 234

Original Doll Artists Council of America (ODACA), 234

Original Paper Doll Artists Guild (OPDAG), 277

Original Wood-Doll Workshop, 166

Originals by Elaine/Parker-Levi, 86

Orillia Doll Hospital, The, 56

Oroyan, Susanna, 152, 292

Orphans in the Attic Doll-Bear-Toy Shows/Sales, 205

Osage County Quilt Factory, 87

P

P.D. Pal, 267, 278

P.G.'s Enchanted Dolls, Inc., 37

Page's Dolls, 87, 293

Pamela's Playthings Doll Hospital, 56

Pam's Paper Dolls and Collectibles, 266, 268

Panek, Marnie, 152

Pannell, Mazie, 153

Paper Doll Queens and Kings of Metro Detroit, 277

Paper Palace, The, 266, 268

Paper Doll Review, 279

Paragon Industries, Inc., 87, 293

Paris Dolls and More Shoppe, 36

Parker, Jim and Sue, 153

Parker People, 153

Patricia Allgeier Barbie Dolls and Collectibles, 36

Patterson, Joyce, 154

Payson Doll Club, 234

Payson Doll Club Annual Doll Show and Sale, 220

Peck, Shirley Hunter, 154

Pedler's Workshop, 165

Pendlebury, Penny, 154

Pennydoll Creations, 154

Perzyk, W. Harry, 155

Peterson, Ellen L., 155

Peterson Original Art Dolls, 155

Pfeifer, Deborah, 155

Pfeifer People, 155

Phillips, Evelyn, 56

Phyllis' Collectors Club, 235

Piecemakers Country Store, 87, 293

Piecemakers Doll Club— Hello Dollies, 234

Pin-Ella-Ps Doll Club, 235

Pittsburgh Area Doll Show and Sales, 220

Pittsburgh Originals, 186

Plum Creek Dollmakers, 88

Pollyanna Doll Show and Sale, 220

Polyform Products Company, 89

Porcelain by Sonja Bryer, 115

Porcelain People, 143

Porcelain Rose, The, 89

Portland Po Henry Supply, 89

Present Idea, 109

Prince Doll Studio, 268, 274

Pritchard, Nancy L., 156

Professional Dollmakers Guild, 235

Q

Q. P. Doll Club, 235

Quality Doll and Teddy Bear Shows, 205

R

R&S Enterprises, 206

Raikes Originals, 156

Raikes, Robert, 156

Rainbows and Things, 160

Ramberg, Jeanette, 157

Rathjen, Jewel L., 273

Rausch, Barb, 274

Real People Dolls, 157

Regina's Doll Heaven, 37

Reitsma, Marianne, 111

Reo, Monica, 158

Reo, Mary, 275

Retägene Hanslïk Dolls, 130

Rhodes, Rosemary, 158

Ribbons and Ringlets, 106

Richard Wright Antiques, 57

Riley, Dawn, 275

Rita's Children, 98, 293

Roanoke Valley Doll Club, 235

Roanoke Valley Doll Club Show and Sale, 220

Robbins, Hope, 158

Robison, Michelle, 159

Robison's Fairy Folk, 159

Rockford Spring Toy, Doll and Bear Show and Sale, 221

Rogue Valley Cloth Doll Club, 235

Romină Creations, 139

Rosalie Whyle Doll Museum, 249

Royal-T Cleaners and Laundry, 300

Royzman, Alexander and Marina, 159

Royzman, Alexander, 301

Rueger, Julia, 159

Russian and American Dollmakers Association (and Friends), Inc. (RADA), 236

Russian Collection, 186

S

S&S Doll Hospital, 57, 90, 206

Sandy Dolls, Inc., 186

Sandy's Dream Dolls, 57

Santa Fe Doll Festival, 221

Sara Bernstein Dolls and Bears, 90

Scarlett, Christine, 275

Schlegel, Bobbie and Bill, 160

Schmidt, Jennifer, 160

Schreeder, Nancy Jo, 220

Schwellenbach, D., 161

Scogin, Susan, 161

Sculpting and Mold Making Seminars (CA), 293

Sculpting and Moldmaking Seminars (OR), 293

2nd Time Around Doll Shop, 37, 57

Seeley's, 90

Seonda's Birthday Party, 221

Sew Beautiful, 279

Seymour Mann, Inc., 187, 236

Shackelford, Iva, 275

Shanahan, Sue, 275

Shellie's Miniature Mania, 37

Sherrod, Myra, 162

Shumaker, Gail J., 162

sigikid, 187

Simpson's Liberty Doll Supply, 90

Singer, Jeanne, 162

Sirkis, Susan, 275

Sirocco Historical Doll Videos, 301

Sirocco Productions, Inc., 206

Sissy and Me, 130

Small Wonders Antique, 57

Society of the Permain Basin Doll Artisans, The, 236

Sonja Hartmann Originals, 132

South Forty Farms, 91

South Jersey Dolls and Toys Club, 236

Southern Oregon Pottery Supply, 91

Sparkling Star, The, 299

Special Joys Dolls and Toy Museum, 249

Special Occasions, 38

Spell, Louise, 163

Spencer, Barb, 163

Spencer, Paul, 164

Spencer Wooden Originals, 164

Spring Blossoms Doll Show, 221

Stafford, Joyce R., 164

Starchild Toy Co., 147

Steilacoom Doll Club, 236

Stellwagon, Linda L., 164

Stevens, RH, 268

Stewart, Brenda, 165

Stone Fence Doll Shoppe, 38

Stoney Point Creations, 167

The Strong Museum, 250

Studio 206, 136

Summertime With Barbie, 221

Sun, Sand and Sea, 277

Sunday's Child, 123

Sundstrom, Mary Lee, 165

Sunnie Andress Designs, 105

Sunny Stansbury— Heartcraft Puppets and Dolls, 294

Susan Scogin Editions, Ltd., 161

Sweet Dreams, 92

T

Tayo's Doll Club, 237

Texas Doll Show and Sales, 222

Theriault's, 57, 59

Thomas Boland and Co., Inc., 187

Thompson, Carla, 165

Tidewater Teddy Bear and Doll Show, 222

Tierney, Tom, 275, 294

Timeless Treasure Doll Club, 237

Timeless Treasures, 121

Timmerman, Ann, 166

Tinius, Ingeborg, 166

Tinseltown Barbie Doll Collectors Club, 237

Toy & Miniature Museum of Kansas City, 250

Treffeisen, Ruth, 166

Treffeisen U.S.A., 92, 166, 188

Truebite Inc., 92, 294

Tryon Treasures Doll Club, 237

Tucson Threadheads, 237

Twickenham Doll Club, 238

Twickenham Doll Club

Antique to Modern Doll Show and Sales, 222

Twin Pines of Maine, Inc., 58, 92, 294

2 JP Ranch, 93

U

Unique Doll Artistry by Lorrie, 149

Unique Products, 93

Uniquely Yours, 106

United Federation of Doll Clubs, Inc., 238

Upper Peninsula Doll and Teddy Bear Show and Sale, 222

V

Van Cleve, Nancy, 167

Vanderpool, Sandra, 268, 276

Victorian Doll Museum, 250

Victorian Replicas, 93

Victorian Tradition, The, 127

Victoria's Paper Dolls, 270

Vinyl Goddess Club of Dallas, 238

Virginia Killmore Dolls, 139

W

Wahl, Annie, 167

Walmsley, Kathryn, 167

Walnut Valley Doll Show, 223

Washington Dolls' House and Toy Museum, 250

Watts, Mary, 168

Waugh, Carol-Lynn Rössel, 168, 276, 294, 301

Wee Three, Inc., 93

Weefoke Empire, 38

Wehrley Dolls, 120

Welker, Lauren, 169, 276, 292

Wellman, Loraine, 276

Wemmitt-Pauk, Christina, 168, 294

Wenham Museum, 251

Westrich, "LoLo," 169

Westside Printing, 93

Whimsical Cloth Doll Creations, 94

Wild Spirit Doll Studio, 38, 94, 294

Wild Spirit Sculpture Studio, 156

Wilder's Doll Center, 94

Wilensky, Jan, 170, 294

Wilensky One of a Kind, 170

Wilfert, Judi, 169

Williams, Tracy Jane, 276

Willis, Loretta, 269, 277

Wilson, Barbara, 170, 295

Wimbledon Collection, 171, 188

Wimpory, Patricia, 170

Windsor Heirloom Collection, 188

Wolff, Gustave "Fritz," 171

Wolter, Marcia Dundore, 171

World Wide Dollmakers, 238

Wyatt, Melissa, 171

Y

Yellow Brick Road Doll and Toy Museum, The, 251

Yesterday's Memories, 143

Young at Heart Doll Shop, 39

Z

Zaklyn Dolls, 104

Zawieruszynski Originals, 172

Zawieruszynski, Zofia and Henry, 172

Zeller, Fawn, 172

Zip's Toys to Go, 39

Geographic Index

ALABAMA

Doll Artists
Carla Thompson Art Dolls, 165
Timmerman, Ann, 166
Wilson, Barbara, 170

Shows
Twickenham Doll Club
Antique to Modern Doll
Show and Sales, 222

Organizations
Twickenham Doll Club, 238

Paper Dolls
Sew Beautiful, 279

Additional Opportunities
Wilson, Barbara, 295

ALASKA

Doll Artists
Dorothy Allison Hoskins
Original Dolls, 133
Frank, Mary Ellen, 125
Hoskins, Dorothy Allison, 133
Kuskokwim Traditional
Dolls, 157
Pfeifer, Deborah, 155
Pfeifer People, 155
Ramberg, Jeanette, 157

Paper Dolls
Northern Lights Paper Doll News, 278

ARIZONA

Antique Doll Dealers
Heirloom Doll, Customs
and Restoration, 54
Sandy's Dream Dolls, 57

Doll Artists
Cartmill, Michael, 119
Michael Cartmill Creations, 119
Raikes Originals, 156
Raikes, Robert, 156

Shows
Payson Doll Club Annual
Doll Show and Sale, 220

Organizations
Payson Doll Club, 234
Tucson Threadheads, 237

Museums
Arizona Doll and Toy
Museum, 247

Paper Dolls
N.M.P., 267, 275
Shackelford, Iva, 275

ARKANSAS

Shows
Christmas in July and
Holiday Doll Shows, 209

CALIFORNIA

Retail Stores
Alcove, The, 21
Blevins Plates 'n' Things, 22
Charlene's Dolls and
Collectibles, 25
Dollmakers, The, 28
Dollsville Dolls and
Bearsville Bears, 29
Shellie's Miniature Mania, 37

Antique Doll Dealers
Barbie Attic, The, 49
Billie Nelson Tyrell's Doll
Emporium, 49
Chatty Cathy's Haven, 50
Christensen Auctions, 58
Doll Attic, The, 51
Fashion Doll, The, 53

Supplies, Clothing and Accessories
All for a Doll, 66
Anthony's of Solvang, 68
Baily, Elinor Peace, 68
Dustmagnet, 76

Hamilton Eye Warehouse, 79
Hedy Katin Cloth Doll
Patterns, 80
Judith Howe Inc., 81
Kemper Doll Supplies, 84
Material Things, 85
Monique Trading Corp., 85
Piecemakers Country Store, 87
Porcelain Rose, The, 89
Victorian Replicas, 93
Wee Three, Inc., 93
Whimsical Cloth Doll
Creations, 94

Doll Artists
American Beauty Dolls, 154
Angélique, Lawan, 105
Baran, Shirley, 108
Blu Frogg Gardens, 110, 128
Brohmer, Earline Maples, 113
California Dolls, 169
Christie Cummins Dolls, 121
Classics in Wood, 165
Creations By Earline, 113
Cummins, Christie, 121
Deb Bonham Art Dolls, 111
Dianne Carter and Molly
Kenney Fantasy Doll
Works, 118
Elena Collectibles, 126
Friends Forever, 108
George, Elena, 126
Gleason, Karen, 127
Gonzales, Ralph and Mary
L., 128
Hanslïk, Retägene, 130
Hei Mana Creations, 132
Hello Dolly, 168
Hornick, Yoshiko, 133
Housley, Sherry, 134
Ibarolle, Joan, 134
Jenkins, Barbara, 135
Jennifer Schmidt Dolls, 160
Julia Rueger, Ltd., 159

Karabay, Adnan Sami, 137
Katin, Hedy, 137
Kelsey, Sharleen, 138
Lyons, Sylvia, 143
McGoodwin-Young, Sara, 145
O'Connor, Bill, 151
Original Wood-Doll
Workshop, 166
Peck, Shirley Hunter, 154
Pendlebury, Penny, 154
Pennydoll Creations, 154
Perzyk, W. Harry, 155
Porcelain People, 143
Retägene Hanslïk Dolls, 130
Robbins, Hope, 158
Rueger, Julia, 159
Schmidt, Jennifer, 160
Sundstrom, Mary Lee, 165
Tinius, Ingeborg, 166
Victorian Tradition, The, 127
Watts, Mary, 168
Westrich, "LoLo," 169
Wilensky, Jan, 170
Wilensky One of a Kind, 170
Wilfert, Judi, 169

Manufacturers
Great American Doll
Company, 184
Muscovy Company Inc., 186
Windsor Heirloom
Collection, 188

Shows
Antelope Valley Dolls,
Bears and Miniatures
Show, 207
Barbara Peterson's Show
and Sale Featuring
Barbie, 198
Bohler Enterprises Inc., 198
China Doll Shows, 200
4 Dolls Co., The, 216
Golden Gate Shows, 202
Nancy Jo's Doll Sale, 204

Old Mother's Cupboard, 205

Pollyanna Doll Show and Sale, 220

Schreeder, Nancy Jo, 220

Organizations

Association of People Who Play With Dolls, 226

Barbie Collector's Club of San Diego, 226

Fabulous Flitters, 229

Frisco Floozies, 229

Gals & Dolls Club, 229

Imitation of Life Construction Company, a Dollmakers Guild, 231

Lawtons Collectors Guild, 232

National Cloth Doll Makers Association (NCDMA), 233

Piecemakers Doll Club— Hello Dollies, 234

Tayo's Doll Club, 237

Tinseltown Barbie Doll Collectors Club, 237

World Wide Dollmakers, 238

Museums

Helen Moe Antique Doll Museum, 248

Paper Dolls

Cornerstones, 277

Felker, Erik, 272

Gathings, Evelyn, 271

Hoover, Bonnie, 272

Illustroplay, 272

Lewis, Marcy, 273

Nathan, Charlott, 274

Noble, John Darcy, 274

Rausch, Barb, 274

Additional Opportunities

Baily, Elinor Peace, 287

Blu Frogg Gardens, 287, 299

C&T Publishing, 299

California Dolls, 287

Hanslik, Alan, 290

Himstedt Times, The, 298

Hoover, Bonnie, 290

Keeping You in Stitches Newsletter, 298

Piecemakers Country Store, 293

Royal-T Cleaners and Laundry, 300

Sculpting and Mold Making Seminars, 293

Wilensky, Jan, 294

COLORADO

Supplies, Clothing and Accessories

Dol-Lee Shop, The, 75

South Forty Farms, 91

Doll Artists

Joel's Creations, 148

Martóne, Joel M., 148

Shows

Hello Dollies of Longmont Doll Sale and Show, 216

Organizations

Hello Dollies of Longmont, 230

Museums

Denver Museum of Miniatures, Dolls and Toys, 247

Paper Dolls

Colorado Paper Doll Collectors Club, 277

Vanderpool, Sandra, 268, 276

CONNECTICUT

Retail Stores

Bear-A-Dise Landing, 22

Dolls by Jim, 27

Young at Heart Doll Shop, 39

Antique Doll Dealers

Kate Smalley's Antique Dolls, 54

Pamela's Playthings Doll Hospital, 56

Supplies, Clothing and Accessories

J. Schoepfer, Inc., 80

K.C. Dolls, 83

Master Eye Beveler, 84

Manufacturers

McAslan Doll Company, 186

Shows

Doll Show and Sale, Annual, 213

Maven Company, Inc., The, 204

Museums

Special Joys Dolls and Toy Museum, 249

DELAWARE

Retail Stores

Empress Doll Boutique, 29

DISTRICT OF COLUMBIA

Museums

Washington Dolls' House and Toy Museum, 250

FLORIDA

Retail Stores

Celia's and Susan's Dolls and Collectibles, 24

Doll Gallery, The, 26

Marl and Barbie, 34

P.G.'s Enchanted Dolls, Inc., 37

Antique Doll Dealers

S&S Doll Hospital, 57

Supplies, Clothing and Accessories

Doll Adventure, The, 73

Doll Studios, 75

Originals by Elaine/Parker-Levi, 86

S&S Doll Hospital, 90

Treffeisen U.S.A., 92

Unique Products, 93

Doll Artists

Banks, S. Kaye, 107

Condon, Judith L., 120

Edna Hibel Gallery, 132

Hibel, Edna, 132

Katie-Did Orignals, 107

McNichols, Ann, 146

McNichols Dolls and Gallery, 146

Oglesby, Sandra Thomas, 152

Treffeisen, Ruth, 166

Treffeisen USA, 166

Wehrley Dolls, 120

Zeller, Fawn, 172

Manufacturers

Doll Factory, Inc., The, 182

Treffeisen U.S.A., 188

Shows

Barbie Goes to Shows, 198

Ceramic Enterprises— CEFI, 200

Cerexpo Inc., 200

Doll and Toy Show, 211

Doll, Bear and Miniature Show and Sale, 201

Doll Show and Sale, 214

Hill, Margaret, 203

Naber Kids Convention, 220

S&S Doll Hospital, 206

Summertime With Barbie, 221

Organizations

Original Doll Artists' Association, 234

Paper Dolls

Barrett, Janie, 266

Stevens, RH, 268

Sun, Sand and Sea, 277

Additional Opportunities

Doll Adventure, Inc., The, 288

Doll Studios, 289

GEORGIA

Retail Stores

Doll World and Surroundings, 27

Supplies, Clothing and Accessories

Bear Threads, Ltd., 68

Beauty-Stone Stands, 68

Doll Artists

Cely, Antonette, 119

Paper Dolls

Loretta's Place Paper Doll Newsletter, 278

Willis, Loretta, 269, 277

Additional Opportunities
Collectors United, 295

HAWAII
Paper Dolls
Green, Yuko, 271

IDAHO
Doll Artists
Antelope Mountain
    Designs, 116
Calvert, Cheri, 116
Cartmill, Gennie, 118
Gennie Cartmill Creations,
    118

Shows
Doll and Bear Show and
    Sale, 210
Hello Dollie Sale and Show,
    217
Les Boise Doll Club, 217
Magic Valley Doll Show
    and Bear Show, 218

Organizations
Boise Treasure Doll Club,
    227
Les Boise Doll Club, 232
Timeless Treasure Doll
    Club, 237

ILLINOIS
Retail Stores
Dolls by Dyan, 27
Dolls Unlimited, 28
Kinder Haus—Retail and
    Wholesale, 31
Paris Dolls and More
    Shoppe, 36

Antique Doll Dealers
Doll Doctor, The, 51

**Supplies, Clothing and
    Accessories**
Alice's Doll Workshop, 66
Doll Place, The, 75
Dolls by Dyan, 75
Eager Plastics Inc., 77
Kathryn's Productions, 83
Polyform Products
    Company, 89
Sweet Dreams, 92

Doll Artists
Barry-Hippensteel, Kathy,
    109
Cunningham, Norma, 121
Dundore Dolls, 171
Hippensteel Dolls, Inc., 109
Jackson, Ann, 135
Jacobsen, Johni, 135
Johni Jacobsen Studio, 135
Joyce Stafford Original
    Dolls, 164
Kendall, Penny McIntire,
    138
Stafford, Joyce R., 164
Wolter, Marcia Dundore,
    171

Manufacturers
Ashton-Drake Galleries,
    181
Thomas Boland and Co.,
    Inc., 187

Shows
Audrey Willmann Shows,
    198
Belleville Doll, Toy and
    Teddy Bear Fair, 207
Black Doll Art and
    Collectible Show and
    Sale, 208
Doll Show, 212
Gigi's Dolls and Sherry's
    Teddy Bears, 202
International Collectible
    Exposition, 203
Jo Ann Reynolds, 206
Rockford Spring Toy, Doll
    and Bear Show and Sale,
    221
Spring Blossoms Doll
    Show, 221

Organizations
Goodenough Group, The,
    230
Madame Alexander Doll
    Club, 232

Paper Dolls
Butterfly Cat Studios, 270
Hopf, Jeanne, 272
Lake, Linda, 273
Shanahan, Sue, 275

INDIANA
Antique Doll Dealers
Dolly Heaven, 53

Doll Artists
Kathryn Walmsley Dolls
    and Toys, 167
Pedler's Workshop, 165
Stewart, Brenda, 165
Walmsley, Kathryn, 167

Shows
Doll Show and Sale, 212
Dolls Unlimited, 201

Paper Dolls
Fancy Ephemera, 270
Henry, Marilyn, 271
Knutsen, Vanessa L., 273
Lucas, John S., 273
Mattox, Brenda Sneathen,
    270
Meehan, Norma Lu, 274
Mrs. Knutsen's Victoria,
    273
*Mrs. Knutsen's Victorian
    Sampler*, 278
Paper Doll Review, 279

IOWA
**Supplies, Clothing and
    Accessories**
CR's Crafts, 72

Shows
Dora Pitts, 202
Iowa Kate Shelley Doll
    Club Annual Doll and
    Toy Fair, 217

Organizations
Iowa Kate Shelley Doll
    Club, 231

KANSAS
**Supplies, Clothing and
    Accessories**
Osage County Quilt
    Factory, 87

Doll Artists
Brandon, Elizabeth, 112
Dey, Peggy, 121
Elizabeth Brandon
    Porcelain Originals, 112
Timeless Treasures, 121

Shows
Walnut Valley Doll Show,
    223

Organizations
Pin-Ella-Ps Doll Club, 235

KENTUCKY
Retail Stores
Stone Fence Doll Shoppe,
    38

Doll Artists
King, Rosemary, 139
Rominā Creations, 139
Wimbledon Collection, 171
Wolff, Gustave "Fritz,"
    171

Manufacturers
Wimbledon Collection, 188

Shows
Bright Star Promotions,
    Inc., 198

Organizations
Naber Kids Collector's
    Club, 233

Additional Opportunities
Sparkling Star, The, 299

LOUISIANA
**Supplies, Clothing and
    Accessories**
Masterpiece Eye Co., 84

Doll Artists
Babin, Sandra F., 106
Ribbons and Ringlets, 106
Scogin, Susan, 161
Susan Scogin Editions,
    Ltd., 161

Manufacturers
Gambina Dolls, 184

MAINE
Antique Doll Dealers
Doll Gallery, The, 52
Doll'tor Jean's Doll
    Hospital, 52
Twin Pines of Maine Inc.,
    58

**Supplies, Clothing and
    Accessories**
Doll Gallery, The, 74
Portland Po Henry Supply,
    89

Twin Pines of Maine, Inc., 92

Doll Artists
Adams, Melissa, 104
Carolyn's Creations, 125
Dolls by DAL, 142
Folsom, Carolyn, 125
Gervais, Janet, 126
Giguere, Barb, 127
Griffin, Judith, 129
J. Gervais Portrait Heirloom Dolls, 126
Law, Deborah A., 142
Maple Nook Designs, 129
Memories and Smiles, 127
Waugh, Carol-Lynn Rössel, 168
Zaklyn Dolls, 104

Organizations
Maine Society of Doll & Bear Artists, Inc., 232

Paper Dolls
OPDAG News, 278
Original Paper Doll Artists Guild (OPDAG), 277
Waugh, Carol-Lynn Rössel, 276

Additional Opportunities
Twin Pines of Maine, Inc., 294
Waugh, Carol-Lynn Rössel, 294, 301

MARYLAND
Retail Stores
Bodzer's Collectibles, 23

Antique Doll Dealers
Aunt Emily's Doll House, 48
Linda's Antiques, 55
Small Wonders Antique, 57
Theriault's, 57, 59

Doll Artists
Dolls, Dolls, Dolls, 151
Dottie Dunsmore Originals, 123
Dunsmore, Dottie, 123
Klosko, Marilyn, 140
Magustine Arts and Collectibles, Inc., 140
Manning, Emily, 147

Manning, Mary Lou, 147
Mary Lou Manning Studio, 147
Ogden, Barbara I., 151
Starchild Toy Co., 147

Shows
Bellman Corp., 198
Doll and Toy Show, 212
Needlearts Adventures, L.L.C., 204

Organizations
Crooked Tree Hollow Rag Doll Club, 228
Russian and American Dollmakers Association (and Friends), Inc. (RADA), 236

Paper Dolls
Christopherson, Victoria, 270
Hobby House Press, 266
Victoria's Paper Dolls, 270

Additional Opportunities
Crooked Tree Hollow Rag Doll Club, 288
Manning, Emily, 292
NeedleArts Adventures, L.L.C., 292

MASSACHUSETTS
Retail Stores
Carriage House Collectibles, 24
Little Shoppe of Dolls and Things, 32
Mann Gallery, the Art of the Doll, 34
"My Dolls" Dolls of Color, 35
Dorothy A. McGonagle, 55

Supplies, Clothing and Accessories
Create an Heirloom, 72
Ironstone Yarns, 80
Kate Webster Company, 82
National Nonwovens, 86

Doll Artists
Bowling, Carole, 111
Bunker, Kat, 116
Carole Bowling Dolls, 111
Dorier, Jacques, 122

Fair, Robbie F., 123
Jacques Dorier Washi Dolls, 122
McAuliffe, Lois K., 143
Peterson, Ellen L., 155
Peterson Original Art Dolls, 155
Sunday's Child, 123

Museums
Wenham Museum, 251

Additional Opportunities
Jacques Dorier Washi Dolls, 290

MICHIGAN
Supplies, Clothing and Accessories
Brown House Dolls, 69
Cascade Doll Shoppe, 70
Page's Dolls, 87
Wilder's Doll Center, 94

Doll Artists
Abel, Monie, 104
Brown, Gladys, 114
Byerly, Mary Alice, 116
Creations in Porcelain, 158
Mary Byerly Originals, 116
McCrory, Melissa A., 144
Melissa Originals, 144
Messina, Lorrie, 149
Monie Abel's Dolls, 104
Parker, Jim and Sue, 153
Parker People, 153
Reo, Monica, 158
Unique Doll Artistry by Lorrie, 149

Manufacturers
Johannes Zook Originals, 185

Shows
Doll Show and Sale, 213
In Celebration of the Doll: The Figure in Cloth, 223
Jean Canaday, 199
Michigan Doll Makers Guild, 218
Upper Peninsula Doll and Teddy Bear Show and Sale, 222

Organizations
Michigan Doll Makers Guild, 233

Paper Dolls
Johnson, Judy M., 272
Judy's Place, 267, 272
McBurnett, Rosemary, 267
Original Paper Doll Artists Guild (OPDAG), 277
Paper Doll Queens and Kings of Metro Detroit, 277
Reo, Mary, 275

Additional Opportunities
Cascade Doll Shoppe, 287
Contempory Doll Collector, 296
Creative Interest, 288
Doll Crafter, 296
Page's Dolls, 293

MINNESOTA
Retail Stores
Dolls From the Heart, 28
Kmitsch Girls, 31
Leslie's American Heritage, Inc., 32

Antique Doll Dealers
Ann Christina's Remember When Collectibles & Auctions, 58
Hart, Kari, 54

Supplies, Clothing and Accessories
Fancywork and Fashion, 77

Doll Artists
Art Room, The, 167
Brown, Laurel, 115
Jilane Originals, 142
Laurel Brown Originals, 115
Legus, Jilane, 142
Stoney Point Creations, 167
Van Cleve, Nancy, 167
Wahl, Annie, 167
Zawieruszynski Originals, 172
Zawieruszynski, Zofia and Henry, 172

Shows
Barbie and Friends
    Extravaganza, 207
Dolls, Teddy Bears, Toys
    and Miniatures Sale, 214
Forever Young Doll Show/
    Sale, 215
Miss USA Doll Pageant
    Show and Sale, 219

Organizations
After 5 Barbie Doll Club of
    Minnesota, 226
Minnesota Valley Doll
    Club, 233
Northwoods Doll Club, 233

Additional Opportunities
Fancywork's Best News,
    297

MISSISSIPPI
Doll Artists
Johnson, Patti, 136
Spell, Louise, 163
Studio 206, 136

MISSOURI
Antique Doll Dealers
Fraser's Doll Auction, 59

*Supplies, Clothing and
    Accessories*
Gallery Collection Molds,
    78

Doll Artists
Anderson Creations, 105
Anderson, S. Catherine, 105
Ashcraft, Janie, 106
Born Yesterday Dolls, 162
Enchanted Attic, The, 163
Malerich, Norma J., 147
Sherrod, Myra, 162
Spencer, Barb, 163
Uniquely Yours, 106

Manufacturers
Sandy Dolls, Inc., 186

Organizations
Phyllis' Collectors Club,
    235
United Federation of Doll
    Clubs, Inc., 238

Museums
Toy & Miniature Museum
    of Kansas City, 250

Paper Dolls
Anderton, Johana Gast, 269

Additional Opportunities
Doll News, 296
Enchanted Attic, The, 299
Johana Gast Anderton
    Lectures, 291

MONTANA
Retail Stores
Montana Dolls and
    Collectibles, 34

Doll Artists
"The Brown Brats," 114
Brown, Jean, 114

NEBRASKA
Retail Stores
Deere Crossing, 25

Organizations
Mad Dollmakers, The, 232

NEVADA
Retail Stores
Fantasia Dolls, 29

*Supplies, Clothing and
    Accessories*
Donna's Doll Factory, 76
2 JP Ranch, 93

NEW HAMPSHIRE
Retail Stores
140 Doll Works, 36

Antique Doll Dealers
Ruth A. Messier, 56

*Supplies, Clothing and
    Accessories*
Center Stage Emporium, 70

Doll Artists
Grampa's Girl Originals,
    146
McKenzie, Deborah Keyes,
    146

Manufacturers
Annalee Mobilitee Dolls
    Inc., 181
Russian Collection, 186

Organizations
Academy of American Doll
    Artists, 226
Annalee Doll Society, 226
Happy Hobby Doll Club,
    230

Paper Dolls
Paper Palace, The, 266, 268

NEW JERSEY
Retail Stores
Cedar Chest Doll Shoppe,
    24

Antique Doll Dealers
Berton Auctions, 58
Debra's Dolls, 50

*Supplies, Clothing and
    Accessories*
Mimi's Books and Patterns
    for the Serious
    Dollmaker, 85
Sara Bernstein Dolls and
    Bears, 90

Doll Artists
Benzell, Joan, 109
Cohen, Marci, 120
Happe, Jeannine, 131
Jeannine Happe Originals,
    131
Jill's Microcosmos, 150
Joan's Bisque Be'Be's, 109
Long, Helga Walker, 143
Marci Cohen Studio, 120
Nemirow-Nelson, Jill, 150
Rainbows and Things, 160
Schlegel, Bobbie and Bill,
    160
Yesterday's Memories, 143

Manufacturers
Effanbee Doll Co., 183

Shows
Brimfield Associates Inc.,
    199
Doll and Bear Show and
    Sale, 210
"Dollmakers, The", 214

Organizations
Chatty Cathy Collectors
    Club, 227
Les Bebes of Southern NJ,
    232
South Jersey Dolls and Toys
    Club, 236

Museums
Newark Museums, The, 249
Yellow Brick Road Doll and
    Toy Museum, The, 251

Paper Dolls
Frey, Pat, 267, 271
Joffee, Priscilla, 267
Scarlett, Christine, 275

Additional Opportunities
Dollmaker's Community
    College, 289
*Let's Talk About
    Dollmaking Magazine*,
    298
Mimi's Books and Patterns
    for the Serious
    Dollmaker, 300
Nemirow-Nelson, Jill, 292

NEW MEXICO
Antique Doll Dealers
Hersh, Mary, 54

Shows
International Celebration of
    Innocence Show and
    Sale, An, 217
Santa Fe Doll Festival, 221

Organizations
Creative Dollmakers
    Society of New Mexico,
    228

Additional Opportunities
Sunny Stansbury—
    Heartcraft Puppets and
    Dolls, 294

NEW YORK
Retail Stores
A Century of Dolls, 24
Honeydoll's Collectibles,
    30

Antique Doll Dealers

Antique Treasurers & Toys, 48

Century of Dolls, A, 50

Christies, 50

Christies, 58

Doll Hospital, The, 52

Grandma's Attic, 54

Kindler, Joan, 55

New York Doll Hosptial Inc., 56

Phillips, Evelyn, 56

Supplies, Clothing and Accessories

Andaco, 67

Buffalo Batt & Felt, 69

Doll Hair Etc., 74

Grandma's Dollings, 78

Linda J. Kays, 83

Seeley's, 90

Truebite Inc., 92

Doll Artists

Baker, Betsey, 107

Betsey Baker Dolls, 107

Dunsmore, Lee, 123

Finch, Margaret, 124, 125

Hanson, Gisele, 131

Jeanne Singer Dolls, 162

Kays, Linda J., 138

Kertzman, Linda S., 139

Killmore, Virginia, 139

Lee Dunsmore Originals, 123

Lindenfolk, The, 139

MAR Creations, 159

Royzman, Alexander and Marina, 159

Singer, Jeanne, 162

Virginia Killmore Dolls, 139

Manufacturers

Camp Venture Inc., 182

FPC International, Inc., 183

Seymour Mann, Inc., 187

sigikid, 187

Shows

"Childhood Dreams" Doll Show and Sale, 208

Christmas Delight, 209

Doll and Teddy Bear Show and Sale, 211

Doll Study Club of Long

Island Annual Show and Sale, 214

Morrisville Doll Show and Sale, 219

Seonda's Birthday Party, 221

Organizations

Barbie and Ken New York Doll Collector's Club, 226

Doll Artisan Guild, 228

Doll Study Club of Jamestown, NY, 229

Foothills Rag Doll Club, 229

Seymour Mann, Inc., 236

Museums

The Strong Museum, 250

Victorian Doll Museum, 250

Paper Dolls

B. Shackman Publishers Inc., 266

Dover Publications, 266

Kleindinst, Sylvia, 273

Tierney, Tom, 275

Additional Opportunities

Antique Doll World, 295

Doll Artisan, 296

Doll Artisan Guild, 288

Dolls—The Collector's Magazine, 297

D'Onofrio, Karen, 289

Linda J. Kays, 291

Royzman, Alexander, 301

Tierney, Tom, 294

Truebite Inc., 294

NORTH CAROLINA

Retail Stores

Judy's Doll Shop, 31

Antique Doll Dealers

Auctions by Nancy, 58

Judy's Doll Shop, 54

Supplies, Clothing and Accessories

All That Glissons, 67

Judy's Doll Shop, 82

Doll Artists

All That Glissons, 127

Brown, Doc and Tasi, 114

Debra's Darling Dolls, 141

Glisson, Theresa A., 127

Lamkin, Debra, 141

Native Sun Studios, 114

Wemmitt-Pauk, Christina, 168

Shows

"A Day With . . ." (a nationally known speaker), 206

C.S.R. Promotions, 199

Doll Show, 212

Fall Festival of Dolls Show, 215

Maas, Marian, 203

Roanoke Valley Doll Club Show and Sale, 220

Organizations

G.I. Joe Collectors' Club, 229

Jerri Collector's Society, 231

Roanoke Valley Doll Club, 235

Tryon Treasures Doll Club, 237

Paper Dolls

Davis, Martha, 270

Sirkis, Susan, 275

Additional Opportunities

All That Glissons, 287

Judy's Doll Shop, 291

Master Collector, 298

Wemmitt-Pauk, Christina, 294

OHIO

Retail Stores

L.M. Crossroads, 32

Linda's Lov-Lez House of Dolls and Bears, More, 32

Love of Country, 33

Mid-Ohio Historical Museum, 34

Antique Doll Dealers

Cobb's Doll Auctions, 59

McMasters Doll Auctions, 59

McMasters, 56

Supplies, Clothing and Accessories

Simpson's Liberty Doll Supply, 90

Doll Artists

Bryer, Sonja, 115

Gail J. Shumaker Originals, 162

Gullett, Deanna, 130

Henry, Linda, 132

Linda Henry Originals, 132

Porcelain By Sonja Bryer, 115

Robison, Michelle, 159

Robison's Fairy Folk, 159

Shumaker, Gail J., 162

Sissy and Me, 130

Manufacturers

Lee Middleton Original Dolls, 185

Lloyd Middleton's Royal Vienna Collection, 185

Mattel, Inc., 185

Shows

Cleveland Doll Club Doll and Bear Show and Sale, 209

Mid-Ohio's Largest Doll Show and Sale, 218

Midwest Ceramic Show, 219

Organizations

Columbia Doll Club, 228

Ohio Barbie™ Doll Collectors Club, 234

Museums

Mid-Ohio Historical Museum, Inc., 249

Paper Dolls

Axe, John, 269

Additional Opportunities

Childhood Treasures, 288

OKLAHOMA

Shows

Dallas Expo, 201

Additional Opportunities

Goodnow, June, 290

OREGON
Retail Stores
Julia's The Ultimate
  Collection, 31
Special Occasions, 38

Supplies, Clothing and Accessories
Ann's Dolls, 67
Best Dressed Doll, 69
Doll Fashions Northwest,
  74
Georgie's Ceramics and
  Clay Art Pak, 78
Kezi's Premier Cloth Doll
  Patterns, 84
Southern Oregon Pottery
  Supply, 91

Doll Artists
Bates, Jeanie, 109
Brown, Ruth Alden, 115
Fabricat Design, 152
Hiddleston, Kate, 133
Kezi Works, The, 149
Lady, Barbara J., 141
Matthews, Kezi, 149
Nielsen, Marlena H., 157
Ochoco Originals, 141
Oroyan, Susanna, 152
Present Idea, 109
Real People Dolls, 157

Shows
Quality Doll and Teddy
  Bear Shows, 205

Organizations
Rogue Valley Cloth Doll
  Club, 235

Paper Dolls
Fairchild, Carol, 271
Riley, Dawn, 275

Additional Opportunities
Doll Fashions Northwest,
  299
Fabricat Design/Book and
  Patterns, 300
Lady, Barbara J., 291
Oroyan, Susanna, 292
Sculpting and Moldmaking
  Seminars, 293

PENNSYLVANIA
Retail Stores
Anna's Collectibles, 21

Doll and Mini Nook, 26
Nanalee's Dolls and Gifts,
  35
Patricia Allgeier Barbie
  Dolls and Collectibles,
  36
Zip's Toys To Go, 39

Antique Doll Dealers
Ann Lloyd—Antique Dolls,
  48
Demsey & Baxter, 51
Doll Express, Inc., The, 51,
  59
Richard Wright Antiques,
  57

Supplies, Clothing and Accessories
Dynasty Doll Collection, 76
Gipe, Dwaine E., 76
Handcraft Designs, Inc., 79
Newark Dressmaker Supply
  Inc., 86
Plum Creek Dollmakers, 88

Doll Artists
Berg, Suzanne, 110
Bloom, Amy Albert, 110
Chesapeake Bay Dolls, 164
Dolls of Original Design,
  137
Glowacki, Kristin, 128
Good-Krüger Dolls, Inc.,
  128
Good-Krüger, Julie, 128
Hartmann, Sonja, 132
Justiss, Sandra Wright, 137
Sonja Hartmann Originals,
  132
Stellwagon, Linda L., 164
Welker, Lauren, 169
Wyatt, Melissa, 171

Manufacturers
Dynasty Doll Collection,
  Inc., 183
Pittsburgh Originals, 186

Shows
Doll Show and Sale/
  Sleeping Angel
  Productions, 213
Pittsburgh Area Doll Show
  and Sales, 220
R&S Enterprises, 206

Organizations
Doll Express, The, 228
International Doll Doctor's
  Club, 231
Original Doll Artists
  Council of America
  (ODACA), 234

Museums
Mary Mettitt Doll Museum,
  249

Paper Dolls
Bloom, Amy Albert, 269
DiFonso, Don, 270
Welker, Lauren, 276

Additional Opportunities
D&B Antiques, 299
Doll Artisan Guild, 289
Doll Reader, 297
Doll Seminars, Workshops
  and Lectures, 289
Lauren Welker's Doll Diary,
  298
Lifetime Career Schools,
  292
Welker's Doll Making
  Workshops, Lauren, 292

RHODE ISLAND
Retail Stores
Wild Spirit Doll Studio, 38

Antique Doll Dealers
Dollworks, 53

Supplies, Clothing and Accessories
Wild Spirit Doll Studio, 94

Doll Artists
Carole Ann Creations, 146
Dolan, Shirley Townsend,
  122
Maddocks, Carole, 146
Pritchard, Nancy L., 156
Wild Spirit Sculpture
  Studio, 156

Museums
Doll Museum, The, 247

Additional Opportunities
Wild Spirit Doll Studio, 294

SOUTH CAROLINA
Doll Artists
Bro, Lois B., 112
Brooks, Patricia Ryan, 113
LBro Original Designs, 112

Shows
Coastal Doll Collectors'
  Show and Sale, 210
Myrtle Beach SC Annual
  Doll Show and Sale, 220

Organizations
Coastal Doll Collectors
  Club of South Carolina,
  228

Paper Dolls
Williams, Tracy Jane, 276

SOUTH DAKOTA
Supplies, Clothing and Accessories
Heartwarmers, 79

Doll Artists
Doneaud ("Nini"), Doina,
  122
"Nini" Dolls, 122

Museums
Enchanted World Doll
  Museum, 248

TENNESSEE
Retail Stores
Magic Moment, 33
Orange Blossom, The, 36

Supplies, Clothing and Accessories
Jones Mold Co. Inc., 81

Paper Dolls
Pam's Paper Dolls and
  Collectibles, 266, 268

TEXAS
Retail Stores
Doll Hospital, Inc., The, 26
For the Love of Dolls, Inc.,
  30

Antique Doll Dealers
Barbara's Dolls, 49

Supplies, Clothing and Accessories
Childhood Fantasies, 70
Dixon, Jean, 81
Jackson Ranch, 81
Just Her Style, 82
Nana's Dolls, 86
Paragon Industries, Inc., 87
Westside Printing, 93

Doll Artists
Anastasia's Porcelain Dolls, 153
Ardis of Starcross, 106
Fabricimages, 154
Pannell, Mazie, 153
Patterson, Joyce, 154
Spencer, Paul, 164
Spencer Wooden Originals, 164

Manufacturers
Daddy's Long Legs, 182

Shows
Annual Bluebonnet Bebes of Houston Doll Show and Sale, 208
Golden Spread Doll Show, 216
Huff, Jean, 203
Metro Plex Annual Doll Show, 218
Texas Doll Show and Sales, 222

Organizations
Golden Spread Doll Club, 230
Jan Hagara Collectors Club, 231
Just Dollinks, 231
Society of the Permain Basin Doll Artisans, The, 236
Vinyl Goddess Club of Dallas, 238

Paper Dolls
Prince Doll Studio, 268, 274
Prince, Dwayne or Karen, 274

Additional Opportunities
Chambers, Karen B., 299

Paragon Industries, Inc., 293

UTAH
Antique Doll Dealers
Cat's Cradle, 50

Supplies, Clothing and Accessories
Jane's Original Art Doll Supplies, 81

Doll Artists
Cannon, Margery, 117
"D" Originals, 129
Greenwood, Dessa Rae, 129
Johnston, Jack, 136
Johnston Original Art Dolls, 136
Margery Cannon Originals, 117
Martindale, Diana, 148
Martindale Originals, 148

Shows
Crossroads Doll, Bear and Toy Show, The, 201

Organizations
Professional Dollmakers Guild, 235

Museums
McCurdy Historical Doll Museum, 248

Additional Opportunities
Johnston Original Art Doll Seminars, 291
Johnston Original Art Dolls, 300

VERMONT
Doll Artists
All Hearts Come Home for Christmas, 112
Andress, Sunnie, 105
Barrie, Mirren, 108
Brochu, Joan L., 112
Finch-Kozlosky, Marta, 125
Sunnie Andress Designs, 105

Paper Dolls
Barrie, Mirren, 269

VIRGINIA
Retail Stores
Angie's Doll Boutique, Inc., 21
Biggs Limited, 22
C&W Enterprises, 23
My Doll House of Hilltop, 35
2nd Time Around Doll Shop, 37

Antique Doll Dealers
Melton's Antique Dolls, 56
2nd Time Around Doll Shop, 57

Supplies, Clothing and Accessories
Angie's Doll Boutique, Inc., 67
Dolls Delight, Inc., 75

Doll Artists
Canton, Jennifer, 117
Characters by Bill Nelson, 150
Nelson, Bill, 150

Manufacturers
Kish and Company, 185

Shows
Sirocco Productions, Inc., 206
Tidewater Teddy Bear and Doll Show, 222

Organizations
Q P Doll Club, 235

Paper Dolls
Faraone, Jim—P.D. Pal, 271
P.D. Pal, 267, 278

Additional Opportunities
Angie's Doll Boutique, Inc., 287
McKinley Books and Tapes, 300
Sirocco Historical Doll Videos, 301

WASHINGTON
Retail Stores
Doll Gallery, The, 26
Dolls and Friends, 27
Heavenly Dolls, 30

Regina's Doll Heaven, 37
Weefoke Empire, 38

Antique Doll Dealers
Annette's Antique Dolls, 48
Clark's Antique Dolls, 50
Doll Gallery, The, 52

Supplies, Clothing and Accessories
Collectible Doll Company, 71
Doll Gallery, The, 74
Donna Lee's Sewing Center, 76
Gabriele's Inc., 77
Heavenly Dolls, 80

Doll Artists
Cindy M. McClure Ent. Ltd., 144
Classic Image, A, 158
Faville, Donna, 124
Faville Original Dolls, 124
Gray, Scott R., 129
Harding, Trish, 131
Iverson Design, 134
Iverson, Thom and Renée, 134
Lemmon, Denise, 142
McClure, Cindy M., 144
Mountain Babies Doll Factory, 142
Not Just Another Pretty Face, 129
Oak, Thorn and Ash Collection, 131
Rhodes, Rosemary, 158

Organizations
Steilacoom Doll Club, 236

Museums
Rosalie Whyle Doll Museum, 249

Paper Dolls
Burdick, Loraine, 266, 270
Cedar Rose Studio, 272
Hines-Pinion, Sharon, 272
Lou Rathjen's Designs, 273
Rathjen, Jewel L., 273

Additional Opportunities
Celebrity Doll Journal, 295
Doll Gallery, The, 289
Heavenly Dolls, 290

Jean Nordquist's Collectible Doll Academy, 290
Miller's Barbie Collector, 298
Miller's Market Report for Barbie Collectors, 299
Natural Fiber Identity Labels, 300

WISCONSIN
Doll Artists
Baierl, Kim Diane, 107
Clarke, Kathi, 119
D. Schwellenbach—Artist's Dolls, 161
Fantasy at Your Fingertips, 149
Fayette Knoop/Original Character Dolls, 140
Kathi Clarke Originals, 119
Knoop, Fayette, 140
Morley, Karen A., 149
Schwellenbach, D., 161

Shows
Enchanted Doll Club of Eagle River Doll Show, 215
Fox Valley Area Doll Show, 216
Loving Memories Doll,

Bear, Toy and Miniature Show, 217
Madison Area Doll Club Show, The, 218
Orphans in the Attic Doll-Bear-Toy Shows/Sales, 205

Organizations
Dolly Follies, The, 229
Loving Memories Doll Club, 232

Additional Opportunities
Barbie Bazaar, 295
Dollmaking—Projects and Plans, 297
Fantasy at Your Fingertips, 290

CANADA
Retail Stores
Browns Gallery, 23
Country Sampler, The, 25

Antique Doll Dealers
Marilyn's Forest of Dolls, 55
Orillia Doll Hospital, The, 56

Supplies, Clothing and Accessories
Rita's Children, 89

Doll Artists
Allen, Clara M., 104

Boers, Martha, 111
Celtic Images, 170
Colston, Deborah, 120
Doll Maker, 140
La Haise, Angelika, 140
Lamb, Jaine, 141
Little People, 145
MacInnis, Christine, 145
Maciak, Heather Browning, 145
Marnie's World of Dolls Inc., 152
Panek, Marnie, 152
Reitsma, Marianne, 111
Wimpory, Patricia, 170

Manufacturers
Avonlea Traditions Inc., 181
Carousel Canada Inc., 182

Shows
Brockville Doll, Miniature and Teddy Bear Show And Sale, 208
Doll and Teddy Bear Festival and Sale, 211
Doll Festival and Sale, 212
M.A.D. Shows, 204

Paper Dolls
Dodington, Judith, 270
Jones, Bruce Patrick, 272

Wellman, Loraine, 276

Additional Opportunities
Canadian Doll Journal, 295
Dodington, Judith, 288
Lamb, Jaine, 291
Rita's Children, 293

GERMANY
Antique Doll Dealers
Käthe Kruse Puppen Gmbh, 55

Manufacturers
Käthe Kruse Puppen Gmbh, 185

THE NETHERLANDS
Museums
Käthe Kruse Puppen Museum, 248

UNITED KINGDOM
Organizations
British Doll Artists' Association, 227

Additional Opportunities
Doll Magazine, 296

Brand Name Index

ALEXANDER
Angie's Doll Boutique, Inc., 21
Anna's Collectibles, 21
Bear-A-Dise Landing, 22
Biggs Limited, 22
Blevins Plates 'n' Things, 22
Bodzer's Collectibles, 23
C & W Enterprises, 23
Celia's and Susan's Dolls and Collectibles, 24
A Century of Dolls, 24
Deere Crossing, 25
Doll and Mini Nook, 26
Doll Gallery, The (FL), 26
Doll Hospital, Inc., The, 26
Doll World and Surroundings, 27
Dolls and Friends, 27
Dolls by Jim, 27
Dolls Unlimited, 28
Empress Doll Boutique, 29
For the Love of Dolls, Inc., 30
Judy's Doll Shop, 31
Kmitsch Girls, 31
Little Shoppe of Dolls and Things, 32
Mid-Ohio Historical Museum, 34
Montana Dolls and Collectibles, 34
My Doll House of Hilltop, 35
P.G.'s Enchanted Dolls, Inc., 37
Shellie's Miniature Mania, 37
Weefoke Empire, 38
Young at Heart Doll Shop, 39

ANNALEE
Anna's Collectibles, 21
Charlene's Dolls and Collectibles, 25
Zip's Toys to Go, 39

ANNETTE HIMSTEDT
Alcove, The, 21
Angie's Doll Boutique, Inc., 21
Biggs Limited, 22
Browns Gallery, 23
Celia's and Susan's Dolls and Collectibles, 24
Deere Crossing, 25
Doll Gallery, The (FL), 26
Dolls by Jim, 27
Dollsville Dolls and Bearsville Bears, 29
Little Shoppe of Dolls and Things, 32
Young at Heart Doll Shop, 39

ARNETT COUNTRY THINGS
"My Dolls" Dolls of Color, 35

ARTIST COLLECTIBLES
Young at Heart Doll Shop, 39

ASHTON-DRAKE
Anna's Collectibles, 21
Blevins Plates 'n' Things, 22
Bodzer's Collectibles, 23
Browns Gallery, 23
Celia's and Susan's Dolls and Collectibles, 24
Dolls and Friends, 27
Dollsville Dolls and Bearsville Bears, 29
Empress Doll Boutique, 29
For the Love of Dolls, Inc., 30
Honeydoll's Collectibles, 30
Kmitsch Girls, 31
Little Shoppe of Dolls and Things, 32
Love of Country, 33
Orange Blossom, The, 36

P.G.'s Enchanted Dolls, Inc., 37
Shellie's Miniature Mania, 37

ATTIC BABIES
Special Occasions, 38

BABY CUDDLE-KINS BY BEAR NECESSITIES
L.M. Crossroads, 32

BARBIE
Alcove, The, 21
Angie's Doll Boutique, Inc., 21
Anna's Collectibles, 21
Blevins Plates 'n' Things, 22
C & W Enterprises, 23
A Century of Dolls, 24
Deere Crossing, 25
Doll Gallery, The (FL), 26
Doll Gallery, The (WA), 26
Dolls by Jim, 27
Dollsville Dolls and Bearsville Bears, 29
Kmitsch Girls, 31
Linda's Lov-Lez House of Dolls and Bears, More, 32
Little Shoppe of Dolls and Things, 32
Marl and Barbie, 34
Mid-Ohio Historical Museum, 34
Montana Dolls and Collectibles, 34
My Doll House of Hilltop, 35
P.G.'s Enchanted Dolls, Inc., 37
Wild Spirit Doll Studio, 38

BELLE DOLLS
"My Dolls" Dolls of Color, 35

BERJUSA
Deere Crossing, 25
Doll Hospital, Inc., The, 26
Doll World and Surroundings, 27
Dolls and Friends, 27
Dolls Unlimited, 28
Kmitsch Girls, 31
Young at Heart Doll Shop, 39

BOLDEN
Biggs Limited, 22

BRADLEE
Bear-A-Dise Landing, 22

BRADLEY
Dolls and Friends, 27
Young at Heart Doll Shop, 39

COLLECTABLES, THE
Wild Spirit Doll Studio, 38

COROLLE
Dolls and Friends, 27
Kmitsch Girls, 31
My Doll House of Hilltop, 35

CREES AND COE
A Century of Dolls, 24

DADDY'S LONG LEGS
Alcove, The, 21
Angie's Doll Boutique, Inc., 21
Anna's Collectibles, 21
Country Sampler, The, 25
Dolls Unlimited, 28
Julia's The Ultimate Collection, 31
L.M. Crossroads, 32
"My Dolls" Dolls of Color, 35
Orange Blossom, The, 36

Special Occasions, 38

DAKIN
Young at Heart Doll Shop, 39

DELTON
Angie's Doll Boutique, Inc., 21

DESTINY
Linda's Lov-Lez House of Dolls and Bears, More, 32

DOLL FACTORY, THE
Charlene's Dolls and Collectibles, 25

DOLLMAKERS ORIGINALS
L.M. Crossroads, 32
Wild Spirit Doll Studio, 38

DOLLS BY JERRI
Dolls by Jim, 27
For the Love of Dolls, Inc., 30
Kmitsch Girls, 31

DYNASTY DOLL COLLECTION
Angie's Doll Boutique, Inc., 21
Doll Gallery, The (WA), 26
Doll Hospital, Inc., The, 26
Dolls and Friends, 27
Shellie's Miniature Mania, 37
Weefoke Empire, 38
Young at Heart Doll Shop, 39

EFFANBEE
Bear-A-Dise Landing, 22
Browns Gallery, 23
C & W Enterprises, 23
Celia's and Susan's Dolls and Collectibles, 24
A Century of Dolls, 24
Doll and Mini Nook, 26
Doll Hospital, Inc., The, 26
Doll World and Surroundings, 27

Dollmakers, The, 28
Dolls and Friends, 27
Dolls by Jim, 27
Dolls From the Heart, 28
Dolls Unlimited, 28
For the Love of Dolls, Inc., 30
Judy's Doll Shop, 31
L.M. Crossroads, 32
Linda's Lov-Lez House of Dolls and Bears, More, 32
Love of Country, 33
P.G.'s Enchanted Dolls, Inc., 37
Shellie's Miniature Mania, 37

ELLENBROOKE
Dollsville Dolls and Bearsville Bears, 29

ENESCO
Celia's and Susan's Dolls and Collectibles, 24

EUROPEAN ARTIST DOLLS
A Century of Dolls, 24
Young at Heart Doll Shop, 39

FAITH WICK
C & W Enterprises, 23
Dolls Unlimited, 28

FAYZAH SPANOS
Biggs Limited, 22
Browns Gallery, 23
Doll and Mini Nook, 26
L.M. Crossroads, 32
Linda's Lov-Lez House of Dolls and Bears, More, 32
Nanalee's Dolls and Gifts, 35
Wild Spirit Doll Studio, 38

FEDERICA
Dollsville Dolls and Bearsville Bears, 29

FIBA
Dolls by Jim, 27

Paris Dolls and More Shoppe, 36

FRANKLIN
Weefoke Empire, 38

FURGA
Dolls and Friends, 27
Young at Heart Doll Shop, 39

GADCO
Carriage House Collectibles, 24
Honeydoll's Collectibles, 30
Little Shoppe of Dolls and Things, 32
Weefoke Empire, 38
Young at Heart Doll Shop, 39

GEORGETOWN
Angie's Doll Boutique, Inc., 21
Blevins Plates 'n' Things, 22
Bodzer's Collectibles, 23
Browns Gallery, 23
Celia's and Susan's Dolls and Collectibles, 24
A Century of Dolls, 24
Charlene's Dolls and Collectibles, 25
Dolls and Friends, 27
Dolls by Jim, 27
Dolls From the Heart, 28
For the Love of Dolls, Inc., 30
Honeydoll's Collectibles, 30
L.M. Crossroads, 32
Little Shoppe of Dolls and Things, 32
Love of Country, 33
Montana Dolls and Collectibles, 34
Nanalee's Dolls and Gifts, 35
Weefoke Empire, 38

GLOBAL
Weefoke Empire, 38

GOEBEL
Young at Heart Doll Shop, 39

GOOD-KRÜGER
Browns Gallery, 23
Carriage House Collectibles, 24
Cedar Chest Doll Shoppe, 24
A Century of Dolls, 24
Charlene's Dolls and Collectibles, 25
Deere Crossing, 25
Doll and Mini Nook, 26
Dolls by Jim, 27
Dolls From the Heart, 28
Dollsville Dolls and Bearsville Bears, 29
Kmitsch Girls, 31
L.M. Crossroads, 32
Little Shoppe of Dolls and Things, 32
Nanalee's Dolls and Gifts, 35
Orange Blossom, The, 36
P.G.'s Enchanted Dolls, Inc., 37
Paris Dolls and More Shoppe, 36
Young at Heart Doll Shop, 39
Zip's Toys to Go, 39

GÖTZ
Angie's Doll Boutique, Inc., 21
Bear-A-Dise Landing, 22
Browns Gallery, 23
Carriage House Collectibles, 24
Cedar Chest Doll Shoppe, 24
Charlene's Dolls and Collectibles, 25
Doll Gallery, The (FL), 26
Dolls and Friends, 27
Dolls From the Heart, 28
For the Love of Dolls, Inc., 30
Judy's Doll Shop, 31
Kmitsch Girls, 31
Linda's Lov-Lez House of Dolls and Bears, More, 32

Paris Dolls and More
 Shoppe, 36
Regina's Doll Heaven, 37
Young at Heart Doll Shop,
 39
Zip's Toys to Go, 39

GREAT AMERICAN DOLL CO.

Charlene's Dolls and
 Collectibles, 25
Doll World and
 Surroundings, 27
Dolls and Friends, 27
Dolls by Jim, 27

GUND

C & W Enterprises, 23

GUSTAVE AND GRETCHEN WOLFF DESIGNER DOLLS

Stone Fence Doll Shoppe,
 38

HAGARA

Dolls by Jim, 27

HAMILTON

Angie's Doll Boutique, Inc.,
 21
Blevins Plates 'n' Things,
 22
Bodzer's Collectibles, 23
Browns Gallery, 23
Celia's and Susan's Dolls
 and Collectibles, 24
Doll Gallery, The (FL), 26
Honeydoll's Collectibles,
 30
Love of Country, 33
Montana Dolls and
 Collectibles, 34
Nanalee's Dolls and Gifts,
 35
Young at Heart Doll Shop,
 39

HANTEL

C & W Enterprises, 23

HEIDI OTT

Bear-A-Dise Landing, 22
Doll and Mini Nook, 26
Dolls and Friends, 27

Dolls Unlimited, 28
L.M. Crossroads, 32

HILDEGARD GUNZEL

Cedar Chest Doll Shoppe,
 24
Doll Hospital, Inc., The, 26
Dolls by Jim, 27
Dolls Unlimited, 28
Nanalee's Dolls and Gifts,
 35
P.G.'s Enchanted Dolls,
 Inc., 37
Young at Heart Doll Shop,
 39

HOLLYWOOD

Dolls and Friends, 27

HORSEMAN

Browns Gallery, 23
P.G.'s Enchanted Dolls,
 Inc., 37

JAN MCLEAN

Celia's and Susan's Dolls
 and Collectibles, 24

JECKEL-JANSEN

Bear-A-Dise Landing, 22
Deere Crossing, 25
Regina's Doll Heaven, 37
Wild Spirit Doll Studio, 38

JOHANNES ZOOK

Bear-A-Dise Landing, 22
Biggs Limited, 22
Browns Gallery, 23
Cedar Chest Doll Shoppe,
 24
Doll and Mini Nook, 26
Doll World and
 Surroundings, 27
Dolls and Friends, 27
Dolls From the Heart, 28
Dollsville Dolls and
 Bearsville Bears, 29
For the Love of Dolls, Inc.,
 30
Kmitsch Girls, 31
L.M. Crossroads, 32
Little Shoppe of Dolls and
 Things, 32
Nanalee's Dolls and Gifts,
 35

Paris Dolls and More
 Shoppe, 36
Weefoke Empire, 38
Wild Spirit Doll Studio, 38

JULIE RUEGER

Browns Gallery, 23

KÄTHE KRUSE

A Century of Dolls, 24
Deere Crossing, 25
Dolls and Friends, 27

KATRINA

Biggs Limited, 22

KEWPIE

C & W Enterprises, 23

KINGSTATE

Angie's Doll Boutique, Inc.,
 21
Blevins Plates 'n' Things,
 22
Dolls and Friends, 27
Dolls Unlimited, 28
Honeydoll's Collectibles,
 30
L.M. Crossroads, 32
"My Dolls" Dolls of Color,
 35
P.G.'s Enchanted Dolls,
 Inc., 37
Wild Spirit Doll Studio, 38
Young at Heart Doll Shop,
 39

KISH AND CO. (HELEN KISH)

Alcove, The, 21
Carriage House
 Collectibles, 24
Deere Crossing, 25
Dolls and Friends, 27
P.G.'s Enchanted Dolls,
 Inc., 37
Paris Dolls and More
 Shoppe, 36
Regina's Doll Heaven, 37
Shellie's Miniature Mania,
 37

KVK

For the Love of Dolls, Inc.,
 30

LAWTON

Biggs Limited, 22
Blevins Plates 'n' Things,
 22
Bodzer's Collectibles, 23
Celia's and Susan's Dolls
 and Collectibles, 24
A Century of Dolls, 24
Dolls and Friends, 27
Dollsville Dolls and
 Bearsville Bears, 29
Kmitsch Girls, 31
Little Shoppe of Dolls and
 Things, 32
Montana Dolls and
 Collectibles, 34
P.G.'s Enchanted Dolls,
 Inc., 37
Zip's Toys to Go, 39

LEE MIDDLETON

Bear-A-Dise Landing, 22
Browns Gallery, 23
A Century of Dolls, 24
Doll World and
 Surroundings, 27
Dolls From the Heart, 28
L.M. Crossroads, 32
Montana Dolls and
 Collectibles, 34
Nanalee's Dolls and Gifts,
 35
P.G.'s Enchanted Dolls,
 Inc., 37
Paris Dolls and More
 Shoppe, 36

LEGACY

Young at Heart Doll Shop,
 39

LENCI

Dolls by Jim, 27

LET'S PLAY DOLLS

Doll Hospital, Inc., The, 26

LISSI

Dolls and Friends, 27
Dolls Unlimited, 28

LIZZIE HIGH

Special Occasions, 38

LL KNICKERBOCKER
Linda's Lov-Lez House of
    Dolls and Bears, More,
    32

LLOYD MIDDLETON
Honeydoll's Collectibles,
    30
L.M. Crossroads, 32
Paris Dolls and More
    Shoppe, 36

MAGIC ATTIC
Love of Country, 33

MARIE OSMOND
L.M. Crossroads, 32

MATTEL
Browns Gallery, 23
Celia's and Susan's Dolls
    and Collectibles, 24
Deere Crossing, 25
Doll and Mini Nook, 26
Dollmakers, The, 28
Dolls and Friends, 27
For the Love of Dolls, Inc.,
    30
Montana Dolls and
    Collectibles, 34
Patricia Allgeier Barbie
    Dolls and Collectibles,
    36
Wild Spirit Doll Studio, 38
Young at Heart Doll Shop,
    39

MIDDLETON
Anna's Collectibles, 21
Cedar Chest Doll Shoppe,
    24
Doll and Mini Nook, 26
Doll Hospital, Inc., The, 26
Dollmakers, The, 28
Linda's Lov-Lez House of
    Dolls and Bears, More,
    32
Little Shoppe of Dolls and
    Things, 32
Young at Heart Doll Shop,
    39

MONIKA
Biggs Limited, 22

NABER KIDS/BABIES
Magic Moment, 33

NASCAR
Browns Gallery, 23

OPT 4 KIDS
"My Dolls" Dolls of Color,
    35

PARADISE GALLERIES
Honeydoll's Collectibles,
    30
Young at Heart Doll Shop,
    39

PAUL CREES
Browns Gallery, 23
Celia's and Susan's Dolls
    and Collectibles, 24

PAULINE
Dollmakers, The, 28
Dolls and Friends, 27
Love of Country, 33
Zip's Toys to Go, 39

PHYLLIS PARKINS
Dolls From the Heart, 28

**PITTSBURGH
ORIGINALS**
Doll and Mini Nook, 26
Dollsville Dolls and
    Bearsville Bears, 29
Linda's Lov-Lez House of
    Dolls and Bears, More,
    32
Montana Dolls and
    Collectibles, 34

**PRECIOUS
HEIRLOOMS**
Dolls From the Heart, 28
Montana Dolls and
    Collectibles, 34
Young at Heart Doll Shop,
    39

PRECIOUS MOMENTS
Deere Crossing, 25
Dollmakers, The, 28
Love of Country, 33

R. JOHN WRIGHT
A Century of Dolls, 24

ROBERT TONNER
Biggs Limited, 22
Carriage House
    Collectibles, 24
Dolls and Friends, 27
Dollsville Dolls and
    Bearsville Bears, 29
P.G.'s Enchanted Dolls,
    Inc., 37
Regina's Doll Heaven, 37

ROBIN WOODS
Dollmakers, The, 28
P.G.'s Enchanted Dolls,
    Inc., 37

**ROBIN WOODS FOR
HORSEMAN**
Doll Hospital, Inc., The, 26

ROTTENKIDS
Bear-A-Dise Landing, 22

ROYAL VIENNA
Charlene's Dolls and
    Collectibles, 25
Doll Gallery, The (FL), 26
Doll Hospital, Inc., The, 26
Nanalee's Dolls and Gifts,
    35

RUTH TREFFEISEN
Alcove, The, 21
Celia's and Susan's Dolls
    and Collectibles, 24
Regina's Doll Heaven, 37

SANDI MCASLAN
Wild Spirit Doll Studio, 38

SANDY DOLLS
Dollmakers, The, 28
"My Dolls" Dolls of Color,
    35

SARAH'S ATTIC DOLLS
Country Sampler, The, 25

SASHA
C & W Enterprises, 23

SEYMOUR MANN
Alcove, The, 21
Angie's Doll Boutique, Inc.,
    21
Anna's Collectibles, 21
Blevins Plates 'n' Things,
    22
Doll and Mini Nook, 26
Doll Gallery, The (FL), 26
Dollmakers, The, 28
Dolls and Friends, 27
Honeydoll's Collectibles,
    30
L.M. Crossroads, 32
Love of Country, 33
"My Dolls" Dolls of Color,
    35
Paris Dolls and More
    Shoppe, 36
Wild Spirit Doll Studio, 38
Young at Heart Doll Shop,
    39

SIGIKID
Carriage House
    Collectibles, 24
Charlene's Dolls and
    Collectibles, 25
Dolls by Jim, 27
For the Love of Dolls, Inc.,
    30
Honeydoll's Collectibles,
    30
Kmitsch Girls, 31

SONJA HARTMAN
Deere Crossing, 25
Dolls by Jim, 27

STEIFF
C & W Enterprises, 23

SUSAN WAKEEN
Alcove, The, 21
Bear-A-Dise Landing, 22
Carriage House
    Collectibles, 24
A Century of Dolls, 24
Charlene's Dolls and
    Collectibles, 25
Doll and Mini Nook, 26
Dolls From the Heart, 28
For the Love of Dolls, Inc.,
    30
Nanalee's Dolls and Gifts,
    35

Young at Heart Doll Shop, 39

SWEETMMS
Deere Crossing, 25

TAHTI
Julia's The Ultimate Collection, 31

TENDER TOUCH
Young at Heart Doll Shop, 39

TIMELESS CREATIONS—MATTEL
Paris Dolls and More Shoppe, 36

ULTIMATE
Young at Heart Doll Shop, 39

VERA SHOLTZ
Nanalee's Dolls and Gifts, 35

VICTORIA
Dollmakers, The, 28

VIRGINIA TURNER
Cedar Chest Doll Shoppe, 24
Deere Crossing, 25
Dolls From the Heart, 28
Nanalee's Dolls and Gifts, 35

VOGUE GINNY
Angie's Doll Boutique, Inc., 21
Deere Crossing, 25
Doll Hospital, Inc., The, 26
Dollmakers, The, 28

For the Love of Dolls, Inc., 30
Linda's Lov-Lez House of Dolls and Bears, More, 32
P.G.'s Enchanted Dolls, Inc., 37

WHITE HORSE WOMAN
Paris Dolls and More Shoppe, 36

WIMBLEDON COLLECTION
Dolls Unlimited, 28
Stone Fence Doll Shoppe, 38

WORLD
Young at Heart Doll Shop, 39

WPM
Doll World and Surroundings, 27

YOLANDO BELLO ORIGINALS
Browns Gallery, 23
Celia's and Susan's Dolls and Collectibles, 24

ZAPF
Doll Gallery, The (FL), 26
Doll World and Surroundings, 27

Supplies and Accessories Index

ARMATURES
Alice's Doll Workshop, 66
All for a Doll, 66
Angie's Doll Boutique, Inc., 67
Ann's Dolls, 67
Anthony's of Solvang, 68
Cascade Doll Shoppe, 70
Center Stage Emporium, 70
Childhood Fantasies, 70
Collectible Doll Company, 71
Create an Heirloom, 72
CR's Crafts, 72
Doll Adventure, The, 73
Doll Gallery, The (ME), 74
Dol-Lee Shop, The, 75
Dolls by Dyan, 75
Donna's Doll Factory, 76
Georgie's Ceramics and Clay Art Pak, 78
Grandma's Dollings, 78
Handcraft Designs, Inc., 79
Heartwarmers, 79
Heavenly Dolls, 80
Jane's Original Art Doll Supplies, 81
Judith Howe Inc., 81
Judy's Doll Shop, 82
K.C. Dolls, 83
Kemper Doll Supplies, 84
Monique Trading Corp., 85
Plum Creek Dollmakers, 88
Rita's Children, 89
Simpson's Liberty Doll Supply, 90
Sweet Dreams, 92
Truebite Inc., 92
Wild Spirit Doll Studio, 94
Wilder's Doll Center, 94

BODIES
Alice's Doll Workshop, 66
All for a Doll, 66
Angie's Doll Boutique, Inc., 67
Ann's Dolls, 67
Cascade Doll Shoppe, 70
Center Stage Emporium, 70

Childhood Fantasies, 70
Collectible Doll Company, 71
CR's Crafts, 72
Doll Adventure, The, 73
Doll Gallery, The (WA), 74
Doll Place, The, 75
Dolls by Dyan, 75
Donna's Doll Factory, 76
Gallery Collection Molds, 78
Georgie's Ceramics and Clay Art Pak, 78
Grandma's Dollings, 78
Heartwarmers, 79
Heavenly Dolls, 80
Jane's Original Art Doll Supplies, 81
Judy's Doll Shop, 82
Kemper Doll Supplies, 84
Newark Dressmaker Supply Inc., 86
Page's Dolls, 87
Plum Creek Dollmakers, 88
Rita's Children, 89
Seeley's, 90
Sweet Dreams, 92
Wild Spirit Doll Studio, 94
Wilder's Doll Center, 94

BUTTONS
Bear Threads, Ltd., 68
Best Dressed Doll, 69
CR's Crafts, 72
Georgie's Ceramics and Clay Art Pak, 78
K.C. Dolls, 83
Kate Webster Company, 82
Newark Dressmaker Supply Inc., 86
Plum Creek Dollmakers, 88
Porcelain Rose, The, 89
Simpson's Liberty Doll Supply, 90
Wilder's Doll Center, 94

CLAYS
All for a Doll, 66
All That Glissons, 67

Angie's Doll Boutique, Inc., 67
Cascade Doll Shoppe, 70
Center Stage Emporium, 70
Collectible Doll Company, 71
CR's Crafts, 72
Doll Adventure, The, 73
Doll Gallery, The (ME), 74
Donna's Doll Factory, 76
Georgie's Ceramics and Clay Art Pak, 78
Grandma's Dollings, 78
Handcraft Designs, Inc., 79
Heavenly Dolls, 80
Jane's Original Art Doll Supplies, 81
Judy's Doll Shop, 82
Kemper Doll Supplies, 84
Plum Creek Dollmakers, 88
Polyform Products Company, 89
Portland Po Henry Supply, 89
Rita's Children, 89
Southern Oregon Pottery Supply, 91
Sweet Dreams, 92
Wild Spirit Doll Studio, 94
Wilder's Doll Center, 94

CLOTHING (READY-MADE)
Alice's Doll Workshop, 66
All for a Doll, 66
Angie's Doll Boutique, Inc., 67
Ann's Dolls, 67
Beauty-Stone Stands, 68
Best Dressed Doll, 69
Childhood Fantasies, 70
Collectible Doll Company, 71
CR's Crafts, 72
Doll Adventure, The, 73
Doll Fashions Northwest, 74
Doll Place, The, 75
Doll Studios, 75

Dolls Delight, Inc., 75
Donna Lee's Sewing Center, 76
Donna's Doll Factory, 76
Dynasty Doll Collection, 76
Grandma's Dollings, 78
Heartwarmers, 79
Heavenly Dolls, 80
Judy's Doll Shop, 82
Just Her Style, 82
Monique Trading Corp., 85
Nana's Dolls, 86
Newark Dressmaker Supply Inc., 86
Page's Dolls, 87
Plum Creek Dollmakers, 88
Rita's Children, 89
S&S Doll Hospital, 90
Simpson's Liberty Doll Supply, 90
Treffeisen U.S.A., 92
Wilder's Doll Center, 94

DOLL-RELATED COLLECTIBLES
Angie's Doll Boutique, Inc., 67
Center Stage Emporium, 70
Collectible Doll Company, 71
Doll Gallery, The (ME), 74
Doll Gallery, The (WA), 74
Donna's Doll Factory, 76
Dynasty Doll Collection, 76
Gallery Collection Molds, 78
Just Her Style, 82
Kate Webster Company, 82
Plum Creek Dollmakers, 88
Treffeisen U.S.A., 92

EYES
Alice's Doll Workshop, 66
All for a Doll, 66
Angie's Doll Boutique, Inc., 67
Ann's Dolls, 67
Cascade Doll Shoppe, 70
Center Stage Emporium, 70

Childhood Fantasies, 70
Collectible Doll Company, 71
Create an Heirloom, 72
CR's Crafts, 72
Doll Adventure, The, 73
Doll Gallery, The (ME), 74
Doll Gallery, The (WA), 74
Doll Studios, 75
Dolls by Dyan, 75
Donna's Doll Factory, 76
Georgie's Ceramics and Clay Art Pak, 78
Grandma's Dollings, 78
Hamilton Eye Warehouse, 79
Heartwarmers, 79
Heavenly Dolls, 80
J. Schoepfer, Inc., 80
Jane's Original Art Doll Supplies, 81
Judith Howe Inc., 81
Judy's Doll Shop, 82
K.C. Dolls, 83
Kemper Doll Supplies, 84
Masterpiece Eye Co., 84
Monique Trading Corp., 85
Newark Dressmaker Supply Inc., 86
Page's Dolls, 87
Plum Creek Dollmakers, 88
Rita's Children, 89
Simpson's Liberty Doll Supply, 90
Sweet Dreams, 92
Truebite Inc., 92
Wild Spirit Doll Studio, 94
Wilder's Doll Center, 94

FABRICS FOR CLOTH DOLLS
All for a Doll, 66
All That Glissons, 67
Cascade Doll Shoppe, 70
CR's Crafts, 72
Gabriele's Inc., 77
National Nonwovens, 86
Newark Dressmaker Supply Inc., 86
Osage County Quilt Factory, 87
Page's Dolls, 87
Wilder's Doll Center, 94

FABRICS FOR DOLL CLOTHING
Alice's Doll Workshop, 66
Bear Threads, Ltd., 68
Cascade Doll Shoppe, 70
CR's Crafts, 72
Donna Lee's Sewing Center, 76
Kate Webster Company, 82
National Nonwovens, 86
Newark Dressmaker Supply Inc., 86
Osage County Quilt Factory, 87
Page's Dolls, 87
Plum Creek Dollmakers, 88
South Forty Farms, 91
Wilder's Doll Center, 94

FABRICS FOR HAIR
Alice's Doll Workshop, 66
Angie's Doll Boutique, Inc., 67
Cascade Doll Shoppe, 70
Center Stage Emporium, 70
Collectible Doll Company, 71
CR's Crafts, 72
Doll Adventure, The, 73
Doll Hair Etc., 74
Dolls by Dyan, 75
Gabriele's Inc., 77
Georgie's Ceramics and Clay Art Pak, 78
Handcraft Designs, Inc., 79
Heavenly Dolls, 80
Ironstone Yarns, 80
Jackson Ranch, 81
Jane's Original Art Doll Supplies, 81
Kays, Linda J., 83
Monique Trading Corp., 85
Newark Dressmaker Supply Inc., 86
Originals by Elaine/Parker-Levi, 86
Osage County Quilt Factory, 87
Plum Creek Dollmakers, 88
Seeley's, 90
Simpson's Liberty Doll Supply, 90
South Forty Farms, 91
Sweet Dreams, 92
2 JP Ranch, 93
Wild Spirit Doll Studio, 94

Wilder's Doll Center, 94

FIBERS/THREADS
CR's Crafts, 72
Donna Lee's Sewing Center, 76
Kate Webster Company, 82
Newark Dressmaker Supply Inc., 86
Plum Creek Dollmakers, 88

FURNITURE
Andaco, 67
Angie's Doll Boutique, Inc., 67
Ann's Dolls, 67
Collectible Doll Company, 71
Create an Heirloom, 72
CR's Crafts, 72
Doll Adventure, The, 73
Doll Gallery, The (WA), 74
Dynasty Doll Collection, 76
Grandma's Dollings, 78
Heavenly Dolls, 80
Judy's Doll Shop, 82
Kathryn's Productions, 83
Page's Dolls, 87
Plum Creek Dollmakers, 88
Rita's Children, 89
Treffeisen U.S.A., 92
Unique Products, 93
Victorian Replicas, 93
Wilder's Doll Center, 94

LACE
Alice's Doll Workshop, 66
All for a Doll, 66
All That Glissons, 67
Bear Threads, Ltd., 68
Cascade Doll Shoppe, 70
CR's Crafts, 72
Doll Gallery, The (WA), 74
Donna Lee's Sewing Center, 76
Georgie's Ceramics and Clay Art Pak, 78
Kate Webster Company, 82
Newark Dressmaker Supply Inc., 86
Plum Creek Dollmakers, 88
Wilder's Doll Center, 94

LASHES
Alice's Doll Workshop, 66
All for a Doll, 66

Angie's Doll Boutique, Inc., 67
Ann's Dolls, 67
Cascade Doll Shoppe, 70
Center Stage Emporium, 70
Childhood Fantasies, 70
Collectible Doll Company, 71
Create an Heirloom, 72
CR's Crafts, 72
Doll Adventure, The, 73
Dolls by Dyan, 75
Donna's Doll Factory, 76
Georgie's Ceramic's and Clay Art Pak, 78
Grandma's Dollings, 78
Heartwarmers, 79
Heavenly Dolls, 80
Judy's Doll Shop, 82
K.C. Dolls, 83
Kemper Doll Supplies, 84
Monique Trading Corp., 85
Newark Dressmaker Supply Inc., 86
Plum Creek Dollmakers, 88
Rita's Children, 89
Simpson's Liberty Doll Supply, 90
Sweet Dreams, 92
Wee Three, Inc., 93
Wild Spirit Doll Studio, 94
Wilder's Doll Center, 94

LEATHER
CR's Crafts, 72
Georgie's Ceramics and Clay Art Pak, 78
Plum Creek Dollmakers, 88
Rita's Children, 89
South Forty Farms, 91

MOLDS
Alice's Doll Workshop, 66
Angie's Doll Boutique, Inc., 67
Anthony's of Solvang, 68
Cascade Doll Shoppe, 70
Center Stage Emporium, 70
Childhood Fantasies, 70
Collectible Doll Company, 71
Create an Heirloom, 72
CR's Crafts, 72
Doll Place, The, 75
Dol-Lee Shop, The, 75
Dolls by Dyan, 75

Donna's Doll Factory, 76
Gallery Collection Molds, 78
Georgie's Ceramics and Clay Art Pak, 78
Heavenly Dolls, 80
Jones Mold Co. Inc., 81
K.C. Dolls, 83
Mimi's Books and Patterns for the Serious Dollmaker, 85
Newark Dressmaker Supply Inc., 86
Originals by Elaine/Parker-Levi, 86
Page's Dolls, 87
Plum Creek Dollmakers, 88
Rita's Children, 89
Seeley's, 90
Wilder's Doll Center, 94

PAINTS

Alice's Doll Workshop, 66
All for a Doll, 66
Angie's Doll Boutique, Inc., 67
Cascade Doll Shoppe, 70
Center Stage Emporium, 70
Collectible Doll Company, 71
CR's Crafts, 72
Doll Adventure, The, 73
Doll Place, The, 75
Doll Studios, 75
Dol-Lee Shop, The, 75
Dolls by Dyan, 75
Donna's Doll Factory, 76
Dwaine E. Gipe, 76
Gallery Collection Molds, 78
Georgie's Ceramics and Clay Art Pak, 78
Grandma's Dollings, 78
Heartwarmers, 79
Heavenly Dolls, 80
Judy's Doll Shop, 82
K.C. Dolls, 83
Newark Dressmaker Supply Inc., 86
Page's Dolls, 87
Plum Creek Dollmakers, 88
Portland Po Henry Supply, 89
Rita's Children, 89
Seeley's, 90

Southern Oregon Pottery Supply, 91
Sweet Dreams, 92
Wilder's Doll Center, 94

PATTERNS FOR CLOTH DOLLS

All for a Doll, 66
Angie's Doll Boutique, Inc., 67
Bailey, Elinor Peace, 68
Brown House Dolls, 69
Collectible Doll Company, 71
CR's Crafts, 72
Doll Gallery, The (ME), 74
Donna's Doll Factory, 76
Gabriele's Inc., 77
Gallery Collection Molds, 78
Georgie's Ceramics and Clay Art Pak, 78
Hedy Katin Cloth Doll Patterns, 80
Jones Mold Co. Inc., 81
Kezi's Premier Cloth Doll Patterns, 84
Mimi's Books and Patterns for the Serious Dollmaker, 85
Osage County Quilt Factory, 87
Plum Creek Dollmakers, 88
Sara Bernstein Dolls and Bears, 90
Sweet Dreams, 92
Westside Printing, 93
Whimsical Cloth Doll Creations, 94

PATTERNS FOR DOLL CLOTHING

Alice's Doll Workshop, 66
All for a Doll, 66
Angie's Doll Boutique, Inc., 67
Ann's Dolls, 67
Anthony's of Solvang, 68
Bailey, Elinor Peace, 68
Best Dressed Doll, 69
Brown House Dolls, 69
Cascade Doll Shoppe, 70
Center Stage Emporium, 70
Collectible Doll Company, 71
Create an Heirloom, 72

CR's Crafts, 72
Doll Adventure, The, 73
Doll Gallery, The (ME), 74
Dolls Delight, Inc., 75
Donna Lee's Sewing Center, 76
Donna's Doll Factory, 76
Fancywork and Fashion, 77
Gabriele's Inc., 77
Gallery Collection Molds, 78
Georgie's Ceramics and Clay Art Pak, 78
Heavenly Dolls, 80
Jones Mold Co. Inc., 81
Judy's Doll Shop, 82
K.C. Dolls, 83
Kate Webster Company, 82
Newark Dressmaker Supply Inc., 86
Originals by Elaine/Parker-Levi, 86
Osage County Quilt Factory, 87
Page's Dolls, 87
Plum Creek Dollmakers, 88
Seeley's, 90
Sweet Dreams, 92
Westside Printing, 93
Wilder's Doll Center, 94

RIBBONS

Alice's Doll Workshop, 66
Ann's Dolls, 67
Bear Threads, Ltd., 68
Cascade Doll Shoppe, 70
CR's Crafts, 72
Donna Lee's Sewing Center, 76
Georgie's Ceramics and Clay Art Pak, 78
Hamilton Eye Warehouse, 79
Jean Dixon, 81
Kate Webster Company, 82
Plum Creek Dollmakers, 88
Wilder's Doll Center, 94

SCALED PROPS/ ACCESSORIES

Alice's Doll Workshop, 66
All for a Doll, 66
Angie's Doll Boutique, Inc., 67
Ann's Dolls, 67
Anthony's of Solvang, 68

Beauty-Stone Stands, 68
Best Dressed Doll, 69
Collectible Doll Company, 71
CR's Crafts, 72
Doll Adventure, The, 73
Doll Gallery, The (WA), 74
Doll Place, The, 75
Donna Lee's Sewing Center, 76
Donna's Doll Factory, 76
Georgie's Ceramics and Clay Art Pak, 78
Grandma's Dollings, 78
Hamilton Eye Warehouse, 79
Handcraft Designs, Inc., 79
Heavenly Dolls, 80
Jane's Original Art Doll Supplies, 81
Judith Howe Inc., 81
Just Her Style, 82
K.C. Dolls, 83
Kate Webster Company, 82
Monique Trading Corp., 85
Newark Dressmaker Supply Inc., 86
Plum Creek Dollmakers, 88
Simpson's Liberty Doll Supply, 90
South Forty Farms, 91
Sweet Dreams, 92
Treffeisen U.S.A., 92

SLIPS

Alice's Doll Workshop, 66
All for a Doll, 66
Angie's Doll Boutique, Inc., 67
Ann's Dolls, 67
Cascade Doll Shoppe, 70
Center Stage Emporium, 70
Collectible Doll Company, 71
CR's Crafts, 72
Doll Adventure, The, 73
Doll Place, The, 75
Doll Studios, 75
Dolls by Dyan, 75
Donna's Doll Factory, 76
Georgie's Ceramics and Clay Art Pak, 78
Grandma's Dollings, 78
Heartwarmers, 79
Jones Mold Co. Inc., 81
Judy's Doll Shop, 82

Page's Dolls, 87
Plum Creek Dollmakers, 88
Portland Po Henry Supply, 89
Rita's Children, 89
Seeley's, 90
Southern Oregon Pottery Supply, 91
Wilder's Doll Center, 94

STUFFING

Ann's Dolls, 67
Buffalo Batt & Felt, 69
CR's Crafts, 72
Heartwarmers, 79
Heavenly Dolls, 80
Newark Dressmaker Supply Inc., 86
Plum Creek Dollmakers, 88
Rita's Children, 89
Sweet Dreams, 92
Wilder's Doll Center, 94

TOOLS

Alice's Doll Workshop, 66
All for a Doll, 66
All That Glissons, 67
Angie's Doll Boutique, Inc., 67
Ann's Dolls, 67
Anthony's of Solvang, 68
Cascade Doll Shoppe, 70
Center Stage Emporium, 70
Collectible Doll Company, 71

CR's Crafts, 72
Doll Adventure, The, 73
Doll Gallery, The (ME), 74
Doll Studios, 75
Dol-Lee Shop, The, 75
Dolls by Dyan, 75
Donna's Doll Factory, 76
Dustmagnet, 76
Dwaine E. Gipe, 76
Eager Plastics Inc., 77
Gabriele's Inc., 77
Gallery Collection Molds, 78
Georgie's Ceramics and Clay Art Pak, 78
Grandma's Dollings, 78
Handcraft Designs, Inc., 79
Heartwarmers, 79
Heavenly Dolls, 80
Jane's Original Art Doll Supplies, 81
Judith Howe Inc., 81
Judy's Doll Shop, 82
K.C. Dolls, 83
Kays, Linda J., 83
Kemper Doll Supplies, 84
Master Eye Beveler, 84
Material Things, 85
Monique Trading Corp., 85
Osage County Quilt Factory, 87
Page's Dolls, 87
Paragon Industries, Inc., 87
Piecemakers Country Store, 87
Plum Creek Dollmakers, 88

Portland Po Henry Supply, 89
Rita's Children, 89
Seeley's, 90
Simpson's Liberty Doll Supply, 90
Southern Oregon Pottery Supply, 91
Sweet Dreams, 92
Truebite Inc., 92
Twin Pines of Maine, Inc., 92
Wilder's Doll Center, 94

TRIMMINGS

Alice's Doll Workshop, 66
All That Glissons, 67
Bear Threads, Ltd., 68
Cascade Doll Shoppe, 70
CR's Crafts, 72
Donna Lee's Sewing Center, 76
Georgie's Ceramics and Clay Art Pak, 78
Hamilton Eye Warehouse, 79
Kate Webster Company, 82
National Nonwovens, 86
Newark Dressmaker Supply Inc., 86
Plum Creek Dollmakers, 88

WIGS

Alice's Doll Workshop, 66
All for a Doll, 66
Angie's Doll Boutique, Inc., 67
Ann's Dolls, 67

Anthony's of Solvang, 68
Cascade Doll Shoppe, 70
Center Stage Emporium, 70
Childhood Fantasies, 70
Collectible Doll Company, 71
Create An Heirloom, 72
CR's Crafts, 72
Doll Adventure, The, 73
Doll Gallery, The (ME), 74
Doll Gallery, The (WA), 74
Doll Studios, 75
Dolls by Dyan, 75
Donna's Doll Factory, 76
Gabriele's Inc., 77
Georgie's Ceramics and Clay Art Pak, 78
Grandma's Dollings, 78
Heartwarmers, 79
Heavenly Dolls, 80
Judy's Doll Shop, 82
K.C. Dolls, 83
Kemper Doll Supplies, 84
Monique Trading Corp., 85
Page's Dolls, 87
Plum Creek Dollmakers, 88
Rita's Children, 89
S&S Doll Hospital, 90
Simpson's Liberty Doll Supply, 90
Sweet Dreams, 92
Wee Three, Inc., 93
Wilder's Doll Center, 94